D1246710

Time and the Biblical Hebrew Verb

Linguistic Studies in Ancient West Semitic

edited by

Cynthia L. Miller-Naudé and Jacobus Naudé

The series Linguistic Studies in Ancient West Semitic is devoted to the ancient West Semitic languages, including Hebrew, Aramaic, Ugaritic, and their near congeners. It includes monographs, collections of essays, and text editions informed by the approaches of linguistic science. The material studied will span from the earliest texts to the rise of Islam.

1. *The Verbless Clause in Biblical Hebrew: Linguistic Approaches*, edited by Cynthia L. Miller
2. *Phonology and Morphology of Biblical Hebrew: An Introduction*, by Joshua Blau
3. *A Manual of Ugaritic*, by Pierre Bordreuil and Dennis Pardee
4. *Word Order in the Biblical Hebrew Finite Clause: A Syntactic and Pragmatic Analysis of Preposing*, by Adina Moshavi
5. *Oath Formulas in Biblical Hebrew*, by Blane Conklin
6. *Biblical Hebrew Grammar Visualized*, by Francis I. Andersen and A. Dean Forbes
7. *Time and the Biblical Hebrew Verb: The Expression of Tense, Aspect, and Modality in Biblical Hebrew*, by John A. Cook
8. *Diachrony in Biblical Hebrew*, edited by Cynthia L. Miller-Naudé and Ziony Zevit

Time and the Biblical Hebrew Verb

The Expression of Tense, Aspect, and
Modality in Biblical Hebrew

JOHN A. COOK

Winona Lake, Indiana
EISENBRAUNS
2012

Copyright © 2012 Eisenbrauns
All rights reserved.
Printed in the United States of America.

www.eisenbrauns.com

Library of Congress Cataloging-in-Publication Data

Cook, John A., Dr.
   Time and the biblical Hebrew verb : the expression of tense, aspect,
and modality in biblical Hebrew / John A. Cook.
      pages cm — (Linguistic studies in ancient West Semitic ; 7)
   Includes bibliographical references and indexes.
   ISBN 978-1-57506-256-3 (hardback : alk. paper)
   1. Hebrew language—Tense.   2. Hebrew language—Verb.
  3. Bible. O.T.—Language, style.   I. Title.
   PJ4659.C66   2012
   492.4′56—dc23
                             2012038996

The paper used in this publication meets the minimum requirements of the American
National Standard for Information Sciences—Permanence of Paper for Printed Library
Materials. ANSI Z39.48-1984.♾™

JKM Library
1100 East 55th Street
Chicago, IL 60615

Contents

Preface ix

Acknowledgments xii

Abbreviations and Symbols xiii

Chapter 1. A Theory of Tense, Aspect, and Modality 1
  1.1. Pre-modern Treatments of Tense and Aspect 1
  1.2. The R-Point and Modern Tense Theory 4
    1.2.1. Jespersen's Universal Tense Theory 4
    1.2.2. Reichenbach's R-Point Theory 7
    1.2.3. Revisions of Reichenbach's R-Point Theory 10
      1.2.3.1. Hornstein: Reducing R-Point Redundancies 10
      1.2.3.2. Bull: Multiple R-Points 12
      1.2.3.3. Comrie: A Compromise R-Point Theory 13
      1.2.3.4. Declerck: A Bifurcated R-Point 15
    1.2.4. Summary: The R-Point and Tense Theory 18
  1.3. A Primer on Aspect 18
    1.3.1. Situation Aspect 19
    1.3.2. Phasal Aspect 25
    1.3.3. Viewpoint Aspect 26
  1.4. The R-Point in Tense-Aspect Theory 28
    1.4.1. M. R. Johnson: The Triadic Relationship of E, R, and S 28
    1.4.2. W. Klein: The R-Point as "Topic Time" 31
    1.4.3. Olsen: Multiple R-Points 33
    1.4.4. Summary: The R-Point and Tense-Aspect Theory 36
  1.5. The R-Point and Discourse 36
    1.5.1. Explaining R-Point Movement with Viewpoint Aspect 37
    1.5.2. Explaining R-Point Movement with Situation Aspect 38
    1.5.3. Explaining R-Point Movement with (Un)boundedness 41
    1.5.4. Summary: The R-Point in Discourse 41
  1.6. A Primer on Modality 42
    1.6.1. Backgrounds of Modality: Grammar, Logic, and
      Speech Acts 42
    1.6.2. Defining Modality 45
    1.6.3. Categorizing Modality 47
      1.6.3.1. Classifications of Modalities 47
      1.6.3.2. Modality and Speech Acts 52
      1.6.3.3. Modality and Mood Systems 53
    1.6.4. Conclusion: Modality and TAM Systems 54

1.7. A Model of Tense, Aspect, and Modality 55
   1.7.1. Semantics and TAM 55
   1.7.2. Time and Space: Temporality and TAM 57
   1.7.3. Aspect and Event Time 57
      1.7.3.1. Situation Aspect and Event Time 58
      1.7.3.2. Phasal Aspect and Event Time 62
      1.7.3.3. Viewpoint Aspect and Event Time 65
   1.7.4. Tense and Unilinear Time 68
   1.7.5. Modality and Alternative Times 70
   1.7.6. The Interaction of Tense, Aspect, and Modality 72
1.8. Conclusion 75

Chapter 2. Tense, Aspect, and Modality in Biblical Hebrew 77
2.1. A Primer on the Biblical Hebrew Verbal System 77
2.2. The Establishment of the "Standard" Theory of the
     Biblical Hebrew Verbal System 83
   2.2.1. Before Ewald and S. R. Driver 83
   2.2.2. Ewald's "Standard" Theory 86
   2.2.3. S. R. Driver's "Extended Standard" Theory 90
   2.2.4. Summary 93
2.3. The Biblical Hebrew Verbal System in Historical
     and Comparative Perspective 93
   2.3.1. The Linguistic Context of the BHVS 95
   2.3.2. East Semitic and the West Semitic Verbal System 97
      2.3.2.1. The Akkadian Verbal System 97
      2.3.2.2. The West Semitic Verbal System in Light
         of Akkadian 99
   2.3.3. Ugaritic and the Northwest Semitic Verbal System 105
      2.3.3.1. The Ugaritic Verbal System 105
      2.3.3.2. The Northwest Semitic Verbal System in Light
         of Ugaritic 107
   2.3.4. Amarna and the Canaanite Verbal System 110
      2.3.4.1. Peripheral Akkadian and the
         Amarna Letters 111
      2.3.4.2. The Canaanite Verbal System in
         Light of Amarna 112
   2.3.5. Summary: The BHVS in Light of
      Historical-Comparative Data 118
2.4. Biblical Hebrew Verb Theory in the Last Half Century 121
   2.4.1. Aspect-Prominent Theory 122
      2.4.1.1. Rundgren's Privative Opposition Theory 122
      2.4.1.2. Meyer's Diachronic *Systemüberlagerung*
         Theory 124
      2.4.1.3. Michel's Synchronic Theory 126
      2.4.1.4. Summary 130
   2.4.2. Tense-Prominent Theory 130

2.4.2.1. Tense and Diachrony 131
2.4.2.2. Tense and Syntax 132
2.4.2.3. Relative Tense and Modality 135
2.4.2.4. Summary 148
2.4.3. Discourse-Prominent Theory 149
2.4.3.1. Discourse Analysis of Biblical Literature 150
2.4.3.2. Discourse Analysis and the Semantics
of the BHVS 156
2.4.3.3. Conclusion 171
2.5. Hebrew Verb Theory at the Beginning of the 21st Century 172

Chapter 3. The Semantics of the Biblical Hebrew Verbal System . . . 176
3.1. Theoretical Considerations 176
3.1.1. Basic Principles 176
3.1.2. Goals of a Semantic Theory 182
3.1.3. Diachronic Typology and Grammaticalization 185
3.1.4 Concluding Remarks and a Look Ahead 190
3.2. The Expression of Aspect in BH 191
3.2.1. Phasal Aspect: The Lexical-Semantic Dimension 191
3.2.2. Situation Aspect: The Stative-Dynamic Opposition 194
3.2.3. Viewpoint Aspect: The Perfective-Imperfective Opposition
and the Progressive 199
3.2.3.1. Perfective *Qatal* 201
3.2.3.2. Imperfective *Yiqtol* 217
3.2.3.3. Participle as Adjectival Encoding of
Event Predicates 223
3.3. The Expression of Modality in BH 233
3.3.1. Word Order in BH: An Overview 235
3.3.2. Directive-Volitive Mood System 237
3.3.3. Realis-Irrealis Mood Opposition 244
3.3.3.1. Irrealis *Yiqtol* 244
3.3.3.2. Irrealis *Qatal* (Including So-Called *Wĕqatal*) 249
3.4. The Expression of Temporality in BH 256
3.4.1. The Past Narrative *Wayyyiqtol* Conjugation 256
3.4.2. The "Default Pattern" of Temporal Interpretation in BH 265
3.5. The TAM System of BH in Diachronic-Typological Perspective 268

Chapter 4. Semantics and Discourse Pragmatics of the
Biblical Hebrew Verbal System 272
4.1. On Discourse-Pragmatic Approaches to BH 272
4.2. Some Elements of Discourse Structure 275
4.2.1. Temporal Succession 275
4.2.2. Foreground-Background 283
4.2.3. The Relationship between Temporal Succession
and Foreground 286
4.3. The Semantics of Temporality in BH Discourse 288

4.3.1. *Wayyiqtol* and Narrative Discourse   289
4.3.2. *Wayyiqtol* in Poetry   298
4.3.3. Irrealis *Qatal* and Non-narrative Discourse   304
4.3.4. Discourse וַיְהִי and וְהָיָה   309
4.4. The Temporal and Modal Interpretation of Discourse   312
4.4.1. 1 Samuel 8 (Prose Narrative)   326
4.4.2. Exodus 12 (Irrealis Instruction)   332
4.5. Conclusion   337

Works Cited 339

Indexes   375
Index of Authors   375
Index of Scripture   380

Preface

A cognate duality marks the coexistence of language and of time. There is a sense, intuitively compelling, in which language occurs in time. Every speech act, whether it is an audible utterance or voiced innerly, "takes time"—itself a suggestive phrase. It can be measured temporally. . . . But this occurrence of language in time is only one aspect of the relation, and the easier to grasp. Time, as we posit and experience it, can be seen as a function of language, as a system of location and referral whose main co-ordinates are linguistic. Language largely composes and segments time. (Steiner 1998: 135–36)

The origins of this book reach back to my dissertation (Cook 2002), though it has grown and morphed significantly in the intervening decade. Some portions of this work bear striking resemblance to its origins, such as the discussion of the history of tense theory in chap. 1 and the discussion of Biblical Hebrew verb theory in chap. 2, which has mainly been expanded to treat recent research. By contrast, the discussion in chap. 3 has been completely revised and rearranged, at times leading to the rejection of my earlier claims; and the latter portion of chap. 4 represents a framework not even conceived of at the beginning of my interest in the Biblical Hebrew verbal system.

The Biblical Hebrew verbal system continues to exercise scholars, and though I have attempted to give an accurate picture of the contours of the discussion, there are undoubtedly various works that I have missed mentioning directly. I trust, however, that I have interacted enough with the range of approaches to the perennial questions on the Hebrew verb to have done them justice. With respect to the perennial questions, my answers may appear deceptively traditional. For instance, my answer to the long-standing debate of "tense or aspect" is not drastically different from Ewald's, though our understanding of the perfective : imperfective opposition encoded in Biblical Hebrew *qatal* and *yiqtol* is distinguished by the century and a half of intervening discussion and the rise of modern linguistics. One distinguishing sign is my employment of the phrase "aspect prominent" (à la Bhat 1999) to describe the Biblical Hebrew verbal system. The framing of the central question as "tense or aspect (or modality)" wrongly implies a mutual exclusivity among these domains of meaning. At the same time, it is unhelpful to claim that they can never legitimately be separated out in the course of analysis: dissection of the system does not necessarily imply that any part of the system can function independently.

The aspect-prominent verbal system of Biblical Hebrew consists of the following forms treated here: a Perfective (*qatal*) : Imperfective (*yiqtol*) opposition; a Past Narrative verb (*wayyiqtol*); a progressive construction consisting of the predicative Participle; irrealis mood expressed by the two central forms exhibiting verb-subject word order, the Irrealis Perfective/*qatal* (i.e., *wĕqatal*) and Irrealis Imperfective/*yiqtol*; and a Directive-Jussive subsystem of irrealis mood, which aligns with the irrealis verb-subject word order. As with almost any of the world's verbal systems, this aspect-prominent system can express a wide range of aspectual, tensed, and modal meanings. The argument of chap. 3 is that all these forms can be semantically identified as listed above and that their expressions of specific aspectual, tensed, and modal meanings are explicable with reference to their general meanings.

Methodologically, I eschew statistical means of validation, pointing out their weaknesses along the way, and draw on diachronic typology and grammaticalization as an "external" means of validating my theory. Linguistic typology consists of collecting data from multiple, genetically unrelated languages and making generalizations about linguistic structures across those languages. Diachronic typology provides a historical dimension by generalizing not simply about language structures but about the types of structural changes that are evident in languages over time. Grammaticalization is an offshoot of diachronic typology that is specifically interested in the structural shift of lexical items to grammatical items or shifts of grammatical items to become more grammatical over time. These fields have provided a wealth of data on verbal systems and diachronic changes to these systems in the world's languages, which serve as an external means of validating my theory of the Biblical Hebrew verbal system: for my theory to be valid, it should accord generally with what is known about verbal systems and the ways that they change over time. Given the inescapable diachronic dimension that is part of studying the ancient, composite corpus of the Hebrew Bible, the findings of diachronic typology with regard to verbal systems is a particularly powerful means of escaping the subjectivity and translation-based approaches of other theories.

Because diachronic changes leave traces on synchronic linguistic structures, some linguists (particularly those working with grammaticalization theory) have argued that the diachronic-synchronic distinction is unhelpful and that a panchronic approach to the linguistic system must be pursued. In this regard, my work here represents a step back from my embracing of grammaticalization theory and panchrony in my earlier work (Cook 2001; 2002). In the intervening decade, I have come to recognize that my theory is neither strictly nor consistently in line with grammaticalization theory and the notion of panchrony. During this time, I have also become convinced that the idea of panchrony is theoretically problematic (Newmeyer 1998: 290) and that the results of an approach of this sort are unhelpful (Andrason 2010; 2011a): the inevitably intergenerational character of language change maintains the legitimacy of the synchronic-diachronic distinction in linguistic analysis (Hale 2007: 33); and the panchronic approach forestalls the important task of distinguishing general and specific meanings by treating all meanings as equally legitimate and available to a linguistic structure. The result of this latter approach, well exemplified in Andrason's articles, is a taxonomy of meanings with no guidance for the Hebrew philologist to decide which is more or less likely in a given syntagm or discourse context.

Having this philological aim in mind, I have framed my discussion not with the central question of "Tense or aspect?" but with the question "What is the range of meaning for a given form, and what sort of contextual factors (syntagm, discourse, etc.) might allow us to narrow this range for a given instance?" While the general meaning may be said to be an abstraction (just as a morpheme or phoneme is an abstraction), its usefulness is in giving us some grasp of the variety of specific meanings a form may express and in what sorts of context these specific meanings may appear.

In order to account for the contextual character of specific meanings, in chap. 4 I address long-standing issues involving interaction between the semantics of verbal forms and their discourse pragmatic functions. More importantly, I propose a theory of discourse modes for Biblical Hebrew. These discourse modes account for various temporal relationships that are found among successive clauses in Biblical Hebrew. Fittingly, my account of this theory of discourse modes ends on an exegetical note with an explication of the interaction of verbs and their discourse context in two passages from the Hebrew Bible, which is the end of this enterprise.

Note to the Reader

Following a now widespread convention, I avoid the use of traditional, semantically laden labels for the BH verb forms in favor a simplified transcription of the unmarked paradigm form (3MS of *QTL* 'to kill', a root traditionally employed in comparative Semitic studies) to refer to each verbal conjugation (more traditional names are given here in parentheses): *qatal* (Perfect), *yiqtol* (Imperfect), *wayyiqtol* (*Waw*-consecutive Imperfect), *wĕqatal* (*Waw*-consecutive Perfect). I have, nevertheless, retained the traditional labels for the Participle, Infinitive, and directive-volitive forms, except for the Cohortative (i.e., Imperative and Jussive); the accuracy and utility of these latter labels is assessed in chap. 3. Throughout the discussion, I follow the oft-used linguistic convention of capitalizing the names of BH and other language-specific verb forms (except for the BH verb forms listed here as referred to by transcription), in distinction from universal semantic categories, which I present in lowercase.

Acknowledgments

I have benefited greatly from colleagues working in cognate areas (e.g., Semitic languages, Rabbinic Hebrew, linguistics, etc.) and on the Hebrew verb specifically, both in published form and in various other interactions with them. I have especially valued feedback from numerous conference papers over the past decade, by means of which I was able to refine my thinking on these matters. I trust that I have adequately and fairly portrayed the viewpoints of my colleagues in these pages.

Several individuals have been especially instrumental in my thinking about these topics and thus deserve specific mention. Cynthia L. Miller-Naudé guided my initial thinking well on these matters as a dissertation mentor. I was fortunate to receive the input of Michael P. O'Connor before his tragic death, both when I submitted my proposal to the LSAWS series and in subsequent conversations with him. Robert D. Holmstedt has been a constant conversation partner in Biblical Hebrew linguistics since our graduate days, and there is little of this book that has not already been the topic of our informal interactions and collaborative enterprises. Also, I would be remiss not to mention the specific help that Joe Salmons of the University of Wisconsin provided me, first through his service on my dissertation committee and subsequently by helping me decipher some particularly difficult eighteenth- and nineteenth-century German passages. Similarly, James Spinti graciously double-checked my translations of Latin passages. Finally, I want to thank Beverly McCoy, whose keen editorial sense has contributed significantly to the readability of this book; and to Jim Eisenbraun and the rest of the Eisenbrauns staff go my thanks for your always-exemplary work producing "good books" of mine and others' manuscripts.

My deepest gratitude is reserved for my family: for my soul-mate Kathy, אשת נעורי ואשת־חיל, without whose support in innumerable ways I could never have begun, much less finished this work; and for our sons, Jared, Colin, Tage, and Evan (כחצים ביד־גבור כן בני הנעורים), who have selflessly allowed this project to accompany me during the majority of their childhood years.

Abbreviations and Symbols

Abbreviations

1	first person
2	second person
3	third person
ACC	accomplishment
ACH	achievement
ACT	activity
adj.	adjective
ASV	Authorized Standard Version (1901)
B.C.E.	before the Common Era
BH	Biblical Hebrew
BHVS	Biblical Hebrew verbal system
COH	cohortative
COND	conditional (protasis)
CS	Central Semitic
DECL	declarative (neutral epistemic)
DIR	directive
DRT	Discourse Representation Theory
DYN	dynamic
EA	El-Amarna
EPIS	epistemic
ES	East Semitic
ET	English translation
EXIST	existential predicate
F	feminine
FIN	final (apodosis/purpose/result)
Fr.	French
FUT	future time/tense
Gk.	Greek
HAB	habitual
IMPV	imperative
IPFV	imperfective aspect
JUSS	jussive
KJV	King James Version (1611)
Lat.	Latin
M	masculine
NAB	New American Bible (1970)

NIV	New International Version (1978)
NJB	New Jerusalem Bible (1985)
NJPS	New Jewish Publication Society (1985)
NRSV	New Revised Standard Version (1989)
NULL	null copula (verbless predication)
NWS	Northwest Semitic
OBL	obligation
P	plural
PAST	past time/tense
PERF	perfect aspect
PFV	perfective aspect
PRES	present time/tense
PRET	preterite
PROG	progressive
PS	Proto-Semitic
PTC	participle
QTL	*qatal*
REB	Revised English Bible (1989)
RH	Rabbinic Hebrew (from approximately 2nd century c.e.)
RSV	Revised Standard Version (1946)
S	singular
SS	South Semitic
STA	state
TAM	tense-aspect-modality (modality includes mood)
VOL	volitive/optative/commissive
WAYY	*wayyiqtol*
WQTL	*wĕqatal*
WS	West Semitic
YQTL	*yiqtol*

Symbols

,	is simultaneous with, e.g., R, E is interpreted "R is simultaneous with E"
?	grammatically awkward or questionable
@	is at, i.e., is located at a given point (see fig. 1.7)
*	unattested or reconstructed (for word forms)
&	conjunction, "and"
→	implicated relationship; e.g., A → B is interpreted "If A then B"
∀	universal quantifier: "for every time . . ."
∈	set membership: "is a member of . . ."
+	positive value for features
+ + . . .	target state (see table 1.14)
+V	plus vector (see fig. 1.2)
±	positive/negative value for features
×	multiplication, e.g., × nucleus is interpreted "multiple nuclei"
=	equivalent relationship (expressions refer to identical event)
=	is equal to

≠	is not equal to
–	negative value for features
– –. . .	source state (see table 1.14)
–V	minus vector (see fig. 1.2)
∩	intersection (used of events with temporal overlap with each other)
~	negator; e.g., ~A is interpreted "not A"
≈	is functionally equivalent to (see chap. 1 n. 30)
≡	strict equivalence (identical reference time for speech and event)
≤	precedes or is equal to (see table 1.9)
«	wholly precedes (see table 1.9)
<	precedence relationship; e.g., A < B is interpreted "A precedes B"
>	becomes, e.g., A > B is interpreted "A becomes B"
⊂	is included in, e.g., A ⊂ B is interpreted "A is included in B"
⊃	includes, e.g., A ⊃ B is interpreted "A includes B"
⊆	inclusion relationship (first event is included within the second)
○	is composed of, e.g., A ○ B is interpreted "is composed of A and B"
□	it is necessary
◇	it is possible
0	zero marking for features
0V	zero vector (see fig. 1.2)
AP	anticipatory point (see fig. 1.2)
C	lengthened (geminated) consonant; e.g., *wa*C-, *ha*C-
C	deictic center
Cl#	clause (see figs. 1.8–9)
C_N	deictic center of the narrator
$C_{pos\#}$	position of deictic center
C_{RF}	deictic center (tense) that serves as reference frame (aspect)
C_S	deictic center of speaker
e	event/situation
E	event time
EF	event frame
F	final point
Farb	arbitrary final point (see fig. 1.13)
Fnat	natural final point (see fig. 1.13)
I	interval of time
I	initial point
m	moment of time
PP	point present (see fig. 1.2)
R	accessibility relation (modality)
R	reference point/time
RAP	retrospective-anticipatory point (see fig. 1.2)
R_C	modal relation of condition
REM	remote (past; see example [4.1])
RF	reference frame
R_H	modal relation of habituality
R_O	modal relation of obligation

RP	retrospective point (see fig. 1.2)
RTO	time of orientation (see example [1.5])
RTR	time referred to (see example [1.5])
S	speech time
SS	source state of 2-state events (see table 1.14)
SV	subject-verb word order
t	segment of time
VS	verb-subject word order
w	world (reference to alternative world/situation)
X-VS	verb-subject word order triggered by some fronted element (X)

Chapter 1
A Theory of Tense, Aspect, and Modality

This chapter introduces the categories of tense, aspect, and modality (TAM), which are most frequently associated with verbal forms in language. The discussion is divided into two parts: the first part is a somewhat historically oriented discussion of these categories, focusing particularly on the role of the "R-point" in tense and tense-aspect theories (§§1.1–6); in the second part of this chapter, I present a theory of TAM based on a central temporal-spatial metaphor and illustrated with fragments of English grammar (§1.7). This chapter provides a general linguistic background for the discussion of the Biblical Hebrew verbal system in chap. 2, and a theoretical-linguistic basis for the analysis of the Biblical Hebrew verbal system in chaps. 3–4.

1.1. Pre-modern Treatments of Tense and Aspect

Tense is closely associated with time, a view reflected in the frequent use of a single term for both in some languages (e.g., Gk. χρόνος, Lat. tempus, Fr. temps).[1] However, tense is not identical with time, thus raising the question of how precisely the two are related. Time is widely conceived of in terms of the triad past, present, and future, yet verbal systems are rarely, if ever, so simply structured.[2] The widespread and widely varying mismatches between the number of verb forms in language and these three categories of time have long exercised grammarians and linguists.

One of the earliest extant grammatical treatises on Greek is the Τέχνη Γραμματική (*Téchnē Grammatikḗ*), ascribed to Dionysius Thrax (around

---

1. Aristotle (*Int.* 3, 16b5–6, trans. Edghill) states that "[a] verb (ῥῆμα) is that which, in addition to its proper meaning, carries with it the notion of time/tense." Robins (1997: 33) cautions that the meanings 'verb' and 'predicate' for ῥῆμα may not yet have been clearly distinguished in Aristotle's day.

2. Binnick (1991: 3–4) remarks that "[t]his notion of three times was already old in the time of the ancient Greeks. . . . We find references to 'the Three Times' in all periods and nearly all the various branches of the Indo-European language family." The unique status of the present in this tripartite division was discussed as early as Aristotle (*Phys.* 6.3, 233b33–234a4, trans. Hardie and Gaye), who took the view that the present does not really take up any time but is an indivisible point that acts as a "boundary" between the past and future.

100 B.C.E.).[3] In the *Téchnē*, the Greek verb forms are reconciled with the three times by categorizing the Imperfect, Perfect, Pluperfect, and Aorist forms as 'variants' (Gk. διαφοράς) of the past.[4] Although the Greek tenses are merely listed in the *Téchnē*, without commentary, the names given to the variants of past tense are revealing, as shown in [1.1].[5]

[1.1] Imperfect = παρατατίκος 'extended'
Perfect = παρακείμενος 'lying near'
Pluperfect = ὑπερσθντέλικος 'more than perfect/complete'
Aorist = αόριστος 'indefinite,' or 'undefined'

The influence of the treatment of the Greek verb in the *Téchnē* on later grammatical theory is mediated by Priscian Caesariensis (fifth to sixth century C.E.). Priscian clarifies and extends what is implied in the *Téchnē*'s label for the Perfect, παρακείμενος ('lying near'), by defining three of the *Téchnē*'s four variant past forms in terms of their temporal distance from the present: the Imperfect denotes events that have begun but have not yet been completed (thus may extend into the present), the Perfect denotes events that occurred recently, and the Pluperfect denotes events that occurred a long time ago (Binnick 1991: 11, 466 n. 50). Priscian's interpretation of the *Téchnē* became the model for subsequent European relative-tense theories, the hallmark of which was their distinction of verb forms in terms of their relative temporal distance.

Stoic grammarians (from ca. 300 B.C.E.) proposed a different resolution of tense and time in Greek that incorporated an early concept of aspect defined in terms of (in)completion (see Robins 1997: 36).[6] The Stoic schema paired the Greek verb forms based on the morphological similarity of their stems

---

3. The *Téchnē* is ascribed to Dionysius Thrax, although much discussion has been devoted over the years to questions about the authenticity of this ascription for at least portions of the work (see Robins 1995; Swiggers and Wouters 1998: xv–xxxi).

4. The Present and Future verb forms were naturally associated with present and future time, respectively, while the Future Perfect was left out of the catalog, perhaps because it was rare and regarded by Greek grammarians as peculiar to the Attic dialect (so Robins 1997: 36).

5. The passage in question (ιγ' περὶ ῥήματος), along with Kürschner's German translation, reads (1996: 198–99):

χρόνοι τρεῖς, ἐνεστώς, παρεληλυθώς, μέλλων. τούτων ὁ παρεληλυθὼς ἔχει διαφορὰς τέσσαρας, παρατατικόν, παρακείμενον, ὑπερσυντέλικον, ἀόριστον. Es gibt drei Tempora (Zeiten): Präsens (Gegenwart), Präteritum (Vergangenheit), Futur (Zukunft). Von diesen hat das Präteritum vier Sorten: Imperfekt (sich erstreckend), Perfekt (nahe stehend), Plusquamperfekt (mehr als vollendet), Aorist (nicht begrenzt).

6. Thus Robins; but Binnick (1991: 22–24) notes that scholars have interpreted the Stoic idea of (in)completion in various ways, some of which do not involve aspect at all but relative tense: completed events lie mostly in the past, and incompleted events lie mostly in the future.

Table 1.1. Stoic Schema of the Greek Verb
(adapted from Binnick 1991: 17)

Aspect \ Tense	Past	Present/Future	
Incomplete	ἔλυον (Imperfect) 'I was loosing'	λύω (Present) 'I loose/am loosing'	(both are built from the present stem)
Complete	ἐλελύκη (Pluperfect) 'I had loosed'	λέλυκα (Perfect) 'I have loosed'	(both are built from the reduplicated stem)
Indeterminate	ἔλυσα (Aorist) 'I loosed'	λύσω (Future) 'I will loose'	(both are built from a *sigmatic* stem)[a]

a. Sigmatic stems are named for the characteristic Greek letter σ/*sigma* (Eng. *s*) in their tense sufformative.

Table 1.2. Stoic-Varronian Schema of the Latin Verb
(based on Binnick 1991: 22 and Robins 1997: 65)

Aspect \ Tense	Past	Present	Future
Incomplete	*amābam* (Imperfect) 'I was loving'	*amō* (Present) 'I love/am loving'	*amābō* (Future) 'I shall love'
Complete	*amāveram* (Pluperfect) 'I had loved'	*amāvī* (Perfect) 'I have loved'	*amāverō* (Future Perfect) 'I shall have loved'

and defined the tenses in terms of two times (past versus present/future or non-past) and three aspects (incomplete, complete, and indefinite), as shown in table 1.1.[7]

The Roman grammarian Marcus Terentius Varro (116–27 B.C.E.) adapted this Stoic schema for Latin, separating the present and future times and eliminating the indeterminate aspect, because Latin has no equivalent to the Greek Aorist (the Latin Perfect expresses the sense of both the Greek Perfect and the Aorist). The Varronian schema of the Latin verb is given in table 1.2.

Versions of both the relative-tense and the tense-aspect approaches persisted in Classical and European grammatical traditions up until the twentieth century, as illustrated by the alternative models of the Latin verb offered by the contemporary Latin grammars of Madvig (1895) and Allen and Greenough (1931; 1st ed. 1888). Madvig's relative-tense model of the Latin verb, shown

---

7. Some scholars have proposed that Dionysius Thrax was influenced by Stoic theories, because he also organized the Greek conjugations based on their morphological similarities (Robins 1997: 37). The passage in question (the immediate continuation of the passage in n. 5), along with Kürschner's German translation (1996: 198–99), reads:

ὧν συγγένεια τρεῖς, ἐνεστῶτος πρὸς παρατατικόν, παρακειμένου πρὸς ὑπερσυντέλικον, ἀορίστου πρὸς μέλλοντα. Drei von ihnen sind miteinander verwandt: das Präsens mit dem Imperfekt, das Perfekt mit dem Plusquamperfekt, der Aorist mit dem Futur.

Table 1.3. Madvig's Schema of the Latin Verb
(adapted from 1895: 289)

	praesens	*praeteritum*	*futurum*
[in praesenti][a]	*scrībō* 'I write'	*scrīpsī* 'I have written/wrote'	*scrībam* 'I will write'
in praeterito	*scrībēbam* 'I was writing'	*scrīpseram* 'I had written'	*scrīpturus eram/fuī* 'I was on the point of writing'
in futuro	*scrībam* 'I shall write'	*scrīpserō* 'I shall have written'	*scrīpturus erō* 'I shall be on the point of writing'

a. Following tradition, Madvig does not label this first row of tenses, though logically the terms must be understood as expressing present, past, and future in-the-present (see Binnick 1991: 42).

in table 1.3, is the product of a long, slow process of modification of Dionysius's and Priscian's theories (Binnick 1991: 38).

It is almost a fully relative-tense theory in that events are located past, present, and future within all three times (in-the-past, in-the-present, and in-the-future) without necessarily referencing the present point of speaking, as earlier relative theories had done (e.g., the Greek Perfect lies near the present). Madvig's model of intersecting times thus contains nine relative-tense categories. By contrast, Allen and Greenough's tense-aspect treatment of the Latin verb, given in table 1.4, follows fairly closely the Varronian tense-aspect schema given in table 1.2 above (p. 3).

1.2. The R-Point and Modern Tense Theory

The decisive break with Priscian's relative-tense theory came with Jespersen's critique of Madvig's model of the Latin verb (Binnick 1991: 38). Although Jespersen's own model of tense was not widely accepted, it was an impetus for Reichenbach's relative-tense theory, from which all modern relative-tense theories derive. Modern relative-tense theories feature in common Reichenbach's innovative "reference time" (R-point)—that is, a temporal location in addition to that of the event and that of the speaker's present (time of speaking), the ordering of which with respect to the latter two temporal locations defines the various tenses.

1.2.1. Jespersen's Universal Tense Theory

Jespersen's work is important as a bridge between traditional grammar and modern linguistics (Binnick 1991: 54). Jespersen offered the first modern critique of relative tense and, although ultimately his alternative model has proven inadequate, his research advanced tense theory by prompting later

Table 1.4. Allen and Greenough's Schema of the Latin Verb
(based on 1931: 293–303)

	Incomplete	*Complete*
Present	*scrībō* 'I write/am writing'	*scrīpsī* 'I have written/wrote'
Past	*scrībēbam* 'I was writing'	*scrīpseram* 'I had written'
Future	*scrībam* 'I shall write'	*scrīpserō* 'I shall have written'

scholars to address the areas that his own theory did not adequately treat (Binnick 1991: 110).

Jespersen employed Madvig's relative-tense model of the Latin verb as a foil for his universal tense model (see table 1.3). He offered three criticisms of Madvig's schema (Jespersen 1924: 255–56). First, there are redundancies in Madvig's model that obscure differences in meaning between various verbal forms and categories. On the one hand, the Future verb form *scrībam* occurs twice, once as future-in-the-present and again as present-in-the-future, on the basis of which other categories, such as present-in-the-past and past-in-the-present, might likewise be treated as equivalent. Yet the verb forms in these categories (i.e., Perfect *scrīpsī* and Imperfect *scrībēbam*) are clearly not equivalent. On the other hand, two verb constructions appear in a single category—the future-in-the-present—that are not synonymous: *scrīptūrus eram* (with the Imperfect form of the copula verb) and *scrīptūrus fuī* (with the Perfect form of the copula verb). Second, Jespersen objected to Madvig's tripartite division of present time on the basis that, like Aristotle (*Phys.* 6.3, 233b33–234a4), Jespersen treated the present as an indivisible boundary between past and future times. Third, Jespersen thought that a one-dimensional model of tense, reflective of a linear conception of time, was preferable to Madvig's two-dimensional model of intersecting times.

On the basis of these criticism's of Madvig's schema of the Latin verb, Jespersen (1924: 277) proposed the universal model of tenses schematized in fig. 1.1.[8] Because he treated the present as an indivisible point or boundary, his model includes only seven categories of tense, thus eliminating the redundancy and ambiguity that he drew attention to in Madvig's schema. For all his criticism of Madvig's relative-tense model, Jespersen's "before-" and "after-" categories were derived from relative-tense theory. However, by presenting

---

8. To be more precise, Jespersen's model features universal times, which are associated with tense forms in a one-to-one fashion (see Binnick 1991: 61).

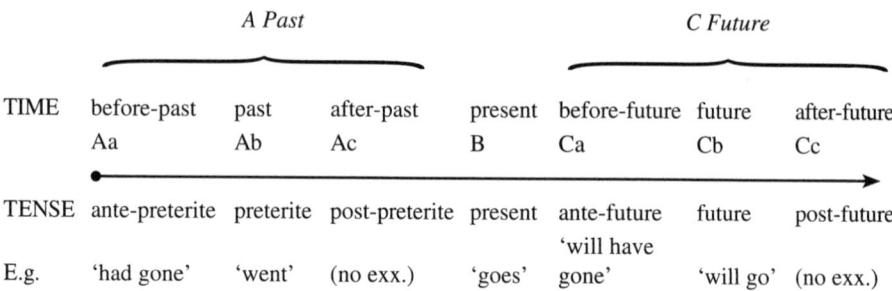

	A Past				C Future		
TIME	before-past Aa	past Ab	after-past Ac	present B	before-future Ca	future Cb	after-future Cc
TENSE	ante-preterite	preterite	post-preterite	present	ante-future 'will have	future	post-future
E.g.	'had gone'	'went'	(no exx.)	'goes'	gone'	'will go'	(no exx.)

Figure 1.1. Jespersen's model of universal tense categories with English examples (adapted from 1924: 257).

the tense categories linearly, anchored to a central present point, Jespersen essentially absolutized relative tense by relating all categories to the present, either directly or indirectly. Tenses that, according to Madvig's relative-tense theory, were located relatively within the past, present, or future, were located a fixed number of units to the right or left of present on Jespersen's timeline (Binnick 1991: 61–62).

Ironically, but not unexpectedly given the above critique, Jespersen's theory suffers from similar inadequacies to the inadequacies for which he criticized Madvig's theory. On the one hand, his model has an after-past category and an after-future category, which do not seem to be realized in any language.[9] On the other hand, Jespersen's model lacks a place for the (present) perfect. In defense of this, Jespersen (1924: 269) stated,

> The system of tenses given above will probably have to meet the objection that it assigns no place to the perfect, *have written, habe geschrieben, ai écrit*, etc., one of the two sides of Lat. *scripsi*, and in Latin often called the perfectum absolutum or "perfect definite." This however, is really no defect in the system, for the perfect cannot be fitted into the simple series, because besides the purely temporal element it contains the element of result. It is a present, but a permansive present: it represents the present state as the outcome of past events, and may therefore be called a retrospective variety of the present.

Jespersen's "rather vague" explanation of present perfect as "a retrospective variety of the present" has been unconvincing to some (Reichenbach 1947:

---

9. Jespersen (1924: 262–63) remarks about the after-past: "I know of no language which possesses a simple tense for this notion"; and on the after-future, he comments: "This has chiefly a theoretic interest, and I doubt very much whether forms like *I shall be going to write* (which implies nearness in time to the chief future time) . . . are of very frequent occurrence."

290 n. 1). However, there appear to be two other, more crucial reasons why Jespersen could not fit the perfect tense into his system. First, because Jespersen adhered to the Aristotelian notion of the present tense as an indivisible point,[10] he could not divide the present as he did the past and future, which would have allowed a "before-present" time slot, which would be the logical position for the perfect (Binnick 1991: 62). Second, and relatedly, Jespersen could not allow such a before-present category in order to maintain the generalization that tense back-shifting in constructions such as indirect speech or hypothetical statements (e.g., *He said, "I am rich" > He said that he was rich*; *I am rich > If I were rich*) involve just one step backwards (Binnick 1991: 64). Thus, as Binnick observes (Binnick 1991: 61–62), Jespersen's absolutized tense model founders in the very cases that a relative-tense model, such as Madvig's, handles most elegantly:

> It was Jespersen's rejection of relative tenses as such that prevented him from recognizing that the retrospective (perfect or ante-) tenses—including the present perfect—can be viewed simply as pasts relative to the main divisions of past, present, and future; and similarly, that the prospective (post-) tenses—including the conditional—can be viewed as futures relative to those same main divisions. Many uses of such tenses in subordinate structures, which a relative-tense theory can account for directly, are at best handled indirectly in Jespersen's theory.

However, it was just such shortcomings in Jespersen's theory that served as the catalyst for Reichenbach's R-point relative-tense theory (see Reichenbach 1947: 290 n. 1).

1.2.2. Reichenbach's R-Point Theory

Reichenbach's (1947: 287–98) briefly outlined relative-tense theory, dubbed the "R-point" theory, is deceptively simple when compared with its explanatory power and the almost universal influence that it has had on subsequent relative-tense theories. The genius of Reichenbach's R-point theory is that, instead of defining tense in terms of a temporal relationship between an event and the present (as Jespersen), tense is defined by means of a three-place temporal ordering of the (present) "point of speech time" (S), the "point of event time" (E), and an abstract "point of reference time" (R). Relationships among these points are formalized through the use of the sigla *less than* (<) for temporal precedence and *comma* (,) for simultaneity, as shown in table 1.5. Reichenbach's system has superficial similarities to both Madvig's schema

---

10. Aristotle (*Phys.* 4.13, 222a10–33, trans. Hardie and Gaye) already realized problems with a strict understanding of the present as the boundary between the past and future and therefore distinguished between the present 'now' and an extended use of 'now', which Binnick (1991: 4) terms "proper 'now' " and "derivative 'now'." Jespersen (1924: 258) also recognized that *now* can be of an appreciable duration; however, his model does not reflect this fact.

**Table 1.5. Reichenbach's List of Possible Tenses,
with English Examples**
(adapted from Reichenbach 1947: 297; see Declerck 1986: 307)

Structure	New Name	Traditional Name	English Example
E < R < S	anterior past	past perfect	'I had done it'
E, R < S	simple past	simple past	'I did it'
R < E < S			
R < S, E	posterior past	—	'(She did not think) I would do it'[a]
R < S < E			
E < S, R	anterior present	present perfect	'I have done it'
S, R, E	simple present	present	'I do it'
S, R < E	posterior present	simple future	'I shall do it'
S < E < R			
S, E < R	anterior future	future perfect	'I shall have done it'
E < S < R			
S < R, E	simple future	simple future	'I shall do it'
S < R < E	posterior future	—	'I shall be going to do it'[b]

a. Reichenbach (1947: 298) notes that the English conditional, although it expresses posterior past, is usually classified as a mood, not as a tense.

b. Reichenbach (1947: 297) suggests the example *I shall be going to see him* as posterior future, which speaks "not directly of the event E, but of the act of preparation for it." However, out of context it is unclear whether *be going (to)* is the main verb or the future auxiliary (see Hopper and Traugott 2003: 1–3). The combination of the English future auxiliaries *will/shall* and *be going to* is grammatical, though uncommon (e.g., *Please be here right at 3 o'clock, because I shall be going to the airport at that time*). Reichenbach (1947: 297) notes that languages such as Latin have a more direct expression of the posterior future in their first periphrastic conjugation, constructed of the Future Participle plus the Future of the verb *to be*: *abiturus ero* 'I will be one of those who will leave'. See also Allen and Greenough (1903: 107), *amaturus ero* 'I will be about to love'.

of intersecting times (i.e., both feature nine tense categories, equally divisible into past, present, and future species) and Jespersen's linear model (i.e., Reichenbach also conceives of time linearly). What particularly distinguishes Reichenbach's theory from Jespersen's is that it does not locate events on the time line absolutely with respect to the present time of speaking but always relatively, mediated by the point of reference time R. This is reflected in Reichenbach's (1947: 297) suggested tense names (second column in table 1.5, above), in which "past," "present," and "future" refer to the temporal placement of R relative to S, and "anterior," "simple," and "posterior" refer to the temporal placement of E relative to R. No direct relationship between E and S is entertained by Reichenbach's model. Hence, multiple orderings in which only the temporal relationship of S and E are in question are irrelevant (e.g., posterior past and anterior future): "Further differences of form result only when the position of the event relative to the point of speech is considered; this position, however, is usually irrelevant" (Reichenbach 1947: 296).

Despite the redundancy of multiple orderings of S and E and the fact that, like Madvig, future tense occurs twice in Reichenbach's system, the explanatory power of his theory is impressive. This can be appreciated best by examining its handling of subordinate clauses, the issue on which Jespersen's theory foundered (see quotation from Binnick 1991: 61–62 in §1.2.1 above). Reichenbach (1947: 293) claimed that tense-shifting in subordinate clauses could be explained with his R-point theory in terms of the principle of "the permanence of the reference point," instead of having recourse to a complicated and often violated sequence of tense rules: "We can interpret these [sequence of tense] rules as the principle that, although the events referred to in the clauses may occupy different time points, the reference point should be the same for all clauses—a principle which, we shall say, demands the *permanence of the reference point.*"[11] This principle may be illustrated by the analyses in [1.2] (based on Reichenbach 1947: 293), in which the "permanence" of the reference points is indicated by the vertical alignment of R (the time of speaking, S, also remains permenantly positioned).

[1.2] a. ₁[And when she <u>had tired</u> herself out with trying], ₂[the poor little thing <u>sat down</u>] ₃[and <u>cried</u>]. (Carroll 2000: 24–25)

first clause: $E_1 < R_1$ $< S$ (anterior past)

second clause: $R_2, E_2 < S$ (simple past)

third clause: $R_3, E_3 < S$ (simple past)

b. ₁[I <u>have</u> not <u>decided</u> ₂[which train I <u>shall take</u>]]. (Reichenbach 1947: 293)

first clause: $E_1 < S, R_1$ (anterior present)

second clause: $S, R_2 < E_2$ (posterior present)

c. ₁[She <u>felt</u> sure ₂[she <u>would catch</u> a bad cold]]. (Carroll 2000: 34)

first clause: $R_1, E_1 < S$

second clause: $R_2 < E_2 < S$

Unfortunately, the validity of this principle of the permanence of the reference point has been questioned. Allen (1966: 166–67) argued, "It is not true that the reference point remains permanent throughout; rather, each E . . . serves as the reference point for the E on the next lower level. This is probably a more

---

11. *Sequence of Tense* rules were developed by Roman grammarians and have been commonplace in grammars on Classical and Indo-European languages even into the twentieth century. The Sequence of Tense rules attempt to explain the choice of tense in subordinate sentences based on the tense in the main sentence (e.g., a primary tense follows a primary tense and a secondary tense follows a secondary tense). There are, however, many exceptions to these rules (see Binnick 1991: 86–93).

generally followed principle than Reichenbach's principle of the permanence of the reference point." In Allen's example, given in [1.3], the hypothetical event *she wouldn't eat it* (third clause) is located after the event (E_2) of her promising (second clause), not after the reference point (R_2).

[1.3] $_1$[I <u>had</u> it wrapped in tissue paper $_2$[because she <u>had promised</u> me $_3$[that she <u>wouldn't eat</u> it $_4$[till we <u>got</u> home]]]]. (Allen 1966: 166)

first clause:	R_1, E_1	< S
second clause:	E_2 < R_2	< S
third clause:	R_3	< E_3 < S
fourth clause:	$R_4, E_4 < S$	

Furthermore, Prior (1967: 13) pointed out that complex sentences such as *I shall have been going to see the queen* appear to require more than one reference point. And if this is the case, observes Prior, then "it becomes unnecessary and misleading to make such a sharp distinction between the point or points of reference and the point of speech; the point of speech is just the *first* point of reference. . . . This makes pastness and futurity *always* relative to *some* point of reference—maybe the first one . . . or maybe some other." These criticisms of Reichenbach's R-point theory raise key issues such as how exactly to define the point of reference, particularly with respect to S and E, and whether multiple reference points are required to account fully for tense. These issues as well as the redundancies of Reichenbach's theory have been the focus of subsequent tense theories.

1.2.3. Revisions of Reichenbach's R-Point Theory

Although numerous tense theories have adopted, adapted, or otherwise included elements of Reichenbach's theory, I focus here on four studies that take Reichenbach's theory as their starting point and have made significant and/ or influential contributions to relative-tense discussions. My interest is particularly with how they have addressed the three concerns regarding Reichenbach's theory mentioned above (§1.2.2): the redundancies of Reichenbach's orderings of S, E, and R; the question whether multiple reference points are required to account for certain tenses; and the question how to define the point of reference (the R-point).

1.2.3.1. Hornstein: Reducing R-Point Redundancies

Hornstein's work (1990) recasts Reichenbach's tense theory within a government and binding framework (see Chomsky 1981). However, what is most germane to the present study is his solution to the redundancies of S, E, and R orderings in Reichenbach's list of tenses. Hornstein's approach to the problem of redundancies begins with demonstrating that there are many more order-

**Table 1.6. Hornstein's List of Temporal Orderings of E, R, and S
for Reichenbach's Tenses**

(adapted from 1990: 87–88; Reichenbach's names are given in brackets
for comparison with table 1.5, p. 8)

past perfect [anterior past]	E < R < S
past [simple past]	E, R < S R, E < S
future in past [posterior past]	R < S, E R < E, S R < S < E R < E < S
present perfect [anterior present]	E < S, R E < R, S
present [simple present]	S, R, E S, E, R R, S, E R, E, S E, S, R E, R, S
proximate future [posterior present]	S, R < E R, S < E
future perfect [anterior future]	S < E < R S, E < R E < S < R E, S < R
future [simple future]	S < R, E S < E, R
distant future [posterior future]	S < R < E

ing redundancies than Reichenbach's presentation admits—in all, there are
24 possible orderings for Reichenbach's 9 tenses (versus Reichenbach's 13
orderings), as shown in table 1.6.

Hornstein (1990: 89) applied two principles to pare down this list. The
first is the distinction between intrinsic and extrinsic ordering: E, R, and S
are intrinsically ordered only if their linear order is reflected in their temporal
interpretation; otherwise, they are extrinsically ordered. [12] For instance, in the
simple past formula (E, R < S or R, E < S) the order of E and R is extrinsic,
whereas the order of E and R with S is intrinsic since the temporal priority of
R to S is reflected in the temporal interpretation. Wherever the order of R, E,
or S is extrinsic, ordering differences may be ignored. The second principle
Hornstein (1990: 108) used is compositionality: the relationship between R, E,
and S is compositional—that is, it is composed of an R-E relationship and an
S-R relationship (see Reichenbach 1947: 297). Thus, for instance, the ordering
of points for present tense (E, R, S) should not be interpreted as E relative R
relative S, but as composed (○) of (E relative R) ○ (S relative R).

By applying these two principles (as well as rejecting Reichenbach's posterior future category), Hornstein reduced the possible orderings from 24 to
the 11 listed in table 1.7. Hornstein still allowed for alternative extrinsic orderings for the present tenses (marked i and ii), though he theorized that only
one order will be used in any given language (however, it is unclear how the
difference between these alternative extrinsic orderings could be realized in

---

12. The concept of *intrinsic* and *extrinsic* ordering appears in discussions about the ordering of rules in generative rule-based syntactic and phonological theories: two rules are
intrinsically ordered when some formal or logical property demands that they be ordered in
a certain sequence (e.g., if the output of rule A provides the necessary input of rule B, they
must be intrinsically ordered A-B); two items are extrinsically ordered if there is no formal
or logical constraint on their ordering, but they must simply be sequenced in some order for
the purpose of carrying out the transformation (see Crystal 2008: 183, 253).

Table 1.7. Hornstein's List of Possible Tenses
(adapted from 1990: 118–19; Reichenbach's names are
given in brackets for comparison with table 1.5, p. 8)

| past perfect [anterior past]
past [simple past]
future-in-the-past [posterior past]
present perfect [anterior present]

present [simple present]

proximate future [posterior present]

future perfect [anterior future]
future [simple future] | $(R < S) \circ (R < E) = E < R < S$
$(R < S) \circ (E, R) = E, R < S$
$(R < S) \circ (R < E)$
$(S, R) \circ (E < R) = E < S, R$ (i)
$(R, S) \circ (E < R) = E < R, S$ (ii)
$(S, R) \circ (R, E) = S, R, E$ (i)
$(R, S) \circ (E, R) = E, R, S$ (ii)
$(S, R) \circ (R < E) = S, R < E$ (i)
$(R, S) \circ (R < E) = R, S < E$ (ii)
$(S < R) \circ (E < R)$
$(S < R) \circ (R, E) = S < R, E$ |

a language, since, by definition, these ordering differences do not affect the temporal interpretation).

The importance of Hornstein's solution to the redundancies of Reichenbach's system are two: first, the distinction between extrinsic and intrinsic ordering provides a more justified dismissal of ordering redundancies than Reichenbach's comment (1947: 296) that they are simply "irrelevant"; second, his potrayal of the orderings as compositional highlights the fact that S and E are never directly related temporally in Reichenbach's R-point theory (see Reichenbach 1947: 297).

1.2.3.2. Bull: Multiple R-Points

Bull's tense theory (1960) contributed to the developing R-point theory in two significant ways. First, by distinguishing between "personal (the subjective division of) time" and "public (the objective division of) time," Bull offered a definition of the reference point as the position from which a person "views" a situation in personal time; in other words, the reference point is the speaker's viewpoint. Second, Bull treated S, which he labeled "point present (PP)," as the first of a possibly infinite number of reference points, each of which establishes a new "axis of orientation" on which E is located before, simultaneous with, or after the reference point (note Prior's subsequent criticism of Reichenbach on precisely this issue, §1.2.2, above).[13]

In Bull's graphic representation of his theory, reproduced in fig. 1.2, S creates a "point present" axis (PP), which may be related via subsequent reference

---

13. Bull (1960: 23) notes that, although theoretically, languages may use an infinite number of R-points, most languages will require only four at the most. Comrie (1985: 122 n. 1), who criticizes Bull's schema for allowing only two reference points, appears to have overlooked this statement.

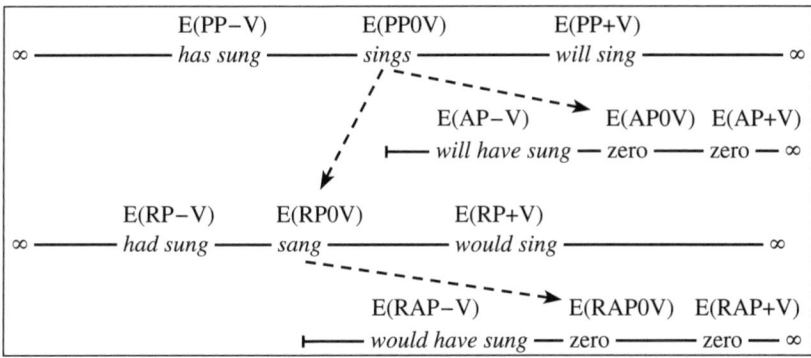

Figure 1.2. Bull's model of universal tense categories (adapted from Bull 1960: 31).

points to an "anticipatory point" axis (AP), a "retrospective point" axis (RP), and a "retrospective-anticipatory point" axis (RAP). The relationship between E and R on each axis is expressed by "minus vector $(-V)$" for E < R, "zero vector $(0V)$" for E, R, or "plus vector $(+V)$" for R < E.

Because Bull's theory allows for multiple reference points, his theory has more explanatory power than Reichenbach's. This is illustrated by the English Perfect Conditional tense example *would have sung* in fig. 1.2, which lies along the retrospective-anticipatory axis (RAP). Its relationship to S (= PP "point present") is mediated by two reference points (represented by the arrows between axes).

At the same time, Bull's allowance of multiple reference points makes his theory too powerful, allowing for tense categories that are unrealized (marked "zero" in fig. 1.2). As Binnick (1991: 118) observes, "Bull's system . . . fails to adequately capture the notion of possible tense, because no distinction is built into the theory between slots which *happen not* to be filled and those which *in principle cannot* be." For instance, McCoard (1978: 95) pointed out that there is no reason why Bull's theory could not include an "anticipatory-retrospective point" axis; it just happens not to have one. In addition, despite the advantages of multiple temporal axes, "Bull's tactic of separating all the axes one from the other . . . brings with it a certain artificiality of its own" (McCoard 1978: 95–96). In other words, how are the axes and their respective reference points related to each other in time and in the speaker's mind?

1.2.3.3. Comrie: A Compromise R-Point Theory

Comrie's tense model (1985: 122 n. 1) has connections with Jespersen's, Reichenbach's, and Bull's. His central innovation is his categorization of the tenses as absolute, relative, or absolute-relative tense, as illustrated in table 1.8.

Table 1.8. Comrie's Taxonomy of Tenses with His English Examples
(1994: 4559–61)

Absolute tense		
past	E < S	*John ate an apple.*
present	E, S	*John is eating an apple.*
future	S < E	*John will eat an apple.*
Relative tense		
relative past	E < R	*Those having sung were asked to leave the stage.*
relative present	E, R	*Those singing were told to be quiet.*
relative future	R < E	*Those about to sing were asked to go onto the stage.*

(In all three above examples, R is contextually [*were asked/told*] located before S: *R < S*.)

Absolute-relative tense		
pluperfect	E < R < S	*Mary had left by six o'clock.*
future perfect	S < E < R	*Mary will have left by six o'clock.*
future in the future	S < R < E	*At six o'clock Mary will be about to leave.*
future in the past	R < E < S	*Mary left at six o'clock. She would return an hour later.*
(= conditional)		
future perfect in the past	$R_2 < E < R_1 < S$	*Mary left home at eight o'clock; she would return an*
(= perfect conditional)		*hour later, by which time her son would have left for*
		school.

Comrie defined *absolute tenses* as the tenses that "use the present moment [S] as their reference point [R]" (1985: 36; see 1994: 4559). *Relative tense* includes a reference point (R) that is contextually determined, often by an absolute tense in an adjacent clause (1985: 56; see 1994: 4560), as illustrated in table 1.8 above. Finally, "absolute-relative tense" possesses the combined temporal denotation of an absolute and a relative tense: "[A] situation is located in time relative to some contextually given reference point, while this reference point is in turn located relative to the present moment, *all of this being done by means of a single tense*" (1994: 4561, italics added; see 1985: 65).

Reminiscent of Jespersen, Comrie's taxonomy conspicuously lacks the present perfect, which he claimed (Comrie 1976: 52) differs not temporally but aspectually from the simple past: "The perfect indicates the continuing present relevance of a past situation." He explains:

> In terms of location in time, however, the perfect is not distinct from the past. The past tense locates an event in time prior to the present moment. If one were to provide an analysis of the perfect analogous to that of the pluperfect and the future perfect, then one would say that the reference point for the perfect is simultaneous with the present moment, rather than being before the present moment (as for the pluperfect) or after the present moment (as for the future perfect). The situation in question would then be located in time prior to this reference point. In terms of location in time, however, this would give precisely

the same result as the past, which also locates a situation as prior to the present moment. Thus, however perfect differs from past, it is not in terms of time location. (Comrie 1985: 78)

Comrie's theory is effectively a reply to Prior's criticism (1967: 13) that Reichenbach's theory "is at once too simple and too complicated": on the one hand, it allows for multiple reference points; on the other hand, it eliminates the reference point whenever it is coterminus with the speech time. However, Reichenbach's claim (1947: 294) that temporal adverbs do not directly modify events, but their reference times, demands that even simple tenses include a reference point for the mapping of such modifiers. Revising this claim of Reichenbach's, Hornstein (1977: 524; 1990: 32) argued that the upward limit of *two sites* for temporal modifiers is evidence that modifiers may be mapped onto both R *and* E, and that, therefore, a reference point (R) is required even for simple tenses (see also Heinrichs 1986). His argument is illustrated by the sentences in example [1.4][14] (adapted from Hornstein 1977: 524–25).

[1.4] ?A week ago, John, yesterday, left for Paris at six o'clock.
A week ago yesterday John left for Paris at six o'clock.

$$E, R < S$$
$$\updownarrow \quad \updownarrow$$

a week ago   at 6 o'clock
yesterday

1.2.3.4. Declerck: A Bifurcated R-Point

Declerck's (1986: 320) relative-tense theory takes Reichenbach and Comrie as its starting point and focuses particularly on the nebulous reference point: "What is striking in Reichenbach (1947), Comrie (1985), and most other treatments of tense is that this notion [of the reference point] never receives an adequate technical definition." Declerck's theory not only corroborates Reichenbach's argument that a reference point is present for all tenses (so also Hornstein; see example [1.4]) but clarifies that multiple reference points are necessary, and that these reference points may serve dual roles. Declerk's theory effectively makes explicit ideas about the reference point that are already implicit in Bull's model (see §1.2.3.2).

According to Declerck (1986: 320), the reference point, of which multiple instantiations may occur, has a dual role: it constitutes the "time of orientation (R_{TO})," from which viewpoint another time, the "time referred to (R_{TR})," is temporally fixed as before (past), simultaneous with (present), or after. This dual role may be illustrated using example [1.5] (based on Declerck 1986: 323).

---

14. A question mark (?) placed at the beginning of a sentence indicates a grammatically awkward or questionable construction (see also the list of symbols in the front matter).

[1.5] [$_{E1}$Jared arrived at five o'clock] [$_{E2}$after the others had left at four.]

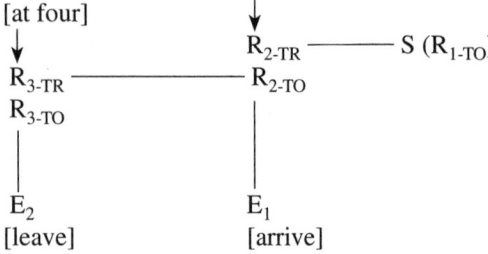

In this example, there are three reference points: R_1 is the speech time S, which serves as the time of orientation ($R_{1\text{-}TO}$) for R_2, which it locates or refers to as before S ($R_{2\text{-}TR}$; also temporally modified by the adverbial phrase *at five o'clock*); at the same time, R_2 serves as the time of orientation($R_{2\text{-}TO}$), locating E_1 [arrive] simultaneous with it, and R_3 before it ($R_{3\text{-}TR}$; like R_2, also modified by an adverbial phrase, *at four*); finally, R_3 serves as the time of orientation ($R_{3\text{-}TO}$), locating E_2 [leave] simultaneous with it (Declerck 1986: 323).

Declerck's understanding of the reference point presents another approach to explaining the compositional nature of tense (cf. Hornstein's theory, §1.2.3.1), a conception that is implicit even in Reichenbach's R-point theory (1947: 297): S and E are never directly temporally related to each other; rather, R (as an R_{TR}) is temporally fixed with respect to S, and R (as an R_{TO}) temporally fixes E (see table 1.7, p. 12). At the same time, Declerck's theory formalizes what is grapically implicit in Bull's model (see fig. 1.2, p. 13)—namely, that the speech time (S; Bull's PP) is simply the first R (so also Prior 1967: 13, quoted in §1.2.2. above), which serves as the point of view (i.e., an R_{TO}) from which another reference time is temporally fixed (i.e., an R_{TR}); this latter reference point may then serve as a new point of view (i.e., a new R_{TO}; Bull's 0V on a new axis) from which to fix yet another temporal point.

Consistently fixing E temporally from the vantage point of an R_{TO} removes logical inconsistencies of an absolute-tense treatment such as Comrie's, in which R is eliminated when it is coterminus with S. For example, an absolute-tense analysis of *Tage was home* locates the event of [be home] as before the speech time (i.e., E < S); however, this analysis is invalidated should Tage remain at home beyond the time of speech. Alternatively, tense in *Tage was home*, analyzed according to Declerck's theory, locates the event [be home] as simultaneous with a temporal viewpoint (i.e., an R_{TO}), which is fixed via an R_{TR} as prior (past) to the speech time S (the first R_{TO}). Hence, the state [Tage be home] may continue to hold past the time of speech without any logical inconsistency, since the event is only indirectly located with respect to the speech time.

Table 1.9. Declerck's Taxonomy of Tenses
(adapted from 1986: 362–63)

past perfect	$E, R_1 < R_2 \ll S$
past tense	$E, R \ll S$
conditional	$R_2 < E, R_1 \ll S$
conditional perfect	$R_3 < E, R_1 < R_2 \ll S$
present perfect	$E, R \leq S$
present tense	E, R, S
future tense	$S < E, R$
future perfect	$S < E, R_1 < R_2$
past perfect	$E, R \ll S$
past tense	$E, R_1 < R_2 \ll S$
conditional	$R_2 < E, R_1 \ll S$
conditional perfect	$R_3 < E, R_1 < R_2 \ll S$
present perfect	$E, R \leq S$
present tense	E, R, S
future tense	$S < E, R$
future perfect	$S < E, R_1 < R_2$

A final innovation of Declerck's theory is his refinement of the temporal relationships "simultaneous with" and "before" that may hold among S, E, and R. "Simultaneous with" may designate three types of temporal relationships:

'T. S. simul T. O.' [= E, R] means that the two times coincide in one of the following ways: (a) both occupy the same point of the time line (as in *At that moment a shot was fired*), (b) both occupy (roughly) the same section of the time line (as in *I was in London yesterday*), or (c) the section occupied by T. S. [= E] is part of the section occupied by T. O. [= R] (as in *I left yesterday*) or vice versa (as in *I was home at 4 o'clock*). In the latter case T. S. [= E] extends beyond T. O. [= R] and there is nothing to prevent it from extending to the present or into the future. (Declerck 1986: 326)

Similarly, "before" can have two distinct temporal meanings: it may signify that one time is "wholly before" another or "before and up to" another time (Declerck 1986: 362). According to Declerck, this distinction between two senses of "before" corresponds to the distinction between past tense and present perfect, respectively. According to Declerck (1986: 350), contra Comrie (see §1.2.3.3), the past and present perfect can be differentiated in terms of tense. Declerck's taxonomy of tenses in table 1.9 (translated into Reichenbach's sigla) indicates a threefold distinction for "before": for wholly before ($\ll$), for before and up to ($\leq$), and before ($<$), which is ambiguous with respect to the former two interpretations.

1.2.4. Summary: The R-Point and Tense Theory

The relative-tense theories of Hornstein, Bull, Comrie, and Declerck have all contributed to the refinement of Reichenbach's R-point theory in important ways. First, all four theories have demonstrated that multiple reference points are required for the interpretation of certain tenses. Second, Hornstein and Declerck refined the temporal relationships among S, E, and R to eliminate redundancies in Reichenbach's theory, whereas Comrie's theory represents a significant departure from Reichenbach by eliminating R in tenses where it does not contribute to the temporal interpretation (i.e., where it is coterminus with S or E).

Third, the theories of Hornstein, Bull, and Declerck explore and thus revise Reichenbach's concept of the reference point. Among their findings, the most important are the following: R always mediates the relationship between E and S; R serves as a temporal viewpoint from which E is temporally evaluated (i.e., located); and S is merely the first of a series of Rs, each of which serves as the temporal viewpoint for the evaluation (i.e., location) of any subsequent R. These ideas not only inform subsequent relative-tense theories but are adapted with significant results by the tense-aspect theories surveyed below (§1.4).

1.3. A Primer on Aspect

An adequate understanding of verbal aspect is hampered by the convoluted course of its discussion in Western grammar.[15] Although aspect was recognized in classical grammar (e.g., the Stoic-Varronian model of Latin, table 1.2), the introduction of Slavic aspect into linguistic disucssion in the nineteenth century, in terms of a morphologically marked opposition between perfective and imperfective, caused confusion. Binnick (1991: 140) claims that the concept was not well established in linguistic discussion until the work of Jakobson (see Jakobson 1932), and in 1940 Goedsche (1940: 189) observed that "in spite of a great amoung of research, a wide divergence of opinion prevails today regarding the character of aspect and regarding the fundamental principles to be pursued in that study."

This confusion has stemmed in part from the fact that several distinct, though related phenomena are regularly referred to by the term *aspect* and are often not sufficiently differentiated from each other. In turn, the terminology employed in aspectual discussions varies widely, and terms such as *Aktionsart* and *Aspekt* have been inconsistently applied (see Bache 1982; Binnick 1991: 135–49).[16] This problem of nomenclature is compounded by the fact

---

15. According to Binnick (1991: 135–36), the term *aspect* entered Western European linguistics in the early part of the nineteenth century but only became part of the "linguistic tradition" at the end of that century; the *Oxford English Dictionary* (2nd ed., s.v. "aspect") dates the entrance of the term into English to 1853.

16. Bache (1982) criticizes Lyons (1977) and Comrie (1976) for collapsing the categories *Aspekt* and *Aktionsart*.

Table 1.10. Comparison of Aspect Labels

My Labels[a]	*Bache (1995)*	*Dahl (1994)*	*Olsen (1997)*	*Smith (1997)*	*Binnick (1991)*
Situation	} Action	Lexical	Lexical	} Situation	Aristotelian aspect
Phasal		Derivational	} Grammatical		*Aktionsart*
Viewpoint	Aspect	Grammatical		Viewpoint	Aspect

a. These terms are also employed by Michaelis (1997).

that *aspect* has been analyzed variously in terms of lexical, grammatical (morphological or syntactic), and semantic distinctions (Binnick 1991: 144). These inconsistencies and divergences are still evident in recent linguistic works on aspect, as illustrated in table 1.10. *Situation aspect*, *phasal aspect*, and *viewpoint aspect* are introduced in turn below.

1.3.1. Situation Aspect

Situation aspect describes differences in the temporal structure of events. The recognition of structural differences among events goes back to Aristotle's observations in *Metaphysics*:

> Of these processes, then, we must call the one set movements [κίνησις], and the other actualities [ἐνέργεια]. For every movement is incomplete—making thin, learning, walking, building; these are movements, and incomplete at that. For it is not true that at the same time a thing is walking and has walked, or is building and has built, or is coming to be and has come to be, or is being moved and has been moved, but what is being moved is different from what has been moved, and what is moving from what has moved. But it is the same thing that at the same time has seen and is seeing, or is thinking and has thought. The latter sort of process, then, I call an actuality and the former a movement. (*Metaph.* 9.6, 1048b27–34, trans. Ross)[17]

The Aristotelian distinction between κίνησις and ἐνέργεια served as the starting point for modern philosophical discussions of event structure (Ryle 1949; Vendler 1957; 1967; Kenny 1963). The most influential of these discussions are those by Vendler, in which he made a four-way distinction among states, activities, achievements, and accomplishments, as shown in table 1.11.[18]

17. In *Nichomachean Ethics* (6.4.1140a1–24, trans. Ross), Aristotle appears to treat πρᾶξις 'doing' and ποίησις 'making' as synonyms of ἐνέργεια 'acting' and κίνησις 'motion', respectively, as defined in the above quotation from *Metaphysics*. In addition, Aristotle distinguishes ἔχειν 'to have' (= state) and ἐνεργεῖν 'to act' (= activity) in *De Anima* 2.5, 417a30–417b2, trans. Smith (see Binnick 1991: 172).

18. Dowty (1979: 51) refers to this model of situation types as the Aristotle-Ryle-Kenny-Vendler model. Ryle (1949: 149–53) made the important contribution of distinguishing between accomplishments and achievements, though Kenny (1963: 171–86) ignored Ryle's distinction, returning to Aristotle's three-way, referring to the category accomplishment/ achievement as "performances."

Table 1.11. Vendler's Aspectual Categories with English Examples
(adapted from 1967: 97)

States	Activities	Accomplishments	Achievements
desire	run	run a mile	recognize
want	walk	walk to school	find
love	swim	paint a picture	win a race
hate	push a cart	grow up	stop/start/resume
know/believe	drive a car	recover from an illness	be born/die

The relationships among these situation aspects may be represented in a number of ways (see Binnick 1991: 179–83). Four types of schemata are strict hierarchy, partial ordering (i.e., tree diagram), hinge ordering, and cross-classification (i.e., feature chart), illustrated in parts a–d of fig. 1.3, respectively.

Besides the formal variety exhibited by these representative schemata, they illustrate the various ways in which the relationships among the situation aspects may be conceived. For instance, Hatav's hierarchy in fig. 1.3a groups states and activities together as "distributive" situations, and accomplishments and achievements as "events," a distinction that is analogous to Aristotle's ἐνέργεια and κίνησις in *Metaphysics* (see quotation above). By contrast, Mourelatos's tree-diagram in fig. 1.3b distinguishes states from the other situation aspects, and then activites from accomplishments and achievements, relating the latter two in a way that combines Kenny's and Vendler's models (Verkuyl 1993: 50; see n. 18 on Kenny's taxonomy). Verkuyl's model in fig. 1.3c is tripartite, treating accomplishments and achievements together as "events," based on the parameters of dynamicity (defined in terms of progression [±ADD TO]) and telicity (defined in terms of whether the NP contains a specified quantity [±SQA]).[19]

Among the schemata illustrated here, perhaps C. S. Smith's feature chart in fig. 1.3d best captures the complexity of the relationships among the different situation aspects. It singles out states with the feature [+static], paralleling Mourelatos's tree diagram (fig. 1.3b); but it also makes a distinction between states and activities, on the one hand, and accomplishments and achievements, on the other, with the feature [±telicity], thus capturing the hierarchical division in Hatav's model (fig. 1.3a). However, Smith's feature chart lacks linguistic elegance, insofar as it allows for feature combinations that are not realized by any situation aspects (e.g., [+static, +durative, +telic]; see Rothstein's [2004:

---

19. Chung and Timberlake (1985: 214–18) similarly treat both accomplishments and achievements as "telic process[es]," in contrast to activities, which are "atelic process[es]"; both types of processes are distinguished from states with the feature dynamicity. In Timberlake's article (2007: 284–85) in the new edition, he employs the alternate term "liminal" to classify accomplishments ("liminal processes") and achievements ("liminal states").

a. Strict Hierarchy (adapted from Hatav 1997: 43)

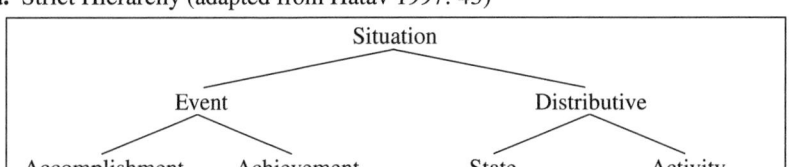

b. Partial Ordering (Tree Diagram) (adapted from Mourelatos 1981: 201; cf. Bach 1986: 6)

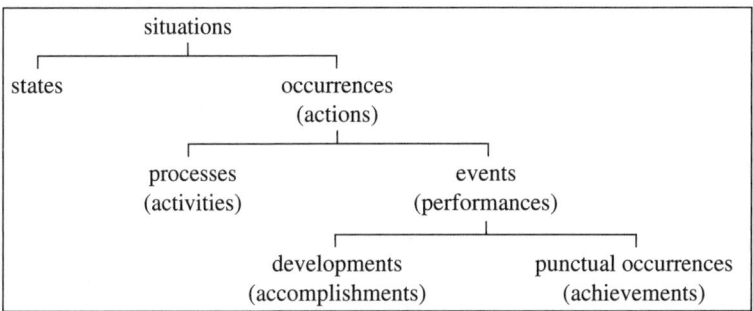

c. Hinge Ordering (adapted from Verkuyl 1993: 19)

NP	[–SQA]		[+SQA]
	STATE	PROCESS	EVENT
	state of change	state of change	change of state
V	[–ADD TO]		[+ADD TO]

d. Cross-Classification (Feature Chart) (adapted from C. S. Smith 1997: 20; cf. Olsen 1997: 51, table 1.16)[a]

Situations	Static	Durative	Telic	Examples
State	+	+	–	*know, be have*
Activity	–	+	–	*run, paint, sing*
Accomplishment	–	+	+	*destroy, create*
Achievement	–	–	+	*notice, win*
Semelfactive	–	–	–	*wink, tap, cough*

a. See also the feature chart based on the discussion of Van Valin and LaPolla (1997: 93) in Butler (2003: 353). Particularly noteworthy is Dik's feature chart (1997: 115) in that it presents a partial ordering relationship within a feature chart format: [±dynamic] distinguishes between situations and events; [±control] (i.e., whether the agent is in control of the situation) distinguishes between states and position as subcategories of situation, and process and action as subcategories of event; [±telic] distinguishes between dynamism and change as subcategories of process, and activity and accomplishment as subcategories of action. For a comparative discussion of situation analyses in functional grammar, see Butler 2003: 337–448.

Figure 1.3a–d. Varieties of models of situational types.

Table 1.12. Rothstein's Feature Chart for Situation Aspect
(adapted from 2004: 12)

Situation Aspect	[±Stages]	[±Telic]
State	−	−
Activity	+	−
Accomplishment	+	+
Achievement	−	+

28–29] remarks).[20] The four situation aspects can instead be adequately differentiated on the basis of just two features, as Rothstein's feature chart in table 1.12 demonstrates.[21]

Rothstein's chart distinguishes accomplishments and achievements from states and activities with the feature [+telic], just as in Smith's chart (fig. 1.3d): *telic* events are characterized by an inherent endpoint (Depraetere 1995: 2–3). The concept *stages* has been used to explain dynamicity (see Smith 1997: 19; Olsen 1997: 35; Verkuyl 1993: 15); however, in Rothstein's chart, the feature [+stages] distinguishes activities and accomplishments from both states and achievements, in contrast to Smith's chart, in which the feature [+static] (= [−dynamic]) distinguishes states from the other three situation aspects (see fig. 1.3d). In Smith's approach, a third feature, [+durative], is needed to differentiate accomplishments from achievements, which unfortunately leads to unrealized feature combinations. Rothstein (2004: 12) classifies both states and achievements as [−stages] because they lack a sense of progression, though for different reasons: states, "because they are inherently non-dynamic," and achievements, "because they are near instantaneous."

Linguists have employed various linguistic "tests" to demonstrate the semantic differences among situation aspects, such as incompatibilities, entailments, and (dis)allowed temporal modifications (see Dowty 1979: 51–71; Binnick 1991: 173–78; Verkuyl 1993: 33–68; C. S. Smith 1997: 39–48; Rothstein 2004: 14–28). For example, stative situations do not generally occur in progressive constructions, as illustrated in example [1.6].

---

20. The same criticism applies to Olsen's feature chart in table 1.16 (see p. 35 below), despite the fact that both Smith and Olsen recognize more situation aspects than Vendler's four (see discussion below this section).

21. Though termed differently, these features are comparable to Verkuyl's [±SQA] and [±ADD TO] (see fig. 1.3c). However, Verkuyl's model lacks elegance (similarly to Smith's and Olsen's) in that Verkuyl distinguishes only three situation types with these two features, while up to four types can be distinguished with the two (there is no realization of [+SQA, −ADD TO] in Verkuyl's model, which would correspond with Rothstein's definition of achievement).

[1.6] a. ?Jared is knowing the answer (STA).
      b. Colin is walking (ACT).
      c. Tage is building a house (ACC).
      d. Evan is winning the race (ACH).

This stative-progressive incompatibility is explained on the basis that states do not "progress" ([−stages]) and hence cannot be portrayed in the progressive. Although achievements likewise lack progression or stages according to Rothstein, they nevertheless can occur in the progressive, as shown in [1.6d]. However, since achievements are instantaneous, the progressive does not express stages of the event itself but the time leading *up to* the event. The question *How long?* applied to an accomplishment predicate, as in [1.7a], can be interpreted as referring to the time before the event or (more naturally) to the duration of the event itself, as shown by [1.7b]; by contrast, *How long?* asked of an achievement predicate, as in [1.7c], can only be interpreted as referring to the time before the achievement, as the paraphrase of [1.7c] in [1.7d] illustrates (see Rothstein 2004: 23).

[1.7] a. How long did it take Jared to read *The Lord of the Rings* (ACC)?
      b. How long did it take before Jared read/for Jared to read *The Lord of the Rings* (ACC)?
      c. How long did it take Evan to win the race (ACH)?
      d. How long before Evan won the race (ACH)?

The progressive (or imperfective) may also be used to distinguish between telic and atelic situation aspects through entailment (known as the imperfective paradox): activites [−telic] in the progressive (or imperfective) entail their perfect or perfective counterpart, whereas accomplishments and achievements, both [+telic], do not have this entailment, as shown by [1.8].

[1.8] a. Colin is walking ENTAILS Colin has walked/walked (ACT).
      b. Tage is building a house DOES NOT ENTAIL Tage has built/built a house (ACC).
      d. Evan is winning the race DOES NOT ENTAIL Evan has won/won the race (ACH).

Other situation aspects besides the four in Vendler's taxonomy have been identified by linguists, but the status of these other situation aspects alongside the four basic ones is disputed. Smith includes *semelfactives* in her feature chart (C. S. Smith 1997: 20; fig. 1.3d, p. 21; see also Olsen 1997: 51; table 1.16, p. 35), defined as [−static, −durative, −telic]. Semelfactives are dynamic, instantaneous events with no natural endpoint, such as *knock* or *wink*; their instantaneous character is evident from their compatibility with *at a time* temporal expressions, as in *Kathy knocked on the door at 6 o'clock*.

However, Rothstein (2004: 28–29) has argued that the inclusion of se- melfactives in a feature chart is problematic because it would require a third feature, which in turn would demand eight situation aspects to account for all the possible feature combinations. Maintaining that the two features are adequate to account for the variety of situation types, Rothstein (2004: 29) instead proposes that semelfactives may be described as "miminal event types of activities" on the basis that "every semelfactive has a homynym which is an activity," as for example, *Kathy knocked/was knocking on the door for an hour* (ACT).

In addition to the four basic situation aspects and semelfactive, Olsen in- cluded stage-level states in her taxonomy (Olsen 1997: 51; table 1.16, p. 35). Stage-level states refer to properties that are transitory or "accidental," in con- trast to individual-level states (referred to simply as "states" in Olsen's chart), which portray "essential, permanent properties" of an entity (Fernald 2000: 4). For example, being happy (*Bill is happy*) is a transitory, stage-level property, compared with the individual-level situation of having brown hair (*Bill has brown hair*).

Unfortunately, there seems to be little justification for adding stage-level states to the list of situation aspects. First, the distinction between stage-level and predicate-level is distinct from the four basic situation aspects in that the distinction can be applied not just to states but to other predicates (see Kratzer 1995; Fernald 2000). Second, even with Olsen's six situation types, her three- feature model is still too powerful, allowing for unrealized feature combina- tions. Thus, it does not appear justified to expand the basic four situation types by the addition of either semelfactive or stage-level predicate as a distinct situation type.

A more important issue than possible expansions to the list of four situation types is the question of the syntactic level to which these classifications refer. For instance, a verb such as *build* can head a telic or an atelic VP (verb phrase), as illustrated in [1.9].

[1.9]   a. Tage built. (ACT)
        b. Tage built a house. (ACC)
        c. Tage built houses. (ACT)

Examples of this sort demonstrate that situation aspect might better be thought of as a property of VPs rather than verbal lexemes. However, in this case the principle of compositionality still requires an analysis of the verbal lexeme in terms of its semantic contribution to the VP. Olsen (1997) has suggested that the types of VPs a verb may head can be predicted through the distinction of semantic and implicature properties of VPs (see below, §1.4.3); a less rigid approach has been offered by Rothstein (2004: 33), who treats the aspectual categorization of verbal lexemes as providing constraints on the types of VPs they may head (see below, §1.7.3.1).

1.3.2. Phasal Aspect

Phasal aspects refer to alterations to one or another of the phases of development through which a situation progresses. Phasal aspect includes specifically defined types such as those given in [1.10].[22]

[1.10] a. Focus on initial phase:
        Inchoative: beginning of a state, e.g., *Tage became sick.*
        Inceptive: beginning of a non-state, e.g., *Colin began writing.*

      b. Focus on final phase:
        Cessative: end of a [−telic] event, e.g., *Colin stopped writing.*
        Completive: completion of a [+telic] event, e.g., *Colin finished writing his report.*

      c. Alteration of middle phase(s):
        Iterative: repetition of a minimal activity event, e.g., *Jared knocked for five minutes.*
        Habitual: regular pattern of repetition of an event, e.g., *Evan (always) walks to school.*
        Continuative: continuation of an event without a pause, e.g., *Jared continued knocking.*
        Resumptive: resumption of an event after a pause, e.g., *Colin resumed studying his lesson.*

Early treatments of phasal aspect, often termed *Aktionsarten* or *modes d'action*, varied widely due to the fact that some linguists approached these aspects in terms of morphology and/or syntax, while other linguists understood them in semantic terms (so Binnick 1991: 144). These alternative approaches stemmed from the object languages being studied. Thus, for example, Forsyth (1970: 29–30) was able to relate phasal aspects or "procedurals" to specific affixes in Russian that signify various nuances such as iterativity, inceptivity, durativity, terminativity, and so on (see also Binnick 1991: 145). However, because phasal aspect is "nongrammatical, optional, and unsystematic" (Binnick

---

22. Iterative is treated here as the repetition of a minimal activity event rather than the repetition of a semelfactive, following Rothstein's analysis (2004: 28–29), on which, see above (§1.3.1). For other taxonomies, see Binnick 1991: 202–7.

1991: 170), it is necessary to define the nuances semantically as metalinguistic categories.

The different approaches taken to phasal aspect appear to have contributed to the failure to distinguish consistently between phasal aspect and situation and/or viewpoint aspect in the literature. In addition, the status of phasal aspect as an independent category suffers from the fact that some phasal aspectual distinctions appear to be derivative, arising from certain semantic combinations. For example, Smith (1997: 49) observed that the natural inceptive interpretation of *They ate dinner at noon* (i.e., *They began to eat dinner at noon*) is derived from the combination of an accomplishment verb phrase [eat dinner] and a momentary adverbial [at noon]. Similarly, the iterative reading of *Jared was knocking* appears to arise from the combination of the minimal activity type (or semelfactive) situation [knock] and an imperfective viewpoint aspect (see C. S. Smith 1997: 50).

However, explanations of this sort cannot account for every type of expression listed above. In addition, certain phasal aspects may be combined with a variety of situation aspectual values (e.g., *Jared continued talking* [ACT], *Colin continued painting a picture* [ACC]) and viewpoint aspects (e.g., *Tage began to play* [≈PFV], *Evan was beginning to cry* [≈IPFV]). These interactions with the other types of aspect support the conclusion that phasal expressions comprise an independent aspectual type.

1.3.3. Viewpoint Aspect

Comrie's (1976: 3) definition of aspect is frequently cited with regard to viewpoint aspect: "Aspects are different ways of *viewing* the internal temporal constituency of a situation" (italics added; see also Bache 1985: 5–6). Viewpoint aspect, which has to do with viewpoints on events, thus contrasts in an important way with situation aspect, which has to do with the structure of events. The aspectual understanding that derives from the Stoic-Varronian theory of Latin has often led to confusion in this regard (see table 1.2, p. 3), since the usual understanding of completion is more easily associated with event location than viewpoints on events.[23] It is felicitous, then, that the Stoic-Varronian terminology of complete : incomplete has been displaced by perfective : imperfective, which is derived from Slavic grammar (*Oxford English Dictionary*, 2nd ed., s.v. "aspect").

The adoption of nomenclature from Slavic grammar is a reflection of the frequent view that Slavic is "the prototypical examplar of aspectual systems," with perfective and imperfective being obligatorily marked categories of the verb (Binnick 1991: 136). This terminological dependence on Slavic has in turn led to concerns about whether the categories of perfective and imper-

---

23. The difference is reflected in the aspectual and relative-tense interpretation of the Stoic model of the verb (see p. 18 n. 16).

fective are indeed applicable to non-Slavic languages (Jespersen 1924: 287). However, Bache (1982: 58) has pointed out that the presence of these categories in Slavic alone requires that perfective and imperfective aspect be defined as metalinguistic categories; it is these metalinguistic categories that linguists have found applicable to a wide array of the world's languages.[24]

It is helpful to explain such an abstract notion as viewpoint aspect with metaphor. The metaphor of the focal length of camera lenses is particularly appropriate for viewpoint aspect.[25] The imperfective is comparable with the view through a high focal-length lens (i.e., a telephoto lens), which gives a close-up view of the subject while sacrificing breadth of scope. Thus, the imperfective aspect presents a view of the segments of time over which a situation progresses while leaving the endpoints of the situation beyond its purview. By contrast, the perfective viewpoint is comparable to a low focal-length lens (i.e., a wide-angle lens), which provides a wide scope but at the expense of detail. Thus, the perfective presents a wide enough view of a situation to include its endpoints in its scope but does not discern in detail the segments of time (i.e., stages) over which the situation progresses.

This metaphor of camera lenses attempts to convey the properties of the perfective : imperfective opposition that account for the different senses of the statements in example [1.11].

[1.11] a. She was rambling on [≈IPFV] in this way when she reached [≈PFV] the wood. (Carroll 2000: 156)

      b. She rambled on [≈PFV] in this way when she reached [≈PFV] the wood.

The event of reaching the wood [1.11a] is interpreted as occurring within the time during which she was rambling; this overlap is overtly signaled by the temporal conjunction *when*. By contrast, when the verb [reach] is made perfective, as in [1.11b], the sentence resists an overlapping reading despite the conjuction *when*; instead, it is more naturally interpreted as indicating that

---

24. As metalinguistic categories, perfective and imperfective viewpoint aspect may be illustrated in any number of languages. Thus, although it is questionable whether any English verbs primarily encode either of these aspects, these aspectual nuances can be inferred, as when Simple Past and Past Progressive constructions are juxtaposed (see Binnick 1991: 296, 372; Bybee, Perkins, and Pagliuca 1994: 241). Accordingly, English Simple Past and Past Progressive are employed to illustrate the perfective : imperfective opposition in the following discussion, though they are marked as ≈PFV and ≈IPFV to distinguish them from verb forms in other languages that are marked primarily for these values.

25. Focal length is defined as the distance from the principal point of a lens to the principal focus. Focal length is measured in millimeters for camera lenses: the normal lens for a 35 mm camera is 50 mm; longer than 70 mm is considered telephoto; shorter than 35 mm is considered wide angle.

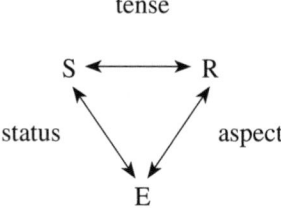

tense

Figure 1.4. M. R. Johnson's schema of the relationships between E, R, and S (adapted from 1981: 149).

after she reached the wood she started rambling—two events in temporal succession.

Although the perfective : imperfective opposition is central to the discussion of viewpoint aspect, the perfect and progressive are also types of viewpoint aspects.[26] They interact with tense and the other aspectual types in similar ways as the perfective : imperfective pair, yet they are semantically distinct from the latter. The distinction between the perfect and perfective, on the one hand, and the progressive and imperfective, on the other, is explored below (§1.7.3.3).

1.4. The R-Point in Tense-Aspect Theory

The functional similarity of viewpoint aspect and the R-point as the "viewpoint" from which an event is temporally evaluated has not escaped the attention of linguists working with tense-aspect models of the verb. Declerck's theory, with its ubiquitous R-point, lends itself especially well to a tense-aspect scheme since tense is determined solely by precedence relationships among R-points that are associated with an S or an E, thereby making the E-R relationship otiose to the interpretation of tense. The tense-aspect theories discussed here, while differing in other important respects, all reinterpret the E-R relationship as determining viewpoint aspect, and the R-S relationship as determining tense.

1.4.1. M. R. Johnson: The Triadic Relationship of E, R, and S

M. R. Johnson's 1981 article, based on her earlier dissertation (1977), presents one of the earliest tense-aspect reinterpretations of the R-point, based on her study of the verb in the Bantu language of Kikuyu. She posited the triadic relationship among E, R, and S, illustrated in fig. 1.4: the E-R relationship determines viewpoint aspect; the R-S relationship determines tense; and the

---

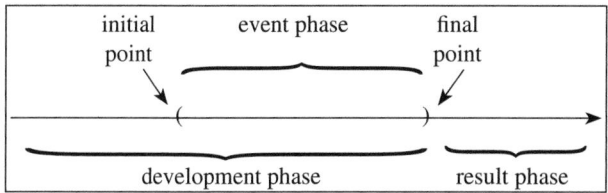

Figure 1.5. M. R. Johnson's event model (adapted from 1981: 152).

S-E relationship determines (existential) status—i.e., whether the "status" of the event in real time is past, present, or future with respect to S.

In order to explain how E and R interface to determine viewpoint aspect, Johnson developed a model in which events are analyzed as comprising "a series of temporal 'phases,'" as illustrated in fig. 1.5: the "development phase" is the time prior to the end of the event; the "event phase" is the interval of the event itself, inclusive of its initial and final endpoints; and the "result phase" is the time following the end of the event.

An important advancement on Reichenbach's R-point tense theory is Johnson's use of interval semantics. She defined E "as occurring at an interval of time" rather than a moment of time (M. R. Johnson 1981: 148; compare with Reichenbach's E as "point of the event time," in §1.2.2 above).[27] However, Johnson followed the Reichenbachian tradition in treating S as a point (i.e., moment), which creates difficulties with respect to whether R should be defined in terms of interval or moment:

> Given that S is a moment of time and E is an interval of time, how should we view R, the reference time? In order to allow for the possibility that R is identified with E, we take R also to be an interval of time. However, we have characterized R intuitively as a point of reference that functions for the speaker as an alternative to the time of speaking, in the sense of being the time of some situation other than his own that the speaker might want to describe. Hence, it seems reasonable to view R as a moment of time whenever the semantics of an utterance does not explicitly require us to do otherwise. (Johnson 1981: 150)

Using the interval event model in fig. 1.5 to define E, Johnson analyzed three morphologically marked viewpoint aspects in Kikuyu: Completive (= perfective), Imperfect (= imperfective), and Perfect. These viewpoint aspects are

---

27. *Interval semantics* was developed by Bennett and Partee (1978) most directly in response to the imperfective paradox (see §1.3.1) and has become standard in linguistic discussion. According to interval semantics, the truth value of an event is defined relative to an *interval* of time rather than a *moment* of time (Dowty 1979: 138–39); moments of time are considered primitives by which an interval is measured as consisting of an ordered set of moments (Cann 1993: 233–35; see further the event model in §1.7.3 below).

a.   R, E for Completive Aspect

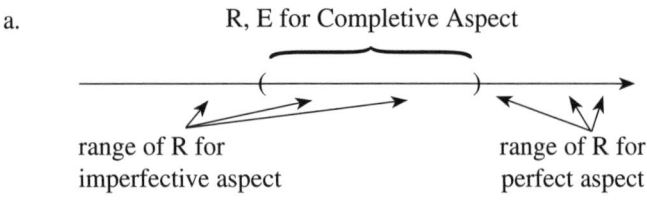

        range of R for   range of R for
        imperfective aspect   perfect aspect

b. Completive: R, E   e.g., *he built a house*
    Imperfect: $R < E$ (partially)[a]   *he was building a house*
                           (time prior to completion)
    Perfect: $E < R$ *he had built a house* (time
                           after house was completed)[b]

a. This is a translation of Johnson's definition (1981: 154): "For some *t* in E, R (<) {t}" (the symbol (<) is equivalent to <); in other words, R precedes some *t* of E.
   b. These examples are taken from the glosses of Johnson's Kikuyu examples (1981: 154–55), which are all in the Kikuyu "near past tense."

Figure 1.6. M. R. Johnson's model of Kikuyu aspectual types (adapted from 1981: 154–55).

distinguished from each other in terms of their distinct "range" of R with respect to one or more phases of E. This is illustrated graphically in fig. 1.6: the Completive has a range of R that is coterminous with the event phase; the range of R for the Imperfect corresponds to the development phase; and the range of R for the Perfect corresponds to the result phase.

While Johnson's analyses of the Kikuyu Perfect and Completive aspects correspond to standard treatments of perfect and perfective, respectively (see §1.7.3.3 below and §1.3.3 above), her analysis of the imperfective is somewhat unique. Rather than defining the imperfective as excluding both endpoints of the event, she associates R for imperfective with the development phase, which extends prior to the initial endpoint of the event (cf. §1.7.3.3 below and §1.3.3 above).

Johnson's treatment of S, R, and E with respect to tense and aspect is typical of the tense-aspect revisions of the R-point theory. By contrast, her inclusion of an S-E relationship is singular, motivated by the presence of a morphologically marked distinction in Kikuyu between "imminent action" and "manifest action" (M. R. Johnson 1981: 161–62). Unfortunately, Johnson did not explore the role of the S-E relationship as a universal feature of tense-aspect systems. However, in a review of W. Klein's tense-aspect model (see §1.4.2 below), Dahl (1997: 425) argues that the sentences in example [1.12] provide evidence that the temporal ordering of S and E may determine tense choice in English.

Table 1.13. W. Klein's Schema of 1-State Events Illustrated for Past Time
(based on 1994: 102–5)[a]

a.	I . . [. . .] . . F	R ⊆ E (and R < S)	e.g., *She was sleeping.* (≈ IPFV)
b.	[I . . . . F]	R ∩ E (and R < S)	*She slept.* (≈ PFV)
	I . . . . [. . . F]		no example
	[I . . .] . . . . F		no example
c.	I . . . . . F [ ]	E < R (and S ⊆ R)	*She has slept.* (PERF)
	[ ] I . . . . . . F	R < E (and R < S)	*She was about to go to sleep.*

a. The tenses in Klein's examples are past (denoted as a simple precedence relationship between R and S) and perfect (denoted as having an R that includes the time of S within it).

[1.12] a. Today, my office hours are from ten to twelve.

b. Today, my office hours were from ten to twelve.

Before twelve o'clock, the statement in [1.12a] would be appropriate, but after that, the statement in [1.12b] would be used; yet the reference time (R), which is fixed by the adverb *today*, has not changed. The only thing that has changed is the temporal order of E and S: before twelve o'clock, at least part of E lies after S; after twelve o'clock, E lies wholly before S.

1.4.2. W. Klein: The R-Point as "Topic Time"

W. Klein developed a comprehensive tense-aspect theory that takes into account both viewpoint aspect and situation aspect along with tense. As is the case with all of the tense-aspect theories discussed here, Klein (1994: 24) analyzed tense in terms of an R-S relationship and viewpoint aspect in terms of an R-E relationship. The most important contributions of Klein's theory have to do with his conceptualization of R and the complexity of its relationship with E.

Klein (1994: 24) relabels R "topic time," defined as the "time for which the speaker wants to make an assertion." Because Klein treats both E and R as intervals of time, he describes viewpoint aspect in terms of the degree of overlap between the intervals of E and R, as illustrated using set-theory sigla in table 1.13 ([brackets] = R; I . . . F = Initial and Final endpoints of E): R can be included in E (table 1.13a); R can partially overlap E at the beginning, end, or both (i.e., E is included in R; table 1.13b); or R can wholly precede or follow E (table 1.13c).

Klein takes some account of situation aspect by distinguishing among 0-state, 1-state, and 2-state situation types (cf. individual-level states, stage-level states, and dynamic events). He employs the idea of "topic time contrast" to distinguish the ways in which R overlaps with these different situation types, as illustrated by the examples in [1.13]: (a) with 0-state situations, there is no

Table 1.14. W. Klein's Schema of 2-State Events Illustrated for Past Time
(based on 1994: 105–9)

a.	$-[---]-+++++$	R ⊂ SS of E (R < S)	e.g., *He <u>was closing</u>* (≈ IPFV) *the door.*
b.	$-[----+++]++$	R ∩ SS of E (R < S)	*He <u>closed</u>* (≈ PFV) *the door.*
c.	$-----++[++]+$	SS of E < R (S ⊂ R)	*He <u>has closed</u>* (PERF) *the door.*
	$[\ \ ]---+++++$	R < SS of E (R < S)	*He <u>was about to close</u> the door.*

topic time contrast, since there is no R (topic time) that exists outside the situation (E); (b) with 1-state situations, there is an "external" topic time contrast, since another R may lie outside the situation (E); (c) finally, with 2-state situations, there is an "external" topic time contrast as well as an internal contrast between the "source state" and the "target state" of the situation (E).

[1.13] a. The book is in Russian (0-state event, no topic time contrast, R is always in E)

b. The book is on the table (1-state event, R contrasts with an R when the book is not on the table)

c. He put the book on the table (2-state event, R contrasts with another R, as in b, *and* the source state [book not on the table] contrasts with the target state [book on the table] in the same R)

Klein (1994: 105) claimed that, with respect to 2-state events, English happens to overlap the topic time R with the source state as opposed to the target state, overlap with which is presumably a possibility. Thus, as shown in table 1.14, R may overlap with the "source state" (SS) of 2-state events (marked by −; + is "target state") in the same way that it overlaps with E in 1-state events, illustrated above, in table 1.13 (p. 31).

Unfortunately, Klein's notion that languages may choose to overlap topic time R with either the source state or target state in 2-state events is problematic. First, such a distinction could theoretically only apply in the case of the imperfective (table 1.14a): according to Klein, the topic time R for perfective includes a portion of both the source state and the target state (table 1.14b), and the perfect and prospective tenses are defined by the scope of topic time R following or preceding the source state (table 1.14c), respectively.

Second, in the case of an imperfective example such as in table 1.14a, a topic time overlapping with the target state would be nonsensical. As Dahl observed in his criticism of Klein's model, the more conventional view of 2-state events is that they consist only of a transition from one state to the other, not initial (source) and resultant (target) states themselves. Citing the example

Table 1.15. Mari Olsen's Feature Chart for Tense
(adapted from 1997: 130)

Privative Tense Features	Past	Future
a. Past tense (R < C)	+	0
b. Present tense (C, R)	0	0
c. Future tense (C < R)	0	+
d. ?Non-present tense (R ≠ C)	+	+

Burton left Mecca, Dahl (1997: 420) states that "it is hard to see how Burton may be leaving Mecca after he has crossed the line."

1.4.3. Olsen: Multiple R-Points

Olsen (1997) constructed a universal tense-aspect model illustrated with respect to the verbal systems of English and Koine (New Testament) Greek. While Olsen treated the E-R relationship as defining viewpoint aspect (cf. §§1.4.1–1.4.2), she presented a more complex analysis of tense by allowing the presence of multiple R-points (see §1.2.3). In particular, she employed the notion of a contextually determined "deictic center" (C; compare with Declerck's R_{TR}, §1.2.3.4 above), which is movable and has S as its default position. The relationship between this deictic center C and R, rather than simply S and R, determines tense in Olsen's theory, as illustrated in table 1.15. Thus, Olsen's theory combines the advantages of treating the R-E relationship as aspect without losing the power of relative-tense theories to analyze tense in subordinate structures, such as those in example [1.14] (subscripts refer to multiple Rs but multiple positions of C): R_1 (*ate*) lies before C_{pos1} (at S), but R_2 (*had cleaned*) lies before C_{pos2} (at R_1).

[1.14]   Before they ate ($R_1 < C_{pos1}$ = S) breakfast, Jared and Colin had cleaned ($R_2 < C_{pos2}$ = R_1) their room.

With regard to the E-R relationship, Olsen (1997: 52, 57 n. 33) used an event model consisting of a nucleus and a coda—terms derived from the phonetic and phonological study of syllables. R intersects E at the nucleus for imperfective aspect and at the coda for perfective aspect, as illustrated in fig. 1.7. The possibility that R should be analyzed as an interval rather than a moment is not addressed by Olsen.

Olsen (1997: 51–52) incorporated situation aspect into this event model by associating the situational features [+telic] with the event coda, and [+dynamic] and [+durative] with the event nucleus. These three features distinguish the six different situation types shown in table 1.16 (Olsen 1997: 48–50; on semelfactive and stage-level states, see §1.3.1 above).

a. *Imperfective aspect:* [E ∩ R] @ nucleus

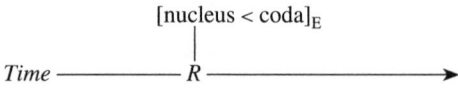

b. *Perfective Aspect:* [E ∩ R] @ coda

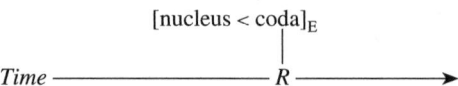

Figure 1.7. Mari Olsen's formalized notation for viewpoint aspect (adapted from 1997: 63).

By comparison with other feature charts (e.g., C. S. Smith's in fig. 1.3d above), Olsen analyzed situations in terms of monotonic privative opposi-tions.[28] With this analysis of situation types, Olsen argues that shifts among situation types, of the sort illustrated by the examples in [1.15] (repeated from [1.9], p. 24; see §1.3.1), can be explained in terms of semantic meaning versus pragmatic implicature.[29]

[1.15]   a.   Tage built. (ACT)
         b.   Tage built a house. (ACC)
         c.   Tage built houses. (ACT)

---

28. *Monotonic* is used in mathematics to refer to the unidirectional relationship be-tween members. *Privative opposition* stands in contrast to *equipollent opposition* and *scalar opposition*. All three concepts are derived from Prague School phonological theory (see Trubetzkoy 1958, ET 1969). *Privative* opposition occurs when the members are asymmetri-cal—one member is marked with a feature that the other lacks (e.g., [+feature A] and [0fea-ture A]). *Equipollent* opposition occurs when the members are logically equivalent but have opposite values; they are marked by a binary +/− notation (e.g., [+feature A] and [−feature A]). *Scalar* (or gradual) opposition occurs when members are contrasted on the basis of a scale (e.g., front vowels, which range along a scale of vowel height from high to low; see Crystal 2008: 172, 217, 386–87).

29. *Pragmatic* or *Conversational Implicature* derives from Grice's theory about seman-tics and pragmatics in the use of natural language. The central premise of the theory is that conversation or discourse proceeds according to four principles that are subsumed under the central *principle of cooperation*: "make your contribution such as is required, at the stage at which it occurs, by the accepted purpose or direction of the talk exchange in which you are engaged" (Grice 1975: 45). When conversation does not proceed according to this principle, hearers still presume that they are being followed at some level and thus draw implica-tional meanings from the conversation, which are termed *conversational implicatures* (see Levinson 1983: chap. 4). Grice (1975: 57–58) offers four linguistic tests for conversational implicature: (1) cancelability (or defeasibility), (2) nondetachability, (3) calculability, and (4) nonconventionality (see also Levinson 1983: 119).

Table 1.16. Mari Olsen's Feature Chart for Situation Aspect
(adapted from 1997: 51)

Aspectual Class	Telic	Dynamic	Durative	Examples
State	0	0	+	*know, be, have*
Activity	0	+	+	*run, paint, sing*
Accomplishment	+	+	+	*destroy, create*
Achievement	+	+	0	*notice, win*
Semelfactive	0	+	0	*wink, tap, cough*
Stage-level state	+	0	+	*be pregnant*

For example, Olsen argued that the atelic (activity) property of a statement such as [1.16a] is demonstrably an implicature meaning because it is cancelable through the addition of a singular direct object, *a mile*, which makes the statement [+telic] (accomplishment) statement. By contrast, she argued that a [+telic] statement is not cancelable, demonstrated by the effect of the addition of the durational phrase *for a week* in [1.16b]: the statement is interpreted as iterative—Jared swam a mile multiple times during a week.

[1.16]   a.   Jared <u>swam</u> (a mile). (unmarked for [+telic])
         b.   Jared <u>swam</u> a mile (for a week). (marked for [+telic])

The case for privatively marked [+durative] and [+dynamic] is analogous: these values are not cancelable, whereas events unmarked for these values may nevertheless be interpreted as durative or dynamic by implicature.

Although Olsen's privative treatment of situation types presents some valuable insights to the contributions of verbs and their complements in determining situation aspect, her arguments are not fully convincing. For example, if the complement *a mile* in [1.16b] above is made plural (*Jared swam miles*), the [+telic] value is canceled, making the VP an activity. Olsen (1997: 33), however, would presumably explain the effect of the plural *miles* in the same way as the addition of *for a week* in [1.16b] above: the resultant VP is not properly an activity but an iteration of accomplishments. Although this explanation is plausible in the case of *for a week* in [1.16b], it is less convincing for *Jared swam miles*, given that the verb is transitive, and therefore the noun phrase *miles* completes the valency frame of the verb. Similarly, Olsen's claim (1997: 47) that semelfactives may be read as durative is unconvincing: she paraphrases the example *John coughed (once) for 5 seconds* as *It took John 5 seconds to cough once.* At the very least, one would need to judge a construction of this sort as extremely rare and as requiring explicit marking to avoid an iterative interpretation (see C. S. Smith 1997: 53).

Another weakness of Olsen's theory is her treatment of perfective aspect. First, she confused perfective and perfect, as is evident from her analysis of the perfective in fig. 1.7 (R intersecting E at the coda), which is analgous with Johnson's model of the Kikuyu Perfect (see fig. 1.6, p. 30: range of R corresponds with the result phase of E). In her treatment of English, Olsen (1997: 172–76; cf. p. 27 n. 24) claimed that the English Perfect tenses are a manifestation of perfective aspect. Second, Olsen's definition (1997: 83) of perfective aspect as denoting an event as "having reached an end" is arguably incorrect and misleading in that it confuses perfective viewpoint with the concept of completion (see Comrie 1976: 18).

1.4.4. Summary: The R-Point and Tense-Aspect Theory

The three tense-aspect theories examined here share the innovation of re-interpreting the R-E relationship as determinative of viewpoint aspect. They each develop some sort of event model in order to explicate the various ways in which R might be temporally related to E, thus differentiating among viewpoint aspects. All three employ interval semantics in their event model, but they differ in their treatment of R: Olsen's theory apparently retains the Reichenbachian view of R as a point; M. R. Johnson's allows R to be a point when associated with the instant S or an interval when associated with the interval E; and W. Klein's theory consistently treats R as an interval of time.

Each of these theories contributes uniquely to tense-aspect R-point theory. Johnson's raises the question whether an S-E relationship should be taken into account in a universal tense-aspect model. Klein's clarifies R as being the interval of time for which one wants to make an assertion. Finally, Olsen's adopts the notion of multiple R-points from relative-tense theory within her tense-aspect theory of R-E, thus presenting the most fully integrated model of relative tense and tense-aspect of the three surveyed here.

1.5. The R-Point and Discourse

Reichenbach argued that the analysis of each tense form requires one and only one R-point. Subsequent relative-tense theories have posited, first, that multiple R-points are required to analyze certain tense constructions—particularly subordinate clause constructions in which there were multiple Es; and, second, that S itself may simply be the first in a series of R-points (see §1.2.3 above). Alternatively, some linguists have argued that, rather than there being multiple Rs, there is one transient R-point (cf. Olsen's movable "deictic center" related to R, §1.4.3). This proposal was first advanced by linguists working on analyzing tense-aspect in narrative discourse, where it is problematic to evaluate the tense of each E directly with respect to S. A theory that temporally locates each E independently with reference to S is unable to distinguish the different meanings given to the two sentences in [1.17], since the relative temporal location of each E with respect to S is crucially important to the interpretation of the discourse fragment.

[1.17] a. She married and became pregnant.
 b. She became pregnant and married.
 (Brown and Yule 1983: 125)

Thus, linguists have employed the concept of a transient R-point to explain the operation of tense and/or aspect in narrative discourse, in which the temporal progression of the discourse may be measured in terms of R-point movement. However, linguists have proposed several different semantic factors as accounting for the movement of R.

1.5.1. Explaining R-Point Movement with Viewpoint Aspect

Discourse representation theory (DRT) was developed in response to the inherent inadequacies of Montague semantics already illustrated by example [1.17] (on DRT, see Kamp 1981; Kamp and Reyle 1993; Kamp, van Genabith, and Reyle 2011; on Montague semantics, see Montague 1974; Cann 1993; Janssen 2006). Montague semantics is only capable of analyzing individual sentences in isolation, whereas many sentences require reference to their discourse context in order to be correctly interpreted. As discourse progresses, the semantic representation must be updated to reflect shifts in situation and participants as well as temporal changes. In an early application of this approach, Kamp and Rohrer (1983) examined the French *Imparfait* and *Passé Simple* with DRT, employing Reichenbach's notion of an R-point to elucidate the temporal dynamics of discourse.

Kamp and Rohrer's central argument (1983: 250) is that "the main function of these tenses [French *Imparfait* and *Passé Simple*], and in fact of all tenses generally, is to signal to the recipient of the sentence in which the tense occurs how he should incorporate the information the sentence brings him into the representation which he has already formed of the preceding sections of the text or discourse of which the sentence is part." They explained that the R-point is reevaluated at each stage of the discourse (i.e., with the addition of each clause). When the perfective *Passé Simple* is employed, the R-point is transferred to the next event introduced into the discourse (1983: 253–54). By contrast, when the imperfective *Imparfait* is used, the R-point is not transferred; instead, the *Imparfait* reports an event that spans the temporal period of the previous event, which retains the reference point (1983: 254–55).

Kamp and Rohrer (1983: 253) illustrated their analysis with the contrastive sentences in [1.18], which correspond to the schematic figs. 1.8 and 1.9, respectively.

[1.18] a. [$_{E1}$Quand Pierre entra (*Passé Simple*)], [$_{E2}$Maria téléphona (*Passé Simple*)].
 When Pierre entered (PFV), Marie telephoned (PFV).
 b. [$_{E1}$Quand Pierre entra (*Passé Simple*)], [$_{E2}$Marie téléphonait (*Imparfait*)].
 When Pierre entered (PFV), Marie was telephoning (IPFV).

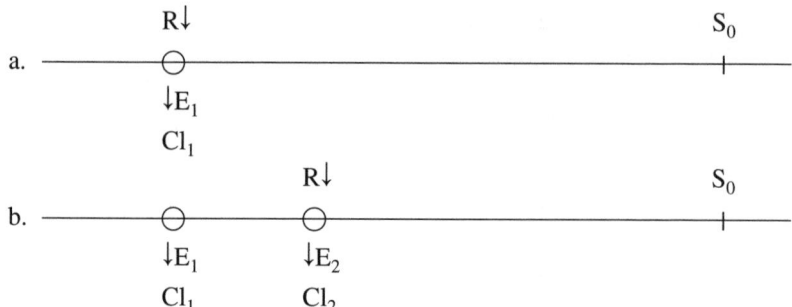

Figure 1.8. Transference of the reference point (adapted from Kamp and Rohrer 1983: 254).

The *Passé Simple* verb *téléphona* in [1.18a] transfers the R-point forward to the subsequent event, as graphically illustrated in fig. 1.8 ($Cl_\#$ = clause). The natural interpretation is that Maria telephoned directly after Pierre entered.

By contrast, the *Imparfait* verb *téléphonait* in [1.18b] does not move the R-point but presents a situation that temporally spans the time of the *Passé Simple entra*, as illustrated in fig. 1.9. Thus, Maria is portrayed as being in the process of telephoning at the time Pierre enters.

Thus, Kamp and Rohrer (1983: 255) concluded that "the reference point about which Reichenbach speaks is established by context" and that, rather than there being multiple reference points, there is just one transient reference point, the movement of which is effected by viewpoint aspect: a perfective aspect verb transfers the R-point, whereas an imperfective aspect verb does not.

1.5.2. Explaining R-Point Movement with Situation Aspect

In contrast to Kamp and Rohrer's viewpoint-aspectual explanation of temporal movement, many of the early semantic studies of discourse explained the movement of the R-point in terms of situation aspect: achievements and accomplishments move the R-point forward, whereas states and activities do not (e.g., Dry 1981; Partee 1984; Reinhart 1984; Dowty 1986; Heinrichs 1986). A more recent scholar to take this tack is ter Meulen, whose dynamic aspect theory (1995) uses insights from situation semantics.[30] The basis of her theory

---

30. *Situation semantics* is a theory developed by Barwise and Perry (1983) as an alternative to model-theoretic (Montague) semantics. At the heart of the theory is its analysis of sentences in terms of situations—consisting of a location, a relation, and a truth value—rather than truth conditions. Situation semantics takes context into account to a greater degree than Montague semantics (Akman 2006; Dekker 1994).

Figure 1.9. Retaining the reference point (adapted from Kamp and Rohrer 1983: 255).

is her treatment of activities, accomplishments, and achievements as "holes," "filters," and "plugs," respectively:

> If we interpret a given clause describing an event as a *hole*, then we interpret the information expressed in the next sentence of the text as describing of [*sic*] a temporal part of that event, as if the information flows through the hole. . . . If we interpret a given clause describing an event as a *filter*, then it restricts the information that flows through it to describing whatever else happened simultaneously. . . . Filters create a choice between interpreting the next clause as describing a later event and interpreting it as describing an event temporally included in the filter. . . . If we interpret a given clause describing an event as a *plug*, then it blocks all information about whatever happened at the same time. No new information can flow through it, so to speak, so it forces the context to redirect its temporal focus, interpreting the next sentence as describing another, later event. (ter Meulen 1995: 7)

Ter Meulen (1995: 43–46) employed "dynamic aspect trees" to illustrate her system. Every tree consists of a "root" node (○) representing the entire episode, and a "source" node (•) representing the point of speech (S). Each event is successively placed as the "current node" on the tree (i.e., the "current node" refers to the location of the R-point). If the event is a plug (•), the following event forms a "sister" node to it; if it is a hole (○), the following event forms a "daughter" node to it. States (as well as perfect and progressive tenses) are placed as "stickers" on the current node if it is a plug, and on the following node if it is a hole (1995: 51).

For example, the situation in [1.19a] consists of three sentences: the verbs in the first and third are plugs, forming two successive events; the second sentence contains a past perfect verb, which is placed as a "sticker" on the preceding plug node to signify that the event of the train's leaving is prior to Pam's arrival at the station. By contrast, [1.19b] consists of a plug followed by a series of holes. The first hole is placed as a sister node to the initial plug, but the following holes are interpreted as part of the situation expressed by the first hole—*was so happy*.

[1.19] a. Pam <u>arrived</u> at the station. The train <u>had left</u> already. She
            sat <u>down</u> on the bench.

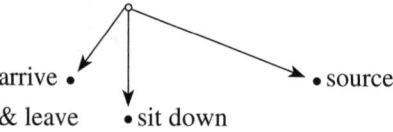

        b. Bill <u>won</u>. He <u>was</u> so <u>happy</u>. He <u>danced</u> around, <u>shouted</u>, and
            <u>clapped</u> his hands.

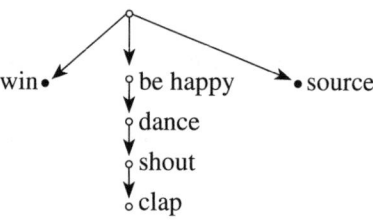

As explained in the above quotation by ter Meulen, a "filter" presents a
choice between interpreting an event as a plug (•) or a hole (○). This ambiguity
is illustrated by ter Meulen's example in [1.20] (1995: 47), which can be represented by two different trees, depending on whether the filter event *attempted
to decipher the message* is interpreted as a plug or hole: either *looked at her
watch* is temporally included in the event of *attempted to decipher the message*
(hole interpretation in a), or—more naturally—it follows it (plug interpretation
in b).

[1.20] Jane <u>felt ill</u>. She sat <u>down</u>, <u>attempted to decipher</u> the message,
        and <u>looked</u> at her watch. She <u>sighed</u>. It <u>was</u> not even noon yet.

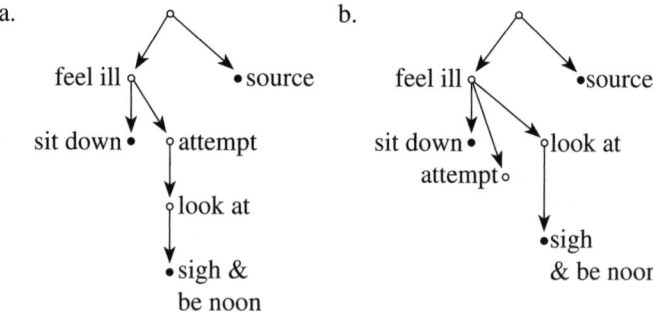

1.5.3. Explaining R-Point Movement with (Un)boundedness

Alongside these studies (§§1.5.1–2) that have tried to explain R-point movement in discourse by recourse to either viewpoint or situation aspect, a number of studies have argued that R-point movement is determined by (un)boundedness (e.g., Dry 1983; Hatav 1989; Depraetere 1995; C. S. Smith 1999). "It is in fact (un)boundedness which determines whether or not the action is pushed forward" (Depraetere 1995: 15): bounded events—those described as having reached an endpoint or temporal bound—advance the R-point, while unbounded events do not advance the R-point. Depraetere's understanding of (un)boundedness represents an advance over earlier studies, which referred to both the initial and the final endpoints of events (Dry 1983: 28; see Hatav 1989: 493), because boundedness has to do only with the linguistic expression of the final endpoint of an event.

Depraetere's explanation of (un)boundedness accounts for the observations made about both viewpoint aspect and situation aspect with respect to the advancement of R. Kamp and Rohrer argued that perfective aspect advances the R-point (§1.5.1), which makes sense when the definition of perfective is compared with boundedness: the scope of perfective aspect includes the endpoints of an event (see §1.3.3; this explains why early studies spoke about both initial and final points as having to be within the scope of R). Thus, it appears that perfective aspect may serve to make events bounded. At the same time, Depraetere's article (1995: 2–3) focuses the similarity between (un)boundedness and (a)telicity: the former "relates to whether or not a situation is described as having reached a temporal boundary," while the latter "has to do with whether or not a situation is described as having an inherent or intended endpoint" (see also Declerck 1989: 277). Thus, the similarity between between (un)boundedness and (a)telicity would appear to mean that telic events (i.e., accomplishments and achievements) make events bounded, whereas activities and states do not (see §1.5.2; see also §1.7.3.1).

These correlations between (un)boundedness and viewpoint and situation aspects explains how earlier theories relating R-point movement to viewpoint or situation aspect were partially *successful*. However, they were only *partially* successful because (un)boundedness cannot be fully correlated with either perfective aspect or telic situation types. Various factors may contribute to an event's being described as bounded, including both viewpoint aspect and situation aspect, and temporal adverbs and pragmatic implicature (see C. S. Smith 1999; 2003; Cook 2004b: 251–54). Further discussion of (un)boundedness and the movement of R in discourse is presented in chap. 4.

1.5.4. Summary: The R-Point in Discourse

While tense-aspect theories reinterpreted R-point in terms of viewpoint aspect, semantic theories of discourse have enriched the temporal value of

R-point so that it plays a role in the temporal determination, not only of E with respect to R, but of each E with respect to previous Es in the discourse. This conception of E is nascent in Declerck's relative-tense theory, in which "time referred to" R can be temporally determined by "time of orientation" R (§1.2.3.4 above).

These discussions of the semantic factors that effect the movement of R have led to an increasing appreciation of the complexities of R-movement in discourse. Neither viewpoint aspect nor situation aspect can fully account for R-point movement, and, although the single factor of (un)boundedness accounts for R-point movement, the determination of (un)boundedness is itself complex (see §4.2 below).

1.6. A Primer on Modality

With the topic of modality, the triad of features commonly associated with verbal systems is complete—tense, aspect, and modality (TAM). Modality is a sprawling category to such an extent that Palmer (1986: 224) expressed doubts in his early study of the topic that he had been able to demonstrate a unified typological category of modality. It is perhaps for this reason that Portner (2009: 1) advocates a practical means of discovering what modality is as beginning with some feature or features of language that obviously involve modality and then attempting to apply one's understanding of those modal features to others. A key reason for the hesitant approaches to modality is the numerous background concepts that resulted in a recognition of the category and shaped the various conceptualizations of it.[31] For this reason, it seems best to begin with a brief excursion into these background concepts of the traditional grammatical category of mood, the basics of modal logic, and speech act theory.

1.6.1. Backgrounds of Modality: Grammar, Logic, and Speech Acts

Jespersen's treatment (1924) of English is a suitable representative of the role that modality, expressed by mood, has traditionally played in grammatical theory. In keeping with Latinate classical grammar study, Jespersen (1924: 313) recognized the primary categories of mood as the indicative, subjunctive, and imperative, explaining that they "express certain attitudes of mind of the speaker towards the contents of the sentence, though in some cases the choice of mood is determined not by the attitude of the actual speaker, but by the character of the clause itself and its relation to the main nexus on which it is dependent." Jespersen (1924: 320–21) further provided a tentative listing of subcategories of mood, grouped by those that include an element of the speaker's will (e.g., jussive *Go*, permissive *You may go*, optative *May he still be alive!*, and intentional *In order that he may go*) and the categories that lack an element of the speaker's will (e.g., assertive *He is rich*, dubative *He may*

---

31. A good example of this hesitancy is Portner (2009: 1), who opens his book entitled *Modality* with the statement "I am not too comfortable trying to define modality."

be rich, necessitative *He must be rich*, potential *He can speak*, and conditional *If he is rich*).

Modal logic was developed in the early twentieth century in order to analyze sentences featuring modal verbs (e.g., *can, could, might, may, must*) or modal adverbs (especially *possibly* and *necessarily*). Sentences employing these and other modal modifiers refer to multiple potential states of affairs, as in [1.21].

[1.21] It may snow.

In this example, multiple states of affairs are potentially in view: one in which it snows, one in which it sleets, one in which it is sunny, and so on. These multiple states of affairs are standardly referred to as "possible worlds," meaning all the logically possible (or in some way non-anomalous) states of affairs that can be imagined. However, because not all logically possible worlds are equally likely, logicians deal with "alternative (or accessible) worlds," left vaguely defined as the worlds that are relatively possible or non-anomalous with respect to the "actual world" (see Cann 1993: 269–70, 276–78; McCawley 1993: 372–76).

The precise character of the relationship between the actual world and alternative/accessible worlds is defined by the modal category in operation, of which there are a number of modes, traditionally referred to by Greek terminology: alethic (or logical), epistemic (having to do with knowledge), deontic (having to do with obligation), boulomaic (having to do with desire), doxastic (having to do with belief), and existential (or temporal; see G. H. von Wright 1951: 1–2; Allwood, Andersson, and Dahl 1977: 111–12; McCawley 1993: 372–73, 378). So with respect to alternative/accessible world relations, all possible worlds are accessible in alethic modality. By contrast, for epistemic modality, only the worlds that share certain known facts with the speaker's world are considered accessible worlds; and in the cases of deontic, boulomaic, and doxastic modalities, the worlds that are consistent with the moral obligations, desires, and beliefs of the speaker, respectively, are accessible. Finally, accessible worlds in existential modality share the same temporal features as the speaker's world (see Kiefer 1987: 71; McCawley 1993: 376).

Modal logic, narrowly defined, focuses on the modal operators "necessarily" ($\square$) and "possibly" ($\lozenge$): a proposition is necessarily true in a particular world if it is true in *all worlds* that are accessible to the actual world; similarly, a proposition is possibly true in a particular world if it is true in *some world* that is accessible to the actual world. These two operators manifest themselves differently in the various modal categories. For example, while they represent logical necessity and possibility in alethic modality, they express obligation and permission, respectively, in the deontic realm. These two operators are also clearly interrelated, as illustrated by the conditions in example [1.22] (McCawley 1993: 379; see Allwood, Andersson, and Dahl 1977: 110; Lyons 1977: 787).

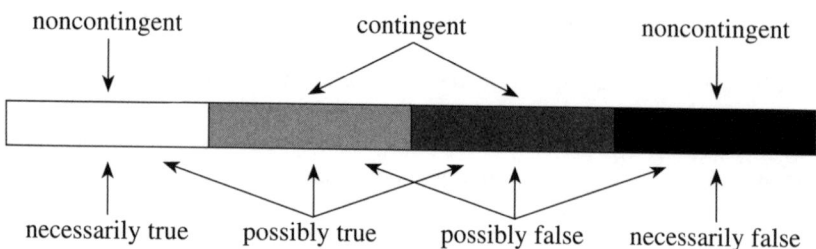

Figure 1.10. Necessity and possibility (adapted from Cann 1993: 271–72).

[1.22] a. □A if and only if ~◇~A
        b. ◇A if and only if ~□~A

These conditions are to be translated as follows: [1.22a] states that A is necessarily true if and only if it is not true that A is possibly not true; [1.22b] states
that A is possibly true if and only if it is not true that A is necessarily not true.
Another helpful conceptualization of the relationship between necessity and
possibility is illustrated by fig. 1.10, which depicts how the two notions *necessity* and *possibility* can be analyzed in terms of *contingent* and *noncontingent
truth/falsity.*

Speech act theory was developed by Austin (1962) against a background of
logical positivism, which, among other tenets, holds that only sentences that
can be verified (i.e., judged true or false) are meaningful (see Lyons 1977:
725–28; Levinson 1983: 226–28). In his posthumously published lectures,
Austin sought to incorporate nonverifiable sentences into a philosophy of language. Speech act theory analyzes utterances in three parts: the "locutionary
act" is the production of a meaningful utterance; the "illocutionary act" refers
to the way in which the locutionary act is used, such as informing, questioning,
or commanding; finally, the "perlocutionary act" is the effect achieved by the
illocutionary act (Austin 1962: 94–101).[32] Thus, the locutionary act of saying
Catch him! may be accompanied by an illocutionary act of urging, advising,
ordering, etc., and a perlocutionary act of persuading the addressee to chase
and catch him (Austin 1962: 101).[33]

---

32. For detailed discussions of the Austin-Searle speech act theory from the perspective of linguistics, see Lyons 1977: 725–45; Levinson 1983: 226–83; and McCawley 1993:
290–325.

33. Hare's distinction of phrastic (proposition content), neustic (speaker commitment),
and tropic (factuality of propositional content) components of speech acts (1952; 1970) derives from a parallel philosophical tradition originating with Frege's distinction between
thought and judgment (so Levinson 1983: 242). Initially, Hare (1952: 17–20) distinguished
between *phrastic* and *neustic*, making the latter essentially equivalent to illocutionary force,

Table 1.17. Types of Illocutionary Force
(Searle 1983: 166; cf. Austin 1962: 150–63)

assertives	where we tell our hearers (truly or falsely) how things are
directives	where we get them to do things
commissives	where we commit ourselves
declarations	where we bring about changes in the world with our utterances
expressives	where we express our feelings and attitudes

Austin's primary concern was to distinguish the illocutionary "force" from the meaning (locution) and the effect (perlocution) of an utterance. It is just at this point that modality (mood, in particular) intersects with speech act theory, since mood markings appear often to coincide with particular illocutionary forces (e.g., imperative mood for commands). However, unlike mood, there are numerous, if not limitless types of illocution, simply judging by the number of performative verbs in English (e.g., *promise, declare, demand, forgive, pronounce,* etc.). Lyons (1977: 745) attempted to find some common ground by treating mood against the backdrop of speech act theory and under the three broad categories of statements, questions, and demands. Searle's taxonomy of five types of illocutionary force, provided in table 1.17, is standardly cited, though Levinson (1983: 240) has noted that it lacks any principled basis (see Lyons 1977: 736–37).

1.6.2. Defining Modality

Concepts from grammar, logic, and philosophy of language intersect in the linguistic discussion of modality. Against these backdrops, the defining of *modality* has proceeded in two directions. The first, earlier approach, which emerged mainly from the backgrounds of grammatical mood and speech act theory, focused on the role of the speaker in using propositions. For example, Palmer (1986: 2), drawing on Lyons (1977: 452), defined modality as having to do with the " 'attitude or opinion' of the speaker." Bybee (1985: 192) defined mood as "any markers that indicated what role the speaker meant the proposition to play in the discourse."

The other approach, which has overtaken the first to some extent (cf. Palmer 1986: 1–2; 2001: 1–2), draws on modal logic to define modality has having to do with the means to talk about alternative situations or situations that are not necessarily real (Chung and Timberlake 1985: 241; Kiefer 1987: 90; Palmer 2001: 1; Timberlake 2007: 315; Portner 2009: 1). Early on, Givón (1984: 272)

---

but in a subsequent article (Hare 1970: 20–21) he identified the speaker's "sign of subscription" with neustic and the "sign of mood" with tropic, thus making illocutionary force the product of the neustic and tropic components (see Lyons 1977: 750). Lyons (1977: 797–800) used this neustic : tropic division to distinguish between objective : subjective modality.

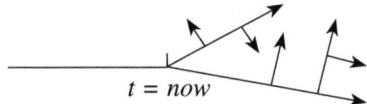

Figure 1.11. Branching timeline (see Hatav 1997: 119; Portner 2009: 233).

provided interrelated definitions for tense, aspect, and modality in terms of the unifying feature of time: whereas tense has to do with the *temporal location* of an event, and aspect has to do with the *temporal structure* of the event, modality has to do with the *temporal existence* of an event—whether it exists at a particular time, has no existence, has potential existence, etc. (see Chung and Timberlake 1985: 256).[34] This temporal concept of modality can be visualized in terms of a timeline with branching vectors that signify alternative or potential times (on which are located alternative situations), as illustrated in fig. 1.11. Modality has to do with the linguistic means by which situations or propositions are related to alternative situations (i.e., situations lying to the right of time *t* 'now').[35]

Modality may operate at a number of levels: Palmer (2001: 22) distinguishes propositional from event modality (see §1.6.3.1, below); Portner (2009: 4–8) lists types of sentence (e.g., modal auxiliaries, verbs, and adverbs, generics and habituals, tense-aspect irreal expressions, and conditionals), subsentence (e.g., modal adjectives and nouns, propositional attitude verbs and adjectives, and verbal mood), and discourse modality (e.g., evidentiality, clause type, and sentential modals). Modality in this sense is a (notional and typological) semantic domain consisting of the virtually limitless number of modal nuances that may be expressed by human languages, such as jussive, deliberative, dubitative, reportative, exclamative, etc. (see Bybee and Fleischman 1995: 2).[36]

By contrast, these various modalities may be expressed in languages in a number of different ways, including notably modal systems, mood systems, and evidential systems. Modal systems express different types of modality using "a single system of commuting terms" (Palmer 2001: 6), such as the modal verb system in English (cf. German): the English modal verbs *may, must*, and *will* express complimentary degrees of epistemic judgments about propositions and deontic modality operating on events. Mood traditionally has referred to

---

34. In modal logic terms, instead of "existence" we should speak of "the set of linguistically relevant accessibility relations" (Kiefer 1987: 90).

35. Similarly, note Kiefer's definition (1987: 90): "[T]he essence of modality consists in the relativization of the validity of sentence meanings to a set of possible worlds."

36. Palmer (2001: 19–21) cautions against terminological confusion among (1) the typological categories (i.e., semantically defined categories common to various different languages), (2) the notional features that justify the distinct typological categories, and (3) the grammatical markers associated with the typological categories.

the expression of modality through verbal morphology and/or morphosyntax (e.g., indicative, subjunctive, imperative), but mood is expressed in some languages by clitics or particles (see Palmer 2001: 19, 150). Most importantly, mood systems are "basically (prototypically) binary," expressing a distinction of realis : irrealis (typologically equivalent to indicative : subjunctive, also labeled declarative : nondeclarative, real : unreal, factual : unfactual, assertive : nonassertive; Palmer 2001: 1, 4).[37] Evidential systems provide ways in which speakers may assess their grounds or basis for saying something (Portner 2009: 263). Evidential expressions may be analyzed in terms of whether the ground is reportative or sensory, as illustrated by Palmer's examples in [1.23] (2001: 36). I will not discuss evidential systems any further because of their irrelevance to Biblical Hebrew, which lacks any indications of this sort related to its verbal system.

[1.23]   a.   Reported evidential:
          ŋindu-dhan   *girambiyi* (Palmer 2001: 36)
          you + NOM-LING.EVID sick + PAST
          'You are said to have been sick' (linguistic evidence)
      b.   Sensory evidential:
          ŋindu-gara   *girambiyi* (Palmer 2001: 36)
          you + NOM-SENS.EVID sick + PAST
          'One can see you were sick' (sensory evidence)

1.6.3. Categorizing Modality

The complexity of modality has resulted in a variety of approaches to categorizing modalities and their expressions. At the root of these varieties lie different analyses of the traditional categories of epistemic, deontic, and dynamic, particularly with respect to how other distinctions cross-cut these categories (e.g., propositional versus event modality and subjective versus objective modalities). In this section, I begin with a discussion of these differences (§1.6.3.1). This discussion is supplemented by a further exploration of the relationship of modality to speech acts (§1.6.3.2) and to mood systems (§1.6.3.3).

1.6.3.1. Classifications of Modalities

The traditional classification of modality is into epistemic, deontic, and dynamic categories, as illustrated by the English modal system in the examples in [1.24] (subcategories based on Palmer 2001: 22).

---

37. Portner (2009: 1) also appears to embrace an underlying binary system in defining modality as means of grammatically referring to non-real events (versus real events), although he goes on (2009: 258–63) to discuss mood in terms of verbal, notional, and sentence mood.

[1.24] a. Epistemic

Speculative: *But it may rain outside* [a possible conclusion].
(Carroll 2000: 168)

Deductive: *There must be a thunderstorm coming on* [the
only possible conclusion based on the available evidence].
(Carroll 2000: 171)

Assumptive: *All the ashes will get into it* [a reasonable conclusion based on what is known]. (Carroll 2000: 135)

b. Deontic

Permissive: *You may try it if you like.* (Carroll 2000: 209)

Obligative: *And here I must leave you.* (Carroll 2000: 213)

Commissive: *I shall never, never forget.* (Carroll 2000:
135)

c. Dynamic

Ability: *I can explain all the poems that were ever invented.*
(Carroll 2000: 189)

Volitive: *You will observe the rules of battle, of course?*
(Carroll 2000: 206)

Simplistically characterizing these modal domains: epistemic consists of
evaluative expressions (possibility, necessity, probability, etc.), deontic encompasses modalities involving obligation, and dynamic includes modalities
of ability and volition. Portner (2009: 134–40) departs from this traditional
taxonomy in some significant ways. First, he moves away form the notion of
"obligation" to "priority," which encompasses deontic, bouletic (wish), and
teleological varieties of modality. He (Portner 2009: 135) explains: "[T]he
idea behind the term 'priority' is that such things as rules, desires, and goals
all serve to identify some possibility as better than, or as having higher priority than, others." Second, Portner (2009: 136) adds generic expressions to the
dynamic category, noting that expressions such as *Spiders can be dangerous*
and *Spiders will be dangerous* represent modal expressions that quantify over
individuals—the generic *spider* in this case.

For Palmer (2001), the crucial distinction within the taxonomy in [1.24]
is between propositional and event modalities: epistemic modality deals with
assessment of a proposition, whereas deontic (or priority) and dynamic assess
events. The distinction can be illustrated by paraphrasing several of the epistemic and deontic examples from [1.24] as in [1.25] (the underlined portions
represent the propositions [a–b] and events [c–d] on which the modalities
operate).

[1.25] a. *But it may rain outside.* (i.e., But it may be the case that it
will rain outside)

b. *There must be a thunderstorm coming on.* (i.e., It must be
the case that a thunderstorm is coming on)

c. *You may try it if you like.* (i.e., You are allowed to try it)

d. *And here I must leave you.* (i.e., I am obliged to leave you
here)

Another distinction that cross-cuts the traditional categories of epistemic, deontic (or priority), and dynamic is the subjective-objective distinction: subjective indicates that the modal force or assessment derives from the speaker, whereas objective modality is based on some speaker-external source. However, these labels are not consistently applied with these basic meanings. Rather, at one end of the spectrum, subjective may indicate the category of modality as a whole in the cases in which modality is defined in terms of the *speaker's* assessment of propositions or situations (e.g., Palmer 1986: 2). On the other end of the spectrum, Portner (2009: 137) prefers a limited application of the terms to the subjective-objective distinction within epistemic modality, as introduced by Lyons (1977: 797–99). Between these extremes stand the discussions regarding the way that the subjective-objective distinction cross-cuts all three tradition categories of epistemic, deontic, and dynamic (Verstraete 2001; Butler 2003: 463–79).[38] For example, Verstraete (2001: 1525), based on his survey of previous theories as well as an analysis of grammatical criteria, concluded that epistemic is always subjective, that dynamic is always objective, and that deontic may be either subjective or objective.

Lyons (1977: 797) introduced the idea of subjective versus objective epistemic modality with the contrastive pair of interpretations in [1.26b–c] for the sentence in [1.26a] (see Portner 2009: 122–23). In the subjective interpretation, the modal force derives from the speaker him/herself regarding the proposition that Alfred is unmarried; in the objective interpretation, the modal possibility is included within the proposition stated by the speaker and thus outside the speaker's assessment in contrast to the subjective interpretation.

[1.26] a. Alfred may be married.

b. Subjective: POSS + it-is-so + [Alfred is unmarried]

c. Objective: I-say-so + POSS + [Alfred is unmarried]

---

38. Functional linguists particularly have given attention to this distinction in the context of their analysis of utterances as multilevel. Subjective and objective modality are understood as operating on different levels of the utterance (similar to the distinction between proposition and event modality; e.g., Dik 1997: 241–43).

A more nuanced view of this distinction is proposed by Nuyts (2001: 33–39), who replaces Lyons's "objective" category with "intersubjective," referring to a modal basis shared by speaker and addressee alike (see also Portner 2009: 122–29). Nuyts (2001: 36) points to parenthetic phrases in English such as *in my view/opinion/mind, if you ask me, to me* (subjective) versus *it is well known, you know* (intersubjective) as useful paraphrases of the distinction between the two types of epistemic expression.

By contrast, the subjective-objective distinction applied to deontic modality differs from this epistemic distinction (so Verstraete 2007: 36–38). Verstraete (2007: 32–35) explains that two features contribute to the subjective-objective distinction in deontic modal expressions: one is the presence or absence of a deontic source of obligation in the expression, and the other is whether this source of obligation is identified with the speaker or not. Thus, three types of deontic expression are possible, as illustrated by the examples in [1.27]: a subjective in which the source of obligation is the speaker; an objective with a specified source of obligation outside the speaker; and an objective with unspecified source of obligation.

[1.27]   a. Subjective deontic: *For taking my sister's life, and all the other lives, too, she must be locked up forever.* (Verstraete 2007: 32)

     b. Objective deontic, specified source of obligation: *But Ramadan means more than just physical deprivation. It has spiritual and moral obligations, too. Followers must refrain from bad thoughts, words and actions, perform special acts of charity and spend even more time than usual in worship.* (Verstraete 2007: 33)

     c. Objective deontic, unspecified source of obligation: *But to reach orbit an object must accelerate to a speed of about 17,500 miles per hour in a horizontal direction.* (Verstraete 2007: 33)

A distinction interrelated with the above is Portner's concept of performativity (2009: 137–38). While he expresses some hesitation at the idea of performativity in epistemic expressions (2009: 172–77), he finds it a productive distinction in deontic expressions (2009: 188–96). Performative deontic expressions are those that perform an additional speech act besides the simple assertion, as illustrated by example [1.28].

[1.28]   *You must not steal.* (performative expression: *Don't steal!*)

Portner (2009: 137–38) notes that his concept of performativity echoes Palmer's (1986: 102–4) category of subjective deontics and is somewhat different from Nuyts's (2001: 39) conception of performativity as reflecting the speaker's commitment to the proposition. Portner's understanding of performativity might be usefully combined with Verstraete's delineation of deontic modality (2007) by proposing that performativity is related to the distinction between objective deontic expressions with a specified source of obligation and those without: the former are performative, whereas the latter are not (see examples [1.27b–c]).

An alternative sort of taxonomy, as illustrated in [1.29], is represented by Bybee, Perkins, and Pagliuca (1994: 176–80): the subjective-objective distinction discussed above intersects with traditional grammatical moods associated with deontic modality, manifest as "speaker-oriented" versus "agent-oriented" modalities (see also Bybee and Fleischman 1995: 6).

[1.29] Taxonomy of modalities related to mood-based categories (based on Bybee, Perkins, and Pagliuca 1994: 176–80)

a. Epistemic modality ("applies to assertions and indicates the extent to which the speaker is committed to the truth of the proposition" [1994: 179])

Possibility: *But it may rain outside.* (Carroll 2000: 168)

Probability: *I shouldn't know you again if we did meet.* (Carroll 2000: 194)

Necessity: *There must be a thunderstorm coming on.* (Carroll 2000: 171)

b. Speaker-oriented modality ("allows the speaker to impose conditions on the addressee" [Bybee, Perkins, and Pagliuca 1994: 179])

Imperative: *Go and order the drums to begin.* (Carroll 2000: 200)

Prohibitive: *Now don't interrupt me!* (Carroll 2000: 128)

Hortative: *Kitty, dear, let's pretend.* (Carroll 2000: 130)

Admonitive: *Beware the Jabberwock, my son!* (Carroll 2000: 137)

Permissive: *You may rest a little now.* (Carroll 2000: 146)

c. Agent-oriented modality ("reports the existence of internal and external conditions on an agent with respect to the completion of the action expressed in the main predicate" [Bybee, Perkins, and Pagliuca 1994: 177])

Obligation (external, social conditions): *We must have a bit of a fight.* (Carroll 2000: 170)

Necessity (physcial conditions): *I must get a thinner pencil.*
I can't manage this one a bit. (Carroll 2000: 136)
Ability (internal enabling conditions): *I can explain all the*
poems that were ever invented. (Carroll 2000: 189)
Desire (internal volitional conditions): *She wanted to hear*
the news too. (Carroll 2000: 198)
Willingness: *You will observe the rules of battle, of course?*
(Carroll 2000: 206)
Permission (from root possibility): *You may try it if you like.*
(Carroll 2000: 209)

Palmer (2001: 84–85) notes, however, that Bybee, Perkins, and Pagliuca's division between speaker-oriented and agent-oriented modalities is "slightly strange." For instance, it groups semantically disparate modalities together in the agent-oriented category: while permission and obligation involve conditions external to the agent, desire and ability have to do with internal conditions. Palmer also notes the apparent redundancy of having a speaker-oriented "permissive" alongside an agent-oriented "permission." Nevertheless, Bybee, Perkins, and Pagliuca's taxonomy helpfully illustrates the manner in which the traditional categories of modality might be realized in categories of grammatical mood.

1.6.3.2. Modality and Speech Acts

The distinction of performativity discussed above and the illocutionary basis of Bybee, Perkins, and Pagliuca speaker-oriented modalities (see Bybee and Fleischman 1995: 6) raise the question of the precise relationship between modality and speech acts. Despite the speech-act background in the study of modality, opinions differ regarding the nature of the relationship between modality (particularly grammatical mood) and illocutionary force. To illustrate two widely different positions on this topic, Lyons (1977: 745) made a direct connection between modality in grammatical mood and illocutionary force in his discussion: the illocutionary force of a statement is associated with the declarative mood; the illocutionary force of a question is associated with the interrogative mood; and the illocutionary force of a command is associated with the imperative mood (see also Dik 1997: 303). By contrast, Kiefer (1987: 87) concluded from his investigation that "illocution is alien to the notion of modality."

The relationship between illocutionary force and modality, especially as expressed in mood, appears to lie between these two views. On the one hand, Austin (1962: 58–59) demonstrated that performative speech acts do not exhibit any unique grammatical structure. Therefore, it is potentially misleading to draw too close a connection between illocutionary moods and their regularly associated grammatical moods, as Lyons did. On the other hand, one cannot fail to observe an almost exclusive connection between particular moods and illocutionary forces, such as the imperative mood for commands. The asymmetrical relationship between illocutionary force and grammatical structure along with the inherent focus of speech act theory on the social function of language leads to the conclusion that illocutionary force belongs more to the domain of pragmatics than semantics (modality). That illocutionary force is more properly treated by pragmatics is underscored by the fact that it may be conveyed by pragmatic or conversational implicature. For example, the illocutionary (pragmatic) force of a polite command is often conveyed by an interrogative (semantic) mood or grammatical structure: *Would you like to close the door?* (as a polite command to the addressee to enter as opposed to the grammatical meaning of querying the addressee's desires).

1.6.3.3. Modality and Mood Systems

Portner (2009: 258–63) distinguishes verbal mood, notional mood, and sentence mood. Verbal mood is of primary interest, given the focus of this study on verbal systems. Portner's notional mood includes phenomena such as infinitives and dependent clauses, while his sentence mood refers to clause types and has connections with Lyon's linking of moods with speech acts (Lyon 1977: 745; see §1.6.3.2). Despite these varieties of mood phenomena, as already stated (§1.6.2; Palmer 2001: 4), mood systems are prototypically binary, exemplified by Indo-European languages' featuring an indicative : subjunctive distinction, or the realis : irrealis marking in Native American languages and the languages of Papua New Guinea (e.g., Chafe 1995; Romaine 1995). The latter *realis : irrealis* is preferable terminology for the typological category of verbal mood inasmuch as it has the advantage of clearly being a technical term (so Palmer 2001: 4) and not being subject to confusion with the grammatical categories of a particular language, as *indicative* and *subjunctive* are (see Portner 2009: 258). In addition, although Palmer (2001: 5) has claimed that "strictly, there is no typological difference between indicative/subjunctive and realis/irrealis," he recognizes that the binary characterization is really not wholly appropriate of indicative : subjunctive systems, since other verbal moods such as imperative and jussive stand outside the indicative : subjunctive opposition. Palmer (2001: 5) goes on to note a number of differences in the "distribution and syntactic functions" of the realis : irrealis and indicative : subjunctive. For one, the subjunctive, in contrast to the irrealis, is mostly found in subordinate clauses (hence the name *subjunctive*). A second difference is that the irrealis marker often co-occurs with other grammatical markers that are in complementary distribution with the indicative : subjunctive marking, such as imperative. A third is that both irrealis and subjunctive markers are often redundant but for different reasons: the irrealis because it co-occurs with other grammatical markers, and the subjunctive because its occurrence in subordinate clauses is usually determined by the type of complementizer. Finally, in contrast to indicative : subjunctive systems, realis : irrealis systems do not generally co-occur with tense systems; rather, past and present will usually be marked as realis, and future marked as irrealis.

As a semantically based typological (or metalinguistic) category, the binary realis : irrealis category is difficult to establish and has been criticized as generally unhelpful (so Bybee 1998). Part of the difficulty lies in the syntactic basis of the distinction in certain cases, such as a irrealis or subjunctive mood being determined by the particular complementizer. Nevertheless, the general association of realis as referring to real or actualized events or assertions versus irrealis's association with events that are not necessarily real or actualized, or are nonassertions remains widely applicable (Mithun 1999: 173; Palmer 2001: 111–12; Portner 2009: 1).[39]

The lack of cross-linguistic uniformity in particular has raised doubts concerning the validity of the typological category realis : irrealis (so Bybee, Perkins, and Pagliuca 1994: 236–40). However, Mithun (1999: 173) has pointed to the relativity of the binary opposition of realis : irrealis in that, while there is a unifying semantic distinction between realis and irrealis, the expression of this semantic distinction in different TAM systems varies. This approach also seems to obviate Bybee's (1998: 269) objection to the category *irrealis*, concluding that it "is simply too general to be useful." While this criticism may be valid with regard to its notional use (in which it may apply across the entire range of modalities; see, e.g., Palmer 2001: 163–68), the term is useful as almost a meta-modality category that recognizes a certain affinity among a wide range of modalities that may be expressed by a single grammatical mood, though the alignment of modalities and the binary-mood distinction may vary to some extent among languages.[40]

1.6.4. Conclusion: Modality and TAM Systems

The sprawling character of modality, the lack of strong uniformity of its categories across languages, and the relative recency of its study versus tense and aspect make it difficult to draw firm conclusions from the preceding overview. Relevant to the theoretical discussion in the following section is that the categories of TAM may all be analyzable in terms of temporality, thus pro-

---

39. Mithun (1999: 173) describes the distinction as follows: "the realis portrays situations as actualized, as having occurred or actually occurring, knowable through direct perception. The irrealis portrays a situation as purely within the realm of thought, knowable only through imagination" (see also Mithun 1995: 386).

40. An example is generic expressions, which Portner (2009: 4–5) classifies as a modal (i.e., irreal) expression but which lacks uniformity across languages; in Biblical Hebrew genericity is mainly expressed with realis mood constructions (see Cook 2005; Holmstedt 2005).

viding a unifying characteristic through which to explain interactions among these categories. In terms of the analysis of modality in Biblical Hebrew (or any specific language), it seems well to follow the advice of Portner (2009: 1):

> As a practical matter, the right way to discover modality is to begin with some of the features of language which most obviously involve modality, to understand these as well as possible, and then to see whether that understanding is also fruitful when applied to new features of language.

Although Portner is referring to the typological study of modality across languages, the lack of uniformity across languages makes it advantageous to approach modality in specific languages in the same way, such as looking for obviously modal expressions (e.g., Biblical Hebrew Imperative and Jussive verbs) and then seeing what other expressions share common features with these modalities.

1.7. A Model of Tense, Aspect, and Modality

In the second part of this chapter, a model of TAM illustrated with grammatical fragments from English is presented. There are several aims in constructing this model. First, it provides opportunity to distill some of the important contributions to understanding TAM that were noted in the survey in the first part of this chapter. Second, it enables further exploration of the interaction between the parameters of TAM. While it was valuable to treat these three parameters separately, as in the preceding surveys, they must also be understood in their dynamic interaction in natural language. Finally, this discussion aims at providing a modest formalization of TAM, thus providing a useful metalanguage for analyzing the object language of BH in subsequent chapters.

1.7.1. Semantics and TAM

Linguistic semantics is the field of linguistics that studies meaning in natural language. The field encompasses intersecting interests and ideas from both logical semantics and philosophical semantics (or philosophy of language; see Crystal 2008: 428). The most common approach to semantics continues to be *Montague semantics* (see Janssen 2006: 7.244–55), named after its originator, Richard Montague (1974). Montague argued that the semantics that was developed for the purpose of interpreting formal languages (i.e., mathmatical and logical languagues) is equally suitable for providing precise interpretations of natural language expressions (see Cann 1993: 2).

There are three important principles underlying Montague semantics that are especially important to introduce here as a backdrop to the semantic theory of TAM to follow. The first of these is the principle of *compositionality*, attributed to the German philosopher Gottlob Frege, which states that "the meaning of an expression is a function of the meaning of its parts" (Cann 1993: 3). Thus, a compositional semantic theory will explain the meaning of larger expressions by reference to the contribution of the individual parts of the expressions. The theory constructed here is compositional in that it begins by examing the parameters of TAM individually, then their isolated interaction, and finally their contribution to full linguistic expressions. This "bottom-up" approach is likewise taken in the move from analyzing BH grammar fragments in chap. 3 to analyzing discourse in chap. 4.

The second principle also derives, at least in part, from the philosophical writings of Frege but is also prominent in the writings of the logician Alfred Tarski (see Chruszczewski 2006; Cann 1993: 17) and has roots reaching back to the ancient Greek philosophers. This principle, referred to as the *correspondence theory of truth*, states that "a statement in some language is true if, and only if, it corresponds to some state-of-affairs" (Cann 1993: 15). The importance of the correspondence theory of truth is in its definition of *meaning*—meaning is truth-conditional; that is to say, to know the meaning of an utterance is to know the conditions under which the utterance would be true (Cann 1993: 15). A drawback to this approach is its apparent limitation to utterances that are descriptive of states of affairs; however, the concept of *alternative futures* provides a means of applying this approach to both descriptive and nondescriptive sentences (see §1.6.1 above and §1.7.5 below).

The third principle, *model-theoretical interpretation*, is closely related to truth-conditional semantics: while truth-conditional semantics states that a statement is true if it corresponds to some state of affairs, model-theoretical interpretation provides a means for representing the individuals and relations among them that make up the state of affairs in question as well as rules for interpreting expressions in natural language with respect to any arbitrary model (Cann 1993: 18). Thus, a central task of a semantic theory built on these three principles must be to "provide an account of the relation between linguistic expressions and the things that they can be used to talk about" (Cann 1993: 1).

In Montague semantics, analysis of meaning is not carried out on the sentences of the object language themselves but on a logical (meta)language into which the object language has been translated. By this means, the inherent ambiguity and inaccuracy in the natural object language is resolved. While the benefits of this approach are indisputable (see Cann 1993: 17, 24), the nature of the logical language(s) of semantics makes such analyses more inaccessible to nonspecialists (hence the need for guides to logical language such as Allwood, Andersson, and Dahl 1977; and McCawley 1993). In the theory of TAM presented here, I attempt to steer a middle course. On the one hand, it is desirable to analyze TAM with a certain degree of formalization, particularly in order to escape the ambiguity and imprecision that an English paraphrase of the object language (BH) presents. An analysis of verbal TAM in an object language may too easily devolve into an analysis of the TAM of a natural metalanguage. On the other hand, it is unwieldy to introduce a logical language and model-theoretical interpretation for entire sentences in every instance. Thus, the following theory, while drawing on the concept of alternative situations and presenting a moderate degree of formalization of TAM, does not present a full model-theoretical interpretation of TAM. It is my hope that this approach avoids the inaccuracies of a natural metalanguage (as opposed to a logical metalanguage) while at the same time preserving a large degree of accessibility for nonspecialists.

1.7.2. Time and Space: Temporality and TAM

Tense has long been recognized as associated with temporality (§1.1). The preceding discussion of TAM also notes that linguists have related all three parameters frequently associated with the verb (TAM) to temporality (§1.6.2), thus vindicating Aristotle's early observation that the verb carries with it the notion of time (p. 1 n. 1 above). The model developed here is based on this unifying feature of temporality in TAM.

It is almost universal to speak of time in spatial terms: we look at time as a line upon which we stand in the now (present); we may look back on the past or forward toward the future.[41] The spatial metaphor of time envisioned as taking up linear space, proceeding from the left (past time) to the right (future time), is the basis of the following discussion. However, a simple unilinear conceptualization based on the time-space metaphor is only adequate for the analysis of tense; this metaphor will require modification to include the notion of "event time"—that is, the internal temporal constituency of events—in order to analyze *aspect*, as well as expansion to incorporate the idea of "alternative times" to account adequately for *modality*. The following discussion is organized around these various time-space metaphorical conceptions.

1.7.3. Aspect and Event Time

The temporal character of aspect can be captured with a model of events. Foundational to constructing a model of this sort is the notion of intervals, introduced by Bennett and Partee (1978; see p. 29 n. 27 above). Since most events extend over multiple moments, and many of these sorts of events also

---

41. There is a rich array of spatiotemporal metaphors perserved in idiomatic expressions, such as "walking" or "stepping into" the future, or being unable to "go back" to one's past. Alternatively, we can conceive of time as moving: past events have "passed" us by, we wait to "meet" our future, "time flies." This alternate conception of time as moving presents the opposite viewpoint to the linear, stationary view of time: the past lies "before" us, while (future) "time is catching up with us." This latter conception of time was common among ancient Greeks and Romans, as is evident from the spatial and temporal use of Latin and Greek prepositions: for example, Latin *post* and Greek ὀπίσω spatially mean 'behind' or 'backward' but temporally 'after' and 'afterward'; Latin *ante* and Greek πρό(σω) spatially mean 'in front of' but are used with the temporal meaning 'before' earlier events (see Liddell and Scott 1940: 1239, 1532; see Traugott 1978 for a discussion of spatial expressions of tense and aspect).

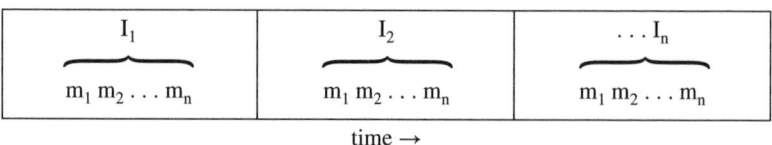

time →

Figure 1.12. An interval model of event time (I = interval, m = moment).

[onset]	[I nucleus F]	[coda]
	I_1	
preparatory phase	$m_1\ m_2\ m_3\ m_4 \ldots m_n$	resultant phase

time →

Figure 1.13. A model of events (I = initial point, F = final point, $I_\#$ = interval, $m_\#$ = moment).

do not occur during every moment of their duration, evaluating the truth-conditional value of an event at a particular moment in time is inadequate. According to *interval semantics*, events must be evaluated at intervals of time, which comprise primitive moments of time ordered by a precedence relationship (<) (see Cann 1993: 234–35). Interval semantics prevents the evaluation of examples such as *Kathy worked all day in the garden* as true at the interval *all day* from being invalidated by the possibility that Kathy took periodic breaks through the day (see Dowty 1977: 50). A model of event time based on interval semantics may be schematized as in fig. 1.12.

A model of event time is not identical with a model of events. In order to be able to model events in terms of their location and progression in event time, one must have a means of designating phases of events. One way of doing this is to analyze event structure using terminology from syllable phonology: an event consists of an *onset*, a *nucleus*, and a *coda* (cf. Olsen's use of nucleus and coda, §1.4.3). The onset refers to the preparatory phase of an event, and the coda to the resultant phase. The nucleus refers to the event proper, which consists of at least one interval (except in the case of achievements; see §1.7.3.1) and is bounded by an I(nitial) endpoint and a F(inal) endpoint. This event model is portrayed in fig. 1.13.

1.7.3.1. Situation Aspect and Event Time

Rothstein's feature chart, presented above (table 1.12, p. 22) and repeated here (table 1.18), is the starting point for the following analysis of *situation aspect*. As mentioned earlier (§1.3.1), the strength of Rothstein's feature chart is its linguistic elegance: only two features are used to distinguish the four situation types, thus leaving no feature combinations unrealized.

Table 1.18. Rothstein's Feature Chart for Situation Aspect
(adapted from 2004: 12)

Situation Aspect	[±Stages]	[±Telic]
State	−	−
Activity	+	−
Accomplishment	+	+
Achievement	−	+

In contrast to other feature charts, Rothstein's uses the feature [±stages] in-stead of [±dynamicity] or [±stativity] (cf. Olsen's chart in table 1.16, p. 35, and C. S. Smith's chart in fig. 1.3d, p. 21; see Smith 1997: 19 on dynamic events' having "stages"). This approach implies a localist understanding of dy-namicity, such as Verkuyl (1993: 15) presents: dynamic (or [+stages]) events feature progress, defined as the movement of a theme from a source to a goal.[42] This progression may be more or less metaphorical. For example, in *John bi-cycled home (from the office)*, the progress is fairly literal, expressible in terms of the location of John along the way home: initially, he is still at the office $< t_0$, office>, then he proceeds past the library $< t_1$, library>, then past the park $< t_2$, park>, and the last point is at home $< t_n$, home> (see Verkuyl 1993: 218). By contrast, the progress in an event such as *Colin ate three sandwiches* is more metaphorical; we can conceive of the progress in terms of Colin moving along a "path" of sandwich eating: $< t_0$, no sandwiches eaten>, $< t_1$, half a sandwich eaten>, . . . $< t_n$, three sandwiches eaten> (see Verkuyl 1993: 239).

Rothstein's [±stages] represent more than simply a terminological differ-ence with other feature charts in that she does not identify [+stages] as a prop-erty of achievements (cf. Olsen's chart in table 1.16, p. 35; Smith's chart in fig. 1.3d, p. 21; Verkuyl's schema in fig. 1.3c, p. 21). This approach is crucial to the linguistic elegance of her chart, because otherwise, achieve-ments and accomplishments would be indiscernible. Rothstein's reason for not identifying achievements as [+stages] is "because they are near instantaneous" (Rothstein 2004: 12; see also fig. 1.14d, p. 63).

The property [±telic] is a feature of virtually all discussions of situation as-pect: accomplishments and achievements are [+telic] because they have an in-herent or intended endpoint (Depraetere 1995: 2–3).[43] The [±telic] distinction is rooted in Aristotle's observations on ἐνέργεια and κίνησις (see quotation in §1.3.1), and has been discussed in the literature in terms of the imperfective

---

42. The localist theory of aspect argues, partially on the basis of the pervasiveness of spatiotemporal metaphors discussed above (p. 57 n. 41), that temporal relationships are in-herently spatial (see Anderson 1973).

43. The atelic : telic distinction is also expressed as homogeneous : heterogeneous and cumulativity : quantization in the literature (see Rothstein 2004: 8–10).

paradox and subinterval property.[44] Situations defined as [− telic] possess the subinterval property: if [− telic] situations are evaluated as true at an interval of time, then they are also true at any subinterval of that interval. For example, if the stative VP in *Evan was asleep* is true at some interval I_1 (e.g., from 2 p.m. to 4 p.m.), then it is true of any subinterval of I_1 (i.e., at any time between 2 p.m. and 4 p.m.). By contrast, if the accomplishment VP in *Tage built a house* is true at some interval I_1, it does not entail a true evaluation at any subinterval of I_1, because the inherent endpoint (of completion) has not been reached until the end of the interval.

This association between the subinterval property and (a)telicity and has been questioned in recent literature (esp. Depraetere 1995; C. S. Smith 1999). Rather than (a)telicity being the determining factor in whether a situation possesses the subinterval property, (un)boundedness is the determining factor (see §1.5.3). While (a)telicity refers to whether an event has an inherent endpoint, (un)boundedness has to do with whether an event has reached a temporal boundary (Depraetere 1995: 2–3). Thus, even though the stative VP in *Evan was asleep* possesses the subinterval property, when temporal bounds are linguistically expressed for the state, as in *Evan was asleep from 2 p.m. to 4 p.m.*, the VP no longer possesses the subinterval property: *Evan was asleep from 2 p.m. to 4 p.m.* can only be true when the endpoint of the interval, the temporal bound defined by 4 p.m., has been reached; it is not true of any subinterval of that interval.

The association of the subinterval property with (a)telicity is also problematic because the subinterval property does not apply to states and activities in the same manner. Dowty (1986: 42) observes that, if a state is true at a certain interval, then it is true in all of its subintervals; but, if an activity is true at a certain interval, then it is true at all of its subintervals, "down to a certain limit in size." In other words, if *Evan was asleep* is true from 2 p.m. to 4 p.m., then it is true at *every* subinterval between 2 p.m. and 4 p.m.; but, if *Kathy worked* is true from 9 a.m. to 5 p.m., it is true only down to a certain level of subinterval. The activity is not considered falsified if, for instance, Kathy takes a half-hour lunch break, even though for that half-hour subinterval *Kathy worked* is not literally true. The interaction of (un)boundedness, situation aspect, and viewpoint aspect is discussed with respect to the temporality of discourse in chap. 4 (§4.2).

The features of [±stages] and [±telic] are properties of the entire VP. Therefore, the argument structure and not only the verbal lexeme determines the situation type of the VP. A longstanding problem that arises is how to define

---

44. The imperfective paradox is illustrated by the examples in [1.8], above (p. 23). The term "subinterval property" was coined by Bennett and Partee (1978) in their treatise on interval semantics, which was conceived in part to address the difficulties of the imperfective paradox; Hatav (1989; 1997) employs the term "distributive property."

the contribution of the verbal lexeme itself. By understanding the aspectual features as privative oppositions (see p. 34 n. 28 above), Olsen claimed to be able to predict what sort of shifts in situation type can or cannot occur from changes in the VP's argument structure. However, as was pointed out above (§1.4.3), Olsen's approach does not always produce convincing results.

It may not be possible fully to predict shifts in situation type, as Olsen attempted to do. Instead, a more reasonable argument is Rothstein's claim (2004: 33) that the situation type of the verbal lexeme (i.e., the verbal lexeme with minimally grammatical or no arguments) provides constraints on what sorts of VPs the verb may head. These constraints are exploited in linguistic tests to distinguish among situation types (see §1.3.1). Understanding the behavior of situation aspect in linguistic tests as constraints underscores their value in explicating the semantic characteristics of the situation types, without demanding that shifts among situation types be fully predictable. For example, states do not generally combine with progressive aspect in English: *?Bill is knowing the answer* (taken from example [1.6a], p. 23). Although Olsen (1997: 36–37) claimed that the examples she produced invalidate the test, it is better to understand this behavior as a constraint, which informs us that that these sorts of construction, though possible, will be nonstandard and relatively infrequent. More importantly, the behavior of states with progressive aspect in English tells us something about the semantic character of the property [±stages] and progressive aspect: the reason that states are ungrammatical or nonstandard when combined with progressive aspect is because they lack the property of [+stages], which progressive aspect requires in the verbal lexeme to which it is applied since the progressive has the sense of being in the process of some activity (Bybee, Perkins, and Pagliuca 1994: 133).

Similarly, it has been noted that accomplishment and achievment VPs are only marginally acceptable with temporal prepositional phrases headed by *for* but fully acceptable with those headed by *in*, as illustrated by the pairs of examples in [1.30]–[1.31] (cf. example [1.7] above, p. 23). By contrast, the reverse behavior is found in activity VPs, as shown by the pair of examples in [1.32].

[1.30] a. ?Colin <u>fixed the car</u> (ACC) *for* an hour.
       b. Colin <u>fixed the car</u> (ACC) *in* an hour.

[1.31] a. ?Tage <u>won the race</u> (ACH) *for* 5 minutes and 35 seconds.
       b. Tage <u>won the race</u> (ACH) *in* 5 minutes and 35 seconds.

[1.32] a. Evan <u>walked</u> (ACT) *for* an hour.
       b. ?Evan <u>walked</u> (ACT) *in* an hour.

Though these tests do not enable us fully to predict the shifts among situation types, they are important because of what they tell us about the semantic character of the feature [±telic]: one does not talk about reaching an inherent endpoint (the feature of telicity) over a period of time (for α time) but within a particular time (in α time).

The temporal characteristics of particular situation types can be illustrated using the event model introduced above in fig. 1.13 (p. 58). While the situation types are distinguished by the features [±stages, ±telic], which apply to the nucleus of the event model (with the exception of achievements), these feature distinctions may be reflected in the event structure itself, as illustrated by fig. 1.14a–d. Other than the notation of a [−stages, −telic] nucleus, the event model for states in fig. 1.14a is identical with the basic event model in fig. 1.13.

The event model for activities in fig. 1.14b has a [+stages, −telic] nucleus. The [−telic] feature is reflected in the nucleus's arbitrary final endpoint (F_{arb}): one does not finish an activity but stops at some arbitrary point.

By contrast, the event model of accomplishments in fig. 1.14c has a [+stages, +telic] nucleus and thus a natural final endpoint (F_{nat}), which when reached makes the accomplishment finished.

Finally, the event model for achievements in fig. 1.14d lacks a nucleus through the combination of features [−stages, +telic]. Since there are no stages or progression leading up to the natural final endpoint, the final endpoint becomes a near instantaneous transition from the preparatory phase to the resultant phase of the event (see Dahl 1997: 420).

1.7.3.2. Phasal Aspect and Event Time

Phasal aspect was defined above as introducing alterations to one or another of the phases of development of a situation (§1.3.2). The particulars of these alterations can now be explicated using the event model developed above (§1.7.3): phasal aspects act upon one of the three phases of an event (the onset, the nucleus, or the coda) or one of the transitions between those phases (i.e., onset-nucleus, nucleus-coda, or onset-coda in the case of achievements); phasal aspects transform a given portion of the event into an activity subevent, and in the case of phasal aspects that act on the nucleus, they also alter the progression of the event in some way (see example [1.11], p. 27).

Other differences between types of phasal aspect have to do with the event phases and the type of situations to which they apply. For example, one type of phasal aspect applies to the onset-nucleus transition (or onset-coda for achievements), illustrated by example [1.33]: the incohative refers to this alteration of states, whereas the inceptive refers to this alteration of dynamic [+stages] events.

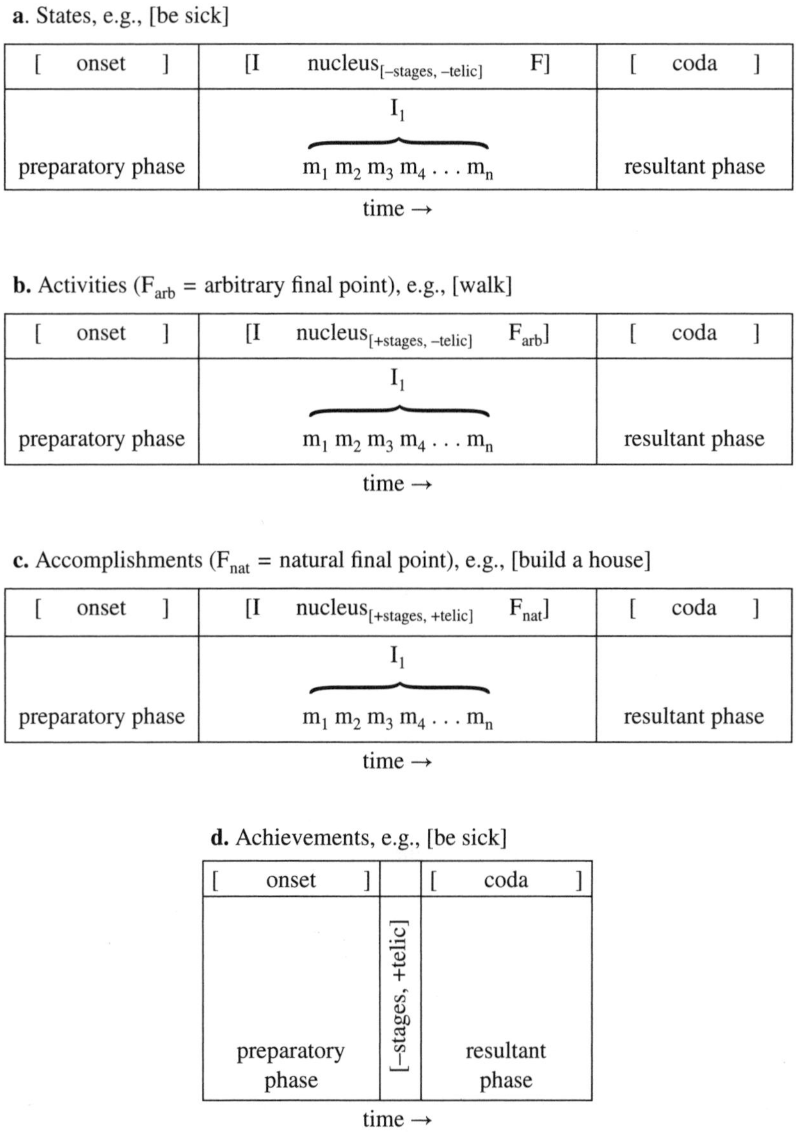

a. States, e.g., [be sick]

[onset]	[I nucleus$_{[-stages, -telic]}$ F]	[coda]
	I$_1$	
preparatory phase	$\overbrace{m_1\ m_2\ m_3\ m_4\ \ldots\ m_n}$	resultant phase

time →

b. Activities (F$_{arb}$ = arbitrary final point), e.g., [walk]

[onset]	[I nucleus$_{[+stages, -telic]}$ F$_{arb}$]	[coda]
	I$_1$	
preparatory phase	$\overbrace{m_1\ m_2\ m_3\ m_4\ \ldots\ m_n}$	resultant phase

time →

c. Accomplishments (F$_{nat}$ = natural final point), e.g., [build a house]

[onset]	[I nucleus$_{[+stages, +telic]}$ F$_{nat}$]	[coda]
	I$_1$	
preparatory phase	$\overbrace{m_1\ m_2\ m_3\ m_4\ \ldots\ m_n}$	resultant phase

time →

d. Achievements, e.g., [be sick]

[onset]		[coda]
	$_{[-stages, +telic]}$	
preparatory phase		resultant phase

time →

Figure 1.14. Event models for situation types (I = initial point, F = final point, I = interval, m = moment).

[1.33] Onset Phasal Aspects

    a. *Incohative* (with states):

       The whole place around her <u>became alive</u>. (Carroll 2000: 117)

       (onset-nucleus$_{[-stages, -telic]}$ > subevent$_{[+stages, -telic]}$)

    b. *Inceptive* (with activities and accomplishments, [+stages] events):

       All the guest <u>began drinking</u> it directly. (Carroll 2000: 232)

       (onset-nucleus$_{[+stages, -telic]}$ > subevent$_{[+stages, -telic]}$)

    c. *Inceptive* (with achievements):

       Alice <u>began to remember</u> that she was a pawn. (Carroll 2000: 148)

       (onset-coda$_{[-stages, +telic]}$ > subevent$_{[+stages, -telic]}$)

Another type of phasal aspect applies, by contrast, to the nucleus-coda transition (onset-nucleus for achievements) of the situation, as illustrated by examples [1.34a–b]: cessative refers to this alteration of [−telic] events, while completive refers to this alteration of [+telic] events.

[1.34] Coda Phasal Aspect

    a. *Cessative* (with activities or states, [−telic] events):

       Tweedledum and tweedledee <u>stopped fighting</u>.

       (nucleus$_{[+stages, -telic]}$-coda > subevent$_{[+stages, -telic]}$)

    b. *Completive* (with accomplishments or achievements, [+telic] events):

       Alice <u>finished reading the poem</u>.

       (nucleus$_{[+stages, +telic]}$-coda > subevent$_{[+stages, -telic]}$)

The accompanying formalizations for examples [1.33]–[1.34] denote (1) the phase of the situation to which the phasal aspect applies (onset-nucleus, nucleus-coda, or onset-coda transition), (2) the situation type (defined in terms of [±stages, ±telic]), and (3) the fact that phasal aspect transforms the situation (>) into an activity subevent (subevent$_{[+stages, -telic]}$).

    Phasal aspects that apply to the nucleus possess an added feature in that they alter the progression of the situation nucleus, through either the repetition of intervals (denoted by ×) or their extension (with or without pause: [±pause]). Iteratives denote the repetition specifically of minimal activity events, which are denoted in [1.35a] as having of a single nucleus interval consisting of just one moment: $I_1 = m_1$ (see Rothstein 2004: 28–29). By contrast, habituals, illustrated by example [1.35b], express the patterned repetition of any type of event. Similarly, continuative and resumptive phasal aspects, illustrated in

[1.35c–d], form a pair: both express the extension of an event nucleus, but the resumptive presumes a pause of unexpressed duration before the event is continued ([+pause]).

[1.35]   Nucleus Phasal Aspect

a. *Iterative* (repetition of minimal activity event):
Alice <u>knocked</u> and <u>rang</u> in vain for a long time. (Carroll 2000: 227)

(nucleus$\{I_1 = m_1\}_{[\text{+stages, }-\text{telic}]} > \times$ subevent$_{[\text{+stages, }-\text{telic}]}$)

b. *Habitual* (regular pattern of repetition of an event):
It <u>always makes one</u> a little <u>giddy</u> at first. (Carroll 2000: 174)

(nucleus$_{[\text{+stages, +telic}]} > \times$ subevent$_{[\text{+stages, }-\text{telic}]}$)

c. *Continuative* (extension of an event without a pause):
The Red Queen <u>continued shaking</u> her head.

(nucleus$_{[\text{+stages, }-\text{telic}]} > {}_{[-\text{pause}]}$subevent$_{[\text{+stages, }-\text{telic}]}$)

d. *Resumptive* (extension of an event after a pause):
Humpty Dumpty <u>resumed explaining</u> the poem.

(nucleus$_{[\text{+stages, }-\text{telic}]} > {}_{[+\text{pause}]}$subevent$_{[\text{+stages, }-\text{telic}]}$)

1.7.3.3. Viewpoint Aspect and Event Time

Viewpoint aspect was defined above as presenting different viewpoints on situations (§1.3.3). The tense-aspect theories that drew on R-point tense theory used the R-E relationship to define viewpoint aspect (§1.4). Klein's theory is of particular importance since he defined both R and E in terms of intervals (§1.4.2). The understanding of viewpoint aspect in the tense-aspect theories is the basis of the approach to viewpoint aspect here. Specifically, here, viewpoint aspect is defined by the temporal relationship between the *reference frame* (RF) and the *event frame* (EF)—the event frame referring to the temporal span of some portion (usually the nucleus) of the event model introduced above (§1.7.3).[45] I treat four different viewpoint aspects: the perfective : imperfective opposition, the perfect, and the progressive.

The opposition between perfective and imperfective viewpoint aspects was described above using the metaphor of the focal length of camera lenses: perfective is like a wide-angle lens, while the imperfective view is like a telephoto lens (§1.3.3). This metaphor involving scope and distance (i.e., focal length) may now be translated into spatiotemporal terms defining the relationship between the reference frame and the event frame. *Scope* refers to how much of

---

45. Chung and Timberlake (1985: 218) employ the term "event frame" in the way I am using "reference frame."

a. Perfective viewpoint   b. Imperfective viewpoint

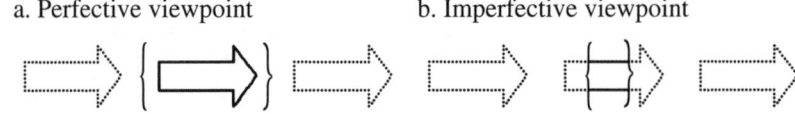

Figure 1.15. Gestalt illustration of perfective and imperfective viewpoints.

the event frame is included in the reference frame. In the case of the perfective, the reference frame includes an entire interval of the event frame nucleus.[46] By contrast, the reference frame of the imperfective viewpoint aspect is included within an interval of the event frame nucleus; it excludes the initial and final endpoints of the interval (see Hatav 1993).

It is important that the relationship between the event frame and reference frame defining perfective and imperfective aspect be defined in terms of a single interval of the event frame in order to avoid the mistaken correlation between perfective : imperfect aspects and the notion of complete(d) : incomplete(d) events. These mistaken implications may be accounted for, and so avoided, by drawing on *Gestalt theory*[47] and conceptualizing the situation spatially as in fig. 1.15: each arrow represents an interval of the event frame; the brackets represent the reference frame for each viewpoint.

Perfective aspect includes an entire interval in its reference frame, as the brackets in fig. 1.15a illustrate; thus, it gives the impression that the event is complete(d). However, the interval in the reference frame is not necessarily the only interval for which the situation holds, as shown by the broken-line arrows outside the brackets. By contrast, imperfective aspect excludes the beginning and end of an interval from its reference frame, represented by the placement of the brackets in fig. 1.15b. As Gestalt theory predicts, when the brackets are placed over the arrow as in fig. 1.15b, one will mentally construct the endpoints of the arrows, represented by the broken lines, thus perceiving that the arrow (or event) projects beyond the reference frame.

Distance refers to whether the event frame interval(s) is/are "discerned" within the reference frame. If an interval is "discerned" within the reference frame, this more easily allows for another event to be portrayed as occurring within that same interval. The perfective aspect has a distant reference frame,

---

46. This way of defining the relationship between RF and EF avoids the over-richness produced by Klein's less precise definition of perfective simply as R ∩ E (see table 1.13, p. 31, above).

47. *Gestalt psychology* (as it relates to the discussion here) deals with the processes of perception. It maintains that images are perceived as whole patterns rather than as distinct parts and formulates principles to explain the perceptual processes, such as the principles discussed here. However, it is a widespread misconception that Gestalt psychology is only concerned with a psychology of perception (see Kanizsa 1979: 55–71).

while the imperfective has a near reference frame. The effect of this difference in distance is found in the fact that the imperfective lends itself more naturally to serve as an event frame for another event taking place within the same interval of time. This is illustrated by example [1.36], repeated from [1.11].

[1.36] a. She was rambling on [≈IPFV] in this way when she reached
             [≈PFV] the wood. (Carroll 2000: 156)
        b. She rambled on [≈PFV] in this way when she reached [≈PFV]
             the wood.

The example with the English progressive construction (≈imperfective) in [1.36a] reports two overlapping events: Alice reached the woods during one of the intervals of time that she was rambling. By contrast, example [1.36b] has a temporally successive default reading: Alice rambled on in this way after the interval of time when she reached the wood.

The perfective : imperfective opposition may be formalized using symbols from set theory, as illustrated in example [1.37]: the perfective is defined as RF ⊃ EF—that is, the reference frame includes an interval of the event frame; the imperfective is defined as RF ⊂ EF—that is, the reference frame is included in an interval of the event frame. A far focal distance is invariably associated with the wide scope RF ⊃ EF of the perfective, while a near focal distance is likewise associated with the scope RF ⊂ EF of the imperfective.

[1.37] a. She was rambling (≈IPFV). RF ⊂ EF(nucleus)
        b. She rambled (≈PFV). RF ⊃ EF(nucleus)

The notation "(nucleus)" in the examples refers to the fact that the perfective and imperfective aspects have a default focus on the nucleus of an event (as opposed to the onset or coda; cf. the perfect below); this default focus may of course be altered by phasal aspects (§1.7.3.2).

Perfect (also referred to as anterior) is treated here as a viewpoint aspect, although it is unique compared with the other viewpoint aspects (Comrie 1976: 52). On the one hand, the perfect allows for tense distinctions (e.g., *had run, has run, will have run*); on the other hand, it may combine with progressive viewpoint aspect (e.g., *has been sleeping*). The ability of the perfect to combine with the progressive may be explained by analyzing the reference frame of the perfect as relating in scope and distance to the coda of the event frame rather than the nucleus (so M. R. Johnson 1981; W. Klein 1994; see fig. 1.6, p. 30, and table 1.13c, p. 31). Hence, the perfect focuses on the resultant phase of a prior event nucleus, as illustrated in example [1.38]: the event [promise] is prior to the reference frame in which *the king has promised*. The reference frames of the nonprogressive perfect and progressive perfect contrast with respect to the event frame coda in the same way as the perfective and imperfective reference frames relate to the event frame nucleus (i.e., in terms of scope and distance), as illustrated by the analyses of examples [1.38a–b] (cf. [1.37]).

[1.38]   a.   The king <u>has promised</u> (PERF) me. (Carroll 2000: 184)
RF ⊃ EF(coda)

b.   The kitten <u>had been having</u> (PERF-PROG) a grand game of romps. (Carroll 2000: 127)
RF ⊂ EF(coda)

The strength of this analysis is that it captures the current relevance characteristic of the perfect (Binnick 1991: 264), but at the same time it avoids the problems created by interpreting the event nucleus as extending into the reference frame (so Hatav 1993: 220; see W. Klein 1994: 104; and table 1.14, p. 32). The perfect focuses on the resultant (or implied) state of a past event. The resultant state is sometimes semantically connected to the perfect verb (e.g., *He has died* [event] > *He is dead* [state]); oftentimes, however, the resultant event must be determined by real world knowledge (e.g., *We can't come to your party. The police have arrested my wife* [event]; thus, *My wife is indisposed.* [state]) (see Moens 1987: 71–72).

Progressive is analyzed here as a viewpoint aspect. However, it has been treated variously as a tense, a viewpoint aspect, a phasal aspect, a discourse-pragmatic verb, and a modality (see Binnick 1991: 281–90; Dik 1997: 225; Dowty 1977). Aspectually, the progressive is apparently identical with the imperfective (see p. 27 n. 24). Nevertheless, there are cross-linguistic features that differentiate the two verb forms. First, progressives often are or develop from periphrastic constructions and/or are based on nominal forms (Bybee, Perkins, and Pagliuca 1994: 130; Dahl 1985: 91). Second, progressives are more restricted than imperfectives: they generally do not occur with stative predicates, and they generally have a narrower future time use, expressing either an "expected" event (Comrie 1976: 33–34; Bybee, Perkins, and Pagliuca 1994: 249–50) or an element of intention (Binnick 1991: 289). Third, the perfective : imperfective opposition is often correlated with the tensed past : nonpast opposition, whereas the progressive is freely used for past, present, and future time reference (Dahl 1985: 92–93). Hence, although the imperfective and progressive are semantically indistinguishable, they can be differentiated based on consistent cross-linguistic characteristics.

1.7.4. Tense and Unilinear Time

Tense is defined by temporal precedence relationships, thus requiring a simple unilinear spatial metaphor of time. The defining characteristic of the tense-aspect R-point theories surveyed above is that they use the notion of a reference point/time for both tense and viewpoint aspect (§1.4). A difficulty encountered with this approach is that R is defined differently for analyzing aspect and for analyzing tense. In particular, M. R. Johnson's theory encountered difficulties over whether to treat R as an interval of time or a point (moment) of time or both, depending on whether it is associated with the interval E or the moment S (§1.4.1).

What is required to overcome this difficulty is a model that associates an interval R, whose relationship with the event time determines viewpoint aspect, with a momentary R, whose precedence relationship with S determines tense. The solution adopted here draws on Declerck's bifurcation of R into R_{TR} (R "time referred to") and R_{TO} (R "time of orientation"; see §1.2.3.4) and Olsen's concept of a "deictic center" (C; see §1.4.3): tense is determined by a precedence relationship between S and C, the latter of which is associated with a relevant RF (denoted as C_{RF}), whose relationship with EF determines viewpoint aspect. Thus, analysis of the basic tense distinctions may be expressed as in example [1.39] (taken from table 1.8, p. 14).

[1.39]   a.   John <u>ate</u> an apple (PAST). C < S

b.   John <u>is eating</u> an apple (PRES). S,C

c.   John <u>will eat</u> an apple (FUT). S < C

However, Dahl has criticized the R-point tense-aspect approach for neglecting the temporal relationship between the event time and the speech time, which had been the basis for defining tense prior to the R-point theory (see §1.4.1). Dahl (1997: 425) introduced the contrastive examples [1.40a–b] to argue that the event time–speech time relationship can be determinative in tense choice. An adequate analysis of these examples requires that tense be defined compositionally (∘) as consisting of a C_{RF}-S precedence relationship and an EF-S precedence relationship, as illustrated by the analyses accompanying examples [1.40a–b].

[1.40]   a.   Today, my office hours <u>are</u> from ten to twelve.

[C_{RF}(*today*), S] ∘ [S ≤ EF(*ten to twelve*)]

b.   Today, my office hours <u>were</u> from ten to twelve.

[C_{RF}(*today*), S] ∘ [EF(*ten to twelve*) < S]

In these examples, the C_{RF}-S relationship remains constant (defined precisely by the temporal adverb *today*), whereas the EF-S relationship contrasts in the two examples, explaining the variation in tense choice. In order to handle tense adequately in expressions requiring multiple R-points, the deictic center must be defined as a transient time that is initially located relative to the speech time and ultimately associated with a reference frame but meanwhile may be located by the tense at some other temporal position.

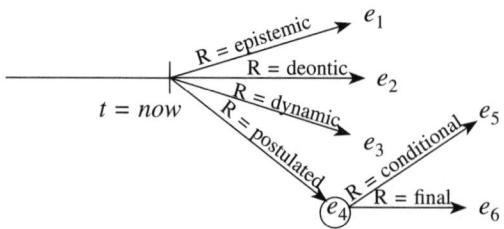

Figure 1.16. Alternative situations (R = accessibility relation; e = alternative situation).

Another difficulty that confronts both R-point tense and tense-aspect theories is the issue of multiple R-points (see §1.2 above). The function of this transient deictic center in defining tense may be illustrated on the subordinate conditional constructions in example [1.41]. The conditional *would* denotes the event [walk] as occuring *after* some time determined by the context—namely, the past tense verb *said* of the matrix clause. Thus, the deictic center is initially located left by the past tense *said* (C_{pos1}); from there, the conditional *would walk* locates C rightward to a position between C_{pos1} and S, where it is associated with RF (C_{RF}) (EF is related to RF to determine viewpoint aspect: RF ⊃ EF).

[1.41]   He said he <u>would come in.</u> (Carroll 2000: 225)

$$C_{pos1} < C_{RF} < S \text{ \& } RF ⊃ EF$$

1.7.5. Modality and Alternative Times

In keeping with a unified analysis of TAM in terms of temporal relationships, we defined modality in terms of the temporal *existence* of an event or with respect to alternative situations (§1.6.2). For the purposes of this book, it is unnecessarily complicated to introduce a full modal logic model (for which, see Allwood, Andersson, and Dahl 1977: 108–24; McCawley 1993: 372–416; Portner 2009: 9–46); however, the principles of modal logic underlie the following simplified formalization of modality in terms of sentential operators. Most basically, the discussion assumes that modality is explicable in terms of accessibility relations and the necessity and possibility modal operators (see Portner 2009: 31).[48]

---

48. For example, a modal logic expression of the truth conditions for *It may snow* might be formulated as follows: A = [snow]; ◇A is true in a world w if for some w', such that $R_K w w'$, A is true in w'. (R_K stands for an epistemic [K = knowledge] accessibility relation between alternative worlds or situations.)

Table 1.19. Taxonomy of Modalities

Absolute modalities		
Declarative (neutral epistemic)	DECL	general expression of speaker knowledge
Epistemic	EPIS	qualification of speaker knowledge
Obligation	OBL	general expression of obligation
Directive	DIR	imposition of speaker will on addressee
Volitive/optative/commissive	VOL	expression of speaker will
Dynamic	DYN	expression of ability
Relative modalities		
Conditional (protasis)	COND	alternative event(s) contingent on a postulated condition
Final (apodosis/purpose/result)	FIN	the outcome of a postulated or real event

The concept of alternative situations was graphically represented above (fig. 1.11, p. 46) as a branching time line, whereby alternative vectors to the right (future) of the present interval of time represent alternative times. Based on this graphic idea, the relationships established by modality between the speaker's present situation and alternative potential situations may be represented as in fig. 1.16 (based on Cook 2008b: 10). Based on this illustration, it is clear that modality may be used to speak about alternative situations from the present ("now") or about the relationship among multiple alternative situations (usually limited to two); these latter types may be grouped together as contingent or relative modalities,[49] which include those listed in the basic taxonomy of modalities in table 1.19.

This taxonomy is meant to be suggestive of the main types of modality in language, somewhat anticipating the categories that will be useful in analyzing TAM in Biblical Hebrew (chap. 3). Assuming the principle of modal logic that a necessity or possibility operator is present in each modality, we can think in terms of the former as the "default" operator and so avoid having to include a NEC or PROB operator for each modality listed above. The distinction between OBL, on the one hand, and DIR and VOL, on the other, is intended to clarify objective and subjective deontic modalities, respectively; similarly, the mention of speaker for DECL and no speaker mentioned for DYN is indicative of the

---

49. The distinction of absolute and relative modality made here is driven by analogy with the distinction between absolute and relative tenses, the latter of which expresses events once (or more) removed (in terms of temporal precedence) from the speech time (see §1.2.3 above).

view that DECL is always subjective and DYN never (see §1.6.3.1).[50] The use of DIR and VOL attempts to capture the distinction between speaker-oriented and agent-oriented deontic modalities as given in example [1.29] above (p. 51). In contrast to my previous presentation (Cook 2008b: 10), here I have excluded causal and concessive from the relative (or contingent) modalities because unlike conditional and final clauses the postulated situation is often realis, though it does not need be, as illustrated by the the following realis and irrealis causal expressions in examples [1.42a–b].

> [1.42] a. We called him Tortoise <u>because</u> he taught us. (Carroll 2000: 91)
>
> b. I wonder what will become of my name when I go in? I shouldn't like to lose it at all—<u>because</u> they'd have to give me another, and it would be almost certain to be an ugly one. (Carroll 2000: 156)

Finally, the distinction between propositional and event modality (see §1.6.3.1) can be captured by combining operators as illustrated in example [1.43] (see Kiefer 1987: 83). In [1.43a] the epistemic PROB operator applies directly to the event, whereas in example [1.43b] the operator is applied to the proposition (DECL) *The three little sisters are ill.*

> [1.43] a. The three little sisters are probably ill. PROB [The three sisters are ill]
>
> b. It is probable that the three little sisters are ill. PROB, DECL [The three sisters are ill]

1.7.6. The Interaction of Tense, Aspect, and Modality

The preceding three sections (§§1.7.3–1.7.5) have treated each component of the TAM constellation in isolation. There is obviously some artificiality to this, since TAM are frequently associated in a single predicate (hence, TAM systems). Example [1.44] illustrates how a unified analysis of TAM may be carried out based on the preceding discussion.

> [1.44] It <u>might have been written</u> a hundred times, easily, on that enormous face. (Carroll 2000: 183)
>
> $C_{RF} < S$ & $RF \supset EF(coda)_{ACT}$ & POSS DYN (e')
>
> e' = [Be written a hundred times, easily, on that enormous face]

---

50. I am restricting dynamic modality to statements of ability, in contrast to Palmer's (2001: 22) classification of both ability and volitive as dynamic; see example [1.24], p. 48.

The formal analysis of example [1.44] defines the TAM values in turn, separated by ampersand (&): the tense is marked as past ($C_{RF} < S$) by the past auxiliary verb *might* (see §1.7.4); the viewpoint aspect is perfect (the *been* indicating passive and not progressive here), so that the RF includes within its scope the coda of the activity EF (RF $\supset$ EF(coda)$_{ACT}$) (§1.7.3);[51] the modal verb *might* (past tense of *may*) relativizes the truth of the event (*e'*) in terms of ability (dynamic modality) with respect to some alternative situation (§1.7.5).

Linguists have drawn attention to certain constraints on the interaction of TAM values. Bache (1995) has presented one of the most comprehensive theoretical discussions on the interaction among tense, viewpoint aspect, and situation aspect. He worked with taxonomies of three tenses (past, present, future), two aspects (perfective and imperfective), and an idiosyncratic partial ordering of situation types (Bache 1995: 194–204, 313–19). In addition, he allowed that expressions may lack any of these paramters (i.e., –tense, –viewpoint aspect, –situation aspect). On the one hand, Bache's discussion draws attention to the semantic irregularlities that arise from certain combinations, which is helpful to the extent that it furthers our understanding of these particular TAM values. On the other hand, Bache has made claims regarding the incompatibility of certain TAM values that need to be assessed critically.

To begin with, Bache (1995: 285–86) claimed that minimal activity events (or semelfactives) default for imperfective aspect, resulting in an iterative event; C. S. Smith (1997: 53) also pointed out this phenomenon. This combination is notable in that it shows that iterative phasal aspect may often be derivative, brought about through the combination of a particular situation (sub)type and viewpoint aspect. However, it is misleading to say that behaviorally minimal activity events default for imperfective aspect, because iterative activities may also be expressed by perfective verbs (e.g., *Jared knocked for five minutes*, example [1.10c], p. 25). A more accurate claim would be that minimal activity events cannot be expressed in combination with imperfective aspect without being interpreted iteratively. This claim stands over and against Olsen's claim (1997: 47), criticized above (§1.4.3), that minimal activity events may be interpreted duratively, as in *John coughed (once) for 5 seconds*, interpreted as *It took John 5 seconds to cough once*. This phenomenon of interaction between viewpoint aspect and minimal activity events is related to the constraint on achievements and imperfective viewpoint: because achievements lack any event intervals (i.e., the [–stages, +telic] event type consists of an instantaneous transition from a preparatory state to the result state), the imperfective viewpoint focuses on the preparatory interval(s)—for example, *He was winning the race* focuses on the preparatory period up until the moment of the winning (achievement).

---

51. A situational aspect label ACT may be used in place of the feature description [+stages, –telic] of the nucleus or coda (cf. examples [1.30–1.32], p. 61).

Another claim that Bache (1995: 284) made is that states (which he identifies as −situation aspect) cannot combine with viewpoint aspectual distinctions; hence, −situation aspect (=state) combines with −viewpoint aspect. This also, however, is too strong a claim. While it is true that one linguistic test for states is that they do not normally appear in the English progressive, this is not a strict incompatibility, as examples [1.45a–b] demonstrate (see Olsen 1997: 36–37 for other examples).

[1.45] a. Digory <u>was disliking</u> (STAT + PROG) his uncle more every minute. (Lewis 1955: 20)

 b. Yes, we should <u>be knowing</u> their judicial philosophy. We should <u>be knowing</u> their legal form of reasoning. (Sen. Charles Schumer, interview by Tim Russert, *Meet the Press*, 10 July 2005).

In addition, Bache's claim is inapplicable beyond English because incompatibilities or constraints on combinations of states with various viewpoint aspects appear to be a parameter of language (C. S. Smith 1997: 40).

Bache (1995: 289) along with other linguists (Bhat 1999: 17; Bybee, Perkins, and Pagliuca 1994: 126; C. S. Smith 1997: 185) has claimed that there is an incompatibility between perfective aspect and present tense. He (Bache 1995: 305–8) explains this incompatibility in spatiotemporal terms as being due to the fact that a certain minimal "temporal distance" is required to encompass the entire event frame within the reference frame of the perfective viewpoint; this minimal temporal distance is not afforded by the present tense. However, it may be more accurate to describe this phenomenon as a constraint than an incompatibility since there is the notable exception of "reportative speech," familiar in the setting of sports (especially radio) announcers (e.g., *Jones runs to third base*; C. S. Smith 1997: 185). The status of forms like the Simple Present in English is uncertain (e.g., *Jared helps around the house*). These constructions are generally interpreted as habitual or gnomic, which may be expressed by perfective forms in some languages and imperfective forms in others: "in speaking of a repeated total event one can use a pf. [perfective] verb, thus stressing each individual total event, or use an ipf. [imperfective] verb, which means that the stativeness of unlimited repetition takes precedence" (Dahl 1985: 79). C. S. Smith (2008: 235) approaches this phenomenon from the other direction when she proposes a temporal location default pattern whereby bounded events are temporally located in the past, and unbounded are located in the present. Perfective aspect, which makes events bounded (C. S. Smith 2008: 238; see table 4.1, p. 282), therefore defaults for past temporal interpretation and is constrained from normally being interpreted as present.

Bache's positing of a negative viewpoint aspect (−viewpoint) raises the more general question of whether there are possible constraints that might lead to having no (or neutral) viewpoint aspect and tense. Smith (1997: 77–78) introduced the notion of a "neutral viewpoint" aspect to describe "aspectually vague sentences." Most of the cases of neutral viewpoint that Smith (1997: 78–80) cites, are temporal clauses, which represent subordinate modality, and thereby may offer an explanation for their viewpoint neutrality. Is it possible that the alternative world status of modal expressions in some way constrains viewpoint aspect?

Although Bache does not include modality in his discussion, there is a long-standing disagreement among linguists as to whether future expressions can ever be non-modal, tensed expressions, or whether they are always modal (see Palmer 2001: 104–6). Although there is ample evidence connecting future expressions with modality (see Lyons 1977: 816–17; Palmer 2001: 104–6), one can argue that future expressions that refer to the "actual" future are properly tense. The distinction between the "actual future" and alternative situations (or alternative futures), as McCawley (1993: 432–34) observes, can be found in the fact that tensed statements made about the actual future may be judged true or false.

Unfortunately, these questions regarding the interaction of TAM can only been raised in a preliminary way within this theoretical discussion. Some of these constraints may be parameters of language, and therefore, they must be examined in more detail with respect to the object language, BH, in chap. 3.

1.8. Conclusion

The first part of this chapter introduced the parameters of TAM from a historical perspective, focusing particularly on the innovative R-point with respect to tense and aspect. The R-point provided linguists with a means of distinguishing certain tenses (e.g., simple past and present perfect) that were indistinguishable when defined in terms of a temporal relationship between the speech time (S) and the event time (E) (§1.2). From this starting point, the R-point was widely adopted and then adapted to other ends. Tense-aspect theories reinterpreted the relationship between reference time and event time (R-E) in terms of viewpoint aspect (§1.4), and discourse-focused studies of tense and aspect employed R-point nomenclature to explain the movement of time in discourse (§1.5). Modality was introduced by examining its roots in grammatical mood, modal logic, and speech act theory. A brief discussion of the major divisions in the typological category was offered as well (§1.6).

The second part of the chapter presented a mildly formalized model of TAM. The model was based on the unifying factor of temporality in TAM: situation aspect and phasal aspect were defined in terms of event time and structure, while viewpoint aspects were understood as presenting different views of

the event structure (§1.7.3); tense was defined in terms of precedence relationships between the speech time and the event time, mediated by a transient deictic center (§1.7.4); finally, modality was defined in terms of alternative times
and their relationship with the actual time (§1.7.5). Possible constraints on
the interaction of the parameters of TAM were also briefly examined (§1.7.6).

The primary aim of this chapter is to provide the requisite background for
the focus of this book, which is the BH verbal system: the first part of this
chapter provides the necessary background for the critical discussion of TAM
in theories of the BH verb in chap. 2; the theory of TAM in the second part of
this chapter is the basis for the analysis of the BH verbal system in chaps. 3–4.

Chapter 2

Tense, Aspect, and Modality
in Biblical Hebrew

This chapter presents an overview of the study of TAM in the BH verbal system (BHVS). It is necessarily limited in scope because it would be impossible to cover thoroughly, even in a book-length treatment, the vast number of works that have treated the BHVS over the years. I begin with the Ewald-Driver "standard" theory, because it forms the general background for almost all of the discussions of the BHVS in the twentieth and even into the 21st century (§2.2). A significant change between the 19th-century and 20th-century discussions of the BHVS is the increased importance of comparative and historical data, of which an overview is given (§2.3). The most substantial section in the chapter focuses on BH verbal theory from the past half century, grouped into aspect-prominent (§2.4.1), tense-prominent (§2.4.2), and discourse-prominent (§2.4.3) approaches. Finally, a concluding section sums up the state of the question on the BHVS at the beginning of the 21st century, setting the stage for the presentation of my theory of the BHVS in chaps. 3–4 (§2.5).

This survey, despite its omissions and limited scope, is justified by the lack of any comparable surveys. The only book-length study of this sort is McFall 1982, which only surveys theories through Thacker 1954 and contains notable gaps in its treatment. Briefer, yet important, surveys appear in Brockelmann 1951; Mettinger 1974; Dempster 1985; Waltke and O'Connor 1990; Endo 1996; Hatav 1997; Goldfajn 1998; and Heller 2004. At the same time, in this survey I do not treat these discussions as a mere historical curiosity (though they are extremely interesting in themselves) but attempt to classify the various approaches and highlight the central persistent issues as preparatory for the presentation of my own theory.

2.1. A Primer on the Biblical Hebrew Verbal System

Before embarking on a grand sweep of history of the study of the BHVS, we must understand some of the basic issues that these studies have attempted to address. While there are various dissenting opinions on how to solve the difficulties inherent in describing the BHVS, there is widespread agreement on just what constitutes the central problems. These problems are faced regularly and recognized as problems by Hebraists, biblical scholars, translators, and novice students of the language of the Hebrew Bible alike. Three problems may be enumerated, in particular. The first problem is that the variety of temporal significations expressed by the forms *qatal* and *yiqtol* appear to defy a singular TAM designation for either form.[1]

The apparently vast range of temporal meanings that *qatal* and *yiqtol* can express is illustrated by the variety of verb forms used to render them in English translations of the Hebrew Bible in examples [2.1a–b].

> [2.1]　a.　English verb forms used to translate *qatal*:
>
> *Simple Past*: 'In the beginning God <u>created</u> (בָּרָא) the heavens and the earth' (Gen 1:1, RSV).
>
> *Past Perfect*: 'Now Jacob did not know that Rachel <u>had stolen</u> (גְּנָבָתַם) them' (Gen 31:32, RSV).
>
> *Present Perfect*: 'They <u>have forsaken</u> (עָזְבוּ) the Lord' (Isa 1:4, RSV).
>
> *Subjunctive*: 'If you had saved them alive, I <u>would</u> not <u>kill</u> (הָרַגְתִּי) you' (Judg 8:19, NRSV).
>
> *Present*: 'The lazy person <u>says</u> (אָמַר), "There is a lion outside!"' (Prov 22:13, NRSV)
>
> *Future*: 'They will not hurt or destroy on all my holy mountain, for the earth <u>will be full</u> (מָלְאָה) of the knowledge of the Lord' (Isa 11:9, NRSV).
>
> *Future Perfect*: 'He shall die in his iniquity; but you <u>will have saved</u> (הִצַּלְתָּ) your life' (Ezek 3:19, NRSV).
>
> *Modal*: 'Awake, my God; <u>decree</u> (צִוִּיתָ) justice' (Psa 7:7[6], NIV).
>
> b.　English verb forms used to translate *yiqtol*:
>
> *Simple Past*: 'Then Joshua <u>built</u> (יִבְנֶה) an altar in Mount Ebal to the Lord' (Josh 8:30, RSV).
>
> *Past Progressive*: 'But a stream <u>was welling up</u> (יַעֲלֶה) out of the earth' (Gen 2:6, NAB).

---

1. Following a now widespread convention, I avoid the use of traditional, semantically laden labels for the BH verb forms in favor a simplified transcription of the unmarked paradigm form (3MS of *QTL* 'to kill', a root traditionally employed in comparative Semitic studies) to refer to each verbal conjugation (more traditional names are given here in parentheses): *qatal* (Perfect), *yiqtol* (Imperfect), *wayyiqtol* (*Waw*-consecutive Imperfect), *wĕqatal* (*Waw*-consecutive Perfect). I have, nevertheless, retained the traditional labels for the Participle, Infinitive, and directive-volitive forms, except for the Cohortative (i.e., Imperative and Jussive); the accuracy and utility of these latter labels is assessed in chap. 3. Throughout the discussion, I follow the oft-used linguistic convention of capitalizing the names of BH and other language-specific verb forms (except for the BH verb forms listed here as referred to by transcription), in distinction from universal semantic categories, which I present in lowercase.

Conditional: 'This is what Job used to always do (יַעֲשֶׂה)' (Job 1:5, NJPS).

Present: 'A wise son makes his father happy (יְשַׂמַּח)' (Prov 15:20, NJPS).

Present Progressive: 'What are you looking (תְּבַקֵּשׁ) for?' (Gen 37:15, NAB)

Future: 'But they will never believe (יַאֲמִינוּ) me' (Exod 4:1, REB).

Modal: 'You shall not kill (תִּרְצָח)' (Exod 20:13, NAB).

The list in example [2.1] reflects fairly well the taxonomies of meaning for *qatal* and *yiqtol* in many of the major grammars (e.g., Bergsträsser 1962: 2.25–36; Gibson 1994: 61–80; Ewald 1879: 1–13; Joüon 2006: §112–13; Kautzsch 1910: 309–21; Waltke and O'Connor 1990: 479–518). The plethora of meanings for *qatal* and *yiqtol* is also illustrated by McFall's statistical listing of translational equivalences for these forms in the Revised Standard Version, presented in table 2.1 (p. 80).

Not only do these data make the determination of a general meaning for each of these forms appear impossible, they make it difficult to draw any contrastive distinction between them. This latter problem is made especially acute by examples such as [2.2]–[2.3], in which the two forms appear to be interchangeable, appearing in parallel contexts.

[2.2] a. Ezek 18:2

אָבוֹת יֹאכְלוּ בֹסֶר וְשִׁנֵּי הַבָּנִים תִּקְהֶינָה

'Fathers eat unripe grapes and the children's teeth become dull'.

b. Jer 31:29

אָבוֹת אָכְלוּ בֹסֶר וְשִׁנֵּי בָנִים תִּקְהֶינָה

'Fathers eat unripe grapes and the children's teeth become dull'.

[2.3] a. Gen 42:7

וַיֹּאמֶר אֲלֵהֶם מֵאַיִן בָּאתֶם

'And he asked them, "Where do you come from?"'

b. Josh 9:8

וַיֹּאמֶר אֲלֵהֶם יְהוֹשֻׁעַ מִי אַתֶּם וּמֵאַיִן תָּבֹאוּ

'And Joshua asked them, "Who are you and where do you come from?"'

**Table 2.1. Statistics for English Verb Forms Used in the RSV
to Translate *qatal* and *yiqtol* (McFall 1982: 186–87)**

qatal forms = 13,874	*yiqtol* forms = 14,299
Past = 10,830	Past = 774
Present = 2,454	Present = 3,376
Future = 255	Future = 5,451
Non-past Modal = 56	Non-past Modal = 1,200
Past Modal = 115	Past Modal = 423
Imperative = 17	Imperative = 2,133
Jussive/Cohortative = 38	Jussive/Cohortative = 789
Non-verbal = 109	Non-verbal = 153

The second problem is that alongside the *qatal* and *yiqtol* verb forms are
two other forms, traditionally called "*waw*-conversive" or "*waw*-consecutive"
forms because of the characteristic presence of the prefixed *waw* ('and') conjunction: *wĕqatal* and *wayyiqtol*. Aside from the phonological peculiarity in
the attachment of the conjunction on *wayyiqtol* (ﬠַ/ﬠַ versus the usual shape of
the conjunction ﬞﬥ), these forms are only superficially and partially distinguishable morphologically from their non-*waw*-prefixed counterparts. The *wĕqatal*
form has an ultimate instead of a penultimate accent in some the 2MS and 1s
forms (e.g., וְשָׁמַרְתָּ/תִּי 'and you/I will keep' versus שָׁמַרְתָּ/תִּי[וְ] '[and] you/I
kept'); but this stress variation is a poor diagnostic because it appears inconsistently on the *wĕqatal* form even within a single passage (e.g., Amos 1:4–5,
7–8). The *wayyiqtol* form exhibits an apocopated shape with roots that have
a glide (*w/y*) in the second or third position (e.g., וַיִּבֶן 'he built' versus יִבְנֶה[וְ]
'[and] he will build') as well as in the Hiphil *binyan* (e.g., וַיַּפְקֵד 'he appointed'
versus יַפְקִיד[וְ] '[and] he will keep'), which is formally equivalent to the Jussive in contrast to *yiqtol* (see Kautzsch 1910: 133–34; Joüon 2006: §47). Thus,
the *waw*-prefixed forms have appeared prima facie to innumerable scholars
through the centuries to consist simply of the *waw* conjunction prefixed to the
qatal and *yiqtol*/Jussive forms.
     However, semantically, *wayyiqtol* (ostensibly *wa*C- + *yiqtol* [C = length-
ened consonant]) corresponds more closely to *qatal* than *yiqtol*, and similarly,
wĕqatal (ostensibly *wĕ*- + *qatal*) aligns semantically better with *yiqtol* than
qatal. This apparent semantic similarity between forms is evident from the
affinities between the grammars' taxonomies for *wayyiqtol* and *qatal*, on the
one hand, and those for *wĕqatal* and *yiqtol*, on the other (e.g., Bergsträsser
1962: 2.36–45; Gibson 1994: 83–102; Ewald 1879: 18–25; Joüon 2006:
§118–19; Kautzsch 1910: 326–39; Waltke and O'Connor 1990: 519–63; and
McFall 1982: 186–87). The semantic similarity between *yiqtol* and *wĕqatal*

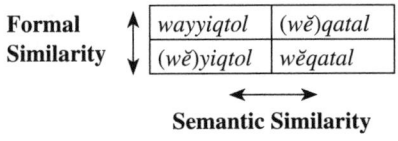

Semantic Similarity

Figure 2.1. Relationships among *qatal*, *yiqtol*, *wĕqatal*, and *wayyiqtol* forms.

is illustrated by verses, such as in example [2.4], in which the two forms are conjoined.

[2.4] Gen 2:24

עַל־כֵּן יַעֲזָב־אִישׁ אֶת־אָבִיו וְאֶת־אִמּוֹ וְדָבַק בְּאִשְׁתּוֹ

'Therefore, a man <u>will leave</u> his father and his mother and <u>will cleave</u> to his wife'.

In the case of a *qatal* and *wayyiqtol* relationship, parallel passages such as those in example [2.5] illustrate the apparent semantic identity of the two forms (cf. also 2 Kgs 18:36 and Isa 36:21).

[2.5] a. 2 Kgs 20:12

בָּעֵת הַהִיא שָׁלַח בְּראֹדַךְ בַּלְאֲדָן בֶּן־בַּלְאֲדָן מֶלֶךְ־בָּבֶל סְפָרִים וּמִנְחָה
אֶל־חִזְקִיָּהוּ כִּי שָׁמַע כִּי חָלָה חִזְקִיָּהוּ:

'At that time, Berodach-baladan son of Baladan king of Babylon sent letters and a gift to Hezekiah, for he <u>heard</u> that Hezekiah was ill'.

b. Isa 39:1

בָּעֵת הַהוּא שָׁלַח מְרֹדַךְ בַּלְאֲדָן בֶּן־בַּלְאֲדָן מֶלֶךְ־בָּבֶל סְפָרִים וּמִנְחָה
אֶל־חִזְקִיָּהוּ וַיִּשְׁמַע כִּי חָלָה וַיֶּחֱזָק:

'At that time, Merodach-baladan son of Baladan king of Babylon sent letters and a gift to Hezekiah; he <u>heard</u> that he was ill and recovered'.

Schematically, the relationship among these four verb forms is illustrated in fig. 2.1, in which the verb forms are shown as being semantically similar across the horizontal axis and formally similar along the vertical axis.

The dilemma that this four-way relationship poses for semantically distinguishing among these forms is trenchantly stated by Binnick (1991: 441):

> If the *waw* adds no temporal (tense or aspect) meaning, then the difference between verbs with *waw* and verbs without *waw* cannot be a semantic one. But apparently it is, for the forms with the *waw* are generally seen as 'reversing' the values the 'tenses' normally have. To reconcile the two, we must assume that the

forms without the *waw* and those with it do not in fact differ in semantics, but the only way this is possible is if the 'tense' forms do not differ from one another in meaning to begin with.[2]

Finally, a third problem is that the division between indicative and non-indicative systems in BH is fuzzy. This feature is not unique to BH; many languages have forms that function both with indicative and various nonindicative meanings. However, in BH this characteristic only exacerbates the problems outlined above. It is not just an issue of the functional diversity of individual forms but the apparently unsystematic mixing of forms. For instance, the *yiqtol* and Jussive forms in BH are often homonymic; nevertheless, even instances of *yiqtol* and Jussive that are morphologically distinct occur with no obvious difference in meaning, as illustrated by examples [2.6a–b].

[2.6] a. Exod 20:10

לֹא־תַעֲשֶׂה כָל־מְלָאכָה

'You <u>shall</u> not <u>do</u> any work/<u>Do</u> not <u>do</u> any work'.

b. Gen 22:12

וְאַל־תַּעַשׂ לוֹ מְאוּמָה

'<u>Do</u> not <u>do</u> anything to him'.

The *wĕqatal* form similarly appears to express both indicative and non-indicative modalities, appearing at times in the same context as indicative *yiqtol* (example [2.4] above) but also conjoined to nonindicative Jussive (including Cohortative) or Imperative forms, as in example [2.7].

[2.7] Ruth 2:7

וַתֹּאמֶר אֲלַקֳטָה־נָּא וְאָסַפְתִּי בָעֳמָרִים אַחֲרֵי הַקּוֹצְרִים

'And she said, "Let me glean <u>and gather</u> into sheaves behind the harvesters"'.

The study of the BHVS is in large part reducible to various attempts to resolve the problems enumerated here. Therefore, the following survey focuses particularly on proposed solutions to these difficulties—namely, the semantic

---

2. Sperber (1943: 199; see also 1966: 591–92) took a resigned approach to the dilemma described by Binnick (above):

> Each of these tenses [*qatal/wĕqatal, yiqtol/wayyiqtol*] may indicate any and every time. . . . The difference that existed between the suffix tense [*qatal*] and the prefix tense [*yiqtol*] was not of a temporal, but rather of a dialectic character. . . . The term *waw consecutivum*, which the grammar had to invent in order to explain the use of an imperfect [*yiqtol*] with the meaning of a perfect [*qatal*], and vice versa, thus becomes obsolete.

For a stringent review of Sperber's grammar, see Blake (1944b) and the response by Edelheit (1944).

distinction between *qatal* and *yiqtol*, the relationship between these forms and their *waw*-prefixed counterparts, and the indicative : nonindicative distinction.

2.2. The Establishment of the "Standard" Theory of the Biblical Hebrew Verbal System

Little justification is required for beginning a survey of theories of the BHVS with Ewald and S. R. Driver. A little more than a quarter century ago McFall (1982: 27) observed that "the majority of scholars [with respect to their views of the Hebrew verb] still go back to two 19th-century theories, those of H. Ewald (1835) and S. R. Driver (1874)." Starting with these theories does not belittle prior contributions but highlights the extraordinary and long-lasting influence that these theories have had on the discussion of the BHVS.

2.2.1. Before Ewald and S. R. Driver

The impact of the theory of the BHVS established by Ewald and S. R. Driver is best appreciated against the immediate backdrop of the state of the field in the early part of the 19th century, just prior to when Ewald introduced his theory into the field. One of the most pervasive theories at that time was the *waw*-conversive theory, which dates back to the Jewish medieval grammarians (as early as the 10th century, according to McFall 1982: 3) and whose influence is still evident in the labels used for the *waw*-prefixed verb forms in some modern grammars.[3] The theory is based on an understanding that BH has three absolute tenses corresponding to the three times, as illustrated in example [2.8] (see discussion in §1.1):[4]

[2.8]   *qatal* = Past (עבר)

Participle = Present (עומד or בינוני)

yiqtol = Future (עתיד)

On this absolute-tense basis, a "conversive" explanation was offered for the two *waw*-prefixed forms—*wayyiqtol* and *wĕqatal*. According to the conversive theory, Hebrew possessed two different *waw* conjunctions—*waw haḥibbûr* and *waw hahippûk* (translated into Latin as *waw conjunctivum* and *waw conversivum*, respectively; McFall 1982: 12). The latter type of *waw*, identified in the *wayyiqtol* and *wĕqatal* forms, was thought to "convert" the tense from past to future or vice versa. One of the clearest expositions of the conversive theory appears in the grammar of Elias Levita (1468–1549), first published in 1518.

---

3. For example, Joüon (2006: §117) labels the *waw*-prefixed forms "inverted tenses"; Lambdin (1971: 108) writes of tense values' being "converted"; and even the recent introductory grammars of Kittel, Hoffer, and Wright (2004: 20) and Pratico and Van Pelt (2001: chap. 17) retain the term "conversive." See survey in Cook 2008b.

4. For discussion of perspectives on the Participle prior to the 19th century, see Dyk 1994: 366–84.

Notice, when you want to convert a past into a future you place a *waw* with a *šewa* in front of it, as in the case of 'keep' in 'And Yhwh **will keep** . . .' [וְשָׁמַר: wqtl.3ms, Deut 7:12], which is like 'and he **will keep**' [וְיִשְׁמֹר: yqtl.3ms]. Likewise, 'And the sons of Israel **shall keep** the Sabbath' [וְשָׁמְרוּ: wqtl.3mp, Exod 31:16]. It is like 'and they **shall keep**' [וְיִשְׁמְרוּ: yqtl.3mp]. And the *waw* is always pointed with *šewa* except before those consonants that cancel it, turning it into a *šureq*, *patah*, or *hireq*, just as is explained in the aforementioned passage.

And if you ask, "How do I know whether this is *waw conjunctivum* or *waw conversivum*?" This (is how): when before it is another past verb, then it is a *waw conjunctivum*; and an example verse is 'Who **has made** and **done** (it)?' [פָּעַל: qtl.3ms, וְעָשָׂה: qtl.3ms, Isa 41:4)]. And the wise one will understand. And likewise the two *waws* in 'And one **called** to another and **said**' [וְקָרָא: qtl.3ms, אָמַר: qtl.3ms, Isa 6:3]. Notice, the two are *waw conjunctiva* because 'And I **saw** the Lord . . .' [וָאֶרְאֶה: wayy.1s, Isa 6:1] is written before them, which is a past verb because the *waw* has a *qames*. And notice that the style in the Bible is to use a past in place of a future and a future in place of a past. And this occurs most often in the words of the prophets, but in historical narrative it occurs very little.

And notice that for second person and first person singular there is another sign to distinguish *waw conjunctivum* from *waw conversivum*: when they have a *waw conjunctivum* they generally have a penultimate accent, which is the rule without the *waw*, as 'and I **ate** the sin-offering today' [וְאָכַלְתִּי: qtl.1s, Lev 10:19] (and) 'I **spoke** by the prophets' [וְדִבַּרְתִּי: qtl.1s, Hos 12:11]. They are pasts since the accent is penultimate but with *waw conversivum* the accent generally turns to ultimate as 'and you **will keep** all his statutes' [וְשָׁמַרְתָּ: wqtl.2ms, Exod 15:26], 'and I **will speak** my judgment, etc.' [וְדִבַּרְתִּי: wqtl.1s, Jer 1:16]. (my translation)[5]

Alongside the prevalent absolute-tense approach of the *waw*-conversive theory were a variety of absolute-relative tense theories in the early 19th century. These theories explained *qatal* and *yiqtol* as absolute tense: *qatal* is past tense, and *yiqtol* is future. The *waw*-prefixed forms, by contrast, were treated as relative tense. Schroeder's Hebrew grammar, first published in 1766, presents one of the earliest expositions of a relative-tense understanding of *wayyiqtol* and *wĕqatal*.

---

5. דע כשתרצה להפך עבר לעתיד תשים ו שואית בראשו כמו כמו מן שמר ושמר יהוה שהוא כמו וישמור. וכן ושמרו בני ישראל הוא כמו וישמרו. ותמיד היא נקודה בשוא זולת המבטלים המהפכים איתה לשורק או לפתח או לחירק כאשר יתבאר בפרק הנזכר.

ואם תאמר במה אדע אי זה היא ו החבור או ו ההפוך. דא כשאים לפניה פעל עבר אחר אז היא ו החבור ופסוק אחד סימן מי פעל ועשה והמעכיל יבין. וכן שני הווין של וקרא זה אל זה ואמר הן שתיהן ו החבור לפי שכתוב לפניהן ואראה את יהוה שהיא פעל עבר בעבור הוו חקמוצה שבראשה. ודע כי דרך המקרא לדבר בלשון עבר במקום עתיד ועתיד במקום עבר וזה לרוב בדברי נבואה אבל בספור דברי מעשה מעט מזער.

ודע כי יש למלות הנוכח והמדבר בעדו ליהיד סימן אחר להכיר ו החבור מן ו ההפוך וזה כשהם עם ו החיבור הם בטעם מלעיל על הרוב כמו שדינם תמיד זולת ו כמו ואכלתי חטאת היום ודברתי על הנביאים הם עברים שהטעם מלעיל אבל עם ו ההפוך ישובו בטעם מלרע על לרוב כמו ושמרת את כל הקיו ודברתי משפטי וגו. (Leo 1818: 226)

Apart from these various usages, the Future [*yiqtol*] has yet another, unique and peculiar to the Hebrews, in that it receives the force of our Past, and designates a matter as truly past; not however by itself nor absolutely, but viewed in relation to some preceding past event. When different events are to be narrated that follow the one from the other in some kind of continuous series, the Hebrews consider the first as past; the others, however, that follow, as future on account of the preceding. Consequently, this describes something that, in relation to another past event, is itself later and future; it may be called the Future *relativum*. (my translation)[6]

Explanations like this were duplicated in subsequent grammars (see McFall 1982: 22).

McFall in his survey distinguishes between "*waw* relative" theories, such as Schroeder's, and "*waw* inductive" theories, exemplified by Bellamy's understanding of the *waw*-prefixed forms. While Bellamy followed the standard relative-tense explanation for *wayyiqtol*, he understood *wĕqatal* as essentially tenseless; its semantic value is conveyed or "inducted" from the initial *yiqtol* form through the *waw*.

When a verb written in the future tense [*yiqtol*] at the head of a subject precedes a verb in the preter tense [*qatal*], which has the ו vau [*waw*], prefixed with the vowel Sheva, then the future time of the first verb is connected by the ו vau [*waw*], and carried to the following verb in the same proposition, though written in the preter form; because it describes an action that takes place future to the verb at the beginning of the subject. (Bellamy 1818: xxxvi–xxxvii)

Philip Gell advanced a more thoroughgoing *waw*-inductive theory the same year as Bellamy's and coined the name of the theory.

When Verbs are connected in Hebrew (the connexion being generally indicated by the sign ו prefixed to the latter), the Power, whether temporal or modal, of the first or Governing Verb is communicated from it, and inducted into the Verb following. And whatever be the power proper to the latter Verb, it still retains its use subordinately; but that which is inducted becomes the prevailing power. If a third Verb follow in connexion, and so on, the power communicated from each successive Verb to that next following, without destroying its proper subordinate power, is the same as was previously inducted into the former. (Gell 1818: 8; quoted in McFall 1982: 25)

---

6. Praeter varios hosce usus, futurum habet adhuc alium plane singularem, et Hebraeis peculiarem, quod illud vim accipit nostri praeteriti, et rem revera praeteritam designat, non tamen per se, et absolute, sed in relatione ad praecedens aliquod praeteritum, spectatam. Quando enim diversae res factae, quae continua quadam serie aliae alias exceperunt, narrandae sunt, Hebraei primam quidem per praeteritum, alias autem subsequentes, quas, ratione praecedentis, tanquam futuras considerant, per futurum exprimunt. Hoc itaque, quia id, quod in relatione ad aliam rem praeteritam posterius et futurum fuit, notat futurum relativum dici potest. (Schroeder 1824: 239–40)

This array of theories formed the immediate backdrop to Ewald's ideas. In some respects, Ewald's theory appears to be quite novel compared with these tensed approaches, but in other respects it clearly was indebted to the insights of its predecessors.

2.2.2. Ewald's "Standard" Theory

Ewald (1803–75) is generally regarded as the first scholar to propose an aspectual theory of the BHVS (Waltke and O'Connor 1990: 463). McFall (1982: 44), however, states that Johann Jahn (1750–1816) was the first to apply the Latin terms *perfectum* and *imperfectum* to the Hebrew verb: "The first aorist presents a perfect [*perfectum*] thing, whether present, or past, or future. The second aorist presents an imperfect [*imperfectum*] thing, whether present, or past, or future" (my translation).[7] In the first edition of his Hebrew grammar (1828), Ewald refers to *qatal* and *yiqtol* simply as I and II Modi ('mood' or 'mode'). However, just a year later, he employed the same terminology as Jahn for the suffix and prefix verbs in his Arabic grammar and then applied them in subsequent editions of his Hebrew grammar (Ewald 1870: 350 n. 1; 1879: 3). The far-reaching influence of this terminological shift by Ewald can be seen in the still-current use of the terms *perfect* and *imperfect* for the *qatal* and *yiqtol* as well as the common use of the term *waw*-consecutive in reference to the *wayyiqtol* and *wĕqatal* forms—a label that Ewald's theory no doubt helped to popularize (Ewald 1847: 385; 1879: 8).[8]

Although no term equivalent to 'aspect' (i.e., *Zeitart, Aspekt, Aktionsart*) appears in his writings, Ewald's description of the *qatal* : *yiqtol* opposition indicates that his terminological shift to *perfectum* and *imperfectum* was based on an aspectual understanding of the BH (and Arabic) verbal system.[9] In one

---

7. "Aoristus primus [*qatal*] sistit rem perfectam, jam praesentem, jam praeteritam, jam futuram. Aoristus secundus [*yiqtol*] sistit rem imperfectam, jam praesentem, jam praeteritam, jam futuram" (from his 1809 *Grammatica linguae Hebraeae*, quoted in McFall 1982: 44; *Aorist* is used here in the general sense of "indeterminate"). Waltke and O'Connor (1990: 463) mistakenly attribute this quotation to Ewald's 1827 Hebrew grammar (*Kritische Grammatik der hebräischen Sprache*). Whether Ewald relied on Jahn for his terminology or arrived at it independently is uncertain, since Ewald does not identify a source, though Samuel Lee accused Ewald of plagiarism in this regard (see McFall 1982: 44).

8. According to S. R. Driver (1998: 72) the term *waw*-consecutive was first suggested by Böttcher in 1827.

9. DeCaen (1996: 132) recently objected to this customary interpretation of Ewald's theory, arguing that it involves relative tense rather than aspect. He claims that the perception of Ewald's theory as aspectual derives from a mistranslation of a key introductory statement in Ewald's grammar (DeCaen 1996: 134). The passage reads: "Die einfachste Unterscheidung der Zeit des Handelns ist aber die daß der Redende zunächst nur die zwei großen Gegensäze unterscheide unter denen alles denkbare Handeln gedacht werden kann" (Ewald 1870: 349). Kennedy, in his 1879 English translation, renders the passage: "But the simplest distinction of time in an action is, that the speaker first of all merely separates between the two grand and opposite *aspects* under which every conceivable action may be

Table 2.2. Stoic-Varronian Schema of the Latin Verb
(adapted from Binnick 1991: 22 and Robins 1997: 65)

Aspect＼Time	Past	Present	Future
Incomplete	*amābam* (Imperfect) 'I was loving'	*amō* (Present) 'I love/am loving'	*amābō* (Future) 'I shall love'
Complete	*amāveram* (Pluperfect) 'I had loved'	*amāvī* (Perfect) 'I have loved'	*amāverō* (Future Perfect) 'I shall have loved'

place, Ewald explained, "Hence, with reference to action, the speaker views everything as either already finished, and thus before him, or as unfinished and non-existent [i.e., not yet existing], but possibly becoming and coming" (1879: 1).[10] Further on, he wrote: "Since, therefore, in virtue of the power and freedom accorded to the imagination, the ideas of completeness and incompleteness may also be used relatively, in such a way that the speaker, in whichever of the three simple divisions of time (past, present, or future) he may conceive of an action, can represent it either as complete, or as going on and coming" (Ewald 1879: 3).[11]

The foundation of Ewald's aspectual treatment of the *qatal* : *yiqtol* opposition appears to be the Stoic-Varronian tense-aspect theory of Latin (DeCaen 1996: 138). As explained in chap. 1 (§1.1), the Stoic-Varronian theory defines the Latin verb forms according to the parameters of tense and aspect (table 2.2, repeated from table 1.2, p. 3). Ewald, however, eschewed the tense parameter since BH has only two primary verb forms; he adopted only the early aspectual conception of complete and incomplete from the Stoic-Varronian model as the distinguishing feature in the *qatal* : *yiqtol* opposition.

Ewald's adoption of the terms *perfectum* and *imperfectum* for *qatal* and *yiqtol* appears to confirm the connection with the Stoic-Varronian theory.

---

regarded" (Ewald 1879: 1, emphasis mine). In light of Ewald's treatment of this opposition, Kennedy's interpretive liberty with the German text appears justified. Nevertheless, DeCaen (1996: 134) argues that Kennedy's use of the term was anachronistic since, as he claims, the term *aspect* was first introduced into Western grammar by Georg Curtius (1846) in his study of the Greek verb. Although the term did not enter the English language until 1853 (so *OED*, s.v. "aspect"), Binnick (1991: 141) notes that Jacob Grimm (1785–1863) earlier had been the first to extend the idea of aspect to non-Slavic languages, employing it in his study of Germanic languages (see above, p. 18 n. 15).

10. "So faßt denn der Redende in Beziehung auf das Handeln alles entweder als schon *vollendet* und so *vorliegend*, oder als *unvollendet* und *nochnichtseiend* möglicherweise aber *werdend* und *kommend* auf" (Ewald 1870: 349).

11. "Da also die Begriffe des Vollendeten und Unvollendeten nach der Kraft und Freiheit der Einbildung auch beziehungsweise (relativ) so gebraucht werden können daß der Redende, in welchem der drei reinen Zeitkreise (Vergangenheit, Gegenwart, Zukunft) er eine Handlung sich denken mag, sie da entweder als vollendet oder als werdend und kommend sezen [*sic*] kann" (Ewald 1870: 350).

Ewald explained the intended sense of his use of the terms *perfectum* and *imperfectum*: "understanding these names, however, not in the narrow sense attached to them in Latin grammar, but in a quite general way" (1879: 3).[12] McFall (1982: 44) explains that, by *allgemein* ('general'), Ewald presumably meant their etymological meaning of 'complete' and 'incomplete', in contrast to their use as labels for specific Latin morphological forms.[13] Thus, Ewald's theory may be understood as an early aspectual type, in the tradition of the Stoic understanding of (in)completion. By "early," I mean to distance Ewald's concept of aspect from the more-recent, Slavic-influenced understanding of aspect that correctly distinguishes perfective and imperfective from the related notions of complete(d) and incomplete(d) (see §1.3.3).

Although Ewald referred to the aspectual pair in temporal terms, he understood the forms to intersect all three times—past, present, and future: "and, on the ground of this most simple distinction of time a multitude of finer distinctions and forms can be made" (Ewald 1879: 3).[14] Ewald's taxonomy (1870: 346–50; 1879: 3–7) of *qatal* includes its use to designate (1) simple past, (2) past in the past (pluperfect), (3) past in the future (future perfect), (4) pres-

---

12. "[D]iese Namen aber nicht in dem engen Sinne der Lateinischen Grammatik sondern ganz allgemein verstanden" (Ewald 1870: 350).

13. DeCaen (1996: 137–38) disagrees with McFall's interpretation, arguing that, "in fact, there is a second, highly technical, 'general' interpretation of the terms *perfectum* vs. *imperfectum* (though usually the latter is termed the *infectum* in Latin studies), referring not to Latin's two so-called 'past' tenses, but to the two Latin *stems* that bear tense inflection. It is equally clear that Ewald intended this technical, comparative Indo-European, 'general' sense." This claim, however, is not supported by Ewald's exposition of the BHVS, nor does DeCaen make any reference to Ewald in his ensuing speculative discussion (DeCaen 1996: 139–40). There is no hint in Ewald's grammar that he wants to parallel the BH verb forms with the Latin stems; rather, DeCaen's view relies on reading more into Ewald's statements than a plain reading (such as McFall has provided) demands.

In truth, DeCaen's disagreement is with the aspectual interpretation of the Stoic-Varronian model of the Latin verb (Robins 1997: 65) more than with Ewald's interpretation of the BHVS: the *imperfectum* (infectum) : *perfectum* distinction in the Stoic-Varronian model "appears to answer to 'relative tense'" (DeCaen 1996: 139). This is a gratuitous assumption not made by other scholars who, nevertheless, disagree with the aspectual interpretation of the Stoic-Varronian model (see Binnick 1991: 20–26).

DeCaen's argument is problematic on still other grounds. He (DeCaen 1996: 137) accuses Ewald of a "morphocentric fallacy" by excluding the Participle from his theory. However, DeCaen (1996: 136 n. 20; see above, §1.1) appears to fall into the age-old error of assuming that the recognition of three times demands that all languages have three corresponding tense forms. DeCaen's accusation (1996: 140–41) that Ewald was misled by German romanticism is likewise unconvincing; if there was an insidious strain in Ewald's treatment of the BHVS that sought to distance it from the Indo-European verbal system, there must have been a more successful way of accomplishing this than analogizing the Hebrew verb with Latin!

14. "[U]nd auf dem Grunde dieser allereinfachsten Zeitunterscheidung [i.e., vollendet: unvollendet] sind eine menge feinerer unterscheidungen und gebilde möglich" (Ewald 1870: 350).

ent, (5) present perfect, and (6) past conditional. His list of meanings for *yiqtol* includes (1) future, (2) present durative, (3) past, (4) present habitual, (5) past habitual, (6) past conditional, and (7) jussive mood (Ewald 1870: 350–58; 1879: 7–13).

Altogether, Ewald recognized six distinct verb forms or "tenses" in BH: two "simple tenses" (*qatal* and *yiqtol*), two "modified tenses" (*wayyiqtol* and *wĕqatal*), and two "reduced tenses" (*waw* plus *qatal* and *waw* plus *yiqtol*). The latter "reduced tenses" are the forms that arose out of the *aufgelösten* ('dissolution') of the modified forms in late BH (Ewald 1870: 842; 1879: 249). The semantic value of *waw* in both the modified tenses and the reduced tenses is that of sequence or consecution of time (1879: 244), including the stronger notion of consequentiality (1870: 841–42; 1879: 247–48; see Waltke and O'Connor 1990: 477).

Beyond these claims regarding the semantics of the *waw*-prefixed forms, Ewald did not greatly advance the understanding of these forms with respect to *qatal* and *yiqtol*. Following the medieval grammarians, Ewald noted the accentual difference between *qatal* and *wĕqatal* in certain forms (Ewald 1870: 600; 1879: 23; see §2.1 and on Levita in §2.2.1 above). With respect to *wayyiqtol*, Ewald (1879: 19) argued that the form is Jussive based, comparing it with the past-tense value of the Arabic Jussive preceded by the negative *lam* (see W. Wright 1962: 2.41). Ewald theorized that the vocalization of the *waw* conjunction on *wayyiqtol* might be explained by the assimilation of the adverb אָז ('then') between the *waw* conjunction and verb prefix, and that it is this peculiar element that "throws an action into the sphere of the past" (Ewald 1879: 19; cf. other theories in McFall 1982: 217–19). [15] Nevertheless, following his predecessors, Ewald continued to assume a basic etymological and therefore semantic identity between *wayyiqtol* and *yiqtol*, on the one hand, and *wĕqatal* and *qatal*, on the other.

At the same time, despite Ewald's efforts to distance his theory from the tense theories of the BHVS, he could not completely escape the influence of the relative-tense explanation of the *waw*-prefixed forms, so popular in his day (§2.2.1). Yet, while he continued to refer to *wayyiqtol* and *wĕqatal* as "bezüglicher Zeiten und Modi" ('relative tenses and moods'; Ewald 1870: 593; 1879: 18), Ewald's explanation may perhaps best be described as relative aspect.

> But as, in creation, through the continual force of motion and progress, that which has become, and is, constantly modifies its form for something new; so, in thought, the new advances which take place (and thus, then) suddenly changes the action which, taken by itself absolutely, would stand in the perfect, into this tense, which indicates becoming—the imperfect. . . . As, therefore, in the combination previously explained [i.e., *wayyiqtol*], the flowing sequence of time or

---

15. "Welches eine Handlung in den Kreis der Vergangenheit verweist" (Ewald 1870: 593).

thought causes that which has been realized, and exists, to be regarded as passing over into new realization; so in the present case [i.e., *wĕqatal*], it has the effect of at once representing that which is advancing towards realization, as entering into full and complete existence. Hence, each of the plain tenses gracefully intersects the other, by interchanging with its opposite. (Ewald 1879: 20, 22–23)[16]

2.2.3. S. R. Driver's "Extended Standard" Theory

While the effect of S. R. Driver's theory[17] on later discussion of the BHVS has been immense (especially among English-speaking students and scholars), its originality and merit have been questioned. A fairly typical portrait of Driver is that he "popularized" Ewald's theory (McFall 1982: 76). A more negative assessment is that he represented a setback with respect to Ewald's theory (Waltke and O'Connor 1990: 464). Both of these portrayals have an element of truth, but they also miss the original contributions that Driver made to the study of the BHVS.

In contrast to Ewald's analysis of the "simple tenses" *qatal* and *yiqtol* as forming a binary opposition, Driver began with a triad of forms, the *qatal*, the Participle, and *yiqtol*. However, while the medieval tense theory had correlated these three forms with the three times—past, present, and future, respectively ([2.8])—Driver interpreted the forms aspectually. Driver claimed, first, that the Hebrew verb designates "kind of action," not the time of the action (i.e., aspect and not tense); and, second, that there are three kinds of action in BH, construed "according to the particular point which he [the speaker] desires to make prominent"—"complete," "continuing," and "incipient." These three kinds of action are associated with *qatal*, the Participle, and *yiqtol*, respectively (Driver 1998: 2). Driver (1998: 5) asserts that "upon these two facts the whole theory of the tenses has to be constructed."

The key to understanding Driver's theory is his treatment of *yiqtol* as incipient action. In addition to "incipient," Driver employed numerous other terms to describe the form's aspectual value: "imperfect" (in the etymological sense), "egressive," "nascent," "progressive continuance," "inchoative," and "incomplete" (Driver 1998: 1 n. 1, 2 n. 1, 5, 27, 119). This terminological variety leads one to suspect that Driver had trouble subsuming all the variegated uses of the *yiqtol* under a single semantic heading. This suspicion appears to

---

16. Wie aber in der Schöpfung durch die ewige Kraft der Bewegung und des Fortschrittes das gewordene und seiende sich stets zu neuem werden umgestaltet, so ändert im gedanken das Einfallende neue fortschreiten (*und so-, da-*) die Handlung welche ansich schlechthin im Perfect stehen würde, plözlich [*sic*] in diese Zeit des Werdens, das Imperfect, um; . . . Wie also in der vorigen Zusammensezung [i.e., *wayyiqtol*] die fließende Folge der Zeit oder des Gedankens die Wirkung hat daß das gewordene und seiende als in neues werden übergehend gedacht wird, so hat sie hier die Wirkung [i.e., *wĕqatal*] daß das wedende sofort als ins seyn [*sic*] tretend gesezt wird, sodaß die schlichten Tempora auf diese Weise anmuthig ein jedes von dem wechsel seines gegensazes [*sic*] durchkreuzt wird (Ewald 1870: 594, 600).

17. See also Garr's introductory essay to the reprint edition (1998).

**Table 2.3. Comparison of
G. Curtius's and S. R. Driver's Verb Models**

Greek	stem:	Aorist	Present	Perfect
		↓	↓	↓
	aspect:	entering/nascent	durative/continuing	completed
		↑	↑	↑
Hebrew	conjugation:	*yiqtol*	Participle	*qatal*

be confirmed by Driver's statement (1998: 29): "an idea . . . however, like that of *nascency, beginning*, or *going to be* is almost indefinitely elastic." Part of Driver's struggle in dealing with *yiqtol* derives from the theoretical basis of his treatment in Curtius's model of the Greek verb (Curtius 1846, 1863, 1870).

Curtius's aspectual model of the Greek verb identifies the Present stem as denoting *dauernd* ('continuous') action, and the Perfect stem as denoting *vollendet* ('completed') action, and the Aorist stem as denoting *eintretend* ('entering') action (Curtius 1863: 173; 1870: 205). Driver's model lines up with Curtius's as shown in table 2.3. As DeCaen (1996: 144) explains, in labeling the Aorist, Curtius was "playing on the slippery ambiguity of the German *eintretend*, which indicates both entry as beginning as well as entry as an endpoint." Curtius's own explanation of *eintretend* is no more clear than Driver's use of nascent:

> The word 'momentary' opens a door to numerous errors. If this term is chosen, we are tempted to measure the distinction between ποιεῖν [Present] and ποιῆσαι [Aorist], νικᾶν [Present] and νικῆσαι [Aorist], ἔβαλλε [Imperfect] and ἔβαλε [Aorist] merely by lapse of time, whereas in reality the distinction is quite different and far deeper. . . . I preferred, therefore, to adopt the terminology of Rost and Krüger, who call the aorist 'eintretend'. The epithet is difficult of translation [*sic*], and cannot be represented in all its bearings by any single English word. It is 'initial' as opposed to 'continued', 'culminating' as opposed to 'preparatory', 'instantaneous' as opposed to 'durative'. An action so qualified is, first of all, quite distinct from a beginning or impending act; it has nothing in common with the *tempus instans* with which it has sometimes been confounded. On the contrary, it is opposed to two other actions. First, to a continuing act. Thus the advent of winter is opposed to its continuance. . . . Secondly, as denoting an incident, it is opposed to an act that is not yet finished. . . . Lastly an act to which this epithet is applied, is invariably an act achieved at one blow, or an act the single moments of which are not to be taken into account. (Curtius 1870: 205–6; trans. Evelyn Abbott)[18]

---

18. Aber abgesehen von dem Fremdwort [momentan], das sich neben einheimischen lass. Es liegt, wenn diese Bezeichnung gewählt wird, nahe den Unterschied zwischen ποιεῖν und ποιῆσαι, νικᾶν und νικῆσαι, ἔβαλλε und ἔβαλε gleichsam nach der Uhr zu messen, während ja doch der Unterschied ein ganz andrer, viel tiefer gegriffener ist. . . . Ich zog es

Despite the novelty of Driver's use of Curtius's aspectual model of Greek, Driver did not present an appreciably different taxonomy for *qatal* and *yiqtol* from Ewald's: the *qatal* can designate (1) simple past, (2) present perfect, (3) performative, (4) gnomic, (5) future (so-called prophetic perfect); the *yiqtol* may designate (1) historical present, (2) present progressive, (3) future, (4) gnomic, (5) volitive, (6) conditional (Driver 1998: chaps. 2–3).

Driver's treatment of the *waw*-prefixed forms advanced little beyond Ewald. Consistent with the assumption of an etymological and semantic connection between the two prefixed forms, he wrote, "[T]he imperfect [*yiqtol*] represents action as nascent: accordingly, when combined with a conjunction connecting the event introduced by it with a point already reached by the narrative, it represents it as continuation or development of the past that came before it. וַיֹּאמֶר [WAYY.3MS] is thus properly not *and he said*, but *and he proceeded-to-say*" (1998: 71–72; cf. Ewald's explanation, §2.2.2 above). McFall (1982: 72) points out the obvious difficulty with Driver's combination of nasceny and continuation in *wayyiqtol*: one must assume not only that *wayyiqtol* indicates the incipience of each event but also its completion before the next *wayyiqtol*, otherwise, "there would be considerable over-lapping of ideas."

Driver did not follow Ewald's connection between the morphology of *wayyiqtol* and the apocopated Jussive ("voluntative") form (Ewald 1870: 19 n. 2). Driver (1998: 72) explained the vocalization of the *waw* as related to the "more original form of the conjunction" (evident in Arabic *wa-*), followed by a doubling in order to preserve the distinction from *waw+yiqtol*. Driver (1998: 75–78) dismissed the morphological similarity between the *wayyiqtol* and the apocopated "voluntative" (Jussive) form as coincidental, arguing instead that the apocopated form was due to the "heavy" vocalization of the *waw* conjunction.

Another departure from Ewald is Driver's adoption of the earlier *waw* inductive theories in his analysis of *wĕqatal* (§2.2.1). By taking this tack, Driver was able to explain the use of the *wĕqatal* following both indicative *yiqtol* and modal verb forms: "To all intents and purposes the perfect [*qatal*], when

---

daher vor mich der Terminologie von Rost und Krüger anzuschliessen, welche die Handlung des Aorists die eintretende nennen. Wer den Gebrauch unsers deutsentlichen Eigenthümlichkeiten der aoristischen Handlung wiederfinden. Eintreten ist zunächst durchaus verschieden von beginnen oder bevorstehen. Die eintretende Handlung hat nichts mit dem tempus instans zu thun, mit welchem man sie irrthümlich verwechselt hat. Eintreten hat vielmehr einen doppelten Gegensatz, einmal das Verweilen an einem Orte. Der Eintritt des Winters ist seiner Fortdauer entgegengesetzt. . . . Zweitens aber ist das Eintreten eines Ereignisses seinen Vorbereitungen entgegengesetzt. . . . Endlich wird mit dem Worte eintreten (vgl. abtreten, vortreten, herzutreten) immer und durchweg eine Handlung ausgedrückt, die auf einen Schlag vollzogen wird, oder deren, wenn auch vorhandene einzelne Momente, nich hervorgehoben, werden sollen. (Curtius 1863: 173)

attached to a preceding verb by means of this *waw* consecutive, loses its individuality: no longer maintaining an independent position, it passes under the sway of the verb to which it is connected" (Driver 1998: 118).

2.2.4. Summary

Virtually all subsequent theories about the BHVS have been consciously presented against the backdrop of the Ewald-Driver "standard" aspectual theory, which arguably has had a greater influence than any other single theory about the BHVS. Despite some dissension, Ewald's theory is properly interpreted as aspectual (Fensham 1978; DeCaen 1996); however, his understanding of aspect, like the classical aspectual theories, is expressed in terms of (in)completion. He popularized the labels *perfect* and *imperfect* for *qatal* and *yiqtol* and popularized the term *consecutive* for the *waw*-prefixed forms. Driver retained Ewald's labels and clarified that the BH verbs designate "kind of action" (i.e., aspect).

Driver, however, departed from Ewald in some significant ways. He rejected parts of Ewald's explanation of the form and etymology of *wayyiqtol* and offered nonparallel explanations for the two *waw*-prefixed forms. Driver also accorded a greater role to the Participle in his model than previous theories had. This innovation may be seen as sort of a compromise, incorporating the three "tenses" of the medieval theories but interpreting them aspectually. It is perhaps a tribute to the power of Ewald's theory, then, that Driver's work is often interpreted as simply an English version of Ewald's aspectual theory

Neither Ewald nor Driver, however, was able to progress beyond the early 19th-century explanations of the *waw*-prefixed forms. Both presumed that the forms were etymologically and semantically related to their non-*waw*-prefixed formal counterparts, and despite their aspectual treatment of the non-*waw*-prefixed forms, they fell back on explanations similar to the relative tense and *waw* inductive theories from the early part of their century in order to explain the semantics of *wayyiqtol* and *wĕqatal*.

2.3. The Biblical Hebrew Verbal System in Historical and Comparative Perspective

Historical and comparative studies of Semitic languages have made some the most important contributions to the understanding of the BHVS in the 20th century.[19] This fact is due to the rapid advancement of knowledge of Semitic languages from approximately the mid-19th to the mid-20th century, instigated specifically by three notable developments. The first was the decipherment of Akkadian in the 1850s, which instigated a new phase of discussions regarding the development of the Semitic verbal system. The second was the discovery

---

19. For an overview of historical and comparative linguistics, see Anttila 1989.

by local bedouins in 1887 of a cache of cuneiform tablets in Tel el-Amarna, the capital and residence of the Egyptian king Akhenaten (Amenhotep IV) (ca. 1353–1336 B.C.E.). The real impact of this discovery on the interpretation of the BHVS was delayed until Moran's 1950 study of the Amarna correspondence that originated in Byblos, in which he demonstrated, among other things, that the TAM system in the letters was almost wholly Northwest Semitic, reflecting the native dialects of the local scribes (Moran 2003: ix). The third important development was the unearthing, beginning in 1929, of clay tablets inscribed with an alphabetic cuneiform writing system from the site of ancient Ugarit. Although our understanding of the Ugaritic language of these tablets is hampered by the largely reconstructed vocalization of the texts, it is nevertheless significant to BH as the only well-attested native language of the Levantine area during the second millennium B.C.E. (Pardee 1997: 131; 2004b: 288). The latter half of the 20th century has also seen important advances, such as the discovery of Eblaite in 1968, the study of which is still (relatively speaking) in its infancy, and a continually growing collection of Northwest Semitic epigraphs (e.g., the Tel Dan inscription, ostraca from the Mousaïeff collection, and the Tel Zayit inscription).

In this section, I begin with an overview of the placement of Hebrew within the Semitic language family (§2.3.1). Following the overview are surveys of the discussions of the BHVS that ensued from the three developments just enumerated above (§§2.3.2–2.3.4). These findings are summarized along with other relevant data in the concluding section (§2.3.5).[20]

---

20. The manner of referring to cognate verb forms varies from language to language with respect to both the root used in paradigms and the semantic labels associated with the conjugations. I employ the following conventions in this discussion in an attempt to avoid confusion. When referring to cognate verbal conjugations, I use the traditional root *QTL* 'to kill' in the 3MS form of the base or G-stem (without any * to designate it as a reconstructed form), ignoring theme vowel variations except where relevant to the immediate discussion; for example, *qatala* stands for West Semitic *qatala~qatila~qatula,* and *yaqtulu* stands for Central Semitic *yaqtulu~yaqtilu~yiqtalu; yaqtul(u),* with the final vowel in parentheses representing both long and short prefix patterns, which were not clearly distinguished in early discussions. When referring to reflexes of cognate verb forms in specific languages, I use a root that is employed as the paradigm form in one or another of the standard grammars of that language; namely, Akkadian *PRS,* Ethiopic *NGR,* Arabic *KTB,* Ugaritic *MLK.* (This approach, however, is not followed for BH, for which *qatal, yiqtol, wĕqatal,* and *wayyiqtol* are employed, as explained above, p. 78 n. 1. I generally avoid employing the semantic labels associated with language-specific forms, because they can be misleading, and there are often multiple labels employed in the literature; for example, Akkadian Durative or Present, Preterit or Past, Permansive or Stative. When I do employ semantic labels, I capitalize them to designate that they are language-specific labels and not notional or typological categories (e.g., Durative vs. durative). For full paradigms of the verb conjugations under discussion, see Moscati 1980: 137, 142; Bergsträsser 1983: 225–35; Bennett 1998: 94–118.

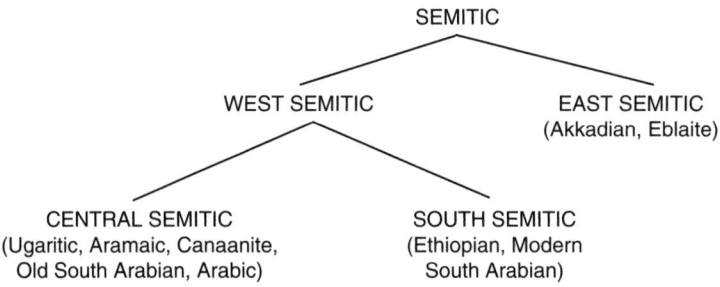

Figure 2.2. Genetic classification of the Semitic language family (based on Huehnergard 2004: 141–42; cf. Voigt 1987: 15; Huehnergard 1992: 157; Faber 1997: 6).

2.3.1. The Linguistic Context of the BHVS

Hebrew is a member of the Semitic language family, which forms a branch of the Afro-Asiatic phylum,[21] alongside Egyptian, Berber, Cushitic, Chadic, and probably Omotic.[22] The traditional subgrouping of the Semitic languages places East Semitic (ES) Akkadian over and against the West Semitic (WS) branch, which is subdivided into a Northwest Semitic (NWS; Canaanite and Aramaic) and a Southwest Semitic (Arabic, Old South Arabian, and Ethi-opic) branch (see Brockelmann 1908–13: 6; Moscati 1980: 4; Bergsträsser 1983: 1; Voigt 1987: 2). The main deficiency of this classification is its lack of an empirical basis; it is based primarily on geographic and ethnic divisions among language speakers (see Moscati 1980: 4; Faber 1997: 5). More-recent classifications of Semitic have been based on shared morphological innova-tions—especially verbal inflection. The results of this shift in approach are illustrated by the tree diagram for Semitic in fig. 2.2.[23] The crucial difference

---

21. The older label for the Afro-Asiatic (or Afrasian) phylum, Hamito-Semitic (or Semito-Hamitic), has been largely abandoned since it is based on the older, mistaken view that the non-Semitic languages in the phylum formed an independent "Hamitic" language family (Diakonoff 1988: 15; Huehnergard 2004: 138; cf. Voigt 2002: 265–66).

22. The extent of the Afro-Asiatic phylum is still being determined: Omotic has only relatively recently been identified as a separate family as opposed to being a subfamily of Chadic (cf. Diakonoff 1965; 1988; see Bender 2007), and similar claims of independent status have been made for other subfamilies within the phylum (see Huehnergard 2004: 139–40).

23. The classifications of both Eblaite and Ugaritic are disputed. Eblaite is well described as a "border language," in that it shares innovations with both WS Amorite and ES Akkadian (see Faber 1997: 8; C. H. Gordon 1997; Huehnergard 2004; Huehnergard and Woods 2004). The place of Ugaritic within WS is uncertain, since it exhibits archaic WS features but also shared innovations with NWS as opposed to Arabic, as well as shared innovations with

from the traditional subgrouping is the addition of the intermediary subgroup
of Central Semitic (CS) and the concommitant reclassification of Arabic and
Old (Epigraphic) South Arabian as CS languages instead of South Semitic
(SS) languages.[24]

The basis for this and similar reclassifications of the Semitic verbal systems
is directly relevant to the present discussion. Voigt (1987: 2) notes that the importance of verb systems for classifying Semitic was raised in the early part of
the 20th century by Christian (1919–20). Arguably, one of the most important
and lasting contributions to this discussion is Rössler's article (1950; ET 1981)
on verb structure and inflection in Afro-Asiatic. Setting aside his broader treatment of Afro-Asiatic, I note that Rössler classifed the Semitic languages based
on the relative stages of development evident in their verbal systems. The "Old
Semitic Stage," represented by Akkadian, features a "nominal" suffix conjugation and two "verbal" prefix conjugations: a "narrative and jussive" form
(*yaqtul*) and a "durative" form with a doubled middle root consonant (*yaqattal*). During the "1st Young Semitic Stage," represented by SS (e.g., Mehri
and Ethiopic), the narrative prefix form (*yaqtul*) was functionally replaced
by a new suffix narrative form (*qatala*) that developed from the Old Semitic
(nominal) suffix conjugation, while the jussive function of the first prefix form
(*yaqtul*) as well as the durative prefix form (*yaqattal*) were retained. Finally,
during the "2nd Young Semitic Stage," represented by CS Arabic, Aramaic,
and Canaanite, not only was the old narrative prefix form (*yaqtul*) replaced by
the new narrative suffix form (*qatala*), but the durative prefix form (*yaqattal*)
was replaced by a new prefix conjugation (*yaqtulu*) with a similar meaning
(Rössler 1950: 467–68, 511–12; ET 1981: 690, 744).[25]

The majority position on the Semitic verbal system aligns with the basic
conclusions arrived at by Rössler—namely, that Proto-Semitic (PS) had three
forms that could be conjugated with person, gender, and number affixes: a
nominal-based suffixed form (*qatala*) that expressed states in copular expressions (i.e., it was not a finite verb); a prefix form (*yaqtul*) that expressed both
perfective aspect and jussive mood;[26] and a second prefix form with doubled

---

Canaanite as opposed to Aramaic. Pardee (1997: 131) suggests that it may be a remnant of
an old Amorite dialect (see also Faber 1997: 10–11; Pardee 2004a).

24. Hetzron (1974; 1976; 1987) was a major advocate for the reclassification of Arabic
as a member of CS; however, his treatment of Canaanite and Arabic as a distinct subbranch
of WS has been criticized and less widely accepted (see Voigt 1987; Huehnergard 1991).

25. Compare Bauer and Leander (1991: 8), who place Hebrew with Akkadian in the
alte Gruppe versus the *jüngere Gruppe*, which consists of Phoenician, Aramaic, Arabic, and
Ethiopic.

26. The relationship between the Past and Jussive *yaqtul* is uncertain: Hetzron (1969)
suggested a stress differentiation between Past *yáqtul* and Jussive *yaqtúl* (cf. Goerwitz 1992);
Huehnergard (1988: 20) uggests that it is pointless to discuss the "relative priority" of the
Past and Jussive *yaqtul*, because both meanings adhered in a single form from an early stage.

middle consonant (*yaqattal*) that expressed present-imperfective aspect (see Rabin 2007: 284; Huehnergard 1991: 283; 2002: 125–26; 2004: 151–52; Müller 1998; Voigt 2002: 283–84).[27] This understanding of the development of the Semitic verb is the basis for the subgrouping of the Semitic languages in fig. 2.2 above: WS is distinguished from ES primarily on the basis of the shared innovation of a dynamic suffix conjugation (*qatala*), and CS is distinct within WS due to the shared innovation of a new prefix form (*yaqtulu*) that displaced the Common Semitic prefix form (*yaqattal*).

2.3.2. East Semitic and the West Semitic Verbal System

The decipherment of Akkadian in the mid-19th century forced a reevaluation of the genetic relationships among the Semitic languages and opened up new approaches to the interminable problems of the BHVS (Barr 1971: 1398). Prior to the establishment of the basic grammar of Akkadian in the 1850s (and for some time afterward), Arabic was treated as most closely resembling its progenitor PS (e.g., Gesenius 1855: 5–6; W. Wright 1962: 1.vi; Barr 1971: 1394).[28] Akkadian, however, exhibited both a more ancient and a notably different verbal system from Arabic, while at the same time providing suggestive new parallels to the *waw*-prefixed forms in BH. Arguably, the weakness of Ewald's and Driver's treatments of the *wayyiqtol* and *wĕqatal* forms was due in large part to the absence of any viable alternatives to etymologically and semantically relating these forms to their non-*waw*-prefixed formal counterparts (Ewald 1879: 21; Driver 1998: 71; see §§2.2.2. and 2.2.3. above).[29]

2.3.2.1. The Akkadian Verbal System

After more than two and a half millennia of use (26th century B.C.E. to 1st century C.E.), first as a spoken language and later as a strictly literary medium, Akkadian was forgotten for over a millennium and a half. European travelers to the Middle East brought back cuneiform tablets to Europe in the 17th century, but scholars were unable to decipher the texts until the publication of a trilingual Akkadian–Old Persian–Elamite text in the 19th century (Huehnergard 2005: xxii). The earliest form of the language is referred to as Old Akkadian, after which two major dialects are recognized—a northern Assyrian dialect

---

27. Voigt (2002: 284) identifies himself as alone subscribing to the view that the Akkadian Perfect (*iptaras*) is a reflex of a PS form and not an ES innovation. Another dissenting view is that of Kuryłowicz (1961; 1972; 1973), who argued that the basic opposition in PS was between *yaqtul* and *yaqtulu* (for his semantic interpretation of these forms, see §2.4.2.3 below) and that Akkadian *iparras* was an ES innovation (see Hamori 1973 for a response).

28. The tenacity of this view is evident in the uniformity in Gesenius's grammar between editions, even after it included Akkadian in its introduction to Semitic languages (cf. Gesenius 1855: 1–6; 1910: 1–8).

29. Notwithstanding Ewald's contention (1879: 21 n. 1) that the *wayyiqtol* is a Jussive-based verb form (see §2.2.2 above), semantically comparable to the Arabic Jussive preceded by the negative *lam* with reference to past events (see W. Wright 1962: 2.41).

Table 2.4. Akkadian Dialects
(based on Huehnergard and Woods 2004: 219)

Old Akkadian Mid-3rd Millennium to Early 2nd Millennium B.C.E.		
Old Babylonian	2000–1500 B.C.E.	Old Assyrian
Middle Babylonian	1500–1000 B.C.E.	Middle Assyrian
Neo-Babylonian	1000–600 B.C.E	Neo-Assyrian
Late Babylonian	600 B.C.E.–100 C.E.	

and a southern Babylonian dialect—for which three broad stages of development may be discerned, as illustrated in table 2.4 (Huehnergard and Woods
2004: 219; Huehnergard 2005: xxiii; see also von Soden 1995: §2; Buccellati
1996: 1–2; 1997: 69; 2003: 57).

In addition, dialects of Akkadian that vary to one degree or another from native Mesopotamian Akkadian are described as "Peripheral Akkadian." In this
category belong, among others, Amurru Akkadian (Izre'el and Singer 1991),
el-Amarna Akkadian (Böhl 1909; Ebeling 1910; Dhorme 1913–14; Knudtzon
1915; Moran 2003; Rainey 1996), and the Akkadian of Ugarit (Huehnergard
1989).[30] Grammatical descriptions have focused primarily on the Old Babylonian dialect, viewed by many as the "classical" stage of the language (Buccellati 1996; 1997: 69; Huehnergard 2005: xxvi).

The verbal system of Akkadian features three indicative prefix verb forms.
The *iparras* form, which is distinguished by the doubling of its middle root
consonant, is described as either Durative (i.e., imperfective) or Present, designating non-past tense (von Soden 1995: §78; Buccellati 2003: 58; Huehnergard and Woods 2004: 253; Kouwenberg 2010: chap. 4). Akkadian *iparras* has
cognates in South Semitic (e.g., Ethiopic *yənaggər*) but lacks any cognate form
in the CS languages;[31] however, its range of meaning is quite close to BH *yiqtol*
(see Buccellati 1996: 100–105; Huehnergard 2005: 98–99; Kouwenberg 2010:
91). The past-perfective *iprus* prefix conjugation is appropriately labeled Preterite or Past (von Soden 1995: §79; Buccellati 1996: 100–105; Huehnergard
2005: 18–19; Kouwenberg 2010: 126–32). Although past-perfective in WS is
predominately expressed by the suffix conjugation *qatala*, the productivity of

---

30. For studies of Peripheral Akkadian dialects, see the bibliographic notes in Izre'el
and Singer (1991: 14) and Huehnergard (1989: 7 n. 6).

31. Attempts to find remnants of a *yaqattal* conjugation in CS Ugaritic and Hebrew
have failed. The main advocate of a *yaqattal* reflex in Ugaritic was Goetze (1938; 1941a–b),
whose arguments have been refuted by Ginsberg (1939) and Fenton (1970). Several scholars
have attempted to find remnants of *yaqattal* in Hebrew, including Meyer (1958), Rössler
(1961; 1962), Rosén (1969), and Siedl (1971); Bloch (1963) and Fitzgerald (1972) refuted
Rössler's arguments in particular. On the *yaqattal* conjugation in Afro-Asiatic and Semitic,
respectively, see Greenberg (1952) and Janssens (1972). Rainey (1975: 423; 1990: 412–13)
has argued that the Amarna Letters provide no evidence for *yaqattal* in WS.

iprus in Akkadian has been crucially important to recognizing cognates in WS, notably in the BH *wayyiqtol* form and in the Arabic negative syntagm *lam yaqtul*. The *iptaras* form is unique to ES and is characterized by *-ta-* infixed after the first root consonant. Although the form exhibits certain dialect- and genre-specific semantic idiosyncrasies, on the whole it is not inaptly termed Perfect since in later Akkadian it begins to supplant the Past tense *iprus*—given the widespread development of past tense from perfect aspect (Huehnergard and Woods 2004: 254; see also von Soden 1995: §80; Buccellati 2003: 58; Huehnergard 2005: 157–58; Kouwenberg 2010: chap. 6).

Akkadian also has a directive modal system consisting of an imperative and jussive form, both patterned on the *iprus* prefix pattern: the Imperative *purus* and the Precative or Desiderative *liprus* (*iprus* plus a prefixed *l-*, except for the 3FS and 1P, before which the particle *lū* appears; von Soden 1995: §81; Buccellati 1996: 180–82; Huehnergard and Woods 2004: 255; Kouwenberg 2010: 133–37, 212–17). The Precative minus the prefixed *l-* is morphologically identical with the Past *iprus* and cognate with the WS jussive forms (e.g., Arabic *yaktub*; Ethiopic *yəngər*, also labeled Subjunctive; Huehnergard and Woods 2004: 252–54).

Straddling the nominal and verbal categories is a Verbal Adjective (often called Stative or Permansive) that may function attributively (with suffixed case, number, and gender agreement markers) or predicatively (with suffixed subject pronouns). The semantics of the Verbal Adjective is determined by the valency and aspect of the verbal lexeme: with stative verbs, the Verbal Adjective expresses a state (e.g., *damqum* '[is] good'); with dynamic-intransitive verbs, it has a resultative meaning (e.g., *wašbum* '[is] seated'); with dynamic-transitive verbs, it has a passive sense (e.g., *ṣabtum* '[is] seized'; von Soden 1995: §77; Buccellati 1996: 165–68; Huehnergard 1987a: 225; 2005: 27, 219–23; Kouwenberg 2010: chap. 7). At the same time, there are a small number of dynamic-transitive verbs that, when conjugated in this verbal adjectival pattern with suffixed subject pronouns, express dynamic-transitive events, often governing accusative objects rather than an expected passive sense (e.g., *bītam ṣabtat* 'she is/was in possession of the house'; Huehnergard 2005: 393–95). The semantic distinctiveness of these forms has led Huehnergard to propose that they are built from a separate base than the Verbal Adjective, which he calls a "Pseudo-Verb" or "Transitive *parsāku*" (Huehnergard 1987a: 232; 2005: 393; cf. Buccellati 1988).

2.3.2.2. The West Semitic Verbal System in Light of Akkadian

The differences between the verbal system of Arabic and the verbal system exhibited by the much older Akkadian evidence prompted a series of articles seeking to establish, in the words of Haupt (1878: 244), which was the "oldest Semitic verb form." For example, Haupt (1878: 244) argued that the geographical and temporal distance between Akkadian and Ethiopic, which both have reflexes of the *yaqattal* form (Akkadian *iparras;* Ethiopic *yanaggar*) in notable contrast to WS Arabic, supports the identification of the form as part of the PS verbal inventory. Hoffman not only argued, similarly to Haupt, that the verbal system of Akkadian more closely reflects the PS verbal system than the WS languages do; he also proposed a developmental connection between the Akkadian Verbal Adjective and WS *qatala:* "Does it signify a loss if the Babylonian system does not know of a encliticized Perfect, or is this Perfect indeed a new formation in Canaan deriving from a Participial-Adjectival form?" (Hoffman 1887: 605; cited in Bauer 1910: 5–6; my translation).[32]

Knudtzon (1892) was apparently the first to propose that the development of WS *qatala* and CS *yaqtul(u)* conjugations might each be found in a confluence of meanings (also Lambert 1893: 52–54). Knudtzon argued that the WS *qatala* developed from the adjectival or nominal pattern *qati/ula*, which expressed a present state (as the Akkadian reflex). This stative meaning was retained in *qatala*, explaining the wide semantic range found in BH (*wĕ)qatal* (1892: 48). He argued that *yaqattal* was the earliest verb form in Semitic, followed by the development of a second prefix form, *yaqtul*. While these forms developed complementary tense meanings in ES (i.e., present-future *iparras*, past *iprus*), these forms and meanings merged in CS *yaqtul(u)*, explaining the contrastive TAM between its BH reflexes *yiqtol* and *wayyiqtol* (Knudtzon 1892: 50).

Building on these early ideas, Bauer presented a theory of the development of the Semitic verb forms, focusing on their reflexes in Akkadian, Hebrew, and Arabic. Bauer (1910: 8) proposed that the most primitive Semitic verbal form was *yaqtul*, constructed through the prefixation of pronominal elements (e.g., *ya-, ta-*) to the base Imperative-Infinitive **qutul* form. He argued that this earliest Semitic verb form expressed neither tense ('subjektiv Zeitstufe') nor aspect ('objektiv Zeitmoment'; Bauer 1910: 10)—thus a true "aorist" (Bauer 1910: 24; see Bauer and Leander 1991: 269). The development of the denominative *qatala*, which by virtue of its origin in a *nomen agentis* expressed primarily a present (participle) meaning, circumscribed the boundless temporal value of the *yaqtul* so that it came to express a complementary perfect (participle) meaning (Bauer 1910: 16–17). These two forms developed in ES Akkadian into the Past (*yaqtul > iprus*) and Present (*qatala > iparras*, with prefixed rather than suffixed pronouns), respectively.[33] However, after the split from ES, the *qatala* verb form underwent further development in WS:

---

32. Bedeutet es Verlust, wenn das Babylonishche kein postfigiertes Perfekt kennt, oder ist dieses Perfekt schon in Kanaan eine Neubildung vom Participial-Adjektive aus?

33. Bauer's connection between *qatala* and Akkadian *iparras* was facilitated by the failure of scholars at that point in time to recognize that the Akkadian Present (or Durative) featured a doubled middle consonant (i.e., *iparas* vs. *iparras*). Greenberg dates the recognition of the doubling in the Akkadian Present to Goetze (1936; 1942), complaining that this view was only slowly accepted by scholars (see Greenberg 1952: 1 n. 2).

Table 2.5. Hans Bauer's Model of the Hebrew Verb
(based on 1910: 35)

Older (PS) Style	Newer (WS) Style
qatalá (> *wĕqatal*)	*qatála* (> *qatal*)
(present participle)	(perfect participle)
yáqtul (> *wayyiqtol*)	*yaqtúl* (> *yiqtol*)
(perfect participle)	(present participle)

In the West-Semitic languages, however, the form *qatala* underwent a further development, by which the whole of the tense relations were completely reshaped. Here, namely, the perfect meaning of the nominal form *qatal*, such as in words like "culprit, winner, murderer," has made a break through and has been spread almost to the whole verbal system. Thereby, the form likewise became suited to serve as a narrative tense, in the way the Perfect of our languages does [i.e., the European languages]; *yaqtul* consequently was relieved of its narrative function and was limited to its other not precisely circumscribed uses, which we can characterize as approximately corresponding to a present participle. Both verbal forms, as one can see, have nearly exchanged their roles compared with Proto-Semitic. (Bauer 1910: 18; my translation)[34]

According to Bauer, this semantic role-reversal of the suffix and prefix forms in WS did not completely obviate their earlier meanings, thus resulting in a system with two "new" verb forms alongside the "old" forms. Bauer argued that these morphologically identical pairs were differentiated by word stress and, within BH in particular, by the requisite prefixed *waw* on the older forms, as shown in table 2.5; thus, Bauer (1910: 10) suggested that, instead of the conventional term "*waw* conversivum," the conjunction on these older verb forms in BH should be termed "*waw* conservativum."

However, Bauer observed that the distinguishing *waw* is sometimes absent from *qatal* in generic (proverbial) sentences, subordinate sentences, and in the poetic representation of future events (i.e., the prophetic perfect), and from *yiqtol* in poetry and following certain particles: אָז 'then', טֶרֶם 'before', עַד 'until'

---

34. In den westsemitischen Sprachen hingegen hat die Form *qatala* eine Weiterentwickelung [*sic*] erfahren, wodurch die gesamten Tempusverhältnisse völlig umgestaltet wurden. Hier ist nämlich die in Wörtern wie "Täter, Sieger, Mörder" liegende perfektische Bedeutung der Nominalform *qatal* zum Durchbruch gekommen und fast auf den ganzen Verbalbestand übertragen worden. Dadurch wurde die Form in derselben Weise geeignet, als Tempus der Erzählung zu dienen, wie das Perfektum unserer Sprachen [i.e., the European languages]; *jaqtul* ward infolgedessen seiner erzählenden Funktion enthoben und auf seine sonstigen, nicht genau umschriebenen Verwendungen eingeschränkt, die wir annähernd als die einem Participium praesentis entsprechenden bezeichnen können. Die beiden Verbalformen haben, wie man sieht, gegenüber dem Ursemitischen ihre Rollen nahezu vertauscht.

(Bauer 1910: 35). The application of Bauer's theory to BH is demonstrated most clearly by Hughes (1955; 1962; 1970; see §2.4.2.1 below).

Bauer's criticism of S. R. Driver's aspectual theory and his alternative description of the BHVS in terms of tense set up his theory as the primary (tense-based) alternative to the Ewald-Driver aspectual theory (see Bauer 1910: 23–25). However, much more importantly, Bauer significantly altered the discussion by turning the conventional wisdom on its head: up until Bauer's study, grammars unanimously portrayed the Jussive *yaqtul* as a shortened or "apocopated" derivative of the long indicative *yaqtulu* form (e.g., Ewald 1879: 16; Driver 1998: 51–52; W. Wright 1962: 1.60; Kautzsch 1910: 130–31). By contrast, Bauer argued that the *yaqtul* was the more primitive form, whose development accounts for the Jussive *yaqtul*, the *yaqtul* with past tense meaning (notably, e.g., BH *wayyiqtol*, Arabic *lam yaqtul*), and the indicative *yaqtulu* through a process of lengthening (*die Verlängerung*; Bauer 1910: 11).

Bauer's proposal that Akkadian *iparras* developed from a Proto-Semitic *qatala* was not taken up by subsequent scholars. Rather, in line with Hoffman's earlier explanation (1887), WS *qatala* has come to be understood as cognate with the Akkadian predicatively employed Verbal Adjective *paris/parsāku* (e.g., Brockelmann 1951: 141; Huehnergard 1992: 156; Kienast 2001: 293). Bauer's less-than-satisfactory treatment of the suffix conjugation opened the way for G. R. Driver's theory (1936) of the Hebrew verbal system, which took the development of the suffix form as its starting point.

G. R. Driver (1936), like Knudtzon (1892) and Bauer (1910), embraced the view that BH is a *Mischsprache* ('mixed dialect') of older and more recent verb meanings and/or functions; however, he proposed an alternative line of development to account for this situation, beginning with the adjectival suffix pattern *qati/ul*. Driver argued that this primitive Semitic form, when predicatively used, has a resultative (stative) sense and thus is ambiguous between a past (tense) event and a present (tense) state (e.g., *qatil* '[he is in a] killed [state]'; i.e., 'he has been killed' ~ 'he is killed'). As a result of this ambiguity, ES developed two complementary prefix forms: a present-future *yaqattal* ('he kills' ~ 'he will kill'), and a past *yaqtul* ('he killed').

By contrast, WS developed a dynamic-transitive *qatala* form (with an *a*-theme vowel to distinguish it from intransitive *qati/ula*—a distinction, Driver hypothesized, necessitated by the loss of case endings) based on the PS *qati/ula* that "became a pure tense restricted almost entirely to the past" (G. R. Driver 1936: 81–83). Due to this semantic development and the failure of CS to retain the *yaqattal* form, the PS *yaqtul* came to describe "incomplete action whether past, present or future" (Driver 1936: 83–84). At the same time, the older, ES meanings associated with the suffix and prefix forms were preserved in BH, distinguished largely by the *waw* prefix as well as word stress (i.e., *qátal* stative-present vs. *qatál* complete-past; *yáqtul* preterite vs. *yaqtúl* incomplete):

Hebrew fully developed *qāṭal* as a transitive form distinguished only by a change of vowel from *qāṭēl* which became tolerably rare and was restricted almost exclusively to stative verbs; in consequence of this development *qāṭal* became a tense descriptive of completed action in past time, but this did not prevent it from retaining a certain amount of the universal force of the primitive *qāṭil* out of which it had been evolved. Thus *qāṭal* continued or rather came to be employed as a present tense in gnomic sentences and in legal or semi-legal phrases which are both apt to be survivals from an older stage of the language. At the same time it preserved the future sense of the old universal *qāṭil* (which also the Accadian permansive state of the same form still in some degree retained), though only in poetry which is wont to preserve archaistic usages, in the prophetic language, which is in its very nature poetical, and in prose when marked by certain safeguards, namely with consecutive *wāw* and certain other particles. Similarly too, although the development of *qāṭal* as a tense describing completed action in past time caused *yiqṭōl* (after the failure to develop *yaqatal/il* in Hebrew) to become the tense of every kind of incomplete action, relics of the purely preterite use of the primitive *yaqtul* (as exemplified in the Accadian preterite *iqtul*) survived in Hebrew sporadically in poetry and normally also in prose after certain particles [i.e., אָז 'then', טֶרֶם 'before' and in *wayyiqtol*]. Again, it is poetry which tends to preserve or to affect archaic language and the fact that *yiqṭōl* was intelligible as a preterite, like *qāṭal* as a future, tense only when it was definitely so marked suggests that it too was a survival from a long-forgotten stage of Semitic speech. (G. R. Driver 1936: 88–89)

Thacker (1954), one of G. R. Driver's students, employed the basic outline of his teacher's theory in his comparative study of Egyptian and Semitic verbal systems.[35] Although Thacker agreed with Driver on most points, evident from his copious references to his mentor's work, he combined ideas from Bauer's theory with Driver's. Thacker (1954: 230) agreed with Bauer, against Driver, that *yaqtul* developed before *yaqattal* in Semitic. By so doing, Thacker was better able to explain the divergent semantics in BH *yiqtol* and *wayyiqtol* as deriving from the universal semantics of *yaqtul* rather than as the result of an expanded incomplete meaning of preterite *yaqtul* (cf. Driver quotation above; see McFall 1982: 165).

Driver and Thacker together helped buttress Bauer's argument that, while ultimately *yiqtol* and *wayyiqtol* may be etymologically related, they are reflexes of two different lines of development in the Semitic verbal system. More importantly, G. R. Driver (see 1936: 15–16 for criticism of Bauer) introduced an important but subtle shift to the treatment of WS *qatala* by rejecting

---

35. Several scholars since Thacker have attempted to explain the Semitic verbal system with respect to Egyptian, which notably lacks any prefix conjugations (Janssens 1972; Loprieno 1986; see Satzinger 2002). By comparing the suffix form in Semitic with the Egyptian Old Perfective (or Pseudo-Participle), the active-transitive meaning of which was dying out in Middle Egyptian (see Moran 2003: 24 n. 58), Thacker sought to buttress G. R. Driver's claim that the suffix form is the oldest Semitic verb form (Thacker 1954: 118).

Bauer's hypothetical *nomen agentis* as an origin and establishing more clearly the form's developmental connection with the precative use of the Verbal Adjective in Akkadian. However, Driver's claim that BH *wĕqatal* in particular preserves the older, ES value of the Proto-form was less convincing.

Andersen (2000) has recently attempted to reintroduce the sort of early *Mischsprache* theory of the BHVS presented by Bauer, G. R. Driver, and Thacker. Like Bauer and G. R. Driver, Andersen (2000: 51–56) argues that both the suffixed pair *wĕqatal/qatal* and the prefixed pair *wayyiqtol/yiqtol* preserve "archaic" meanings, primarily in the *waw*-prefixed forms, in addition to the later meanings associated mainly with the non-*waw*-prefixed forms. In a sort of throwback to these early theories, Andersen (2000: 23, 32) begins from the outdated assumption that both *qatala* and *yaqtulu* are PS verb forms, rather than WS and CS innovations, respectively (see §2.3.1 above). He argues that PS *yaqtulu* was marginalized by the imperfective *yaqattal* form and became a subordinate verb in the languages that featured the *yaqattal* form (Andersen 2000: 23–25).[36] *Qatala*, which originated from a verbal noun (versus the verbal adjective origin for *qatila*) according to Andersen, interacted contrastively with (mostly intransitive) activity predicates and (mostly transitive) achievement and accomplishment predicates: with the former, it yielded a progressive meaning that subsequently developed into an imperfective-future form (e.g., BH *wĕqatal*); with the latter predicates, it had a resultative meaning that developed into a perfective sense, as in BH *qatal* (Andersen 2000: 39–42).

Although Andersen helpfully updates the evidence supporting an etymological distinction between *yiqtol* and *wayyiqtol*, his theory suffers from numerous unsubstantiated claims. These include his outmoded view that *yaqtulu* and *qatala* are both PS forms, along with his concomitant claim that PS had two distinct suffix conjugations—the verbal noun *qatala* and the adjectival noun *qatila* (cf. G. R. Driver 1936: 15–16). Andersen (2000: 40–41) fails to produce any convincing evidence that *qatala* had a split meaning based on the situation aspect of the verbal lexeme, notwithstanding the interesting illustrations of this phenomenon in Japanese and Dravidian. Finally, Andersen wrongly presumes, as many theories of the BHVS have, a semantic symmetry among the *waw*-*prefixed* and *non*-*waw*-*prefixed* forms. In other words, he assumes that *wayyiqtol* is semantically equatable with *qatal* (apart from *wa*C-), while *wĕqatal* is semantically equatable with *yiqtol.*

Theories of the BHVS from the perspective of the East-West division of the Semitic verbal system have ultimately been successful with respect to the prefix conjugations, but unsuccessful with regard to the suffix conjugation. As the most recent garnering of evidence by Andersen demonstrates, it is well-established that *wayyiqtol* and *yiqtol* are reflexes of distinct verb forms in

---

36. Andersen (2000: 23) equivocates on the PS status of *yaqattal*, stating that "*yaqattal* was not a well-established PS conjugation."

WS—*yaqtul* and *yaqtulu*, respectively—regardless of how they may be related at an earlier stage of Semitic (Andersen 2000: 17–20; see also Tropper 1998a: 157–64). Although Driver succeeded in establishing a clear developmental link between WS *qatala* and the predicative use of the ES Verbal Adjective, the *Mischsprache* theories have not gained a following with regard to their explanations of the divergent semantics of *qatal* and *wĕqatal*.

With respect to the TAM of the BHVS, the early East-West discussions ended up highlighting the role of tense in the verbal system, because they were largely cast as reactions to the growing hegemony of the Ewald-Driver aspectual understanding (see Bauer 1910: 23–24; G. R. Driver 1936: 87). In particular, Bauer's theory of the Semitic verb formed the foundation of tense-based theories of the BHVS such as Blake's (1944a; 1946; 1951) and Hughes's (1955; 1962; 1970). G. R. Driver's treatment of the Hebrew verbal forms is more of a compromise between aspect and tense approaches: *qatal* expresses completed-past events; *wĕqatal* expresses present and future in limited contexts; *wayyiqtol* expresses past events; *yiqtol* expresses incomplete events in past, present, or future.

2.3.3. Ugaritic and the Northwest Semitic Verbal System

The importance of the discovery of Ugaritic is underscored by Pardee's statement (1997: 131; 2004b: 288), referred to above (§2.3), that it is the only well-attested native language of the Levantine area in the second millennium B.C.E.[37] As Moran has noted (2003: 197), in the early 19th century Gesenius had lamented the complete lack of historical data for reconstructing earlier stages of Hebrew, and a century later, on the eve of the discovery of Ugaritic, little had changed, as evidenced by a perusal of Bauer and Leander's historical grammar (1991). Despite the inherent difficulties in interpreting the largely un-vocalized texts and the continued disagreements regarding points of grammar, including the verbal system, the Ugaritic tablets have influenced nearly every part of Hebrew and NWS grammar and biblical studies—so much so that one may regularly speak about pre- and post-Ugaritic epochs in these fields (thus Moran 2003: 203).

2.3.3.1. The Ugaritic Verbal System

The vast majority of the over 1,000 well-preserved texts (in addition to numerous other fragments) written in Ugaritic have been excavated from Ras Shamra, the site of the ancient city of Ugarit, which may have controlled an area of approximately 2,000 square km (Pardee 1997: 131; see Yon 2006). Excavated more or less continually by the French since its discovery in 1929, the site has yielded some 50 mythological epic narrative (poetic) texts along with over 1,000 prose texts of various types, including religious, administrative,

---

37. On all facets of Ugaritic studies, see Watson and Wyatt 1999.

and epistolary (Pardee 2004b: 289; Bordreuil and Pardee 2009: 1–20). The texts mostly originated in Ugarit and date to the period of the Late Bronze Age between 1300 and 1190 B.C.E.; the city was destroyed and abandoned in the early 12th century B.C.E. In addition to Ugaritic, texts have been unearthed at Ras Shamra written in Akkadian, the international lingua franca of the period (about 2,000 texts), as well as Sumerian, Egyptian, Luwian, Hittite, Hurrian, and Cypro-Minoan (Pardee 2004b: 289; Bordreuil and Pardee 2009: 8).

While Ugaritic is recognized as a NWS language (e.g., Ugaritic features word-initial /w/ > /y/, which separates NWS from CS Arabic), debate has persisted since its discovery regarding its status within NWS, narrowing to the question whether Ugaritic is Canaanite or a sister NWS language of Canaanite (see fig. 2.2 above; C. H. Gordon 1965: 144–48; see esp. Goetze 1941b; more recently, cf. Tropper 1994 and Sivan 2000). While Ugaritic shares certain isoglosses that place it closer to Canaanite than Aramaic, the other major branch of NWS (e.g., /ḏ/ > /ṣ/; cf. Aramaic /ḏ/ > /q/ or /ʕ/), it lacks certain earmarks of Canaanite, including the Canaanite shift (i.e., /ā/ > /ō/) and a causative *h*-stem or *y*-stem (cf. Ugaritic causative *š*-stem; see Goetze 1941b; Segert 1984: 13–14; Sivan 1997: 2–3). Literarily, Ugaritic poetry strongly resembles biblical poetry formally (parallelism), lexically, and thematically (Gordon 1965: 145; Pardee 2004b: 288). Some of the difficulty in comparing Ugaritic and Canaanite arise from the chronological difference between the second-millennium Ugaritic material and the first-millennium Canaanite texts. Pardee (1997: 131; 2004b: 288) observes that Ugaritic has "features characteristic of old Canaanite and it may be a remnant of a Western 'Amorite' dialect" (similarly Goetze 1941b).

The Ugaritic writing system is consonantal with the crucially important exceptions of the three ʾalep signs *ȧ*, *i*, and *u̇*. These three signs are syllabic, representing a glottal (ʾalep) followed by an *a*, *i*, and *u* vowel, respectively; syllable-final ʾalep is represented by the *i* sign (see Segert 1984: 22–23; Sivan 1997: 9–10; Tropper 2000: 33–39; Pardee 1997: 132; Bordreuil and Pardee 2009: 22). Another important source of information for the vocalization of Ugaritic are texts with Ugaritic words written in Akkadian syllabary (Sivan 1984; Huehnergard 1987b). Together, these sources form the most direct and important knowledge about the vocalization of Ugaritic.

The Ugaritic verbal system manifests an archaic WS verb system (Pardee 2004b: 302) consisting of two basic patterns. One is the suffix conjugation *malaka*, labled Perfect. Internal evidence exists only for a *malika* pattern, i.e., *lìk* = /laʾika/ 'he sent' (see C. H. Gordon 1965: 69; Sivan 1997: 113; Tropper 2000: 469–71), but Ugaritic texts written in Akkadian syllabary attest to some *malaka* forms, e.g., *ṣa-ma-ta* = /ṣamata/ (Huehnergard 1987b: 319–20). The second, a prefix pattern, is the basis for several conjugations, distinguished by suffixation. As with *malaka*, there is evidence for internal ablaut distinguishing dynamic *yamluku* from stative *yamliku* and *yimlaku* patterns: e.g., *àmlk* *ʾamluku/* 'I will reign'; *ilàk* *ʾilʾaku/* 'I will send'; syllabic [*i*]*a-ab-ṣi-ru* /yabṣiru/ (C. H. Gordon 1965: 71; Sivan 1997: 115–17; Tropper 2000: 447–54; Huehnergard 1987b: 219 n. 87). The Imperfect *yamluku* and Perfect *malaka* stand in binary opposition as the only two indicative verb forms in prose texts.

The nonindicative (modal) system features an Imperative, built on the prefix pattern base, **m(u)luk*; a Jussive *yamluk*, which is distinguished from the Imperfect by a zero suffix; a Subjunctive or Volitive *a*-suffixed *yamluka*; and two energic forms with suffixed *-n(n)* (Energic 1 *yaqtulan* and Energic 2 *yaqtulanna*), the meanings of which are not entirely clear but are generally associated with the modal system (see Pardee 2004b: 303–6; C. H. Gordon 1965: 71–73; Segert 1984: 56–63; Sivan 1997: 115–19; Tropper 2000: 497–506). Despite some dissenting opinions (esp. Greenstein 1998; 2006), it is widely recognized that Ugaritic had a reflex of PS prefixed past *yaqtul*, homophonous with the Jussive *yamluk* (Lipiński 2001: 347; Sivan 1997: 98–100; Tropper 2000: 683, 695–97; Pardee 2004b: 303; but cf. Bordreuil and Pardee 2009: 46).

Crucial to the semantic description of the Ugaritic verbal system is the prose : poetry distinction. In prose, the verbal conjugations function analgously to their cognate forms (e.g., BH, Aramaic, Arabic). However, the distribution of the suffix and prefix conjugations in Ugaritic poetic texts "has thus far defied complete description" (Pardee 2004b: 303). Pardee has criticized attempts to describe the Ugaritic verbal system on the basis of the poetic texts or to theorize a system that is equally applicable to prose and poetry, surmising that the poetic texts "reflect an older stage of the language when the zero-ending imperfect form functioned as a preterite, like the Akkadian iprus" (Pardee 2004b: 303; 2003–4: 14; 1997: 13).

2.3.3.2. The Northwest Semitic Verbal System in Light of Ugaritic

Granting the singular importance of the Ugaritic evidence to our knowledge of NWS, we nevertheless find that the contribution of the data on its verbal system is particularly difficult to assess because of several complicating factors.[38] The first is simply the nature of Ugaritic philology: the texts are mostly consonantal, often fragmentary, and many still await authoritative publication (Pardee 2003-4: 1–2). Second, and following naturally on the first point, debate continues unabated regarding the semantics and functions of the Ugaritic verbal forms (e.g., Richardson 1991; Tropper 1991; 1992; 1995; Rainey 1990; M. S. Smith 1995; Sivan 1998; Greenstein 1998: 409–13; 2006). Finally, based on continued debate over the genetic affinities of Ugaritic, scholars' interpretation of its verbal system has often been via the paradigm of related Semitic languages, particularly Hebrew. A case in point is C. H. Gordon's comment

---

38. Emerton (1994b: 54) comments, perhaps somewhat tongue-in-cheek, on the contribution of Ugaritic to our understanding of Hebrew: "Whether it [Ugaritic] has shed more light or raised more problems is a debatable question."

(1965: 68–69) that "in fact *yqtl* is the regular narrative form and we shall often translate it as a historical present." Richardson (1991: 285) surmises that Gordon's puzzling treatment of the form as a historical present stems from his underlying equation of Ugaritic *yamluk(u)* and BH *yiqtol*.

However, Hebrew was not the first framework through which the Ugaritic verbal system was viewed. Goetze, in one of the earliest descriptions of the Ugaritic verbal system, approached it from Akkadian. Goetze (1938: 286) argued that the Ugaritic suffix conjugation should be vocalized *malika*, similar to the Akkadian counterpart *paris/parsāku*, and that it predominately has a "stative connotation" and is therefore not an integral part of the system of "tenses" (Goetze 1938: 289). Goetze (1938: 289–96) identified three different prefix conjugations in Ugaritic: the indicative *yamluku*, regularly used as a narrative past in poetic texts; the nonindicative subjunctive *yamluka*; and the apocopated jussive *yamluk*. On the basis of his semantic description of these three conjugations, Goetze (1938: 296) argued that, because none of the three properly expresses present tense, a present tense *yaqattal* conjugation had been and should be "surmised" for Ugaritic.

Through a series of exchanges between several scholars in the 1960s–1970s, claims to have found reflexes of PS *yaqattal* in Ugaritic and other NWS languages were discredited (see p. 98 n. 30 above). Fenton, who argued forcefully against Goetze's view in this matter (Fenton 1970), subsequently interpreted the BHVS in light of Ugaritic (Fenton 1973). Fenton (1973: 34) stated that "Hebrew and Ugaritic belonged to the same linguistic continuum and their tense systems shared the same history" and drew appropriate lines of developmental connection between the two. In poetry, the BHVS, not surprisingly, appeared to be at a later stage of development than the Ugaritic verbal system in that *qatala* was used more freely as a narrative form alongside the "omnitemporal" *yaqtul(u)* form. By contrast, in prose, the BHVS appears to be the more conservative system since it preserves the *yaqtul* preterite in *wayyiqtol* in contrast to Ugaritic, in which *qatala* is the "exclusive form for recording single past events" (Fenton 1973: 34). Similarly, Held (1962: 282) saw clear parallels in the Ugaritic and BH verbal systems in poetry, except that he argued that, when *yaqtul(u)* appeared parallel with *qatala* in BH or Ugaritic, it was not an omnitemporal verb form but a reflex of the PS Past *yaqtul*.

Fenton (1973: 32) found in the Ugaritic data confirmation of Bauer's (and G. R. Driver's) view of the *wayyiqtol* in BH as derived from an earlier/eastern past *yaqtul*. By contrast and earlier, Harris (1939: 11) had claimed that the Ugaritic evidence countered Bauer's theory in that it showed that the BHVS was no *Mischsprache* of ES and WS dialects but was a native NWS verbal system.[39] In this regard, Ugaritic has provided invaluable data on the early NWS

---

39. Although Harris's work is entitled *Development of the Canaanite Dialects*, it treats Ugaritic on the supposition that it is part of Canaanite; thus his treatment is essentially of NWS languages exclusive of Aramaic (Harris 1939: 10–11).

verbal system: it has confirmed the presence of a short final vowel on *qatala* (like Arabic) in contrast to ES Akkadian *paris/parsāku*, and it establishes the form of the prefix conjugations, the Indicative *yaqtulu*, Jussive *yaqtul*, and Subjunctive *yaqtula* (Harris 1939: 7–8; see Bauer and Leander 1991: 296–300; 307–8). Ugaritic also appears to support the identification of a past prefix form in NWS, though the Ugaritic data led Harris (1939: 46–48) to identify both a *yaqtulu* preterite and a *yaqtul* preterite. Harris claimed that "the outstanding change in morphological structure of Canaanite [i.e., NWS minus Aramaic] was the replacing of the objective aspect [i.e., tense] system by a subjective aspect [i.e., viewpoint aspect] system" through the following developments:

> As the perfect [*qatala*] replaced the preterite [*yaqtul(u)*] in regular speech, the few cases of the preterite which still occurred (in old stereotyped phrases and the like) came to be formulaic, members of an obsolescent form, and were no longer understood as a preterite tense. Now it happened that this petrified verbal form, *yaqtulu*, seemed to have an obvious relation to the other existing forms: as between *yaqatalu* present indicative,[40] and *yaqtul, yaqtula* jussive and subjunctive aspects, this *yaqtulu* had precisely the form which an indicative aspect related to the two modes would have had. It is probable that on this formal analogy the petrified *yaqtulu* forms came to be interpreted as a new imperfect indicative, a category hitherto non-existent. This new imperfect soon became a regular construction, applicable to any root for which there was a jussive or present. . . . Fitting as it did into the now largely "subjective" system of the Canaanite verb, it was favored over the present. In time, the present dropped out of use and Canaanite was left with a practically pure subjective-aspect verb system, the chief remnant of the old tense system being the short preterite in the inland dialects. (Harris 1939: 84–85)

While Harris's early understanding of TAM in the NWS verbal system is understandably no longer credible, TAM in Ugaritic remains unsettled, judging from the grammars. Gordon apparently treated Ugaritic *malaka* and *yamluku* aspectually, as equivalent to their BH cognates, though he assiduously avoided the semantic labels "perfect" and "imperfect" (C. H. Gordon 1965: 68–69; see Richardson 1991: 284–85). Segert (1984: 88–89) explained that Ugaritic opposition *malaka : yamluku* expressed a perfective : imperfective ("constative" : "cursive") opposition at its early strage; these meanings are preserved in poetry, where the forms may function in "all three temporal spheres." By contrast, in prose texts the forms have "temporal character." Sivan (1997: 96–103; 1998), following his teacher Rainey, treats the Ugaritic verbal system in terms of tense: *malaka* expresses past tense, while *yamluku* expresses present-future tense; unfortunately, these tense identifications appear prima facie at odds with his taxonomies of the forms as used alike in all three temporal spheres. Tropper's recent grammar (2000) returns to a more traditional aspectual approach

---

40. Harris (1939: 49) accepted Goetze's argument (1938) for a reflex of Proto-Semitic *yaqattal* in Ugaritic.

to the forms, albeit recognizing also past tense *yaqtul* (versus imperfective *yaqtulu*) in the system (Tropper 2000: 682–84; see also 1992; 1995; 1999: 109). Finally, Greenstein (2006) has recently argued against claims of a prefixed past form in Ugaritic and, further, that the default meanings that *malaka* and *yaqtulu* have in prose, which he identifies as past and present-future, respectively, are "in practice subordinated to all manner of discourse and rhetorical factors" (Greenstein 2006: 78; and Bordreuil and Pardee 2009: 46, who endorse his position). The implication appears to be that it is still impossible to construct a coherent semantic analysis of the Ugaritic verbal system in poetry (see also Greenstein 1988; 1998: 409–13).

2.3.4. Amarna and the Canaanite Verbal System

One of the most important contributions that Ugaritic studies have made to understanding the BHVS is indirect: although discovered in 1887, the Canaanite influences on the Akkadian language of the Amarna correspondences[41] were not fully appreciated until they were viewed in the light of their close contemporary, Ugaritic (see Rainey 1996b: 4; Moran 2003: 6). The Amarna Letters were discovered at el-Amarna, the capital and residence of the Egyptian king Akhenaten (Amenhotep IV; ca. 1353–1336 B.C.E.) and contain diplomatic correspondence from Mesopotamia, Syria, and Asia Minor. Several excavations uncovered over 350 texts (see Moran 2003: 223–25, 237–41, 343–44). While the letters are almost entirely written in Babyonian, the lingua franca of the period (exceptions are some Assyrian, Hurrian, and Hittite letters), they are not written in standard Babylonian but in Akkadian dialects reflective of the native languages of the regions from which the letters originated (Moran 2003: 343). The dialects of Amarna Akkadian along with the dialects of other Akkadian texts found at Ugarit (Ras Shamra, Syria), Emar (Tell Meskeneh, Syria), Nuzi (administrative center of the Mitanni empire; modern Yorgan Tepe, Iraq), Alalakh (Tell Atchana, Turkey), Hattusas (the capital of the Hittite empire; modern Boğazköy, Turkey), and other places are collectively classified as "peripheral Akkadian" (Moran 2003: 237; Huehnergard 2005: xxv).

---

41. In this discussion, *Canaanite* refers to the Semitic dialects spoken in the geographical region of ancient Canaan in the second half of the second millenium B.C.E., in contrast to its more conventional reference to Canaanite dialects of the first millenium as distinct from other NWS dialects (Pardee 2004a: 386). Moran (2003) and Rainey (1996) use the term with this former meaning, although Rainey (e.g., 1996b: 221) freely mixes the term with "West Semitic" and "Northwest Semitic." The Canaanite of Amarna period is clearly CS, based on the presence of the innovative *yaqtulu* verb form. In the following discussion, WS, CS, and NWS are used to refer to the domain of a particular feature exhibited in the Canaanite of the Amarna Letters.

2.3.4.1. Peripheral Akkadian and the Amarna Letters

The standard edition of the Amarna Letters by Knudtzon along with several important studies of the correspondences appeared in the early 20th century (Knudtzon 1915; Böhl 1909; Ebeling 1910; Dhorme 1913–14).[42] After the discoveries at Ras Shamra, Albright began to reexamine the Amarna Letters in the light of Ugaritic (1937; 1942a; 1942b; 1943a; 1943b). More importantly, Albright engaged his student Moran in the reinvestigation (Albright and Moran 1948), and Moran (1950; repr. in Moran 2003) produced his landmark study on the Byblian (Canaanite) dialect as reflected in the Amarna Letters originating at Byblos. Following Moran's lead, scholars have studied other regional dialects reflected in the Amarna Letters as well as in other peripheral Akkadian texts (e.g., Izre'el 1978; Izre'el and Singer 1991; Huehnergard 1989; Cochavi-Rainey 1990; Sivan and Cochavi-Rainey 1992; Pentiuc 2001); however, Rainey's work on the peripheral Akkadian of the Canaanite region is of particular importance because Rainey's goal was its contribution to understanding the BHVS. In addition to publishing extensively on the verbal system in the Amarna Letters (Rainey 1971; 1973; 1975; 1991–93; 1993; 1996), Rainey has reconstructed the early Canaanite verbal system based largely on evidence in the Amarna Letters (Rainey 1986; 1988; 1990; 2003).

The difficulty with extracting information from the Amarna Letters about the Canaanite verbal system is that the scribes rarely wrote purely Canaanite forms. Rainey (1996b: 13) explains that there are three linguistic strands in the language of the Amarna Letters: the first is the Old Babylonian "stock language"; the second is the "colloquialism" brought about by independent developments of the Akkadian stock language in these peripheral areas in which the scribes worked; the third is the influence from the scribes' native dialects. The methodology applied by Moran (2003: 7–8) to isolate the Byblian linguistic strand in 1950 is still generally valid, though there now exists a much more abundant database with which to work: Moran compared elements of the grammar in the Byblian Amarna Letters with the grammar of Babylonian and Assyrian and then with the major caches of peripheral Akkadian at Nuzi and Hattusas (Boğazköy); if no parallels were found in these sources, it was assumed that the grammar was influenced by the native dialect of the scribes, and parallels would be sought in its close congenator Ugaritic and in its presumed descendant BH material. The types of influence that Moran (2003: 237) discovered include Canaanite glosses of Akkadian forms, the use of non-Akkadian (Canaanite) morphemes, the non-Akkadian use of morphemes common to both Akkadian and Canaanite, and non-Akkadian (Canaanite) syntax.

---

42. The texts discovered since Knudtzon's publication have been published by Rainey (1978); up-to-date French and English translations of all the letters have been published (Moran, Collon, and Cazelles 1987; Moran 1992).

These types of WS (and specifically Canaanite) influence in the Amarna Letters may be illustrated by the passages discussed below. An example of the practice of glossing by the native scribes is given in example [2.9]. In this letter from Hazor, in northern Canaan, the scribe glossed the Akkadian Precative (jussive) *liḫsusmi* (*ḫasāsum* 'to be mindful') with a Canaanite equivalent, the WS Jussive *yazkur* (*zkr* 'to remember').

> [2.9] [*u*] ***liḫsusmi*** (*li-iḫ-šu-uš-mi*) ***yazkur*** (*ia-az-ku-ur-mi*) *mi šarrī mimma ša innepušmi eli ḫaṣura ālīka u eli wardīka*
> 'May the king, my lord, **be mindful** (gloss: **take thought**) of all that has been done against Hazor, your city, and against your servant'. (EA 228:18–24; Rainey 1996b: 65)

This glossing example also illustrates one of the most striking WS influences in the letters—the use of the *y*- verbal prefix; in Akkadian, except for late loanwords, word-intial *y*-glide elided (von Soden 1995: §22; Buccellati 1996: 24; Huehnergard 2005: 38). Other non-Akkadian features of the verbal morphology in the Amarna Letters include the *t*- prefix for 3MP verbs (i.e., *taqtulū*[*na*]; cf. Akkadian *iprusū*, BH יִפְקְדוּ; see Moran 2003: 159–64), whose NWS character is confirmed by its presence in Ugaritic (C. H. Gordon 1965: 75; Segert 1984: 60; Sivan 1997: 111–12; Tropper 2000: 432), and the -*ū*(*na*) suffix on 2MP forms (i.e., *taqtulū*[*na*]; cf. Akkadian *taprusā*; see Rainey 1996b: 47).

In contrast to the purely WS Jussive form in example [2.9], the scribes of the Amarna Letters more often applied their native verbal affixes to an Akkadian base, often ignoring the semantics of the base form. For example, the Akkadian Present base of the stative *bašû* ('to be'), *ibašši*, was used as the basis (the "theme," in Rainey's nomenclature) for constructing the Canaanite suffix form *ibaššāti* ('I am'), identifiable by the telltale NWS 1s -*ti* suffix (cf. Akkadian, Geʿez -*ku*; Arabic -*tu*) (Rainey 1996b: 14). The selected prefix verb forms from the Amarna Letters listed in table 2.6 illustrate how this hybrid verbal system worked (note particularly the use of the Present base to construct the preterite in the last two lines of the table).

Besides the morphological peculiarity of these hybrid forms, the syntax and semantics of the forms diverge from standard Akkadian in ways that evidence the Canaanite influence of the native scribes (Rainey 1996b: 15).

2.3.4.2. The Canaanite Verbal System in Light of Amarna

Although his findings were crucially dependent on earlier studies, especially of Ugaritic, Moran must be credited with making the definitive breakthrough in understanding the Canaanite verbal system (Moran 2003: 1–130). Based on an inductive study of the native Canaanite dialect reflected in the Amarna Letters from Byblos, Moran isolated, with varying degrees of certainty, five prefix verbal conjugations as well as a dynamic suffix conjugation. With vary-

Table 2.6. Selected Verbal Forms from the Amarna Letters
(Using the Root *šemû*) (Rainey 1996b: 14–15)

Preterit 1s *iš-me* = $\emptyset$ + **išme** + $\emptyset$
Imperfect 1s *iš-mu* = $\emptyset$ + **išm** + u
Preterit/Jussive 3ms *yi-iš-me* = y + **išme** + $\emptyset$
Imperfect 3ms *yi-iš-mu* = y + **išm** + u
Imperfect 3mp *ti-iš-mu-na* = t + **išm** + ûna
Imperfect Passive 3mp *tu-uš-mu-na* = tu + **šm** + ûna
Preterit 3ms *yi-še$_{20}$-mé* = y + **išemme** + $\emptyset$
Preterit 1s *i-še$_{20}$-me* = $\emptyset$ + **išemme** + $\emptyset$

ing degrees of success, Moran also sought to delineate the semantic range of each conjugation based on its syntactic distribution. Rainey's comprehensive study of the evidence in the Amarna Letters from Canaan has substantiated and supplemented Moran's earlier findings (Rainey 1996b). In particular, Rainey has championed the admittedly meager evidence in the Amarna Letters for a WS prefixed past verb form (i.e., *yaqtul*; e.g., Rainey 1986; 1990; 2003). The findings of Moran and Rainey regarding the Canaanite (proto-Hebrew) verb are summarized here.

Moran's study of the Byblian Amarna evidence confirmed the stative : dynamic theme-vowel distinction already recognized in WS *qatala* (i.e., *qati/ula* : *qatala*) in contrast to the predominance of the *qatil* theme-vowel pattern in Akkadian (Moran 2003: 28–29; Rainey 1996b: 295–96).[43] Importantly, the *qatila* pattern in the Amarna evidence sometimes expresses a passive sense with active (transitive) verbs (Moran 2003: 29; Rainey 1996b: 303–5), just as the Akkadian Verbal Adjective *paris* regularly does (see Buccellati 1988; 1996: 356; Huehnergard 1987a; 2005: §4.3; von Soden 1995: §77); this is illustrated by example [2.10].

[2.10]   *laqiḫū* (*la-qí-ḫu*) *ina ugāri šade* [*ana*] [uru]*ialuna*[ki]
'**They were taken** in the open territory of Ayalon'. (EA 287:56–57; Rainey 1996b: 304)[a]

a. On *ša-de₄-e* [uru]*ia-lu-na*[ki], see Moran 1987: 514 nn. 17–18; 1992: 328; 2003: 259–60.

Moran observed that, in Byblian Canaanite (as in Ugaritic prose), WS *qatala* had largely taken over the past narrative functions of PS *yaqtul* (Moran 2003: 30; Rainey 1996b: 365). In addition, *qatala* appears 33 times with a future sense in the Byblian data: 24 are preceded by *u* 'and', while 8 without *u*

43. Moran referred to the verb classes as "stative" and "active"; Rainey labels them "stative" and "transitive."

occur in the protasis of a conditional clause (Moran 2003: 31). Rainey supplemented Moran's data with similar examples from the other Amarna Letters from Canaan: *qatala* has a future sense in conditional protases and apodoses, in purpose clauses, and when used as a future-optative (Rainey 1996b: 355–65).

Moran, followed by Rainey, drew two main conclusions from this evidence: first, the WS *qatala* in Amarna Canaanite shows an earlier stage of development than BH—a stage at which the stative present meaning of the adjectival-predicative origin of the form is more prominent, and functions typical of the Akkadian Verbal Adjective are still associated with the form (Moran 2003: 35, 216; Rainey 1996b: 365); second, the future sense of *qatala* derives from its generally restricted conditional context, which may point to an optative or precative origin for BH *wĕqatal* (Moran 2003: 31–33, 216; Rainey 1996b: 366). Moran argued that WS *qatala* should be defined, by virtue of its origin in a verbless predication, as a "tenseless aorist"—a form incompatible with either tense or aspect (in the Ewald-Driver sense of complete : incomplete; Moran 2003: 33–34; Rainey 1996b: 365–66).

One of the most significant discoveries in the Byblian Amarna Letters was a clear morphological and semantic distinction between *yaqtulu* and *yaqtul*. Although the difference had already been posited for BH and NWS on the basis of internal (e.g., BH יָקוּם vs. יָקֹם; see Holmstedt 2000) and comparative evidence (Arabic *yaktubu* vs. *yaktub*; Bauer and Leander 1991: 273–74), morphological proof of the distinction in NWS only came with the discovery of Ugaritic, and the semantics of the distinction was clarified only with Moran's study of the forms in Amarna (Moran 2003: 38–39). Although the *-u* suffix appears in the Amarna Letters as the Akkadian subjunctive or subordinate marker (on the form, see von Soden 1995: §83; Huehnergard 2005: 183–84), Moran demonstrated that the final *-u* may also indicate the CS *yaqtulu* conjugation, which has a similar semantic range as the Akkadian *iparras* conjugation (Moran 2003: 41–47). Rainey's study has underscored Moran's earlier conclusions (Rainey 1996b: 195–202).

The semantic range of *yaqtulu* in the Amarna Letters is demonstrated by example [2.11].

[2.11] *miya mārū Abd-aširta ardi kalbi šar māt kašši u šar māt*
*mitan(n)i šunu u **tilqûna** (ti-ìl-qú-na) māt šarri ana šāšum*
*panānu **tilqûna** (ti-ì[l-q]ú[-n]a) ālāni ḫazānīka u qâlāta annû*
inanna dubbirū rābiṣaka u laqû ālānišu ana šāšunu anumma
*laqû āl ullaza šumma ki'ama qâlāta adi **tilqûna** (ti-ìl-qú-na) āl*
ṣumura u tidûkūna rābiṣa u ṣāb tillati ša ina ṣumura
'Who are the sons of ʿAbd-aširta, the slave and dog? Are they the king of the Kassites or the king of the Mitanni that **they take** (*yaqtulu*) the royal land for themselves? Previously **they used to take** (*yaqtulu*) the cities of your governors, and you

were negligent. Behold! now they have driven out (*qatala*)
your comissioner and have taken (*qatala*) his cities for themselves. Indeed, they have taken (*qatala*) Ullaza. If you are
negligent (*qatala*) this way, **they will take** (*yaqtulu*) Simyra
besides, and they will kill (*yaqtulu*) the commissioner and the
auxiliary force which is in Simyra'. (EA 104:17–36; Moran
2003: 43–44, 213–14; Rainey 1996b: 233)

In this passage, the *yaqtulu* form *tilqûna* (with energic *nun*) appears three times,
each with a different semantic nuance: expressing present progressive or habitual; expressing past progressive or habitual following *panânu*; and expressing a future event. From this evidence, Moran concluded that *yaqtulu* expresses
"continued action, the time and particular nuance of continued action (incipi-
ency, repetition, custom, duration) deriving from the context" (Moran 2003:
46; Rainey 1996b: 228). Regarding the use of the form to express future events,
Moran had recourse to S. R. Driver's explanation, which plays off the meaning of the Greek term for future tense τὸ μέλλον 'to be destined': "The same
form [*yaqtulu*] is further employed to describe events belonging to the future:
for the future is emphatically τὸ μέλλον and this is just the attribute specially
expressed by the imperfect. . . . that which is in the process of coming to pass
is also that which is *destined* or *must* [i.e., epistemic necessity] come to pass
(τὸ μέλλον)" (S. R. Driver 1998: 28–29; Moran 2003: 47; Rainey 1996b: 228).

The distinction between *yaqtulu* and *yaqtul* in the letters is confirmed by
Moran's findings regarding the latter form: *yaqtul* regularly has a jussive
meaning, and by contrast, no examples of *yaqtulu* as jussive were found in the
Byblian evidence; in addition, the Canaanite scribes glossed Akkadian preca-
tives with *yaqtul* jussive (see example [2.9] above; Moran 2003: 48; Rainey
1996b: 244–45; see further Izre'el and Singer 1991: 235).

Moran was cautious about the possibility of a past tense meaning for *yaqtul*
in the Byblian evidence, noting that the paucity of examples was due to the use
of *qatala* for historical narration in the letters: "In Byblian the perfect [*qatala*]
was normally used to express a present or historical perfect, though it is impossible to say that *yaqtul* could not, at least in certain circumstances, have a similar use" (Moran 2003: 49). Rainey, drawing on significantly more material than
Moran, has argued vigorously that the Amarna Letters demonstrate that "the
preterite was a living tense form in spoken WS of the time" (Rainey 1996b:
223). Rainey draws attention to passages such as example [2.12], which features the *yaqtul* form *išpur* with a past sense in a subordinate clause that lacks
the Akkadian subordinate marker and that also exibits a contrast between the
short form *išteme* and the long forms *iṣṣuru* and *ištemu*.[44]

---

44. The forms with a *šemû* ('hear') root are either built on an Akkadian Perfect base or,
in the Gt-stem, attested with the root in Ugaritic (see Rainey 1996b: 95–96). For examples

[2.12] *išteme* (*iš-te-mé*) *awâtim ša išpur* (*iš-pu-ur*) *šarru bêlīya ana waradšu uṣurmi rābiṣaka ālanī ša šarri bêlīka annuma iṣṣuru* (*ú-ṣur-mi*) *u annuma ištemu* (*iš-te-mu*) *ūma u mūša awâtim ša šarri bêlīya*
'**I have heeded** the words which the king, my lord, **sent** to his servant, "Guard your commissioner and guard the cities of the king, your lord." Now **I am guarding** and now **I am heeding** day and night the words of the king, my lord'. (EA 297:17–19; Rainey 1990: 409; 1996b: 226)

Nevertheless, the admittedly scant evidence from the Amarna Letters along with the lack of past *yaqtul* in Ugaritic prose have made some scholars more cautious than Rainey: "I am inclined to agree with Moran and to believe that Rainey is looking too hard for a form that surely existed in proto-West Semitic but not necessarily in the fourteenth-century Canaanite prose" (Pardee 1999: 314).

Alongside *yaqtulu* and *yaqtul*, Moran also identified a "subjunctive" *yaqtula* pattern, cognate with the Arabic Subjunctive and BH Cohortative (2003: 84). The identification of this form in the Amarna Letters is complicated by the morphological identity that may prevail between the final -*a* suffix and the Akkadian Ventive -*a*(*m*) (see Rainey 1996b: 202–11) and by the fact that no certain evidence of the pattern has been discovered in Ugaritic (so Segert 1984: 62; Tropper 1999c: 106–7; cf. Sivan 1997: 104–5). On the one hand, Moran thought that the statistics of the Byblian evidence (of the 75 occurences of *yaqtula,* 18 have jussive meanings, 30 appear in purpose or result clauses, and 14 in conditional protases or apodoses; 5 are doubtful because they appear in broken contexts, and 8 may be identified as allatives [i.e., -*a* is the Ventive morpheme]) demonstrated the existence of a Canaanite subjunctive *yaqtula* (Moran 2003: 87, 179–95). On the other hand, Rainey concludes that the Amarna texts "have not given us any conclusive evidence for the existence of a Canaanite *yaqtula* pattern" (Rainey 1996b: 262). Nevertheless, Rainey (1996b: 262–63) argues for the existence of the conjugation, which he labels "volitive," on the basis of comparative evidence from Arabic, BH, and Ugaritic, noting that "it was hardly distinguishable in its nuances from the jussive."

Evidence for an energic subjunctive *yaqtulanna,* cognate with Arabic Energic, is not much more substantial than the evidence for the subjunctive *yaqtula.* However, Rainey notes one clear example from Moran's data in the passage in example [2.13].

---

of short form (*yaqtul*) : long form (*yaqtulu*) contrast in the Jerusalem Amarna Letters (EA 285–91), see Tropper 1998b.

Table 2.7. The Canaanite Prefix Conjugation System
(adapted from Rainey 1986: 4; 1990: 408; 1996b: 221)

Indicative Singular, Plural		Injunctive Singular, Plural	
Preterite	yaqtul, -û	Jussive	yaqtul, -û
Imperfect	yaqtulu, -ûna	Volitive	yaqtula, -û
Energic	yaqtulun(n)a	Energic	yaqtulan(n)a

[2.13] paḫlātī awīlūt ḫupši ul **timaḫ(ḫ)aṣananī** (ti-ma-ḫa-ṣa-na-n[i])
'I am afraid of my tenant farmers **lest they smite me**'. (Rainey
1996b: 263; Moran 2003: 94)

By contrast, the *yaqtulu* form with energic suffix, *yaqtuluna*, was recognized
in the early studies on Amarna, and its NWS character was confirmed by the
Ugaritic materials (Rainey 1996b: 234). Moran's survey of this energic form
demonstrated that while it was not confined to any particular syntagm it never
occurred with the short *yaqtul* form (Moran 2003: 50). He concluded: "Essentially it is an emphatic form of *yaqtulu*, with the precise nuance of emphasis
determined by the context" (Moran 2003: 51). Despite further studies on the
energic forms in Semitic (see Zewi 1999), the meaning of the suffix is still not
well understood.

Rainey, extending Moran's analysis of the Byblian evidence to the Amarna
Letters from Canaan, has proposed the prefix verbal patterns in table 2.7 for
Canaanite (proto-Hebrew). Moran was content to recognize the presence
of these forms in second-millenium Amarna Canaanite (albeit the Preterite
only as theoretically possible, without a clear instantiation); however, Rainey
(1986: 15–16) has attempted to find remnants of these forms in the biblical
text, as in the passage in example [2.14]. Rainey has claimed that the distinction between Preterite/Jussive *yaqtul* and Imperfect *yaqtulu* is found in the
distribution of the BH energic suffixes, which are limited to the *yaqtulu* form
(as expected from Moran's Byblian data). Based on this distinction, Rainey
identifies the bold forms in the passage in example [2.14] as Preterite *yaqtul*
forms (2 of the 9 forms with *wa*C- prefix), and the underlined forms as Imperfect *yaqtulu* forms.

[2.14] When the Most High gave the nations their inheritance, when
he separated the sons of men, **he fixed** (יַצֵּב) the boundaries of
the peoples according to number of the sons of God;[45] [9]because

---

45. Rainey's translation follows the reading of a Qumran manuscript, the LXX, etc. (see
Tigay 1996b: 302–3, 514–15).

the Lord's portion is his people, Jacob is the portion of his inheritance. [10]**He found him** (יִמְצָאֵהוּ) in the steppe land, and in the howling waste of the desert; he continually encircled him (יְסֹבְבֶנְהוּ); **he instructed him** (יְבוֹנְנֵהוּ);[46] he protected him (יִצְּרֶנְהוּ) as the apple of his eye. [11]An eagle stirs up (יָעִיר) its nest, flutters (יְרַחֵף) over its young; **he spread out** (יִפְרֹשׂ) his wings; **he took him** (יִקָּחֵהוּ); **he bore him** (יִשָּׂאֵהוּ) on his pinions. [12]The Lord alone was leading him (יַנְחֶנּוּ), and there was no foreign god with him. [13]**He mounted him** (יַרְכִּבֵהוּ) upon the high plateaus of the earth **and he ate** (וַיֹּאכַל) the produce of the fields; **and he made him suck** (וַיֵּנִקֵהוּ) honey from the rock and oil from the flinty crag. (Deut 32:8–13; translation Rainey 1986: 15)

Moran's assessment of the semantics of the Canaanite and, *mutatis mutandis*, BH verbal forms lacked linguistic sophistication, even for its time: *qatala* (> *qatal*) and *yaqtulu* (> *yiqtol*) do not denote tense or (in)complete aspect but a contrast between "stative fact (or point)" and "moving progression (or continuum)" (Moran 2003: 49). Although Rainey has been an important champion of the WS *yaqtul* background for preterite *yiqtol* and *wayyiqtol* in BH, he has failed to offer any more sophistication than Moran on the matter of tense-aspect: on the one hand, Rainey (1986: 7) insists that "the [BH] verbal system as a whole does indicate tense," and this most notably in the preterite continuative *wayyiqtol*; but on the other hand, Rainey at once vehemently rejects the label "perfect" for *qatal*, implying that it must be past tense by virtue of its coming to replace the preterite *yaqtul* in WS, and accepts "imperfect" as an adequate descriptive label for *yiqtol* (< *yaqtulu*) (e.g., Rainey 1990: 413; 2003: 5). In addition, as late as 2003, Rainey continued to adopt a *waw*-relative view of *wĕqatal* (cf. §2.2.1 above): "It should be noted at the beginning, however, that most of the specific functions of *wᵊqtl* seem to have one feature in common, viz., that they assume the tense and aspectual nuances of the verbal construction in the preceding clause(s). One form, be it indicative (preterit, imperfect) or injunctive (imperative or jussive), sets the tone for the ensuing *wᵊqtl* forms(s)" (Rainey 2003: 6).

2.3.5. Summary: The BHVS in Light of Historical-Comparative Data

The historical-comparative data from Akkadian, Ugaritic, and El-Amarna Canaanite have been revolutionary with respect to the BHVS. The most important conclusion arrived at through the historical-comparative investigations is that WS originally possessed a Past prefix form *yaqtul*. Comparison of the Akkadian Past *iprus* with BH *wayyiqtol* and the Arabic syntagm *lam yaqtul* supported the supposition that a Past prefix form *yaqtul* existed in WS; the Ugaritic data, though not completely clear, appears to exhibit the form; and the Amarna Letters shows evidence of the form in second-millennium Canaanite. To these data may be added others from Amorite onomastica and NWS epigraphs. Although no Amorite texts have survived, the grammar of Amorite can be deduced from onomastics found in Akkadian texts (Gelb 1980). Knudsen (1991: 879) points to the example of the Assyrian king Shamshi-Adad (ca. 1800 B.C.E.), of Amorite stock, who appointed his two sons administrative posts; the older son, *Išme-dagān* ('Dagan heard'), adopted an Akkadian name with a Past prefix *iprus* form, whereas the younger son, *Yasmaᶜ-hadd* ('Hadad heard'), took a WS name with a cognate Past prefix form.

Numerous examples of a WS prefixed Past *yaqtul* form have been discovered in NWS epigraphs—rarely without the prefixed *waw* (e.g., Tel Dan), more frequently with *waw*, as in BH *wayyiqtol*—including Zakir (or Zakkur), Deir Alla, Mesha, and Tel Dan, not to mention the examples of the form in the Hebrew epigraphs (see Garr 2004: 184–86; M. S. Smith 1991: 18–19).[46] Garr (2004: 186) concludes: "[T]his distribution suggests that the consecutive imperfect [i.e., *wa(y)yiqtol*] was a common NWS verb form."

The impact of historical-comparative investigations on the understanding of the BH *qatal* is no less dramatic. The late-19th-century suggestion by Knudtzon that WS *qatala* (and BH *qatal*) had developed from a verbless construction (specifically, the predicative use of a verbal adjective *qatil/ul* form) has received ample support in data from Amarna and Ebla that link the development of the form to the ES Verbal Adjective *paris/parsāku*. The Amarna Letters show the WS *qatala* functioning with semantic similarities both to Akkadian (e.g., transitive verbs with passive sense; see example [2.10], p. 113) and to later WS texts. In Eblaite, despite its affinities with Akkadian (e.g., *yaqtul* : *yaqattal* opposition), the suffix pattern functions as active dynamic with transitive verbs (e.g., *ba-na-a* 'he built'; Müller 1984: 154–56; Diakonoff 1990: 27; C. H. Gordon 1997: 110; cf. Huehnergard and Woods 2004: 252).

By comparison with the etymological distinction evidenced in the historical-comparative data for *wayyiqtol* : *yiqtol* (i.e., *yaqtul* : *yaqtulu*), no evidence has been forthcoming to sustain the claims of Bauer and others that *qatal* and *wĕqatal* are etymologically distinct. Rather, the investigations have pointed

---

46. Zakir: *wʾšᶜ ydy* 'and I lifted my hands' (A11), *wyᶜnny* 'and he answered me' (A11), *wyʾmr* 'and he said' (A15); Deir Alla: *wyʾtw* 'and they came' (I 1), *wyʾmrw* 'and they said' (I 2), *wyqm* 'and he arose' (I 3), etc.; Mesha: *wʾʾš* 'and I made' (3, 9), *wybn* 'and he built' (10), and *wʾhrg* 'and I killed' (11, 16); Tel Dan: without *waw*: *yssq* 'he went up' (2), *yhk* 'he went' (3); with *waw*: *wyškb* 'and he lay down' (3), *wyᶜl* 'and he entered' (3), *wyhmlk* 'and he made king' (4), *wyhk* 'and he went' (5), *wʾpq* 'and he went out' (5), *wʾqtl* 'and I killed' (6), *wʾšm* 'and I made' (9, 12; see Emerton 1994a; 1997; Muraoka 1995; 1998; Müller 1995a; Sasson 1997; 2001; Tropper 1996); Hebrew epigraphs: *wylkw* 'and they came' (Siloam 4), *wyqṣr . . . wykl* 'and he harvested and he measured' (Yavneh Yam 4–5), *wyᶜlhw* 'he brought up' (Lachish 4.6–7).

to the syntactic environment of (*wĕ*)*qatal* as determinative of its TAM value. Specifically, with or (less commonly) without *waw*, *qatal* exhibits a non-past meaning within conditional clauses in the Amarna texts. This pattern, noticed by Moran, is evidenced in other WS languages as well, including Aramaic (Folmer 1991) and Syriac (Nöldeke 2001: 203–5, 265), Phoenician (Krahmalkov 1986), Arabic (W. Wright 1962: 2.14–17), and Ethiopic (Dillmann 1974: 548; see below, §3.3.3.2). It is unclear how the optative or precative meaning for *qatal* (in conditional clauses) can account for the semantics of *wĕqatal* (contra Moran 2003: 31–33, 216; Rainey 1996b: 366; Joosten 1992: 3).

Alongside these important historical-comparative findings are less-certain claims, such as a NWS subjunctive prefix conjugation (*yaqtula*); as well as unanswered questions, such as the semantic nuance and syntactic distribution of the energic forms. More significant, but with just as little evidence, is the claim that *wĕqatal* developed on analogy with the *wayyiqtol* : *yiqtol* opposition (e.g., Bergsträsser 1962: 2.14; Bobzin 1973: 153; Fenton 1973: 39; M. S. Smith 1991: 6–8; Buth 1992: 101), which led Fenton to suggest renaming the (*waw*-consecutive) form "*wāw* analogicum" (Fenton 1973: 39). Regardless of whether *wĕqatal* is an analogical development (and even more certain if it is), the *waw* cannot be used to account for the form's semantics any more than *wa*C- accounts for the semantics of *wayyiqtol*. Although the origin and significance of the *wa*C- prefix on *wayyiqtol* remains unanswered, the appearance of the Past prefix form without *waw* in similar syntactic environments as *wayyiqtol* (e.g., Tel Dan, Deuteronomy 32, Ugaritic poetry) appears prima facie to invalidate claims that *wa*C- is in any way a determining factor in the form's TAM.

The historical-comparative investigations served to unsettle the Ewald-Driver approach to TAM in the BHVS. Bauer's theory was seen as "the most devastating attack" on the Ewald-Driver aspectual theory (Moran 2003: 33 n. 77) and thus instigated a revival of tense explanations of the BHVS tied to historical-comparative data (e.g., Driver 1936; Blake 1944a; 1946; 1951; Hughes 1955; 1962; 1970). Nevertheless, the diachronic explanations in Bauer (1910) are not inherently incompatible with the Ewald-Driver aspectual approach, and Cohen successfully combined the two: while accepting that the *waw*-prefixed forms in BH were archaisms (Cohen 1924: 19; he described the *waw*-prefixed forms as being "en rôle" of the other forms with which they are semantically similar), Cohen describes the *yaqtulu* : *qatala* opposition in Semitic as one of "l'inaccompli" versus "l'accompli" (Cohen 1924: 10–12, 286).

2.4. Biblical Hebrew Verb Theory in the Last Half Century

The previous sections of this chapter largely serve as the groundwork for this section, which is a critical survey of various theories of the BHVS from approximately the past half century. The first section of the chapter (§2.1) intends to

provided an orientation to the debate. The description of the "standard" aspectual theory, established by Ewald and mediated to the English-speaking world by Driver (§2.2), provides necessary background to verb theory of the past half century. Finally, the survey of historical and comparative studies of the Hebrew verb (§2.3) points to one of the most important developments in Hebrew verb theory of the 20th century. One could justly add alongside this latter development the rise of modern linguistic theory as being just as important (or more so) to the advancement of Hebrew verb theory. Although space does not permit a formal introduction to modern linguistics, reference is made in the following survey to its influence on Hebrew verb theory.

Two primary options present themselves for organizing this survey. One is a historical survey in which developments in Hebrew verb theory are traced linearly over the past half century. This is a fascinating story and could fill an entire volume on its own; and frankly, a survey of this sort is a desideratum. However, instead, I have organized this survey in terms of families of theories. The most basic categories of Hebrew verb theory are aspectual theories (§2.4.1), tense theories (§2.4.2), and discourse theories (§2.4.3). In addition, the last two decades have seen the rise of theories that attempt to do justice to the insights of each of these other groups of theories—a point that is treated in the following section (§2.5). Within some of these categories, subdivisions of theories according to "pedigree" may be made (e.g., Longacrean discourse theory vs. the Weinrich-Schneider school). At the same time, my presentation is strongly historical because there are notable trends with respect to the waning and waxing of popularity of certain types of theories.

This "theory families" approach may appear reductionistic. After all, many theories describe the Hebrew verb as a combination of features, and certain theories escape categorization according to this scheme. This approach is justified, however, in that these are the terms in which the debate is regularly cast, and it is therefore expedient to summarize the debate within this familiar framework. At the same time, by qualifying these theory types with the adjective *prominent* (a term borrowed from Bhat 1999), I hope to soften the rigidness with which these categories are often employed in the debate. Few, if any, single-parameter theories of the Hebrew verb exist; however, generally, one or the other of these parameters is identified as most prominent in the system. These shortfalls notwithstanding, this survey presents the "lay of the land" of Hebrew verb theory—a worthy goal in itself and a necessary prerequisite for the presentation of my theory of the Hebrew verb in the following chapters.

2.4.1. Aspect-Prominent Theory

Aspect-prominent theories are heirs of the Ewald-Driver "standard" theory in one form or another. They recognize that the most basic distinctions in the Hebrew verbal system are aspectual. Despite Bauer's concomitant rejection of aspect for tense distinctions in his diachronic analysis of the Semitic verb (Bauer 1910; see §2.3.2.1), it did not take long for scholars to recognize that Bauer's historical conclusions were fully compatible with the "standard" aspectual analysis. For example, while accepting Bauer's contention that the *waw*-prefixed forms were archaisms (Cohen 1924: 19), Cohen argued, contra Bauer, that the forms were aspectual: the "imparfait" (*yiqtol*) and "le parfait en rôle d'imparfait" (*wĕqatal*) are "l'inaccompli," while the "parfait" (*qatal*) and "le imparfait en rôle de parfait" (*wayyiqtol*) are "l-accompli" (Cohen 1924: 10–12, 286). At the same time, a new level of linguistic sophistication can be seen in Cohen's theory, which is evident in the title of his monograph, *Le système verbal sémitique et l'expression du temps*: although the formal system is defined by aspect, he recognized that the verbal forms express a variety of temporal nuances.[47]

A renewed interest in the aspectual analysis of the BHVS appears in the 1950s and 1960s, the beginning of which is marked by Brockelmann's 1951 article, in which he defined the Semitic verb as expressing "subjektiven Aspect" (Brockelmann 1951:1 34; see also 1956: 39; see comments in Mettinger 1974: 65). Significantly, this article represented a reversal of his earlier analysis of the Semitic verbal systems as expressing tense ("Zeitstufen"; Brockelmann 1908–13: 144–51). Equally significant was Brockelmann's departure from Ewald's *perfectum* : *imperfectum* terminology in his introduction of the alternative Latinate terms "konstatierend Aspekt" (Lat. *constare* 'stand still, exist') and "kursiv Aspekt" (Lat. *cursus* 'running, coursing'; Brockelmann 1951: 146; see also 1956: 39). This terminology was subsequently adopted by other European scholars, notably Rundgren (1961; 1963) and Meyer (1960; 1964; 1966; 1992).

2.4.1.1. Rundgren's Privative Opposition Theory

Rundgren's theory is constructed on the linguistic principles of synchrony and privative oppositions. Although his theory draws on historical-comparative research, he chose to treat the BH data as deriving from a single synchronic entity (Mettinger 1974: 74). The concept of privative oppositions derives from phonological theory in the Prague school of linguistics (see p. 34 n. 28). The concept can be illustrated in the realm of semantics by the example of English *bitch* and *dog*, which are distinguished by the feature of [+female], which the former term has and the latter lacks. *Dog* can express two values with respect to [+female] *bitch*, to which it stands in privative opposition: (1) it may express the negative counterpart of male canine [+male], or (2) it may express the neutral meaning of canine [±female] or [±male] (a similar example is the opposition *drake* : *duck*).

---

47. On the linguistic distinction between form and substance (meaning), see de Saussure 1959: 111–22; Lyons 1968: 54–70.

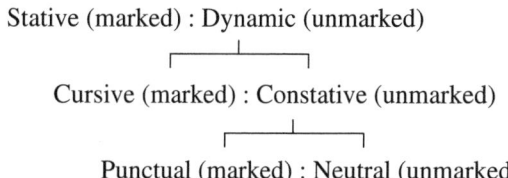

Stative (marked) : Dynamic (unmarked)

Cursive (marked) : Constative (unmarked)

Punctual (marked) : Neutral (unmarked)

Figure 2.3. Rundgren's model of privative oppositions in Semitic (1961: 109–10).

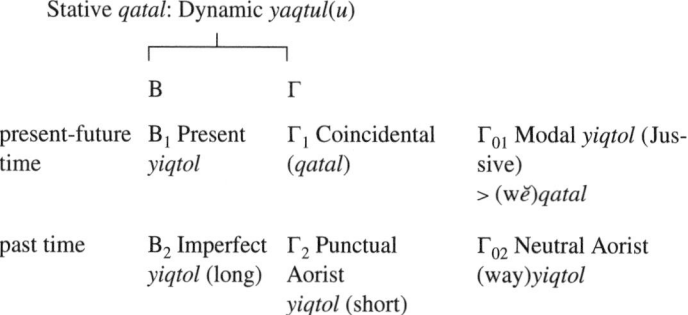

Stative *qatal*: Dynamic *yaqtul(u)*

	B	Γ	
present-future time	B$_1$ Present *yiqtol*	Γ$_1$ Coincidental (*qatal*)	Γ$_{01}$ Modal *yiqtol* (Jussive) > (wĕ)*qatal*
past time	B$_2$ Imperfect *yiqtol* (long)	Γ$_2$ Punctual Aorist *yiqtol* (short)	Γ$_{02}$ Neutral Aorist (way)*yiqtol*

Figure 2.4. Rundgren's model of the BHVS (based on 1961: 109–10).

Rundgren proposes a series of nesting privative oppositions, illustrated in fig. 2.3, to describe the Semitic verb system. He maps the suffix and prefix forms of BH onto this system of privative oppositions, distinguishing two temporal levels—a present-future time level and a past time level. This is illustrated by fig. 2.4.

According to Rundgren, the most basic distinction is between Stative *qatal* and the Dynamic prefix conjugation(s). The latter bifurcates into a marked Cursive value for both present-future time (B$_1$ Present) and past time (B$_2$ Imperfect) and a neutral Constative value. This Constative unmarked value is in turn divided into yet a tertiary-level privative opposition between a marked value in present-future (Γ$_1$ Coincidental; neutralized with Present B$_1$) and past (Γ$_2$ Punctual Aorist = remnants of the prefix preterite without *waw*) time, and a neutral value also represented in both present-future time (Γ$_{01}$ Modal forms, including modal *wĕqatal*) and past time (Γ$_{02}$ Neutral *wayyiqtol*; see Rundgren's description, 1961: 105–6).

Although Rundgren's model is based to a degree on a deductive "idealization," it recognizes the messiness of the Hebrew verbal system in that categories were collapsed (i.e., Γ$_1$ with B$_1$), and Stative *qatal* encroached on the domains of the prefix form, both at an early stage (Rundgren proposes [1961:

105] that *qatal* early on might have had the same punctual past meaning as preterite [*way*]*yiqtol*) and at the BH stage (i.e., modal *wĕqatal*).

Rundgren's model has been praised as a convincing aspectual model of Hebrew (Mettinger 1974: 74), and it has remained current in Scandinavian studies of BH, being adopted by his students in their studies of related aspects of Hebrew grammar (Isaksson 1987; Eskhult 1990). However, Rundgren's model is problematic, most of all because *qatal* does not always or even mostly express stative events—a fact that Rundgren admits but explains as being due to the encroachment (of sorts) of *qatal* into semantic domains that are dominated by the dynamic prefix conjugation(s).[48] In addition, Rundgren's model is "idealized" to the degree that he must "force" the BH verbs into categories that are not clearly distinguished by the data. For example, it is not clear what the semantic difference is between Punctual *yiqtol* and Neutral *wayyiqtol*.

2.4.1.2. Meyer's Diachronic *Systemüberlagerung* Theory

In contrast to Rundgren's deductive, synchronic treatment of the Hebrew verbal system, the contemporary theory by Meyer is preeminently determined by the historical and comparative data. Meyer's theory is largely an attempt to resolve the data from Afro-Asiatic and Semitic (particularly East Semitic) comparative investigations (notably Rössler 1950, ET 1981) and Ugaritic and Amarna Canaanite studies (see §2.3 above).

Based on the evidence of a Semitic-wide prefix-form opposition of *yaqtul* : *yaqattal* (see Rössler 1950) and the narrative use of *yamluku* in Ugaritic epic, Meyer reconstructed the Old Canaanite (including Ugaritic) verbal system as consisting of five prefix forms based on the Common Semitic *yaqtul/qtul* (i.e., Preterite/Jussive *yaqtul* and Imperative/Infinitive *qtul*; Meyer 1960: 310–13; 1992: 96–103):

    1. Preterite/Jussive *yaqtul* (basis of the "Imperfect Consecutive" *wayyiqtol* form)
    2. Narrative (Indicative) *yaqtulu* (based on *yamluku* in Ugaritic epic narrative)
    3. Durative *yaqattal* (based on evidence of its widespread presence in Semitic)
    4. Finalis (subjunctive) *yaqtula*
    5. Energic *yaqtulan(nā)*

The central opposition in this system was between narrative (indicative) *yaqtulu* and durative *yaqattalu*, which Meyer posited on the basis of Rössler's work (1950), in particular, and which he described with Brockelmann's terminology (1951; see §2.4.1 above) as "konstatierenden Aspekt" versus "kursiven Aspekt" (Meyer 1960: 311–12). Meyer's understanding of the BHVS centers on his understanding of the direct and concomitant effects of the development

---

48. The effect of seeing the stative as not merely earlier but the more basic meaning for *qatal* is evident in Isaksson's study (1987: 75–92) of the form in Qoheleth, about which Schoors (1992: 174) criticizes him for his tendency "to multiply the instances of a perfect tense with a present force" (see Cook forthcoming).

of fientive (dynamic) *qatala* in West Semitic from the Common Semitic stative *qatila* form against the background of this Old Canaanite verbal system—the overlay of a "younger" system on the "older" one (Meyer 1960: 313–14). This "mile-stone" development (so Mettinger 1974: 71) precipitated three effects in the Canaanite verbal system. First, the new *qatala* form appropriated some of the past-narrative ("präterital-erzählende") and jussive functions of the Preterite/Jussive *yaqtul*, as well as the narrative-past ("erzählend-präterital") function of the narrative (indicative) *yaqtulu* (Meyer 1960: 314). Later on, in the form of the "Perfect Consecutive," it also assumed present-future functions (Meyer 1960: 316). Second, concurrently the Durative *yaqattal* fell into disuse, due in part to its formal similarity with the Semitic (*Intensiv*) D-stem (1960: 315). Third, the *yaqtulu* was in turn confined primarily to present-future functions and fell together with the Finalis *yaqtula* when final short vowels were elided throughout the system (Meyer 1960: 316).

Although Meyer's view of the BHVS is superficially similar to Bauer's *Mischesprache* theory, Meyer appears to view the development of *qatala* as an unwelcome intrusion into the Old Canaanite verbal system. Meyer's theory also has several obvious problems. For one, the idea that Canaanite ever possessed a reflex of the *yaqattal* form is now thoroughly discredited (see p. 98 n. 31 above) but is a major component of Meyer's Old Canaanite verbal system (and a feature for whose neglect he criticized Rundgren's theory; Meyer 1964: 123). The other difficulty with Meyer's theory is what it leaves unexplained. For instance, what is the relationship between the past-narrative *yaqtul* and narrative-past *yaqtulu* meanings? It seems clear in hindsight that Meyer's theory, in that it attemps to give due attention to the Ugaritic evidence and the comparative Semitic data, is forced. The difficulty seems primarily to lie in his uncritical acceptance of how *yamluku* functions in Ugaritic epic narrative, given how unsettled this issue remains (see Greenstein 2006).

Müller's more recent work on the Semitic and BH verb represents a continuation (with certain revisions) of Meyer's theory (Müller 1983; 1986; 1991; 1998). Müller, like Meyer, takes a diachronic approach, explaining the BHVS in terms of the effects of a *Systemreduktion* in the collapsing of the distinction beteween *yaqtul* and *yaqtulu*, and a *Systemüberlagerung* in the development of *qatal* (Müller 1983: 56; 1998: 151). However, Müller remedies the major weaknesses in Meyer's theory by (a) downplaying the presence of the *yaqattal* conjugation in West Semitic (1983: 44; 1986: 373; 1998: 150) and (b) shifting the center of his theory to the West Semitic opposition between the short and long prefix forms, *yaqtul* : *yaqtulu*: the former of these had a preterite-narrative function (> BH *wayyiqtol*) as well as a jussive meaning, while the latter expressed imperfective or durative aspect and present-future tense (Müller 1983: 37–38; 1986: 370–71; 1998: 147–49).

Müller describes the BH (and Semitic) verbal system in terms of subjective aspect ("subjektiven Aspekte"), objective aspect ("objektiven Aspekt" [*Aktionsarten*]), and tense (Müller 1983: 52) as follows, setting aside the undisputed Jussive and Imperative forms (1983: 55–56; 1998: 147–49):

1. *wayyiqtol* (< *yaqtul*) expresses perfective aspect (*Aspekt*), momentary-punctual action (*Aktionsart*), and past tense
2. *qatal* expresses perfective aspect, punctual action, and past tense; also (usually with *wĕ-* conjunction) present-future and modal meanings (Müller 1986: 385)
3. *yiqtol* (< *yaqtulu*) expresses imperfective aspect, durative action, and present-future tense

Müller explains that the Hebrew verbal system moved toward a purely tensed system in the late and postbiblical periods, creating a three-conjugation tense system of *qatal* (past), Participle (present), and *yiqtol* (future) (Müller 1998: 150–51).

Two peculiarities may be noted about Müller's treatment of the BHVS. The first is his denial of a semantic distinction between the waC- and wĕ-morphemes (Müller 1991), emphasizing that the morphological distinction between *wayyiqtol* and *wĕyiqtol* reflects the historical opposition between short *yaqtul* and long *yaqtulu*, respectively (Müller 1983: 40). The other peculiarity is his division between subjective *Aspekt* and objective *Aktionsart*, reflected in the distinction between perfective and momentary-punctual and between imperfective and durative. Yet these terms are often used interchangeably, thus making it difficult to determine the significance of Müller's distinction between these categories (see Binnick 1991: 139–49).

2.4.1.3. Michel's Synchronic Theory

Michel approached the BHVS with an inductive, synchronic approach, in conscious opposition to historical and comparative theories. He objected that comparative linguistics is only possible if the languages being compared are understood in their own right (Michel 1960: 14). Examining the verbal system in the book of Psalms, and rejecting diachronic evidence, Michel concluded that there was virtually no distinction between the *waw*-prefixed forms and their non-*waw*-prefixed counterparts: *qatal* (including *wĕqatal*) represents situations as "selbstgewichtig," whereas *yiqtol* (including *wayyiqtol*) presents situations as "relativ" to some other event (Michel 1960: 254). While he does not recongize any semantic difference between *yiqtol* and *wayyiqtol*, based on his close attention to syntax Michel claims that *wayyiqtol* represents a situation that is in closer relation to what precedes than *yiqtol* (Michel 1960: 47, 132). In addition, Michel distinguishes the prefix pair and the suffix pair in terms of how they relate their subject to the action: with the *qatal* (and *wĕqatal*), the action has an "akzidentiellen Charackter" with regard to the subject, whereas the *yiqtol* (and *wayyiqtol*) has a "substantiellen Charakter" (Michel 1960: 110, 127). Although Michel's explanation appears prima facie to be quite different from anything preceding it, it does have points of connection. On the one hand, Michel uses terms remincent of earlier aspectual treatments when he describes the *qatal* form in isolation or at the beginning of a sentence as expressing "konstatiert es ein Faktum" (Michel 1960: 47). On the other hand, Waltke and O'Connor (1990: 473) point out the similarity between Michel's description of the Hebrew verb opposition and Turner's 19th-century theory: [49]

> It might be said that the first [*qatal*] is the more abstract, the second [*yiqtol*] the more concrete,—the one the more objective, the other the more subjective. . . . Perhaps the most proper words which our language affords for the expression of the distinction are these,—the Factual and the Descriptive. The one makes statements, the other draws pictures; the one asserts, the other represents; the one lays down positions, the other describes events; the one appeals to reason, the other to imagination; the one is annalistic, the other fully and properly historical. (Turner 1876: 384) [50]

Michel's theory produces valuable observations on the verbal system in Psalms, and at times Michel offers insights that are more broadly applicable (e.g., Waltke and O'Connor [1990: 473] note his important demonstration that *wayyiqtol* may "signify consequence or dependence"; cf. Ewald, §2.2.2 above). However, his basic understanding of the BHVS is clearly invalid for the entire corpus of BH. To note the most obvious, his theory cannot adequately explain the clear semantic and discourse-pragmatic differences between the *waw*-prefixed forms and the non-*waw*-prefixed forms in biblical narrative. Similarly, the inductive, synchronic analysis of *waw* + *yiqtol* and *waw* + *qatal* of B. **Johnson** (1979: 30, 96), despite its adherence to Brockelmann's constative and cursive aspects terminology, arrives at the untenable conclusion that there

---

49. Waltke and O'Connor (1990: 474–75) also note the similarity of Kustár's conclusions to Michel's, though Kustár uses different terminology, describing the opposition between *qatal* (including *wĕqatal*) and *yiqtol* (including *wayyiqtol*) in terms of determining ("determinierend") and determined ("determiniert") action, respectively (Kustár 1972: 45–46, 55).

50. McFall (1982: 77) offers the following succinct description:

> The essence of Turner's theory is that *qtl* expresses the action or state as the attribute of the person or thing spoken of; the *yqtl* form expresses or represents the verbal action as in or of the subject, the produce of the subject's energy, the manifestation of its power and life, like a stream evolving itself from its source. Whereas the first represents the act or state as an independent thing: the Factual; the second expresses the same act or state as a process, and one that is passing before our very eyes: the Descriptive.

is no semantic difference between the the *waw*-prefixed forms and their formal non-*waw*-prefixed counterparts.[51]

The most recent permutation of this type of theory comes from **Furuli** (2006), who claims based on his examination of all the verb forms in the Hebrew Bible, Ben Sira, and the Dead Sea Scrolls that there are only two conjugations: a perfective suffix conjugation (*qatal* and *wĕqatal*) and an imperfective prefix conjugation (*yiqtol* and *wayyiqtol*; Furuli 2006: 4). He concludes that a diachronic approach is problematic and unnecessary, since (1) there is no evidence of a prefix preterite in Northwest Semitic or Akkadian, and (2) there is no evidence in his corpus of any semantic change in the Hebrew verbal forms (Furuli 2006: 147).

Furuli's approach is based on two premises that he claims are not taken into account by any earlier theories. This first is the systematic distinction between past time reference and past tense. Although it is a sound principle, Furuli uses this premise to dismiss out of hand any and every tense explanation of Hebrew and Semitic (e.g., Furuli 2006: 32, 98). Furuli claims that context "can fix the temporal reference of a verb" and then refuses to acknowledge any other possible means of fixing temporal reference—that is, tense (Furuli 2006: 100).

His second principle is that aspect (viewpoint aspect, in particular) in Hebrew is of a different sort than English aspect, which he claims informs most previous understandings. Unfortunately it is unclear to me the basis for his claim because the only explanation he offers is, "because aspect is a kind of viewpoint, it is not obvious that it has the same nature in the different aspectual languages of the world" (Furuli 2006: 49).

A full survey of Furuli's work would take too long and yield too little of value (see the reviews of Kummerow 2007 and Cook 2010). Here I mention the two fundamental difficulties with his theory that are most germane to this discussion: his treatment of *wayyiqtol* and his analysis of aspect. A major if not the central focus of Furuli's work is to show that *wayyiqtol* is not a distinct prefix form from *yiqtol* (and *wĕyiqtol*) but is an invention of the Masoretes. He recognizes that a major obstacle to his argument is that 93.1% (according to his analysis) of *wayyiqtol*s in the Bible refer to past events, which accounts for the majority view that the form has developed from a Semitic prefixed preterite form. He argues, however, that, "because of the problem of induction, confirmatory examples can never confirm a hypothesis, but contradictory ones can even falsify it" (Furuli 2006: 73). Thus, Furuli admits that he allows 6.9% of the evidence to drive his semantic theory of *wayyiqtol*! The obvious protest to this is that Hebrew is an ancient language, attested only in a composite and re-

---

51. Janssens (1980: 74) in his review disparagingly states, "I have the impression that Johnson's work is not a progress as compared with the traditional grammar, a good description of which can be found in Joüon's *Grammaire de l'Hébreu biblique*."

dacted text that has been vocalized (which is the distinguishing factor between *wayyiqtol* and *wĕyiqtol*) only hundreds of years after the stabilization of the text. But this point aside, Sapir's dictum that "grammars leak" certainly applies here. Further, Furuli's argument that the Masoretes created the *wayyiqtol* form and that they made mistakes in writing the form appears prima facie to cancel out the significance of his 6.9% of counterexamples: these data are simple "errors" introduced by the Masoretes; but even so, if the form is simply a Masoretic invention, how can any of the examples be deemed either erroneous or representative of the actual language of the texts? In addition, Furuli (2006: 459) admits that his theory is completely at odds with the typological data on TAM but dismisses those findings, stating that: "we should not force modern views upon a dead language." This comment betrays a lack of understanding of not only typology but the nature of languages and language universals!

Aside from the unsubstantiated claim that (viewpoint) aspect in Hebrew differs from the modern linguistic universal and that elements of metaphor for understanding viewpoint aspect in Hebrew are open to criticism (see Cook 2010), Furuli's approach to aspect is fundamentally flawed and contradictory. First, although he claims that modern views should not be foisted on a dead language such as ancient Hebrew, he admits that his own analysis is based on English translations (Furuli 2006: 417). Although by this statement he intends simply to underscore the lack of native-speaker knowledge for a dead language, it seems all too apparent that his English translations (some quite wrong) determine his analysis of the Hebrew verbal forms.

Second, his discussion of discourse linguistics is quite illuminating when immediately followed by his alternative semantic analysis. Having examined several passages in which the context (adverbial phrases, etc.) affects the aspectual interpretation of the verb form, Furuli (2006: 186) concludes "that it is impossible to know the semantic meaning of most verbs in the Tanakh by analyzing the clauses and contexts in which they occur." On the following page (2006: 187), he continues his argument, stating that "[O]ur only hope is to find situations where no other factors than the verb conjugation can cause a particular characteristic." As an example, he offers his analysis of וַיִּבֶן (a *wayyiqtol* form) in 1 Kgs 6:1, which he translates 'he began to build': "The verb is durative and dynamic, the verb phrase is telic, and the adverbial fixes the time. But it seems that the small part of the progressive action that is made visible is caused by the verb form alone, because the only other information apart from the verb form that is needed is a knowledge of the world (that it took more than one year to build the temple)" (Furuli 2006: 187). In other words, Furuli's analysis of aspect has little to do with the linguistic portrayal of events; instead, it relates to his preconceived ideas of the character of the events themselves in the Bible.

2.4.1.4. Summary

The aspectual theories of the past half century all have their roots to some degree in the Ewald-Driver "Standard" theory and have all dealt to one degree or another with issues arising from this theory and the advance of knowledge (both of Semitic and linguistics). One issue is how to explain *aspect* adequately. Brockelmann (1951: 146) jump-started the discussion by his espousal of an aspecual analysis using the Latinate terms *constative* and *cursive*—terms that were widely used among European scholars in the decades following his work. However, B. Johnson's (1979: 30) multiplication of adjectives and metaphors alongside these terms illustrates their limited success.

The other issue is *methodogical*—namely, how should a theory of the BHVS be constructed and how should it deal with the growing body of historical and comparative data. The theories examined above have taken different tacks with respect to this issue. Rundgren embraced the maturing ideas of linguistics, drawing on historical and comparative data, but intentionally aiming to describe the BHVS as a synchronic system. By contrast, Meyer made comparative and historical data paramount, to the point where his theory became untenable because of his attempt to do justice to all of the sundry and (at points) equivocal data. Michel and similar scholars writing about synchronic theories, in contrast to Rundgren, chose to ignore completely all historical and comparative data, describing the BHVS based simply on an inductive study of the forms. Unfortunately, concomitant with synchronic approaches of this sort has been the assumption of a one-to-one correspondence between form and meaning. The result is that the possibility of (partial) homonymy (e.g., *yiqtol*, *wayyiqtol*, and Jussive) among the BH verbal forms is never entertained in these "synchronic" studies in the way that it has been considered by diachronic studies (see, e.g., §2.3.4.2). Instead, in the authors' efforts to deal with the broad range of meanings for a reduced set of verbal conjugations—because of their collapsing of the *waw*-prefixed and non-*waw*-prefixed forms—these synchronic-theory advocates have led to sometimes farfetched explanations of the verb forms that at once entail concepts from semantics, psychology, and discourse-pragmatics.

2.4.2. Tense-Prominent Theory

Despite the hegemony of the Ewald-Driver aspectual theory in the 20th century, the understanding of the Hebrew verbal forms as tense based was not wholly abandoned. Joüon (1923) was one of the notable champions of tense theory in his grammar (the term "future" for *yiqtol* is retained in Muraoka's translation [Joüon 2006: 114, 325]). The combination of diachronic interests with an understanding of the Semitic verb as tensed in Bauer (1910) helped renew interest in tense-based theories of the Hebrew verb, inspiring the studies of Blake (1951) and Hughes (1955), which are discussed in §2.4.2.1.

Others have dismissed the diachronic approach as being of little value for informing the way that the BHVS works as a *"synchronic"* system. Prominently taking this point of view are scholars who, in a series of studies, have explained verb choice in BH with reference to syntax, pointing to the obvious syntactic restriction of the *waw*-prefixed forms. This line of approach is examined in §2.4.2.2 below.

The rise of relative-tense theory in the mid-20th century (i.e., Reichenbach 1947) inspired a new approach to the BHVS as relative tense. This in turn has led to more-recent permutations of the *relative-tense* theory that identify relative tense and modality as the defining parameters of the BHVS. The development of the relative-tense approach is examined in §2.4.2.3 below.

2.4.2.1. Tense and Diachrony

Blake (1944a; 1946; 1951) sought to draw out the implications of Bauer's tense theory of Semitic for BH in particular (Bauer 1910; see §2.3.2.2 above). Like Bauer, Blake was dissatisfied with the Ewald-Driver aspectual theory, stating that "[t]he whole [standard aspectual] treatment presents a picture strongly characterized by complexity, obscurity and artificiality" (Blake 1951: 1). Therefore, he "resurveyed" the list of verb meanings found in the standard treatments in S. R. Driver (1998) and Gesenius (Kautzsch 1910), associating each meaning with either the older or the newer Semitic tense forms. Although he admitted that the verbs could express certain "aspectual" nuances, he claimed that these significations were always "subordinate" to their primary tensed meanings (Blake 1951: 2). Blake's inability to surpass the "complexity, obscurity and artificiality" of the Ewald-Driver aspectual theory is patently obvious from his confused concluding paragraph:

> The imperfect may denote any tense or mood. . . . The perfect may denote past tenses but also present or future. . . . Verb forms immediately following ו [*waw*] have in most cases meanings equivalent to that of the preceding verb. Converted imperfects and converted perfects may be used independently of any leading verb. Converted imperfects are regularly past. . . . Perfects with ו [wĕ] may have any of the normal meanings of the imperfect (present-progressive past-future-modal), but in many cases they are ordinary perfects with past meaning. (Blake 1951: 73)

Hughes's study (1955; see also 1962; 1970) was also based on Bauer's theory (1910), but his aim was less confrontational than Blake's: he sought to illustrate Bauer's old and new tense forms in the Hebrew Bible by investigating the syntactic contexts in which the old tense forms might appear—taking his lead from Bauer (1910: 27). Thus Hughes focused on the verbs that appear after particles such as אָז, טֶרֶם,טְרֶם, אֲשֶׁר, כִּי,פֶּן, and אִם in Genesis–2 Kings:

> It is our thesis that all the Imperfects in past time are vestiges of an old preterite tense of the preformative type (which was found in two forms: *yaqtulu*

and *yaqtul*) and are consequently found in stereotyped constructions. They have
been preserved simply because they are in construction with certain particles and
other elements. The preteritive use of the Imperfect is not restricted to instances
with *waw* consecutive and other particles such as *ʾāz* and *ṭérem*: additional particles are also used with the Imperfect in a preterite sense. Also, we postulate that
all Perfects in future time are straight (aoristic) future tenses and, like the Imper-
fects in past time, are to be regarded as archaisms. This futuristic use harks back
to the time when the old affirmative verb *qatil* (*qatal*) was employed in future
situations. Hence the Perfect is found in future time in stereotypic construction
with other elements—not simply with *waw* consecutive but with other particles
as well. It would seem then that the *Zeitpunkt* does come under consideration in
an evaluation of the usage of the forms and is indicated by factors external to the
verb. (Hughes 1955: 142–43)

Aside from a historical interest, neither Blake nor Hughes adds much to our
understanding of tense in BH. Blake's tense system seems as convoluted as
he envisioned the aspectual theory being, and Hughes assumes the validity of
Bauer's thesis a priori, so his results really only serve an illustrative end. Both
theories, however, illustrate how difficult tense explanations of the BHVS were
becoming as the level of linguistic sophistication progressed (e.g., cf. Blake
1951 and Brockelmann 1951; or Hughes 1955 and Meyer 1953).

2.4.2.2. Tense and Syntax

Blau in a brief note on the alternation of the *waw*-prefixed and non-*waw*-
prefixed verbal forms signaled a new approach to the question of verb choice
in BH:

> To summarize: Biblical prose exhibits a verbal system that denoted tenses, since
> the alternation of *qâṭal*/*wayyiṭqol* and *yiqṭol*/*wǝqâṭal* is due to the syntactic en-
> vironment (the impossibility/possibility of the use of *wâw* copulative). Accord-
> ingly, one will assume a similar system in the spoken language. Deviations in the
> usage of verbs in biblical poetry have to be interpreted as intentional archaism.
> Since it is impossible to reconstruct such an intricate system as the verbal system
> is, from mere archaic features (including, no doubt, pseudo-archaic ones), noth-
> ing certain can be inferred from them as to the nature of the Proto-Hebrew verbal
> system. (Blau 1971: 26; likewise 2010: 190)

About the same time, **Silverman** (1973) made similar comments, that *qatal*
and *wayyiqtol* are syntactic varieties of past tense, and that *yiqtol* and *wĕqatal*
are likewise both future tense. But he also hinted that this approach could yield
more far-reaching explanations of the BHVS: "It is then conceivable that the
more widely studied aspects of completeness (perfect) versus incompleteness
(imperfect) would also be indicated by the placement of the verb within the
clause, and not by its morphology" (Silverman 1973: 175).

Revell (1989) has adopted a syntactic explanation for verb choice as suggested by Blau and has attempted to ground it in historical evidence by arguing

that, in light of the evidence for a tense system in pre-BH (i.e., preterite *yaqtul*; see §2.3) and in post-BH (e.g., Mishnaic Hebrew), "[I]t seems likely, a priori, that the system of the intervening period would also have been one of tense" (1989: 3).[52] From this assumption of tense prominence, Revell extends the syntactic explanation not in the direction of aspect, as Silverman had suggested, but toward modality: modal *yiqtol* is clause initial, while indicative (tensed) *yiqtol* is non–clause initial, and exceptions to this basic pattern represent "nonstandard" uses of modal *yiqtol* (Revell 1989: 14). Although Revell was not the first to observe this syntactic pattern of modality (e.g., Rosén 1969; Niccacci 1987; Voigt 1990), the idea has become more widely disseminated through Revell's students (DeCaen 1995 [see §2.4.2.3]; Shulman 1996; Gentry 1998 [see §2.4.3.2]). With his incorporation of this modal distinction, Revell (1989: 21) is able to add a new dimension to the syntactic explanation: *wĕqatal* developed as a syntactic alternative to clause-initial indicative *yiqtol*, which would be indistinguishable from modal *yiqtol* in this position.

Zevit (1988; 1998) has been a proponent of the view that the BHVS primarily indicates tense: *qatal* is past tense, and *yiqtol* is present-future tense (Zevit 1988: 26). At the same time, Zevit takes a different approach to each of the *waw*-prefixed forms. With respect to *wayyiqtol*, he accepts the historical-comparative argument that it derives from a prefix preterite *yaqtul* form but demurs at the notion that examples of preterite *yaqtul* may be found in the Hebrew Bible, because the consequent omnitemporal character of *yiqtol* would "short-circuit" the tensed verbal system of BH (Zevit 1988: 30; contra especially Rainey 1986). Instead, he explains *yiqtol* forms in past contexts as a sort of "historical present" use of the form (see Smyth 1956: 422 for this category in Greek): "[I]t [the *yiqtol* in past context] actualizes a situation by projecting it into the real time of the speaking voice either for dramatic effect or for emphasis" (Zevit 1988: 31). Zevit (1998: 15) explains the significance of *wĕqatal* within the context of his broader treatment of syntax and the *qatal* form, in which he proposes that the syntagm *waw*-subject-*qatal* following a *wayyiqtol* or a *qatal* clause expresses a past- or present-perfect meaning.

The greatest difficulty with Zevit's theory is simply that it is not borne out by the data (e.g., on *waw*-subject-*qatal*, see Gen 4:2–3). More pertinent to this discussion, however, are the methodological difficulties in Zevit's approach. First, his position on the use of historical-comparative data is conflicted. While

---

52. Although Revell does not employ the term *relative tense*, he nevertheless recognizes that tense in Hebrew is not *absolute*: "It is important to note that the time reference of the two categories in relation to the speaker/narrator is not absolute, but is conditioned by the time reference of the context in which the verb form is used" (Revell 1989: 4). I treat Revell in this section (versus §2.4.2.3), however, because of the importance of his syntactic approach. His student, DeCaen (1995: 232, 256), follows Revell's lead in recognizing tense as relative (see §2.4.2.3).

he states that historical-comparative (etymological) studies "are inadequate as descriptions of how this system works" (Zevit 1988: 27), he nevertheless accepts the argument that *wayyiqtol* is distinct from *yiqtol* based on the hypothesis that the former derives from preterite *yaqtul*. Second, Zevit's rejection of examples of *yiqtol* with past temporal reference is not only unconvincing (compare with the widespread recognition of *yiqtol* with past progressive and habitual meanings in the grammar) but poorly motivated. If, as he claims, the past tense meaning of *yiqtol* would "short circuit" the verbal system, we must ask how the "historical present" use of *yiqtol* in a past context is nevertheless permissible without having the same destructive effect on the system? In other words, regardless of how Zevit defines *yiqtol* in a past context, he recognizes that it is functioning distinctly from its "normal" non-past meaning; otherwise, he would have no basis for identifying examples of *yiqtol* as "historical presents." He has not successfully obviated the contradictory character of these *yiqtol* examples in past context for a tensed theory of the BHVS. Finally, Zevit's typological arguments are faulty: first, he claims that no languages are tenseless (Zevit 1988: 26; see on Kuryłowicz and Joosten in §2.4.2.3), whereas linguists have documented several tenseless (i.e., no morphological tense marking) languages (Binnick 1991: 444–45; Comrie 1976: 82–84); second, Zevit cites Bybee's claim (1985: 160) that any language that has an anterior (i.e., perfect) verb has a tensed verbal system, but he fails to distinguish that Bybee is referring to morphologically marked anterior verb forms, not syntactically signaled anterior constructions, as Zevit is arguing for in BH.

Peckham (1997) proposed an elaborate model of the BHVS that at once lies firmly in the camp of syntactic tense theory—"tense, in short, is due to verb movement, not to verb form" (Peckham 1997: 139) and also shares characteristics with relative-tense and modality theories (see §2.4.2.3 below), in that he treats both tense and mood as "relative" based on the syntagm in which the verb form appears. Peckham constructed his model on the supposition of two basic verb forms, *qatal* and *yiqtol*, which may appear in five distinct syntagms: consecutive *qatal* (= *wayyiqtol*) and consecutive *yiqtol* (= *wĕqatal*), disjunctive (*waw* + x + *qatal/yiqtol*), paratactic (*waw* + ∅ + *qatal/yiqtol*; i.e., *wĕqāṭal/ wĕyiqṭōl*), conjunctive (clauses with a conjunction not attached to the verb), and asyndetic (clauses without any conjunction). These syntagms intersect with three different word orders: subject or subject modifiers first, object or object modifiers first, and verb or verb modifiers first (Peckham 1997: 142–43). The resultant model is shown in table 2.8.

Peckham also examines the effects of interclausal relationships on the TAM of *qatal* and *yiqtol*. He concludes that *qatal* and *yiqtol* can both be either indicative or modal, depending on the type of clause in which they appear (Peckham 1997: 155–60) and that, when they appear in their consecutive syntagm (i.e., *wayyiqtol* and *wĕqatal*), they "maintain the tense of the lead clause" (Peckham 1997: 164; cf. *waw* inductive theory in §2.2.1 above).

Table 2.8. Peckham's Syntactic Tense-Aspect Model of BH
(modified from 1997:145)

	qatal (*Relative Time, Punctual Aspect*)	yiqtol (*Absolute Time, Continuous Action*)	
Word Order	*Tense (Time)*	*Tense (Time)*	*Clause Type*
Subject First	perfect past perfect (prior)	past (durative/habitual)	Asyndetic and Disjunctive
Object First	preterite (complete)	imperfect (repeated/distributive)	Asyndetic and Disjunctive
Verb or Modifiers First	present perfect present (simultaneous)	present (incomplete/ progressive)	Asyndetic and Disjunctive
Subject First	present perfect present (simultaneous)	present (incomplete/ progressive)	Conjunctive
Object First	preterite (complete)	imperfect (repeated/ distributive)	Conjunctive
Verb or Verb Modifiers First	perfect past perfect (prior)	past (durative/habitual)	Conjunctive
Verb First	preterite (complete)	imperfect (repeated/ distributive)	Consecutive and Paratactic

Peckham's theory attempts to take into account innumerable factors affecting the determination of the TAM of the BH verbal forms (e.g., he briefly discusses the TAM in parallel lines with ellipsis: Peckham 1997: 160), but it also places too much emphasis on syntax as the determinative feature for TAM distinctions. As a result, his theory introduces more confusion than clarity, and it stretches one's imagination that a system such as this could ever have existed in a living language (see Tropper 1999b). Beneath the clutter of intersecting syntagms, however, Peckham's theory shares features in common with a broad range of theories of the BHVS, including the tense and syntax theories discussed above in this section (i.e., tense is determined by word order), the relative-tense and modality theories discussed in §2.4.2.3 (i.e., *qatal* and *yiqtol* may both express either indicative or modal senses), and even some discourse-prominent theories that associate both tense and aspect with the *qatal* and *yiqtol* forms (see §2.4.3.2 below).

2.4.2.3. Relative Tense and Modality

Modern relative-tense theory begins with Reichenbach (1947). One of the earliest relative-tense models for BH was developed by Barnes (1965) and is strongly reminiscent of Bull's relative-tense theory (Bull 1960; see §1.2.3.2):

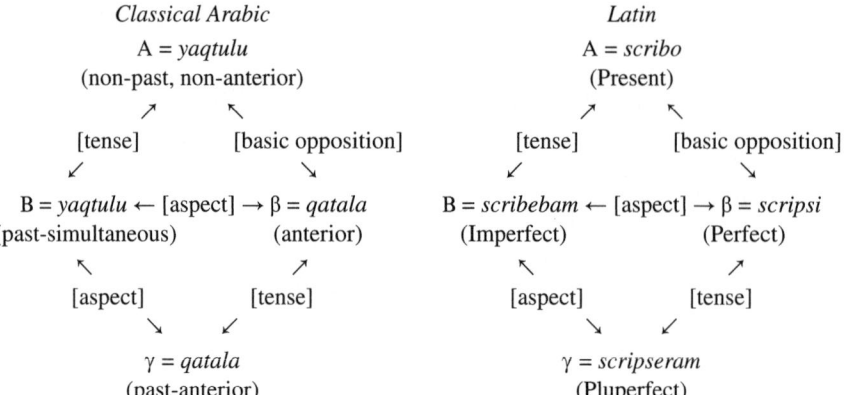

Figure 2.5. **Kuryłowicz's schemata of Classical Arabic and Latin verb oppositions** (adapted from 1973: 116).

events may be evaluated from multiple points in time, including the actual present, or "positional present 1" in the actual past, or "positional present 2" in the actual future (Bull 1965: 131; cf. Bull's schematic, fig. 1.2). Relative to these temporal evaluation points, *qatal* and *wĕqatal* both denote an event "already fulfilled before one's eyes," while *yiqtol* and *wayyiqtol* equally denote events "not in the course of fulfillment" (Bull 1965: 7). In like manner to the tense theories surveyed in §2.4.2.2, Barnes collapses any perceived semantic distinction between the *waw*-prefixed forms and their non-*waw*-prefixed counterparts.

The linguist Kuryłowicz (1972; 1973) proposed a model of the Semitic verbal system that has become influential in relative-tense-and-modality theories of the BHVS and that raises important questions about the relative status of tense and aspect in the verbal systems of the world's languages. His basic argument is that the core of the Semitic verbal systems consists of a privative opposition between a verb, the primary meaning of which "is simultaneous with the moment of speaking," and another, the primary meaning of which "is action anterior to the moment of speaking" (Kuryłowicz 1973: 115; cf. Barnes's definition of *qatal/wĕqatal* and *yiqtol/wayyiqtol* above).[53] Illustrating his point using Arabic as representative of West Semitic (see fig. 2.5), Kuryłowicz argued that "[a] binary system like Ar[abic] *yaqtulu* : *qatala* excludes not only the category of aspect, but also the category of tense. . . . The fundamental relation A [*yaqtulu*] : β [*qatala*] is neither one of aspect nor one of tense. Its correct definition is simultaneity (or non-anteriority) versus an-

---

53. On privative oppositions, see Crystal 2008: 342, 386–87; and above, p. 34 n. 28.

Table 2.9. Kuryłowicz's Taxonomy of West Semitic Verbal Functions
(adapted from 1972: 86; 1973: 118)

	Secondary Functions (Tense)	*Teriary Functions (Aspect)*
of *yaqtulu*	imperfectum	imperfective preterit
	futurum	imperfective future
of *qatala*	plusquamperfectum	perfective preterit
	future exactum	perfective future[a]

a. The aspect "perfective future," in contrast to the tense "futurum exactum" (= future perfect), correlates with the so-called prophetic perfect function of BH *qatal* (Kuryłowicz 1972: 87; 1973: 118).

teriority" (Kuryłowicz 1973: 115). Rhetoric like this was meant to distance his understanding of the Semitic verbal system from both the Slavic notion of aspect and the Indo-European concept of tense (1973: 118).[54]

In contrast to the range of morphologically expressed TAM values in the Indo-European languages, Kuryłowicz (1973: 116) argued that the West Semitic verbal system expressed the same range of TAM values by context-conditioned functions of the basic binary pair. These functions are illustrated by the contrasts in fig. 2.5, which compares Arabic and Latin. Arabic's (and, by extension, BH's) basic binary opposition between *yaqtulu* and *qatala* (A:β) expresses relative tense, non-anterior versus anterior; each form of this pair has secondary functions that create (absolute) tense contrasts with its basic relative-tense functions (A:B and β:γ), as well as aspectual contrasts between these secondary functions (B:γ) and between the secondary tense function of *yaqtulu* and the primary relative-tense meaning of *qatala* (B:β). Hence, Kuryłowicz concludes (1972: 86) that "genuine aspect is in Sem[itic] a tertiary function of the verbal forms." The TAM of each of these secondary and tertiary functions in West Semitic is illustrated in table 2.9.

---

54. Kuryłowicz's rhetoric has created difficulties in categorizing his theory, illustrated by Binnick's comment (1991: 435, 438) in one place that Kuryłowicz's theory is "relative tense" and in another, that he treats the Semitic "aspects" as "absolute time." Kuryłowicz's terminology is a mix of absolute and relative tense: "the relation [of Polish] *pisze : pisał* like that of *il écrit : il écrivait* is an opposition of mere tense (simultaneity with the *moment of speaking : simultaneity with a moment of the past*)" (i.e., absolute tense; Kuryłowicz 1973: 114); and "the only non-modal opposition of personal verb forms is *yaqtulu : qatala* equal to simultaneity (or non-anteriority): anteriority, tense being context conditioned" (i.e., relative tense) (Kuryłowicz 1973: 116). His preference for the labels "anteriority" and "simultaneity" adds to the difficulties, because they are also regularly applied to perfect and progressive viewpoint aspects, respectively (see Bybee, Perkins, and Pagliuca 1994: 54, 133–34; Binnick 1991: 285–86).

a. Kuryłowicz's tense-aspect model   b. Bybee and Dahl's tense-aspect model
         past : non-past   perfective : imperfective

              /\   /\

     perfective : imperfective   past : non-past

Figure 2.6. Kuryłowicz's and Bybee and Dahl's tense-aspect models.

Kuryłowicz's model exhibits some notable oddities. First, even though Kuryłowicz recognizes a tertiary aspectual opposition in Semitic, applying appropriate labels (see table 2.9), he also defines this opposition with relative-tense labels: *qatala* (β) expresses "action prior to the moment of speaking," whereas *yaqtulu* (B) denotes "simultaneity with a moment of the past" (Kuryłowicz 1973: 115). Second, his comparison with Latin leads to some puzzling alignments among forms. In particular, his hypothesis that, at an earlier stage of West Semitic, the preterite **yaqtul* functioned in γ in his model means that **yaqtul* is correlated with the Latin Pluperfect form (see fig. 2.5, p. 136), a correlation less plausible than *qatala* and the Latin Pluperfect. Third, Kuryłowicz hypothesized that at an earlier stage West Semitic had a morphological opposition between anterior *qatala* (β) and past-anterior **yaqtul* (γ) (Kuryłowicz 1973: 119).[55] However, despite this recognition of a West Semitic preterite **yaqtul*, he did not relate it to BH *wayyiqtol* but instead adopted S. R. Driver's century-old explanation of the *waw*-prefixed forms (see §2.2.3):

> The *waw*-"imperf." denotes an action simultaneous with or ensuing from an action mentioned (generally expressed by a "perf.") or inferred. . . . The *waw*-"perf." is formally determined, as regards tense, by the preceding verbal form, generally an "imperf." or its equivalent (e.g., the participle *qātil*). Its value corresponds in the majority of instances to a secondary function of the "perf.": state or result of previous action (corresponding to the function of the perfect in the classical sense). The relation between *qatala* and the preceding *yaqtul(u)* is often consecutive or final (result). (Kuryłowicz 1972: 88)

By his claim that tense is always presupposed in a verbal system that expresses aspect, Kuryłowicz raised an important typological question: Which is more basic in the world's verbal systems, tense or aspect? This is an especially

---

55. Kuryłowicz also hypothesized that Akkadian may at one time have had morphological distinctions throughout its verbal system, though these oppositions were skewed through semantic shifts of certain forms, notably the Subjunctive: Present *iparras* (A), Subjunctive *iprusu* (B), Perfect *iptaras* (β), and Preterit *iprus* (γ) (Kuryłowicz 1973: 119–20; cf. Latin in fig. 2.5, p. 136). However, Kuryłowicz's hypothesis assumes that the Subjunctive form is basic to the Akkadian verbal system (i.e., a distinct conjugation), a view that is now rejected by most Assyriologists (see §2.3.2.1).

pertinent question because the universal model of tense and aspect underlying Kuryłowicz's Semitic tense theory is the exact reverse of the model proposed by Bybee and Dahl (1989: 83), as illustrated in fig. 2.6.

Three pieces of evidence argue against Kuryłowicz's universal tense model and in favor of Bybee and Dahl's (see also Cook 2006a). First, Bybee and Dahl's (1989: 83) model of tense and aspect is based on an extensive cross-linguistic typological study of verbal systems and represents the most common type of verbal system found in their data. Second, Dahl (1985: 81–84) observes that the relative priority of aspect versus tense in verbal systems is evident from the fact that tense forms show more morphological similarity with each other within verbal systems than aspectual forms do. This is illustrated by the Arabic examples in [2.15] (from Dahl 1985: 83), in which the grammatical constructions that create a past : non-past opposition are morphologically related, whereas the aspectual distinction is expressed by morphologically distinct forms.

[2.15]   Perfective: *kataba* 'he wrote'
Imperfective: *yaktubu* 'he is writing'
Past Imperfective: (*kana*) *yaktubu* 'he was writing'

Third, based on her hypothesis that "the degree of morphophonological fusion of an affix to a stem correlates with the degree of semantic relevance of the affix to the stem" (relevancy defined as "the extent that the meaning of the category directly affects the lexical content of the verb stem"), Bybee concludes that the category of aspect "is most directly and exclusively relevant to the verb" and that its relevancy is reflected in the high degree of fusion between aspectual morphemes and verb stems cross-linguistically (Bybee 1985: 4, 15, 21, 24). Aspect is directly relevant to the temporal character of an event and alters the meaning of a predication at a more basic level than tense, which relates to the whole proposition in terms of location in time. Bybee's point is likewise illustrated by the Arabic verb forms in example [2.15], in which aspectual distinctions are expressed by bound verbal morphology, while tense is expressed through a periphrastic construction.

The modal component in relative-tense-and-modality theories stems particularly from the contribution of **Zuber** (1986), which he characterized as "bringing tense and mood/modality into right relation" (1986: 29).[56] Zuber argued that the Hebrew verbal system has a binary tense-modality division between "recto-Formen," consisting of *qatal* and *wayyiqtol,* and the "obliquo-Formen" *yiqtol* and *wĕqatal*: the recto forms express indicative mood and past tense (though Zuber stresses mood more than tense); the obliquo forms express

---

56. Mein Beitrag dürft lediglich darin bestehen, Tempus und Modus ins richtige Verhältnis zu bringen.

nonindicative mood and future tense, understanding the meaning of these two
categories as intertwined (Zuber 1986: 27; on the interrelationship of future
tense and modality, Zuber [1986: 15] cites Lyons [1968: 310]). Zuber reluctantly falls back on the medieval *waw-hahippuk* theory to explain the *waw*-
prefixed verb forms, thus interpreting the forms in each group (i.e., recto and
obliquo) as semantically identical and interchangeable (Zuber 1986: 27–28).[57]

Zuber's methodology consists in analyzing the forms used to translate the
Hebrew verbs in the Septuagint and Vulgate. He argues that the translators'
understanding of the Hebrew verb forms will bring us close to the understanding of the Hebrew verbal system in the Qumran period (Zuber 1986: 38), and
he is persuaded that his statistical examination has sufficiently demonstrated
his thesis (Zuber 1986: 77). However, Zuber never sufficiently addresses other
factors that might contribute to translational agreement between the Septuagint
and Vulgate (e.g., dependency) or the issues involved in analyzing translation
technique between languages with different verbal systems. For example, the
fact that both the Greek and Latin translators employ a Future form to render
yiqtol does not mean that *yiqtol* is a future tense verb; it merely means that
Future (in such passages) was thought the best equivalent in the Greek and
Latin verbal systems for *yiqtol*.

Nevertheless, Zuber correctly recognizes that the greatest challenges to his
theory lie in the expression of present tense and past imperfective. In the case
of present tense, the use of both recto and obliquo forms are problematic:
the recto are properly past tense, and therefore their use for present tense is a
makeshift ("Nötlosung") use of the forms (Zuber 1986: 89); and Zuber (1986:
89) concedes that the use of the modal-future obliquo forms for indicative present tense presents difficulties for his theory. Similarly, although the translation
of indicative recto forms with Greek and Latin Imperfect (past tense) forms is
perfectly acceptable, the similar rendering of future-modal obliquo forms presents a difficulty for Zuber's theory, though he attempts to obviate the problem
by arguing that such instances must be understood as "modal oder dubitativ"

---

57. Loprieno (1986) and Rattray (1992) present two notable variations to Zuber's model,
both combining this indicative : modal opposition with aspect instead of tense. Loprieno's
model features modality (+real : –real) intersecting with the privative modal oppositions
from Rundgren's theory (§2.4.1.1): unmarked neutral, marked (perfective), and unmarked
negative (imperfective). The +real values are realized by (*way*)*yiqtol* (unmarked neutral),
qatal (marked), and *yiqtol* (unmarked negative), and the –real values are expressed by the
Imperative (unmarked neutral), the Subjunctive Cohortative (marked), and the Jussive (unmarked negative; Zuber 1986: 110, 180). Rattray's model is more similar to Zuber's, with
the opposition of *realis* (immediate reality) : *irrealis* (nonimmediate reality) intersecting a
perfective (or nonprogressive) : *imperfective* (or progressive) opposition. Thus four categories are realized: realis-perfective *qatal* and *wĕqatal*; realis-imperfective Participle; irrealis-
perfective Imperative (including Jussive and Cohortative); and irrealis imperfective *yiqtol*
and *wayyiqtol* (Rattray 1992: 149–50).

Table 2.10. Joosten's Relative-Tense-and-Modality Model of the BHVS
(adapted from 1999: 16)

Indicative	(Nonindicative) Modal	
	Nonvolitive (Modal)	*Volitive (Modal)*
wayyiqtol = contemporaneity with a moment in the past *qatal* = anteriority with the moment of speaking Participle = contemporaneity with the moment of speaking	*yiqtol* and *wĕqatal* = future-modal	Imperative, Jussive, and Cohortative

and, most significantly, that "Iterativ" should be understood as properly expressed by the future-modal forms (Zuber 1986: 101–2).

One of the most influential scholars in the relative-tense-and-modality camp is **Joosten**, who has presented his ideas in numerous articles (1989; 1992; 1997a; 1997b; 1999; 2002; 2005; 2006). The clearest presentation of his theory appears in Joosten 1997a and 2002, the latter with which I have interacted at length (Cook 2006a). In his 2002 article, which is directed particularly against the dominant aspectual theories of the BHVS, Joosten makes his alignment with Kuryłowicz's relative-tense theory particularly evident, claiming with the latter that "a language needs to express tense before it can express aspect" (Joosten 2002: 51). However, already in his 1997a article, his terminology for the BH verbal forms illustrated his familiarity and favorable disposition toward Kuryłowicz's relative-tense theory: *wayyiqtol* expresses "contemporaneity with a moment in the past," *qatal* expresses "anteriority . . . with the moment of speaking," and the Participle "expresses contemporaneity with the moment of speaking" (Joosten 1997a: 60). In the latter article, Joosten also acknowledges the influence of Zuber on his thinking (Joosten 1997a: 57 esp. n. 21; see also 1992: 1 n. 1). On these two bases—Kuryłowicz's relative-tense theory and Zuber's modal division of BH—Joosten constructs his theory of the BHVS, illustrated in table 2.10.

One of the foremost challenges to Joosten's model of the BHVS is that it is typologically unparalleled, consisting, as it does of "a past (*wayyiqtol*) : perfect (*qatal*) opposition, a perfect (*qatal*) : present (participle) opposition (a present tense form that is likewise used for past and future expressions), and two future/modal forms (*yiqtol* and *wǝqatal*)" (Cook 2006a: 27). Not only have no other verbal systems like this been documented in the world's languages, viewed from the perspective of diachronic typology, there is no way Joosten's system can be explained in terms of the previous or subsequent configurations of the Hebrew verbal system (e.g., Joosten [2002: 63] identifies *yiqtol* as imperfective in proto-Hebrew; elsewhere [1989: 156], he speaks of a "historically earlier use" of *yiqtol* as present tense).

In three other articles (1989; 1992; 1999), Joosten has addressed the same issues that Zuber recognized as problematic for his tense-and-modality theory. In the earliest of these articles, Joosten advances the claim that "in Biblical Hebrew the present tense is properly the domain of the predicative participle" (Joosten 1989: 128). He claims that both Subject-Participle and Participle-Subject word order "refer positively to the grammatical present, i.e., they represent an action as contemporary with the moment of speaking" (Joosten 1989: 129), in opposition to the widespread view that the participle may appear in any temporal domain (past, present, or future). Joosten tempers this claim by noting (1) that the participle may express events that are past or that are still future as if they are present (i.e., "historic present" and *futurum instans*," respectively); and (2) that the past temporal reference of circumstantial participles (e.g., Gen 19:1) "is due to the specific type of subordinate clause (the circumstantial clause), not to the participle" (Joosten 1989: 129). The focus of the remainder of the article is on demonstrating his thesis that Subject-Participle word order indicates "actual present" (i.e., "an action as actually going on at the moment of speaking"), whereas Participle-Subject word order indicates "factual present" (i.e., "action represented as fact"; Joosten 1989: 130).

Setting aside his word order argument, Joosten's association of the predicative Participle with present tense is prima facie problematic in light of the obvious and plentiful examples of the participle with past and future temporal reference. His attempts to nuance his position with respect to such data are unsuccessful: given that the grammars agree with him that the temporal reference of Participles derives from its context, all that Joosten seems to be claiming is that the Participle defaults for present time. But in this case, the temporal reference of the predicative participle is still derived from its context, and his claim that the present tense is in some way the "proper domain" of the predicative Participle is at best unhelpful for understanding its role in the BH verbal system.

In his 1992 article, Joosten argues that the "main function" of BH *wěqatal* "is the expression of modality" (1992: 3), a syntactic alternative (i.e., semantically identical) to *yiqtol* (1992: 13). Central to his argument are the following points: (1) *wěqatal* "should be considered as a separate formal category with its own function" (1992: 7); (2) its use to express "iterativity" in the past should be viewed as "an extension of its modal function" (1992: 7), analogous with the use of English modal "would" for past iterative (i.e., habitual). While I welcome Joosten's championing of Zuber's view that *wěqatal* expresses modality, I also have several criticisms. First, he cites Zuber with respect to *wěqatal*'s modal functions' being "to express obligation, potentiality or prediction" (Joosten 1992: 3), yet Joosten has never delineated the exact range of modality expressed by *wěqatal* or how the different meanings relate to each other diachronically and/or semantically. Relatedly, Joosten's use of English "would" as an analogy is problematic because modal "would" and past habitual "would" may in fact be unrelated in English (i.e., homonyms), as some linguists have argued (e.g., Bybee, Perkins, and Pagliuca 1994: 238–39; but cf. Boneh and Doron 2008; 2010). Finally, I am not persuaded that *wĕqatal* should be treated as a separate conjugation from *qatal*, either etymologically or functionally (see §3.3.3.2 for discussion of all three issues).

Finally, in his 1999 and 2002 articles, Joosten particularly addresses the problem of *yiqtol* with past temporal reference. In the earlier article, Joosten surveys typical modal uses of *yiqtol* with past temporal reference, including "prospective" (i.e., future-in-the-past), various nuances of epistemic modality, and "iterative" (or habitual) actions. After also examining several problematic cases, he concludes that, "[a]lthough the relatively large number of iterative instances could be explained as imperfective [cf. Comrie 1976: 25], the absence of clear examples of durative *yiqtol* (in the past) and the presence of prospective and modal functions show it preferable to ascribe a basic modal function to this verb form synchronically" (Joosten 1999: 25). This conclusion is paralleled in his 2002 study, in which he examines possible cases of *yiqtol*'s expressing durative or imperfective action in the present ("real present") and the past ("attendant circumstances in the past"): "The most prominent features attached to the imperfective in recognized aspect languages are the expression of real present and of attendant circumstances in the past. Since neither of these functions is regularly expressed by *yiqtol* in BH there is no point in classifying *yiqtol* as imperfective (Joosten 2002: 53).

Despite Joosten's treatments of these problematic data—*yiqtol*'s expressing imperfective action in the past or in the present—his approach is consistently dismissive: ". . . these are modal uses. The seemingly indicative functions of *yiqtol* can on closer inspection be explained as being modal as well" (Joosten 1997a: 58); "the examples that have been invoked to argue that *yiqtol* does express the real present can practically all be contested" (2002: 54); "instances where *yiqtol* could be held to express attendant circumstance are infrequent and generally doubtful" (2002: 57). However, the greater problem with Joosten's argument in these two articles (1999 and 2002) is his assumption that if he debunks the identification of imperfective *yiqtol* he will likewise defeat the aspectual theory of the entire verbal system (see Cook 2006a: 27). In fact, such a result does not necessarily follow a debunking of imperfective *yiqtol*, nor do his special pleadings with respect to the difficult data assure that he has successfully disproved the imperfective identification of *yiqtol* (i.e., he is forced to admit that imperfective values are at times expressed by *yiqtol*, though he wants to see these as marginal uses only).

Several recent dissertations have followed Joosten's lead that the BHVS is modality- and tense-prominent and that syntax has semantic significance. **DeCaen**'s theory (1995) is particularly eclectic, using Rundgren's privative opposition model to define TAM (see §2.4.1.1), adopting his teacher Revell's tense model (see §2.4.2.2) but expanding it by combining Revell's syntactic observations with Zuber's and Joosten's binary modal distinction (above, this section), all within a government-and-binding formalist syntactic framework (Chomsky 1981).

DeCaen's basic schema for TAM is provided in three ternary models—one for each parameter: *tense* = past : non-past (present : subjunctive); *aspect* = perfective : imperfective (perfect : progressive);[58] and *modality* = real : irreal (epistemic : deontic; DeCaen 1995: 205, 210, 218). DeCaen rejects *aspect* as an inflectional category in BH: all forms default for perfective aspect, and imperfective is expressed by the progressive Participle (1995: 221–22). He associates nonindicative modality with verb-first (versus verb-second) word order: irreal = *wĕqatal*; irreal deontic = Imperative, Jussive, and Cohortative; irreal epistemic = *wayyiqtol* (1995: 296–98). Finally, DeCaen claims that the BH verbal forms are inflected for tense, as illustrated by his model in fig. 2.7, which he notes is in agreement with the model given by Rundgren's student Eskhult (1990).

DeCaen offers several important innovations in his study of the verbal system. Most notable is his analysis of word order within a formalist syntactic framework. Until DeCaen's analysis, BH verbal theories, if they took word order into account at all, described word order in linguistically unsophisticated ways. DeCaen has brought the proper focus to bear on the order of the subject and verb and on verb movement within the clause, effected by overt or covert complementizers (DeCaen 1995: chap. 9).

DeCaen's other contribution is more problematic than his analysis of word order: DeCaen posits a second prefix conjugation that includes the Imperative, Jussive, and Cohortative forms, as well as *wayyiqtol*, on the basis of morphological and syntactic similarities. The difficulty with this analysis lies in the mismatched semantics of the deontic Imperative, Jussive, and Cohortative forms and the past narrative *wayyiqtol* form. DeCaen's solution to this is to posit "tense neutralization" for *wayyiqtol*, whereby it is a "sequential" form that derives its TAM from the "head" verb in the sequence (DeCaen 1995: 284–92). Unfortunately, this analysis falls under the same censure that 19th-century sequential and inductive theories fall under: (1) *wayyiqtol* is not obviously "underspecified," as sequential verbs generally are; (2) *wayyiqtol* manifestly does not require a "head" verb, and DeCaen (1995: 286) recognizes that " 'headness' is crucial to [his] account of the Hebrew constructions";

---

58. DeCaen either does not fully appreciate the import of Rundgren's privative opposition model, or he is just careless in his terminology. He correctly labels the unmarked (neutral) category in opposition to perfective aspect as "nonperfective," in one instance (1995: 46), but elsewhere he calls it "imperfective" (e.g., 1995: 32), which results in the incoherent classification of perfect aspect as a subcategory of imperfective!

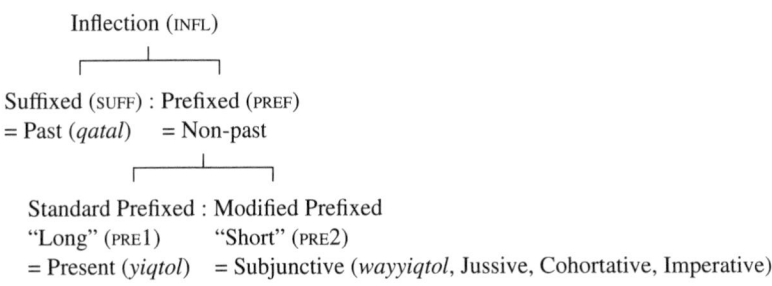

Figure 2.7. DeCaen's ternary model of the BHVS (based on 1995: 105, 282).

(3) he fails to engage the possibility of partial homonymy among the prefix forms, i.e., morphological and syntactic identity are interpreted as indicating a single form (cf. Driver [1892] 1998: 77).

At the same time, DeCaen's work suffers because of his neglect of semantics, which is illustrated by his comment in his 1999 essay that, "the precise semantic interpretation of this formal model is still an open question" (DeCaen 1999: 125). DeCaen's lack of clarity with regard to the semantics of *wĕqatal* (i.e., verb-first *qatal*) seems to be one symptom of his neglect of semantics: he defines the form as "relative past" in one part of his discussion (1995: 232, 256), but elsewhere he associates it with "irreal" modality (1995: 293, 297; 1999: 124).

DeCaen fails to appreciate the semantic interaction among categories of TAM. For example, he claims that the forms default for perfective aspect, and that therefore *qatal* will have a perfective reading except "with unbounded event structures" (1995: 256). However, as linguists have pointed out for languages in general (e.g., C. S. Smith 1999), and I have noted with respect to BH in particular (Cook 2004b: 253), perfective aspect itself makes events bounded. Similarly, linguists have argued that perfective aspect is incompatible or canceled when combined with present tense (Bache 1995: 289; Bybee, Perkins, and Pagliuca 1994: 126), yet DeCaen (1995: 222) claims that the BH verbal forms default for perfective aspect in every temporal sphere. DeCaen's failure to grapple with the semantic interaction among TAM categories also undermines his refutation of the aspectual theory of the BHVS: because he envisions tense and aspect as completely independent categories (DeCaen 1995: 181), he finds incompatibilities between aspectual forms and certain temporal adverbs "wholly unexpected" (1995: 58). In fact, a decade prior, Dahl (1985: 79) had already identified past temporal reference as a secondary feature of perfective verbs, invalidating DeCaen's conclusion that the aspectual theory is problematic because there is no pathway of development from perfective aspect in BH to past tense in RH (DeCaen 1995: 182–83).

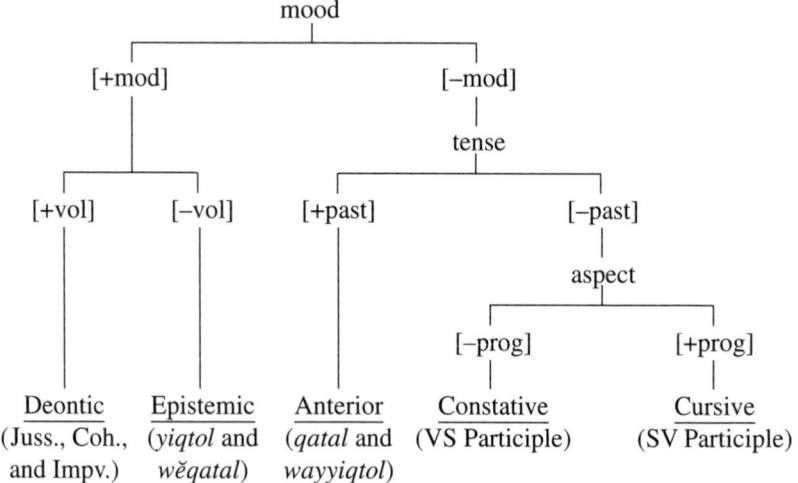

Figure 2.8. Warren's modality-tense-aspect ordering of the BHVS (based on 1998: 68, 99).

Finally, by adopting a tense theory, DeCaen encounters the same deficiency in his model as Joosten: the need to incorporate the Participle as an integral part of the verbal system to express nonperfective aspect and "true present" (DeCaen 1995: 222, 264–65). However, DeCaen's (1995: 222) theory is less problematic than Joosten's in his attention to the role of the copula in constructing periphrastic participial constructions.

In his dissertation on modality in Psalms, **Warren** (1998: 65) adopts the relative-tense-and-modality theory of the Hebrew verb: "I understand the Hebrew verbal system primarily in terms of relative tense (Kuryłowicz, DeCaen) and mood (Joosten)." A distinctive of Warren's study is his attention to the relative order of TAM distinctions, which he argues is properly modality-tense-aspect; however, Warren's precise understanding of what this order entails is unclear. On the one hand, he cites personal communication with Ljungberg, who states that modality stands "outside the core [of the verbal system]," while "aspect is the innermost" (Warren 1998: 67). This view would accord with the arguments by Dahl and Bybee that aspect is more "basic" than tense in verbal systems (above, this section). However, Warren does not see any conflict between Ljungberg's stated view of TAM and his own adoption of Kuryłowicz's, DeCaen's, and Joosten's theories, all which rest on the prioritization of tense over aspect in language. Instead, Warren confusingly concludes that the Hebrew verbal system "iconically (i.e., with surface structure reflecting deep structure) distinguishes verbal forms first by mood, then by tense, then by aspect" (Warren 1998: 68), leading to the ordering model for the the BHVS given in fig. 2.8.

Besides this peculiarity, a detailed discussion of Warren's theory is made unnecessary by its derivational status. His reliance on Joosten's ideas (and Zuber's and Kuryłowicz's as mediated by Joosten) is particularly evident from his distinction between volitive (Jussive, Cohortative, and Imperative) and nonvolitive (*yiqtol* and *wĕqatal*) modality (cf. Joosten 1999: 16); by his constative : cursive distinction, signaled by subject-Participle word order (cf. Joosten 1989); and by his choice of labels, such as "anterior" for *qatal* and "contemporaneous" for the Participle (cf. Joosten 1997a: 60). Although DeCaen's theory is not completely consonant with Joosten's, Warren (1998: 78) notes that it is "highly susceptible to a modal interpretation of *yiqtōl*" (cf. DeCaen 1995). However, he is somewhat uneasy about his acceptance of DeCaen's explanation of the *waw*-prefixed verbs as "continuation" forms: "Our adoption of DeCaen's argument for why the continuation forms should cross-match with the main-clause forms remains problematic. DeCaen does not show clearly how he has moved from mood-neutralization to the ascription of new modal values to *wĕqāṭal* and *wayyiqṭōl*" (Warren 1998: 94). In any case, the value of Warren's theory does not lie in his understanding of the TAM of the BHVS but in his empirical investigation of the range of modality and its expression in BH, which may be drawn upon without partaking of the weaknesses in his adoption of the ideas of Joosten, Kuryłowicz, and DeCaen.

Penner (2006) focuses on the Qumran verbal system, using as a foil the claims of "most standard textbooks" that BH "primarily grammaticalizes aspect" and that MH "primarily grammaticalizes tense" (Penner 2006: 211). Based on his synchronic, empirical, statistical analysis of the verbal forms in a number of sectarian writings from Qumran, Penner concludes that, though there is a strong correlation between the verb forms and both absolute tense and modality (recto and obliquo), Qumran Hebrew is mainly tense-prominent: "Under this hypothesis, past events and present states are expressed using *qatal* or a *waw*-prefixed verb following a *qatal*, and future events and present actions are expressed using *yiqtol* or a *waw*-prefixed verb following a *yiqtol*" (Penner 2006: 213).

Although Penner concludes that absolute tense and modality are prominent in Qumran Hebrew, he is nevertheless quite dependent on the relative-tense-and-modality theories for many of his ideas: his use of Zuber's modal categories of recto (*qatal* and *qatal+wyqtl*) and obliquo (*yiqtol* and *yiqtol+wqtl*) (Penner 2006: 170–71);[59] and his classification of future as properly modality, using arguments similar to Joosten's against an aspectual view of *yiqtol* (Penner 2006: 177). At the same time, he draws on more recent theories,

---

59. Penner notes (2006: 21) that Zuber's conclusions may well be more applicable to Qumran Hebrew than BH (see Zuber 1986: 38).

notably Hatav's (1997; see §2.4.3.2 below) for ideas concerning modality and sequentiality (e.g., Penner 2006: 96–97, 22–25).

Besides the fact that Penner's theory partakes of the weaknesses of Joosten's and the other relative-tense-and-modality theories, as described above, his empirical method is suspect when compared with Furuli's contemporary study (based on a broader database that includes Qumran Hebrew; see §2.4.1.3), which arrives at very different conclusions: both Furuli and Penner attempt an empirical, statistical analysis of the verb forms in "context" (Furuli 2006: 186–87; Penner 2006: 101–2) and arrive at contradictory results, Furuli positing some unique form of aspect for Hebrew (with just two main conjugations—prefix and suffix), and Penner proposing tense-prominence in Qumran Hebrew (Furuli 2006: 462–64; Penner 2006: 212–13). It appears prima facie that both Furuli and Penner have found what they were looking for; that is, their interpretation of the data was guided by what they expected a priori to find, which accounts for their very divergent results based on overlapping data sets.

2.4.2.4. Summary

The modern revival of tense theory of the BHVS against the background of the hegemonic Ewald-Driver aspectual theory has been widely influential because of two significant insights in particular. First, modern tense theory has brought to bear an ever-more-sophisticated analysis of the syntax of the BHVS, theorizing that certain TAM distinctions may in fact be syntactically rather than morphologically marked. Second, modern tense theory has been instrumental in bringing modality into the TAM discussions of the BHVS. One of the most important insights, not yet fully explored in the literature, is the modal status of *wĕqatal*.

At the same time, however, modern tense theories suffer from several shared weaknesses. First, an absolute tense theory appears prima facie to be an impossible model for the BHVS, because the forms clearly function in all three temporal spheres, even if there are certain notable patterns in their distribution. Second, modern tense theories have largely protested the diachronic theories of the BHVS, and like the synchronic aspectual theories, thereby miss the possibilities of homonymy in the BHVS (see §2.4.1.4). The results are semantically implausible explanations for explaining the broad range of meanings for particular forms (e.g., DeCaen's tense-neutralization of modal *yiqtol* to explain past-narrative *wayyiqtol*). Third, modern tense theory is most problematic when viewed from a typological perspective. This is recognized by tense theorists themselves, who have all struggled to some extent to explain the use of "modal" *yiqtol* as past and present imperfective. Generally, however, the data have not been sufficiently explained, the typological data have been selectively used (e.g., see Cook 2006a: 26–28 on Joosten's use of typological data), and statistical analyses have been used to dismiss the relevant data as negligible (e.g., see Cook 2006a: 28–29 on Joosten's use of statistics; see comments above, p. 148, on Penner's and Furuli's inductive, statistical approach). However, the faulty efforts of modern tense theories serve as important guides to a sound analysis of the BHVS. First, the BHVS must be analyzed as a system rather than in terms of individual verb forms in order to avoid proposing arbitrary and typologically unparalleled TAM models for BH, such as are found in tense theories (e.g., Joosten, DeCaen) or in the assumption that understanding the system rests solely in explaining *yiqtol* (e.g., Joosten 2002 and my response, Cook 2006a). Second, statistical analysis is not as crucial to the argument as sound typological analysis.[60] Inductively and systematically examining the verb forms according to context has been unsuccessful for both aspectual and tense theories (e.g., Furuli and Penner): this approach seems to "discover" what the scholar a priori assumes is there, whether tense, aspect, modality, or none of these. Instead, a theory of the BHVS should be judged by whether it presents a "typologically credible" model of the verbal system in light of the abundance of data on verbal systems in the world's languages. With reference back to Kuryłowicz's theory, which pointedly raised the typological question of the relative priority of tense and aspect in the verbal systems—the tense theories examined here have already been shown to be typologically less credible than an aspectual model of the BHVS.

2.4.3. Discourse-Prominent Theory

Discourse analysis entered linguistic terminology with Harris's 1952 articles by this title (1952a; 1952b).[61] He used the term in a fairly restricted sense to refer to the analysis of discourse through breaking it up into its fundamental elements. Now, however, the term "is without a doubt one of the most widely used and loosely defined terms in the entire field of linguistics" (Prince 1988: 164). Nevertheless, most approaches to discourse analysis, and particularly those interacted with below, share two general characteristics. First, they are unified by a common object of inquiry—a discourse/text as the verbal representation of a communicative act (Brown and Yule 1983: 6). This characterization entails two common assumptions of discourse analysis: linguistic analysis should not be restricted by the traditional grammatical boundary of the sentence but should extend beyond this to the "discourse" level; discourse is a social (communicative) act, not simply an artifact.[62] Second, the general goal

---

60. The data must, of course, be interacted with. Andrason's recent spate of articles (2010; 2011a; 2011b; 2011c; forthcoming) falters on his obvious lack of acquaintance / discomfort with the Hebrew text, aside from the theoretical deficiencies of his semantic foundation (compare with my approach in §3.1).

61. *Text-linguistics* is the more commonly employed term among European linguists.

62. Although discourse analysis (as linguistics generally) has tended to give normative status to the study of spoken discourse, analyses of written discourse are becoming more

of discourse analysis is to discern patterns in the discourse that make possible meaningful communication from speaker/writer to listener/reader. The dominant methodology for reaching this goal is to begin with discourse-pragmatic functions and correlate them with certain linguistic forms or patterns, and it is here where we find tension between discourse-pragmatic theory and semantic theory: while discourse analysis generally favors a top-down approach, analyzing discourse-pragmatic functions and correlating them with linguistic forms, semantics operates in a bottom-up fashion, beginning with an analysis of linguistic forms prior to explicating their meaning and possible discourse-pragmatic functions. Although semantic theory and discourse analysis are not mutually exclusive but complementary, a fundamental issue is the priority of one type of analysis over the other. I critically discuss this issue in §4.1; here in chap. 2, however, I simply introduce the discourse analysis of biblical literature (§2.4.3.1), examine the development of discourse-prominent theories of BHVS and their interaction with semantic analyses of the verbal forms (§2.4.3.2), and present some general criticisms that anticipate the discussion in chap. 4 (§2.4.3.3).

2.4.3.1. Discourse Analysis of Biblical Literature

Because of the diversity within the field of discourse analysis, the limited contact between the field and biblical studies, and the specific interests of the latter discipline, discourse analysis of biblical literature has several unique characteristics. First, discourse analysis of biblical literature has largely been presented in contrast to traditional philological analyses—particularly source criticism (e.g., Bodine 1995: 5–7; Longacre 2003: 3–18). As a result, discourse analysis of biblical literature has come to signify a "holistic" or "final form" interpretation of the biblical text, in contrast to the fragmenting traditional higher-critical approaches. Unfortunately this view threatens to confuse discourse analysis—the examination of discourse features of BH—with exegesis of the Hebrew Bible—the interpretation of specific biblical passages (see Talstra 1992: 282–83; O'Connor 2002). This point is important because, just as discourse linguistics in biblical studies has come to serve as an escape from the fragmenting analysis of traditional biblical criticism, so also discourse-prominent analysis of the BHVS seems to serve for some as an escape from the morass of traditional semantic and (predominantly) diachronic approaches (see Cook 2001: 117).

Second, a particularly important point of contact between general discourse theory and discourse analysis of biblical literature is a cluster of correlated distinctions: foreground-background, temporal succession ("chronological sequencing"), and perfective-imperfective aspect. Hopper (1979) posited the foreground-background distinction as a universal feature of narrative discourse

---

frequent. Even in the case of written discourse, however, the text is treated as a communicative act (see the discussion of dialogue versus monologue in Longacre 1996: 123–27).

Table 2.11. Discourse Correlations for Perfective and Imperfective Aspect
(based on Hopper 1979: 126; Molendijk 1994: 23;
Hopper and Thompson 1980: 252)

Perfective	Imperfective
chronological sequencing	simultaneity or chronological overlapping
narrative, dynamic events	descriptive, non-action situations
foreground information	background information
high transitivity	low transitivity
punctual; view of event as a whole	nonpunctual/durative; view of a situation or happening not necessarily complete
subject identity consistent, presupposed	frequent change of subject
human topics	nonhuman topics
realis	irrealis
affirmative	negative

and correlated it with temporal succession (i.e., foreground is temporally successive; background is not). In turn, Hopper (1979: 214) viewed temporal succession as effected by perfective aspect, leading to a three-stage correlation: foreground is temporally successive and is marked by perfective aspect; background is not temporally successive and is indicated by imperfective aspect (see also Hopper 1982).[63] In another influential article, Hopper and Thompson correlated foregrounding with transitivity: "The grammatical and semantic prominence of Transitivity is shown to derive from its characteristic discourse function: high Transitivity is correlated with foregrounding, and low Transitivity with backgrounding" (Hopper and Thompson 1980: 251). These correlations among discourse functions and verb forms, illustrated in table 2.11, form an important foundation for the discourse analysis of the BHVS and explain the predominant focus on foreground-background and temporal succession in these theories.

Third, and a logical outcome of the previous two characteristics, discourse analyses of biblical literature have emphasized the importance of describing verbal forms in terms of the discourse-pragmatic functions. For a segment of the field, this approach derives from Weinrich's discourse theory of European languages (2001: 43; 1st ed. 1964), in which he argues that syntax should be described in terms of providing a preliminary sorting ("Vorsortierung") of the

---

63. I should note that Hopper's understanding of temporal succession and his simplistic (in retrospect) association of it with the perfective-imperfective aspectual distinction is merely indicative of the time period in which he wrote, during which investigations into temporal succession and the semantic components that contribute to its expression were still nascent (see discussion in §1.5). For an up-to-date discussion of temporal succession and its role in BH, see Cook 2004b; and §4.2 below, and the references cited there.

discourse world for the speaker and listener. This preliminary sorting is defined by the distinctions between speech ("Besprechen") and narrative ("Erzählen"), between between background and foreground ("Relief"), and among backward, neutral, or forward "Perspektiv"—that is, temporal reference (Weinrich 2001: chaps. 2–4).

Longacre, who's ideas have been influential especially among Bible translators, shares the same basic perspective as Weinrich: "I posit here that (*a*) every language has a system of discourse types (e.g., narrative, predictive, hortatory, procedural, expository, and others); (*b*) each discourse type has its own characteristic constellation of verb forms that figure in that type; (*c*) the uses of given tense/aspect/mood form are most surely and concretely described in relation to a given discourse type" (Longacre 2003: 57). By "most surely and concretely," Longacre means to set his discourse theory in contrast to traditional semantic theory; but as Talstra (1997: 86) states, the debate over whether to describe the verbal forms at the discourse-pragmatic level or semantic level "is not one of principle, but one of priority." Although Talstra argues for the priority of a discourse-pragmatic analysis and that "the categories of 'tense', mood' and 'aspect' operate only within the limits of the textual organization as it is created by text-grammatical categories," he also states that "it is important to remain open to the possibility of relating text-level and clause-level categories to each other within one system of grammatical analysis" (Talstra 1997: 85–86). In Niccacci's theory, TAM values are correlated with specific discourse functions: "We can affirm that verb forms have fixed temporal reference when they are verbal sentences and/or indicate the mainline of communication both in narrative and in direct speech. On the other hand, they have a relative temporal reference when they are nominal clauses and indicate a subsidiary line of communication" (Niccacci 1994b: 129).

All of these approaches, however, are subject to the criticism of an unhealthy circularity because of their notable lack of any semantic foundation: correlations between discourse functions and specific verbal forms presume the independent determination of the semantic value of the verbal forms; otherwise, how can we know what is being correlated with a given discourse function? This inherent circularity when discourse analysis is given priority over semantic analysis has been noted with respect to both Weinrich's discourse theory (Bache 1985: 22) and Longacre's discourse studies of BH (Hatav 1997: 21; see also Heimerdinger 1999: 98) and is discussed in detail in §4.1 below.

Although there are a variety of approaches to discourse analysis of biblical literature, there are two particularly influential "schools": the Longacre school and the Schneider school.[64] Longacre's discourse analysis, which has been widely used in the analysis of previously unstudied languages and for Bible

---

64. Not surprisingly, the Longacre school has predominated among American scholars, while the Schneider school has been more influential in European scholarship.

Table 2.12. Longacre's Taxonomy of Discourse Types
(adapted from 1996: 10)

	+*Agent-Orientation*	−*Agent-Orientation*	
+*Contingent* *Succession*	NARRATIVE	PROCEDURAL	
	Prophecy	How-to-do-it	+*Projection*
	Story	How-it-was-done	−*Projection*
−*Contingent* *Succession*	BEHAVIORAL	EXPOSITORY	
	Hortatory Promissory	Budget proposal Futuristic essay	+*Projection*
	Eulogy	Scientific paper	−*Projection*

translation, stems from Pike's tagmemic theory (Pike 1967; Waterhouse 1974). The approach is empirical and functional—that is, language is part of human behavior (Dawson 1994: 75–76). The central concepts of tagmemics (not restricted to its application to discourse) are *slot* and *filler* and the *hierarchical* character of language. Slot and filler or class and set refer to the paradigmatic (or associative) and syntagmatic relationships in language (see de Saussure 1959: 122–27), referred to in tagmemic theory as *tagmemes* and *syntagms*: tagmemes combine at various levels of language structure to create syntagms. Thus, Longacre (2003: 302) explains that the two create a correlative relationship: tagmemes are "expounded" by their role in syntagms, and syntagms are composed of various tagmemes. This "part-whole" relationship occurs at each level of language structure, usually by employing syntagms of a lower level as tagmemes at the next level up, forming a hierarchy of morpheme, word, phrase, clause, sentence, paragraph, and discourse (Longacre 2003: 302; Dawson 1994: 82).

Longacre's tagmemic-based discourse analysis begins with the assumptions that identifiable linguistic patterns exist at the discourse level and can be described, and that "text-type" is the stongest determining factor at the discourse ("macro-syntactic") level of tagmemes lower in the hierarchy (i.e., "micro-syntactic" level; Dawson 1994: 23; see Longacre 2003: 57, quoted above this section). A difference of some importance for the present study is that Dawson, in the exposition of his Longacre-based theory, states that correlating "micro-syntactic" tagmemes with "macro-syntactic" roles "in no way lessens the micro-syntactic identities" (Dawson 1994: 23). By contrast, Longacre, quoted above, argues that verb forms are "most surely and concretely described" in terms of their role in a particular text-type (Longacre 2003: 57). This uncertainty about the status of micro-syntactic versus macro-syntactic constructions is exacerbated within discourse studies of BH because of the existing challenges involved in describing the verbal system.

Table 2.13. Longacre's Saliency Cline for English Narrative
(adapted from 1996: 24)

Band 1: Storyline	Past (Subject/Agent) Action, (Subject/Agent/Patient) Motion Past (Subject/Experiencer) Cognitive events (punctiliar adverbs) Past (Subject/Patient) Contingencies
Band 2: Background	Past Progressive (Subject/Agent) background activities Past (Subject/Experiencer) Cognitive states (durative adverbs)
Band 3: Flashback	Pluperfects (events, activities which are out of sequence) Pluperfects (cognitive events/states that are out of sequence)
Band 4: Setting *(expository)*	Stative verbs/adjectival predicates/verbs with inanimate subjects (descriptive) "Be" verbs/verbless clauses (equative) "Be"/"Have" (existential, relational)
Band 5: Irrealis *(other possible worlds)*	Negatives Modals/Future
Band 6: Evaluation *(author intrusion)*	Past tense (cf. setting) Gnomic present
Band 7: Cohesive Band *(verbs in preposed/* *adverbial clauses)*	Script determined Repetitive Back reference

The core of Longacre's theory is the positing of several universal "notional" text-types, initially based on the two parameters of [±agent-orientation] and [±contingent succession], to which later was added [±projection], as illustated in table 2.12 (see also Dawson 1994: 95, 98).

For each major text-type, Longacre has proposed "verb-rank clines" based on the two major classifying features of (1) "main-line" and "off-line" (i.e., temporal succession), and (2) "foreground" and "background," illustrated by his cline for English narrative discourse in table 2.13. Longacre has proposed clines for narrative (2003: 79), predictive (2003: 106), hortatory (2003: 121), and instructional discourse text-types (1995: 47) in BH, and he and others have made initial observations regarding verb ranking in procedural (1992: 181) and expository text-types (2003: 111; see also Dawson 1994: 116).

The Schneider "school" of discourse analysis of biblical literature derives from Schneider's (1982; 1st ed. 1974) application to BH of Weinrich's (2001; 1st ed. 1964) discourse theory of European languages. Because Schneider's work is a student grammar, he does not discuss his theoretical basis at length. However, Talstra, a prominent follower of Schneider's approach, has discussed the theory behind Schneider's grammar in a number of essays (Talstra 1978; 1982; 1992). Talstra argues that Schneider's theory is more sound than other discourse theories because it proceeds from form to function, rather than the

Table 2.14. Application of Weinrich's Discourse Categories to BH
(adapted from Talstra 1992: 272; see Schneider 1982: 208)

	Narrative		Speech		
Foreground	*wayyiqtol*		*yiqtol*/Imperative		
Background	x-*qatal*	x-*yiqtol*	x-*qatal*	*qatal*	*wĕqatal*
	backward	forward	backward	zero	forward

reverse (Talstra 1992: 284). However, this is problematic in that Schneider's neglect of semantics (Tasltra 1978: 174) results in an insecure understanding of the forms prior to correlating them with specific functions.

Schneider's theory is framed as a study of syntax, but it is evident from his shared assumptions with Weinrich that it is properly a discourse theory: syntax should describe structures above the level of clause and sentence; language should be studied as a means of human communication (Talstra 1992: 269). Weinrich argued that verbal forms should not be described in terms of their temporal reference outside the text world or in terms of their aspectual character, in terms of completion, but with reference to their "syntactic" role of providing a preliminary sorting ("Vorsortierung") of the discourse world of the communication situation (Weinrich 2001: 43). This preliminary sorting, Weinrich argued, is effected with respect to three parameters: "Sprachhaltung" or speaker orientation (narrative vs. direct speech); "Relief (foreground vs. background material); and "Perspektiv" (backward vs. zero vs. forward with respect to the temporal location of the communicative situation; Weinrich 2001: chaps. 2–4; see table 2.14). For example, Weinrich (2001: 19) observed that in European languages the verb forms could be divided into two groups based on their dominance within narrative or direct speech: German *Präterium*, *Plusquamperfektum*, and *Konditional* and French *Passé Simple*, *Plusque-Parfait*, *Imparfait*, and *Conditionel* belong to the narrative group; whereas German *Präsens*, *Perfekt*, and *Futur* and French *Présent*, *Passé Composé*, and *Futur* compose the direct speech group.

Although Longacre's and Schneider's theories are sufficiently distinct, they are also relatively similar. Of course, both give precedence to describing the verbal forms in terms of their discourse-pragmatic functions rather than their semantic meanings. In addition, however, Longacre's three parameters for determining discourse types and Weinrich's three parameters by which discourse is preliminarily sorted are tolerably comparable: Longacre's [±contingent succession] corresponds to Weinrich's "Relief" distinction; Longacre's [±agent-orientation] correlates with Weinrich's difference of "Sprachhaltung"; and Longacre's [±projection] is functionally equivalent with Weinrich's "Perspektiv."

2.4.3.2. Discourse Analysis and the Semantics of the BHVS

Summarizing the treatment of the BHVS by discourse analyses is a deceptively simple task because prima facie there appears to be a great deal of uniformity in the conclusions reached by discourse analyses of BH with regard to the functions of the verbal forms. In fact, the differences among the various discourse analyses are with respect to emphasis more than content, and confusion arises primarily from unstated and unrecognized correlations among discourse-pragmatic parameters. For example, the Longacre school focuses on the association of sequentiality (i.e., temporal succession) and foreground with the *waw*-prefixed forms. By contrast, the Schneider, instead of multiplying text-types, focuses on the broad narrative-speech distinction. But in fact, this difference of focus breaks down at a certain level, because narrative discourse is characterized by sequential (i.e., temporally successive) events versus various other types of temporality in direct speech. Therefore, what we find lying behind most discourse analyses of the BHVS is a constellation of related, and sometimes undifferentiated, correlated phenomena: narrative, sequentiality, and foregrounding versus speech, nontemporal succession, and background. Of course, this is an oversimplification, because discourse analyses distinguish foreground and background in both narrative and speech (and other text-types); however, this fact only serves to illustrate the confusing nature of the field at a certain level. Thus, after surveying some of the major contributions to the field below, I examine in particular the treatment of "sequentiality" (variously defined)[65] and the narrative-speech distinction.

Niccacci has published prolifically on his discourse theory of the BHVS (1987; 1989; 1990; 1993; 1994a; 1994b; 1995; 1996; 1997; 1999; 2006). Niccacci's theory clearly belongs to the Schneider school of discourse analysis, a fact that is evident from the centrality given to Weinrich's three parameters, "linguistic attitude," "emphasis," and "lingusitic perspective" (as they are termed in the English translation of Niccacci's book, 1990: 20). At the same time, Niccacci gives a more substantial place to word order than Schneider, though he follows the latter's peculiar syntactic distinction between verbal and nominal clauses, rooted in Arabic grammar: clauses with verbs in first position are "verbal," while clauses with something other than a verb in first position (regardless of whether their predicate is verbal or not) are "nominal" (Niccacci 1994b: 119; see Schneider 1982: 163–67; Tasltra 1978: 169). Niccacci, however, elevates the importance of "first position" to the discourse level in his identification of two types of *wayyiqtol*: "narrative *wayyiqtol*" and "continuative *wayyiqtol*":

---

65. For most of this survey I am employing *sequential* as a cipher for a number of undifferentiated phenomena, which I will clarify toward the close of this section and discuss in more detail in §4.2.

Wayyiqtol is a narrative form when it occurs at the beginning of an independent unit of text and when it belongs to a chain of identical narrative forms. . . . *Wayyiqtol* is a continuation form when it belongs to a text which begins with a non-*Wayyiqtol* construction. . . . It is clear, therefore, that the essential difference is the following: a narrative *Wayyiqtol* is in first position whereas a continuation *Wayyiqtol* is in second position. For this reason the continuation *Wayyiqtol* has no linguistic level or tense of its own but acquires the tense of the preceding construction. (Niccacci 1990: 177–78)

Niccacci, in contrast to Schneider, also accords a greater place to semantics—the neglect of which Talstra criticized Schneider's theory (Talstra 1978: 174; see Niccacci 1990: 21–22). Unfortunately, Niccacci's attempt to combine discourse-pragmatics and semantics has been characterized as "muddled categories and mixing paradigms" (Exter Blokland 1995: 23), because it is unclear in Niccacci's theory how Schneider's discourse model of the Hebrew verb (see table 2.14, p. 155) and his own semantic distinctions, which derive from Bartelmus (1982; see Niccacci 1990: 165 and 205–6), are related. Not only this, but it is unclear which takes precedence in defining the BHVS, and even Niccacci's description of the semantic categories is unclear. In one place he states, "[T]he function of the verb form or a grammatical construction is dependent on its morphology and meaning. Context, style and literary composition have also to be taken into account since they combine to determine the meaning of a text" (Niccacci 1990: 163). Two pages later, he refers back to this statement, explaining:

We have already stated that semantics is of importance, even if only secondary, in determining the function of a verb form or grammatical construction. Further clarification is now required. In fact, in the account given so far the following criteria based on semantics and interpretation have emerged which play a part in the choice of verb forms or constructions in texts: simultaneous or prior action, single or repeated action, emphasis (mode of action, 'Aktionsart'). (Niccacci 1990: 165)

And in a subsequent publication, he makes the following statement: "We can affirm that the verb forms have fixed temporal reference when they are verbal sentences and/or indicate mainline of communication both in narrative and in direct speech. On the other hand, they have a relative temporal reference when they are in nominal clauses and indicate a subsidiary line of communication" (Niccacci 1994b: 129).

Niccacci's conclusions on the finite verbal clauses in BH are summarized in the following condensed version of his summary statement (see also Niccacci's tabular summary, 1990: 168):[66]

---

66. Baayen (1997) clothes the Schneider theory in new terminology but does not differ appreciably from its adherents in his conclusions (see esp. Baayen 1997: 267): *wayyiqtol*

1. *Wayyiqtol* is the narrative tense (linguistic attitude), it denotes foreground (emphasis), and denotes zero degree (linguistic aspect). Narrative *wayyiqtol* occurs at the beginning of an independent unit of text and within a series of other narrative *wayyiqtol* forms, all marking the foreground with a fixed simple past tense. Continuative *wayyiqtol* appears in texts headed by non-*wayyiqtol* forms, and retains the tense and linguistic perspective of the preceding form (1990: 175–80).
2. *Qatal* is neutral with respect to the lingusitic-attitude distinction narrative-speech and is principally retrospective (linguistic aspect), which also means that it does not denote foreground in narrative. However, in reportative speech, *qatal* can function in an analogous way to *wayyiqtol*, developing into the foreground tense of "narrative discourse." Because of *qatal*'s neutrality to the narrative-speech distinction, it is not properly a "tense" (as defined within the Schneider school of discourse analysis; 1990: 180–81).
3. *Yiqtol* is the tense of speech (linguistic attitude), corresponding to *wayyiqtol*'s role in narrative. Thus, it denotes foreground in speech (emphasis), whether in first position as "jussive" or in second position as "indicative." In either position, it may express either zero or anticipatory degree (linguistic perspective) and only rarely is used to express repeated action in the past in narrative (1990: 181–82).
4. *Wĕ-qatal* expresses future or repetition (usually in the past) in either narrative or speech and always in second position (linguistic attitude). In discourse, it denotes foreground or anticipated information, depending on the preceding construction, whereas in narrative it always expresses background and repetition (emphasis and linguistic perspective), being distinguished from *qatal* by this latter function (1990: 182–86).
5. *Wĕ-yiqtol* continues a volitive form (Jussive, Cohortative, Imperative), expressing purpose as opposed to simple future, but it may also follow a jussive (first-position) *yiqtol* coordinately (1990: 186–87).

Heller's study (2004) of "clause function" in the Joseph "novella" (Genesis 37–47) and David's succession narrative (2 Samual 9–1 Kings 2) is one of the most recent contributions within the Longacre school of approach, although Heller gives primary credit for his approach to Lambdin (Heller 2004: 25). Heller argues for six distinct discourse types in BH, including narrative and

---

and *yiqtol* are foreground verbs ("tight linkage") in narrative and speech, respectively, while *qatal* is a backgrounding verb ("loose linkage"). Like Niccacci, Baayen sees word order as determinative, especially because he folds *wĕqatal* into *qatal* as a single conjugation: VS order belongs to foreground, whereas background is SV order. Finally, correlative with foregrounding, *wayyiqtol* is a narrative verb ("disfocal referential concern") whereas *yiqtol* is a speech verb ("focal referential concern"). Baayen illustrates an extreme discourse-pragmatic approach when he concludes: "[T]he *qāṭal* is a tense form that has a pragmatic function without having a semantic value of its own. To my knowledge, this is exceptional for verb forms" (Baayen 1997: 281). The exceptionality of his conclusion should have alerted him to his error in disallowing *qatal* any semantic value.

five direct discourse varieties: narrative (i.e., embedded in direct discourse), predictive, expository, interrogative, hortatory (Heller 2004: 25). With respect to narrative, Heller argues that the "basic narrative story line" in BH is indicated by "chains" of *wayyiqtol* forms, while the other finite verb forms (*qatal*, *yiqtol*, and *wĕqatal*) indicate "either nonsequential, 'background' information or episode boundaries" (Heller 2004: 26). With regard to the five types of direct discourse, Heller (2004: 27) argues that within each type the verbal forms "are consistent in their meaning." The bulk of Heller's work is a chapter-by-chapter analysis of the text in terms of these discourse types and the functions of the verbal forms within each.

Regardless of the insights Heller sometimes has to offer on particular passages, his theory ultimately fails because, first, discourse-pragmatic functions are an insufficient basis for distinguishing the BH verbal forms; and, second, his vague relating of discourse-pragmatic functions of the verbal forms to their semantics undercuts his discourse-pragmatic treatment (see Cook 2006c). With respect to the first point, Heller's difficulties stem from his central discourse-pragmatic distinction in narrative: first, he associates both sequentiality and foreground with *wayyiqtol* clauses, though how these two are related is not entirely clear: "the use of WAYYIQTOL clauses in uninterrupted syntactical chains consistently implies sequentiality of action in the narrative" (Heller 2004: 430). Conversely, and wrongly, he argues that sequential action cannot be expressed by other verb forms in narrative and, therefore, neither can foregrounded events. The prime counterexamples to these claims are the instances where two corresponding, equally salient events are portrayed by *wayyiqtol* and *qatal* clauses (e.g., Gen 4:3–4). Heller, however, argues that the *qatal* clauses in these sequences in his corpus present background events compared with the foregrounded *wayyiqtol* events (see Gen 40:23; 2 Sam 13:19; 1 Kgs 1:9–10; and his discussion, 2004: 93, 281, 406). Such examples require that at the very least *wayyiqtol*'s foregrounding opposition with *qatal* be characterized as privative: *wayyiqtol* always expresses foreground, while *qatal* is neutral with respect to the opposition, thus allowing for its expression of both background and foreground events (so Cook 2006c: 117; 2004b: 264).

Heller's treatment of the semantics of the BHVS is vague and ad hoc. In the previously quoted passage, he states that a syntactic chain of *wayyiqtol* forms "*implies* sequentiality of action in the narrative" (Heller 2004: 430; italics added). However, sequentiality or, better, successivity of events is ultimately a semantic characteristic (see §4.2.1). In practice, Heller associates both this semantic parameter and the discourse-pragmatic function of foreground with *wayyiqtol*. Similarly, Heller (2004: 428) makes passing reference to "the normal aspectual connotations that the various Hebrew verbal forms imply," leaving the reader to wonder about what exactly he thinks about the semantics of the BH verbal forms. This vague use of semantics is helpful, however, where it can be called upon to shore up his insufficient discourse-pragmatic explanations of verb choice. Thus, when faced with explaining several examples of *wĕqatal* as "terminal paragraph markers," in place of the more usual *qatal* with this function, he explains that "the narratological reason why these clauses were used instead of the more usual QAṬAL terminal clause is related to their inherent semantic and aspectual meanings, since discourse pragmatics and the semantic fields of the verbs work together to provide the sense of the clauses" (Heller 2004: 439: n. 17). Given this sort of statement, it is a wonder that only in such instances does Heller find it necessary to say anything about the semantics of the verbal forms, and even then his statements are of the vague and uncertain character of this quotation (e.g., Heller 2004: 311 n. 44, 324 n. 48).

Del Barco's recent discourse study (2003) has connections with both Longacre and Niccacci: following Longacre, del Barco posits notional discourse types, such as narrative and predictive; at the same time, his taxonomy for *qatal* and *yiqtol* is organized on the basis of word order—a particular focus of Niccacci's work. The primary distinctive of del Barco's work is that he has chosen for his database the preexilic minor prophets (Hosea, Amos, Micah, Nahum, Habakkuk, and Zephaniah). As a result, his emphases differ from prose-narrative-based discourse analyses. This is seen in his more extensive treatment of the *wĕqatal* form than other studies vis-à-vis his treatment of *wayyiqtol* (Barco del Barco 2003: chap. 3) and in his identification of discourse types that are particular to prophetic speech: predictive, exhortative, descriptive (or expository, lamentive, discursive narrative, and discursive interrogative-rhetorical (2003: 236–41).

In line with previous discourse theories, del Barco distinguishes *wĕqatal* and *wayyiqtol* from the non-*waw*-prefixed forms primarily in terms of sequentiality of events. The primary function of *wĕqatal* is the expression of sequential events in predictive discourse, in which it has a future temporal reference. However, the form may appear as well in predictive discourse without a sequential sense, often following a lead *yiqtol* form (Barco del Barco 2003: 89). Outside predictive discourse, *wĕqatal* may appear in descriptive types of discourse (e.g., expository, lamentive) without an explicit temporal reference (2003: 97). Del Barco's (2003: 126) analysis of *wayyiqtol* is also similar to previous studies: when the form appears in prophetic discourse, it is usually headed by *qatal* and expresses past tense, sequential narrative events, usually embedded in speech.

Del Barco discovers the same sorts of variation in function/meaning for the non-*waw*-prefixed forms as may be found in previous studies. He emphasizes that interpreting the function/meaning of *qatal* and *yiqtol* depends on paying attention both to the discourse context and to their position within the clause (Barco del Barco 2003: 158). *Qatal* appears independently (i.e., not headed by *waw* or subordinating conjunction) with an anterior or perfect meaning, rarely

Table 2.15. Basic TAM-Discourse Model
(cf. Gropp 1991: 57; Buth 1992: 104; Bentinck 1995: 26; Endo 1996: 321)

	±Modal		
	±Tense-Aspect		
±Discourse-pragmatic	*qatal*	*yiqtol*	IMPV-JUSS-COH/*yiqtol*
	wayyiqtol	*wĕqatal*	W+IMPV-JUSS-COH/*wĕqatal*

appears with *waw* (which would be indistinguishable from *wĕqatal*), and may appear with a variety of functions/meanings following subordinate conjunctions (2003: 158). *Yiqtol* has three different functions/meanings clause initially: a modal form (i.e., jussive), the antecedent of a chain of *wĕqatal* forms, and at the head of either clause in a protasis-apodosis construction or parallel bicola (2003: 194–95). *Yiqtol* prefixed with *waw* shows a close functional/ meaning connection with the preceding clause, often with a continued jussive sense. Finally, *yiqtol* functions variously following subordinate conjunctions, similarly to the case of *qatal* (2003: 195).

Given the similarity of treatment in del Barco with the other discourse theories surveyed here, it is open to the same or similar criticisms (see Cook 2004a). I offer an example from his work to illustrate the difficulties inherent in his approach. Del Barco identifies the occurrence of *wĕqatal* and *yiqtol* in the midst of a past-tense narrative sequence in Amos 4:7–8 as an atypical case ("un caso atipico"), because the forms generally belong to predictive discourse where they have a future temporal reference. Hence, he reluctantly concludes that these forms express future tense in a predictive discourse that intrudes in the midst of a past-tense narrative discourse (Barco del Barco 2003: 88–89). However, the traditional semantic approach to the BHVS has no such problem with the occurrence of these forms in narrative discourse, since it recognizes as part of their semantic makeup the expression of past habitual (or "customary") action (Waltke and O'Connor 1990: 533–34). As with other discourse analyses, del Barco runs into problems because the BH verbal forms do not align with discourse functions as uniformly as he expects. When deviations from their expected functions are encountered, discourse analysts have no recourse to semantics except in vague and ad hoc ways (see on Heller, above), and if a semantic explanation is rejected, they can deduce, as does del Barco, conclusions that are directly counter to what traditional grammars have long recognized.

In the final decade of last century, there was a confluence of opinions on the Hebrew verb that resulted in a flurry of publications, all seeking to refine a basic shared model of the BHVS, illustrated in table 2.15. This basic model consists of two or three parameters by which the BH verbal forms are distinguished: a tense-aspect semantic distinction, a discourse-pragmatic distinction, and in some models a modal semantic distinction between indicative and nonindicative. One of the earliest models of this sort is by **Gropp** (1991), which quite closely resembles the generic model in table 2.15 (p. 161). He defines the tense-aspect distinction as relative tense (±anterior) and distinguishes between the *waw*-prefixed forms and non-*waw*-prefixed forms (including volitives: indirect versus direct) in terms of ±sequential, which he understands in terms of "contingent temporal succession," following Longacre (Gropp 1991: 50; see Longacre 1996: 8–9); and he includes a third, modal distinction (±volitive) to differentiate the indicative and nonindicative forms, as defined in the traditional grammars (for "direct" and "indirect" volitives, see Joüon 2006: §§114, 116).

Besides the criticism of distinguishing forms in terms of discourse-pragmatic function (±sequential), Gropp creates difficulties by defining both *qatal* and *wayyiqtol* as [+anterior] (relative tense), because *wayyiqtol* "almost always implies anteriority to the moment of speaking" (i.e., absolute tense; 1991: 55). His solution is ad hoc: "In order to account for the relationship between the perfect [*qatal*] and the narrative [*wayyiqtol*] we need to posit a semantic rule such that +ANTERIOR in the context of +SEQUENCE, is to be interpreted as +PAST, or in other terminology, the interaction between +RELATIVE PAST and +SEQUENCE converts the form semantically to an +ABSOLUTE PAST" (Gropp 1991: 55). Similarly, Gropp's distinction between direct and indirect volitives in terms of ±sequential is less than perfect, because the semantic range of indirect volitives is arguably greater than just contingent temporal succession (see Waltke and O'Connor 1990: 575–76), not to mention that Muraoka (1997a) has called into question the validity of this volitive distinction.

Buth's model (1992) is an example of the two-parameter variation of the basic model in table 2.15. In contrast to Gropp's form-meaning correspondences, Buth understands these parameters to be functional categories. This is evident from his preliminary remark that, "Like any human language, Hebrew is able to make time and aspect distinctions. Reports to the contrary can be ignored" (Buth 1992: 96). His functional approach is further evidenced in the broadness with which he defines these parameters. He characterizes the tense-aspect parameter in terms of "verb forms for *definite* events (that is, past or perfective or decisive or contrary to fact) versus verb forms for *indefinite* events (future or imperfective or potential or repetitive)" (Buth 1992: 103). Buth refers to the discourse-pragmatic parameter as "thematic continuity," which encompasses both temporal succession and foregrounding: the *waw*-prefixed forms signal thematic continuity, whereas the non-*waw*-prefixed forms signal discontinuity" (1992: 101–4). Unfortunately, the broad, functional basis of Buth's model eschews the very questions we are attempting to answer—namely, the semantic notional categories marked by the BH verbal forms. Buth addresses neither the question of semantic-functional correspondences (i.e., why certain verb forms are preferred for some functions and rejected for others) nor that of distinguishing functions (e.g., how we determine whether a form is expressing tense, aspect, or something else in a given instance). It is also interesting to note that, while Gropp and Buth differ from each other, it is not due to Gropp's "self-consciously synchronic approach" (Gropp 1991: 46) versus Buth's explicitly diachronic model (Buth 1992: 98). In fact, the conclusions of each would appear more compatible with the approach of the other: Gropp's attempt to distinguish *wayyiqtol* semantically (especially from *qatal*) is unconvincing (Gropp 1991: 55; see above) but could be bolstered by an examination of the historical development of *wayyiqtol*, which Buth carries out (1992: 100–101); by contrast, there is no inherent reason that Buth's historical discussion is necessary to his functional model of the BHVS, in which the semantic development and identity of the forms play little or no role (see Bentinck 1995 for an application of Buth's theory to Bible translation).

Endo's study (1996) is one of the first monograph-length treatments of the BHVS to embrace the three-parameter model in table 2.15 (p. 161). His model differs from Gropp's only in that he makes the *wĕqatal* form do double duty, expressing both sequential, non-past indicative and volitive (in place of Gropp's indirect volitive category; Endo 1996: 321). These similarities, however, are only superficial, because Endo's understanding of the parameters is quite different from other proponents' understanding of this basic semantic-discourse model (for my earlier assessment, see Cook 2003b). First, his use of both tense and aspect labels ("past" and "complete" versus "non-past" and "incomplete") for the semantic parameter is nothing more than terminological variety:

> Though one cannot be sure which category presupposes the existence of the other, there may not be much difference between these oppositions [i.e., past : non-past and complete : incomplete] in describing the function of, particularly, the freestanding conjugations [i.e., *qatal* and *yiqtol*]. A state of affairs which is complete can be viewed as past, one which is incomplete can be viewed as either present or future. (Endo 1996: 64, 320–21; quotation from p. 320)

Endo's understanding of aspect, as reflected in this quotation, is quite different from the understanding found in the great majority of linguistic works. Although aware of Comrie's advocacy for the terms perfective : imperfective instead of complete : incomplete (Comrie 1976: 18), Endo (1996: 320) rejects this suggestion but then proceeds to confuse complete : incomplete with the significantly different opposition of completed : incompleted; this is evident from the fact that he treats perfective : imperfective and complete : incomplete as distinct categories (e.g., Endo 1996: 55; cf. Comrie 1976: 18–19, who equates them) and at the same time views complete : incomplete as functionally indistinguishable from past : non-past (cf. Comrie 1976: 18, whose

discussion implies that the completed : incompleted pair may easily be confused or equated with the past : non-past temporal distinction in just the sort of
way that Endo confuses tense and aspect categories).

Second, Endo's description of the parameter of sequentiality is impenetrable. Although he does not offer a definition, he clearly intends to distinguish sequentiality as a syntactic relation at the discourse level (i.e., between
clauses) from the more customary understanding of sequentiality in biblical
discourse linguistics as temporal/logical succession of events: "the parameter
of sequentiality and non-sequentiality is purely syntactical, relating to the flow
of the story as discourse function: the non-sequential form stops the flow of
the story, whereas the sequential form lets the story flow on" (Endo 1996:
70). Endo argues that it is the verb form itself in the *waw*-prefixed forms that
has this syntactic marking of sequentiality, rather than being effected by the
conjugation, based on the diachronic argument, going back to Bauer (1910),
that Hebrew had two sets of suffix and prefix conjugations, distinguished by
stress placement:

> Biblical Hebrew may be of the kind [of language] where sequentiality in the
> verb form is clearly distingiushd [*sic*] from the function of the conjugations.
> That is, it seems to have particularly sequential verb forms, since, . . . it is highly
> probably that biblical Hebrew has two sets of conjugations in each temporal-
> aspectual distinction: QATAL and (waY)YIQTOL for past (complete); YIQTOL
> and (wə)QATAL for non-past (non-complete). The latter conjugations usually
> appear in the sequential context. (Endo 1996: 68)

Neither does word order have any semantic significance; rather, Endo classifies all word-order variation as related to the pragmatic feature of "topicalization" (Endo 1996: 320). Finally, Endo also rejects the widespread view
(generally concomitant with the temporally successive understanding of sequentiality) that verb forms distinguish anything like foreground and background in discourse (Endo 1996: 322). The uncertainties regarding Endo's
syntactic understanding of sequentiality underscore the confusion that abounds
regarding this parameter (see further below).

Gentry's model (1998) of the BHVS represents a culmination of the generic semantic and discourse-pragmatic theory in table 2.15 (p. 161). His
model, given in table 2.16, includes four parameters in total: two semantic
parameters (modal and tense-aspect), and two discourse parameters (sequentiality, and narrative versus direct speech). In addition, he incorporates the
patterns of negation that interact with word order and restrictions on modal
forms (Gentry 1998: 157).

Gentry's understanding of the BHVS combines insights from several quarters. First, he accepts the diachronic argument that *yiqtol* and (*way*)*yiqtol* derive
from two separate prefix conjugations in West Semitic (Gentry 1998: 10–13;

Table 2.16. Gentry's TAM-Discourse Model of the BHVS
(adapted from 1998: 39)

	Assertive Modality		Projective Modality	
	Perfective ±Past	Imperfective ±Non-past	Perfective	Imperfective
Nonsequential (Negative)	[x] *qatal* (לֹא + *qatal*)	[x] *yiqtol* (לֹא + *yiqtol*)	Jussive (אַל + Jussive)	*yiqtol* (לֹא + *yiqtol*)
Sequential	*wayyiqtol*	*wĕqatal*	*waw* + Jussive	*waw* + *yiqtol/* (*wĕqatal*)
	Narrative			
	Conversation (direct speech)			

see §2.3.4.2 above); he argues that both diachronic and synchronic analysis of the verbal system are necessary (Gentry 1998: 9). Second, he argues that the verb forms morphologically indicate an aspectual opposition of perfective : imperfective, while tense is indicated by the combination of verb form and discourse context; for example, in direct speech, the perfective "normally" expresses past tense, and the imperfective forms non-past tense (Gentry 1998: 14–20). Third, Gentry closely follows Buth in his understanding of sequentiality as a discourse-pragmatic parameter. Thus, the sequential verb forms "are employed to encode continuity or to foreground information in the discourse" (Gentry 1998: 13). Fourth, Gentry follows his teacher Revell and the work of other Revell students (notably Shulman 1996) in his treatment of modality (assertive/indicative versus projective): only the Imperative morphologically marks projective modality; otherwise, the modal opposition is signaled by word order—projective modality being marked by "initial position" in the clause (Gentry 1998: 21–24).

Gentry helpfully interacts with many of the previous theories of the BHVS, making it quite easy to determine the relationship of his model to others, both previous and contemporary. For example, he credits Hendel (1996) with his definitions of aspect and modality and cites Gropp's definition of tense (Gentry 1998: 14, 21). As already mentioned, he derives his understanding of sequentiality from Buth (1992) and his syntactic treatment of modality from Shulman's study of volitives (1996). In addition, Gentry distances his model from previous theories of the BHVS, noting that the tense-aspect parameter is unconnected with the sequence of verb forms (Gentry 1998: 20; compare 19th-century *waw*-inductive theories, above, §2.2.1). He also departs from the "consensus" view that the ה-suffix on the Cohorative is a marker of projective modality, preferring instead to identify the Cohorative ה with the ה on other forms (notably the 99 instances of *wayyiqtol* with final ה) as a single morpheme related to the Akkadian Ventive *-a* (Gentry 1998: 25–30; see above, §2.3.4.2).

At the same time, Gentry's attempt at comprehensiveness results in an unhelpful category confusion similar to the confusion that permeates many models of this variety (i.e., those akin to the basic model in table 2.15 above): the model mixes together parameters defined by semantic meaning with parameters of discourse-pragmatic functions and, in some cases, syntactic distinctions, without adequately distinguishing these linguistic levels. This sort of confusion seems to lie at the root of protestations such as the humorous quip by Rainey (1986: 7) that "[t]he ancient Israelite farmer certainly knew when to milk his cow and his language was adequate to explain the routine to his son," to which an apt reply would be Buth's remark, cited above: "Like any human language, Hebrew is able to make time and aspect distinctions. Reports to the contrary can be ignored" (Buth 1992: 96). Semantics (meaning) must be distinguished from syntax and, above all, discourse pragmatics (function) in the analysis of the BHVS.

A major distinctive feature of discourse-prominent theories of the BHVS is *sequentiality*, which has been defined (or not defined) in various ways, notwithstanding the general consensus that it involves the notions of temporal succession and foreground. However, there has been a good deal of confusion over sequentiality, evident in works such as Endo's (see above) and Li's (1999), due to a lack of rigorous definition (e.g., Endo) or due to confusion between similar phenomena related to sequentiality (see Cook 2004b: 248). Li's definitions illustrate the potential for confusion:

> It may be useful to bring three definitions together. An *iconic* clause is one that occurs in the temporal and/or logical order of the events represented in the narrative. A *sequential/consecutive* clause is an iconic clause that is marked for sequence. A *narrative* clause is the least marked iconic syntagm in the narrative, and normally also the most frequently occurring iconic syntagm. (Li 1999: 4, italics added)

This definition sets up Li's study as virtually incomprehensible. Is he dealing with the iconicity, sequentiality, or narrative clause structure, and how much difference would this determination make since iconicity is assumed in his definitions of both sequentiality and narrative clause? What is a "marked" narrative clause, given that Li has defined narrative clause in the previous sentence as "unmarked"? Presumably, he is using (un)marked in two different senses here. His conclusion is no clearer when he discusses "the employment of the narrative clause in non-iconic functions" and that "though a sequentially marked syntagm is consistently iconic, its iconicity does not need to be exceptionless" (Li 1999: 227). These statements appear to run counter to his initial definitions, in which iconicity is an integral part of both sequentiality and narrative clause. Several approaches to the issue of sequentiality are illustrated here.

Dempster (1985) attempts to avoid just the sort of confusion that Li seems to encounter by distinguishing between *syntactic* sequentiality ("sentence sequencing") and *semantic* sequentiality ("predicate sequencing"): sentence sequencing refers to the *wa*-clause connecting, whereby a clause prefixed with *wa*- presupposes a previous clause with which it is in "sequence" (Dempster 1985: 40); predicate sequencing presupposes sentence sequencing, but further indicates that the predication in the clauses so connected present a "coherent sequence of past events" (Dempster 1985: 33, 51). Dempster further identifies the sequencing constraint as interactive with word order variation: "The normal pattern in which the prefixed verb occurs is used to present the majority of verbal predications. If it is removed narrative ceases to exist. Two formal conditions regulate the use of the prefixed verb in this pattern: sentence position (first) and sentence sequence (*wa*). This verb is restricted to linguistic contexts in which it is the first grammatical constituent of syndetic sentences" (Dempster 1985: 68–69). Thus, speaking of *wayyiqtol* versus *qatal*, Dempster states that the "verbs themselves in the different patterns do not signal any significant semantic difference . . . but the pattern itself is the primary signal of the semantic consecution" (Dempster 1985: 68, 96). In other words, the syntax is the marker of both sentence sequencing and predicate sequencing.

Dempster's discourse study focuses on four "supra-sentential" constraints, derived from Gleason's class lectures on discourse analysis: sequencing, theme, reference, and lexical cohesion (Dempster 1985: 38 n. 1). **DeRouchie** (2007) has adapted these four constraints in his discourse study of Deuteronomy 5–11, though otherwise, DeRouchie's study is quite different from Dempster's in that DeRouchie primarily follows Longacre's discourse theory and incorporates a semantic component based on Cook (2001; 2002; 2004b) in an effort to avoid the pitfalls of simple form-function correlations (see DeRouchie 2007: 25–28). With regard to Dempster's sequencing constraint, DeRouchie explains:

> What the present study terms "text logic" and "foregrounding," Dempster used the term "sequencing" and distinguished between sentence sequencing (i.e., connection) and predicate sequencing (i.e., semantic succession). But as has been recently argued by J. A. Cook [Cook 2004b], not only is sequencing to be distinguished from temporal succession, but also temporal succession is most appropriately seen as a context-determined feature and not a grammaticalized one. (DeRouchie 2007: 78 n. 62)

Several questions and problems are raised by these statements. First, DeRouchie's wording implies that he is equating his text logic category with Dempster's sentence sequencing, and foregrounding with Dempster's predicate sequencing category. However, as stated above, Dempster's predicate sequencing is the equivalent of temporal succession, which DeRouchie seems

Table 2.17. Hatav's Semantic Feature Model of the BHVS
(adapted from 1997: 29)

	wayyiqtol	*wǝqatal*	*yiqtol*	*qatal*	*qotel* (Participle)
Sequentiality	+	+	−	−	−
Modality	−	+	+	−	−
Progression	−	−	−	−	+
Perfect	−	−	−	+	−

to recognize in his parenthetical definition of predicate sequencing in the quotation above.

Second, and relatedly, it is unclear what DeRouchie means by "sequencing" when he states (with reference to my argument) that sequencing should be distinguished from temporal succession, because at least part of Dempster's category of sequencing, which he adopts, is equivalent to temporal succession, though DeRouchie himself eschews the term *sequencing*, as he here explains. Third, he misconstrues my argument when he states that temporal succession is "a context-determined feature and not a grammaticalized one." Rather, based on Fregean's compositional principle of semantics, I argue that temporal succession is determined by the interaction of a number of semantic features, including the situational aspect of the verbal lexeme, the grammaticalized TAM marking(s), and adverbial modifiers. Context becomes a determining factor in the interpretation of temporal succession only rarely and in cases involving select types of semantic combinations (on which, see C. S. Smith 1999). Despite the uncertainty of DeRouchie's comments, the net result of his combining of Dempster and my ideas is that sequencing (his text logic) is strictly syntactic, while temporal succession is viewed as "the default interpretation of narrative texts" (DeRouchie 2007: 152) rather than as being marked by any particular syntactic pattern.

By contrast, in **Hatav**'s theory of the BHVS (1997; 2004), sequentiality is strictly semantic—that is, temporal succession. Unfortunately, Hatav's contribution to the semantic understanding of sequentiality is much more significant than is her application of her theory to the BHVS. Hatav's understanding of the BHVS, illustrated by the feature chart in table 2.17, has close affinities with Joosten's theory (see §2.4.2.3 above), except that there is no apparent underlying relative tense theory to Hatav's understanding: (1) both *yiqtol* and *wǝqatal* are modal, distinguished from each other by the sequential feature of *wǝqatal* (Hatav 1997: 123–38); (2) *qatal* is a perfect form and therefore incapable of expressing sequential events or advancing the reference time (Hatav 1997: 175–88); (3) the Participle (*qotel*) plays an integral part of the verbal system, expressing progressive aspect, the defining feature of which is "inclusion"—that is, the ability to include other events in its reference time (Hatav 1997: 89); finally, (4) *wayyiqtol* is defined by sequentiality and the absence of Hatav's other feature.

Wayyiqtol (and to a lesser extent *wĕqatal*) and sequentiality are the central concerns of Hatav's theory. Interacting with semantic theories regarding the movement of reference time (see §1.5 above), Hatav (1997: 6) defines the *waw*-prefixed forms as always presenting bounded events and therefore advancing the reference time in discourse. Hatav's relating of temporal succession (sequentiality) to boundedness is no doubt correct (see Hatav 1989; Depraetere 1995); however, her strict association of boundedness in BH with the *waw*-prefixed forms and her opposing claim that *qatal* never expresses boundedness denies both the complexity and sometimes the indeterminacy of boundedness (see C. S. Smith 1999) as well as the obvious counterexamples in the biblical text, both of *wayyiqtol* without boundedness and of *qatal* expressing boundedness (Cook 2004b: 251–67). Hatav has mollified these claims in a more recent article (2004), allowing that *qatal* may express bounded events by "borrowing" its reference time from another clause in the context, having its reference time determined by an adverbial phrase, or taking the speech time as a default reference time (Hatav 2004: 513–18). Thus, Hatav begins to sound more and more similar to writers who make a narrative : speech distinction between *wayyiqtol* and *qatal* (cf. Gropp's statements on the reference time of these two forms, above; and Goldfajn and Kawashima, below this section).

However, a problem that persists in Hatav's recent compositional treatment of *wayyiqtol* and sequentiality (2004) is her identification of the underlying prefix form in *wayyiqtol* as modal *yiqtol*, when the historical and comparative evidence points to separate origins for these two conjugations (see §2.3 above). She argues that *wayyiqtol*'s semantics arises from the restricting of its modal meaning by two prefixed morphemes: the doubling *ay* morpheme acts similarly to the definite article in a noun phrase, anchoring the verbal event in "the familiar actual world" (Hatav 2004: 500–7); the *wa* morpheme effects sequentiality by creating a new reference time (Hatav 2004: 510–12). This analysis is simply a more linguistically sophisticated and semantically oriented revision of DeCaen's earlier analysis of the form (1995), on which, see my critique above (§2.4.2.3).

Alongside sequentiality, the other major trait of discourse-prominent theories is their distinction between *narrative and (direct) speech*, although this distinction may be more or less covert in some theories (e.g., Gropp's distinction between *wayyiqtol* and *qatal* may be correlated with the reference-time distinction between narrative and direct speech, above), or it may be obscured by subcategories within each (e.g., Heller, above). **Goldfajn**'s theory (1998), notably, makes the narrative-speech distinction centrally important: narrative and speech correlate with sequential and nonsequential temporality, explained within a framework informed by relative–tense ideas from Reichenbach (see §1.2.2) and Kuryłowicz (see §2.4.2.3). Goldfajn argues that speech has a default reference point of the speech time (R, Ts), whereas narration has a reference point that is determined by the narration (R<Tn) (Goldfajn 1998: 114; Ts = speech time, and Tn = narrative time; for Riechenbach's notation system, see §1.2.2). Thus, *wayyiqtol* is past-sequential and belongs particularly to the domain of narrative, while *wĕqatal* is future-sequential and, contrastingly, appears more frequently in speech (Goldfajn 1998: 71). *Qatal* and *yiqtol* differ from the *waw*-prefixed forms by their nonsequentiality "unbounded" character, explained in terms of nonadvancement of the reference point. *Qatal* can express repetition, simultaneity, or anteriority with respect to a preceding event (reference time), whereas *yiqtol* often refers to future events in speech and past posterior (i.e., past conditional) events in narrative (Goldfajn 1998: 115).[67]

A different approach to the narrative-speech distinction appears in **Kawashima**'s (2004) work on the innovation of biblical narrative in the ancient world. Drawing on Benveniste's discourse theory (1966; ET 1971), filtered through the more philosophical-literary work of Banfield (1982), Kawashima finds a correlation between BH *wayyiqtol* and *qatal* and French *Passé Simple* and *Passé Composé*: "while the perfect [*qatal*] locates events deictically with respect to the speaker, the consecutive [*wayyiqtol*] co-occurs with non-deictic temporal markers" (Kawashima 2004: 39). Kawashima proceeds to (unsuccessfully) excuse *wayyiqtol* in direct speech and explain *qatal* in narration as a variety of perfect aspect (often pluperfect), drawing on Zevit's theory (see §2.4.3 above) in the latter case (see my critique, Cook 2006b).

Kawashima is at pains to distinguish his theory from the Weinrich-based discourse theories of BH, but his conclusions are not appreciably different from them. Although he adopts Banfield's notion of "unspeakable" sentences to differentiate narration from speech as nondeictic discourse (i.e., the reference time is not anchored to a speaker as with speech), Goldfajn's analysis of narrative (R<Tn) versus speech (R, Ts) captures the same distinction within a Reichenbachian and Weinrich's framework (above). In fact, the distinction between objective and subjective time (i.e., narrative and speech in discourse theory) seems to have both (1) semantic dimensions, related to the anchoring of reference time (see Lyons 1977: 688), and (2) philosophical dimensions, related to the way we metaphorically conceive of time (see Radden 2004; see Cook 2006b: 441–42), which I discuss in further detail in chap. 4.

---

67. Goldfajn (1998: 100) also find significance in word order changes that accompany verb alternation as signaling temporal shifts, for example, the subject-verb order with *qatal* as interrupting the narrative flow of verb-subject *wayyiqtol* (see §2.4.2.2. above).

2.4.3.3. Conclusion

Discourse-prominent theories as a whole have been among the most influential force in the discussion of the BHVS. In this concluding section, I want to underscore some distinctive features of these theories and provide a preliminary critique of discourse-prominent theory vis-à-vis semantic theory, which will provide a starting point for the much more extensive discussion in chap. 4.

The central features in discourse-prominent analyses of the BHVS are the oppositions of sequentiality : nonsequentiality, foreground : background, and narrative : speech. Unfortunately, these phenomena are not consistently defined—especially sequentiality—if they are defined at all, and they are often assumed to be coterminus with each other; that is, sequential events are foregrounded events in narrative, whereas direct speech features nonsequential and often background events (versus the surrounding narrative material). The first portion of chap. 4 (§4.1–2) is therefore devoted to examining these phenomena and their interrelationship.

Despite a large degree of uniformity among discourse-prominent theories, different conclusions emerge depending on whether the model takes as its starting point the Longacre approach or the Schneider. The most notable difference is that the Schneider school focuses on the narrative-speech distinction, whereas the Longacre school works with a variety of text-types. The latter is open to criticism with respect to both the utility (see Niccacci 1994b: 119) and the soundness of the determination of these text-types. It is especially unclear how such notional text-types are to be distinguished from literary genre (so Michael O'Connor, private communication, 2006). The result of these different starting points is subtle but important: in the Schneider school, the major divide in the BHVS comes between *wayyiqtol* and *yiqtol* (or in some cases *qatal*), the former belonging to narrative as the latter does to speech; by contrast, in the Longacre school, the primary distinction made is between the temporally successive *waw*-prefixed forms and the other forms. What appears evident here is that Longacre's approach places Ewald's 19th-century "consecutive" theory on a new foundation of "discourse analysis." This assessment is confirmed by Longacre's semantic understanding of the *waw*-prefixed forms (e.g., he begins with GKC and faults it not for being erroneous as much as for being incomplete; Longacre 1994: 50; 2003: 62); and studies such as Gross's (1976), in which he argues for a consecutive understanding of *wayyiqtol* in a more sophisticated linguistic framework than Ewald.

My central critique of discourse-prominent theory with regard to the BHVS, which has arisen at various points throughout the preceding survey, is that the functional identifications of the verb forms apart from attention to semantics is methodologically problematic. In the most extreme cases, a semantic component of certain verbal forms is denied altogether (e.g., Baayen 1997 on *qatal*). More often, however, the theories proceed from discourse-pragmatic functions to forms but fail to persuade because of the numerous exceptions to their function-form correlations. Talstra (1992: 284) lauded Schneider's theory as more sound than other discourse theories because he proceeded instead from form to function, but Talstra (1978: 174) likewise recognized that Schneider's theory suffered from a neglect of semantics. DeRouchie (2007), having heeded my earlier criticism of discourse theories on this point (Cook 2004b), has attempted a corrective in which semantics is seen as a necessary first step to sound discourse-pragmatic analysis. In chap. 4, I present a semantics-based approach to these discourse-pragmatic issues, based on my theory of the BHVS presented in chap. 3.

To take this criticism further: the correlations between function and form by discourse linguists fail for several reasons, each of which will be elaborated on in chap. 4. First, they are inadequate as the sole means of distinguishing forms, because the correlations do not hold up consistently. It is not a viable solution to hold that the correlations do not need to be consistent (e.g., Talstra 1992: 284; Li 1999: 227); statements of this sort only demonstrate the inadequacy of discourse function to distinguish among verbal forms. Second, the correlation between functions and forms is problematically circular in that the correlated form and function are mutually identifying (e.g., *wayyiqtol* belongs to narrative discourse because it denotes sequential, foregrounded events, and these are sequential, foregrounded events in narrative discourse because they are expressed by *wayyiqtol*). This sort of analysis must presume that each (the form or the function) is determined independently of its correlation, but this cannot be the case when semantics is eschewed and replaced with discourse-pragmatics.

2.5. Hebrew Verb Theory at the Beginning of the 21st Century

The preceding survey has illustrated how several methodological issues have featured centrally in the debate over the BHVS throughout the past half century. Therefore, these issues serve as a ready agenda for the methodological discussion in chap. 3 and generally as cruces that must be addressed by any successful theory of the BHVS. The first of these is the *diachrony versus synchrony* debate: should the BHVS be studied as a system of a single language stage, or should comparative and historical materials inform our understanding of the meanings of the forms? This debate was brought about in large measure by the extraordinary advances in comparative and historical grammar of the Semitic languages in the first half of the 20th century along with the hegemonic rise of structuralist linguistics (notably after de Saussure) and its view that diachrony and synchrony are two separate approaches to be kept distinct at all times. The effects can be seen in the fact that theories up through the 1950s–60s tended without exception to allow diachronic data to inform their analyses, but the trend since the 1970s has been toward analyzing the BHVS "as a (sychronic) system," thus marginalizing if not altogether dismissing diachronic data. The verbal forms that lie at the center of this debate are *wayyiqtol* and *yiqtol*, because of the great importance often attached to the diachronic evidence for a short **yaqtul* and a long **yaqtulu* underlying these two forms, respectively.

Unfortunately, Hebraists, just as much as biblical scholars, have yet to resolve the question how to apply a "synchronic" approach to a composite (i.e., temporally disparate) text such as the Hebrew Bible. More pointedly, however, the perspective that lies at the center of this debate is problematic. In earlier studies, I objected to the terms of this debate—that diachrony and synchrony are mutually exclusive options for the analysis of the BHVS—on the basis of criticism of de Saussure's strict distinction between diachrony and synchrony, and I pointed out that Hebraists have failed to remain consistently synchronic even when they have consciously sought to take this sort of approach (see Cook 2001: 122; 2002: 191–94). Since then, I have come to recognize that the problem with the synchrony-diachrony debate lies at a more basic level of linguistic understanding: Hebraists have generally incorrectly assumed that *wayyiqtol* must be construed as related both formally and semantically to *yiqtol* if diachronic data is made inadmissible. However, "synchronic" studies (cf. Michel 1960; Kustár 1972) as well as diachronic demonstrate that these forms differ in meaning and function to such a degree as to make them distinct though partially homonymous (disregarding for the moment the *wa*C- prefix) conjugations regardless of their etymology. An argument for homonymy does not need to rest on any diachronic data but can to be supported by a synchronic analysis of the distribution of the two forms.

The second issue, closely correlated to the first, is *meaning versus function* in the description of the BHVS. Concomitant with the shift from diachronic to synchronic description, there has been a movement away from description of meaning (often based on etymology) to the function of verb forms (within a synchronic system). This reflects to some degree the development in linguistics generally (from a concern for semantics to pragmatics) and is represented by the move toward discourse analysis, which is concerned more with the function of the verb forms within a discourse than the meaning attached to the individual form itself.

Objections to the abandonment of meaning for verb forms in favor of "functional" analyses have been raised by linguists (e.g., Comrie 1985) and Hebraists (e.g., Joüon [and Muraoka] 2006: xviii–xix) alike on the grounds that verbs have a discernible meaning apart from their discourse context. Although context crucially informs the meaning/function of words, to deny thereby that a word has any discernible meaning or a fuzzy meaning at best goes against the well-established Fregean principle of compositionality that meaning is a product of the contribution of individual components. What is the contribution of the verbal morphology to the interpretation of the form in context—whether word-level, sentence-level, or discourse-level? Word-level semantic analysis of the BHVS is therefore valid, even if discourse-level functional analysis is important. Instead of either-or, the real debate is with regard to the priority of semantic (meaning) versus pragmatic (functional) analyses, which I address in chap. 4.

However, even when there is not an actual eschewal of meaning, confusion between form and meaning has often permeated the rhetoric about the BHVS. Remarks such as those of Rainey and Buth, quoted above (§2.4.3.2), illustrate the confusion, and Hendel's essay (1996) on the BHVS illustrates the end result. Although Hendel's study provides important clarifications of all the TAM notional categories that may be expressed by the BHVS, he fails to grapple fully with the questions which category or categories are morphologically marked by each verb form and how do the morphologically marked TAM values interact with the various expressions of TAM in the text. Approaches such as Hendel's are "functionalist" inasmuch as they are satisfied with simply providing a taxonomy of TAM categories that may be expressed by the various verb forms, without taking the additional step of explaining which categories are associated with each verb form in which contexts. Andrason's recent publications (2010; 2011a; 2011b; 2011c; forthcoming) are especially egregious in this regard, because he argues that, as long as the many meanings for a form can be related to each other in some typologically coherent way, the problem of the BHVS is "solved." An approach of this sort makes it meaningless to ask whether the BHVS is tense, aspect, or modality, simply because *functionally* it is all of these! More seriously, however, such approaches at once insist that the forms have a breadth of meaning dependent on context while not bothering to explain the semantics that the verb forms contribute to the context. It appears that word-level semantics remains a valid question if the discourse-pragmatic functions of these verbal conjugations are to be fully understood.

The third issue is the *problem of induction*, by which I mean the difficulty in verifying meaning or function based simply on an inductive examination of the text. The never-ending debates are in large part due to the lack of any external means of evaluating the verb data in the Hebrew Bible. It is no coincidence that, for example, speakers of tensed languages (particularly of Modern Hebrew) generally view BH as a tensed language. Rather, it is an almost unavoidable outcome of the inductive study of the BHVS that the structure of the research language is imposed on the ancient Hebrew language.

In linguistic analyses of modern languages, native-speaker intuition goes a long way toward correcting this problem. Obviously, however, there exists no such corrective for ancient languages. Instead, statistics have been perceived as a means of bolstering one theory over competing theories in BH verb discussions. Unfortunately, statistics too often lead to a false sense of "objectivity," when in fact statistics are only raw data in need of interpretation through a more or less successful theoretical lens. How then are competing theories to be judged? As with all interpretation, the questions that they must answer are: Does this theory explain more data more satisfactorily than any other? But to whose satisfaction? Generally, each interpreter's theory is to his/her own satisfaction the best theory, so there needs to be some objective means by which competing models may be judged. In chap. 3, I argue that typology appears to be invaluable for evaluating competing models, because it asks in light of the ever-increasing data from the world's languages whether a particular theory is typologically "believable/reasonable" or "anomalous."

Typology, therefore, appears to be an especially useful tool for the study of ancient languages, because it provides an external means of judging the results of inductive study—namely: Is the model of the language typologically believable or is it typologically anomalous? The value of typology has already been shown preliminarily in my criticism of relative-tense theories above: they are typologically anomalous (§2.4.2.3). A typological approach suited particularly to the chronologically disparate writings of the Hebrew Bible is presented in chap. 3.

Chapter 3

The Semantics of the
Biblical Hebrew Verbal System

The preceding two chapters have been groundwork for the semantic and discourse-pragmatic treatments of the BHVS presented in this and the subsequent chapter, respectively. I began in chap. 1 with a historically oriented discussion of TAM, concluding with a modest formalization of the TAM parameters most relevant to the semantic discussion in this chapter. In chap. 2, I sketched the history and *status quaestionis* of the BHVS, which provided both the requisite "background knowledge" for the proceeding discussion and hinted at the direction a successful semantic theory of the BHVS might take.

Before discussing the BH data themselves, I need to clarify and justify the particular approach I am taking here. This discussion necessarily entails a pretheoretical discussion of terms and concepts basic to linguistic semantics.

3.1. Theoretical Considerations

Several issues must be discussed up front regarding my approach to the BHVS. These can be organized conveniently against the backdrop of three fundamental Saussurean structuralist distinctions: language (*la langue*) versus speech (*parole*); synchrony versus diachrony; and signal (*signifiant*) versus signification (*signifé*; see Matthews 2001: 10–20). This discussion is followed by a more specific description of the approach I take to the BHVS in this and the following chapter.

3.1.1. Basic Principles

Saussure distinguished within *langage* ('language') between *la langue* ('the language system') and *parole* ('speech'): "from the very outset we must put both feet on the ground of language [*la langue*] and use language as the norm of all other manifestations of speech [*langage*] to it" (Saussure 1959: 9).[1] The "substantialist" approach to language (particularly typology) presents a challenge to the Saussurean emphasis on structure.[2] In their study of TAM in the world's languages, Bybee, Perkins, and Pagliuca (1994: 1) state:

---

1. "[I]l faut se placer de prime abord sur le terrain de la langue et la prendre pour norme de toutes les autres manifestations du langage" (Saussure 1995: 25).

2. Taylor (2003: 7) notes that prototype theory (discussed below) likewise rejects this structuralist dictum that languages should be studied as closed systems of oppositions.

We do not take the structuralist position that each language represents a tidy system in which units are defined by the oppositions they enter into and the object of study is the internal system the units are supposed to create. Rather, we consider it more profitable to view languages as composed of substance—both semantic substance and phonetic substance. Structure or system, the traditional focus of linguistic inquiry, is the product of, rather than the creator of, substance.

However, in contrasting the structuralist and substantialist approaches to TAM, Lindstedt (2001: 770) rightly points out that "the traditional structuralist approach retains part of its value; the notion of opposition especially cannot be dismissed. The perfective and imperfective aspect, for instance, cannot be conceived of without each other, and obviously a language with only one tense gram would have no tense grams."

It seems that some sort of compromise position is required, and indeed compromise seems eminently possible. The position that Bybee, Perkins, and Pagliuca (1994) take is a reaction to structuralism's view that language structures are noncomparable between languages. And so they argue that, while the structures may vary, the substance is comparable—with which I agree in regard to categories of TAM. But their disregarding of system can be attributed largely to their focus on TAM categories *across the world's languages*. By contrast, my interest is in using these sorts of typological data to analyze a *particular language's* TAM system. Therefore, even if language-internal systems such as the BHVS are "epiphenomenal," as Bybee, Perkins, and Pagliuca (1994: 1) claim, they require attention within a descriptive linguistic account of the grammar of a particular language. I also eschew the extreme functionalist position of teleological arguments for form, and here I am in full agreement with Bybee, Perkins, and Pagliuca (1994: 297), who state, "Our approach to explanations differs from that of some other researchers examining grammaticalization in that we do not appeal to motivations or to functional teleology. That is, we do not subscribe to the notion that languages develop grammatical categories because they NEED them."

Another important Saussurean distinction is the distinction between synchrony and diachrony, which follows from the previous distinction. Given that the focus of linguistics is on the *state* of a language system (*la langue*), "the linguist who wishes to understand a state must discard all knowledge of everything that produced it and ignore diachrony" (Saussure 1959: 81).[3] Disputes over the usefulness of this distinction have arisen in part through different interpretations of Saussure's distinction. Reflecting on Heine, Claudi, and Hünnemeyer's (1991:1) characterization of structuralism as claiming that "linguistic description must be strictly synchronic," Newmeyer (1998: 290) writes, "Perhaps Heine et al. mean that generativists believe that synchrony

---

3. "[L]e linguiste qui veut comprendre cet état doit-il faire table rase de tout ce qui l'a produit et ignorer la diachronie" (Saussure 1995: 117)

and diachrony can be *understood* in total isolation from each other. But this too is incorrect. A particular synchronic stage of a language is, in part, a product of children's reanalyses of an earlier synchronic stage. In that way, synchrony and diachrony are inseparable." On reconsideration of the matter, I reject my earlier endorsement of Heine, Claudi, and Hünnemeyer's "panchronic" rhetoric (Cook 2001: 122; 2002: 191–94) and adopt the argument that, unless language systems change through some means other than "cross-generational and cross-lectal transmission," the notion of panchronic is nonsense (Joseph and Janda 1988: 194).[4]

All this said, it is not surprising that typology has long embraced a diachronic dimension of analysis (see Greenberg 1978), given its empirical methods and association with functionalism's substantialist approach to language. Bybee, Perkins, and Pagliuca (1994: 3–4) list four reasons for their taking a diachronic approach to typology of the TAM categories, three of which I list here by way of endorsement. First, diachrony increases the explanatory power of the theory. This is affirmed by the more recent comment on causal explanations in typology by Moravcsik (2007: 39): "[T]here is no need to choose between synchronic and diachronic accounts: synchrony is what diachrony explains." Second, given that language is constantly changing, it is unnecessarily limiting to examine "only a thin synchronic slice" (Bybee, Perkins, and Pagliuca 1994: 4). Rather, and third, "[S]imilarities among languages are more easily seen from a diachronic perspective." I would add to these arguments that the diversity of the data for the BHVS (i.e., cross-generational as well as cross-lectal) argue in favor of attention to diachronics. Arguably, in the absence of native speaker linguistic tests, diachronics (and particularly diachronic typology) remains the only truly viable external "control" on the analysis of BH grammar.[5]

Finally, Saussure distinguished between *signal* ("signifiant") and *signification* ("signifé") unified in the idea of the sign: "I call the combination of a concept and a sound-image a sign. . . . I propose to retain the word *sign* [*signe*] to designate the whole and to replace concept and sound-image respectively

---

4. Andrason's recent (2010; 2011a; 2011b; 2011c; forthcoming) advocacy for panchronic explanations of the BHVS only underscore the weakness of such an approach, which pays little attention to the BH verbal system *as a system* and is content with a taxonomy of unranked functions for individual forms.

5. I have made this case in Cook 2012, where I explore the possibility that the use of diachronic typology as an external control may enable us to date portions of the Hebrew Bible relatively based on the development of the verbal system, among other things. This approach using diachronic typology as the means of validation is directly in contrast to the statistics-based approach followed in recent years, aided especially by computer databases (see chap. 2).

by *signified* [*signifié*] and *signifier* [*signifiant*]" (Saussure 1959: 67).[6] While Saussure's mentalist view of the sign (i.e., the sign signifies a "concept") is an important development,[7] his simplistic understanding of an immediate relation between signal and signification required revision. Jespersen (1924: 56), for example, noted that the multiplicity of meanings for a given form could be dealt with by positing a "function" that would mediate between the "form" and its many meanings, which he termed "notions." Similarly, Jakobson (1936), in his study of cases in Russian, distinguished between a general meaning ("Gesamtbedeutung") for each case and individual meanings ("Sonderbedeutungen") that could be explained by reference to the general and specific contexts in which they appear.[8]

In this way, both Jespersen and Jakobson sought to preserve categorical discreteness and invariability of meaning that constitutes the classical approach to categorization. Taylor (2003: 21) summarizes the classical approach to categorization as having four basic assumptions: (1) categories are defined in terms of a conjunction of necessary and sufficient features; (2) features are binary; (3) categories have clear boundaries; (4) all members of a category have equal status. In recent years, the "prototype" theory, rooted in Wittgenstein's idea of "family resemblances," has been presented as a significant alternative to the

---

6. "Nous appelons *signe* la combinaison du concept et de l'image acoustique. . . . Nous proposons de conserver le mot *signe* pour désigner le total, et de remplacer *concept* et *image acoustique* respectivement par *signifié* et *signifiant*" (Saussure 1995: 99).

7. Frege's distinction (1892) between "Sinn" (sense) and "Bedeutung" (reference) betrays the earlier thinking in philosophy that reference was most basic to semantics (compare with the alternative opposition in German between *Bedeutung* ['meaning'] and *Bezeichnung* ['designation']; see Lyons 1977: 199). Compare the related distinction made by Mill (1843) between *connotation* and *denotation*, which has affinities with the more recent *intensional-extensional* distinction (see Lyons 1977: 175–76).

8. Jakobson used markedness theory to explain individual meanings with reference to general meanings. The usefulness of markedness theory in preserving the invariability of meaning for a category can be seen by comparing Jakobson's approach with Dahl's discussion of the difficulties of determining "basic meaning" of a word or form (Dahl 1985: 9–10). Dahl notes that *dog* defined extensionally or prototypically refers to the species *Canis canis*, but defined intensionally, according to the most narrow meaning, it refers to the male member of the species. By contrast, treating the issue in terms of markedness leads us to posit a privative marked opposition between *dog* and *bitch*, whereby the latter refers to the female member of the species and the former is unmarked for sex, thus referring to either the male member of the species or the entire species regardless of sex (see Jakobson 1932 for a parallel example using the Russian terms for 'donkey'; and Matthews 2001: 123 for another parallel using *drake* and *duck*, based on Jakobson's study). Lindstedt (2001: 769) points out a weakness of markedness (particular privative oppositions) for semantic theory based on Dahl's remarks (1985: 19): to call a form "unmarked" for some feature essentially means that it is semantically empty and thereby not subject to testable hypotheses since any unexpected uses can be interpreted in terms of "neutralization."

classical model.[9] Unfortunately, it has too often been characterized as the only real alternative to the classical model (for a critique, see Wierzbicka 1990; 1996: 148–69) and as the inevitable choice of theory for functionalists:

> It might be expected, then, that functionalist accounts of language would reject the classical, Aristotelian concept of classification, under which entities can be classified in terms of sets of necessary and sufficient features, in favour of some version of the approach to non-discreteness which, prompted by Wittgenstein's philosophical observations on "family resemblance" models of meaning, have been developed, largely by psychologists, into what is now generally known as "prototype theory." (Butler 2003: 28)[10]

The approach I take here to the meaning of TAM categories, however, is much closer to the classical model than any sort of prototype theory (cf. Cook 2002: 198–200; Dahl 1985: 3–19). In particular, I view TAM categories as discrete and their meanings as invariable. With regard to discreteness, the prototype theory to my mind has not successfully addressed the argument of Frege (1980: 159) based on the principle of the excluded middle: "To a concept without sharp boundary there would correspond an area that had not a sharp boundary-line all round, but in places just vaguely faded away into the background. This would not really be an area at all; and likewise a concept that is not sharply defined is wrongly termed a concept." With regard to invariability, Aristotle's distinction between defining and accidental properties remains a powerful principle. For example, in contrast to Dahl (1985: 9), who sees perfective aspect simply as the more "dominant" feature alongside past tense in defining the category of Perfective, using Aristotle's distinction we can distinguish perfective aspect as the defining property, while past tense is an accidental property that can be explained in terms of implication (e.g.,

---

9. The relevant passage in Wittgenstein follows (2009: §66–67; see Taylor 2003: chaps. 3–4):

If you look at them you will not see something in common to all, but similarities, affinities, and a whole series of them at that. . . . I can think of no better expression to characterize these similarities than "family resemblances"; for the various resemblances between members of a family—build, features, colour of eyes, gait, temperament, and so on and so forth—overlap and criss-cross in the same way.

Denn, wenn du sie anschaust, wirst du zwar nicht etwas sehen, was *allen* gemeinsam wäre, aber du wirst Ähnlichkeiten, Verwandtschaften, sehen, und zwar eine ganze Reihe. . . . Ich kann diese Ähnlichkeiten nicht besser charakterisieren, als durch das Wort "Familienähnlichkeiten"; denn so übergreifen und kreuzen sich die verschiedenen Ähnlichkeiten, die zwischen den Gliedern einer Familie bestehen: Wuchs, Gesichtszüge, Augenfarbe, Gang, Temperament, etc. etc.

10. Newmeyer (1998: 289) makes the point that linguists working with grammaticalization often confuse data and analysis (i.e., grammar) with consequent effects on categorization. That is, they mistake the historical development of forms across categories to mean that categories are not discrete. However, with a grammar (i.e., analysis) of those data at any particular synchronic level, the categories are discrete.

C. S. Smith [2006] explains the default past time implication of perfective verbs as due to the property of "boundedness," which perfective aspect effects; see further chap. 4). An extension of this principle from Aristotle is found in the "two-level" approach to lexical semantics (see Bierwisch and Schreuder 1992), which distinguishes between linguistic and encyclopedic or conceptual meaning.[11] This sort of approach is consonant with the modular view of grammar that likewise informed Jakobson's general-individual meaning distinction. To illustrate, note the English Past Tense specimen cited by Matthews (2001: 121–22) as an example of a non–past tense use of the form: *If I planted a tree tomorrow*. Although the form does not express past temporal reference here, its specific meaning can be explained by reference to its general meaning and its syntactic context. Specifically, the meaning of the past tense form is extended via the past time–irrealis metaphor to denote an unreal condition within the syntactic context of a conditional protasis.[12]

At the same time, I question the usefulness of the classical binary features with regard to categories of TAM. Rather, Wierzbicka (1996) has made a convincing case that discrete semantic primes exist as the building block of language meaning without recourse to binary features inherited from phonological theory. In treating TAM categories, I define them in detail and with a modest degree of formalism in chap. 1 but not in terms of binary features. These categories are treated as the primes of TAM in the world's languages by Dahl (1985), Bybee and Dahl (1989), and Bybee, Perkins, and Pagliuca (1994). On analogy with Wierzbicka's primes, I consider the TAM "gram-types" to be the basic building blocks of TAM systems such as the BHVS, and thus I concur with Lindstedt's observation (2001: 770) that classifying certain forms as tense or as aspect or as modality (or as tense-prominent, etc.)

---

11. Taylor (2003: 162–64) criticizes the two-level approach on the empirical basis that it requires the view that we store only highly abstract representations of words rather than specific, context-rich meanings. In his remarks he moves from objecting to abstract representations to admitting that perhaps both sorts exist, so that language acquisition proceeds horizontally (relatedness among specific meanings) and vertically (ever increasing abstraction as more data is learned). In so doing, he reveals a basic weakness of his critique: if the specific meanings are stored as part of a language system, why would we ever need to abstract meanings? In other words, he has admitted that abstract meanings exist in the mind without assigning them a cognitive role. This weakness may derive in large part from his focus on language *acquisition* rather than linguistic structure. In any case, his learning model does not seem to be a serious objection to the general claim that linguistic meaning is abstracted from its context-specific uses so that language users can see the connection between otherwise disparate looking meanings. For an example of a learning model that rejects fuzzy categories, see Sassoon 2005.

12. With respect to prototypical theory, I am sympathetic with Wierzbicka's observations (1990: 347–67]) that "In too many cases, these new ideas have been treated as an excuse for intellectual laziness and sloppiness. In my view, the notion of prototype has to prove its usefulness through semantic description, not through semantic theorizing."

is relatively unimportant, given that perfective, past, subjunctive, and so on are seen as the real building blocks of TAM systems, not the supercategories of tense, aspect, and modality. Given this background, I want to be clear that in my use of perfective, imperfective, directive-volitive, and so forth to describe the various BH conjugations I am associating these conjugations with cross-linguistic gram-types, a purpose that serves to validate the identification and explicate the functions associated with the conjugation.[13] Further, the use of diachronic typology means that my use of these labels is intended to associate a given conjugation with a particular diachrony (e.g., resultative-perfective or progressive-imperfective).

3.1.2. Goals of a Semantic Theory

A fairly uncontroversial statement is that a successful semantic analysis of the BHVS should identify the meaning of each of the various verbal conjugations as they are used to refer to states of affairs in linguistic expressions and should delineate the systematic meaning relationships among the conjugations, including explaining semantic ambiguities among them. These goals, which are adapted from Cann's (1993: 1) description of the requirements of a semantic theory, presume the principles of compositionality and correspondence theory of truth that were introduced in §1.7.1 (see there for discussion) and are listed again here:

1. *The principle of compositionality*: The meaning of an expression is a monotonic function of the meaning of its parts and they way they are put together. (Cann 1993: 4)

---

13. This point needs to be made forcefully because of traditional terms of the debate, in which the identification of a form as "perfective" (or some other label) assumes that the form is barred from expressing anything but that narrowly defined semantic value. Andrason (2010: 22 n. 30) correctly notes, referencing Dahl (2000), that a *gram* (an abbreviated reference to *grammatical structure*, used in order to avoid the restrictiveness of traditional categories, such as *verb*; see Bybee, Perkins, and Pagliuca 1994: 2) is made up of an amalgam of meanings associated with its diachronic path of development. However, this should not be taken to mean, as Andrason implies by his critique of my "dominant" value labeling of the forms, that we can dispense with discrete, universal categories altogether, which would leave us at an extreme position of categorical particularism that bars any typological comparison with the BH verbal conjugations. While Andrason's approach to associating the conjugations with a particular diachrony alleviates some of the difficulties he finds with maintaining discrete categories, he correctly recognizes (Andrason 2010: 33 n. 48) that I have taken this approach in my work. But even this association of conjugation with a given diachrony does not obviate the value of determining a cross-linguistically valid gram-type for a given conjugation, nor is it any less important to discern between more dominant and less dominant functions/meanings for a form in order to place it accurately along its diachrony. This point also clearly distinguishes the task of semantically formalizing tense, aspect, and modality in chap. 1 and the identification, in light of the understanding afforded by this analysis, of the BH conjugations with a given gram-type, each of which represents an amalgam of TAM values.

2. *The correspondence theory of truth*: A statement in some language is true if, and only if, it corresponds to some state-of-affairs. (Cann 1993: 15, 18)

My restatement of goals assumes the preceding discussion about meanings and categories. Thus, my theory needs to identify an invariable "general" meaning for each conjugation from among the various discrete TAM categories (see chap. 1), and it also must describe "specific" meanings that can be accounted for in terms of the general invariable meaning and contextual factors, either syntactic or pragmatic.

More difficult than determining the goals of a semantic theory of the BHVS is determining the methods for reaching these goals. I begin by explaining why some approaches are unsuccessful followed by an introduction to the approach taken here. The approach of generative grammar, which sees the first goal of a grammar as to adjudicate between grammatical (or well-formed) and ungrammatical (ill-formed) sentences, has lead to the widespread use of linguistic tests and native-speaker intuition to determine grammaticality. An approach of this sort seems inherently problematic for trying to describe a grammar of an ancient language represented only in a closed corpus of texts, such as BH is. We have no recourse to native-speaker intuitions, and linguistic tests are difficult to create and often must assume what they are trying to prove or else they fail to take into account other factors besides the factors in focus. For example, we do not seem to get very far devising a test to determine the grammaticality of *yiqtol* or the Participle to describe a state of affairs ongoing at the time of speaking (e.g., אני עומד פה vs. אעמוד פה 'I am standing here'). The fact is that we cannot mimic native-speaker intuition well enough to evaluate fully why the participle or *yiqtol* might be more grammatical in this context. Consider the parallel contrast in English between *I am standing here* and *I stand here.* Although a native English speaker will choose the former to describe a state of affairs ongoing at the time of speaking, the test of a simple choice fails to capture the essence of the distinction between the English Simple Present and Present Progressive in terms of the former's having an implication of habituality. Should the English Simple Present by this comparison be excluded from the category of present tense? The answer appears to be "no" in light of its reference to events ongoing at the time of speaking, albeit within the narrow sociolinguistic context of play-by-play reportative speech at sporting events (see C. S. Smith 1997: 185).

We must be content, then, with taking a *purely descriptive* approach with respect to the grammaticality of the sentences found in the corpus of BH. We must, of course, balance the premise of grammaticality with a healthy suspicion of the text due to its long transmission history and belated explicit marking of vocalization. A case in point is the distinction between *wayyiqtol* and *waw + yiqtol* in the Masoretic Text: this distinction was not denoted (with vowel points and *dagesh*) in manuscripts until long after the former conjugation had fallen out of use. As a result, the possibility that the text has been altered (by scribes or the Masoretes) through grammatical misunderstanding (not to mention inadvertent changes) must always remain open. (This seems to be especially true in Psalms, where the temporal reference of many portions is ambiguous, and therefore the context is less helpful in deciding the cases.) Cases such as these are especially problematic when we are dealing with unvocalized texts, such as the Dead Sea Scrolls, where an analysis of the prefix forms may presume a priori in which contexts each form is grammatically acceptable—a seemingly problematic assumption (Penner 2006).

A similar sort of a priori understanding of the BHVS seems to underlie the widespread and favored use of statistics (e.g., Furuli 2006; Penner 2006). The use of statistics provides a misleading sense of objectivity and definitiveness to the enterprise, because it mimics empirical science. However, in the end the statistics only serve as a tally of the interpreter's subjective and often predetermined semantic interpretation of the forms of the BHVS. Statistics cannot serve to validate semantic interpretation, which still partakes of human enterprise. Statistics are only valid when they tally objectively measurable things, such as the number of times a distinctly Jussive form of the verb appears clause initially (e.g., Shulman 1996). Statistical studies are even unnecessary for gathering the requisite data for analysis, because their results are readily available in the standard reference grammars, old and more-recent, including examples of both "standard" meanings (e.g., Waltke and O'Connor 1990; van der Merwe, Kroeze, and Naudé 1999) and "inexplicable" uses (e.g., Gesenius 1910; Joüon 1923). The real challenge, then, is validation: How can one validate a theory of the BHVS?

One answer to this question is to avoid it and settle instead for a taxonomy of syntactic and discourse "uses" of the verb forms. The approach of syntactic taxonomy as theory can be traced back to Moran (2003) and seen in the works of Rainey (e.g., 2003a) and his students (e.g., Zewi 1999). Not only do these taxonomies fail to provide a theory of linguistic structure, they lead to unwarranted implications that the correlation between form and syntactic context is causal (i.e., this specific meaning can be explained as contingent on this particular syntactic context). This is the case because they ultimately can only offer a list of "specific" meanings for forms when what is desired is a "general" meaning for each form to which the specific meanings can be reasonably related.[14] The same criticism may be leveled at discourse studies, which merely

---

14. Despite his employing a much more sophisticated semantic theory, a similar criticism can be leveled at Andrason (2010; 2011a; 2011b; 2011c; forthcoming), who is content with a taxonomy of meanings for each BH verb form that is "cognitively coherent" without any concern for either relating the varied functions to a general meaning or ranking the meanings in any way for a given form. Thus, he essentially advocates the abandonment of any sort of general-specific distinction in meaning (e.g., Jakobson) in favor of an amalgam

replace sentence syntax with discourse-pragmatic context as their taxonomic basis (e.g., Heller 2004). The correlative *observations* of these studies cannot replace the need for *explanations* in terms of the general meaning that each verbal conjugation contributes to the various syntactic and discourse contexts (Frege's principle of compositionality). In this chapter, the interaction of semantics with syntax is addressed, while discourse context is treated in chap. 4.

3.1.3. Diachronic Typology and Grammaticalization

Turning back to the knotty issue of how a theory of the BHVS may be validated, we reach a presentation and justification of the particular approach in this book, an approach built on the ideas and data from diachronic typology and grammaticalization studies of the world's verbal systems. The preceding observations about the inadequate means of validation in other approaches is adequate justification for turning to diachronic typology and grammaticalization studies. Given competing analyses of a grammatical construction (here the BHVS and/or its individual components), there is no real alternative but to turn to factors that are "external" to the language system itself, such as language change, or what other TAM systems look like, in order to arbitrate between the competing descriptions. As Haspelmath (2004: 574) succinctly states it: "What I am saying here is that external evidence is the only type of evidence that can give us some hints about how to choose between two different observationally adequate descriptions." In this section, I provide an introduction to diachronic typology and grammaticalization studies, anticipating their role in elucidating and validating the following analysis of the BHVS, and I provide additional justification for the approach along the way.

Typology may be described in terms of its two main procedures: the classification of languages in terms of a given linguistic structure, and the development of generalizations regarding the pattern of a given linguistic structure across languages. These two phases, though complementary, should not be seen as strictly ordered. They may be referred to conveniently, following Croft (2003: 1), as *typological classification* and *typological generalization*. The typological classification of TAM systems in the world's languages (e.g., Dahl 1985; Bybee and Dahl 1989; and Bybee, Perkins, and Pagliuca 1991) provides an important tool for assessing models of the BHVS in lieu of native speakers by providing "statistical tendencies" regarding types of TAM systems in the world's languages (Newmeyer 1998: 350). Historically, the study of the BHVS has suffered from idiosyncratic analyses that find no support among the recent typological classifications (e.g., the *waw hahippuk* theory of the *waw*-prefixed verbal forms).

---

of meaning, the distribution or ranking of which is unknown nor of interest. Although approaches of this sort may be theoretically sound, they are practically useless to the philological task of understanding the language of the Hebrew Bible.

Bickel (2007) notes that in recent years typology has escaped its narrow confines of being merely another tool for determining universals of grammar and shifted its focus from the former question of "what's possible?" to "what's where why?"[15] Because of the long-standing conviction that typological distributions are "historically grown," this shift of inquiry has brought with it a concomitant increased interest in historical explanations and what is referred to as *diachronic typology* (so Croft 2003: chap. 8). Croft (2003: 233) explains: "In diachronic typology, synchronic language states are reanalyzed as stages in the process of language change." Diachronic typology therefore seeks not simply to classify language types but shifts between types, because language states "are seen as the product of type transitions and diachronic processes in general" (Bickel 2007: 239). Thus, as Moravcsik (2007: 39) states, "[T]here is no need to choose between synchronic and diachronic accounts: synchrony is what diachrony explains."[16]

A field closely associated with diachronic typology (it "emerged from" the latter according to Croft 2003: 253) is *grammaticalization*. The term *grammaticalization* refers to both a type of diachronic change in language—wherein lexical items become grammatical items or grammatical items become more grammatical—and a framework for examining diachronic changes (Hopper and Traugott 2003: 1–2). The process of grammaticalization has been recognized for almost a century; the term was coined by Antoine Meillet in 1912 (Fr. *grammaticalisation*; see Hopper and Traugott 2003: chap. 2). However, the more recent development of "grammaticalization theory," composed of various "principles" recognized with respect to grammaticalization processes (see Hopper 1991; Bybee, Perkins, and Pagliuca 1994: 9–22), has increasingly been severely criticized (see esp. Newmeyer 1998: chap. 5). Campbell (2001: 113) has noted that grammaticalization has only a "derivative" status, because it can be reduced in every instance to a combination of diachronic processes known independently from grammaticalization theory (e.g., reanalysis and analogy). For this reason, grammaticalization theory has, at best, a "heuristic" value within diachronic typological research (Campbell 2001: 158). Similarly, Newmeyer (1998: chap. 5) has argued that grammaticalization is "epiphenomenal" and not properly a "theory." More importantly, he criticizes the circularity of constructing a theory of grammaticalization based on reconstructions that presume the validity of the theory. My use of grammaticalization studies in

---

15. This shift in inquiry is complete enough to prompt Nichols (2007: 232) to write: "Typological theory is almost entirely unconcerned from distinguishing possible from impossible languages."

16. To illustrate her case, Moravcsik (2007: 37) cites Dryer (2007: 246), who notes that, although language function often describes typological explanations for language structure, this is simply a loose way of saying that language function reflects diachrony, which in turn explains language structure (see there for his examples).

constructing a theory of the BHVS is limited to drawing on their data, which exhibit important statistical tendencies with respect to the way that TAM systems develop.

Each of these three successively more-narrow areas of study—linguistic typology, diachronic typology, and grammaticalization studies—contribute to the framework, tools, and data for the following description of the BHVS. To begin with, the wealth of data on the world's verbal systems provides an external means of validation of a model of the BHVS, by placing restrictions on what constitutes possible and impossible verbal systems. [17] In other words, below, I use typological arguments (generalizations) based on the various typological classifications of the world's TAM systems to argue for the most "plausible" semantic identification of the various verb forms in the BHVS. The two main sorts of typological generalization are the *unrestricted* and the *implicational*: unrestricted generalizations hold across all languages (e.g., all languages have vowels); implicational generalizations connect otherwise unrelated phenomena in languages (e.g., if a language has nasal vowels, then it has oral vowels; see Croft 2003: 52–59). All generalizations of this sort have to do with the distribution of linguistic properties—both the diversity and the uniformity of languages; they inform us not only of what is possible but what is probable and what is necessary in language (Moravcsik 2007: 29, 36). Importantly, these generalizations are not *causal* explanations. Rather, the only causal explanation for the typological distribution of properties is diachronic: "Indeed, the only possible causal explanation for a language system is by reference to history: how a given system evolved from something else" (Moravcsik 2007: 38). This reasoning applies equally to an individual TAM system such as the BHVS: we may *describe* the distribution and interaction among forms, but if we want to *explain* the system we must have recourse to its development. Further, given the ancient and temporally varied character of the textual witnesses to ancient Hebrew, I argue that we have little chance of understanding it simply through a description of the system without attention to its development (see discussion of the synchrony-diachrony distinction in §3.1.2 above).

This last point favors an approach from diachronic typology and use of the data from grammaticalization studies to explain the BHVS. These areas of study offer several interrelated principles of language change that help us explain the character of the BHVS. The two most important principles are that the change between languages stages is a step-by-step process that can be classified just as language states can be, and that change tends to be unidirectional or irreversible, so that a return to the original state takes place through a cyclical

---

17. Notwithstanding Nichol's comment (2007: 232; cited above, n. 15). Croft (2003: 239) notes that within diachronic typology this focus is shifted to one of "more probable vs. less [probable] language states."

| | Pre-Latin | Latin | French |
| | *? | | |

*?

*kanta bʰ umos > cantabimus

cantare habemus > chanterons allons chanter > ?

Figure 3.1. Development of Latinate futures (from Hopper and Traugott 2003: 9).

Early Old English	Old–Middle English	Present-Day English
wolde 'wanted' >	*wolde* 'wanted'	
	wolde (auxiliary) >	*would* (auxiliary)

Figure 3.2. Grammaticalization of English *wolde/would* (based on Hopper and Traugott 2003: 48).

process or renewal (Croft 2003: 253).[18] This latter process can be readily illustrated in the tendency of languages to develop new periphrastic expressions that may exist for a time alongside older synthetic forms, as in the case of the Latinate futures, the development of which is schematized in fig. 3.1.

Another way in which new constructions may develop is through divergence, in which a form develops a new grammatical meaning without immediately discarding the older function for the form: "When a form undergoes grammaticalization from a lexical to a grammatical function, so long as it is grammatically viable some traces of its original lexical meanings tend to adhere to it, and details of its lexical history may be reflected in constraints on its grammatical distribution" (Hopper 1991:22). This development is especially well illustrated in the case of the grammaticalization of English *wolde/would*, schematized in fig. 3.2.

In the intermediate stage of this change, we find the following rare example, [3.1], of both the past inflected meaning of the form and its auxiliary function in a single passage.

[3.1] þa   Darius geseah þæt he overwunnen beon **wolde**, þa
       when Darius saw   that he overcome   be   **would**, then
       wolde   he hiene selfne on ðæm gefeohte forspillan.
       wanted he him   self   in that battle   kill:inf
       'When Darius saw that he **would** be overcome, he **wanted** to
       commit suicide in that battle'. (Hopper and Traugott 2003: 48)

---

18. Moreno Cabrera (1998: 224) argues that the principle of unidirectionality is better described as "irreversibility."

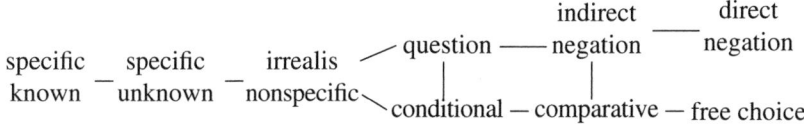

Figure 3.3. Conceptual space for indefinite pronouns (Croft 2003: 135).

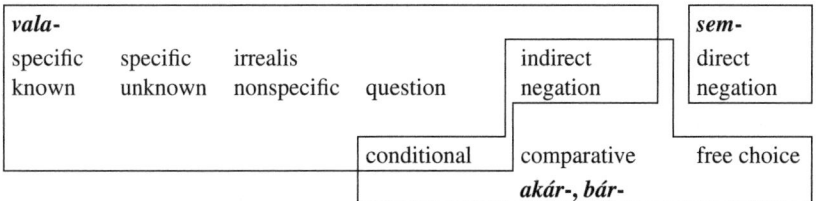

Figure 3.4. Semantic mapping of Hungarian indefinite pronouns (from Croft 2003: 137).

In both cases—that of renewal and that of divergence—the synchronic results of diachronic process is the same—namely, layering: "Within a broad functional domain, new layers are continually emerging; in the process, the older layers are not necessarily discarded, but may remain to coexist with and interact with new layers" (Hopper 1991: 22; Hopper and Traugott 2003: 125). This competition among layers can lead to specialization of one or another forms, "conditioned by semantic types, sociolinguistic contexts, discourse genre, and other factors" (Hopper and Traugott 2003: 116). This last point demonstrates how the layered characteristic of language stages creates a particular challenge for explaining the BHVS, because we have no native speakers to explain all the different types of motivation for using one or another layered alternative within each broad functional domain.

We may, however, elucidate the overlap among alternative verb forms in BHVS by creating a semantic map. Semantic maps are one of the most important innovations in typology for representing the relationship between an individual language and language universals (see Croft 2003: 133–39; 2007: 83–89). A semantic map consists of "mapping" the relevant forms in a language onto a "conceptual" space, as illustrated by figs. 3.3–3.4, in which the Hungarian pronouns (*vala-, sem-, akár-, bár-*) are mapped onto the conceptual space (functionally or semantically defined) of indefinite pronouns.

Analogous with this semantic mapping within diachronic typology are universal paths of development that represent the unidirectional stages of development within broad semantic domains. In this case, the "conceptual

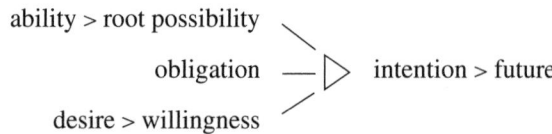

Figure 3.5. Paths of development of agent-oriented modality into futures (based on Bybee, Perkins, and Pagliuca 1994: 256, 263, 266).

space" will be conceived of diachronically, in that the relationship between the parts is represented as stages of development. In their study of grammatical-ization of TAM systems, Bybee, Perkins, and Pagliuca (1994) have proposed a number of universal paths of this sort, one of which is illustrated in fig. 3.5, and others that are discussed below in connection with my analysis of the BHVS.

The importance of the insights from diachronic typology and grammatical-ization studies for validation lies in the way that they demonstrate "statistical tendencies" and therefore demonstrate more- or less-probable TAM systems. Hence, a semantic model of the BHVS should not be anomalous as compared with the sorts of TAM systems found in other world languages. A second, more specific contribution that these studies provide is implicational typologi-cal arguments. Whereas the interpretation of a given conjugation is to a degree subjective, if something more objective can be tied to its interpretation, then the interpretation gains weight.

3.1.4 Concluding Remarks and a Look Ahead

Here I reiterate the main conclusions from this section. First, I am adopt-ing neither an extreme formalist/structuralist position nor a thoroughgoing functionalist/substantialist stance. Rather, I draw freely on insights from both camps. Second, I eschew the in-vogue prototype approach to categories, insist-ing that with tools such as markedness theory it is possible to discern one gen-eral meaning for a given linguistic form and reasonably to relate this meaning to the various specific meanings that the form may have, based on recourse to the syntactic and pragmatic contexts of the specific meanings. Third, logically following on the previous point, the goals for my semantic theory are the dem-onstration, description, and validation of (1) a general meaning for each TAM form in BH and (2) the specific meanings that these forms may express in the BH text. The descriptive side of this goal assumes the principle of composi-tionality and correspondence theory of truth; the validation side of these goals draws on the insights and data from (diachronic) typology and grammaticaliza-tion studies of the world's TAM systems.

Despite the obvious focus on individual verb forms in these stated goals, I have not organized the discussion around an analysis of each individual form in turn (cf. Cook 2001) or around some morphological or diachronic patterning (cf. Cook 2002). Rather, a persuasive theory must succeed in explaining not simply the general and specific meanings of each verb form but how they work together *as a system*. This system—and not merely the analyses of individual forms—must then be validated on diachronic(-typological) bases. Thus, I have organized my analysis in terms of the central unifying and distinguishing feature of TAM systems: time. All three domains of TAM that are associated with verbal expression in the world's languages relate language to time and time to language. However, their precise relationship to time distinguishes among the domains: *tense* has to do with the *location of situations in time*; the various types of *aspect* treat the *structure of situations in time*; finally, *mood* refers to *alternative situations in relationship to time*. This terse characterization is based on the discussion in §1.7.2 and is illustrated with respect to the BHVS in the following discussion.

3.2. The Expression of Aspect in BH

Of the TAM triad, aspect is the most difficult element to define. In part, this is because there are several quite different types of "aspect" and in part because the lack of uniform terminology has only contributed to confusing these distinct types. In §1.3, I introduce three distinct categories that (following the lead of a number of linguists) I label *phasal aspect*, *situation aspect*, and *viewpoint aspect*. These are treated in turn below.

3.2.1. Phasal Aspect: The Lexical-Semantic Dimension

In §1.7.3.2, I define *phasal aspect* as creating an activity subevent out of one of the three phases (onset, nucleus, or coda) of an event. The most common types of *onset*-applying phasal aspects are inchoative and inceptive, which are distinct only in that the first refers to the alteration of the onset of a state and the second to the alteration of the onset a dynamic event. In BH, onset phasal aspects of both types (stative and dynamic events) are expressed lexically by the verb חלל ('to begin') with a complementary Infinitive, as illustrated in examples [3.2a–b].[19]

[3.2] a. Gen 10:8b

הוּא הֵחֵל לִהְיוֹת גִּבֹּר בָּאָרֶץ

'He <u>began to be</u> a hero in the land'.

  b. Jonah 3:4a

וַיָּחֶל יוֹנָה לָבוֹא בָעִיר מַהֲלַךְ יוֹם אֶחָד

'Jonah <u>began to enter</u> into the city, a three day's journey'.

---

19. Gen 4:26; 6:1; 10:8; 11:6; 41:54; Num 25:1; Deut 2:31; 3:24; 16:9; Judg 10:18; 13:5, 25; 16:19, 22; 20:31, 39–40; 1 Sam 3:2; 14:35; 22:15; 2 Kgs 10:32; 15:37; Jer 25:29; Jonah 3:4; Esth 6:13; 9:23; Ezra 3:6; Neh 4:1; 1 Chr 1:10; 27:24; 2 Chr 3:1–2; 31:7, 10; 34:3.

The relative rarity of this construction (i.e., חלל plus infinitive) with stative roots[20] may be explained by the freedom with which stative roots express an inchoative based on the logic of the discourse context, as illustrated in example [3.3].[21]

[3.3] Neh 13:19

וַיְהִי כַּאֲשֶׁר צָלֲלוּ שַׁעֲרֵי יְרוּשָׁלַם לִפְנֵי הַשַּׁבָּת וָאֹמְרָה

'Then, when the gates of Jerusalem <u>became shaded/darkened</u> prior to the sabbath, I said . . .'.

The *coda* phasal aspects, which express the discontinuation of a situation, include the cessative (with [–telic] events) and completive (with [+telic] events). Both of these are marked lexically in BH with the same sort of infinitival construction as the onset phasal aspects: cessative aspect is expressed by חדל or שבת ('cease'), and completive aspect uses כלה ('finish'), as illustrated in examples [3.4a–b].[22]

[3.4] a. Gen 18:11

וְאַבְרָהָם וְשָׂרָה זְקֵנִים בָּאִים בַּיָּמִים חָדַל לִהְיוֹת לְשָׂרָה אֹרַח כַּנָּשִׁים

'Abraham and Sarah (were) old, advanced in days; the manner of women <u>had ceased to be</u> for Sarah'.

b. 1 Kgs 9:1a

וַיְהִי כְּכַלּוֹת שְׁלֹמֹה לִבְנוֹת אֶת־בֵּית־יְהוָה וְאֶת־בֵּית הַמֶּלֶךְ

'Then, when Solomon <u>finished building</u> the house of Yhwh and the house of the king . . .'.

Phasal aspects that apply to the **nucleus** of the event structure affect the progress of a situation, through either repetition (iterative and habitual) or extension with or without a pause (resumptive and continuative). The expression of these aspects in BH is less uniform than in the cases of the other phasal

---

20. I have found only two stative and one passive examples: with the Infinitive of היה (Gen 10:8; 1 Chr 1:10) and with a Niphal Infinitive of סתם ('be stopped up'). Gen 9:10 features a (stative) verbless clause as the complement of חלל.

21. Other inchoative examples are: Gen 26:13 (גדל 'become great'); Deut 32:15 (שמן 'become fat'); Judg 1:30, 33, 35, etc. (היה 'become'); 1 Sam 4:1 (רפה 'become slack'); Ezek 31:5 (גבה = גבא 'become high'; רבה 'become many'; ארך 'become long'); Neh 13:19 (צלל 'become overshadowed').

22. Examples with חדל: Gen 11:8; 18:11; 41:49; Exod 23:5; Num 9:13; Deut 23:23; 1 Sam 12:23; 23:13; 1 Kgs 15:21; Isa 1:16; Jer 44:18; 51:30; Ps 36:4; Ruth 1:18; 2 Chr 16:5. Examples with שבת: Jer 31:36; Ezek 34:10; Hos 7:4 (with Participle instead of Infinitive). Examples with כלה: Gen 17:22; 18:33; 24:15, 19, 22, 45; 27:30; 43:2; 49:33; Exod 5:14; 31:18; 34:33; Lev 16:20; 19:9; 23:22; 26:44; Num 7:1; 16:31; Deut 7:22; 20:9; 26:12; 31:24; 32:45; Josh 8:24; 19:49, 51; Judg 3:18; 15:17; 1 Sam 10:13; 13:10; 18:1; 24:17; 2 Sam 6:18; 13:36, 39; 1 Kgs 1:41; 3:1; 7:40; 8:54; 9:1; 2 Kgs 10:25; Is 10:18; Jer 5:3; 26:8; 43:1; 51:63; Ezek 43:23; Amos 7:2; Ruth 3:3; Dan 9:24; 12:7; 1 Chr 16:2; 2 Chr 4:11; 7:1; 29:29.

aspects discussed above. The adverb עוֹד infrequently expresses continuative aspect, as in example [3.5]; usually, it has the sense of *to do again* (e.g., Gen 30:7). While this latter meaning is very similar to the idea of resumptive aspect, it differs by denoting a new interval of action as opposed to a resumption of the same, left-off interval.[23] So far, I am unaware of a clear example of resumptive aspect in BH.

[3.5] Gen 25:6b

וַיְשַׁלְּחֵם מֵעַל יִצְחָק בְּנוֹ בְּעוֹדֶנּוּ חַי

'He sent them away from Isaac, his son, while he (was) still alive'.

Iterative and habitual are semantically similar but refer to the application of patterned repetition to a minimal event type and any event type, respectively. Although I have not found a clear iterative example in the Hebrew Bible, habitual expressions are numerous and may be expressed in a variety of ways. In most cases, the logic of the way the situation fits within the discourse context leads to a habitual interpretation of *yiqtol* or *wĕqatal*), as in example [3.6] (see additional discussion in chap. 4).[24]

[3.6] Gen 29:2b–3

כִּי מִן־הַבְּאֵר הַהִוא יַשְׁקוּ הָעֲדָרִים וְהָאֶבֶן גְּדֹלָה עַל־פִּי הַבְּאֵר: וְנֶאֶסְפוּ־
שָׁמָּה כָל־הָעֲדָרִים וְגָלְלוּ אֶת־הָאֶבֶן מֵעַל פִּי הַבְּאֵר וְהִשְׁקוּ אֶת־הַצֹּאן
וְהֵשִׁיבוּ אֶת־הָאֶבֶן עַל־פִּי הַבְּאֵר לִמְקֹמָהּ:

'. . . because from that well they would water the flocks. Now the stone was large that was upon the mouth of the well, and all the flocks would gather there and they would roll the stone from upon the mouth of the well and they would water the flock and they would return the stone that was upon the mouth of the well to its place'.

In other instances, temporal adverbial expressions disambiguate and/or reinforce the habitual interpretation of the *yiqtol* or *wĕqatal* forms, as in examples [3.7a–b].[25]

---

23. One could argue that *again* represents yet another type of phasal aspect, such as "repetitive," since there is no agreed-upon list of possible phasal aspects (see chap. 1 n. 27). However, given the specific definition of phasal aspect in §1.7.3.2, *again* does not qualify, and it seems preferable to retain the stricter definition rather than allowing every adverbial modification of a situation to become a type of phasal aspect.

24. Other habitual expressions are: with *wĕqatal*, Exod 33:7; 1 Sam 7:15–16; 2 Sam 17:17; 2 Kgs 3:4; Amos 4:7–8 (on the latter, see comments in Cook 2004a: 337); with *yiqtol*, Gen 2:6; 31:39; Exod 33:7; 40:36; 2 Sam 15:32; Num 9:18.

25. See also 1 Sam 1:7; 2:19; 7:16; 1 Kgs 5:25.

[3.7] a. Job 1:5

כָּכָה יַעֲשֶׂה אִיּוֹב כָּל־הַיָּמִים

'This is what Job <u>would do all the time</u>'.

  b. 1 Sam 1:3

וְעָלָה הָאִישׁ הַהוּא מֵעִירוֹ מִיָּמִים יָמִימָה לְהִשְׁתַּחֲוֹת וְלִזְבֹּחַ לַיהוָה
צְבָאוֹת בְּשִׁלֹה

'Now that man <u>would go up</u> from his city <u>periodically</u> to
worship and to sacrifice to Yhwh Sabaoth in Shiloh'.

The confusing issue that arises with regard to a habitual expression is deciding whether it is a matter of phasal aspect or irrealis or nonindicative mood.
Although logically, it makes some sense to consider habituals acting on predicates to be phasal aspect, this classification is also motivated by the origin of
the study of phasal aspects in Slavic languages (see §1.3.2). The absence of a
system of phasal affix markers in BH and recent arguments connecting habituality to irrealis mood make a modal analysis of habituality in BH preferable
to a phasal aspectual analysis. Below (§3.3.3), I analyze habitual *yiqtol* and
wĕqatal as irrealis mood.

A full treatment of phasal aspect is beyond the scope of this book and less
to the point than an examination of the semantics of verbal marking itself (i.e.,
verbal morphology and syntax versus lexical expression of TAM). The brief
preceding overview illustrates well how the expression of phasal aspect fits
with other parts of the BHVS, especially with respect to its interaction with
situation aspect, to which I turn next.

3.2.2. Situation Aspect: The Stative-Dynamic Opposition

Situation aspect classifies situations in terms of their internal temporal constituency. In chap. 1, I discuss the development of this category from Aristotle's comments on types of action and from some of the classifications of
situation aspect that have been developed (§1.3.1). In constructing my model
of TAM, I have adopted Rothstein's minimal classification of four situation
types distinguished by two features ([±stages], [±telic]; Rothstein 2004;
§1.7.3.1). However, the practice of classifying BH situations in relation to
this model is much more difficult than the distinction of situation types in the
abstract. In addition to the difficulties already endemic to classifying situation
types (see §1.3.1 for discussion), the lack of native speakers hampers the use of
linguistic acceptability tests to distinguish among types. This is especially the
case in distinguishing accomplishments ([+stages, +telic]) from achievements
([–stages, +telic]).[26]

---

26. For example, are the verbs יִקַּח וְשָׂם ('he will take . . . in order to place') in 1 Sam
8:11 accomplishments (the plural locations, 'with his chariots and with his horsemen', imply
[+stages]) or achievements (the verbs 'to take' and 'to place' are generally [–stages])?

Most relevant to the theory I am constructing is the morphological distinction in BH between (as it has traditionally been understood) stative and dynamic (i.e., activity, accomplishment, achievement) situations. In brief, in the Qal *binyan* (which is the only *binyan* in which the distinction is observable) in the suffix-pattern, *qatal*-conjugation dynamic verbs have an *a* theme vowel (e.g., שָׁמַר 'he kept') while stative verbs have an **i* (> *e*) or **u* (> *o*) theme vowel (e.g., זָקֵן 'he is old' and קָטֹן 'he is small'); correspondingly, in the prefix-pattern conjugations (*yiqtol*, *wayyiqtol*, Jussive-Imperative) dynamic verbs have a **u* (> *o*) theme vowel (e.g., יִשְׁמֹר 'he will keep/is keeping'; שְׁמֹר 'keep!') while stative verbs have an *a* theme vowel (e.g., יִזְקַן 'he is becoming/will be old'; יִקְטַן 'he is becoming/will be small'; see G. R. Driver 1936: chap. 7 for a full listing of stative roots).[27] Several semantic characteristics accompany this morphological pattern, reinforcing the identification of the pattern as a dynamic-stative distinction. First, stative verbs generally lack an active Participle form but instead may be encoded either verbally (i.e., verbal inflection), or adjectivally (the MS form is identical with the Qal 3MS *qatal*). Second, the stative verbs show a distinct pattern of interaction with the *qatal* and *wayyiqtol* conjugations: conjugated in *qatal*, stative verbs default to a present stative meaning, whereas conjugated in *wayyiqtol,* they always express past states. (Context may dictate an inchoative meaning for statives in either *qatal* or *wayyiqtol*.) All these issues have significance for understanding the development and meaning of the BHVS and are discussed in turn.

By contrast to my above characterization of these morphological and semantic patterns as having a dynamic (or fientive or active) : stative distinction (so Joüon 2006: §§41, 112), other labels for this distinction have been suggested (both for Semitic in general and BH in particular), including transitive : intransitive (so Gesenius 1910: 118–19; see W. Wright 1962: 1.28 regarding Arabic) and active voice : passive/middle voice (Tropper 1998a: 182; Joosten 1998: 207). The reason for so many competing explanations is the interaction of voice, transitivity (and valency), and situation aspect and the patterns of correlation among such parameters and the vowel pattern in BH (and Semitic). To clarify the situation adequately (though not completely), it is helpful to

---

27. The dynamic-stative vowel pattern is regularly obscured in verbs with a pharyngeal or largyngeal consonant in the second or third positions of the verbal root, which tend to effect an *a* theme vowel, regardless of the underlying vowel pattern (e.g., גָּבַר 'be strong'; cf. גָּבְרוּ in pause, 2 Sam 1:23; יִשְׁלַח 'he stretches/will stretch out x'), and in verbs with final glide consonants that undergo contraction (e.g., **rabiya > rɔbɔʰ*, רָבָה 'it was numerous'; cf. **galaya > gɔlɔʰ*, גָּלָה 'he uncovered'). This pattern is part of a larger observable pattern, referred to as the "Barth-Ginsburg law" (see Joüon 2006: §41 n. 12), involving vowels of both the suffix-pattern and the prefix-pattern conjugations: dynamic verbs have *a-a* suffix vowel patterns and *a-u* prefix vowel patterns; stative verbs have *a-i/u* suffix vowel patterns and *i-a* prefix vowel patterns (in the Masoretic tradition, the attenuation of *a*-vowel in a closed, unstressed syllable levels the distinction in the prefix vowel).

have in place some basic definitions for dynamic and stative situation aspect, transitivity and intransitivity, and active, middle, and passive voice. These are given in example [3.8].[28]

[3.8] a. The *dynamic* : *stative* opposition classifies verbs/predicates according to their situation aspect: either they express a state or some variety of dynamic event, such as activity, accomplishment, or achievement. In addition to states' being used dynamically, such as when they are combined with certain phasal aspects, such as inchoative (e.g., *He was old* > *He became old*), certain verbs are naturally stative and dynamic, such as 'smell': *He smelled* (*the roses*).

b. The *transitive* : *intransitive* opposition categorizes verbs/predicates according to the number of "inner participants" that they require: intransitive (subject), transitive (subject and object), ditransitive (subject, object1, and object2). Stative verbs are mostly intransitive, but there are regular exceptions, such as *love* (BH אהב) and *hate* (BH שׂנא) as in *Jack loves/hates Jill*.

c. The *active* : *passive* opposition classifies verbs/predicates according to the role of the subject—whether agent or patient. The subject of an active predicate is the agent, whereas the subject of a corresponding passive predicate is the patient, as in *The wind struck the house* versus *The house was struck* (*by the wind*). The middle has elements of both the active and passive voices in that the grammatical subject is both agent and patient.

The interaction among these parameters is evident in Klaiman's (1991) study of grammatical voice. However, a comparison between the vowel-pattern marked distinction in BH and the systems that Klaiman examines (ergative-absolutive, active/dynamic-stative, and active-middle) makes it evident that BH distinguishes dynamic and stative. On the one hand, it is readily apparent that the class of verbs with *i/u* theme vowel in BH is neither consistently passive nor consistently intransitive, and Joosten's argument (1998) that this class of verbs is middle voice is based on the view that middle voice is essentially intransitive (see Klaiman 1991: 45). While the majority of the *i/u* class of verbs

---

28. Transitivity is a narrower category than valency in that as it deals entirely with the "inner participants" familiar from traditional grammar: direct objects and indirect objects. While a verb may only license one of each type of inner participant (multiple noun phrases will be construed as compounds), it may require (semantically and/or grammatically) any number of "free participants" (e.g., locative prepositional phrase with certain verbs of motion); valency treats both types of participant.

are intransitive, there are notable exceptions (e.g., אָהֵב 'he loves' and שָׂנֵא 'he hates'). On the other hand, the *i/u* class of verbs in BH exhibit several characteristics of dynamic-stative systems. For one, as in other dynamic-stative systems (Klaiman 1991: 128), BH has a means of augmenting its class of statives in the *binyanim* system—namely the stative, passive Niphal *binyan* (see Benton 2009). For another, the variation between agent-encoding and patient-encoding intransitive stative verbs in BH is typical of dynamic-stative systems (see Klaiman 1991: 107–8, 123–24). For example, זָקֵן 'he is old' encodes the patient ("undergoer") as grammatical subject, whereas קָרֵב 'he is near' encodes the agent as grammatical subject.[29] Not surprisingly, some of the agent-encoding type verbs tend toward a dynamic interpretation quite frequently in BH (e.g., קָרֵב 'he is drawn near' > 'he draws near'). Similarly, BH grammar tends to treat transitive statives as more dynamic than the other statives, which is evident in the occurrence of active Participle forms for some (e.g., אֹהֵב 'loving' and שֹׂנֵא 'hating'). These moves toward a more dynamic interpretation of certain stative forms are part of the larger move away from the stative-adjective class altogether in Semitic (Joüon 2006: §41b; Stassen 1997: 495–96)[30] and contribute to a broader typological argument regarding the "drift" of the BH verbal system from being aspect-prominent to tense-prominent (Cook 2008a: 13–16; see below, §3.2.3.3). By the end of the Tannaitic period (ca. 200 C.E.),

---

29. This variation of agent- and patient-encoding found with statives is the basis for Andersen's criticism (2000: 34) of the reconstruction of West Semitic dynamic *qatala* conjugation as developed from a stative *qatila* pattern (see §2.3): "[I]n Proto-Semitic . . . *qatala *'anta* would have meant 'you (are) killed', with the subject as patient, not agent. It is unclear how this could have evolved into **qatalta* meaning 'you have killed'" (Andersen 2000: 34). However, the association of this variation with aspect prominence and the general shift toward tense prominence evident in Semitic may make such a patient-to-agent encoding shift more plausible. Two pieces of evidence are suggestive in this direction: first, a shift from an originally ergative-absolutive to a nominative-accusative system has been posited for Semitic (see Diakonoff 1988: 59–61; Müller 1995b; Tropper 1999a); second, Klaiman (1991: 129) notes that languages regularly exhibit split ergative systems based on the distinction of "completive" and "incompletive" TAM categories of the verb. In an early ergative system, the agent of an intransitive (e.g., **qariba *'anta* 'you are drawn near') and the patient of a transitive (e.g., **'ahiba *'anta* 'you are loved') presumably would have been marked identically, thus allowing for a "reanalysis" of the patient as the agent for intransitives when the system began to shift from ergative-absolutive to nominative-accusative (see §2.3.2.1). Thus, the development of West Semitic dynamic **qatala* was a gradual process of reanalysis, probably led by the intransitives that required no reanalysis for a dynamic interpretation: **qariba *'anta* 'you are drawn near' > **qarib(a)ta* 'you have drawn near'.

30. Thus, G. R. Driver's (1936: 48–49) approach is sound in assuming an original or etymological stative sense for *i/u* theme vowel roots in BH even when they no longer exhibit stative meanings in the biblical text. In many cases of this sort, the verbs are inconsistent morphologically, alternating between *i/u* and *a* theme vowels, e.g., 3MS קָרַב, but 3FS קָרְבָה in pause (Zeph 3:2), and comparative data supports a stative origin (Koehler et al. 1994: s.v. קרב).

the *qatal* conjugation was restricted to past temporal reference even with stative roots (Segal 1927: 150; Kutscher 1982: 131).[31]

Another typological argument tied to the dynamic-stative analysis not only
serves to confirm the dynamic-stative analysis of the theme-vowel alternation
presented here but contributes to the analysis of the verbal conjugations (particularly, *qatal* and *wayyiqtol*; see §§3.2.3.1 and 3.4.1). The argument is based
on the observable pattern of interaction between stative verbs and the *qatal*
and *wayyiqtol* conjugations: stative verbs default to present temporal reference
when conjugated with *qatal*; that is, absent contextual indicators otherwise,
stative verbs are interpreted as present states.[32] By contrast, stative verbs conjugated in *wayyiqtol* consistently show a past temporal reference. This contrast
is substantiated by a statistical analysis of 49 stative verbs:[33] conjugated in

---

31. Segal (1927: 150) states that in the Mishnah *qatal* with stative roots is restricted to
expressing past states, and the conjugation no longer exhibits any future temporal reference.
Kutscher's statement (1982: 131) that "the perfect now [i.e., in RH] denotes only past action"
is consonant with Segal's earlier assessment. Nevertheless, Pérez Fernández (1997: 108)
objects that "M. H. Segal overstates his claim that forms like יָדַעְתִּי can never have a present
significance in R[abbinic] H[ebrew] [i.e., I know vs. I knew], for in fact, we find in rabbinic
literature certain idiomatic turns of phrase, such as אַתָּה אָמַרְתָּ, in which the present is clearly
signfied." However, none of Pérez Fernández's examples (see 1997: 116–17) involve stative
roots. Ridzewski (1992:160) offers an example of a stative root in *qatal*, which he categorizes as *Präsens*: אֲנַחְנוּ אָשַׁמְנוּ. However, he translates it with a past inchoative sense ('wir
luden Schuld auf uns'), which is consistent with the above assessment that *qatal* is restricted
to past temporal reference even with stative roots. While these examples, therefore, do not
contradict the claim that *qatal* is restricted to past temporal reference in Rabbinic Hebrew,
they do illustrate the complexity of the verbal semantics.

32. Joüon (2006: §112a) characterizes the present temporal reference of statives in *qatal*
as their "primary meaning."

33. The selection is based on the lists in Joüon (2006: §41) and G. R. Driver (1936:
46–47). An attested stative meaning was the primary parameter for selection; thus some
very common stative roots were included despite an attested active Participle (these are designated by ptc. in the list); those with verbal adjective are marked with adj. and the predominant dynamic meanings in some forms is glossed as a development (>) of the original stative
meaning: אָהֵב (ptc.) 'love'; גָּבַה (adj. גָּבֹהַּ) 'be high'; גָּבַר/גָּבֵר 'be strong' > 'prevail'; גָּדַל (adj.
גָּדוֹל) 'be great'; דָּבַק/דָּבֵק (adj. דָּבֵק) 'cling'(?); דָּלַל (adj. דַּל) 'be low'; דָּשֵׁן (adj.) 'be fat'; זָקֵן
(adj.) 'be old'; חָזַק (adj.) 'be strong' > 'prevail'; חָמֵץ 'be leavened'; חָנֵף (adj.) 'be polluted';
חָסֵר (adj.) 'be lacking'; חָפֵץ (adj.) '(be) delight(ed) in/with'; חָפֵר 'be ashamed'; חָרַד (adj.
חָרֵד) 'be terrified' > 'tremble'; טָהֵר 'be clean'; טוֹב (adj.) 'be good'; טָמֵא (adj.) 'be unclean';
יָבֵשׁ (adj.) 'be dry'; יָגֹר (adj.) 'be afraid'; יָכֹל (adj.) 'be able'; יָעֵף (adj.) 'be weary'; יָרֵא (adj.)
'be afraid'; יָשֵׁן (adj.) 'be asleep' > 'fall asleep'; לָבֵשׁ (ptc.) 'be clothed' > 'clothe'; כָּבֵד (adj.)
'be heavy'; כָּשֵׁר 'be advantageous', 'be proper'; מָלֵא (adj.) 'be full' > 'fill'; נָבֵל 'be foolish';
נָעֵם 'be pleasant'; עָצַם/עָצֵם 'be vast'; עָשֵׁשׁ 'be moth-eaten' > 'waste away'; פָּחַד 'be in dread'
> 'dread'; צָמֵא (adj.) 'be thirsty'; קָדֵשׁ 'be consecrated'; קָטֹן (adj.) 'be small'; קָלַל (adj.) 'be
slight'; קָמֵל 'be decayed'; קָרַב/קָרֵב (adj.) 'be near' > 'draw near'; רָבָה 'be much'; רָחַק
(adj. רָחוֹק) 'be far'; רָעֵב (adj.) 'be hungry'; רָעַע (adj. רַע) 'be evil'; שָׂבַע/שָׂבֵעַ (adj. שָׂבֵעַ) 'be
sated'; שָׁכַל/שָׁכֵל 'be bereaved'; שָׁמֵם (adj.) 'be desolated'; שָׂמַח/שָׂמֵחַ (adj.) 'be glad' > 'rejoice'; שָׂנֵא (ptc.) 'hate'; שָׁפֵל (adj. שָׁפָל) 'be low'.

qatal they have a present temporal reference in 54 percent of the cases (326 times out of 606 occurrences) versus a past temporal reference in the other 46 percent (279 occurrences). More importantly, when the discourse context is delimited by examining only instances of direct speech, which have a separate deictic center from the surrounding discourse (see Miller 2003: 131), the statistics shift even more favorably toward a default present temporal reference for stative verbs in *qatal*: 78 percent (227 of 290 occurrence) show a present temporal reference versus 22 percent with past temporal reference.

The significance of this patterning in BH is that it is typical of stative verbs with perfective aspect and past tense conjugations in other languages (so Bybee, Perkins, and Pagliuca 1994: 92; e.g., Schuh 2007: 606, with reference to Bade's "completive" verb). Thus, not only does it confirm the above dynamic-stative interpretation of the *a-i/u* theme vowel distinction, it presents a strong typological argument that *qatal* is a perfective verb form and *wayyiqtol* is past tense.

3.2.3. Viewpoint Aspect: The Perfective-Imperfective Opposition and the Progressive

Most of the time when the term *aspect* comes up in discussions of the BHVS, viewpoint aspect is what is intended. As discussed at some length in §§1.3.3 and 1.7.3.3, viewpoint aspect has to do with the way in which language can encode different viewpoints on a situation, distinct from the temporal constituency (situation aspect) and temporal location (tense) of the situation. The debate over viewpoint aspect in the BHVS has traditionally been a two-way debate between tense and aspect, and more recently a three-way argument among tense, aspect, and mood or modality. Traditionally, this debate has centered on how to characterize the opposition between *qatal* and *yiqtol*. The reason for this is that, despite other disagreements over the BHVS, most scholars still concur with the traditional view that *qatal* and *yiqtol* form a central (if not *the* central) opp̲_____n within the BHVS. This position is fairly self-evident when one c_̲_____restrictions placed on the other verb forms: *wayyiqtol* is larg̲_____o prose narrative; the Jussive-Imperative constitutes a directi̲_____ subsystem of irrealis mood in the BHVS; and the Participle, as ̲_____predicate, is not fully integrated into the finite verbal system. ̲_____either *qatal* nor *yiqtol* is restricted to certain types of literature ̲_____e versus poetry), or types of discourse (e.g., narrative versus discourse), or even certain genres (e.g., story, wisdom sayings, prophetic speech, etc.).

The few scholars who demure from the traditional view that the *qatal* : *yiqtol* opposition is central to the BHVS sometimes posit a more abstract opposition that includes a number of verb forms. For example, Joosten (1999: 16) characterizes the system as constituting a primary opposition between indicative and nonindicative modality (for summary and critique, see §2.4.2.3). Others object that the entire tense-versus-aspect debate is problematic because these parameters cannot be distinguished adequately in any TAM system (e.g., Buth 1992). Although there is some validity to these remarks, which I addressed above (§3.1.1), by and large this sort of criticism is simply unhelpful because it represents a retreat from meaning. This results in an unclassified taxonomy of meanings/functions for the BH verb forms that is useless to the philological task for which it was presumably developed (see the especially egregious case of Andrason 2010; 2011a; 2011b; 2011c; forthcoming). This objection must in part be rejected when it entails entirely banning questions about the precise semantic identity of individual grams, such as *qatal* and *yiqtol*.

I am defending here the traditional views that *qatal* and *yiqtol* form a central opposition of the TAM system of BH and that this opposition is best described as perfective (*qatal*) and imperfective (*yiqtol*) viewpoint aspect. Granting this position (substantiated below), it is legitimate and helpful to employ Bhat's (1999) terminology of the "aspect-prominence" of the BHVS. Not only this but, while the focus of this book remains the semantics of the individual grams that make up the BHVS (of which there are tense grams, aspect grams, and mood grams), identifying the BHVS as aspect-prominent and the central opposition of *qatal* : *yiqtol* as perfective : imperfective viewpoint is useful from the perspective of making typological comparisons and arguments. For instance, the presence of a distinct class of stative verbs in BH (see above) and the absence of tense shifting (see Endo 1996: 300) aligns the BHVS with aspect-prominent TAM systems versus tense-prominent systems (Bhat 1999: 40, 150).

From the perspective of diachronic typology, the BHVS appears more aspect-prominent than mood-prominent. Not only are TAM systems with a primary realis : irrealis (cf. Joosten's indicative : nonindicative/modal opposition) opposition rare in the world's languages (Bybee, Perkins, and Pagliuca 1994: 237–38), they usually develop into non-future : future tense–prominent systems (so Bhat 1999: 17; see also Comrie 1985: 50). This is in contrast to Hebrew, about which there is general agreement that in the postbiblical period it developed into a past : non-past opposition, tense-prominent system (Segal 1927: 150).

Complementary to these negative typological arguments, several arguments in favor of an aspect-prominent analysis have already been touched on and can be rehearsed here as a general segue to the detailed analyses of the *qatal* and *yiqtol* conjugations and the predicatively used Participle. First, a TAM system with a core binary opposition of perfective : imperfective viewpoint aspect is eminently probable based on the extensive typological studies of Dahl (1985) and Bybee (1985; also Bybee, Perkins, and Pagliuca 1994) and their combined study (Bybee and Dahl 1989). Bybee and Dahl (1989: 83) note that TAM systems with a core binary opposition of perfective : imperfective viewpoint aspect constitutes the most frequent type of TAM system in their data and "seems to occur in about every second language in the world" (see fig. 2.6b in §2.4.2.3, p. 138).

Second, buttressing these findings are the arguments of Bybee (1985) and Dahl (1989) regarding the "basic-ness" of aspectual oppositions versus tensed oppositions, which I have already rehearsed in §2.4.2.3 in my critique of Kuryłowicz's theory of the Semitic verb. The integration of TAM morphology with the discontinuous-root morphology of the Semitic (and BH) verb in contrast to the periphrastic means of denoting tense in some Semitic languages (e.g., Classical Arabic Past Imperfective with *kana yaktubu* 'he was writing', cited in example [2.15], p. 139)[34] make it much more plausible that the *qatal* : *yiqtol* opposition is one of viewpoint aspect and not tense or mood.

Third, as already discussed in the previous section (§3.2.2), the pattern of interaction of *qatal* versus *wayyiqtol* with stative roots is mutually confirming of the dynamic-stative analysis of the *a-i/u* theme-vowel distinction as well as a perfective analysis of *qatal* and past tense analysis of *wayyiqtol* (see below). Bybee, Perkins, and Pagliuca (1994: 91–92) note that this interaction with stative roots is an important means of distinguishing perfective aspect verbs and past tense verbs, the semantics of which are closely intertwined (e.g., Dahl [1985: 79] characterizes past tense as a "secondary meaning" of perfective verbs).

Fourth, despite the intermingling of meanings between past tense and perfective aspect, the predominate past temporal reference for *qatal* can be accounted for within an aspectual analysis in light of Smith's analysis of "default temporal interpretation" of aspectual forms (C. S. Smith 2006; 2008; see §§1.7.6 and 3.4.2). Fifth, and finally, as will be demonstrated in the following subsections, the viewpoint-aspect analysis of the *qatal* : *yiqtol* opposition is consonant with the diachronic data and contributes to a coherent and typologically feasible TAM system for BH.

3.2.3.1. Perfective *Qatal*

A helpful starting point to my argument that *qatal* is a perfective aspect conjugation (i.e., a perfective gram) is the summary of the typical taxonomy of meanings for the form given in the standard grammars: the *qatal* may express (1) present or past state (with statives), (2) simple past, (3) past perfect, (4) present perfect, (5) present (gnomic), (6) performative, (7) future perfect, (8) counterfactual, (9) so-called prophetic perfect, and (10) optative/precative (see Bergsträsser 1962: 2.25–29; Davidson 1901: 58–63; S. R. Driver 1998: 13–26; Gibson 1994: 60–70; Joüon 2006: §112; Kautzsch 1910: 309–13;

---

34. By contrast, and more similar to Hebrew, Aramaic developed periphrastic progressive past using the participle rather than imperfective finite verb form (for Syriac, see Nöldeke 2001: 216–18; and Muraoka 1997b: 68; for Babylonian Jewish Aramaic, see Khan 2007: 114).

Waltke and O'Connor 1990: 486–95).[35] The range of temporal reference evident in this taxonomy forms the strongest objection to a past tense analysis of
qatal,[36] because it is difficult to explain the full range of temporal reference for
a form, the general meaning of which is identified as past tense. Indeed, Bybee,
Perkins, and Pagliuca (1994: 95) note that a distinguishing feature between
perfective verbs and past tense is the ability of the former to appear with present or future temporal reference. Attempts to explain the perfect meaning for
qatal based on its syntactic context are unsuccessful (e.g., Zevit 1998; see my
critique above, §2.4.2.2), and recourse to Reichenbach's relative tense theory
is problematic inasmuch as Reichenbach ignored the aspectual dimensions of
the perfect (see Comrie 1976: 52; and above, §1.7.3.3).

Theories that identify the *qatal* conjugation as realis or indicative mood
versus irrealis or nonindicative conjugations likewise falter in dealing with the
basic taxonomy of meanings for the conjugation. In particular, such a theory
cannot incorporate counterfactual examples such as example [3.9].[37]

[3.9] Gen 26:10

כִּמְעַט שָׁכַב אַחַד הָעָם אֶת־אִשְׁתֶּךָ וְהֵבֵאתָ עָלֵינוּ אָשָׁם
'One of our people might have lain with your wife so that you
would have brought guilt upon us'.

Finally, discourse-pragmatic theories that contrast the *qatal* conjugation
with *wayyiqtol* in terms of the former's inability to introduce a new reference
time (e.g., Hatav 1997; Goldfajn 1998; see §2.4.3.2 above) likewise falter in

---

35. These grammars identify *qatal* as 'perfect' (= perfective) aspect in every case except
two. Joüon (1923: 292; 2006: §111) claims that trying to explain the BHVS in terms of completed (*l'achevé*) and incomplete (*l'inachevé*) action is inadequate. Therefore, although he
characterizes the BH verb as tense-aspect, he stresses that the forms primarily express tense
distinctions, most of the aspectual distinctions being determined by the semantics of the
verbal root (i.e., situation aspect; Joüon 1923: 290–92; 2006: §111). However, Joüon (1923:
290; 1993: §111) confusingly retains the Ewald-Driver terminology of 'perfect' (*parfait*) for
qatal but employs the tense label 'future' (*futur*) for *yiqtol*. Gibson (1994), in his revision
of Davidson (1901), departs from the latter's adherence to the Ewald-Driver standard theory
and appears to endorse German scholarship's characterization of the *qatal* : *yiqtol* opposition as a constative : cursive aspectual opposition (e.g., Brockelmann 1956; Meyer 1992;
Rundgren 1961; see §2.4.1): *qatal* "identifies a situation or event as static or at rest," whereas
yiqtol identifies a situation "as fluid or in motion" (Gibson 1994: 60).

36. Anstey's argument (2009: 827) that *qatal* is a past tense conjugation because that is
its "default interpretation in narrative and reported speech" is simplistic both in its adoption
of the majority use as the conjugation's defining meaning and its failure to grapple with the
variety of non-past meanings that *qatal* has in narrative (versus reported speech).

37. Other examples, mostly introduced by the counterfactual conditionals לוּ or לוּלֵא,
include Gen 43:10; Num 20:3; Deut 32:29; Josh 7:7; Judg 8:19; 13:23; 14:18; 1 Sam 25:34;
2 Sam 2:27; 19:7; 2 Kgs 13:19; Isa 1:9; Zech 10:6; Ps 27:13; Job 3:13; 6:2; 10:19.

the face of clear examples, such as [3.10], of *qatal*'s advancing the reference time (see §1.5; for additional criticism, see Cook 2004b; and chap. 4).[38]

[3.10]   Gen 4:18

וַיִּוָּלֵד לַחֲנוֹךְ אֶת־עִירָד וְעִירָד יָלַד אֶת־מְחוּיָאֵל וּמְחִיָּיאֵל יָלַד אֶת־
מְתוּשָׁאֵל וּמְתוּשָׁאֵל יָלַד אֶת־לָמֶךְ

'Irad was born to Enoch, and Irad <u>begat</u> Mehujael, and Mehu-jael <u>begat</u> Methusael, and Methusael <u>begat</u> Lamech'.

In contrast to these unsuccessful approaches, in the remainder of this section I make my case for perfective *qatal* based first on a diachronic-typological examination of the form, followed by a discussion of the way that the various indicative meanings of the conjugation relate to its general perfective meaning (see §3.1.1 for justification of this approach). Part of this argument will entail identifying morphologically the so-called *wĕqatal* conjugation with *qatal*, but since (as I argue) this is a syntactically signaled realis : irrealis distinction within the *qatal* conjugation (see §3.3.1 below), I am choosing to treat the irrealis meanings of the conjugation separately below (see §3.3.3).

The development of the BH *qatal* conjugation is relatively undisputed in Semitic studies (see §§2.3.2.1–2). Its origin is identified as a Common Semitic verbal adjective **qatil*.[39] As evidenced in Akkadian, this verbal adjective came to be combined with the encliticized subject pronoun to express null-copula predications (e.g., **qarib ʾanta > *qarib-ta* 'you are drawn near'; see von Soden 1995: §77; Kuryłowicz 1972: 64–65; Huehnergard 2005: §22.1; Kouwenberg 2010: §7).[40] This construction became further grammaticalized in West Semitic, where the subject pronouns were reduced to inflectional suffixes and the theme vowel of the pattern was changed from the "stative" *i*-class to a "dynamic" *a*-class (**qarib-ta > *qarabta*; Bergsträsser 1983: 11 note s; Diakonoff 1988: 90; Huehnergard 1992: 156; Lipiński 1997: 341; Moscati 1980: 133; Tropper 1998a: 182).[41] At the other end of the spectrum is the fact that the verbal system of Hebrew underwent dramatic changes in configuration

---

38. Examples of this sort, though not frequent, can quite easily be multiplied: Gen 10:24; 17:20; 29:34; 30:8; Deut 5:27; 1 Chr 1:18; 2:48–49; 2 Chr 7:12.

39. Note, however, that a dynamic perfect *qatal* is posited for East Semitic Eblaite: e.g., *a-kà-al-ma-lik* 'Malik has devoured'; *da-na-il* 'Il has judged' (Müller 1984: 157–58).

40. This predicative use of the Verbal Adjective in Akkadian (as Huehnergard 2005 refers to it) is referred to as the *Stative* (e.g., Borger 1979: 170; see Huehnergard 1987; 1988; Kouwenberg 2000 for discussion; the older term *Permansive* has largely been abandoned).

41. Like the stative : dynamic distinction in BH (see §3.2.2), the semantic distinction between the **qati/ula* and **qatala* patterns was not consistently observed in West Semitic: Müller (1983: 38) claims that originally the stative **qatila* pattern was not limited to present time reference or to an active or passive sense (similarly, G. R. Driver 1936: 80); both verb patterns occur with a dynamic meaning in Eblaite (Müller 1984: 157–58); and some roots in EA occur in both patterns (Rainey 1996b: 303).

Table 3.1. Development of Hebrew *Qatal* Conjugation

Common Semitic (see Akkadian)	West Semitic (e.g., El Amarna)	Biblical Hebrew	Rabbinic Hebrew (e.g., Mishnah)
*qariba ʾanta > *qarib-ta	*qarabta	qɔraḇtɔ	qɔraḇtɔ

between the end of the biblical writings (ca. 2nd century B.C.E.) and the end of the Tannaitic period of rabbinic literature (ca. 200 C.E., the date generally assigned to the Mishnah). Most obvious is the loss of the *wayyiqtol* form, which affected the distribution of the *qatal* conjugation, and thus the form became generally restricted to past temporal reference.[42] Thus, we can reconstruct the *qatal* conjugation as in table 3.1.

While this reconstruction of the form of the *qatal* conjugation is widely agreed on, a case must be made for the TAM meaning of the conjugation at each stage. One approach to this task would be to analyze each relevant occurrence by way of translation into a natural metalanguage (e.g., English), compile statistics, and identify the conjugation's meaning as that which appears in the majority of instances. I reject this sort of approach (see above, §3.1.2) because it lacks an objective means of validation. A more promising tack is to ask what type of development of verb forms can be seen in the typological data that would best explain the development of this form. The starting point for this comparison is the major characteristics of the conjugation rehearsed above: (1) the origin of the form is a verbal adjective used as the predicate of a null copula; (2) the most basic functions of the form in the Hebrew Bible are to denote perfective, perfect, and past events (see taxonomies of standard grammars); (3) by the end of the Tannaitic period, the conjugation becomes restricted to past temporal reference, even with stative roots. Even more importantly, the patterning of *qatal* with stative predicates in BH and RH strongly disposes one to identify the TAM of *qatal* as perfective aspect in BH and past tense in RH. Given all of these data, the most relevant path of development is the perfective/past development proposed by Bybee, Perkins, and Pagliuca (1994: 105) and provided in fig. 3.6.

Variations within this path of development may occur at either end. At the front end, verb forms may originate in either a *resultative* (a state brought

---

42. There are isolated instances in which *wayyiqtol* in the Samuel–Kings source text is replaced with *qatal* in the Late BH narratives of Chronicles: e.g., 1 Kgs 8:4 and 2 Chr 5:5; 2 Sam 24:4 and 1 Chr 21:4; 1 Kgs 5:1 and 1 Chr 1:26; 1 Kgs 12:16 and 2 Chr 10:16 (corrupt text); 1 Kgs 15:13 and 2 Chr 15:16; 2 Kgs 8:27 and 2 Chr 22:3; 2 Kgs 15:5 and 2 Chr 26:20; 2 Kgs 16:17 and 2 Chr 28:16. These may be evidence of *qatal*'s shift from perfective to simple past (see Sáenz-Badillos 1993: 120; Polzin 1976: 57; see Kienast 2001: 315). However, there are also passages in which the opposite phenomenon is observable (e.g., 1 Kgs 14:21 and 2 Chr 12:13; 1 Kgs 22:41 and 2 Chr 20:31; 2 Kgs 18:4 and 2 Chr 31:1).

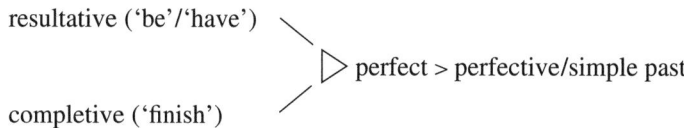

Figure 3.6. Grammaticalization paths for perfective/simple past verbs (adapted from Bybee, Perkins, and Pagliuca 1994: 105).

about by a past action) or a *completive* (to do something thoroughly or to completion) construction (for definitions, see Bybee, Perkins, and Paglicua 1994: 54). Besides the semantic distinction, the lexical sources for these two forms are quite distinct: completive constructions derive from dynamic verbs or directions, while resultatives derive from stative verbs used with some non-finite verb form (Bybee, Perkins, and Paglicua 1994: 59). At the other end, perfect verbs may develop into either perfective or simple past verb forms, an option that Bhat (1999: 182) argues may be determined by whether the verbal system as a whole is aspect- or tense-prominent. However, Bybee, Perkins, and Pagliuca (1994: 92) also hypothesize that verb forms that have developed from perfect to perfective may develop into simple past verbs as an additional rather than optional step along this development path.

Examples of verbs developing along this path are manifold in Germanic and Romance languages. A ready illustration of the resultative > perfect change in English is found in a comparison of Bible translations: *For he is gone down this day* (1 Kgs 1:25, KJV 1611; also ASV 1901); *For today he has gone down* (1 Kgs 1:25, NRSV 1989). The perfect > perfective/simple past development is evident in the French *passé composé* (e.g., *j'ai écrit* 'I have written' ~ 'I wrote') and German *Perfekt* (e.g., *Ich habe geschrieben* 'I have written' ~ 'I wrote') forms, which have all but replaced the older perfective/simple past forms (i.e., the French *passé simple*, e.g., *j'écrivis*; and the German *Imperfekt*, e.g., *Ich schrieb*) in all but formal and literary registers. These latter examples illustrate well the layering effect of grammaticalization, introduced above (§3.1.3): the forms coexist within the language, exhibiting a particular distribution that is not semantically based.[43]

If we attempt to align the reconstruction of the Hebrew *qatal* conjugation given in table 3.1 with the development path of perfective/simple past verbs given in fig. 3.6, we find that there is ample evidence for identifying the TAM of the *qatal* conjugation at each stage of its development. First, as with the resultative verbs in Bybee, Perkins, and Pagliuca's data, the origin of Hebrew *qatal* is a stative construction (null copula) with a nonfinite verb form (a verbal adjective). Thus, a reasonable hypothesis is that the *qatal* conjugation

---

43. Whether the French and German forms in question are identified as perfective or simple past is not germane to my argument.

developed from a resultative (versus a completive) construction (i.e., *qarib-at* 'You are drawn near'). T. D. Andersen (2000: 34) has recently objected to a resultative origin for *qatal*, arguing that "in Proto-Semitic . . . *qatala ʾanta* would have meant 'you (are) killed', with the subject as patient, not agent. It is unclear how this could have evolved into *qatalta* meaning 'you have killed'" (Andersen 2000: 34). The confusion in Andersen's objection aside (How could *qatala* ever have had a passive sense?)[44]—resultatives are more restricted than perfects, and thus *qatala* would have combined initially only with *intransitive* predicates (which Andersen apparently confuses with passive voice).[45] Presumably then, the development of the dynamic *qatala* conjugation in Semitic originally occurred with intransitive verbs and subsequently spread to transitives (see p. 197 n. 29). This explanation accords with Huehnergard's discussion (2005: §4.3; see also Kouwenberg 2010: 165–74) of the predicative use of the Verbal Adjective in Akkadian, which has a *passive* sense with transitive verbs and a *resultative* meaning with intransitive verbs. It is also consonant with Haug's (2008) recent discussion of this shift in ancient Greek. Haug (2008: 294–95) argues that "the crucial step" in the resultative > perfect shift is the inferential identification of the subject of the main verb with the agent of the participle, which becomes conventionalized so that the construction spreads to other predicate types besides those to which the resultative is confined. Haug (2008: 295–302) makes his case for the correctness of this surmise for ancient Greek from the development of the Greek Perfect with middle and active voices. Despite the lack of similar evidence, we can reasonably hypothesize that a similar sort of conventionalization and spread from intransitive predicates to all predicates accompanied the theme-vowel shift from *qatil-ta* to *qatalta* and was coincident with the reanalysis of the construction as a finite, dynamic verb form (versus enclitic pronoun, null copula, and adjectival complement).

Second, and proceeding from the first point, we would expect West Semitic *qatala* to exhibit a primary perfect meaning, and so Daniels (in Bergsträsser 1983: 21 note ac) surmises. Data in support of this contention may be fewer

---

44. T. D. Andersen (2000: 34) also confuses resultative and perfect in his discussion, claiming that the functional equivalent in English of the Semitic resultative construction is *have* + Past Participle. However, it is clear from Bybee, Perkins, and Pagliuca's discussion (1994: 63–67) that resultatives in English are constructed of *be* + Past Participle (e.g., *He is gone*). After identifying the Dravidian Present Perfect as a perfect, Andersen (2000: 41) translates the form with an English resultative construction: *The lights are turned on*. This confusion perhaps accounts for his objection to a resultative > perfect shift for transitive verbs in Semitic alongside his proposal that *qatala* "tended to have a resultative meaning" with achievement and accomplishment verbs, which are mostly transitive (T. D. Andersen 2000: 41–42).

45. Haug (2008: 294) states it this way: "Resultatives are lexically restricted to verbs with defined resultant state, whereas Anteriors [= perfects] can in general be formed from any verbs."

than desirable but nevertheless sufficient. In the El-Amarna letters, a perfect meaning for Canaanite *qatala* is statistically dominant (100 of 175 instances), versus a perfective/simple past sense, according to Moran's study (2003: 30), and this dominance of the perfect meaning has been substantiated by Rainey's (1996b: 281–366) more recent study of the Canaanite verb.

Third, the real point of contention comes with the BH data, in which *qatal* exhibits both a perfect and a perfective/simple past meaning, begging the question whether the form should be identified as a perfect, perfective, or simple past conjugation. The simplest explanation for the concurrence of the perfect and perfective/simple past meanings in BH *qatal* is to explain the perfect as a meaning that persists from the earlier stage when it was its primary meaning. This explanation is on analogy with the persistence of lexical meanings, illustrated earlier (§3.1.3 and especially in the discussion of fig. 3.2), but contrary to Bybee, Perkins, and Pagliuca's (1994: 78) category of "old anteriors," which they explain "represent an intermediate stage between pure anterior and past or perfective. These grams have anterior as a use but also have other uses suggestive of more grammaticalized meanings." Although BH *qatal* might be fitted into their "old anterior" category (the ubiquitous nature of the perfective/simple past meaning of BH *qatal* might challenge their notion of "suggestive" uses), it is more in keeping with the strong tendencies of grammaticalization (e.g., persistence of lexical meaning, irreversibility of meaning) to identify BH *qatal* as perfective/simple past with a persistent perfect meaning.

Evidence to distinguish *qatal* as a perfective aspect gram instead of simple past is amply supplied by its appearance in present and future temporal spheres, as illustrated by the performative and future perfect examples in [3.11],[46] and the contrastive interaction of *qatal* and *wayyiqtol* with stative predicates, demonstrating that *qatal* is a perfective verb while *wayyiqtol* is a simple past (see §§3.2.2 and 3.2.3; for further discussion, see §3.4.1 below).

[3.11] a. 2 Sam 19:30

אָמַרְתִּי אַתָּה וְצִיבָא תַּחְלְקוּ אֶת־הַשָּׂדֶה

'I say, you and Ziba will divide the field'.

b. Gen 28:15

כִּי לֹא אֶעֱזָבְךָ עַד אֲשֶׁר אִם־עָשִׂיתִי אֵת אֲשֶׁר־דִּבַּרְתִּי לָךְ

'Indeed, I will not abandon you until (the time) when I will have done that which I have told you'.

---

46. Examples of *qatal* with a future perfect sense are plentiful in the grammars: e.g., Gen 43:14; Num 32:17; Deut 8:10; 1 Sam 20:22; Isa 11:9; Jer 8:3; 29:14, 18; Amos 9:15; Mic 5:2; Ruth 2:21; 1 Chr 14:15, etc. Performative *qatal* is likewise well recognized in the grammars: e.g., Gen 14:22; 22:16; Deut 8:19; Ruth 4:9; 2 Sam 17:11; 19:30; 24:22–23; Song 2:7; etc.

Table 3.2. Development of Hebrew *Qatal* Conjugation

Common Semitic (see Akkadian)	West Semitic (e.g., EA)	Biblical Hebrew	Rabbinic Hebrew (e.g., Mishnah)
resultative	> perfect	> perfective	> simple past
*qariba 'anta > *qarib-ta	*qarabta	qɔraḇtɔ	qɔraḇtɔ

The performative example in [3.11a] in particular provides an additional typological argument: while languages are not limited to a specific verb form for performative expressions, the choice of verb to express performatives is not haphazard; rather, in languages where tense is grammaticalized, a present-tense form is used (e.g., English), but in languages where aspect is grammaticalized, perfective aspect grams are used, as in BH (see Dobbs-Allsopp 2004–7: 52, 57–58).

Fourth, based again on the distinctions between perfective and simple past verbs given in Bybee, Perkins, and Pagliuca (1994: 91–95), we can identify *qatal* in post-BH (i.e., the Mishnah and beyond) as a simple past verb. The data that have already been discussed above (§3.2.2, especially n. 31) are the mirror image of the data for BH *qatal*; namely, RH *qatal* is restricted to past temporal reference, and it does not exhibit a distinctive present-stative meaning with stative predicates. The disappearance of *wayyiqtol* at the same time as this perfective > simple past shift of *qatal* both explains the shift and buttresses the semantic identification of the form in the post-BH period.[47]

Thus, to conclude this section, I propose the reconstruction of forms and TAM of Hebrew *qatal* given in table 3.2. This reconstruction has been argued, not based on statistical analysis of individual examples, but primarily on the basis of typological arguments along with the consensus views regarding the primary meanings of the conjugation in each period.

A final issue in this reconstruction of *qatal* that remains to be addressed is the status of the so-called *wĕqatal* conjugation. Since at least the medieval grammarians, *wĕqatal* has been treated as a separate conjugation from *qatal*, based on semantic, morphological, and morphophonemic differences between the two forms: semantically, the meaning of *wĕqatal* parallels more closely *yiqtol* than *qatal*, analogous to the semantic parallel apparent between *qatal* and *wayyiqtol*; morphologically, the *waw* conjugation appears obliga-

---

47. The expression of perfect by *qatal* in RH (see Pérez Fernández 1992: 116–17; e.g., אם לא עלה עמוד השחר 'if the pillar of dawn has not risen' in *m. Ber.* 1:1) cautions against too simplistic a picture of the verbal system in RH. However, this feature does not overturn the weight of the other evidence for past tense *qatal* in RH, and further exploration of the RH verbal system is beyond the scope of this book.

torily prefixed to the *wĕqatal* form, just as it appears to be with *wayyiqtol*; and the *wĕqatal* form is frequently distinguished morphophonemically by its ultimate stress pattern in forms that are stressed penultimately in *qatal* (e.g., 1s וְשָׁמַרְתִּי versus שָׁמַרְתִּי; 2ms וְשָׁמַרְתָּ versus שָׁמַרְתָּ; see §§2.1–2.2). These differences along with the apparently analogous semantic relationship of the two pairs of *waw*-prefixed : non-*waw*-prefixed forms (i.e., *wayyiqtol* : *yiqtol* and *wĕqatal* : *qatal*) has led to the theory that *wĕqatal* developed on analogy with *wayyiqtol* in ancient Hebrew (e.g., Bergsträsser 1962: 2.14; Bobzin 1973: 153; Fenton 1973: 39; M. S. Smith 1991: 6–8; Buth 1992: 101). Unfortunately, the relationship between these pairs is not analogous—either semantically or developmentally, and comparisons of this sort seem only to hinder an accurate assessment of all of the conjugations. Most importantly, Ewald (1879: 23) rightly observed that, in contrast to *wayyiqtol* (see below), there is no evidence in the Semitic languages for a *wĕqatal* conjugation. Despite attempts to make a case based on comparative-historical grounds (e.g., Bauer 1910), no convincing evidence is forthcoming.

T. D. Andersen's article (2000) represents a recent attempt to distinguish two morphologically independent conjugations in *qatal* and *wĕqatal*. Andersen (2000: 30–34) argues that *qatala underwent a semantic split, creating an imperfective (*wĕ*)*qatal* and a perfective *qatal* conjugation in BH. This split was effected by the contrastive interaction of the *qatala conjugation with intransitive and transitive verbs:

> [A]t a certain stage of Proto-Semitic, the *qatala conjugation had similar semantics to the *te-iru* aspect marker in Japanese or the Present Perfect tense in some Dravidian languages. With activity verbs, most of which are intransitive, it had a progressive meaning. With achievement verbs and accomplishment verbs, most of which are transitive, it tended to have a resultative meaning, which later developed into perfect meaning. (Andersen 2000: 41–42)

Aside from other misunderstandings in Andersen's argument,[48] the most obvious objection is that there is no evidence that (West Semitic) *qatala at any of its stages was limited to particular types of predicate (e.g., transitive, intransitive).

The morphophonemic argument is perhaps the most well-established argument for a distinct *wĕqatal* conjugation. However, it faces several problems.

---

48. Andersen's analysis contains numerous misunderstandings and inaccuracies, from his confusion of resultative and perfect (see n. 44) and claim that *qatala is a Proto-Semitic form (a marginal view at best; see §2.3) to his classifying stative under imperfective aspect (2000: 28). He also misreads Bybee, Perkins, and Pagliuca when he claims based on their data that perfective and simple past verbs rarely function in conditional statements—in contrast to the frequent use of *wĕqatal* in conditional clauses (Andersen 2000: 38; citing Bybee, Perkins, and Pagliuca 1994: 207). Andersen has overlooked the conditional functions of old anteriors and perfectives listed elsewhere in Bybee, Perkins, and Pagliuca (1994: 79, 93).

First, the ultimate stress on *wĕqatal* forms is limited within the paradigm (only 1s and 2ms exhibit the variation, the other forms already showing ultimate stress in *qatal*). Second, even for these forms, there is a good degree of variation so that many apparently *wĕqatal* forms (on the basis of the *waw* conjunction and nonperfective meaning) that should show ultimate stress do not, even within the immediate context of others that do show the expected stress pattern (e.g., Amos 1:4, וְשִׁלַּחְתִּי and Amos 1:5, וְשָׁבַרְתִּי). As a result, scholars have questioned whether this stress pattern could even be formulated as a morphophonemic "rule" (e.g., C. H. Gordon 1938; Blake 1944a; Sheehan 1970).

Revell's examination (1984; 1985) of the stress pattern on the *wĕqatal* represents an important argument against the morphophonemic interpretation. Revell examines the variation in the presence or absence of the ultimate stress and concludes that it is subject to prosodic forces: "Stress position in the perfect forms with *waw* consecutive is, then, conditioned by the intonation patterns characteristic of speech units into which the text was divided according to the syntactic, (other) semantic, and rhythmic factors described" (Revell 1985: 299; see p. 280). More importantly, he argues that "the distinguishing mark of the semantic category '*waw* consecutive perfect' almost certainly arose after this form had ceased to be used even in contemporary literature, and probably arose within the biblical reading tradition" (Revell 1984: 440). Thus, it represents at most a retrospective grammatical analysis and not an organic development within BH grammar.

In conclusion, there is no evidence that *qatal* and *wĕqatal* represent distinct and independent developments in Hebrew, and therefore I am eschewing the continued use of *wĕqatal* along with the misunderstandings it conveys. Nevertheless, the perceived semantic and syntactic distinctions between *qatal* and *wĕqatal* are undeniable, and it may be possible even to argue that they are separate conjugations if one can demonstrate how *wĕqatal* branched off from *qatal* (the reverse direction of divergent development is unlikely enough not to merit entertaining it) and that the two are now (in BH) sufficiently distinct. Below (§3.3), I argue that the difference between *qatal* and the so-called *wĕqatal* is a syntactically signaled mood distinction: *qatal* as realis mood, *wĕqatal* as irrealis mood.

What follows is not intended simply as a taxonomy of meanings—meanings that are already available in the standard grammars. Rather, it is further support for the argument that BH *qatal* is marked for perfective aspect. To support my argument, I pose the question at every step in the taxonomy whether the particular meaning for the *qatal* conjugation can persuasively be explained with reference to a basic meaning of perfective aspect. As with the earlier part of my argument, here too, we have recourse to typological data: to the extent that the range of meanings for *qatal* lines up with the range of meanings generally associated with perfective verbs in other languages, my argument is strengthened.

The irrealis meanings will be examined separately, below (§3.3.3.1); the realis meanings for BH *qatal* are relatively few and have already been touched upon above (this section). Examples [3.12]–[3.14] illustrate the most frequent meanings for *qatal* in BH. Examples such as [3.12] I am analyzing as perfective aspect with past temporal reference as opposed to a simple past (tense) verb, based on the preceding arguments (this section).

[3.12] 2 Sam 5:5

בְּחֶבְרוֹן מָלַךְ עַל־יְהוּדָה שֶׁבַע שָׁנִים וְשִׁשָּׁה חֳדָשִׁים וּבִירוּשָׁלַם מָלַךְ
שְׁלֹשִׁים וְשָׁלֹשׁ שָׁנָה עַל כָּל־יִשְׂרָאֵל וִיהוּדָה

'In Hebron <u>he reigned</u> seven years and six months and in Jerusalem <u>he reigned</u> thirty-three years over all Israel and Judah'.

The question remains how to explain the close association between these two notions, given that perfective *qatal* is largely confined to past temporal reference. To argue that, in some instances, perfective aspect is more salient and, in other cases, past tense is better is simply to sidestep the issue or deny that there is any such notion as "basic meaning" in terms of TAM forms. Dahl (1985: 79) concluded from the correlation of perfective aspect and past temporal reference that past tense is simple a "secondary meaning" of perfective verbs. While perhaps accurate, his claim fails to explain why this is so. More promising is C. S. Smith (2006: 92; 2008: 35), who argues that in languages with aspectual conjugations there is a "default" temporal interpretation assigned to the verbs based on the parameter of boundedness (on boundedness, see §1.5.3 and chap. 4): unbounded situations are located in the present, and bounded situations are located in the past. Because perfective aspect is one way to effect boundedness, the temporal location of perfective events is constrained by this default pattern, resulting in the close association between the notions of perfective aspect and simple past tense. This default temporal interpretation is central to explaining the expression of temporality in BH (see §3.4.2).

The stative interpretation of stative predicates with perfective *qatal* has already been discussed at some length in this and the previous section, where it is shown that this interaction differs from the interpretation of stative predicates with simple past verbs. Because stative verbs are unbounded, the default in temporal interpretation is present (see example [3.13a]). However, within past-time accounts, the unbounded state is delimited to the past by the temporal deixis of the narrative discourse, thereby yielding a past stative meaning (see example [3.13b]; see additional discussion in chap. 4).

[3.13] a. Josh 23:2

וַיֹּאמֶר אֲלֵהֶם אֲנִי זָקַנְתִּי בָּאתִי בַּיָּמִים

'He said to them, "I am old, I have advanced in days"'.

  b. Gen 48:10

וְעֵינֵי יִשְׂרָאֵל כָּבְדוּ מִזֹּקֶן לֹא יוּכַל לִרְאוֹת

'They eyes of Israel were heavy from old age; he could not see'.

The perfect (or anterior) meanings for perfective *qatal* were accounted for above (this section) as the persistence of the conjugation's earlier perfect meaning. As with the temporal distinction of stative predicates with *qatal* (present or past), the temporal interpretation of perfect verbs is determined by the deictic characteristics of the discourse in which they appear.

[3.14] a. Deut 1:10

יְהוָה אֱלֹהֵיכֶם הִרְבָּה אֶתְכֶם וְהִנְּכֶם הַיּוֹם כְּכוֹכְבֵי הַשָּׁמַיִם לָרֹב

'Yhwh your God has increased you, and look, you
(are) today as the stars of the heavens with regard to
numerousness'.

  b. Gen 5:24

וַיִּתְהַלֵּךְ חֲנוֹךְ אֶת־הָאֱלֹהִים וְאֵינֶנּוּ כִּי־לָקַח אֹתוֹ אֱלֹהִים

'Enoch walked with God and he was no more, because God
had taken him'.

  c. 1 Chr 14:15

וִיהִי כְּשָׁמְעֲךָ אֶת־קוֹל הַצְּעָדָה בְּרָאשֵׁי הַבְּכָאִים אָז תֵּצֵא בַמִּלְחָמָה
כִּי־יָצָא הָאֱלֹהִים לְפָנֶיךָ לְהַכּוֹת אֶת־מַחֲנֵה פְלִשְׁתִּים

'When you hear the sound of marching at the tops of
the baca trees, then you shall go out into battle, for God
will have gone out before you to strike the camp of the
Philistines'.

For instance, in example [3.14a], the present perfect interpretation is determined in part by the deictic connection to the speaker (as opposed to anchoring to a previous narrative event) of direct speech and in part by the explication of the resultant state of the *qatal* event in a verbless clause that defaults for the present deictic center of the speaker. Similarly, the past perfect interpretation of *qatal* in [3.14b] can be explained by reference to the narrative deictic center of the immediate context (i.e., the preceding *wayyiqtol* form), which determines a past temporal interpretation of the resultant state ('he was not') of the *qatal*, resulting in a past perfect interpretation of the event. Finally, the future perfect interpretation in [3.14c] is, again, determined by the deictic character of the context. Here the temporal adverbial אָז with the directive *yiqtol* expressing God's command to David places the deictic center in the future so that the perfective *qatal*, expressing a bounded event, is interpreted as future perfect. These are just brief illustrations of the way that the temporal character of a given discourse context determines the precise interpretation of perfective *qatal*. I provide a much more detailed discussion in chap. 4, after the semantic groundwork of the default temporal interpretation has been explicated in §3.4, below.

Of the other meanings listed in the summary of standard taxonomies at the beginning of this section, the counterfactual and optative/precative are discussed below under the category of irrealis mood (§3.3.3.1). Three other categories of realis mood *qatal* remain to be discussed here: the performative use, the employment of the form in gnomic expressions, and the category traditionally referred to as "prophetic perfect" because of its association with prophetic oracular literature.

The performative use of *qatal* has been introduced above in example [3.11a] as evidence that it is a perfective gram and is further illustrated by example [3.15a] below: the performative use of this gram demonstrates that the conjunction may be used with a non-past temporal reference, and the regular choice of this verb instead of the *yiqtol*, for example, for performative points to the crucial characteristic of the gram in this function to be its instantaneousness—that is, its perfective aspect value. Other present- or future-time expressions with *qatal* represent extensions of the performative, from which they are usually not distinguished (see S. R. Driver 1998: 17; Joüon 2006: §112g; Waltke and O'Connor 1990: 489). The commissive, by which "we commit ourselves to do things" (Searle 1983: 166), is distinct from the performative only by a perceived temporal gap between the statement and action, as illustrated by example [3.15b]. Waltke and O'Connor's (1990: 489) commissive analysis (they label it "perfect of resolve") of the performative example [3.15a] illustrates the close similarity between these meanings. Finally, the epistolary use of the *qatal*, illustrated in [3.15c], differs from performative and commissive by yet another temporal gap—the gap between the writing and the reading of the correspondence.[49] The semantics of the *qatal* form remains constant in all three examples, namely, [C_{RF}, S & PFV & DECL] (i.e., present temporal reference, perfective aspect, and declarative mood); the discourse-pragmatic context disambiguates them.

---

49. Other commissive examples include Gen 23:13; 17:20; Judg 1:2; 2 Chr 12:5. Another epistolary example is 2 Chr 2:12 (for others, see the epigraphic examples in Pardee 1983).

[3.15] a. Gen 23:10–11

וַיַּעַן עֶפְרוֹן הַחִתִּי אֶת־אַבְרָהָם . . . הַשָּׂדֶה נָתַתִּי לָךְ וְהַמְּעָרָה אֲשֶׁר־
בּוֹ לְךָ נְתַתִּיהָ לְעֵינֵי בְנֵי־עַמִּי

'Ephron answered Abraham, "The field I (hereby) give to
you, and the cave that is in it to you I (hereby) give it in the
sight of my people'.

b. Gen 17:20

וּלְיִשְׁמָעֵאל שְׁמַעְתִּיךָ הִנֵּה בֵּרַכְתִּי אֹתוֹ וְהִפְרֵיתִי אֹתוֹ וְהִרְבֵּיתִי אֹתוֹ
בִּמְאֹד מְאֹד

'As for Ishmael, I have heard you: behold, I (promise to)
bless him, with the result that I will make him fruitful and
will multiply him very greatly'.

c. 1 Kgs 15:19

הִנֵּה שָׁלַחְתִּי לְךָ שֹׁחַד כֶּסֶף וְזָהָב

'Herewith, I send you a gift of silver and gold'.

An accurate assessment of *qatal* in gnomic (better termed "generic") expressions requires clarifying because it is still a poorly understood category
(for more details, see Cook 2005, on which the following discussion is based).
First, generics do not refer to particular situations but are probability statements characterizing the properties of certain states of affairs. For this reason,
they are often referred to as "omnitemporal." Second, languages do not use any
particular linguistic means of marking generics; therefore, their interpretation
is often ambiguous, both with respect to a generic or nongeneric expression
and with respect to different sorts of generic descriptions (e.g., habitual, descriptive, normative). Third, languages tend to use a minimally marked verb
form or some form of present/imperfective verb in generic expressions. For
this reason, traditional treatments of generic expressions in the Hebrew Bible
have advocated translating them with general present tense verbs (e.g., S. R.
Driver 1998: 17). Thus, the use of BH *qatal* in generic expressions presents a
challenge both for scholars who argue that the form is a simple past (e.g., Rogland 2003) and for my argument here that the form is perfective aspect. However, as both Rogland (2003) and I (Cook 2005) have show in some measure,
the appearance of *qatal* in generic expressions is not nearly as prevalent as is
sometimes supposed (see Cook 2005: 124), and it is too often misunderstood.
I have expressly argued (Cook 2005), based on the data of Proverbs, that TAM
distinctions are retained within generic expressions in BH (see Dahl [1985:
100], who makes a general claim to this effect).

Thus, the *qatal* form in examples such as [3.16] should not be analyzed as
having a present or omnitemporal reference but should be given the sort of

interpretation we would expect based on the default temporal interpretation introduced above and illustrated in my translation of the example as a past-time anecdotal proverb.

[3.16]   Prov 21:22

עִיר גִּבֹּרִים עָלָה חָכָם וַיֹּרֶד עֹז מִבְטֶחָה:

'A wise man <u>went up</u> to a city of mighty men and brought down (its) strong fortification'.

Similarly, other meanings expressed by *qatal* in other contexts (above) are exhibited likewise in generic expressions, including present states [3.17a], perfect events [3.17b], and types of irrealis mood (see §3.3.3.1; see also Cook 2005: 131–33).

[3.17]   a. Prov 12:21

לֹא־יְאֻנֶּה לַצַּדִּיק כָּל־אָוֶן וּרְשָׁעִים מָלְאוּ רָע

'No harm will befall the righteous, but the wicked <u>are full</u> of evil'.

b. Prov 20:12

אֹזֶן שֹׁמַעַת וְעַיִן רֹאָה יְהוָה עָשָׂה גַם־שְׁנֵיהֶם

'An ear that listens and an eye that sees—Yhwh <u>has made</u> both of them'.

In cases of alternation between *qatal* and *yiqtol* in Proverbs, the usual TAM distinctions of the conjugations are retained, as illustrated by the examples in [3.18].

[3.18]   a. Prov 14:1

חַכְמוֹת נָשִׁים בָּנְתָה בֵיתָהּ וְאִוֶּלֶת בְּיָדֶיהָ תֶהֶרְסֶנּוּ

'Wisdom <u>has built</u> her house, but folly <u>will tear it down</u> with her own hands'.

b. Prov 6:8

תָּכִין בַּקַּיִץ לַחְמָהּ אָגְרָה בַקָּצִיר מַאֲכָלָהּ

'It <u>will prepare/prepares</u> its food in the summer, it <u>has gathered</u> its produce in harvest'.

The same holds for some examples in Psalms, as in example [3.19a]. However, other examples appear to fit Held's explanation (1962); he argued that the *yiqtol* forms in cases such as [3.19b] represent the prefixed simple past conjugation (> *wayyiqtol*) and not imperfective *yiqtol* (see further §3.4.1).

[3.19] a. Ps 2:2

יִתְיַצְּבוּ מַלְכֵי־אֶרֶץ וְרוֹזְנִים נוֹסְדוּ־יָחַד עַל־יְהוָה וְעַל־מְשִׁיחוֹ

'The kings of the earth <u>are setting</u> themselves and the
rulers <u>have taken council</u> together, against Yhwh and his
anointed'.

b. Ps 24:2

כִּי־הוּא עַל־יַמִּים יְסָדָהּ וְעַל־נְהָרוֹת יְכוֹנְנֶהָ

'For he <u>has founded</u> it upon waters, and upon streams he
<u>established it</u>'.

The category "prophetic perfect," which has been used to describe examples
[3.20a–d], among others (see C. L. Klein 1990; Rogland 2003: 53–113), clearly
lies in the "margins" of the verbal system (to borrow Hendel's phrase [1996]).

[3.20] a. Isa 5:13

לָכֵן גָּלָה עַמִּי מִבְּלִי־דָעַת וּכְבוֹדוֹ מְתֵי רָעָב וַהֲמוֹנוֹ צִחֵה צָמָא

'Assuredly, My people <u>will suffer exile</u> for not giving heed,
its multitude victims of hunger and its masses parched with
thirst'. (NJPS)

b. Isa 11:9

לֹא־יָרֵעוּ וְלֹא־יַשְׁחִיתוּ בְּכָל־הַר קָדְשִׁי כִּי־<u>מָלְאָה הָאָרֶץ</u> דֵּעָה אֶת־
יְהוָה כַּמַּיִם לַיָּם מְכַסִּים

'In all of My sacred mount nothing evil or vile shall be
done; for the land <u>shall be filled</u> with devotion to the Lord
as water covers the sea'. (NJPS)

c. Isa 19:7

עָרוֹת עַל־יְאוֹר עַל־פִּי יְאוֹר וְכֹל מִזְרַע יְאוֹר יִיבַשׁ <u>נִדַּף</u> וְאֵינֶנּוּ

'And the Nile papyrus by the Nile-side and everything sown
by the Nile shall wither, <u>blow away</u>, and vanish'. (NJPS)

d. Jer 48:41

נִלְכְּדָה הַקְּרִיּוֹת וְהַמְּצָדוֹת נִתְפָּשָׂה וְהָיָה לֵב גִּבּוֹרֵי מוֹאָב בַּיּוֹם הַהוּא
כְּלֵב אִשָּׁה מְצֵרָה

'Kerioth <u>shall be captured</u> and the strongholds shall be
seized. In that day, the heart of Moab's warriors shall be
like the heart of a woman in travail'. (NJPS)

C. L. Klein's (1990) description of the category makes it suspiciously ad hoc.
He insists that a prophetic statement must be textually clear, in realis (indicative) mood, and have a clear future temporal reference in order to qualify as
a prophetic perfect. Likewise, my (Cook 2002: 222–23) explanation in terms

of a new category called "immediate future," created on the basis of slight typological data seems, in hindsight, unconvincingly ad hoc.

In addition, the standard grammars present a confusing picture in regard to whether the prophetic perfect is a grammatical category or a rhetorical device (so Joüon 2006: §§112h, 118s; see Rogland 2003: 53–54).[50] If it is a rhetorical device, it might be seen as analogous to the "historical present" (e.g., Matt 4:10, τότε λέγει αὐτῷ ὁ Ἰησοῦς . . . 'Then Jesus said [PRES] to him . . .'). However, there is notably more agreement among scholars with respect to identifying historical presents than prophetic perfects, and it is not clear that the prophetic perfect examples are all to be explained in the same way.

Rogland (2003: 58–113) has argued that many of the examples are misidentified and that the *qatal* is functioning with much more "normal" senses (i.e., past and perfect expressions) that are missed by scholars because they overlook the possibility of future perfect expressions ('this will have happened') or temporal shifts such as quoted speech or visionary narratives. Examples [3.20a–d] are no less susceptible to explanations of this sort. For example, גלה in [3.20a] may be as easily analyzed along the lines of Kautzsch's "perfectum confidentiae" (see p. 213 n. 49): 'My people *are gone into exile*', with a meaning of assurance that the exile is as good as happened already. The stative מלא in [3.20b] might reasonably be treated as irrealis or future perfect following a temporal כי: 'when the land is filled/will have been filled with the knowledge of Yhwh'. Although problematic passages remain (so Rogland 2003: 113), and some of Rogland's arguments in an effort to explain away the category are questionable, a good deal of doubt is cast on the category. At the least, examples of the so-called prophetic perfect serve as reminders of how much we have yet to grasp of the grammar of the prophets.

3.2.3.2. Imperfective *Yiqtol*

The case that *qatal* and *yiqtol* conjugations form an aspectual opposition has already been presented in the discussion of *qatal* in the previous section (§3.2.3.1). The imperfective identity of *yiqtol* follows almost inevitably from the case made for perfective *qatal* based on this implicational typological generalization: perfective grams develop only in languages that already possess

---

50. The explanation in Kautzsch (1910: §106n) comes across as some sort of psycholinguistic explanation: the *qatal* is used "to express facts which are undoubtedly imminent, and, therefore, in the imagination of the speaker, already accomplished." This description encompasses more than just prophetic perfects, however, including those that are clearly rhetorical in character: for example, the "perfectum confidentiae" (e.g., הֵן גָּוַעְנוּ אָבַדְנוּ כֻּלָּנוּ אָבָדְנוּ 'Behold, we perish, we are undone, we are all undone'; from Kautzsch 1910: §106n) is more a matter of rhetoric than grammatical tense. That is, stating "Behold, we have perished, we have been undone, we have all been undone" while one is still alive (to be able to say it) would assure that there was no confusion for the hearer regarding the time of death, but it precludes all possibility of escape from it.

an imperfective gram, with which the perfective stands in opposition (Bybee, Perkins, and Pagliuca 1994: 91). However, substantiating this imperfective identification of *yiqtol* is more difficult than the perfective case for *qatal* was, for two reasons. First, *yiqtol* exhibits a more even distribution of meanings among all three temporal spheres and between realis and irrealis mood (see table 2.1). This is exemplified by the typical taxonomy for *yiqtol* in the standard grammars: *yiqtol* may express (1) past progressive, (2) past habitual/iterative, (3) present progressive, (4) present gnomic, (5) general future, (6) future past (= English Conditional), (7) deontic modality, (8) contingent modality, and (9) simple past (with certain adverbs; Bergsträsser 1962: 2.29–36; Davidson 1901: 64–69; S. R. Driver 1998: 27–49; Gibson 1994: 70–80; Joüon 2006: §113; Kautzsch 1910: 313–19; Waltke and O'Connor 1990: 502–14).

Two main alternative identifications of the *yiqtol* gram have been proposed in light of the form's distribution over temporal and modal domains: *yiqtol* is a nonvolitive modal form (Joosten 2002; see §2.4.2.3); or it is a non-past tense gram (Anstey 2009). Both of these proposals give preference to the majority meanings of *yiqtol* as a basis for identifying the gram. However, in taking this tack, the theories are unable to account sufficiently for the wide-ranging semantics of the form. With regard to the nonvolitive modal identification, the expression of indicative past and present imperfective by *yiqtol* is problematic (see examples in [3.21]).[51]

[3.21] a. 1 Sam 13:17–18 (past imperfective *yiqtol*)

וַיֵּצֵא הַמַּשְׁחִית מִמַּחֲנֵה פְלִשְׁתִּים שְׁלֹשָׁה רָאשִׁים רָאשִׁים הָרֹאשׁ אֶחָד יִפְנֶה
אֶל־דֶּרֶךְ עָפְרָה אֶל־אֶרֶץ שׁוּעָל: וְהָרֹאשׁ אֶחָד יִפְנֶה דֶּרֶךְ בֵּית חֹרוֹן
וְהָרֹאשׁ אֶחָד יִפְנֶה דֶּרֶךְ הַגְּבוּל הַנִּשְׁקָף עַל־גֵּי הַצְּבֹעִים הַמִּדְבָּרָה:

'The raiding party departed from the camp of the Philistines in three companies: one company <u>was turning</u> the way of Oprah towards the land of Shual; another company <u>was turning</u> the way of Beth-horon; and another company <u>was turning</u> the border road that overlooks the valley of Zeboim in the direction of the wilderness'.

b. 1 Sam 22:23 (present imperfective *yiqtol*)

שְׁבָה אִתִּי אַל־תִּירָא כִּי אֲשֶׁר־יְבַקֵּשׁ אֶת־נַפְשִׁי יְבַקֵּשׁ אֶת־נַפְשֶׁךָ

'Stay with me; do not be afraid, for whoever <u>is seeking</u> my life <u>is seeking</u> your life'.

---

51. Other past imperfective examples include: Gen 6:4; Exod 8:20; 19:19; Judg 9:38; 1 Sam 1:10; 2 Sam 15:37; 23:10; 1 Kgs 6:8; 20:33; Isa 1:21; Hos 2:1. As Joosten's discussion (1999) illustrates, distinguishing past imperfective (realis mood) from habitual (irrealis mood) can be difficult (e.g., Isa 1:21 and Hos 2:1 both might be past habitual or past imperfective). Other present imperfective examples include: Gen 16:8; 37:15; Josh 9:8; etc. In Bybee, Perkins, and Pagliuca's view (1994: 126), all present-time indicative *yiqtol* examples would be by definition imperfective, but this seems to overstate the case (see §1.7.6).

Joosten (1999; 2002) accepts the premise that these meanings for *yiqtol* are at variance with his nonvolitive modal identification; hence, he attempts to explain them as nonindicative modal meanings. The individual faults in his argument aside (see Cook 2006a), his overall approach has two weaknesses. First, in order to explain examples such as [3.21] as modal, he must make the category "modal" endlessly elastic, such as by the claim that "there is something inherently modal about questions" (Joosten 2002: 54). If *yiqtol* is a modal gram, the precise extent of modal should be more clearly delineated than he has hitherto done. Second, given his admission that *yiqtol* was at an earlier stage an imperfective (Joosten 2002: 63) or present-future (Joosten 1989: 156; 2007: 58), his theory needs to account more clearly for the way that this form became modal—beyond simply claiming that the change is common (so Joosten 2007: 58).

The weakness of the non-past tense identification is even more serious insofar as the examples of *yiqtol* with past temporal reference are inherently at odds with identifying the form as an opposite, tensed gram. Zevit's claim (1988: 30) that examples of preterite *yiqtol* (< **yaqtul*) in the biblical text would "short circuit" the verbal system is equally valid with respect to the non-past gram identification of *yiqtol* and *yiqtol*s with past temporal reference.

A somewhat different objection to the imperfective identification of *yiqtol* is the argument of Waltke and O'Connor (1990: 476–77) that, as the unmarked member in privative opposition with perfective *qatal*, it is better labeled "nonperfective." Essentially, Waltke and O'Connor have reclothed earlier "aorist" identifications of *yiqtol* in the garb of markedness theory:

> In this form the notions of aspect and time both blend (imperfective aspect in past and present time) and separate (aorist in future time). Sperber [1943; 1966] and Hughes [1955; 1970] are partially right in describing it as a universal tense. And it may signify more than a blending of tense and aspect or pure tense; it may also signify either real or unreal moods—the indicative as well as degrees of dubiety and volition. In short: a form that can signify any time, any mood, and imperfective aspect (but not perfective), is not imperfective but nonperfective, "a more than opposite" of the suffix [*qatal*] conjugation. (The term "aorist," meaning without limits or boundaries, is not inappropriate.) (1990: 476–77)

Insofar as *yiqtol* is clearly less marked than *qatal* in its aspectual opposition, Waltke and O'Connor are justified. However, given my goal to determine an appropriate cross-linguistically comparable gram identity for *yiqtol*, nonperfective is essentially equivalent to imperfective, understanding (again) that we are not thereby limiting the form to expressing only imperfective aspect (e.g., excluding tense as part of its amalgam of meaning).

The second complication for substantiating imperfective *yiqtol* is that the comparative-historical evidence is simply not as transparent for the form compared with the case for *qatal*. Nevertheless, even given such constraints, diachronic typology is able to shed light on the development and identity of *yiqtol*.

To begin with, the diachronic reconstructions of the Semitic verbs, discussed at length in §2.3, all place the development of *yiqtol* prior to *qatal*, which fits well with the initial implicational argument given above (this section).

Also widely held is the view adopted here that **yaqtulu* is a Central Semitic (CS) innovation (see §2.3), of which BH *yiqtol* is a reflex. Explaining the precise origin of this gram is difficult because of its morphological similarity to the preterite-jussive Proto-Semitic **yaqtul* (e.g., Akkadian *iprus*) and its semantic parallel with the imperfective or present Proto-Semitic **yaqattal* (e.g., Akkadian *iparras*) gram (see Kouwenberg 2010: 91). The majority account of the CS **yaqtulu* is that it derives from the Proto-Semitic **yaqtul* via the addition of an *-u* vocalic suffix (Kuryłowicz 1973:60; Diakonoff 1988:103; T. D. Andersen 2000: 25; Kienast 2001: 338–39; Lipiński 2001: 342).[52] Semantically, this form assumed the meanings of the **yaqattal* form in Central Semitic. The major difficulty with this suggestion is that there is no attested grammaticalization path between the resultative-perfect-perfective path with which **yaqtul* is associated (based on its *iprus* Akkadian reflex) and the progressive-imperfective path with which **yaqtulu* is usually associated.

One way to obviate this difficulty is to combine Bauer's suggestion (1910: 8) that the prefix forms in Semitic originated by adding agreement affixes to the infinitive base form **q(u)tul* with Diakonoff's suggestion that the *u* suffix is perhaps a locative marker (cf. Akkadian *-u(m)*, which may occur on the infinitive form; see von Soden 1995: §66; Huehnergard 2005: §28.3). On this hypothesis, the origin of the CS **yaqtulu* is truly an innovation and is not derived from another form, and its origin is fully in keeping with a common lexical source of progressives: locative constructions involving infinitives (Bybee, Perkins, and Pagliuca 1994: 128; Heine and Kuteva 2002: 202). Competition between this new progressive-imperfective gram and the PS **yaqattal* would presumably account for the absence of the later in CS (see p. 98 n. 31).

Andrason (2010: 41–42) has proposed an analogical explanation, that CS **yaqtulu* is the "direct functional successor" of PS **yaqattal* analogically reshaped to the dominant **yaqtul* morphology. Regardless of whether the analogical explanation is successful, Andrason helpfully draws attention to the undisputed opinion that CS **yaqtulu* semantically corresponds to PS **yaqattal*: both belong to the same path of development, which begins with a pro-

---

52. The explanations are not completely uniform: Kuryłowicz (1972: 60) argued that Akkadian Subjunctive *iprusu* was an old present verb conjugation displaced and then syntactically delimited in East Semitic by the new present *iparras* conjugation (see Andersen 2000: 23–25; Garr 1998: lvi–lvii, whose comments are, at the least, misleading concerning the Akkadian Subjunctive and West Semitic **yaqtulu*); by contrast, Diakonoff (1988: 103) argued that **yaqtulu* originated as a subjunctive form and then spread to independent clauses in West Semitic. The *-u* suffix in this formation is generally related to the subordinating marker in Akkadian (see von Sodon 1995: §66; Kienast 2001: 269; Huehnergard 2005: 183–84), though Diakonoff (1988: 103) suggested it was a nominative or locative marker.

gressive construction that develops into an imperfective gram (Dahl 1985: 93; Bybee, Perkins, and Pagliuca 1994: 141).[53] These two grams are distinguished primarily by the more generalized meaning of the imperfective, which includes progressive expressions along with other meanings such as habitual and gnomic (Comrie 1976: 25; Bybee, Perkins, and Pagliuca 1994: 141; Heine and Kuteva 2002: 93).

However, this progressive-imperfective path of development does not adequately account for the future and irrealis mood meanings that the *yiqtol* conjugation expresses in BH (Andrason 2010: 36 n. 50). In this regard, Haspelmath 1998 represents an important extension of Bybee, Perkins, and Pagliuca's study (1994), which Andrason (2010) applies to BH as a corrective, by way of extension, to my earlier ideas (Cook 2002). Haspelmath surveys a number of "anomalous" grams, such as indicative forms that also express subjunctive mood, futures that may denote present, and grams with both future and habitual meanings and concludes that they can only be explained as originating in "old presents." That is, the "miscellaneous set of functions" (Bybee, Perkins, and Pagliuca 1994: 277) associated with these forms derives from older grams along the progressive-imperfective diachrony that through competition with newer progressive grams have lost their central imperfective/ present function (on overlap of imperfective and present, see Bybee, Perkins, and Pagliuca 1994: 126). These miscellaneous functions, such as future and habitual, regularly appear as "peripheral" meanings of imperfective grams (see Bybee, Perkins, and Pagliuca 1994: 158). But Haspelmath's crucial insight is that, through competition with other grams, these peripheral and seemingly miscellaneous meanings may come to be the more dominant meanings alongside the diminished or lost prototypical imperfective meanings. A shift of this sort would neatly explain the distribution of meanings associated with the BH *yiqtol*: because of competition from the participial progressive gram, imperfective *yiqtol* only infrequently expresses past and present imperfective as "residual" meanings of its earlier prototypical functions (Haspelmath 1998: 36), while (general) future and subjunctive meanings are becoming primary functions of the form. This reconstruction removes the objection that *yiqtol* cannot be an imperfective gram because it expresses general (perfective) future, in that such grams are "anomalous" in part because of the tendency of future and subjunctive expressions to be perfective (Haspelmath 1998: 55; for a similar case in Tigre, see Bybee, Perkins, and Pagliuca 1994:146–47). This sort of proposal fits well with the Rabbinic Hebrew data, which point to irrealis's becoming even more predominantly the central meaning for *yiqtol* (see Pérez Fernández 1997: 108).

---

53. More strongly, Haspelmath (1998: 34 n. 6) states that he knows of no present grams (a "subpart of imperfective" according to Bybee, Perkins, and Paglicua [1994: 141]) that derive from any source other than progressives.

Table 3.3. Development of Hebrew *Yiqtol* Conjugation

Central Semitic	Biblical Hebrew	Rabbinic Hebrew
progressive *ya-qtul-u*	> imperfective *yiqtol*	> irrealis *yiqtol*

A graphic representation of this development for BH *yiqtol* is presented in table 3.3. I have labeled the latest stage *irrealis* based on the case made below (§3.3.3) that mood is basically binary; thus, irrealis accounts for the various subordinate and deontic meanings of the form (some of the latter undoubtedly arising from the merger of the Jussive and *yiqtol* forms) as well as future and habitual. Whether future and/or habitual should be treated as modal (i.e., irrealis) is debated by linguists. The fact that imperfective grams may express these (even though as peripheral meanings) may indicate that they are realis mood. In Cook 2002: 230, I expressed hesitation at identifying habitual expressions as irrealis, though clearly there is a close association between the two in BH (i.e., irrealis *qatal* regularly expresses past habitual); however, further arguments have come forward favoring an irrealis analysis of habituality (Boneh and Doron 2008; 2010). In my treatment to follow, I survey the habitual expression by *yiqtol* under irrealis *yiqtol* (§3.3.3.2.); however, the gram's future meaning is analyzed under tense (§3.4.2.). My reasoning for the later is that the future meaning of *yiqtol* is mainly found in reported speech, where it forms a realis tense opposition with *qatal* (past). Thus, notwithstanding the difference of opinion that prevails regarding the relationship between futurity and modality, it seems reasonable to examine the future functions of *yiqtol* under realis tense.

The development of *yiqtol* along the diachronic path in table 3.3 accounts for the occurrences of past and present imperfective expressions, such as in examples [3.21a–b], and explains their relative paucity versus irrealis expressions by *yiqtol* (see §3.3.3.2). The remaining realis meaning associated with imperfective *yiqtol* is generic or gnomic. Such generic expressions are frequent for imperfective conjugations and unsurprising if one accepts the view of Bybee, Perkins, and Pagliuca (1994: 141) that an imperfective in the present is indistinguishable from a present, which is the most unmarked type of generic expression. However, as I have argued (Cook 2005), the TAM values of verbs in generic expressions are not fully leveled to a general present idea. As illustrated by examples [3.22a–c], *yiqtol* frequently expresses a sense of inevitability, except for the ambiguous examples that might be interpreted as describing either inevitabilities or typicalities.[54]

---

54. Examples of generic *yiqtol* in Proverbs and Qoheleth (see Cook 2005 and forthcoming for discussion): "typical" examples include Prov 10:1; 11:6; 12:25; 13:16; 14:17; 15:1, 2; 16:23; 18:1; 26:24; 29:2, 8; "inevitable" examples include Prov 11:11, 31; 13:13; 14:11;

[3.22] a. Prov 11:4

לֹא־יוֹעִיל הוֹן בְּיוֹם עֶבְרָה וּצְדָקָה תַּצִּיל מִמָּוֶת

'Wealth will not avail on the day of wrath, but righteousness will deliver from death'.

b. Prov 13:20 (*Qere*)

הוֹלֵךְ אֶת־חֲכָמִים יֶחְכָּם וְרֹעֶה כְסִילִים יֵרוֹעַ

'Whoever walks with the wise will become wise, and whoever consorts with fools will suffer harm'.

c. Qoh 3:14

יָדַעְתִּי כִּי כָּל־אֲשֶׁר יַעֲשֶׂה הָאֱלֹהִים הוּא יִהְיֶה לְעוֹלָם

'I know that all that God does, it will be forever'.

3.2.3.3. Participle as Adjectival Encoding of Event Predicates

Treatments of the Participle in studies of the BHVS have been uneven.[55] Although S. R. Driver (1998) included a chapter on the form, no one really followed his lead (Joosten [1989; 2002; etc.] is a notable exception among those
surveyed in chap. 2), and only in recent decades have there been calls for more
attention to the role of the Participle in the BHVS (cf. Hoftijzer 1991; see
further Cook 2008a; Notarius 2010). Hesitancy about treating the Participle
as part of the verbal system is no doubt attributable to its characterization as
"double-natured" or an "intermediate" form, sharing characteristics of both
the verbal and the nominal system (see Andersen and Forbes 2007; Dyk 1994;
A. Gordon 1982; Kahan 1889; Sellin 1889). This characterization is most
clearly illustrated by example [3.23], in which the plural construct form of the
Participle מְשָׁרְתֵי suggests a nominal analysis of the form, whereas the following direct object marker, אֹתִי, appears to require that we treat the participle as
a verb (A. Gordon 1982: 14).

[3.23] Jer 33:22

אַרְבֶּה אֶת־זֶרַע דָּוִד עַבְדִּי וְאֶת־הַלְוִיִּם מְשָׁרְתֵי אֹתִי

I will multiply the seed of David my servant and the Levites,
my servants/who serve me/the ones serving me'.

17:2, 20; 19:5, 9; 21:11; 27:18; 28:18; 29:23; from Qoheleth: 1:3 (or general present), 18
[2×]; 2:3 (or general present), 16, 21 (or future); 3:14 [2×], 15, 17; 4:10 [2×], 11, 12; 5:9
(stative), 11, 17 (or general present); 6:7 (stative), 12; 7:3, 7 [2×], 9, 12, 18, 19, 20 [2×], 26
[2×]; 8:1 [2×], 3 [2×], 5 [2×], 12, 13, 15; 9:4, 11; 10:1 [2×], 8 [2×], 10:9 [2×], 12, 14, 15, 18
[2×], 19 [2×], 20 [2×]; 11:3 [2×], 4 [2×], 5.

55. The discussion in this section is based on Cook 2008a.

Although this is the only such example in the Hebrew Bible, a fact that makes the text suspect to some scholars,[56] there are plenty of examples of plural construct Participles followed by constituents that are semantically complements (e.g., Gen 3:15, יֹדְעֵי טוֹב וָרָע 'knowing good and evil'; Josh 3:14, 15, 17, נֹשְׂאֵי הָאָרוֹן 'those lifting the ark'). The verbal-nominal ambiguity in example [3.23] is analogous to the verbal-nominal split in the stative form, as illustrated by examples [3.24a–c].

[3.24] a. Josh 23:2b

וַיֹּאמֶר אֲלֵהֶם אֲנִי זָקַנְתִּי בָּאתִי בַּיָּמִים

'He said to them, "I am/have become old, I have advanced in days'.

b. Gen 18:11

וְאַבְרָהָם וְשָׂרָה זְקֵנִים בָּאִים בַּיָּמִים חָדַל לִהְיוֹת לְשָׂרָה אֹרַח כַּנָּשִׁים:

'Abraham and Sarah (were) old, advanced in days; the manner of women had ceased to be for Sarah'.

c. Gen 24:1

וְאַבְרָהָם זָקֵן בָּא בַּיָּמִים

'Now Abraham was old/(was) old, he had/(was) advanced in years'.

I submit that the ambiguities described above place both the Participle and the stative alike in the class of *adjective*, which has long held an uncertain position between verbal and nominal classes (see Cook 2008a: 5–6).

At the same time, the Participle when used predicatively overlaps semantically with *yiqtol*, even in close juxtapositioning, as in example [3.25] (see Waltke and O'Connor 1990: 624; cf. S. R. Driver 1998: 27).

[3.25] Gen 37:15–16

וַיִּשְׁאָלֵהוּ הָאִישׁ לֵאמֹר מַה־תְּבַקֵּשׁ: וַיֹּאמֶר אֶת־אַחַי אָנֹכִי מְבַקֵּשׁ

'The man asked him, "What are you looking for?" He said, "I (am) looking for my brothers"'.

Thus, while it is incorrect to classify the Participle as a finite verb form (e.g., Joosten 1989: 128), it is likewise unwarranted to exclude the Participle from discussions of the BH TAM, as previous studies have done (e.g., Ewald 1879).

Examining the status of the adjectival Participle (and stative) in light of typological data on predicate encoding strategies makes it possible to clarify

---

56. Joüon (2006: §121k n. 2) suggests that either the text is in error and we should read מְשָׁרְתַי 'my servants,' as found in the previous verse (vs. 21), or if the text is correct then the construction is analogous with instances of the construct participle before prepositions (see Joüon 2006: §129m), especially given that the two particles (object marker and preposition את) are often confused in the book of Jeremiah.

the precise character of these forms in relation to the TAM system of BH and also to develop strong implicational typological arguments with regard to the diachronic development of this TAM system. Stassen's (1997: 12) typology of intransitive predication encodings, listed in examples [3.26a–d], provides an appropriate framework for this discussion.

> [3.26] Predicate categories of intransitive predication (Stassen 1997: 12):
> a. John walks (event/verbal)
> b. John is a carpenter (class/nominal)
> c. John is in the kitchen (location)
> d. John is tall (property/adjectival)

Stassen finds that the first three of these categories—event, class, and location [3.26a–c]—have cross-linguistically valid "prototypical" encoding strategies, described as follows.

First, event predicates are prototypically encoded according to the verbal strategy [3.26a]. Stassen includes both states and dynamic event types in this category. The verbal strategy is "non-supported"; that is, there is no copula or auxiliary required. In addition, if the language has person-agreement features, the verbal strategy will have person-agreement marking (Stassen 1997: 50, 120). Second, the nominal strategy, which prototypically encodes class-membership predicates [3.26b], in contrast to the verbal strategy, is supported by a nonverbal or zero copula. That is, either the predicate is introduced by an overt copula that does not have the characteristics of a verb, such as a pronoun or particle, or the predicate is juxtaposed with the subject, and the copula is merely implied (Stassen 1997: 120–21). Although English does not exhibit these sorts of copula strategies, examples [3.27a–c] illustrate the strategies.

> [3.27] a. Zero-copula (Stassen 1997: 62)
> *Moskva gorod* (Russian)
> Moscow city
> 'Moscow (is) a city'
> b. Pronominal copula (Glinert 1989: 189)
>
> השעון הוא מתנה
>
> gift PRO clock
> 'The clock is a gift'
> c. Particle copula (Stassen 1997: 79)
> *Rmṯ pw mḥw* (Egyptian)
> man COP Mahu
> 'Mahu is a man'

Third, the prototypical encoding of locative expressions, the locative strategy
[3.26c], features a verbal support element; that is, the copula can be marked for
typical verbal categories of tense, aspect, and modality and, most significantly,
person agreement (Stassen 1997: 55, 120).

By contrast with these first three strategies, Stassen (1997: 30) observes
that property predicates (i.e., adjectives) lack a prototypical encoding strategy
cross-linguistically. Instead, one of the other encoding strategies is adopted to
encode adjectives. This finding is significant on a general and a specific level.
Generally, it affirms and helps explain the noted ambiguities of the adjective
class in language. Specifically, it provides a means of delineating the particular
ambiguities of the Participle and stative in Hebrew.

In Biblical Hebrew, we find evidence of each of the strategies in Stassen's
typology: the finite verb conjugations represent the "non-supported" verbal
strategy, including person-agreement inflection, whereas class (nouns) and
locative predicates are encoded with some "supporting" copula strategy, in
free variation with each other: verbal, pronominal, particle, and zero (examples
[3.28a–d]).[57]

[3.28] Predicate encoding in Biblical Hebrew
   a. Gen 6:4 (verbal copula)

       הַנְּפִלִים הָיוּ בָאָרֶץ בַּיָּמִים הָהֵם

       'The Nepilim <u>were</u> in the land in those days'.
   b. 2 Kgs 19:15 (PRO copula)

       אַתָּה־הוּא הָאֱלֹהִים לְבַדְּךָ

       'You <u>are</u> God alone'
   c. Judg 6:13 (particle copula)

       בִּי אֲדֹנִי וְיֵשׁ יְהוָה עִמָּנוּ וְלָמָּה מְצָאַתְנוּ כָּל־זֹאת

       'Please, my lord, if Yhwh <u>is</u> with us, why has all this hap-
       pened to us?'
   d. Josh 22:34 (zero copula)

       עֵד הוּא בֵּינֹתֵינוּ כִּי יְהוָה הָאֱלֹהִים

       'It (<u>is</u>) a witness between us that Yhwh (<u>is</u>) God'.

---

57. The pronominal copular analysis [3.28b] in Biblical Hebrew is debated. A majority of scholars argue that examples such as יְהוָה הוּא הָאֱלֹהִים should be analyzed as cases of
extrapositioning (traditionally labeled *casus pendens*). That is, they consist of an extraposed
noun (יְהוָה), a resumptive pronoun (הוּא), and predicate noun (הָאֱלֹהִים): 'Yhwh, he is God'
(e.g., Geller 1991; Muraoka 1999b; Zewi 1996; Khan [2006] presents the minority pronominal copula position). However, in the above example from 2 Kgs 19:15, the lack of person
agreement between the fronted element (אַתָּה) and the resumptive pronoun (הוּא) favors a
pronominal copula interpretation. As further support, C. N. Li and Thompson (1977) have
argued that extrapositional equative clauses (as are the clauses mentioned here) are an important source for the development of pronominal copulas cross-linguistically.

Prototypical adjectives or properties (i.e., other than the Participle and stative) use the same copula strategies as nouns and locative expressions, as illustrated in example [3.29].[58]

[3.29] a. Gen 29:31 (zero copula)

וְרָחֵל עֲקָרָה

'But Rachel (was) barren'.

  b. Lam 1:18 (pronominal copula)

צַדִּיק הוּא יְהוָה

'Yhwh is righteous'.

  c. Gen 11:30 (verbal copula)

וַתְּהִי שָׂרַי עֲקָרָה

'Now Sarai was barren'.

By contrast, the stative and the Participle exhibit unique and distinct patterns of predicate encoding. First, the stative allows either verbal or nominal-locative predicate encodings, as illustrated by examples [3.30a–c].

[3.30] a. Gen 48:10 (verbal encoding)

וְעֵינֵי יִשְׂרָאֵל כָּבְדוּ מִזֹּקֶן

'They eyes of Israel were heavy from old age'.

  b. Exod 17:12 (nominal encoding with zero copula)

וִידֵי מֹשֶׁה כְּבֵדִים

'Moses' hands (were) heavy'.

  c. Gen 50:9 (locative encoding with verbal copula)

וַיְהִי הַמַּחֲנֶה כָּבֵד מְאֹד

'The camp was very large'.

Second, the predicative Participle is consistently encoded with nominal-locative strategies; however, it is distinct from prototypical adjectives (which are also consistently encoded with nominal-locative strategies) in that the Participle can encode *an event predicate*, as in examples [3.31a–d].

[3.31] a. 1 Kgs 13:1 (zero copula)

וְיָרָבְעָם עֹמֵד עַל־הַמִּזְבֵּחַ

'Jeroboam (was) standing beside the altar'.

  b. Deut 31:3 (pronominal copula)

יְהוָה אֱלֹהֶיךָ הוּא עֹבֵר לְפָנֶיךָ

'Yhwh your God is passing over before you'.

---

58. Neither [3.29b] nor [3.31b] is as compelling an example of the pronominal copula as example [3.28b], with its lack of person–person agreement. This sort of uncertainty does not affect the larger argument I am making here, however.

c. Gen 43:4 (particle copula)

אִם־יֶשְׁךָ מְשַׁלֵּחַ אֶת־אָחִינוּ אִתָּנוּ נֵרְדָה וְנִשְׁבְּרָה לְךָ אֹכֶל

'If you are sending our brother with us, we will go down and buy food for you'.

d. 1 Kgs 20:39 (verbal copula)

וַיְהִי הַמֶּלֶךְ עֹבֵר

'The king was passing by'.

The "intermediate" character of the Participle may therefore be restated in clearer terms: the Participle represents a "nominal takeover" of event predicates, whereby a nominal predicate encoding strategy is applied to event predicates, which are more prototypically encoded by the verbal strategy. The new gram created through the nominal takeover strategy in turn plays a role in the BH TAM system.[59]

This explanation of the Participle differs markedly from previous approaches, which have tried to discern the point at which the Participle stops being an intermediate form (e.g., A. Gordon 1982) or becomes "reanalyzed" as a finite verb with the copula treated as an "auxiliary" (Dyk 1994). There is no evidence that the Participle stops being adjectival at any time in the history of Hebrew; thus, it continues to be used in both nominal and verbal slots in the grammar. As predicative, it is always "supported" by a copula, whether expressed or implied.[60]

When we draw the stative split-encoding form back into the discussion, it becomes evident that the Participle is part of a cycle of nominal takeovers in Semitic and Hebrew, as delineated in table 3.4. The stative represents an early nominal takeover that eventually developed into a verbal encoding (Huehnergard 1992: 156; Stassen 1997: 494).[61] The split nominal-verbal encoding, which was on the decline in the biblical period, represents an intermediate

---

59. Notarious (2010: 243) sets aside passive participles from her discussion, and admittedly I have focused here on the active participle. The distinction, however, is not really substantive but accidental: given the valency-reducing status of passive participles, their "event" characteristic is much less prominent (i.e., they are intransitive so they have no verbal arguments to govern), and their meaning is more static (on the basis of similarities between stative and passive meanings; on which, see above, §3.2.2).

60. The correctness of this analysis of the zero copula as "implying" a copula is supported by contrastive examples such as 2 Sam 7:16 (כִּסְאֲךָ יִהְיֶה נָכוֹן עַד־עוֹלָם 'your throne will be established forever') versus 1 Chr 17:24 (וּבֵית־דָּוִיד עַבְדְּךָ נָכוֹן לְפָנֶיךָ 'the house of David, your servant, will be established before you'), in which the copula with the adjectival participle, in this instance, is shown to be optional and without effect on the semantic interpretation of the constructions, and no certain conclusions of a diachronic or dialectic contrast can be drawn from these and similar contrastive examples.

61. A parallel grammaticalization process is observable in Aramaic, in which the propensity to use enclitic pronouns with the participle has resulted in the grammaticalization of

Table 3.4. Nominal Takeovers of Event Predicates

Early Semitic	Biblical Hebrew	Rabbinic Hebrew
nominal takeover >	split nominal-verbal encoding >	verbal encoding
*qaribim + ʾattem	qərĕḇim ʾattɛm ~ qĕraḇtɛm	qĕraḇtɛm
'you (are) drawn near'	'you (are)/have drawn near'	'you are/have drawn near'
		split nominal-locative
	nominal encoding >	encoding >
	huʾ holeḵ	hu haya holek ~ hu holek
	'he (is/was) walking	'he was/(is) walking'

stage. This decline is demonstrated by the propensity toward dynamic vowel patterns instead of stative (e.g., *qārēḇ* > *qārab*), evident from comparative data, and the decline of present-stative interpretations for *qatal*-conjugated statives (see Cook 2012). Significantly, in some cases the alternate strategy for expressing present states of these lexemes was the predicative Participle (e.g., יָדַעְתִּי 'I know' > 'I knew', replaced by אֲנִי יוֹדֵעַ 'I know'). The Participle represents a newer nominal takeover that developed unevenly into a split nominal-locative encoding after the biblical period.[62] This split nominal-locative encoding, which was only incipient in BH, patterned according to the "present parameter" (Stassen 1997: 314);[63] that is, the verbal copula (locative strategy) was used with the Participle in past (and some future) expressions, while the zero-copula strategy was employed for present temporal expressions.[64]

---

the enclitic pronouns as verbal inflections in Northeastern Neo-Aramaic: *qaṭel-na* 'I kill (M)' in Babylonian Jewish Aramaic versus *qaṭlen* 'I kill (M)' in Jewish Arbel (Khan 2007: 110).

62. That this shift is uneven can be seen in the following: (1) there was an increased use only of the *yiqtol* of היה with the Participle in Qumran Hebrew versus Biblical Hebrew (see Muraoka 1999a); (2) the use of the *qatal* versus the *yiqtol* of היה with the Participle in Mishnaic Hebrew was both more frequent and more systematic—in part, no doubt, due to the generally higher frequency of past-progressive versus future-progressive expressions in language (Pérez Fernández 1997: 108–9); (3) certain dialects of postbiblical Hebrew moved toward abandoning the use of the Participle for future expressions in favor of the imperfective form (Rabin 2000: 115 n. 2). A. Gordon (1982: 40–41) notes that the locative encoding (with Past היה copula) is required for the predicative Participle used with past temporal reference.

63. The examples of copula plus Participle expressing past progressive in BH are few: Gen 37:2; 39:22; Exod 3:1; Deut 9:24; Josh 5:5; Judg 1:7; 16:21; 1 Sam 2:11; 2 Sam 3:6; Zech 3:3; Job 1:14; Dan 10:2; Neh 1:4 (see Kautzsch 1910: §116r).

64. This split encoding pattern appears also in Modern Hebrew (e.g., *Dan haya holek* 'Dan used to walk'; see Schwarzwald 2001: 62–63), where the copula is treated as an auxiliary (e.g., Shlonsky 1997: 25, 30–31; Glinert 1989: 125–26, 332). Kuteva (2001: 13) discusses the difficulties involved in identifying auxiliaries, noting that there is a good degree of variation with regard to how many features of "canonical auxiliary constructions" a given

Finally, these findings form the basis for an important implicational typological argument based on Stassen's "Tensedness Parameter" (1997: 347–57),
which states that languages that are aspect-prominent tend to encode adjectival predicates according to their verbal strategy, whereas tense-prominent languages tend to encode adjectival predicates according to one or more of their
nominal strategies. Reversing this implication, the shift away the split verbal-
nominal stative encoding and the development nominal encoding—both of
prototypical adjectives and of event predicates in the Participle—indicates that
the drift of Hebrew is from more aspect-prominent to more tense-prominent.

Identification of the predicative Participle construction as a progressive
gram is compelling on the basis of several pieces of evidence. First, given
the above arguments that the *yiqtol* is a gram developing on the progressive-
imperfective path and given the degree of overlap between it and the Participle
(see example [3.25] above), it makes good sense to see the predicative Participle as a younger (progressive) gram developing along the same progressive-
imperfective path. Second, Stassen (1997: 242) notes that all such relationships
of the sort I have posited for *yiqtol* and the predicative Participle (which he
terms "verb switching") "take the form of a contrast between simple verb
forms and periphrastic (or complex) verb forms." This datum lends support to
the view espoused above, that the Participle is always copularly supported. It
also confirms the progressive analysis of the predicative Participle in that periphrastic expressions are a major lexical source of progressive grams (Bybee,
Perkins, and Pagliuca 1994: 127–33).

As a progressive gram, the predicative Participle expresses an agent in the
midst of an activity at the reference time (so Bybee, Perkins, and Pagliuca
1994: 136), which is determined by the discourse context in which the Participle occurs, whether by lexical modification, as in [3.32a–b], by a neighboring
TAM form, as in [3.32c–d], or by the narrative reference time more generally
[3.32d].

---

auxiliary has. These include: (1) change of semantics of the main verb; (2) variation regarding whether or not the construction is used with all verbs in the language; (3) integration of
the structure into the system of paradigmatic distinctions of the language; (4) possibility/im-
possibility of using adverbials between the auxiliary and main verb; (5) particular facts about
gender/number agreement between subject and object and the components of the auxiliary
structure, etc. Points (2) and (3) and possibly (4) argue in favor of an auxiliary analysis of
היה in compound tenses in Modern Hebrew. Dyk and Talstra (1999: 165) attempt to nuance
the case in Biblical Hebrew by arguing that "a difference should be maintained between stating that the formal syntax allows for a participle to be interpreted as being the main verbal
predication and stating that in a particular instance it actually was intended as the main verbal
predication." However, it is unclear what they mean by "actually was intended," nor does
their next comment seem to follow logically: "Obviously, something would be missed if one
were to treat the participle merely as a nominal form in examples such as Jeremiah 7:17."

[3.32] a. Jer 28:3

בְּעוֹד שְׁנָתַיִם יָמִים אֲנִי מֵשִׁיב אֶל־הַמָּקוֹם הַזֶּה אֶת־כָּל־כְּלֵי בֵית יְהוָה

'Within two years I (am) <u>returning</u> to this place all the
vessels of the house of Yhwh . . .'

b. Judg 14:4

וּבָעֵת הַהִיא פְּלִשְׁתִּים מֹשְׁלִים בְּיִשְׂרָאֵל

'Now <u>at that time</u> the Philistines (were) <u>ruling</u> over Israel'.

c. Gen 18:22

וַיִּפְנוּ מִשָּׁם הָאֲנָשִׁים וַיֵּלְכוּ סְדֹמָה וְאַבְרָהָם עוֹדֶנּוּ עֹמֵד לִפְנֵי יְהוָה

'The men turned from there and <u>went</u> towards Sodom; but
as for Abraham, he (was) still <u>standing</u> before Yhwh'.

d. Exod 7:17

כֹּה אָמַר יְהוָה בְּזֹאת תֵּדַע כִּי אֲנִי יְהוָה הִנֵּה אָנֹכִי מַכֶּה בַּמַּטֶּה אֲשֶׁר־
בְּיָדִי עַל־הַמַּיִם אֲשֶׁר בַּיְאֹר וְנֶהֶפְכוּ לְדָם

'Thus says Yhwh: "By this you <u>will know</u> that I am Yhwh:
Look, I (am) <u>striking</u> with the staff that is in my hand the
waters that are in the Nile so that they turn to blood'.

e. Gen 24:30

וְהִנֵּה עֹמֵד עַל־הַגְּמַלִּים עַל־הָעָיִן

'And look, he (was) <u>standing</u> by the camels beside the
spring'.

In example [3.33], all of the above-listed elements contribute to a correct past-
perfect progressive interpretation of the the participle, [$C_{RF} < C_{pos1} < S$ &
$PROG_{ACT}$ & DECL]: the preceding *qatal* forms set the past-temporal context;[65]
the temporal phrase עַד־הַיָּמִים הָהֵמָּה sets a temporal boundary in the past before
which the situation was taking place; finally, the overt *qatal* copula הָיוּ reinforces the past-in-the-past (i.e., past perfect) location of the event.[66]

---

65. Note that a series of *qatal* forms is employed intentionally to avoid the narrative
implication of temporal succession associated with *wayyiqtol*: Hezekiah did each of these
things as part of his reform but not necessarily in this order (see further chap. 4).

66. Examples such as this illustrate well the manner of the development of the "present
parameter" in terms of verbal copular support of the participle (see above in this section): the
overt copula here clarifies the past-perfect progressive interpretation that otherwise would be
ambiguous between a past-perfect and a simple past interpretation. Such ambiguity appears
in two other places in the text: אֲשֶׁר־עָשָׂה מֹשֶׁה is ambiguous between past or past perfect in
Hebrew just as in the English rendering; similarly, and supporting the ambiguous understanding of the preceding, the *wayyiqtol* וַיִּקְרָא continuation from the past-perfect progressive
participle maintains the continued sense of past-perfect temporal interpretation. Probably a
consequential sense is the main motivation for its use here: because they had been burning
incense to the bronze serpent, they had taken to calling it by a proper name, thus personifying

[3.33] 2 Kgs 18:4

הוּא הֵסִיר אֶת־הַבָּמוֹת וְשִׁבַּר אֶת־הַמַּצֵּבֹת וְכָרַת אֶת־הָאֲשֵׁרָה וְכִתַּת נְחַשׁ
הַנְּחֹשֶׁת אֲשֶׁר־עָשָׂה מֹשֶׁה כִּי עַד־הַיָּמִים הָהֵמָּה הָיוּ בְנֵי־יִשְׂרָאֵל מְקַטְּרִים
לוֹ וַיִּקְרָא־לוֹ נְחֻשְׁתָּן

'He [Hezekiah] removed the high places and broke the
standing stones and cut down the Asherah poles and cut up the
bronze serpent that Moses (had) made, for up until those days
the children of Israel <u>had been burning incense</u> to it; (so) he
(had) called it Nehushtan'.

The temporal determination of the progressive by the discourse reference time
points to a default temporal interpretation of present time inasmuch as the default deictic center is the present. Most of the examples with a default present-
time interpretation appear in direct speech, in which events are individually
anchored to the speaker's deictic center (see chap. 4 and example [3.34a]).
This fact should not be overgeneralized so as to claim that participles are present in direct speech and past in narrative, given the default present interpretation in non-narrative, non-speech generic statements, illustrated by [3.34b].

[3.34] a. Gen 24:33

הִנֵּה אָנֹכִי נִצָּב עַל־עֵין הַמָּיִם

'Look, I (am) <u>standing</u> beside the spring of water'.

b. Prov 11:13

הוֹלֵךְ רָכִיל מְגַלֶּה־סּוֹד וְנֶאֱמַן־רוּחַ מְכַסֶּה דָבָר

'A slanderer <u>reveals</u> confidences, but a trustworthy spirit
<u>conceals</u> a word'.

An extension of the present progressive interpretation of the Participle has
been termed *expected future* (Cook 2002: 268, adopting the term from Bybee, Perkins, and Paglicua 1994: 249–50) or *prospective aspect* (see Comrie
1976: 64). The analogous relationship evident between this temporal meaning
and the present perfect (see Comrie 1976: 64) might suggest an analogous
label, such as *present prospective* (cf. present retrospective = present anterior/
perfect): an event in process at the speaker's reference time is fully realized
only at some point after that reference time. In English, these expressions are
generally periphrastic using *going to* or the like, which rendering accords well
with prospective examples in BH.[67] However, a *going-to* rendering is not re-

---

it (this assumes that the subject is impersonal or 'children of Israel', despite the unexpected
singular form).

67. The list of examples includes Gen 6:13, 17; 19:13; 37:30; Exod 9:17–18; 10:4; 17:9;
Josh 11:6; 1 Sam 19:11. See others in the grammars: Kautzsch 1910: §116p; Joüon 2006:
§121e; Waltke and O'Connor 1990: 627–28.

quired to makes sense of these passages: the participle's basic progressive sense remains, and the prospective sense is recoverable from the contextual clues, whether lexical, as in example [3.32a], or logical, as in [3.32d] and [3.35] (i.e., obviously Moses is not yet dead in the example below, since he is still speaking!)

[3.35] Deut 4:22

כִּי אָנֹכִי מֵת בָּאָרֶץ הַזֹּאת אֵינֶנִּי עֹבֵר אֶת־הַיַּרְדֵּן וְאַתֶּם עֹבְרִים וִירִשְׁתֶּם
אֶת־הָאָרֶץ הַטּוֹבָה הַזֹּאת:

'Because I (am) <u>dying/going to die</u> in this land, I am not <u>crossing/going to cross</u> the Jordan, but you (are) <u>crossing/going to cross</u> (it) so that you might take possession of this good land'.

Although the Participle gram clearly overlaps with the *yiqtol* semantically, the Participle is much more restricted in its meanings. In addition, the above diachronic typological analysis that places the two grams on the same line of progressive-imperfective development enables us to distinguish the two in terms of how far they have developed instead of simply performing a semantic analysis: as the older form, the *yiqtol* has largely lost its prototypical imperfective functions to the progressive Participle, such as past, present, and future progressive. This competition may be observed "in process" by comparing the "earlier" wisdom literature in the book of Proverbs with the "later" material in Qoheleth (Ecclesiastes): in generic expressions in Proverbs, *yiqtol* appears much more frequently than the Participle, whereas in Qoheleth, the numbers are reversed, and the Participle is more frequently employed as a generic form than *yiqtol* (cf. Cook 2005: 124; and forthcoming). The change has been independently identified in parts of the prophetic literature (Notarius 2010), a fact that lends weight to the claims made here regarding the change.

3.3. The Expression of Modality in BH

In this section, I discuss the expression of modality by the BHVS, which is to say, I discuss the irrealis mood grams and the range of modalities that they regularly express. There is an almost limitless range of modal nuances available to human language, and there is notable semantic-functional overlap among BH irrealis mood grams. For example, the expression of epistemic possibility by irrealis *yiqtol* is generally signaled by context alone, and often uncertain in a given passage. It is well nigh impossible at this point in our knowledge to be able to predict whether a conditional apodosis might more likely feature an irrealis *qatal* or an irrealis *yiqtol* form. Confronted with these sorts of challenges my goal is to explain how irrealis mood is indicated in the BHVS and what the central correlations are between irrealis grams and expressions of modality.

The discussion here presumes that of §1.6 as background to the analysis of mood in the BHVS. By way of review—modality refers to the conceptual or semantic domain consisting of the theoretically limitless ways in which speakers might choose to relate an event or proposition to alternative situations; however, there is a core group of these gram-type modalities that is attested widely cross-linguistically (Bybee and Fleischman 1995: 2; Bybee 1998: 262). The various modalities may be expressed alternatively, but not mutually exclusively, by modal systems or mood systems. There is no evidence that the former is found at any stage of Hebrew,[68] but BH has mood systems: a syntactically indicated irrealis mood system and a directive-volitive mood subsystem that includes morphologically distinct Imperative and Jussive conjugations in addition to the syntactic distinction.[69]

Despite challenges to the validity or at least value of the category of irrealis mood (see §1.6.3.3), it is an appropriate categorization for this mood system in Hebrew for several reasons. First, although Bybee (1998: 267–69) complains that it is too general to be useful inasmuch as it encompasses a variety of other more specific modalities that should be the real focus of a linguistic description of mood, in BH this mood is indicated by a word order distinction: realis clauses default to subject-verb word order, whereas irrealis clauses exhibit verb-subject word order. Thus, the use of this broad distinction is valid insofar as it is expressed by a particular grammatical construction. This broader category is particularly useful in that it applies not only to the word-order distinction of mood with the two primary conjugations, *qatal* and *yiqtol*, but applies likewise to the directive-volitive mood system: the directive-volitive system also exhibits irrealis mood word order. Thus, irrealis helpfully encompasses the syntactic marking of mood in BH and, including the subcategory of that syntactic mood system, the morphologically distinct directive-volitive mood system.

A second reason that irrealis is appropriate is that the modalities expressed by irrealis *qatal* and irrealis *yiqtol* are indeed quite broad, including subordinate modalities, habituality, volitive, and positive and negative directive meanings. Below, I make the case that at least some of these modal meanings come to be associated with these two irrealis forms (in the narrow sense of the category; i.e., excluding the directive-volitive system) through context-induced reinterpretation or modal contamination through the use in inherently modal

---

68. This is not to deny that Hebrew has modal predicates (e.g., יכל), but it does not seem ever to have had a modal system, as in "a single system of commuting terms" to express modalities (Palmer 2001: 6). Melnik (2010: 1) remarks on modality in Modern Hebrew that, though Modern Hebrew has various modal expressions, they "do not seem to form a coherent set."

69. The partial obscuring of the morphological distinction between the Jussive and *yiqtol* and the status of the so-called Cohortative are discussed in §3.3.2 below.

constructions, such as apodictic/conditional law codes. This idea fits well with Bybee's (1998: 265) characterization of grams that typically are labeled irrealis as denoting situations that are not asserted and frequently derive their meaning from the construction in which they occur. Thus, and third, the category is appropriate because it designates the origin of these grams in modal constructions and their dependence on those constructions to inform their meaning.

Finally, the negative argument is Occam's razor: if the various nonindicative meanings cohere in a single form and can be reasonably related to that form in terms of a single "general" meaning and context-determined "individual" meanings, this is preferable to positing several different grams that "happen" to have the same grammaticalized form. The case is analogous with the case for allomorphs: if the various phonological shapes are all related to a "general" meaning, and the variation can be explained based on phonological context, then it is expedient to posit a morph that represents, albeit as an abstraction, the various allomorphs as a single morphological entity.

3.3.1. Word Order in BH: An Overview

Since the word-order indicated mood distinction encompasses both mood systems (i.e., irrealis and directive-volitive), I begin with an overview of word order in BH. These arguments are not my own, however, but are adopted from colleagues whose work on word order I am endorsing here. Word order necessarily comes into play in any analysis of the BHVS because the *waw*-prefixed conjugations (according to the traditional understanding of them) are almost always clause initial. Variation among these and the *qatal* and *yiqtol* forms have been explained by some scholars as being due to this syntactic restriction and not any semantic difference (see §2.4.2.2). Several other theories surveyed in chap. 2 included attention to word order for understanding the semantics of the BHVS (see §2.4.2.3).

Assessments of word order in BH illustrate a sort of tyranny of the majority in two respects: the overwhelming majority of scholars have held that BH syntax is basically a verb-subject (VS) order because this is statistically the most frequent order. However, given that the *waw*-prefixed forms represent a syntactically constrained clause type and that *wayyiqtol* in particular is additionally restricted to past narrative genre, there should be some healthy suspicion about whether frequency alone is sufficient for determining basic word order in BH. The tyranny of the majority is seen also in the fact that the VS analysis is often assumed, without any defense, to be the very foundation of studies of the pragmatics of word order (e.g., Shimasaki 2002, and the criticisms in Cook 2003a and Holmstedt 2003; Moshavi 2010 and the reaction in Holmstedt 2011).

Suspicions regarding this majority position have been growing and with good reason: SV languages outnumber VS languages by almost six to one

(Dryer 2005: 334–37). Thus, a priori, there is a better chance that BH is SV rather than VS. Joüon (1923; 2006) is one of only a few grammarians to endorse an SV position. However, almost half a century ago now, Rosén (1969) pointed out the statistical tendency for directive-volitive mood verbs (i.e., Imperative, Jussive, and Cohortatives) to head their clauses. Revell (1989) and his students followed up on this observation: Revell argued that the difference between indicative and nonindicative *yiqtol* is indicated by word order, with nonindicative being clause initial. Shulman (1996) examined all of the directive-volitive forms in Genesis through Kings and found that these forms head their clause between 94 and 97 percent of the time.[70] DeCaen (1996) refined these observations by examining them from the perspective of generative grammar. He argued that BH was a verb-second (V2) language—that is, that the basic order in BH is SV but that in subordinate clauses the order is reversed to VS, resulting in the verb's having second position following the subordinating word. Significantly, DeCaen explained the VS order of the *wayyiqtol* in this framework, arguing that an "underspecified" function word assimilated between the conjunction and the agreement affix (i.e., *wa-y-yiqtol*) accounts for the VS ordering within a V2 system.

Holmstedt (2002; 2005; 2009; 2011) argues for SV basic word order in BH from a perspective similar to DeCaen's and thus also uses the idea of constituent movement to account for variation in word order. In each of his analyses of Proverbs (2005: 150–51), Jonah and Ruth, (2009: 124–25), and Genesis (2011: 28), Holmstedt has concluded that Hebrew is best described as a SV/X-VS language: that is, BH finite clauses (i.e., copular expressions are unaffected) have a basic SV word order, departures from which are due to a third constituent (X), including subordinators and negative words, (pragmatically) fronted items (on which, see especially Holmstedt 2009: 126–37), and (irrealis) modality. Important to our mood-based concern with word order, the multiple "third constituents" may interact to obscure the expected word order, as in example [3.36], in which the expected irrealis VS word order with the Jussive is "overridden" by the focus fronting of the subject 'the boy'.

[3.36] Gen 44:33

וְעַתָּה יֵשֶׁב־נָא עַבְדְּךָ תַּחַת הַנַּעַר עֶבֶד לַאדֹנִי וְהַנַּעַר יַעַל עִם־אֶחָיו

'Now, please allow your servant to remain here instead of the boy as a servant to my lord; but the boy let go up with his brothers'.

Space precludes a full exposition of Holmstedt's SV/X-VS theory, and, as Holmstedt (2011: 25) notes, "[A]ny final conclusion about Biblical Hebrew

---

70. Imperative 1454 out of 1515; Jussive 96 out of 102; and Cohortative 192 out of 197 (Shulman 1996: 241, 246, 248).

Table 3.5. Representative Paradigm of BH Prefix Pattern

Qal binyan	PQD	KBD	QWM
yiqtol 3MS	יִפְקֹד	יִכְבַּד	יָקוּם
wayyiqtol 3MS	וַיִּפְקֹד	וַיִּכְבַּד	וַיָּקָם
Jussive 3MS	יִפְקֹד	יִכְבַּד	יָקֹם
Imperative MS	פְּקֹד	כְּבַד	קוּם
Cohortative 1s	אֶפְקְדָה	אֶכְבְּדָה	אֶקוּמָה
Infinitive	פְּקֹד	כְּבַד	קוּם

[word order] as a whole must be delayed until a full study of all the texts has been completed." Yet at this point the case for an SV-realis : VS-irrealis mood opposition makes the best sense of the word order data generally and, as argued below, the BHVS specifically. For this reason, I proceed on the basis of Holmstedt's SV/X-VS theory, drawing particularly on the word-order mood opposition included in his theory. This pattern is justified by the statistical correlation between the morphologically distinct directive-volitive irrealis mood forms and VS order (above) and by claims that the VS-restricted *wěqatal* is essentially an irrealis mood form (Joosten 1989). Here I extend these ideas and argue that, system wide, the BHVS displays a mood-based word order distinction, and that the adoption of this position particularly illuminates the position of *wěqatal* with respect to the rest of the BHVS.

3.3.2. Directive-Volitive Mood System

There are good morphological, syntactic, and semantic grounds for treating the Imperative, Jussive, and Cohortative forms as constituting a distinct directive-volitive subsystem of BH irrealis mood. Morphologically, the three forms are constructed on the "prefix pattern," which they share in common with *yiqtol* and *wayyiqtol*.[71] Thus these conjugations all share a common set of agreement features, and the vowel pattern in the root-and-pattern morphology is consistent throughout the conjugations for each verb (see table 3.5).

However, the Imperative, which is limited to the second person, lacks the agreement prefixes, retaining only gender-number-indicating suffixes (cf. Imperative MP שִׁמְרוּ 'Guard!' versus *yiqtol* or Jussive 2MP תִּשְׁמְרוּ 'You shall guard'). Cross-linguistically, this is similar to some non-pro-drop languages that do not require an overt subject for the imperative (e.g., English *Go!*; see Verstraete 2007: 39).

The Jussive is distinct from *yiqtol* only with certain roots, verbs, and inflectional forms: in the 3MS and 2MS forms (i.e., forms without any inflectional

---

71. The final vowel that distinguishes the *yiqtol* (< **yaqtulu*) has been discussed above (§§2.3; 3.2.3.2), and the case for a distinct *wayyiqtol* conjugation is discussed further below (§3.4.1).

sufformative) in (1) the Hiphil *binyan*, where the Jussive has a different theme vowel (e.g., Jussive 3ms יַקְהֵל 'Let him congregate' versus *yiqtol* 3ms יַקְהִיל 'He will congregate'), or in (2) roots with a glide (*w* or *y*) in the second or third position, in which cases the Jussive has an apocopated singular (e.g., Jussive 3ms יִבֶן 'Let him build' versus *yiqtol* 3ms יִבְנֶה 'He will build'; see Kummerow 2007a).

The Cohortative has traditionally been described as a first-person volitive, distinguished from first-person *yiqtol* by its paragogic הָ-, which, however, does not occur on roots with a glide (י/ו) or glottal (א) in third position or with enclitic object pronouns.[72] Older grammars treat the paragogic הָ- as a lengthening of the Imperfect, in contrast to Jussive, which is a shortening of the same (e.g., Kautzsch 1910: 129). The paragogic הָ- has been understood as contributing some sort of "intensification" (Ewald 1879: 17) or "emphasis" (S. R. Driver 1998: 51) to the verbal action. Moran (1950; 1960, repr. 2003), followed by Rainey (1975; 1986), suggested that BH Cohortative is a reflex of a fuller Canaanite Volitive conjugation **yaqtula* (see Joüon 2006: §117c). However, the modal interpretation of the paragogic הָ- is questionable on several grounds.

First, the EA evidence for a Canaanite Volitive conjugation is equivocal. Rainey (1996b: 262) states that "it is abundantly clear that the EA texts have not given us any conclusive evidence for the existence of a Canaanite *yaqtula* pattern. In spite of Moran's brilliant mustering of the evidence, it is still possible to argue that the *-a* suffix is merely the Akkadian ventive." This view is more strongly stated by Lipiński (2001: 260–61): "This subjunctive in *-a* alternates in the Amarna correspondence with the East Semitic ventive, and its particular use with expressions of wish or expectation, especially in 1s, leave little doubt that the West Semitic subjunctive in *-a* is but a ventive or allative, with some distinctive syntactical features."

Second, although the paragogic הָ- appears on the so-called Cohortative over 500 times,[73] it occurs over 300 times on the Imperative, with which as a modal marker it would seem to be redundant. Shulman has examined the 116 examples of the "long" imperative form (i.e., those with a paragogic הָ-) in Genesis through 2 Kings and has concluded "that the long imperative form is used where the speaker requests an action directed to himself, an action done for him/to him/towards him/with him etc." (Shulman 1996: 66). Shulman discovered that in 112 cases a prepositional idea with reference to the speaker was present (61 times) or implied in the context (51 times), thus re-

---

72. Dallaire (2002: 127 n. 228) notes several exceptions wherein roots with a third-position א exhibit the paragogic הָ-: -Gen 29:21; Judg 15:1; 2 Kgs 19:23; Ps 43:4; Gen 19:8; Judg 19:24; 2 Chr 1:10.

73. The Westminster morphology contains 521 examples of the form out of 2813 first-person *yiqtol* forms (of which the Cohortative is treated as a subcategory).

inforcing the reflexive interpretation of the paragogic הָ. Fassberg reached the same conclusion as Shulman in his study of the imperative with paragogic הָ: "[T]he lengthened imperative קָטְלָה is used in biblical Hebrew when the action of the verb is directed towards the speaker" (1999: 13).[74] Fassberg (1999: 13) contends that the paragogic הָ on the Imperative is semantically similar to the Akkadian ventive, which is related to the dative verb suffixes, especially the 1s -*am* (von Soden 1995: §66).[75]

Third, the paragogic הָ occurs on about 100 (realis) *wayyiqtol* forms, which further argues against a modal interpretation of the morpheme.[76] Gentry (1998: 24) argues that the paragogic הָ in these cases has a locative (*hither/thither*) or reflexive (*myself/for my sake*) meaning. Significantly, all but two of the examples are first person forms, and the locative sense (*here/there, hither/thither*) is more prevalent in the passages from earlier texts, whereas the reflexive sense is more prevalent in the passages from later literature. In most passages in which paragogic הָ is interpreted locatively, there is a locative expression in the immediate context that is antecedent to the paragogic הָ, as in example [3.37] (i.e., 'there' expressed by the paragogic הָ refers back to 'the lodging place').

[3.37] Gen 43:21

וַיְהִי כִּי־בָאנוּ אֶל־הַמָּלוֹן וַנִּפְתְּחָה אֶת־אַמְתְּחֹתֵינוּ וְהִנֵּה כֶסֶף־אִישׁ בְּפִי אַמְתַּחְתּוֹ

'And when we came to the lodging place we opened our sacks there and behold (each) man's sliver (was) in the mouth of his sack'.

The reflexive sense is sometimes difficult to discern, perhaps in part because it appears to have become conventionalized on first-person forms. Suggestive of this explanation is the observation that relatively frequent occurrences of the paragogic הָ with אמר 'say' are entirely restricted to late BH literature except for one example in Judges (Judg 6:10; Dan 9:4; 10:16, 19; 12:8; Ezra 8:28; 9:6;

---

74. Fassberg's count is 288; the Westminster database indicates 306 examples.

75. The three occurrences of paragogic הָ on third-person *yiqtol* forms (Isa 5:19 [2×]; Ezek 23:20) support Shulman's and Fassberg's conclusions.

76. Counts vary: Gentry (1998: 24 n. 67) lists 99 cases, noting that his list varies from the list in McFall 1982: 211–14. A search of the Westminster electronic text yields 104 examples: 95 first-person-singular forms (Gen 32:6; Num 8:19; Josh 24:8; Judg 6:9–10; 10:12; 12:3; 1 Sam 2:28; 28:15; 2 Sam 4:10; 7:9; 12:8; 22:24; Jer 11:18; 32:9; Ezek 3:3; 9:8; 16:11; Zech 11:13; Ps 3:6; 7:5; 69:12, 21; 73:16; 119:55, 59, 106, 131, 147, 158; Job 1:15–17, 19; 19:20; 29:17; Qoh 1:17; Dan 8:13, 15, 17; 9:3–4; 10:16, 19; 12:8; Ezra 7:28; 8:15–17, 24–26, 28; 9:3, 5–6; Neh 1:4; 2:1, 6, 9, 13; 5:7–8, 13; 6:3, 8, 11–12; 7:5; 12:31; 13:7–11, 13, 17, 19, 21–22, 30), 6 first-person-plural forms (Gen 41:11; 43:21; Ps 90:10; Ezra 8:23 [2×], 31), and 2 non-first-person forms (Ezek 23:16, 20).

Neh 5:7; 8:13; 6:11; 13:9, 11, 17, 19 [2×], 21, 22)[77] and often have no evident reflexive sense. A development toward conventionalization of the paragogic הָ‎ on first-person forms is confirmed by the Hebrew of the Dead Sea Scrolls, in which the first-person forms almost always appear with the paragogic הָ‎ (notable exceptions are found in scrolls of the biblical and apocryphal books; Qimron 1997: 177). This conventionalization of the reflexive paragogic הָ‎ on first-person forms may explain its obligatory appearance on first-person directive forms: the attraction of a reflexive sense to a first-person speaker-oriented (or subjective deontic) gram is logical, and the sense of the morpheme is comparable to the "dative of interest" (e.g., Classical Greek; see Smyth 1956: 341).[78]

Finally, some scholars have recently suggested that the paragogic הָ‎ forms an "energic system" with the paragogic נ‎ and energic נ‎ forms (Rattray 1992: 47–49; Testen 1994; Gentry 1998: 21–30).[79] Significantly, the latter נ‎ forms are associated with the realis *yiqtol* form. The comparative data of the EA and Arabic verbal systems suggest the presence of one or more נ‎-terminating conjugations (see table 2.7, p. 117; Moran 2003: 94; W. Wright 1962: 1.62). The suggestion that these form an energic "system" with the paragogic הָ‎ forms arises from the complementary distribution of the morphemes: paragogic הָ‎ following consonant-terminating prefix-pattern forms, paragogic נ‎ following vowel-terminating prefix-pattern forms, and energic נ‎ before pronouns on prefix-pattern forms (e.g., אֶשְׁמְרָה‎ 'I will guard', תִּשְׁמְרִין‎ 'you [F] will guard', and יִשְׁמְרֶנּוּ‎ 'he will guard him/us'; see chart in Rattray 1992: 48, and reproduced in Cook 2002: 245).

Testen (1993; 1994) has argued that all three of these morphemes (i.e., paragogic הָ‎, paragogic נ‎, and energic נ‎) can be traced back to a Proto-Semitic *-am/-nim*. However, while morphologically related, a unifying semantic sense for this "energic" system is difficult to determine. The Proto-Semitic

---

77. The paragogic הָ‎ also occurs frequently (12 times) on the root נתן‎ 'give': Num 8:19; Judg 6:9; 1 Sam 2:28; 2 Sam 12:8 (2×); Ezek 16:11; Ps 69:12; Qoh 1:17; Dan 9:3; Neh 2:1, 6, 9. Polzin (1976: 54) incorrectly states that only 1 example of paragogic הָ‎ (i.e., so-called Cohortative) is found in Chronicles (1 Chr 22:5); there are, in fact, 11 examples (1 Chr 13:2 [2×], 3; 19:13; 21:2, 13; 22:5; 2 Chr 1:10 [2×]; 18:6; 20:9).

78. Shulman (1996) tries to discern a separate nuance for the paragogic הָ‎ on first-person modal *yiqtol* than on the Imperative form: the forms with paragogic הָ‎ express "uncertainty and intention," whereas the forms without the paragogic הָ‎ express "commitment, and determination" (Shulman 1996: 238). This conclusion is less convincing (not to mention less clear) than the conclusion she draws with respect to the paragogic הָ‎ on Imperatives.

79. More specifically, the נ‎ forms are associated almost exclusively with realis *yiqtol*: of the approximately 450 instances of energic נ‎ (Williams 1972: 82), only 5 occur on a *wayyiqtol* form (Judg 15:2; 2 Kgs 9:33; Job 31:15; 33:24; Lam 1:13) and 3 with negative Jussives (2 Sam 13:12; Job 9:34; 13:21; Rattray 1992: 48); similarly, only 9 of the 304 examples of paragogic נ‎ occur on *wayyiqtol* forms (Deut 1:22; 4:11; 5:23; Judg 8:1; 11:18; Isa 41:5; Ezek 44:8; Amos 6:3), and none on Jussives (Hoftijzer 1985: 2–3).

-am/-nim is realized in the Akkadian ventive, which "is essentially a directional element that denotes motion or activity in the direction of, or to a point near, the speaker" (Huehnergard 2005: §15.2). Its connection to the so-called Cohortative הָ- has been outlined above. However, the semantic significance of the נ morpheme(s) is uncertain, despite Rattray's claim (1992: 112) of a similar ventive meaning for them. We still await a full semantic study of the נ forms (cf. Hoftijzer 1985; Zewi 1999).

Despite uncertainties, the above arguments as a whole call into question the validity of treating the first-person directive as a distinct Cohortative form. Rather, it is preferable to treat it as a first-person Jussive. Syntactically, the coherence of this system is apparent from the fact that the directive forms stand in complementary distribution with each other: the Imperative is limited to second-person positive directive and volitive expressions; the Jussive, although it appears in all three persons, is particularly complementary to the Imperative in the second person, which is almost exclusively the negative-directive (using a special negator, אַל) counterpart to the positive-directive Imperative.[80] Conversely to the restriction of second-person Jussives to negative expressions, the first-person Jussives are almost entirely positive.[81] As such, the BH directive-volitive system falls into the minority category of having a minimal and maximal pattern (see van der Auwera, Dobrushina, and Goussev 2005): the Imperative has a unique strategy (no agreement prefixes and limited to second person), so it is the minimal part of the system; the Jussive appears in all three persons, so it is the maximal part of the system.

Semantically, these forms are described in the grammars as expressing imperative, prohibitive (Jussive with negator אַל), hortatory, permissive, and admonitory modalities (Bergsträsser 1962: 2.45–53; Davidson 1901: 86–95; S. R. Driver 1998: 50–69; Joüon 2006: §114; Gibson 1994: 80–83, 105–7; Kautzsch 1910: 319–26; Waltke and O'Connor 1990: 564–79). Determining the most felicitous label for the system per se is difficult. On the one hand, the traditional label "volitive" (e.g., Joüon 1923, 2006; Waltke and O'Connor 1990: 565) understates the central use of the system (especially the Imperative and Jussive) as addressee-oriented modalities (i.e., speaker's will is imposed on the addressee). On the other hand. the typological label of imperative-hortative (van der Auwera, Dobrushina, and Goussev 2005: 294) is too narrowly specific, expressly excluding the prohibitive (i.e., negative directive)

---

80. A search of unambiguous second-person Jussive forms turns up only 3 out of 91 examples lacking an אַל negator (1 Sam 10:8; Ezek 3:3; Ps 71:21). The 2 examples preceded by אַל in the Leningrad Codex (Exod 10:28; Deut 2:9) are in error, judging from manuscript evidence and context.

81. Of 518 occurrences of first-person Jussives with paragogic הָ-, only 9 are negated (with אַל negative): 2 Sam 24:14; Jer 17:18; 18:18; Ps 25:2; 31:2, 18; 69:15; 71:1.

and optative (i.e., expression of speaker will without any imposition on the
addressee) meanings associated with the system. When we examine this system with respect to the taxonomies in the first chapter, this system straddles
the speaker-oriented and agent-oriented categories in example [1.29]—which
is just another fact that highlights the infelicitous character of that taxonomy.
A more useful approach to classifying the system is to adopt Verstraete's category of subjective-deontic modality (2001, 2007). As such, the system encompasses the directive and volitive modalities in my proposed taxonomy in
table 1.19 (p. 71) as directive-volitive. *Directive* here is not limited to positive
commands but also includes negative, prohibitive expressions. This table is especially helpful because it encompasses both the positive-directive Imperative
and the negative-directive (negated) Jussive grams. *Volitive* in my classification does not distinguish between expressions that impose the speaker's will on
the addressee (hortative) and expressions that do not (optative), because both
senses are expressed by the BH directive-volitive system and are sometimes
difficult to distinguish in a given example.

The association of certain meanings as dominant with one or the other form
in the system is a by-product of the complementary distribution of the forms
among persons and numbers. For example, the second-person Imperative and
negated Jussive predominantly express directive modality, as illustrated in examples [3.38a–b]; only rarely does the Imperative express volitive modality,
such as in [3.38c].

[3.38] a. Jonah 1:2

קוּם לֵךְ אֶל־נִינְוֵה הָעִיר הַגְּדוֹלָה וּקְרָא עָלֶיהָ כִּי־עָלְתָה רָעָתָם לְפָנָי

'Get up, go to Nineveh, the great city, and proclaim against
her that their wickeness has risen before me'.

   b. Gen 22:19

וַיֹּאמֶר אַל־תִּשְׁלַח יָדְךָ אֶל־הַנַּעַר וְאַל־תַּעַשׂ לוֹ מְאוּמָה

'And he said, "Do not stretch out your hand against the boy,
and do not do to him anything"'.

   c. Ruth 1:9

יִתֵּן יְהוָה לָכֶם וּמְצֶאןָ מְנוּחָה אִשָּׁה בֵּית אִישָׁהּ

'May Yhwh grant you and may you find:IMPV.FP rest, each
in the house of a husband'.

The first-person Jussive is largely limited to volitive expressions in the singular, because it is difficult to distinguish a reflexive imposition of the speaker's
will (directive or hortatory) from the simple expression of a speaker's will
(simple volitional). By contrast, in the plural the first-person Jussive frequently
has a directive (hortatory) idea because the addressees are broader than just the
speaker. These are illustrated by the examples in [3.39].

[3.39]   a. Ps 9:3

אֶשְׂמְחָה וְאֶעֶלְצָה בָךְ אֲזַמְּרָה שִׁמְךָ עֶלְיוֹן

'I will rejoice and I will exult in you; I will sing about your
name, Elyon!'

b. Gen 37:17

וַיֹּאמֶר הָאִישׁ נָסְעוּ מִזֶּה כִּי שָׁמַעְתִּי אֹמְרִים נֵלְכָה דֹּתָיְנָה

'The main said, "They set out from here, for I heard them
saying, 'Let us go to Dothan'"'.

Finally, the third-person Jussive expresses both speaker-imposition (directive
or hortative)—though frequently as a circumlocution with second-person addresses in the singular—and simple volitive expressions, as illustrated in examples [3.40a–f].

[3.40]   a. Gen 1:3

וַיֹּאמֶר אֱלֹהִים יְהִי אוֹר

'God said, "Let there be light"'.

b. Judg 6:39

וַיֹּאמֶר גִּדְעוֹן אֶל־הָאֱלֹהִים אַל־יִחַר אַפְּךָ בִּי

'Gideon said to God, "Do not let your anger burn against
me."'

c. Gen 47:4

וְעַתָּה יֵשְׁבוּ־נָא עֲבָדֶיךָ בְּאֶרֶץ גֹּשֶׁן

'And now, please let your servants settle in the land of
Goshen'.

d. Ps 25:2

אֱלֹהַי בְּךָ בָטַחְתִּי אַל־אֵבוֹשָׁה אַל־יַעַלְצוּ אֹיְבַי לִי

'My God, in you I have trusted, I will not be put to shame;
do not let my enemies exult over me'.

e. Ps 104:31

יְהִי כְבוֹד יְהוָה לְעוֹלָם יִשְׂמַח יְהוָה בְּמַעֲשָׂיו

'May the glory of Yhwh endure forever and may Yhwh
rejoice in his works'.

f. Job 3:6

הַלַּיְלָה הַהוּא יִקָּחֵהוּ אֹפֶל אַל־יִחַדְּ בִּימֵי שָׁנָה בְּמִסְפַּר יְרָחִים אַל־יָבֹא

'That night—may darkness take it; may it not be joined to
the days of the year; into the number of the months may it
not enter![82]

---

82. Reading יֵחַדְּ 'be joined' instead of the MT's 'rejoice'.

A contingent (purpose/result) modal meaning has been attributed to the directive forms in certain syntactic contexts—namely, when prefixed with the *waw* conjunction and following a clause with another directive form (or irrealis *yiqtol* with a directive meaning). Joüon (1923: 290; 2006: §116) introduced the label *indirect volitive* (Fr. "volitif indirect") for these examples, in contrast to *direct volitives* (Fr. "volitif direct"; see also Niccacci 1990; Gropp 1991; Dallaire 2002; see Muraoka 1997a: 229 n. 6, for a list of others who use these labels). Shulman and Muraoka have both questioned this contingent meaning for directives. Shulman (1996: 221) claimed that the implicated meanings in these cases are contextual. More strongly and clearly, Muraoka (1997a: 240) concluded his discussion as follows:

> In summing up we would say that the syntagm in question does not have a function of normally indicating purpose. A sequence of volitive verb forms is a series of so many expressions of the speaker's or writer's wish and will. The fact that in some cases the second verb can be more elegantly translated as indicating a purpose of the first is essentially a question of pragmatics and translation techniques, and not of descriptive grammar and syntax.

Thus, example [3.38c] is translated literally above, based simply on the syntactic coordination of the two clauses; however, the relationship between the clauses implied by their juxtaposed semantics may justify rendering the verse *May the Lord grant that you might find rest*. This treatment underscores the need to distinguish between the syntactic and semantic relationship between clauses: the *waw* signals a coordinate syntactic relationship, but semantically the clauses may be related in terms of contingent modality, as in the case of the so-called indirect volitive discussed here and frequently with the irrealis *qatal* (§3.3.3.1).

The directive-volitive system is summarized in table 3.6. Morphologically, the forms are constructed on the prefix pattern. Syntactically, they are in complementary distribution among three persons and positive and negative expressions. Semantically, there are tendencies among some persons toward mainly directive (second person) or volitive (first person) expressions.

3.3.3. Realis-Irrealis Mood Opposition

Justification of the term *irrealis* has been given above (§3.3) and the directive mood system, which aligns with irrealis VS word-order, has been examined (§3.3.2). Here the focus is the two primary conjugations, *qatal* and *yiqtol*, and the irrealis meanings that they express in accordance with their VS word order.

3.3.3.1. Irrealis *Yiqtol*

Grammars recognize the various irrealis mood meanings for *yiqtol* (see list of meanings, §3.2.3.2 above); however, explaining how these meanings came

Table 3.6. The BH Directive-Volitive Irrealis Mood Subsystem

	Prefix Pattern		
	Positive	Negative	
First Person	Jussive	(rare)	mostly volitive
Second Person	Imperative	אַל + Jussive	mostly directive
Third Person	Jussive	אַל + Jussive	directive and volitive

to be associated with the imperfective gram is difficult because of lack of data and the complicating factor of the partial homonymy between *yiqtol* and the Jussive (§3.3.2). Although, above, I posited future/subjunctive meaning at the end of the progressive-imperfective diachronic path (§3.2.3.2), it is difficult to attribute to this stage of development the various irrealis meanings associated with *yiqtol* simply because the range of meanings is so broad. Andrason (2010: 36, 45) recognizes this problem and proposes that, early on, *yiqtol* developed out of its primitive iterative sense a modal habitual meaning that initiated a modal (ability) diachrony that ran parallel with the development of progressive-imperfective-future/subjunctive diachrony. However, this sort of development is unattested and *prima facie* is unlikely, given the characterization of ability grams in Bybee, Perkins, and Pagliuca (1994: 188–89, 241–42): in only one case are ability and habituality/frequency combined in a single gram, and ability is infrequently expressed by bound forms, such as *yiqtol*, but instead uses lexical strategies, such as יכל in BH (see §3.2.1).[83]

Negatively, Andrason (2010: 36) concludes from the range of irrealis meanings expressed by *yiqtol* (meanings that appear both early and late in the modal diachronies in Bybee, Perkins, and Pagliuca [1994]) and from the fact that *yiqtol* can express irrealis mood apart from explicitly modal contexts, such as conditional clauses, that

> the gram must be defined as a properly modal diachrony (ability, obligation, desiderative, or intentional path) and not as an outcome of the modal trajectory of contamination. The *yiqtol* is a modal category due to its proper "virtues" and not because of the contextual contamination imposed by other external elements, and thus cannot be understood as an old indicative imperfective-present reduced to modal uses.

However, the logic of this conclusion escapes me. For one thing, this statement is apropos of *yiqtol* in Rabbinic Hebrew, but BH *yiqtol* lies at an earlier stage of the same diachronic path, in which it is not yet "reduced to modal uses" (and thus also not "a proper modal diachrony"). For another, the very

---

83. The fact that *yiqtol* does at times express dynamic aspect without יכל (e.g., Deut 1:12, example [3.44a], p. 248) does not weaken this argument.

nature of modal contamination or "context-induced reinterpretation" is that
once a meaning becomes associated with a form in a given context it then
spreads to other contexts (see Heine, Claudi, and Hünnemeyer 1991: 71–72);
this is therefore no argument against modal contamination. Andrason appears
to oversimplify the matter and draws conclusions that lack a sufficient basis in
the evidence. I doubt whether it is possible completely to untangle the origins
of the irrealis meanings for *yiqtol* beyond the supposition that multiple factors
played a role in their development, among which two factors feature prominently: (1) confusion of / merger between *yiqtol* and Jussive, and (2) the use
of the form in the ancient law code (i.e., context-induced irrealis meanings).
Both of these factors suggest contamination as a more likely explanation than
Andrason's ability modal trajectory.

It is difficult to imagine that the partial homonymy between the Jussive and
yiqtol does not account to some extent for the development of directive meanings for *yiqtol*, especially considering that the Jussive disappears in post-BH,
and its functions are appropriated entirely by *yiqtol* (see Pérez Fernández 1997:
108). It stands to reason that this process of directive-volitive appropriation by
the *yiqtol* was underway already in BH, encouraged by the formal ambiguity of
many paradigm forms, as illustrated by the directive and volitive in examples
[3.41a–b], in which the *yiqtol* is formally identically with the Jussive.

[3.41]   a. Lev 19:2

דַּבֵּר אֶל־כָּל־עֲדַת בְּנֵי־יִשְׂרָאֵל וְאָמַרְתָּ אֲלֵהֶם קְדֹשִׁים תִּהְיוּ כִּי קָדוֹשׁ
אֲנִי יְהוָה אֱלֹהֵיכֶם

'Speak to the entire congregation of the children of Israel,
and you shall say to them, "You shall/must be holy, for I,
Yhwh God, am holy"'.

b. Gen 3:3

וּמִפְּרִי הָעֵץ אֲשֶׁר בְּתוֹךְ־הַגָּן אָמַר אֱלֹהִים לֹא תֹאכְלוּ מִמֶּנּוּ וְלֹא תִגְּעוּ
בּוֹ פֶּן־תְּמֻתוּן

'But of the fruit of the tree that is in the middle of the
garden God said, "You must not eat from it and you must
not touch it lest you die"'.

However, the distinctive directive negator אַל remains a crucial disambiguating feature between the prohibitive (negative directive) Jussive, illustrated in
example [3.38b] above, and the prohibitive *yiqtol*, illustrated in [3.41b]. The
semantic distinction between these two prohibitive expressions has resisted a
clear explanation beyond intuitive statements such as made by Shulman (1996:
128, 187), who states that the Jussive has more "urgency" about it. In a subsequent article, she writes:

The difference between utterances, in which these forms [Jussive and *yiqtol*] occur, is close to the distinction between deontic and epistemic modality. Jussive forms are typically used for expressing deontic modality (wishes, commands and other expressions of volition). The indicative forms, although they may be used for either deontic or epistemic modality, are typically used for epistemic modality. (Shulman 2000: 180)

Shulman's ideas suggest that the difference lies in the speaker's commitment to the obligation: with the Jussive (and the entire directive system), the obligation is speaker originated, whereas the obligation is only described by the irrealis *yiqtol*. The latter is thus similar to epistemic judgment in that epistemic modality only commits the speaker to the proposition in terms of knowledge, not obligation.

Nevertheless, Shulman's introduction of epistemic modality is somewhat confusing. Better suited to describing the difference in question is Verstraete's (2007: 32–35) distinction between subjective and objective deontic expressions: subjective deontics have their source of obligation in the speaker, whereas objective deontics have a source of obligation outside the speaker—whether expressed or left unexpressed. This speaker-oriented source of obligation explains the "urgency" of the directive forms noted by Shulman (above), while the association of irrealis *yiqtol* with epistemic modal expressions, as in example [3.42], explains its suitability for objective deontic modality, hinted at by Shulman (i.e., analogous to epistemic judgment, objective deontic expressions only describe the obligation without making the speaker a source of this obligation).[84]

[3.42]   Gen 24:39

וָאֹמַר אֶל־אֲדֹנִי אֻלַי לֹא־תֵלֵךְ הָאִשָּׁה אַחֲרָי׃

'And I said to my master, "Perhaps the woman will not follow after me"'.

This opposition is a privative one; that is, the directive-volitive system is limited to subjective-deontic expressions (directives and volitives), whereas the irrealis *yiqtol* may express either objective or subjective deontic modalities. Irrealis *yiqtol* expressing subjective deontic permission is illustrated in example [3.43]: the most straightforward reading of this unambiguous *yiqtol* is that the source of permission is the speaker himself, Reuben.

---

84. This explanation rooted in the source of obligation is more convincing to me than Hatav's (2006: 739), who connects the "urgency" that Shulman observed to the deictic character of the directive-system forms, which "always take the speech-time as their reference-time."

[3.43]   Gen 42:37

וַיֹּאמֶר רְאוּבֵן אֶל־אָבִיו לֵאמֹר אֶת־שְׁנֵי בָנַי תָּמִית אִם־לֹא אֲבִיאֶנּוּ אֵלֶיךָ

'Reuben said to his father, "My two sons you <u>may kill</u> if I do
not bring him to you"'.

This privative opposition may well be the result of ambiguity between the
Jussive and *yiqtol* and, at the least, made the takeover of Jussive by the *yiqtol*
easier. This gradual takeover is the simplest explanation for all of the directive-volitive meanings expressed by irrealis *yiqtol*, while the association of
imperfective *yiqtol* with epistemic expressions accounts for the objective :
subjectivedeontic opposition with the prohibitive Jussive.

     The expression of dynamic and habitual modality by irrealis *yiqtol*, illus-
trated in examples [3.44a–b], is associated with epistemic modality, already
illustrated above in example [3.42], in that they all belong more properly to
irrealis *yiqtol* rather than being a result "contamination" from the directive-
volitive system. In each case, the irrealis status of the situation referred to is
evident: epistemic modality describes the probability of situations; dynamic
situation describe potential situations; and habituality describes the regularity
of situations rather than "actual" situations.

[3.44]   a. Deut 1:12

אֵיכָה אֶשָּׂא לְבַדִּי טָרְחֲכֶם וּמַשַּׂאֲכֶם וְרִיבְכֶם

'How <u>can I bear</u> alone your trouble and your burden and
your bickering?'

         b. Gen 29:2

וַיַּרְא וְהִנֵּה בְאֵר בַּשָּׂדֶה וְהִנֵּה־שָׁם שְׁלֹשָׁה עֶדְרֵי־צֹאן רֹבְצִים עָלֶיהָ כִּי
מִן־הַבְּאֵר הַהִוא יַשְׁקוּ הָעֲדָרִים

'He looked and, behold, there was a well in a field and,
behold, three flocks of sheep were lying beside it, because
from that well they <u>would water</u> the flocks'.

Central to the broadening meaning of *yiqtol* discussed above (§3.2.3.2) is, of
course, its use in subordinate expressions. In contrast to irrealis *qatal* (§3.3.3.2
below), the use of irrealis *yiqtol* in subordinate expressions (conditional and
final [purpose/result] in particular) is frequently lexically marked by a subordinating word (e.g., לְמַעַן, פֶּן, כִּי, אִם, etc.),[85] as illustrated by examples [3.45a–b].

---

85. The contrast between irrealis *yiqtol* and irrealis *qatal* with conditional and final subordinating words is notable (see also the remarks by Ferguson 1882: 41): following פֶּן, *yiqtol*
126 times and *qatal* 2 times (2 Sam 20:6; 2 Kgs 2:16); following לְמַעַן, *yiqtol* 113 times and
qatal 2 times (Josh 4:24; Jer 25:7); אִם, *yiqtol* 275 times and *qatal* 100 times. The main exception is counterfactual (positive and negative) conditions, marked with לוּ or לוּלֵא, respec-

[3.45]   a.   Judg 13:16

וַיֹּאמֶר מַלְאַךְ יְהֹוָה אֶל־מָנוֹחַ אִם־תַּעְצְרֵנִי לֹא־אֹכַל בְּלַחְמֶךָ וְאִם־
תַּעֲשֶׂה עֹלָה לַיהֹוָה תַּעֲלֶנָּה

'And the angel of Yhwh said to Manoah, "If you detain me,
I will not eat of your food, and if you make a burnt offering,
to Yhwh you should offer it up"'.

b.   Exod 20:12

כַּבֵּד אֶת־אָבִיךָ וְאֶת־אִמֶּךָ לְמַעַן יַאֲרִכוּן יָמֶיךָ עַל הָאֲדָמָה אֲשֶׁר־יְהֹוָה
אֱלֹהֶיךָ נֹתֵן לָךְ

'Honor your father and your mother in order that your days
might prolong on the land that Yhwh your God is giving to
you'.

Given that subordinating words trigger inversion to VS word order, as does
irrealis modality, the two features of the VS order may have mutually fed one
another; that is, irrealis mood marking with VS was induced by the association
of irrealis mood with subordinate constructions, which are X-VS.

3.3.3.2. Irrealis *Qatal* (Including So-Called *Wĕqatal*)

In the section on perfective *qatal* (§3.2.3.1), I presented the negative argument, that there is no evidence that *qatal* and *wĕqatal* are reflexes of distinct
conjugations in Semitic and that at best one might argue that BH *wĕqatal* has
developed into a distinct gram from *qatal*. In the word order discussion above
(§3.3.1), I have provided a positive argument, that the VS word order exhibited by *wĕqatal*—usually prefixed with a clause-boundary *waw* conjunction—
aligns the form with the irrealis *yiqtol* and directive mood system, suggesting
that it be reanalyzed as irrealis *qatal*. This reanalysis is not simply a change
in nomenclature, because there is not complete coincidence between the traditional category of *wĕqatal* and what I am treating here as irrealis *qatal*. Rather,
the latter category includes all the instances in which *qatal* exhibits VS word
order and irrealis mood.[86] This includes, notably, the *qatal* forms that appear
after אִם, כִּי, לוּ, or לוּלֵא in conditional protases, which are not in the *wĕqatal*
category because the latter has been defined as including the *waw* conjunction
as part of the conjugation, just as in the case of *wayyiqtol*.

---

tively, in which *qatal* predominates (see [3.46], p. 250). By contrast, ו-prefixed *qatal* occurs
6,459 times versus 1,421 ו-prefixed *yiqtol* forms.

86. For example, the *qatal* passages discussed in examples [3.46a–b] and [3.9] are all
treated with the (realis) perfective *qatal* in the standard grammars (e.g., Kautzsch 1910:
§106p; Waltke and O'Connor 1990: §30.5.4), but here I am classifying them as irrealis *qatal*
based on their semantics; word order alone is insufficient, since each has a fronted syntactic
element that may account for the VS order apart from irrealis mood.

The main categories of meaning for irrealis *qatal* include contingent modality (i.e., conditional constructions, broadly defined, and final clauses), directive modality, and habituality.[87] Counterfactual conditional expressions commonly feature grams with a past-temporal reference on the basis of the past-irrealis metaphor: that which is temporally removed from the speaker's present is irrealis (Bybee, Perkins, and Pagliuca 1994: 79; compare with English *Had I known, I would have helped*). In BH counterfactuals, the conditional words לוּ (positive) or לוּלֵא (negative) may be used, as in [3.46], or other general contexts may indicate a counterfactual statement, as in [3.9] (p. 202).

[3.46] a. Judg 13:23

וַתֹּאמֶר לוֹ אִשְׁתּוֹ לוּ חָפֵץ יְהוָה לַהֲמִיתֵנוּ לֹא־לָקַח מִיָּדֵנוּ עֹלָה וּמִנְחָה
'His wife said to him, "If Yhwh had desired to kill us he would not have accepted from our hand a burnt offering and meal offering"'.

b. Judg 14:18

וַיֹּאמֶר לָהֶם לוּלֵא חֲרַשְׁתֶּם בְּעֶגְלָתִי לֹא מְצָאתֶם חִידָתִי
'He said to them, "If you had not plowed with my heifer you would not have discovered my riddle"'.

Although Bybee, Perkins, and Pagliuca (1994: 79, 93) include in the data two cases of perfective verbs that are used to express general "hypothetical" conditions, this usage is an unexpected development for perfective *qatal*, in spite of its unsurprising appearance in counterfactual expressions. As I argued above, it cannot be attributed to a different gram from *qatal*; but comparative evidence shows that cognates of BH *qatal* frequently acquire a non-past temporal reference in conditional structures in many Semitic languages, including Arabic, Ethiopic, Aramaic and Syriac, Phoenician, and EA Canaanite (W. Wright 1962: 2.14–17; Dillmann 1974: 548; Folmer 1991; 1995: 394–415; Nöldeke 2001: 203–5; Krahmalkov 1986; Moran 2003: 31–33; Rainey 1996b: 355–65). In these data, non-past time examples of *qatal* cognates ap-

---

87. The existence of an irrealis optative or precative meaning for *qatal* is even more questionable than the prophetic perfect meaning (§3.2.3.1 above). Note, however, that *qatal* can have an optative counterfactual meaning when lexically marked by לוּ: Isa 48:18; 63:19. G. R. Driver (1965: 60; S. R. Driver 1998: 25-26) has examined candidates for optative or precative *qatal* in the Hebrew Bible and concluded that "on the one hand the optative or precative use of *qtl* is theoretically as possible in Hebrew as in the cognate Semitic languages. . . . On the other hand, all the supposed instances in the Old Testament are doubtful; none are unavoidable and all can be otherwise explained." After examining all the passages he treats, in addition to those referenced by S. R. Driver (1998: 25), I concur with G. R. Driver's assessment (1965): all the examples can be explained in terms of indicative meanings for *qatal* or textual problems (e.g., Ps 4:2; 7:7; in Lam 1:21, the Septuagint renders the *qatal* as an imperative).

pear in conditional protases (as in example [3.47a]), in conditional apodoses (see [3.47b–c]), and in both (as in [3.47d]).

[3.47]   a.   Imperial Aramaic

hn grynk dyn wdbb wgryn lbr bbrh lk wlmn zy ṣbyt lmntn ʾnḥn nntn lk ksp . . .

'If we **institute** against you suit or process or **institute** (suit) against son in/with (scribal error for: or) daughter of yours or (anyone) to whom you desire to give (it), we shall give you silver . . .'. (Porten and Yardeni 1986: B3 4.14–15; see discussion in Folmer 1995: 395)

   b.   El-Amarna Canaanite

allū paṭārima awīlūt ḫupšī u ṣabtū [lú.pl.]GAZ *āla*

'Behold, if the serfs desert, then the Ḫapiru **will capture** the city'. (Moran 2003: 31)

   c.   Phoenician

*wʾm mlk bmlkm wrzn brznm . . . ymḥ šm ʾztwd bšʿr z wšt šm . . . **wmḥ** bʿlšmm wʾl qn ʾrṣ . . . ʾyt hmmlkt hʾ wʾyt hmlk hʾ wʾyt ʾdm hʾ*

'And if a king among kings and ruler among rulers . . . erases the name of Azitawada on this gate and places his name . . . then Baalshamen and El, creator of the earth, **will erase** that kingdom and that king and that man'. (Donner and Röllig 2002: no. 26 III.12–IV.1; see discussion in Krahmalkov 1986: 9)

   d.   Arabic example

*ʾin **qatalum** ṣāḥibayya **qataltu** ṣāḥibaykum*

'If you **kill** my two friends, I will **kill** yours'. (from Peled 1992: 18; see also W. Wright 1962: 2.15)

Peled (1992: 12), treating Arabic specifically, argues that the non-past modal meaning in cases of this sort derives from the modal context of the conditional syntagm.

Given these data, a reasonable hypothesis is that irrealis *qatal* derives from a context-induced reinterpretation of perfective *qatal* from its use in conditional constructions (see the recent argument in this vein by Andrason forthcoming a, b). Heine, Claudi, and Hünnemeyer (1991: 71–72) describe the process as follows:

Stage I: In addition to its focal or core sense A, a given linguistic form F acquires an additional sense B when occurring in a specific context C. This can result in semantic ambiguity since either of the senses A or B may be implied in

context C. Which of the two senses is implied usually is, but need not be, dependent on the relevant communication situation. . . .

Stage II: The existence of a sense B now makes it possible for the relevant
form to be used in new contexts that are compatible with B but rule out sense A.

Stage III: B is conventionalized; it may be said to form a secondary focus
characterized by properties containing elements not present in A—with the effect that F now has two "polysemes," A and B, which may develop eventually
into "homophones."

But beyond simply the contingent conditional protasis–induced modal sense
for irrealis *qatal*, the final (purpose/result) and directive meanings of the form
might also be attributed to this context-induced reinterpretation on the basis of
the appearance of the form in conditional apodoses, especially in conditional
legal formulations (example [3.48]).

[3.48] Num 27:9

וְאִם־אֵין לוֹ בַּת וּנְתַתֶּם אֶת־נַחֲלָתוֹ לְאֶחָיו

'If he has no daughter, then you <u>should give</u> his inheritance to
his brothers'.

At stage 2, in Heine, Claudi, and Hünnemeyer's scheme, these irrealis meanings can be conveyed by VS *qatal* apart from the overt modal contexts that
gave rise to them. Thus, we find final and directive senses of the irrealis *qatal*
appearing outside conditional apodoses, as illustrated by examples [3.49a–b].

[3.49] a. 2 Kgs 5:6

הִנֵּה שָׁלַחְתִּי אֵלֶיךָ אֶת־נַעֲמָן עַבְדִּי וַאֲסַפְתּוֹ מִצָּרַעְתּוֹ

'Look, I have sent to you Na'aman my servant <u>so that</u> you
<u>might deliver</u> him from his leprosy'.

b. Exod 25:8

וְעָשׂוּ לִי מִקְדָּשׁ וְשָׁכַנְתִּי בְּתוֹכָם

'They <u>should make</u> a sanctuary for me <u>that</u> I <u>may dwell</u> in
their midst'.

At the same time, examples [3.46a–b] illustrate the shortcomings of the above
hypothesis: the modal context of conditional constructions does not consistently obviate the default past-time interpretation of irrealis *qatal*. One recent
study (Kaufmann 2005) suggests that the "tenseless" interpretation of verbal
forms in conditional clauses is incorrect and that the TAM of verbal forms
in conditional structures is identical to their interpretation in isolation. This
suggests that the approach to conditional structures may be as wrong-headed
as the general-present interpretation of generic sentences: the TAM of the BH
verbal forms should be interpreted in conditional structures as they would be

in isolation. However, Kaufmann (2005: 265) admits, in keeping with Peled (1992) that the conditional structure itself is responsible for the "forward shift in temporal perspective" that is evident in many conditional clauses. Thus, compare examples [3.50a–c]: a case might be made for a good number of examples of irrealis *qatal* in a consequent (apodosis) clause that the form has a past-in-the-future meaning (i.e., future perfect; see Kaufmann 2005: 275).

[3.50] a. Job 10:14

אִם־חָטָאתִי וּשְׁמַרְתָּנִי וּמֵעֲוֹנִי לֹא תְנַקֵּנִי

'If I have sinned, then you have watched me and from my iniquity you will not acquit me'. (compare NRSV 'If I sin, you watch me . . .')

b. 1 Sam 11:3

וְאִם־אֵין מוֹשִׁיעַ אֹתָנוּ וְיָצָאנוּ אֵלֶיךָ

'And if there is no one who will rescue us, then we will have surrendered to you'.

c. Gen 18:26

אִם־אֶמְצָא בִסְדֹם חֲמִשִּׁים צַדִּיקִם בְּתוֹךְ הָעִיר וְנָשָׂאתִי לְכָל־הַמָּקוֹם בַּעֲבוּרָם

'If I will/may find in Sodom fifty righteous people in the midst of the city, then I will have spared the whole place on their account'.

Of course, more frequently than these past or past-in-the-future interpretations, the irrealis *qatal* in the consequent clause expresses a modal directive sense, as in example [3.48] above. As with the case of irrealis *yiqtol* versus the directive-volitive forms in directive expressions, the distinctive nuance of the irrealis *qatal* in directive expressions has eluded explanation. Two characteristics appear to be crucial to disambiguating among the Imperative/Jussive, irrealis *yiqtol*, and irrealis *qatal* directive expressions. The first has to do with the source of the obligation, already outlined above (§3.3.3.1.): the directive-volitive forms are limited to expressing subjective deontic modality, in which the source of obligation derives from the speaker, while irrealis *yiqtol* directives may locate the source of obligation with the speaker or outside them. The preference of irrealis *qatal* for procedural directives and law codes seem to place it alongside irrealis *yiqtol*'s expression of obligation, which derives from some source other than the speaker. However, the frequent use of irrealis *qatal* in conjunction with subjective directive-volitive forms, illustrated in example [3.51], indicates that irrealis *qatal* like irrealis *yiqtol* may be used for subjective or objective deontic modalities.

[3.51] Exod 9:13

וַיֹּאמֶר יְהוָה אֶל־מֹשֶׁה הַשְׁכֵּם בַּבֹּקֶר וְהִתְיַצֵּב לִפְנֵי פַרְעֹה וְאָמַרְתָּ אֵלָיו
כֹּה־אָמַר יְהוָה אֱלֹהֵי הָעִבְרִים שַׁלַּח אֶת־עַמִּי וְיַעַבְדֻנִי:

'Yhwh said to Moses, "Get up early in the morning and station
yourself before Pharaoh, and (then) say to him, 'Thus says
Yhwh the God of the Hebrews, "Dismiss my people so that
they may serve me"'"'.

The second relevant characteristic is the aspectual distinction between irrealis *yiqtol* and irrealis *qatal* that makes the latter preferable for procedural
directives—that is, directives that require being carried out in a particular order, as illustrated by example [3.52].

[3.52] Exod 25:10–14

וְעָשׂוּ אֲרוֹן עֲצֵי שִׁטִּים אַמָּתַיִם וָחֵצִי אָרְכּוֹ וְאַמָּה וָחֵצִי רָחְבּוֹ וְאַמָּה וָחֵצִי
קֹמָתוֹ: וְצִפִּיתָ אֹתוֹ זָהָב טָהוֹר מִבַּיִת וּמִחוּץ תְּצַפֶּנּוּ וְעָשִׂיתָ עָלָיו זֵר זָהָב
סָבִיב: וְיָצַקְתָּ לּוֹ אַרְבַּע טַבְּעֹת זָהָב וְנָתַתָּה עַל אַרְבַּע פַּעֲמֹתָיו וּשְׁתֵּי
טַבָּעֹת עַל־צַלְעוֹ הָאֶחָת וּשְׁתֵּי טַבָּעֹת עַל־צַלְעוֹ הַשֵּׁנִית: וְעָשִׂיתָ בַדֵּי עֲצֵי
שִׁטִּים וְצִפִּיתָ אֹתָם זָהָב: וְהֵבֵאתָ אֶת־הַבַּדִּים בַּטַּבָּעֹת עַל צַלְעֹת הָאָרֹן
לָשֵׂאת אֶת־הָאָרֹן בָּהֶם:

'They should make an ark of acacia wood—two and a half
cubits its length, a cubit and a half its breadth, and a cubit and
a half its height. And then you should overlay it with pure gold
on its inside, and on its outside you should overlay it. Then you
should make upon it a gold molding round about. Then you
should cast for it four gold rings and place (them) upon its four
feet—two rings on one of its sides and two on the other of its
sides. Then you should make poles of acacia wood and overlay
them with gold and insert the poles into the rings on the sides
of the ark, to lift the ark by them'.

This preference for using irrealis *qatal* for procedural instructions may best be
understood as being grounded in its identity as a perfective gram: perfective
qatal presents events as bounded (see further on boundedness in §4.2.1) and
therefore may effect temporal succession among events (just as realis *qatal*
and *wayyiqtol* effect in temporal succession past narrative texts). Because irrealis mood is "tenseless" (see Verstraete 2007: 42–47), the successiveness
of the bounded perfective irrealis *qatal* is transferred to the sphere of modal
alternative situations: the accessibility of situations is successive (see §§1.6
and 4.3.3).

This hypothesis is in keeping with the view, expressed above, that the TAM
of a verbal gram in isolation is maintained in conditional structures: the argu-

Table 3.7. The Expression of Irrealis Mood in BH

	Irrealis Mood		
Modalities	*Directive-Volitive*	*Irrealis* Yiqtol	*Irrealis* Qatal
directive	(subjective)		(procedural)
volitive		(merger with Directives)	
epistemic			
dynamic			
contingent		(more lexically marked)	(less lexically marked)
habitual			(procedural)

ment here would be that the perfective aspect of the *qatal* gram is maintained throughout its uses, for both realis and irrealis mood expressions. Buttressing this argument is the similar preference for irrealis *qatal* in procedural habitual expressions, as illustrated by example [3.53]: notice the singular use of the ir-realis *yiqtol* (יַשְׁקוּ) in v. 2 to express habituality of the larger situation of water-ing the flocks (cited in example [3.44b] above, p. 248), whereas the discourse shifts to irrealis *qatal* to report the habitual procedures for the watering of the flocks (see further discussion in chap. 4).

[3.53]   Gen 29:2–3

וַיַּרְא וְהִנֵּה בְאֵר בַּשָּׂדֶה וְהִנֵּה־שָׁם שְׁלֹשָׁה עֶדְרֵי־צֹאן רֹבְצִים עָלֶיהָ כִּי
מִן־הַבְּאֵר הַהִוא יַשְׁקוּ הָעֲדָרִים וְנֶאֶסְפוּ־שָׁמָּה כָל־הָעֲדָרִים וְגָלֲלוּ אֶת־
הָאֶבֶן מֵעַל פִּי הַבְּאֵר וְהִשְׁקוּ אֶת־הַצֹּאן וְהֵשִׁיבוּ אֶת־הָאֶבֶן עַל־פִּי הַבְּאֵר
לִמְקֹמָהּ:

'He looked and, behold, there was a well in a field and, behold, three flocks of sheep were lying beside it, because from that well they would water the flocks: all the flocks <u>would gather</u> there, then they <u>would roll</u> the stone from upon the mouth of the well, then they <u>would water</u> the flock, then they <u>would replace</u> the stone upon the mouth of the well'.

By way of conclusion, the irrealis mood forms may be mapped according to table 3.7, which illustrates the complementary and overlapping relationships among the directive system, irrealis *yiqtol*, and irrealis *qatal*.

Directive modality is the primary category shared among directive-volitive forms, *yiqtol*, and *qatal* but, as discussed above, the three differ in their par-ticular nuances: directive-volitive forms express subjective deontic obligation while irrealis *yiqtol* and *qatal* may freely express either subjective or objective deontic obligation; however, irrealis *qatal* expresses deontic obligation pre-dominantly in procedural contexts. The volitive use of *yiqtol* is best understood as a partial and growing takeover of the directive-volitive system, parts of which it supplants in postbiblical Hebrew. The distinction between *yiqtol* and *qatal* in the expressions of contingent modality (i.e., final and conditional clauses) has to do with their use of lexical marking, like subordinating words: *yiqtol* is much more frequently lexically marked than *qatal* is (see n. 85 above).

Finally, the procedural character of habitual expressions with *qatal* distinguishes them from habitual *yiqtol*. Admittedly, these distinctions are crude in that we lack an exhaustive study of the irrealis verb forms, which are deserving of a separate monograph. However, what is crucial to the argument here is that these distinctions are in part related to the underlying semantic evaluation of the grams: for example, imperfective *yiqtol* is the main form for the expression of epistemic and dynamic modalities, and so these characteristics shape its use in directive statements; the irrealis *qatal* is preferred in procedural expressions such as instructions and habitual narratives because of its bounding characteristics associated with its being a perfective aspect gram.

3.4. The Expression of Temporality in BH

One of the most confused issues in studies of the BHVS is temporality. Simply put, there has been an unfortunate confusing of *temporality* and *tense* in discussions of the BHVS. In recent decades, this has elicited calls to clarify the misunderstanding, such as the statement by Rainey (1986: 7) that BH can express *temporality* (i.e., locate events past, present, and future) *apart from* the question of whether it has *tensed* (i.e., grammaticalized locations in time; see Comrie 1985: 9) grams in its TAM system. In this section, I develop the argument that the BHVS expresses temporality both in the tensed gram *wayyiqtol* and via a default pattern of temporal interpretation of the aspectual grams. Lexical means of temporal interpretation are only touched on insofar as they intersect with a description of the TAM system as expressed in the verbal conjugations (e.g., טֶרֶם and אָז with prefix pattern forms). In order to keep clear this crucial distinction between temporal location and tense as a grammaticalized location in time, I will consistently employ *temporality* versus *tense* for these two categories of temporal expression.

3.4.1. The Past Narrative *Wayyyiqtol* Conjugation

The identification of *wayyiqtol* as a past (tense) narrative conjugation appears *prima facie* quite straightforward. In anyone's statistical count, well over 90% of the more than 15,000 occurrences of the form in BH appear in prose narrative with past temporality.[88] The relatively few uniform functions

---

88. Even allowing for extreme skewing of the data due to serious methodological flaws in his approach, Furuli's (2006: 73) identification of 93.1% of *wayyiqtol*s as occurring in a past temporal context is telling—despite the fact that he proceeds to dismiss the form as a past tense gram (see Cook 2010).

assigned to *wayyiqtol* in the standard grammars are in line with these statistics: (1) simple past (usually with the idea of succession); (2) present perfect and past perfect (the latter under restricted circumstances); (3) logical consecution (past or present time), (4) some exceptional (apparently) future uses in prophetic contexts (Bergsträsser 1962: 2.36–45; Davidson 1901: 70–78; S. R. Driver 1998: 70–99; Gibson 1994: 95–102; Joüon 1993: 389–96; Kautzsch 1910: 326–30; Meyer 1992: 2.44–46; Waltke and O'Connor 1990: 543–63).

However, the semantic analysis of *wayyiqtol* has been complicated by the morphological similarity of the conjugation with imperfective *yiqtol*, on the one hand, and the semantic parallels between the conjugation and perfective *qatal*, on the other hand (see §2.1). These seemingly contrary relationships lie directly behind the long-developed view of the form as expressing some sort of "sequentiality" in addition to its semantics, whether this parameter served to distinguish it from *yiqtol* (so S. R. Driver 1998: 72m "and-he-proceeded-to-say"; see §2.2.3) or from *qatal* (Joüon 2006: §118a). But in the century since Bauer's influential theory (1910), in which he posited two distinct prefix conjugations in order to account for the semantic distinctions between (among others) BH *wayyiqtol* and *yiqtol*, this explanation has come to hold hegemonic status in BH studies, though not in the same form as Bauer presented it.[89] Rather, the usual explanation now is that two prefix conjugations, which were originally distinct because of the presence of a final vowel on the one (i.e., **yaqtul* versus **yaqtulu*), partially merged morphologically through the loss of final short vowels (see §2.3 for the full comparative-historical argument). In BH, reflexes of the short **yaqtul* form appear in the Jussive and the *wayyiqtol*, while the long **yaqtulu* form is realized in *yiqtol*. This explanation accounts for the long-observed morphological parallel between the Jussive and *wayyiqtol*, wherein they both exhibit the same apocopated pattern when possible (see discussion of Jussive and prefix pattern in Kummerow 2007a). The question of the relationship between the Jussive and *wayyiqtol* reflexes of **yaqtul* (i.e., whether there are two homonymous **yaqtul* forms or a single polysemous form; Huehnergard 1988: 20) seems both intractable and moot—intractable inasmuch as no clear diachrony between the two reflexes can reasonably be posited given their distinct semantic contrast; and moot, in that, given the wide semantic discrepancy between the reflexes in BH, there is no risk of confusing the forms. Nevertheless, two other issues regarding the morphology of *wayyiqtol* (which in some respects are just as intractable) require comment here: the first is the distinctive *wa*C- prefix; the second is the question whether any reflexes of the preterite **yaqtul* form occur in BH without the distinctive *wa*C- prefix.

---

89. The hegemony of this explanation is evident in its appearance in introductory grammars (e.g., Seow 1995: 225–26), which are generally limited to endorsing widely held grammatical ideas.

The origin and shape of the *wa*C- prefix are a long-standing problem (see list of proposed explanations in McFall 1982: 217–19). Analyses may be classified as one of three types (see Testen 1998: 193–94): first, the prefix consists of the *waw* conjunction plus some other element that has been assimilated into the following consonant to create the geminated prefix (e.g., Ewald [1879: 19], who proposed an assimilated אָז 'then'); second, the prefix is an alternate form of the conjunction with a different meaning (e.g., G. R. Driver [1936: 92], who suggests that the alternate form is analogous to the Akkadian -*ma* suffix on verbs); third, the prefix represents a secondary distinction made simply to disambiguate *wayyiqtol* from the *waw* conjunction plus the imperfective *yiqtol* or Jussive (e.g., S. R. Driver 1998: 72; Müller 1991).

Given that the *wa*C- prefix is universally present on the *wayyiqtol* form in prose narrative,[90] apart from a handful of disputed cases (e.g., יַעֲלֶה in Judg 2:1), it is probably justifiable to identify the prefix as part of the grammatical form of the BH Past Narrative (so Washburn 1994: 40–41). However, at the same time, this third type of approach simply begs the question why the prefix has the form that it has in BH. Testen (1998: 217) has proposed a theory of the first type, that *wa*C- consists of the *waw* conjunction prefixed to a particle that originated as an *l* but became syllabic (*ḷ) in environments without an adjacent vowel.

Testen proposes that this form is the origin of several particles in Semitic, including the definite article (*ha*C-), precative *la*-, asseverative *l*-, which is realized in Akkadian as *lū* (e.g., *lū iqtul* 'may he kill'; see von Soden 1995: §81; Huehnergard 2005: §29.3), the negative *lam* in Arabic (*l* + neg. *mā*; e.g., *lam taf'al* 'you did not do'; see W. Wright 1962: 2.22–23, 41), and the *wa*C- prefix in BH *wayyiqtol*. Testen (1998: 203) traces the *ha*C- definite article and *wa*C- prefix in Hebrew to a common source by analogy with the allomorphs of the definite article in Arabic: (*a*)*l*-/(*a*)C-. He hypothesizes that in Arabic and Canaanite the syllabic *ḷ developed into *a*C- (as seen in Arabic), but because Canaanite did not allow initial vowels, a "paragogic" ה was preposed to the particle. In the case of *wa*C-, that ה has elided with the addition of the conjunction, just as in the case of the *ha*C- definite article with a preposed preposition (e.g., בַּבַּיִת, *babbáyit* 'in the house' < **b*- + *ha*C- + *báyit*).

Testen's etymological explanation, that *wa*C- preserves a particle or function word within the geminated prefix, is preferable syntactically to the other sorts of explanations because it can account for the obligatory VS order for *wayyiqtol* in terms of triggered inversion (so DeCaen 1995: 128; Holmstedt 2009: 125; see §3.3.1).[91] Semantically, the analysis of the *wa*C- prefix is even

---

90. The question whether the conjugation appears in poetry without the *wa*C- prefix is a separate issue (on which, see below this section) in that most scholars treat such instances as "archaic" pasts—i.e., not simply the Past Narrative without the distinctive *wa*C- prefix.

91. DeCaen (1995: 128) also identifies a function word in the prefix *wa*C-, explaining it as a phonologically impoverished (he uses the term "underspecified") subordinating

more difficult. The long-standing "consecutive" explanation is that the prefix adds a sense of sequentiality (i.e., temporal succession) to *wayyiqtol*, which is otherwise synonymous with *qatal*. However, examples such as [3.54] illustrate that *wayyiqtol* does not always express temporal succession (see Cook 2004b and §4.3.1 below for additional examples).[92]

[3.54]   a.   Isa 39:1

בָּעֵת הַהִוא שָׁלַח מְרֹדַךְ בַּלְאֲדָן בֶּן־בַּלְאֲדָן מֶלֶךְ־בָּבֶל סְפָרִים וּמִנְחָה
אֶל־חִזְקִיָּהוּ וַיִּשְׁמַע כִּי חָלָה וַיֶּחֱזָק׃

'At that time, Merodach-baladan son of Baladan, king of Babylon, sent letters and a gift to Hezekiah; he <u>heard</u> that he was ill and recovered'.

   b.   2 Sam 14:5

וַתֹּאמֶר אֲבָל אִשָּׁה־אַלְמָנָה אָנִי וַיָּמָת אִישִׁי

'She said, "Alas, I am a widow; my husband <u>died</u>"'.

In addition to these examples that run counter to the sequential analysis of *wa*C-, in §4.2.1 I demonstrate that temporal succession is dependent on a variety of factors, including aspect and adverbial modification, making it a priori unlikely that the prefix itself indicates temporal succession. We must conclude either that the semantic value of the *wa*C- prefix eludes us or that the function word has become semantically bleached.[93]

Hatav (2004) has recently proposed a semantic explanation for the *wa*C-prefix that builds conceptually on Testen (1998) and DeCaen (1995), though she does not appear to be aware of Testen's theory and only makes passing reference to DeCaen's syntactic explanation of the prefix (Hatav 2004: 498 n. 14). Taking the same tack as DeCaen, she argues that the prefix conjugation in *wayyiqtol* is modal, and similar to Testen, she analogizes the function word in the *wa*C- prefix with the article to argue that it anchors the event in the real world; the *waw* conjunction then adds the sense of sequentiality. The motivations behind her theory are two: first, she is committed to a synchronic explanation in contrast to the comparative-historical proposals that identify the prefix form as a reflex of a preterite or past tense verb (Hatav 2004: 493); second, she is convinced that BH is a "tenseless" language (2004: 523; see Hatav 1997). Both of her motivating arguments illustrate long-standing misunderstandings in discussions of the BH verbal system, which I have referred to in §2.4.1.

---

conjunction. However, DeCaen identifies the verb form to which *wa*C- is prefixed as modal Jussive in order to account for the VS word order.

92. Compare the parallel passage with [3.54a], cited in example [2.5] (p. 81): כִּי שָׁמַע 'because he had heard'.

93. Semantic bleaching refers to the loss of an item's semantic content—either partial or whole—while its grammatical content is retained (see Hopper and Traugott 1993: 87; Lessau 1994: 75).

First, the question whether *yiqtol* and *wayyiqtol* are reflexes of two distinct conjugations is not strictly a diachronic question but a synchronic question, since homonymy by its very definition is a synchronic phenomenon. While comparative-historical data conveniently present evidence for two conjugations, one could just as easily argue from the distribution of the two forms in the biblical text that *yiqtol* and *wayyiqtol* are distinct conjugations. Second, Hatav treats TAM as discrete categories, so that, if BH is "tenseless," it therefore cannot have any tensed grams. Earlier in this chapter (§3.2.3), I adopted Bhat's terminology of "aspect-prominent" (1999) to avoid just such a conclusion as Hatav's, given my argument that *qatal* and *yiqtol* form an aspectual opposition. There are, in fact, aspectual, tensed, and mood grams in BH so, to speak about it as a tense or aspect *or* mood system is problematic except as I have qualified it in terms of the "prominence" of one or the other parameter.

Few scholars any longer dispute that examples of the prefix conjugation that appears in *wayyiqtol* occur without the characteristic *wa*C- in the Hebrew Bible (but see Zevit 1988), as illustrated in example [3.55] by virtue of the parallel passage in which the form has the *wa*C- prefix.[94]

[3.55]   2 Sam 22:16

וַיֵּרָאוּ אֲפִקֵי יָם יִגָּלוּ מֹסְדוֹת תֵּבֵל

'And the channels of the sea appeared; and the foundations of the world <u>were exposed</u>'.

Despite the contrast between the parallel texts of 2 Samuel 22 and Psalm 18, it is inaccurate to think of such examples as simply the *wayyiqtol* without the prefixed *wa*C- in light of the characterization given above. Instead, it is probably best to follow the lead of previous scholars in treating examples of this sort as archaic past forms (e.g., Waltke and O'Connor 1990: §31.1.1; Rainey 1986; Greenstein 1988 on "the prefixed preterite"), in contrast to the more developed and restricted Past Narrative *wayyiqtol*.[95] Unfortunately, because these occurrences are fully homonymous with the Jussive (and therefore partially with *yiqtol*), identifying them as such is mostly ad hoc and often open to dispute.

Alternatively, scholars have long sought to establish the archaic past in specific syntagms in which the prefix form *prima facie* expresses past time: following אָז ('then', 20×) and טֶרֶם ('before', 26×; e.g., Greenstein 1988: 8; Waltke and O'Connor 1990: 498; Meyer 1992: 3.43–44; cf. Rainey 1988: 35). However, the identification of the archaic preterite in these cases is problematic on several grounds: first, the prefix verb exhibits the expected apocopated

---

94. Other possible examples of the archaic past (preterite) are Exod 15:5–6; Deut 2:12; 32:8, 10, 11, 13; Judg 2:1; 2 Sam 22:14 (cf. Ps 18:14); Ps 18:12 (cf. 2 Sam 22:12); 24:2.

95. Compare with the parallel in Ps 18:16, where the form is *wayyiqtol*: וַיִּגָּלוּ. The precise discourse-pragmatic role of *wayyiqtol* in prose and poetry is discussed in chap. 4.

form in only 1 example (1 Kgs 8:1, אָז יַקְהֵל 'then he assembled') out of 18 that
are expected to be apocopated (10 following אָז: Exod 15:1; Num 21:17; Deut
4:41; Josh 8:30; 1 Kgs 8:1; 11:7; 12:18; 15:16; 16:5; 2 Chr 5:2; and 8 following טֶרֶם: Gen 2:5; 1 Sam 3:3; 9:3; 2 Kgs 2:9; Isa 66:7; Jer 47:1; Ezek 16:57; Ps
119:67); further, the single apocopated example is written *plene* in the parallel
passage in 2 Chr 5:2 (יַקְהִיל אָז); finally, 3 of the examples following טֶרֶם are
suffixed with a paragogic or energic נ (Deut 31:21; Josh 2:8; 1 Sam 2:15),
which is associated almost exclusively with the imperfective *yiqtol* rather than
the Jussive or *wayyiqtol* (see p. 241 n. 80).

Alternatively, Rabinowitz (1984: 54) has offered the following explanation
for the prefix forms as imperfective *yiqtol* following אָז:

> Temporal *ʾāz* + perfect always marks a consecution in an uninterrupted narration
> of past actions or events: first so-and-so did such-and-such, then (*ʾāz*) so-and-so
> did (perfect) such-and-such (or: first such-and-such happened, then such-and-
> such). *ʾāz* + imperfect in a past-definite context, on the other hand, is never thus
> strictly sequential. Rather, referring to the foregoing context of narrated past
> events, *ʾāz* + imperfect indicates this context as approximately the time when,
> the time or circumstances in the course of which, or the occasion upon which
> the action designated by the imperfect verb-form went forward: this was when
> (*ʾāz*: i.e., the time or occasion or circumstances mentioned or spoken of in the
> foregoing context) so-and-so did (imperfect) such-and-such. The imperfect verb-
> form is used in these instances because the action is thought of as having taken
> place before the completion of, hence as incomplete relative to, the actions de-
> scribed as completed in the preceding context.

Unfortunately, Rabinowitz's approach suffers from two errors. First, his
basic distinction of temporal succession for אָז plus *qatal* versus simultaneity for אָז plus *yiqtol* is not valid. The sense 'at that time' with reference to
the contextually determined time can be applied to אָז plus *qatal* just as frequently as אָז plus *yiqtol*, as Kautzsch (1910: 314) points out and example
[3.56] demonstrates.

[3.56] Gen 4:26

וּלְשֵׁת גַּם־הוּא יֻלַּד־בֵּן וַיִּקְרָא אֶת־שְׁמוֹ אֱנוֹשׁ אָז הוּחַל לִקְרֹא בְּשֵׁם יְהוָה
'And to Seth also was born a son and he named him Enosh.
<u>Then</u> (people) <u>began</u> to call on the name of Yhwh'.

Second, Rabinowitz's conception of complete versus incomplete action is confused: how can an event that is conceived of as having occurred before another
completed action be conceived of as relatively incomplete with reference to
that complete action?

Rabinowitz's explanation is partially endorsed by Revell (1989: 11) who,
however, reinterprets the approach within his tense model of the BHVS: "An

imperfect introduced by אָז (*'āz*) represents an event which is present relative to its past context." Similarly, Hendel (1996: 159) treats *yiqtol* following both אָז and טֶרֶם as a relative future in which the event (E), portrayed by אָז/טֶרֶם plus *yiqtol*, is placed relatively after (in the future) the reference time (R), which is set by the narrative context or the verb in the main clause. However, this approach works consistently only with טֶרֶם, since, as Hendel (1996: 160) points out, אָז does not require a relative future verb, as does טֶרֶם. Hendel's treatment of טֶרֶם makes good sense of the temporal ordering of events in an example such as [3.57]: the temporal adverbial טֶרֶם specifies that the subordinated event 'finished speaking' (E = C_{RF}) is preceded by the main clause event of 'Rebekah (was) coming out' (R = C_{pos1}). Thus, the *yiqtol* אֲכַלֶּה expresses future-in-the-past (or relative future).[96]

[3.57]   Gen 24:45

אֲנִי טֶרֶם אֲכַלֶּה לְדַבֵּר אֶל־לִבִּי וְהִנֵּה רִבְקָה יֹצֵאת

'Before I <u>would finish</u> speaking in my heart, Rebekah (was) coming out'.

[$C_{pos1} < C_{RF} < S$]

This approach may appear counterintuitive to English-speakers because the subordinated event can appear in the Past Perfect in English, thus giving the impression that the event is *before*, not *after* the reference time. However, this characteristic of English arises from the fact that it, unlike BH, is a tense-shifting language (see Endo 1986: 300): while future in the past is normally conveyed in English by a Conditional construction (*Before I <u>would finish</u> speaking*), in a subordinate construction English opts for a Simple Past (the same tense as the verb in the main clause), or it may back-shift the tense by using a Past Perfect (see Binnick 1991: 64). That this is a syntactic phenomenon in English and not semantic is evident from examples [3.58a–b], in which back-shifting is optional regardless of how the adverb portrays the order of the two situations.

[3.58]   a. *Before* John (had) finished cleaning, Kathy came home.

   b. *After* John (had) finished cleaning, Kathy came home.

---

96. Compare with the narrative account expressed as using טֶרֶם with *qatal*: וַיְהִי־הוּא טֶרֶם כִּלָּה לְדַבֵּר וְהִנֵּה רִבְקָה יֹצֵאת 'It happened, before he <u>had finished</u> speaking, look, Rebekah was coming out' (Gen 25:15). In this case, the discourse וַיְהִי (see §4.3.4) sets the narrative deictic center in the past (C_{pos1}) and the *qatal* in the past context shifts the time back one step further (C_{RF}) to express a past-in-the-past (past perfect): [$C_{RF} < C_{pos1} < S$]. The participle, expressing a progressive event, is then indicated as intersecting the past perfect action by the adverbial טֶרֶם.

Thus, the טֶרֶם-*yiqtol* syntagm does not preserve the *wayyiqtol* past tense form without the *waC*- prefix and should not be interpreted as past perfective. Instead, *yiqtol* in this syntagm in a past context has the sense of a relative future in the past—thus accounting for the three examples with paragogic or energic נ.

As mentioned, Hendel's approach does not explain the use of *yiqtol* following אָז. In fact, אָז does not function like טֶרֶם but temporally locates the event as approximately simultaneous with the preceding narrative context (so Kautzsch 1910: 314). The TAM values of the verb forms following אָז are not limited by the adverb. Thus, we are back to the initial problem created by the 8 examples of אָז + *yiqtol* (i.e., excluding the uncertain 1 Kgs 8:1 and its parallel 2 Chr 5:2), for some of which we can find parallel or analogous passages with *wayyiqtol* (cf. Josh 8:30 and 1 Kgs 11:7 with Gen 8:20 and 1 Sam 14:35; compare Exod 15:1 and Num 21:17 with Judg 5:1). There is no easy explanation for these forms, though on the basis of the semantic comparisons with *wayyiqtol*, they may tentatively be identified as archaic past, which their contexts seem to dictate.[97]

The case for *wayyiqtol*'s being a *narrative* past tense form is discussed in chap. 4. Here, however, is the place to make the case for a past tense identification of the gram. As with the rest of the prefix pattern conjugations, the data do not allow a confident etymological reconstruction; however, the semantic similarity with *qatal* makes it reasonable to hypothesize that *wayyyiqtol* developed likewise along the resultative-perfect-perfective-past diachrony.[98] These verbs' relative placement on this path is evident from their contrastive interaction with stative predicates: *qatal* with stative predicates can express past or (default) present states, whereas *wayyiqtol* consistently exhibits a

---

97. The orthography in 1 Chr 5:2 (יָקֵיל) may indicate that these examples of the archaic past have been altered in the process of transmission, being written *plene* and then reinterpreted as *yiqtol*s.

98. Kouwenberg (2010: 130) and Andrason (2011a: 35) both reason backwards that the form originated from the combination of prefixed pronouns and an adjectival/participle form based on the overwhelming evidence that resultatives derive from such constructions (Bybee, Perkins, and Pagliuca 1994: 67–68). Both scholars (Kouwenberg 2010: 129 n. 11; Andrason 2011a: 48) also point out my misreading of the data in Bybee, Perkins, and Pagliuca (1994) and my erroneous *ya-qrub* reconstruction in my identification of the origin of *wayyiqtol* with the infinitive *q(u)tul* (Cook 2001: 130, 134; 2002: 239), similar to Bauer's reconstruction (1910) of *yiqtol* that I follow (see §3.2.3.2 above). The difference between the reconstructions of these two grams (i.e., *yaqtul* and *yaqtulu*) illustrates the difficulty of being certain about their origins: despite the similarity of form, the two are presumably differentiated by more than simply the final -*u* vowel; in the case of *yaqtulu*, however, we are on firmer ground both in terms of the typological data (see Bybee, Perkins, and Pagliuca 1994: 128–29) and an identifiable infinitive form *q(u)tul* that morphologically resembles *yaqtulu*. By contrast, there is no identifiable "past participle" in Semitic for Kouwenberg's and Andrason's reconstruction of *yaqtul*, and so Kouwenberg (2010: 130) quite appropriately classifies this reconstruction as a matter of "speculating."

past-state meaning with stative predicates (see §3.2.2).[99] This divergent behavior with stative predicates establishes the semantic distinction between perfective *qatal*, which defaults for past temporal expressions (see further §3.4.2) and past tense *wayyiqtol* (including also the aptly termed *archaic preterite* discussed above). The loss of *wayyiqtol* in later Hebrew at the same time that *qatal* was beginning to express past tense points to the competition between these two forms: *wayyiqtol* was the older form on the diachronic path, which had come to be restricted to a narrative role in BH, and later disappeared from the TAM system; *qatal* as the younger form functioned more widely in BH and showed significant semantic overlap with the narrative *wayyiqtol* while maintaining a discourse-pragmatic distinction with it (see chap. 4).

The prototypical simple past meaning of *wayyiqtol* is illustrated in example [3.59].

[3.59]   Josh 19:47

וַיַּעֲל֨וּ בְנֵי־דָ֜ן וַיִּלָּחֲמ֣וּ עִם־לֶ֗שֶׁם וַיִּלְכְּד֨וּ אוֹתָ֜הּ וַיַּכּ֥וּ אוֹתָ֛הּ לְפִי־חֶ֖רֶב וַיִּרְשׁ֣וּ
אוֹתָ֔הּ וַיֵּ֥שְׁבוּ בָ֖הּ אֲבִיהֶֽם

'The sons of Dan <u>went up</u> and <u>fought</u> against Leshem and <u>captured</u> it and <u>struck</u> it with the edge of the sword and <u>took possession</u> of it and <u>dwelt</u> in it'.

Alongside the overwhelmingly dominant simple past meaning, *wayyiqtol* sometimes appears to express a present perfect and past perfect meaning. However, it is not evident that these meanings are basic to *wayyiqtol* or even semantic rather than contextual: a perfect meaning does not apply in enough cases to explain it as a persistence of the form's presumably earlier perfect meaning (cf. *qatal*, §3.2.3.1); in most instances where a perfect meaning seems to be called for, the *wayyiqtol* or a series of *wayyiqtol*s is preceded by a *qatal* that determines the perfect meaning, as illustrated by example [3.60a]; no clear instances have been produced that require a perfect sense (i.e., simple past versus perfect seems optional at best).[100] In poetic material, where the narrative form is exploited for its accretive sense of temporal succession (see §4.4.3), *wayyiqtol* seems to require a consequential sense following a *qatal*, as illustrated in [3.60b] (see Waltke and O'Connor 1990: 477; and §4.3.2 below).

---

99. Based on the roots listed above (p. 198 n. 33), minus the following 14 roots that do not occur in *wayyiqtol*: דָּלַל (adj. דַּל) 'be low'; דָּשֵׁן (adj.) 'be fat'; חָמֵץ 'be leavened'; חָפֵץ (adj.) '(be) delight(ed) in/with'; טוֹב (adj.) 'be good'; יָגֹר (adj.) 'be afraid'; כָּשֵׁר 'be advantageous' 'be proper'; נָבֵל 'be foolish'; נָעֵם 'be pleasant'; עָשֵׁשׁ 'be moth-eaten' > 'waste away'; פָּחַד 'be in dread' > 'dread'; קָמֵל 'be decayed'; שָׁכַל/שְׁכֵל 'be bereaved'; שָׁמֵם (adj.) 'be desolated'.

100. Note the following examples that are treated as perfects by many translations but that are more accurately rendered as simple past: Gen 19:19; 31:9; 32:5; Isa 49:7; Jer 8:6; Prov 7:15.

[3.60] a. Deut 4:33

הֲשָׁמַע עָם קוֹל אֱלֹהִים מְדַבֵּר מִתּוֹךְ־הָאֵשׁ כַּאֲשֶׁר־שָׁמַעְתָּ אַתָּה וַיֶּחִי

'Has a people heard the voice of God speaking from the
midst of the fire as you have heard and lived?'

b. Ps 119:90

כּוֹנַנְתָּ אֶרֶץ וַתַּעֲמֹד

'You (have) established (the) earth and/so that it stood'.

The instances of *wayyiqtol* with a past perfect sense admit a similar explanation, as illustrated by example [3.61], in which the leading *qatal* form
semantically determines the sense: once the narrative time is set as past-in-the-
past (past perfect) by the leading *qatal*, the simple past *wayyiqtol* forms convey
simple continuity within this narrative time (see C. S. Smith 2003: 94; see also
example [4.13] and discussion there).[101]

[3.61] Gen 39:13–14

וַיְהִי כִּרְאוֹתָהּ כִּי־עָזַב בִּגְדוֹ בְּיָדָהּ וַיָּנָס הַחוּצָה: וַתִּקְרָא לְאַנְשֵׁי בֵיתָהּ

'And when she saw that he had left his garment in her hand and
fled outside, she called to the men of her house'.

The examples presented in grammars of *wayyiqtol* as expressing irrealis
mood or non-past events are all suspect. Most should be translated as simple
past or perfect (e.g., Isa 2:9; 5:15, 25; 24:18; 44:12–13; Jer 4:16; 8:16; Mic
2:13; Joel 2:23; Ps 7:13; 20:9; 64:8–10; 94:22–23; Job 14:17) and/or have
textual problems (e.g., Ps 22:30; 49:15; 109:28). The remaining examples that
appear truly problematic are philological rather than linguistic problems (e.g.,
Ezek 33:4, 6; Ps 37:40; Job 5:15–16; 36:7). The fact that there are no indisputable future examples of *wayyiqtol* is another argument that the form is simple
past, since, according to Bybee, Perkins, and Pagliuca (1994: 95), simple past
grams cannot express future events.

3.4.2. The "Default Pattern" of Temporal Interpretation in BH

In his discussion of imperfective *yiqtol*, Rainey (1986: 7) protested against
the conventional wisdom that if the BH verbal forms are aspectual the language is "tenseless" (e.g., Hatav 2004: 523), noting that "the verbal system as a
whole does indicate tense" and that the "communicational context" disambiguates the temporal interpretation. He wryly concluded: "The ancient Israelite
farmer certainly knew when to milk his cow and his language was adequate to
explain the routine to his son." In this section as well as more extensively in

---

101. The issue of *wayyiqtol* and reference time movement entailed by examples such as
these is treated in chap. 4 in terms of subsidiary foregrounds (§4.2.3).

chap. 4, I attempt to delineate precisely what has too frequently been vaguely referred to as the "contextual" temporal interpretation of the BH verbal system.

In this section, I apply C. S. Smith's recent research (2006; 2007; 2008; Smith and Erbaugh 2005) on temporal expression in "tenseless" languages (particularly Mandarin Chinese and Navajo) to BH in order to make a case that the aspectual grams in the BHVS (i.e., *qatal*, *yiqtol*, and the Participle) have a default temporal interpretation, most clearly evident in reported speech, which is in keeping with comparable aspectual forms in other languages.

Smith (2006; 2008) argues that three basic principles can account for how aspectual grams are assigned a "default" temporal interpretation. The most important of these is the deictic pattern of temporal interpretation, listed in [3.62].

[3.62] *The Deictic Pattern of Temporal Interpretation*
        (C. S. Smith 2006: 92; 2008: 235)
        a. Unbounded situations are located in the Present
        b. Bounded situations are located in the Past

Boundedness has been discussed in §1.5.3, has been discussed briefly in §3.2.3.1, and is discussed with reference to temporality in discourse in §4.2.1. Sufficient for the present discussion are the following: first, boundedness refers to whether an event is portrayed as having reached an endpoint or not (Depraetere 1995: 2–3);[102] second, perfective aspect is one means of making an event bounded, while imperfective and progressive aspects are strategies for making an event unbounded. This second point in light of [3.62] explains the oft-noted observations that perfective aspect and past tense are closely related (e.g., Dahl 1985: 79) and that imperfectivity and present time are at times indistinguishable (Bybee, Perkins, and Pagliuca 1994: 126). Smith's second principle, [3.63], is thus simply a corollary of the first:

[3.63] *Bounded Event Constraint* (C. S. Smith 2006: 92)
        Bounded situations may not be located in the Present

The well-recognized exceptions that prove this rule are reportative speech (see §1.7.6) and performatives, which reach their endpoint during the speech interval (see discussion in §3.2.3.1).

Based on these two principles, we can claim with respect to BH that *qatal* and *wayyiqtol* present bounded events, while *yiqtol* and the Participle present unbounded events. Although basically correct, this conclusion requires tempering with Smith's third principle [3.64]:

---

102. Note the distinction that Depraetere (1995: 2–3) makes between boundedness and telicity: the latter refers to whether an event has an "inherent" or "intended" endpoint (see §1.5.3).

[3.64] *Simplicity Principle of Interpretation* (C. S. Smith 2006: 93)
Choose the interpretation that requires the least information
added or inferred.

This third principle, a variation of Grice's pragmatic principle of quantity
(see Lindblom 2006: 176–83), qualifies the deictic pattern of interpretation
in [3.62] as a "default" pattern that may be cancelled, such as by adverbial
expressions that make endpoints or lack of endpoints explicit (for details on
the determination of boundedness, see §4.2.1). The same qualification then
extends to the association of perfective aspect with boundedness and the imperfective and progressive aspects with unboundedness: they default to these
interpretations, which interpretations may be canceled by other factors. These
qualifications explain why the default temporal interpretation is most evident
in reported speech: reported speech is more directly anchored to the canonical
deictic center of the speaker's speech time, discontinuous from the surrounding discourse (see Miller 2003: 74), so there are less complicating temporal
factors in reported speech that might cancel the default interpretation. As C. S.
Smith (2008: 231) puts it, "the speech time is the central orientation for language." This is in part why some complex tense constructions are liable to appear only in literary registers, in which a more complex temporal arrangement
of events appears. By contrast, in reported speech, distinguishing events with
respect to their location respective of the central orientation of the speech time
is paramount.

However, BH presents another complicating factor in the "competition"
between the imperfective *yiqtol* and the progressive Participle. In contrast to
the competitive relationship between *wayyiqtol* and *qatal*, in which the former
is mostly restricted to narrative discourse (i.e., non-speech), both *yiqtol* and
the Participle are unrestricted in register and discourse type. Further, as argued
above, while *yiqtol* continues to be employed for some imperfective expressions, the progressive is the more favored construction for these expressions,
while *yiqtol* is preferred for future and subjunctive (irrealis) expressions, which
tend toward perfective aspect (Haspelmath 1998: 55; and above, §3.2.3.2). As
a result of this, we find the following default temporal interpretation in BH
reported speech, example [3.65].

[3.65] a. 2 Sam 3:24

וַיָּבֹא יוֹאָב אֶל־הַמֶּלֶךְ וַיֹּאמֶר מֶה עָשִׂיתָה

'Joab came to the king, and he said, "What <u>have</u> you <u>done</u>/
<u>did</u> you <u>do</u>?"'

b. Deut 1:30

יְהוָה אֱלֹהֵיכֶם הַהֹלֵךְ לִפְנֵיכֶם הוּא יִלָּחֵם לָכֶם

'Yhwh your God, who is going before you, he <u>will fight</u> for
you'.

c. Gen 37:15–16

וַיִּשְׁאָלֵהוּ הָאִישׁ לֵאמֹר מַה־תְּבַקֵּשׁ: וַיֹּאמֶר אֶת־אַחַי אָנֹכִי מְבַקֵּשׁ

'The man asked him, "What <u>are</u> you <u>looking for</u>?" He said,
"I (am) <u>looking for</u> my brothers"'.

Note that the promiscuousness of *yiqtol* and the Participle in the expression of present and future events is such as to prompt perhaps the default temporal interpretation given in [3.66]:

[3.66] *Default Pattern of Temporal Interpretation in BH*
  a. Perfective *qatal* is temporally interpreted as past.
  b. Imperfective *yiqtol* and progressive Participle are temporally interpreted as non-past.

Recently, Matheus (2011) has argued that the deictic difference between speech and non-speech requires that the BH verbal system be treated separately in each deictic context. While his approach is significant in this respect, it also overstates this situation in a way that is analogous to the way that traditional wisdom overstates the difference in grammar between prose and poetic texts: there is not a fundamentally different TAM system at work in speech and non-speech deictic contexts; rather, the temporal organization of non-speech discourse is less directly related to the canonical speech time than it is (generally) more complicated than the temporal organization of reported speech. For this reason, rather than attempting to construct a separate "default" pattern of temporal interpretation of the BH verbs in non-speech discourse here, I explore in chap. 4 the temporal organization of various modes of discourse with the aim of clarifying the semantic and discourse-pragmatic interaction about the temporal interpretation of the BH TAM.

3.5. The TAM System of BH in Diachronic-Typological Perspective

In the preceding sections, I have presented a semantic theory of the TAM system of BH from the perspective of diachronic typology. I chose this approach as a means of solving the problem of validation of a semantic theory that deals with ancient texts for which we have no native speakers (i.e., we have no sure way of testing for felicitous or grammatical expressions). The theory may be deemed successful to the degree that I am able to map general meanings to specific meanings by recourse to interaction of various parameters' syntagms. This approach is thus far incomplete, and in chap. 4 I extend it to discourse contexts, with specific examples of the way that an analysis of the TAM system in specific passages might proceed.

At the beginning of this chapter, I argued that more-extreme approaches to meaning are unhelpful and are unwarranted by the data (e.g., grammatical-

Table 3.8. Development of the BHVS

		Pre-BH	*Biblical Hebrew*	*Post-BH*
Wayyiqtol	**Resultative**	perfect-perfective	> past (narrative)	> obsolete
Qatal	**Path**	resultative-perfect	> perfect-perfective	> past
Yiqtol	**Progressive Path**	progressive-imperfective	> imperfective-irrealis	> irrealis/future
Participle		progressive (nominal encoding)	> progressive (nominal encoding)	> progressive (split nominal-locative encoding)

ization, panchrony, or prototype theory). I have embraced the balanced view that individual grammars are static and therefore susceptible to synchronic analysis and that language change is strictly intergenerational (see Hale 2007: 33). Given the uncontested intergenerational character of the Hebrew Bible, diachronic typology is particularly well suited to the task, but it is also only a starting point: each artifactual text in the Hebrew Bible attests one or more "grammars" that may be identified and analyzed with ever-increasing sophistication in symbiotic relationship with descriptions of the whole or the "system," as I have sought to do here. It is premature to throw up our hands in despair at the task, and to be content to give a taxonomy of equally available meanings for the BH verbal forms is to sidestep the philological responsibility of linguistic studies of ancient texts: ultimately, a theory of the "system" is judged by its ability to make sense of the various meanings that a form has in the text and to guide philological study toward ever-greater confidence in predicting which meaning is most expected for a given syntagm or discourse context.

By way of summary and conclusion, in this final section I bring together the diachronic-typological explanations (grammaticalization paths) from this chapter, as shown in table 3.8 (based on tables 3.1 [p. 204], 3.3 [p. 222], and 3.4 [p. 229] above). These reconstructed paths of development go beyond simple description to provide explanations for the range of meanings that the individual verbal grams exhibit in the Hebrew Bible and to account for the "competition" evident among certain grams (e.g., *wayyiqtol* and *qatal*; *yiqtol* and the Participle).

I have described the BHVS as a TAM system that has certain prominent oppositions within it, while at the same time being capable of expressing a wide range of distinctions traditionally associated with tense, aspect, and mood and modality. That is to say, the simplistic debate over whether the BHVS is a "tense or aspect" system needs to be put aside and replaced with a recognition that languages have a variety of strategies for expressing TAM distinctions and that, while individual grams may reasonably be associated with oppositions

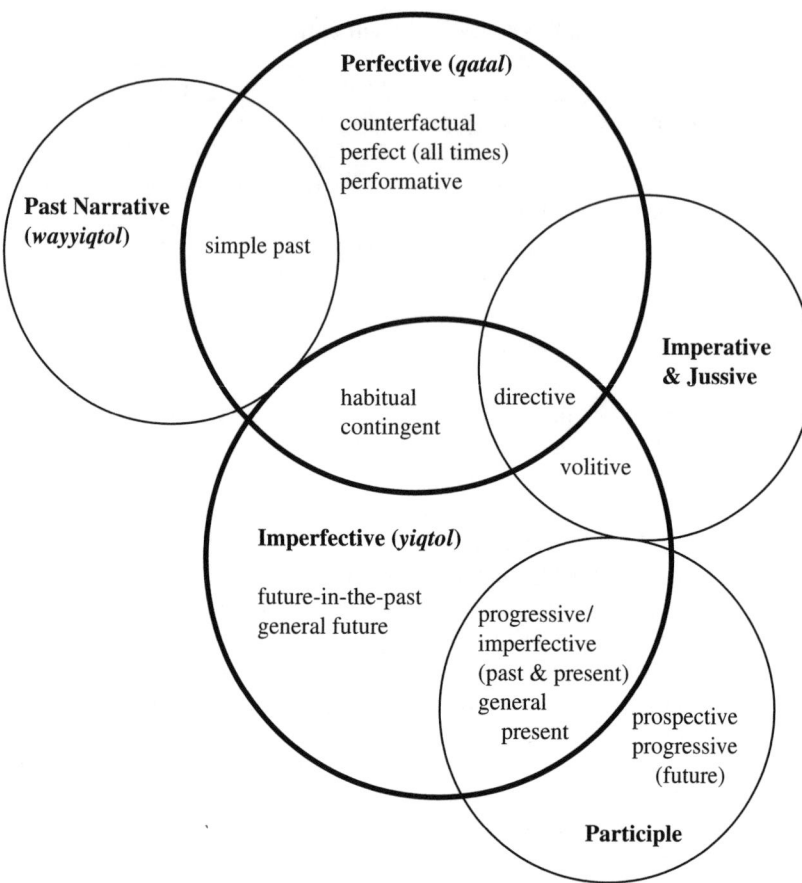

Figure 3.7. Semantic mapping of the BH verbal system.

involving one or the other of these domains, this does not confine these grams
to these domains. The basic oppositions treated in this chapter that constitute
the skeleton of the BHVS are stative : dynamic situation aspect, perfective :
imperfective viewpoint aspect, and realis : irrealis mood. The first of these is
crucial mainly for its role in certain key typological arguments that distinguish
perfective and past grams.

   The other two distinctions are key to understanding the system as such because they cross-cut one other—that is, the perfective and imperfective grams
function in both the realis and the irrealis domains. The system is visually captured in fig. 3.7. The larger, darker-bordered areas of the Perfective *qatal* and
Imperfective *yiqtol* underscore the centrality of their aspectual contrast in the

system. At the same time, the smaller circles encompassing the Past Narrative *wayyiqtol*, Participle, and Imperative and Jussive forms underscore their distinct but less-central position in the BHVS: the Past Narrative is a specialized verb form in BH that becomes obsolete in post-BH; the Participle is not a finite verb but, in a supported copular structure, is a productive progressive gram; the Imperative and Jussive constitute a distinct directive-volitive system. The meanings associated with each gram are cross-linguistic semantic categories that are traditionally associated with TAM systems. Thus, certain distinctions discussed in this chapter are excluded from this diagram. For example, distinctions among various directive expressions discussed above (§§3.3.2–3.3.3) are not included here; commissive is included as part of performative (both entail the speaker's committing to something) inasmuch as it differs, not semantically, but in terms of whether there is a perceived gap in time between the speech and the action (see §3.2.3.1 above). Although generic (or gnomic) expressions prefer null copula, *yiqtol*, and the Participle, they are not restricted to these predicates, and in particular generic anecdotal narratives (see example [3.16]) illustrate that generic is not a semantic category of the same sort as the TAM meanings included here. The strict focus on semantic categories in this mode also means it is unable properly to distinguish among the categories of progressive and imperfective because they differ primarily behaviorally—that is, the imperfective encompasses a broader array of meanings, is more closely associated with non-past time and irrealis mood, and so on.

These limitations inherent in this strictly semantic model set the stage for chap. 4, in which I turn my attention to the question of the discourse function of the BH verbal forms. After investigating the semantic-discourse function interface, I propose there a taxonomy of temporal discourse modes for BH and illustrate a semantic analysis of the BHVS with them in the context of various discourse modes.

Chapter 4
Semantics and Discourse Pragmatics of the Biblical Hebrew Verbal System

In chap. 3, I described the semantics of the BHVS at clause level. But many theories of the BHVS surveyed in chap. 2 posit discourse-pragmatic (temporal succession[1] and/or foreground) rather than semantic distinctions between *wayyiqtol* and *qatal*, on the one hand, and irrealis *qatal* ("*wĕqatal*") and *yiqtol*, on the other hand. Addressing these claims from the perspective of the semantic theory constructed in the last chapter is a central purpose of this chapter (see §§4.2–4.3 below). At the same time, I am more broadly concerned to show how the semantic theory in chap. 3 is a crucial foundation upon which to explain the temporality of BH discourse, illustrating along the way the interaction of TAM grams and coherent form-meaning correlations in BH discourse (see §4.4. below). As a necessary backdrop to this task, I begin in §4.1 with a critique of the methodology of discourse analysis more generally, which was only briefly touched on in chaps. 1–2 (§§1.5 and 2.4.3).

4.1. On Discourse-Pragmatic Approaches to BH

The discourse approaches discussed in §2.4.3 all take a similar tack to TAM in verbs—they either eschew the semantic component or downplay its contribution to the function of verb forms. Weinrich (2001: 43), for instance, claims that the significance of verbal forms is to provide a preliminary sorting ("Vorsortierung") of the world of discourse for the speaker and listener. Similarly, Longacre (2003: 57) claims that verbal forms are "most surely and concretely described" in terms of their saliency levels in different types of discourse. Niccacci and Talstra offer more-nuanced statements: observing that traditional sentence-level grammar alone cannot address the issue of the interaction of verbal forms in discourse, Niccacci (1994b: 118) claims that a discourse approach "is a necessary, even indispensable, starting point" in the study of Hebrew discourse; Talstra (1997: 85–86) states that, while one should "remain open to the possibility of relating text-level [discourse] and clause-level [semantics] categories," discourse concerns must be given priority.

---

1. *Temporal succession* is what is usually intended by the more frequently employed term *sequentiality* in reference to BH (see discussion of these terms in §4.2.1 below).

Thus, in the opinion of discourse analysts, the discourse-pragmatic functions that may be correlated with verbal forms are a priority for understanding a verbal system. This approach creates three methodological problems. First, discourse studies have been criticized for too-quickly making the leap from correlation to causation. Downing (1995: 6) cautions that, "[w]hen particular language structures are used in particular discourse contexts, say, . . . in a passage devoted to storyline development, it is sometimes difficult to determine whether the relationship between the linguistic form and the discourse factor is causal or merely correlational" (see also Tomlin 1995: 545).

The blurring of this line between correlation and causation is evident in some of Paul Hopper's discussions: in an early study of aspect and the foreground-background discourse distinction, Hopper (1982: 15) concluded from the strong correlation between foregrounding and perfectivity that the primary function of perfectivity is to foreground events in discourse. The examination of foregrounding and movement of reference time below (§4.2) makes it clear, however, that perfectivity is only one of many features that contribute to foregrounding events. Slightly differently, Hopper and Thompson (1980: 251) claimed that frequent employment of transitive constructions in the foreground of discourse contributes to transitivity's "grammatical and semantic prominence." However, DeLancey (1987: 54) demurred, claiming that the explanation of transitivity should be semantic rather than discourse-pragmatic.

Second, without a semantic component, discourse-pragmatic claims about verbs are often circular; there is no objective means by which to support or contest such claims. For instance, Hatav (1997: 21) observes an inherent circularity in Longacre's dynamic verb rankings: "The main difficulty with this notion [of dynamic verb ranking] is that it is not defined by objective metalinguistic means, which results in a circular claim (*wayyiqtol* is a dynamic form because the situation it denotes is dynamic, and the situation is dynamic because it is denoted by a dynamic form)." Bache (1985: 22) leveled a similar criticism at Weinrich's discourse approach to European languages:

> First of all, the fact that the theory is "unassailable" (to use Weinrich's own word) makes it rather suspicious. As the saying goes: a theory which cannot be mortally endangered cannot be alive. As it stands, Weinrich's theory fails to offer the rigid set of criteria for determining the validity of its own claims which one would expect of an "unassailable" theory. It simply relies on our intuitive ability to tell discursive communication from narrative communication (of course, independently of tense choice since otherwise the 'unassailable' theory is circular).

Third, and perhaps *the* underlying problem with discourse analyses of verbal systems, is that they present (explicitly or implicitly) their discourse-pragmatic explanations as suitable alternatives to semantic explanations. For instance, many biblical scholars have been content with identifying *wayyiqtol* as a sequential narrative form without examining a possible semantic motivation for its narratival use. However, this is an insufficient substitute for a semantic explanation since one presumes that verb forms generally mean something apart from their discourse context. An extreme example is Baayen's (1997: 245) treatment of *qatal*: "I will argue that *qāṭal* form has no intrinsic semantic value and that it serves a pragmatic function only." Comrie (1986) wrote a brief article claiming that semantics and discourse function are distinct, though related issues. He complains that discourse linguists have confused the two. His concluding thoughts are worth quoting in full.

> I believe that this is an important result [i.e., the distinctness of meaning and discourse function]. At present there is considerable controversy surrounding the relationship between language structure and discourse, with those at one extreme denying any relevance of discourse to studies of language structure (e.g. many formal grammarians) and those at the other extreme attempting to reduce the whole of language structure to discourse factors. While I would not deny that there may be some linguistic items whose meaning is reducible to discourse function, my experience is that there is a wide range of linguistic items for which this is definitely not the case.
>
> With regard specifically to tense, we have for instance the study by Weinrich (1964), which argues for a discourse-based approach to tense, based on the crucial distinction between narration and discussion. I have learned much about the discourse function of tenses, and even about the meaning of tenses, from such works, and from my own studies of how tenses function in discourse. But in nearly every case my conviction remains that the meaning of a tense is independent of its discourse function in any particular context, while the discourse function does depend on the meaning (and also of course, on certain features of the context). More generally, while the study of tenses in discourse is an important methodological aid in coming towards an understanding of the meaning of a tense, a full understanding of the discourse function of a tense has as one of its prerequisites a solid accounting of the meaning of that tense. (Comrie 1986: 21)

In other words, discourse approaches to verbs make valid and helpful *observations* about how verbs function in discourse; however, their *explanations* are inherently circular because of their self-imposed limitation to the realm of discourse-pragmatics. Therefore, I align myself with Fleischman's view (1990: 23) on the relationship between semantics and discourse-pragmatics of verbal systems: "The pragmatic *functions* of tense-aspect categories in narrative are not arbitrary; rather, I see them as motivated extensions of the *meanings* of those categories, extensions that, according to the view of grammar as 'emergent' (Hopper 1987) may ultimately contribute to a reshaping of the basic meanings" (see also Comrie 1985: 26–29).

Although the preceding critique of discourse analysis may appear harsh, it is not intended to be dismissive of the discipline (see e.g., O'Connor 2002). Discourse analyses furnish important, even necessary observations regarding the use of verb forms as a *system* in discourse. In particular, discourse analysis often provides a means of distinguishing verb forms that appear to be synonymous based on a semantic analysis alone, since such semantically overlapping forms may contrast in certain discourse contexts (so Hopper and Traugott 2003: 126).

Nevertheless, the argument here is that discourse analysis is only valuable when it used in conjunction with a semantic analysis, because the discourse functions of verb forms are not unrelated to their semantics (see Fleischman, quoted above). By combining semantics and discourse-pragmatics in this ordered way (i.e., semantic analysis as a prerequisite for discourse analysis), the problems of discourse analyses that eschew semantics are avoided, and our understanding of verbal systems is maximized.

4.2. Some Elements of Discourse Structure

The concepts of *temporal succession* and of *foreground-background* have both been identified as fundamental to narrative discourse (Labov 1972: 360; Reinhart 1984: 787). However, important questions have been raised about each of these concepts. Discussions about temporal succession have clustered around the questions how to define it and what semantic factor(s) contribute to temporal succession (e.g., situation aspect, viewpoint aspect, and transitivity; see §1.5). Complicating the issue is the fact that linguists often fail to distinguish foreground and temporal succession, or they explicitly equate the two (e.g., Dry 1983: 48; Reinhart 1984: 782). The identity of temporal succession and foreground, however, has been called into question (Thompson 1987).

Some linguists have questioned whether the foreground-background distinction is too intuitive to be useful. Thus, in an attempt to elucidate the foreground-background concept, numerous descriptive labels have been offered for each (e.g., foreground has been labeled "skeleton," "main line," "central," "highlighted," "new information," and "gist"; and background has been labeled "old information," "presupposition," and "non-sequential"; see Givón 1987: 176–77; Wald 1987: 486). The following sections (§§4.2.1–4.2.3) distinguish and define the concepts of temporal succession and foreground-background as a foundation for criticizing BH verb theories that apply these labels to the *waw*-prefixed forms.

4.2.1. Temporal Succession

Temporal succession is what is intended by most Hebraists who employ the more well-established term *sequentiality*. The former term is preferable because sequentiality is frequently applied (at least outside biblical studies) to a separate phenomenon (see Longacre 1985: 243–44, 263–67). Sequentiality is used to describe morphologically underspecified verb forms in syntactic chains (e.g., Marchese 1988). Conflation of the two concepts is accounted for by the fact that sequential chains are frequently employed in temporally successive discourse, as illustrated by examples [4.1a–b] (see Longacre 1985: 263–84).[2]

[4.1] *Sequential Chaining in Selepet* (from Longacre 1985: 238)
   a. Kawa ari-*op*   kiap ya taka-*op*
       kawa left:3s REM PAST   patrol officer that arrived:3s REM PAST
       'Kawa left'.   'That patrol officer arrived'.
   b. Kawa ari-*mu* kiap ya taka-*op*
       'Kawa left and that patrol officer arrived'.

When the two statements in [4.1] are expressed separately, as in [4.1a], the verbs 'left' and 'arrived' are both marked with the suffix -*op*, indicating third-person remote past tense. However, because Selepet is a sequential language, when these clauses are expressed in a chain, as in [4.1b], only 'arrived' is inflected for tense, aspect, and mood; 'left' is marked instead by the -*mu* suffix, which only indicates third-person, subject switch. No current theory of the BHVS that I am aware of supports an analysis of the *waw*-prefixed forms as sequential in this sense (there is no evidence that either of the *waw*-prefixed verb forms is in any way "underspecified"); however, the 19th-century *waw*-inductive theories may be interpreted as positing a sequential analysis (see §2.2.1 and McFall 1982: 24–6).[3]

Temporal succession is the natural or default interpretation of narrative texts, whereby, in the absence of any indicators to the contrary, the first-mentioned event is understood as occurring first, the second-mentioned event second, and so on (see Brown and Yule 1983: 125, 144). In other words, the linear ordering of events in texts is implicitly understood to mirror the order of their occurrence in the depicted world (Reinhart 1984: 780). Fleischman (1990: 131), therefore, describes temporal succession as *diagrammatically iconic*: "An iconic *diagram* is a systematic arrangement of signs, none of which necessarily resembles its referent in respect to any prominent characteristic, as in the case with an iconic *image*; rather, it is the relationship of the signs to one another that mirrors the relationships of their referents" (see Hopper and Traugott 1993: 27; 2003: 27). Diagrammatic iconicity of temporal succession is illustrated by contrasting examples [4.2a–b]. In [4.2a], the events are diagram-

---

2. Apropos of the above discussion (§4.1), Longacre (1985: 265) warns that correlations such as these do not invariably warrant a claim of causation.

3. A more convincing "sequential" syntagm in BH is the stringing together of Infinitives Absolute headed by a fully inflected verb (e.g., Zech 7:5; see Rubinstein 1952); Gai (1982) argues that the Infinitives Absolute in such examples in BH and cognate Northwest Semitic languages (esp. Phoenician) should rather be analyzed as underspecified forms that adopt the specifications of the lead verb (i.e., sequential).

matically iconic (i.e., temporally successive), whereas temporal succession is avoided in [4.2b] through the use of the Past Perfect forms (*had bought, had asked*) and subordination (*when . . . , riding . . .*).

[4.2] a. Jared bought a scooter
and he rode it up and down the street;
and Colin saw him
and he asked to borrow it,
and Jared lent Colin his scooter.

b. Jared lent Colin his scooter.
Jared <u>had bought</u> a scooter
and Colin <u>had asked</u> to borrow it
<u>when</u> he saw him
<u>riding</u> it up and down the street.

Labov (1972: 360) defines a narrative text as "a sequence of two clauses which are temporally ordered: that is, a change in their order will result in a change in the temporal sequence of the original interpretation." Thus, clauses that are in temporal succession have what we will call the *irreversibility property*: given clauses A and B, AB ≠ BA. Clauses that have the irreversibility property can often be described as conjoined with an asymmetric *and*, equivalent to 'and then' (Lakoff 1971: 126–31). Thus, notice that example [4.3a] has a different interpretation when the order of clauses is reversed, as in [4.3b].

[4.3] a. Tage drank his milk *and* went to bed.
b. Tage went to bed *and* drank his milk.

Linguists have proposed various theories to explain the semantic factors in temporal succession, some of are surveyed in §1.5: early theories identified either viewpoint aspect (e.g., Kamp and Rohrer 1983) or situation aspect (e.g., Dry 1981; Heinrichs 1986) as the determining element in temporal succession. According to the viewpoint aspect theory of Kamp and Rohrer (1983), events presented with perfective aspect advance the reference time (i.e., are temporally successive), whereas events presented with imperfective do not advance the reference time (see §1.5.1). Dry's (1981) situation aspect approach was just as simplistic: accomplishments and achievements move narrative time (i.e., are temporally successive), whereas states and activities do not (see §1.5.2).

Ter Meulen (1997) and Hatav (1989) present two attempts to refine these early approaches to temporal succession (see §1.5.2–3). Using the metaphorical labels "hole," "filter," and "plug," ter Meulen (1995: 7) claims, in agreement with earlier studies, that states and activities do not advance the reference time ("hole"), allowing a subsequent event to be interpreted as "a temporal part of that [preceding] event," whereas achievements always advance reference time ("plug"). In contrast to earlier theories, however, ter Meulen characterizes accomplishments as a "filter," which can be interpreted as either advancing ("plug") or not advancing ("hole") the reference time based on the context.

Hatav (1989: 499) makes an important departure from earlier studies by arguing that *any* situation aspect may advance reference time when it occurs with a perfective viewpoint and/or with temporal adverbial modifiers, both of which semantically assert the endpoints of the event (i.e., the event is bounded). Hatav's claim that all four Vendlerian situation types may advance reference time under certain circumstances is demonstrated by the discourse in example [4.4], in which the endpoints of each event are semantically asserted through the combination of a perfective viewpoint (illustrated by the English Simple Past) and either a [+telic] situation (i.e., achievement or accomplishment) or a temporal adverbial modifier *(for awhile, for a few minutes)*.

[4.4] Evan walked around for awhile (ACT),
found his blanket (ACH),
and was happy for a few minutes (STA),
then he angrily toppled Tage's tower of blocks (ACC).

As observed by Hatav (1989: 493), the issue of temporal succession, or the movement of the reference time, is actually reducible to a single parameter, (un)boundedness: bounded events are temporally successive (i.e., advance the reference time); unbounded events are not (see §1.5.3). As briefly discussed in §1.7.3.1, (un)boundedness relates most directly to the subinterval property, which can be used as a test for (un)boundedness: unbounded situations have the subinterval property; bounded situations lack the property (see C. S. Smith 1999: 486–88). However, additional discussion is warranted with regard to (un)boundedness and temporal succession since this parameter, which accounts for temporal succession, is related to but cannot be fully correlated with any parameter of situation aspect (e.g., [a]telicity) or viewpoint aspect.

The early attempts to account for temporal succession with perfective aspect or telicity (e.g., achievements and accomplishments) arose because of the frequency with which these semantics values correlate with boundedness. However, further investigation makes it clear that these correlations are simplistic: states, activities, accomplishments, and achievements are not all "bounded" in the same sense; while perfective situations may determine bounded events, imperfective situations may also be bounded by means of temporal adverbs.

As observed by Dowty (1986: 42; see §1.7.3.1), states are not "bounded" in the same way that accomplishments and achievements are bounded (assuming that the language even allows the combination; see Bybee, Perkins, and Pagliuca 1994: 92; Comrie 1976: 50). This is demonstrated by the different entailments that accomplishments and achievements, on the one hand, and states, on the other, have with perfective (expressed here by the English Simple Past) aspect and the adverb *yesterday* in example [4.5] (see Hatav 1989: 495; 1997: 47).

[4.5]   a.   I fixed the car yesterday (ACC). → I am not fixing it now.
        b.   I arrived yesterday (ACH). → I am not arriving now.
        c.   I was at home yesterday (STA). ~→ I am not at home now.

The subinterval-based entailments in [4.5a–b] demonstrate that the accomplishment and achievement are bounded; by contrast, the state is not bounded in [4.5c] but is understood as possibly extending beyond the adverbially-indicated boundary *yesterday*. These different entailments can be explained based on the results of the discussion on perfective aspect and (a)telicity (§§1.7.3.1–2). Since perfective aspect includes an entire interval of the event within its scope (see fig. 1.15), and since by definition the interval of accomplishments and achievements includes an inherent endpoint [+telic], this endpoint must be included in the scope of the perfective, making the situation bounded; by contrast, because states have no inherent endpoint, boundedness is not forced by the perfective aspect or the adverb *yesterday* in example [4.5c].

C. S. Smith (1999: 488) observes that activities differ yet again from states and accomplishments and achievements in terms of their boundedness: activities with perfective aspect and a durational adverbial phrase are bounded and thus do *not* have the subinterval property (e.g., *Kathy worked for two hours* is not true of any subinterval of the two-hour interval); however, when perfective aspect is applied to activities without any adverbial modification, there is an "implicit temporal bound." This implicit temporal bound is exemplified by the contrastive examples of [4.6a–b]: example [4.6a] illustrates that states are not bound by the perfective viewpoint (and adverbial modification); the interval of time during which Colin knows the answer extends beyond the perfective event frame; by contrast, a similar statement of continuation with the perfective activity in [4.6b] implies that another segment of time follows the initial period, during both of which times the same activity occurs (see C. S. Smith 1999: 487–88).

[4.6]   a.   Colin <u>knew</u> the answer yesterday and still knows the answer (STA).
        b.   Jared <u>studied</u> and continued studying without a break (ACT).

In the case of states and activities with perfective viewpoint, the common issue is implicature: states are allowed (though not required) to extend beyond the perfective reference frame, and the default interpretation implies this extension, although the implicature may be canceled (Hatav 1989: 495;

activities are also allowed (though not required) to extend beyond the perfective reference frame, but their default interpretation is that they are included in their reference frame, although again, this implicature may be canceled (C. S. Smith 1999: 488). These conclusions are illustrated by examples [4.7a–b].

[4.7] a. Evan <u>knew</u> the answer yesterday (STA),
                              . . . and he still knows it today.
                              . . . but today he does not know it.

         b. Tage <u>played</u> with his toys (ACT) . . . and ate his cookie.
                              . . . and fell asleep.

Without further context, the state in [4.7a] is interpreted as extending beyond the perfective RF, and the activity in [4.7b] is interpreted as included in the perfective RF. The implicatures may be either reinforced by the context (first clause option), or canceled (second clause option).

    In summary, perfective aspect makes accomplishments and achievements bounded, without the need for adverbial modification, because the inherent endpoint of these situation types is always included in the scope of the perfective viewpoint. Perfective aspect with activities has an implicit temporal bound whereby the default interpretation is that the activity is bounded, but this implicature interpretation may be either reinforced or canceled by the context. Finally, perfective aspects with states are not bounded and are by default interpreted as extending beyond the perfective scope; however, as with activities, this default interpretation is due to implicature and may be either reinforced or canceled by the context.

    By contrast, any situation aspect with imperfective aspect (in a neutral context) is unbounded, as illustrated in example [4.8].[4] In each case, a subsequent event (introduced by the asymmetrical *and then*) in the discourse is understood as *interrupting* the interval of the imperfective event, regardless of the situation aspect.

[4.8] a. Evan was playing (ACT), *and then* he ate lunch.
         b. Tage was building a tower (ACC), *and then* he fell down.
         c. Jared was winning the race (ACH), *and then* he tripped.

These examples also serve to illustrate the distinction between (a)telicity and (un)boundedness, since the accomplishment and achievement events remain [+telic] while being unbounded by their combination with imperfective aspect;

---

4. No example is given of a state because it does not generally occur with the English Progressive (used here to illustrate imperfective aspect), though the combination is common in colloquial English (e.g., *He was loving his job more every day*); states are unbounded in any case (i.e., with perfective or imperfective aspect; see [1.45], p. 74).

their lack of boundedness gives the interpretation that their inherent endpoint has not been reached.

As already alluded to above, temporal adverbial expressions (e.g., *three times, from 10 a.m. to noon, for three hours*, etc.) can be used lexically to effect boundedness in any situation and viewpoint combination. This adverbial strategy is illustrated by examples [4.9a–d] (based on [4.4] and [4.8] above).

[4.9]   a.   Colin was happy for a few minutes (STA), and then he started to cry.

b.   Evan was playing all morning (ACT), and then he ate lunch.

c.   Tage was building a tower this morning (ACC), and this afternoon he fell down.

d.   Jared was winning the race for 30 seconds (ACH), but then he tripped.

Two other factors affecting temporal succession may be mentioned. The first is subordination, whereby temporal succession is explicitly canceled through syntactic rather than semantic means (e.g., *Evan cried when he went to bed*; see Heinrichs 1986; example [4.2b] above). The second is discourse-pragmatic: Dowty (1986: 43) observed that the structure of accomplishments is such that they always allow the inference of "temporally included subevents"; similarly, ter Meulen (1995) labels accomplishments "filters" to describe the contextually determined choice between a temporally successive interpretation and an interpretation in which the following events are understood as being temporally included in the accomplishment. Thus, in example [4.10], the accomplishment *Bill built a house* is understood as consisting of the subsequently described subevents.

[4.10]   Bill built a house (ACC).
         He drew up plans (ACC),
         bought the lumber and hardware (ACC),
         and poured the foundation (ACC).

However, the interpretation of accomplishments as including subevents is based on pragmatic implicature; it is not semantic, since the accomplishment remains properly bounded. By contrast, since activities are only "implicitly bounded," these temporally included subevents would indicate that the activity is unbounded, as in example [4.7b], first option (cf. example [4.14] below). In such cases, the accomplishment event is perhaps best characterized as the "discourse topic" (see Brown and Yule 1983: 71–83).

Thus, in example [4.11], the accomplishment *he did what was upright* is interpreted as consisting of several subsequently reported events: removing the high places, shattering the standing stones, cutting down the Asherah, and

Table 4.1. Determination of (Un)boundedness

Bounded Situations, Temporally Successive	Unbounded Situations, Not Temporally Successive
perfective viewpoint + accomplishment or achievement [4.5a–b]	any viewpoint + state (default interpretation) [4.5c]
perfective viewpoint + activity ("implicitly bound") [4.7b] (second option)	imperfective viewpoint + any situation type [4.8]
any combination of viewpoint and situation aspects with a lexically asserted temporal boundary [4.9]	any combination of viewpoint and situation aspects with a lexically asserted temporal overlay (e.g., subordination) [4.2b]

smashing the bronze serpent. Knowledge about the nature of an event such as *he did what was upright* (i.e., the event is complex) and the subsequent events as being considered "upright" in the discourse context lead to the implicational reading that the latter events compose the former.

[4.11]   2 Kgs 18:3–4

וַיַּעַשׂ הַיָּשָׁר בְּעֵינֵי יְהוָה כְּכֹל אֲשֶׁר־עָשָׂה דָּוִד אָבִיו: הוּא הֵסִיר אֶת־
הַבָּמוֹת וְשִׁבַּר אֶת־הַמַּצֵּבֹת וְכָרַת אֶת־הָאֲשֵׁרָה וְכִתַּת נְחַשׁ הַנְּחֹשֶׁת אֲשֶׁר־
עָשָׂה מֹשֶׁה

'He did (wayy.3ms) what was upright in the eyes of Yhwh, according to all that David his father had done (qtl.3ms). He removed (qtl.3ms) the high places, and he shattered (qtl.3ms) the standing stones and he cut down (qtl.3ms) the Asherah and he smashed (qtl.3ms) the bronze serpent that Moses had made (qtl.3ms)'.

The preceding discussion of (un)boundedness as the determining factor in temporal succession is summarized in table 4.1 (the numbers of relevant examples are given for each). To anticipate the discussion of BH below (§4.3), I draw two preliminary conclusions from this discussion of temporal succession. First, in view of the fact that temporal succession corresponds to the *ordo naturalis* of narrative discourse, it is intrinsically unlikely that this value will be obligatorily marked in language.[5] Instead we should expect to find, and indeed

---

5. Temporal succession is rarely marked regularly in discourse in the languages of the world (so Wald 1987: 488, 507; cf. Cook 2001: 130 n. 18). Wald (1987: 507) concludes from his examination of several African languages that grammatically mark temporal succession that only the Bantu language of Bemba "obligatorily encodes . . . temporal sequence"; the marking is optional in the other languages. The instances of marking of temporal succession that Longacre (1985: 264–69; 1972: 1–25) cites are all within serial/sequential verb constructions. For examples of nonobligatory morphemes used to mark temporal succession (or consecution), see Heine and Kuteva 2002.

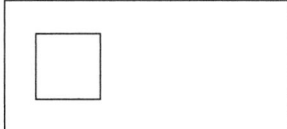

Figure 4.1. Principle of one-sided contour (adapted from Reinhart 1984: 788).

we do find, that most languages only obligatorily mark *departures* from *ordo naturalis* in discourse (i.e., they mark temporal overlay). Second, based on an understanding of the constellation of semantic factors that contribute to temporal succession, it is illogical to suppose that temporal succession is determined solely by a particular verbal conjugation.

4.2.2. Foreground-Background

The concept of a foreground-background distinction is recognized by almost all linguists (but cf. Givón 1987), but defining it has been problematic. Many linguists and virtually all scholars working on BH narrative state the distinction almost as if it were self-evident. DeLancey (1987: 65) observes that some factors involved in the foreground-background distinction are "psychological rather than purely linguistic." Similarly, Erbaugh (1987) has produced psycholinguistic evidence of the universality of foreground-background in oral narratives. Appropriately then, Reinhart (1984) draws on Gestalt theory to demonstrate the psychological reality of foreground-background in discourse (on Gestalt psychology, see p. 66 n. 47); the key conclusions from her study are summarized here.

As already mentioned in §1.7.2, space has long been used as a metaphor for time, as demonstrated by the many temporal concepts that have developed from spatial concepts (e.g., *before*, expressing the spatial idea, is metaphorically extended to express the temporal idea of *priority*; Heine, Claudi, and Hünnemeyer 1991: 48). Because of this metaphorical relationship between space and time, examination of key principles in Gestalt theory is particularly enlightening regarding both the reality and the character of the temporal foreground-background distinction. Reinhart (1984: 787) claims that the foreground-background distinction "is a cardinal principle of the organization of narrative texts" and goes on to argue that this distinction "reflects principles of the spatial organization of the visual field": foreground-background in narrative is analogous with figure-ground in Gestalt theory.

To understand the similarity between foreground-background and figure-ground, consider fig. 4.1. The figure is more readily perceived as a square lying on a rectangle than as a rectangle with a square hole in it. Thus, the square is the *figure*, and the rectangle the *ground*. Figure 4.1 illustrates the Gestalt

Table 4.2. Principles of Figure-Ground and Foreground-Background
(based on Reinhart 1984: 789–805)

Figure-Ground	*Foreground-Background*
1. Law of functional dependency: the figure depends for its characteristics upon the ground on which it appears. The ground serves as a *framework* in which the figure is suspended, and thereby it appears (Koffka 1935: 184).	1. Foreground is functionally dependent on the background.
2. Law of good continuation: shapes with continuous lines are more easily perceived (i.e, will be the figure) than those with broken lines (e.g., circle as opposed to triangle; Koffka 1935: 151–53).	2. Foregrounded events are usually temporally successive.[a]
3. Law of proximity: lines with greater proximity will be treated as units organized into higher units (i.e., as figures against a ground; Koffka 1935: 164–65).	3. Punctual [+telic] events more easily serve as foregrounded events.
4. Law of closure: enclosed areas will be treated as units organized into higher units (i.e., as figures against a ground; Koffka 1935: 167–68).	4. Foregrounded events are usually perfective aspect.

a. On this principle, I depart from Reinhart (1984: 801), who claims that only temporally successive events are candidates for foreground; I explain my position below, in §4.2.3.

principle of the one-sided function of contour: "the contour shapes its inside, not its outside" (Koffka 1935: 181). In other words, the lines of the square more readily define the inside figure as a square than the outside figure as a rectangle with a hole. The prominence of foregrounded events, in contrast to backgrounded events, is analogous to the prominence of the figure over the ground, explained by this Gestalt principle (Reinhart 1984: 803).

Another important analogy between spatial ground and temporal background is that they are both assumed to continue underneath the figure (spatially) or concurrently with the foregrounded event (temporally), even though they are not explicitly seen or depicted (Dowty 1986: 59). Reinhart (1984: 787–88) explains that, if we imagine fig. 4.1 as a square book lying on a rectangular table, we assume that the table top continues behind the book.

Reinhart proceeds from her analogy of foreground-background and figure-ground to apply the four specific principles of the figure-ground relationship by analogy to foreground-background, as shown in table 4.2.

Functional dependency is illustrated by the shapes in figs. 4.2a–b, in which the figure is characterized as a square or a diamond depending on the ori-

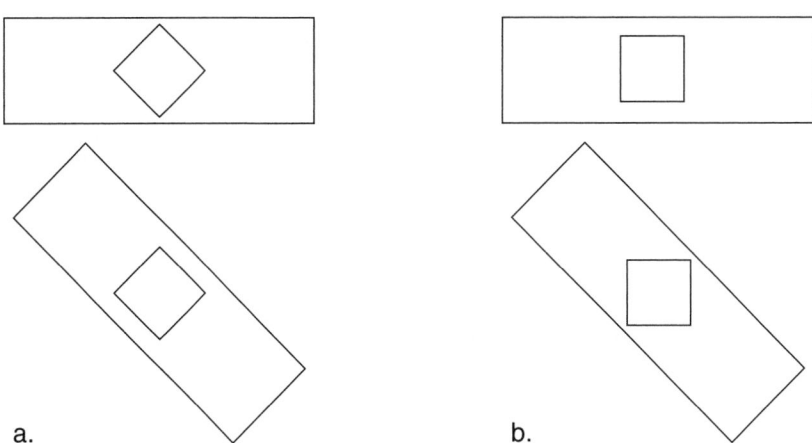

Figure 4.2a. Diamond figure; 4.2b. Square figure (adapted from Koffka 1935: 185; Reinhart 1984:789).

Figure 4.3. Law of good continuation (adapted from Reinhart 1984: 803).

entation of the rectangular ground (Koffka 1935: 185; Reinhart 1984: 789). Functional dependency with respect to the foreground-background relationship explains why the intuitive notion of foreground as the "gist" of a discourse fails: one cannot simply remove the backgrounded events, since they are functionally interdependent with the foregrounded events, just as the figure is functionally interdependent with the ground.

The law of good continuation is illustrated by fig. 4.3. The pattern of a single white horizontal stripe crossing over top of two black stripes is more easily perceived than four black boxes, because the white stripe is the more continuous part of the figure (see Reinhart 1984: 803, for other illustrations). Analogously, foregrounded events, for which temporal succession is the default interpretation, are more prominent in discourse because of their temporal continuity (Fleischman 1990: 133).

Reinhart draws an analogy between the Gestalt principle of proximity and the predominance of punctual (telic) events in the foreground of discourse. The principle is illustrated in fig. 4.4, in which we more readily perceive three thin stripes or pairs of lines, with one extra line to the right, than three wide stripes or pairs of lines, with one extra line to the left (i.e., one perceives the smaller

Figure 4.4. Principle of size and proximity (adapted from Koffka 1935: 164; Reinhart 1984: 804).

Figure 4.5. Principle of closure (adapted from Koffka 1935: 168; Reinhart 1984: 805).

spaces between the lines more readily than the larger spaces). Analogously, a series of punctual events are more salient than durative events.

Finally, Reinhart connects the Gestalt principle of closure with the use of perfective aspect to denote foregrounded events. This principle is illustrated in a comparison of fig. 4.5 with fig. 4.4 above. In fig. 4.5, the effect of the brackets is to reverse the areas of figure and ground in fig. 4.4 by enclosing the larger areas of space between the lines. Similarly, where perfective aspect effects boundedness, the events are viewed as salient. Reinhart's analogy between the principles of the foreground-background distinction in narrative discourse and figure-ground distinction in Gestalt theory support the psychological reality of the distinction as well as explain certain regular correlations between aspect and foreground or background.

4.2.3. The Relationship between Temporal Succession and Foreground

The preceding discussions (§4.2.1 and §4.2.2) may give the impression that foreground is coterminous with temporal succession. In Reinhart's estimation (1984: 801), the two are identical (see also Dry 1981: 19), and she tries to support her equating of the concepts by addressing possible objections. The first objection is raised by examples such as [4.12], in which the backgrounded action expressed by the subordinated clause appears to be temporally successive with the surrounding clauses.

[4.12]   When I strapped on his helmet, Colin ran out to get his bicycle.

In order to account for examples such as [4.12], Reinhart (1984: 797–98) distinguishes between "content criteria" and "linguistic, or sentence-level, criteria" with respect to foreground/temporal succession: while the subordinated clause is temporally successive and, therefore, foregrounded in terms of content, linguistically it is backgrounded because it is expressed by a subordinated clause. However, the definition of temporal succession given above (§4.2.1) makes Reinhart's explanation unnecessary. It is clear that the subordinated clause does not express temporal succession since it does not have the irreversibility property: the order of the subordinated clause with its matrix clause does not affect the interpretation (i.e., *Colin ran out to get his bicycle when I strapped on his helmet*).

The second objection that Reinhart addresses is the presence of temporal succession within a backgrounded section, such as in a flashback, as illustrated by example [4.13].

[4.13]   Slowly in Pippin's aching head memory pieced itself together
and became separated from dream-shadows. Of course: he
and Merry had run off into the woods. What had come over
them? Why had they dashed off like that, taking no notice
of old Strider? They had run a long way shouting—he could
not remember how far or how long; and then suddenly they
had crashed right into a group of Orcs: they were standing
listening, and they did not appear to see Merry and Pippin
until they were almost in their arms. They yelled and dozens
of other goblins had sprung out of the trees. Merry and he had
drawn their swords, but the Orcs did not wish to fight, and
had tried only to lay hold of them, even when Merry had cut
off several of their arms and hands. Good old Merry! (Tolkien
1965: 58)

Reinhart (1984: 785) asserts that there can be successive layers of the foreground-background distinction, so that "the background itself can divide into (subsidiary) foreground and background." Thus, even the flashback story-line, expressed with Past Perfect verbs in [4.13], forms a subsidiary foreground of temporally successive events within the background that is the flashback. The fact that after the initial Past Perfect (*had run*) the subsequent temporally successive events could have been expressed with Simple Past verbs supports the assertion that the events are foregrounded; the periodic return to Past Perfects in [4.13], however, reinforces the fact throughout the section that the storyline is contained in a backgrounded flashback.

Examining these objections to Reinhart's equating of foreground with temporal succession serves to clarify the concepts, but it does not demonstrate that her equation is correct. The parameters used to define temporal succession, on the one hand, and foreground-background, on the other, point to discrete and discontinuous concepts. Temporal succession is a semantic concept that can be defined logically in terms of the principle of irreversibility and (un)bounded-ness. It is determined by a combination of situation aspect, viewpoint aspect, subordination, and temporal adverbial modifiers. By contrast, the foreground-background distinction is defined as a psycholinguistic concept having to do with the discourse processing. Whether events are foreground or background depends on their relative saliency, which is determined by a gestalt of features such as the items listed in table 4.3.[6] While the semantic factors that contribute

6. See also Longacre's salience parameters (1996: 26): (non)substantive, (non)narrative, (ir)realis, (non)dynamic, (non)sequential, and (non)punctiliar.

Table 4.3. Features of the Saliency Continuum
(see Hopper 1979: 129; Hopper and Thompson 1980: 252)

More Salient	*Less Salient*
temporal succession	temporal overlap
perfective	imperfective
dynamic	nondynamic (descriptive)
telic	durative
volitional	nonvolitional
affirmative	negative
realis	irrealis
nonanaphoric	anaphoric
identity of subject maintained	frequent change of subject
human topics	nonhuman topics
agent high in potency	agent low in potency
object totally affected	object not affected
object highly individuated	object nonindividuated

to boundedness (e.g., perfectivity, telicity) are generally "more salient," saliency is a broader and different sort of concept; thus, it cannot be limited solely to the semantic parameters that determined (un)boundedness.

4.3. The Semantics of Temporality in BH Discourse

Having examined the semantics of temporal succession and pragmatics of the foreground-background distinction above (§4.2), I turn back to the question of the relationship between these elements of discourse organization and the *wayyiqtol* and irrealis *qatal*. The argument of this section is to some extent negative, inasmuch as it is framed against and contrasts with the traditional and discourse approaches to these verbal forms. Because of the foil of these other approaches, it is also somewhat disjointed. I begin by addressing the role of *wayyiqtol* in prose narrative discourse (§4.3.1). I follow this up in §4.3.2 with a complementary analysis of the conjugation in poetry, which helpfully clarifies both the narrative function of *wayyiqtol* as well as illustrating the symbiotic interaction of semantic meaning and discourse function (see quotation from Fleischman, above, §4.1). The following section (§4.3.3) turns to the question of irrealis *qatal* and its discourse functions. Here, I especially use Longacre's careful analysis of the form to illustrate the shortcomings of discourse approaches to the form. Finally, I briefly examine the bifurcated functions of the 3MS forms of the copular verb הָיָה in *wayyiqtol* and irrealis *qatal* (§4.3.4), which conveniently illustrate the distinction between semantics and discourse pragmatics. All this is a sort of "clearing of the decks" and sorting out of preliminary issues in preparation for §4.4, in which I present an alternative, semantics-based analysis of temporality of discourse.

4.3.1. *Wayyiqtol* and Narrative Discourse

While it is self-evident that *wayyiqtol* forms the "backbone" of narrative discourse, the longstanding claim that it differs semantically from *qatal* in that it expresses temporal succession (e.g., Ewald [1879: 18] and S. R. Driver [1998: 71–72], who employ the term "consecutive") cannot be valid given the understanding of temporal succession outlined above. Simply put, if temporal succession is determined by a number of semantic factors, including viewpoint and situation aspect and adverbial modification, then a single verbal gram— regardless of how it is identified semantically—cannot fully correlate with temporal succession.

A survey of the BH data is in line with this conclusion, showing that *wayyiqtol* sometimes expresses situations that are not temporally successive (e.g., with stative predicates) and that perfective *qatal* may be used for temporally successive expressions. To begin with the latter cases, the examples cited in chap. 3 ([3.10] and p. 203 n. 38) of temporally successive *qatal* demonstrate that temporal succession cannot be the distinguishing feature between *qatal* and *wayyiqtol*, that *wayyiqtol* cannot be the exclusively used verb for temporally successive expressions, and that temporal succession may be expressed using forms other than *wayyiqtol*.

I turn now to examples of *wayyiqtol* that express events that are not temporally successive; the form appears in contexts with a variety of sorts of temporal overlay as illustrated in examples [4.14]–[4.18]. Since activities are only implicitly bound by *wayyiqtol*, like accomplishments (see [4.10], p. 281) they allow subsequently described situations to be understood as temporally included subevents, as illustrated in [4.14]: while the two *wayyiqtol* forms in each verse are temporally successive (i.e., 'she rose up . . . she returned'; 'she left . . . they set out'), the second pair expresses subevents of the activity 'she returned' in v. 6. The overlay interpretation is confirmed and reinforced by the infinitive in 'they set out to return' in v. 7, which makes it evident that the event of returning has not yet reached a temporal bound.[7]

[4.14]   Ruth 1:6–7

וַתָּקָם הִיא וְכַלֹּתֶיהָ וַתָּשָׁב מִשְּׂדֵה מוֹאָב כִּי שָׁמְעָה בִּשְׂדֵה מוֹאָב כִּי־פָקַד
יְהוָה אֶת־עַמּוֹ לָתֵת לָהֶם לָחֶם: וַתֵּצֵא מִן־הַמָּקוֹם אֲשֶׁר הָיְתָה־שָׁמָּה וּשְׁתֵּי
כַלֹּתֶיהָ עִמָּהּ וַתֵּלַכְנָה בַדֶּרֶךְ לָשׁוּב אֶל־אֶרֶץ יְהוּדָה:

'And she rose and her daughters-in-law and she <u>returned</u> from the steppes of Moab, for she had heard in the steppe of Moab that Yhwh had visited his people by giving bread to them. And

---

7. Other examples include Josh 2:23 ('the two men returned and came down from the hill country . . .') and Deut 8:3 ('he afflicted you and made you hunger'). The example in 2 Sam 11:17 cited in Cook (2004b: 259) is contestable: the sequence of 'fought . . . fell . . . died' could be understood as successive, since each precludes the continuation of the previous situation; however, the plural subjects of the first two events suggest a degree of overlap.

she <u>went out</u> from the place where she had been and her two
daughters-in-law with her and they <u>went</u> on the way to return
to the land of Judah'.

"Implicitly" bound activities allow for a more general type of temporal
overlay that might be termed *coincidental,* as illustrated in example [4.15]
(see also Josh 8:4; 18:8), where Rahab's lowering of the men through her
window and her directions to them cannot be temporally interpreted in that
order; rather, a reasonable understanding would be that the complex activity of
lowering them (i.e., getting the rope, tying it off, etc.) overlaps with her giving
them directions.

[4.15]   Josh 2:15–16

וַתּוֹרִדֵם בַּחֶבֶל בְּעַד הַחַלּוֹן כִּי בֵיתָהּ בְּקִיר הַחוֹמָה וּבַחוֹמָה הִיא יוֹשָׁבֶת:
וַתֹּאמֶר לָהֶם הָהָרָה לֵּכוּ פֶּן־יִפְגְּעוּ בָכֶם הָרֹדְפִים וְנַחְבֵּתֶם שָׁמָּה שְׁלֹשֶׁת
יָמִים עַד שׁוֹב הָרֹדְפִים וְאַחַר תֵּלְכוּ לְדַרְכְּכֶם:

'And she <u>lowered</u> them with a rope through the window, for
her house was in the city wall and she was living in the wall;
and she <u>said</u> to them "Go to the hill-country lest the pursuers
overtake you"'.

Stative predicates cannot be bound by *wayyiqtol,* though frequently they are
interpreted as having an initial temporal bound (i.e., inchoative state *become*).
However, in example [4.16], real-world knowledge tells us that Jacob did not
fall in love (inchoative) during the course of his coversation with Laban (see
Hatav 1989: 496); nor is it appropriate to render the *wayyiqtol* form as past perfect (e.g., *Now Jacob <u>had fallen in love</u> with Rachel*; so the REB, NAB). Rather,
in the course of his month-long stay with Laban, Jacob fell in love and now,
where the fact is important to the story, it is reported that *Jacob loved Rachel*
(so the NJPS, NRSV).

[4.16]   Gen 29:14b–18

וַיֵּשֶׁב עִמּוֹ חֹדֶשׁ יָמִים: וַיֹּאמֶר לָבָן לְיַעֲקֹב הֲכִי־אָחִי אַתָּה וַעֲבַדְתַּנִי חִנָּם
הַגִּידָה לִּי מַה־מַּשְׂכֻּרְתֶּךָ: וּלְלָבָן שְׁתֵּי בָנוֹת שֵׁם הַגְּדֹלָה לֵאָה וְשֵׁם הַקְּטַנָּה
רָחֵל: וְעֵינֵי לֵאָה רַכּוֹת וְרָחֵל הָיְתָה יְפַת־תֹּאַר וִיפַת מַרְאֶה: וַיֶּאֱהַב יַעֲקֹב
אֶת־רָחֵל וַיֹּאמֶר אֶעֱבָדְךָ שֶׁבַע שָׁנִים בְּרָחֵל בִּתְּךָ הַקְּטַנָּה:

'He stayed with him a month. And Laben said to Jacob, "Because you are my kin, should you therefore serve me without
compensation? Tell me what your wage should be?" Now
Laben had two daughters. The name of the older was Leah and
the name of the younger was Rachel. And the eyes of Leah
were soft/weak, but Rachel was lovely and beautiful. Now
Jacob <u>loved</u> Rachel, and he said, "I will serve you seven years
for Rachel, your younger daughter"'.

In example [4.17], Esau's *eating* and *drinking* are simultaneous or alternating. This simultaneous overlap contrasts with the strict temporal succession expressed by the second two *wayyiqtols*—'*and he rose and he left*'.

[4.17]　Gen 25:34

וְיַעֲקֹב נָתַן לְעֵשָׂו לֶחֶם וּנְזִיד עֲדָשִׁים וַיֹּאכַל וַיֵּשְׁתְּ וַיָּקָם וַיֵּלַךְ וַיִּבֶז עֵשָׂו
אֶת־הַבְּכֹרָה:

'Jacob gave to Esau bread and lentil stew, and he <u>ate</u> and he <u>drank</u> and he <u>rose</u> and he <u>left</u>, and Esau despised his birthright'.

Finally, a different sort of overlap exists in the case of verbal hendiadys, in which the verbs refer to the same event. This type of overlap is found especially with verbs of speaking as in example [4.18] (see Miller 2003: 147–57 for other examples involving reported speech).

[4.18]　Exod 6:2

וַיְדַבֵּר אֱלֹהִים אֶל־מֹשֶׁה וַיֹּאמֶר אֵלָיו אֲנִי יְהוָה:

'God <u>spoke</u> to Moses and <u>said</u> to him, "I am Yhwh"'.

The most frequently discussed counterexamples to the claim that *wayyiqtol* is marked for temporal succession are instances in which *wayyiqtol* appears to express a past perfect meaning (see Baker 1973; Buth 1994; Collins 1995). Thus, as in example [4.19], *wayyiqtol* forms may follow a past perfect *qatal* with a past perfect sense (S. R. Driver 1998: 84).[8]

[4.19]　2 Kgs 13:13–20

וַיִּשְׁכַּב יוֹאָשׁ עִם־אֲבֹתָיו וְיָרָבְעָם יָשַׁב עַל־כִּסְאוֹ וַיִּקָּבֵר יוֹאָשׁ בְּשֹׁמְרוֹן
עִם מַלְכֵי יִשְׂרָאֵל: פ וֶאֱלִישָׁע חָלָה אֶת־חָלְיוֹ אֲשֶׁר יָמוּת בּוֹ וַיֵּרֶד אֵלָיו
יוֹאָשׁ מֶלֶךְ־יִשְׂרָאֵל וַיֵּבְךְּ עַל־פָּנָיו וַיֹּאמַר אָבִי אָבִי רֶכֶב יִשְׂרָאֵל וּפָרָשָׁיו:
וַיֹּאמֶר לוֹ אֱלִישָׁע קַח קֶשֶׁת וְחִצִּים וַיִּקַּח אֵלָיו קֶשֶׁת וְחִצִּים: וַיֹּאמֶר לְמֶלֶךְ
יִשְׂרָאֵל הַרְכֵּב יָדְךָ עַל־הַקֶּשֶׁת וַיַּרְכֵּב יָדוֹ וַיָּשֶׂם אֱלִישָׁע יָדָיו עַל־יְדֵי
הַמֶּלֶךְ: וַיֹּאמֶר פְּתַח הַחַלּוֹן קֵדְמָה וַיִּפְתָּח וַיֹּאמֶר אֱלִישָׁע יְרֵה וַיּוֹר וַיֹּאמֶר
חֵץ־תְּשׁוּעָה לַיהוָה וְחֵץ תְּשׁוּעָה בַאֲרָם וְהִכִּיתָ אֶת־אֲרָם בַּאֲפֵק עַד־כַּלֵּה:
וַיֹּאמֶר קַח הַחִצִּים וַיִּקָּח וַיֹּאמֶר לְמֶלֶךְ־יִשְׂרָאֵל הַךְ־אַרְצָה וַיַּךְ שָׁלֹשׁ־
פְּעָמִים וַיַּעֲמֹד: וַיִּקְצֹף עָלָיו אִישׁ הָאֱלֹהִים וַיֹּאמֶר לְהַכּוֹת חָמֵשׁ אוֹ־שֵׁשׁ
פְּעָמִים אָז הִכִּיתָ אֶת־אֲרָם עַד־כַּלֵּה וְעַתָּה שָׁלֹשׁ פְּעָמִים תַּכֶּה אֶת־אֲרָם: ס
וַיָּמָת אֱלִישָׁע וַיִּקְבְּרֻהוּ:

[13]'So Joash lay down (WAYY.3MS) with his fathers, and Jeroboam sat (QTL.3MS) upon his throne; and Joash was buried (WAYY.3MS) in Samaria with the kings of Israel. [14]Now Elisha had <u>become sick</u> (QTL.3MS) with the illness of which he would die, and King Joash of Israel had <u>gone/went down</u> (WAYY.3MS)

---

8. For other examples, see Josh 13:8–33; 2 Kgs 7:6–7, 15–20; and Baker 1973: 23–53.

to him, and (had) wept (WAYY.3MS) before him, and (had) said
(WAYY.3MS), "My father, my father! The chariots of Israel and
its horsemen!" [15]And Elisha (had) said (WAYY.3MS) to him,
"Take (IMPV.MS) a bow and arrows"; so he had taken/took
(WAYY.3MS) a bow and arrows. [16]And he (had) said (WAYY.3MS)
to the king of Israel, "Grasp (IMPV.MS) the bow"; and he (had)
grasped (WAYY.3MS) it. And Elisha (had) laid (WAYY.3MS) his
hands on the king's hands. [17]And he (had) said (WAYY.3MS),
"Open (IMPV.MS) the window eastward"; and he (had) opened
(WAYY.3MS) (it). And Elisha (had) said (WAYY.3MS), "Shoot"
(MS.IMPV); and he (had) shot (WAYY.3MS). And he (had) said
(WAYY.3MS), "The Lord's arrow of victory and the arrow of victory over Aram! For you should fight (QTL.2MS) the Arameans
in Aphek until (you) make an end (INF) (of them)." [18]And he
(had) said (WAYY.3MS), "Take (IMPV.MS) the arrows"; and he had
taken/took (WAYY.3MS) (them). And he (had) said (WAYY.3MS) to
the king of Israel, "Strike (IMPV.MS) the ground"; and he (had)
struck (WAYY.3MS) three times, and (had) stopped (WAYY.3MS).
[19]And the man of God had become/became angry (WAYY.3MS)
with him, and (had) said (WAYY.3MS), "(You should have) struck
(INF) five or six times; then you would have struck (QTL.2MS)
Aram until (you) made an end (INF) (of it), but now you will
strike (YQTL.2MS) Aram only three times." [20]And Elisha (had)
died (wayy.3ms), and they (had) buried him (WAYY.3MS)'.

Notice, however, that in English example [4.13] above, the past-in-the-past
temporal deixis carries through the passage even with the alternation between
Past Perfect and Simple Past verbs. The case in BH is similar: the initial past
perfect is signaled *semantically* by the past-perfect *qatal* חָלָה ('he had become
sick', the meaning of which is clear from the discourse, which moves from
reporting Joash's death to narrating events prior to Joash's death; the *wayyiqtol*
verbs form a subsequent storyline through which the past-in-the-past temporal
frame is maintained (see §3.4.1 and C. S. Smith 2003: 94).

There are other cases in which a flashback storyline expressed by *wayyiqtol*s is signaled by a temporal protasis instead of a past perfect *qatal* (e.g., Gen
19:28–29; 2 Sam 4:4; 1 Kgs 11:15–22). The exigencies of linearly recounting
two parallel storylines (such as overlapping reigns of kings in 2 Kgs 14:1–16)
also implicates a past perfect sense for *wayyiqtol* forms. Both these cases are
illustrated by example [4.20] (see Talmon 1978).

[4.20] 1 Kgs 18:1–5

וַיְהִי יָמִים רַבִּים וּדְבַר־יְהוָה הָיָה אֶל־אֵלִיָּהוּ בַּשָּׁנָה הַשְּׁלִישִׁית לֵאמֹר לֵךְ
הֵרָאֵה אֶל־אַחְאָב וְאֶתְּנָה מָטָר עַל־פְּנֵי הָאֲדָמָה: וַיֵּלֶךְ אֵלִיָּהוּ לְהֵרָאוֹת
אֶל־אַחְאָב וְהָרָעָב חָזָק בְּשֹׁמְרוֹן: וַיִּקְרָא אַחְאָב אֶל־עֹבַדְיָהוּ אֲשֶׁר עַל־
הַבָּיִת וְעֹבַדְיָהוּ הָיָה יָרֵא אֶת־יְהוָה מְאֹד: וַיְהִי בְּהַכְרִית אִיזֶבֶל אֵת נְבִיאֵי
יְהוָה וַיִּקַּח עֹבַדְיָהוּ מֵאָה נְבִאִים וַיַּחְבִּיאֵם חֲמִשִּׁים אִישׁ בַּמְּעָרָה וְכִלְכְּלָם
לֶחֶם וָמָיִם: וַיֹּאמֶר אַחְאָב אֶל־עֹבַדְיָהוּ לֵךְ בָּאָרֶץ אֶל־כָּל־מַעְיְנֵי הַמַּיִם וְאֶל
כָּל־הַנְּחָלִים אוּלַי נִמְצָא חָצִיר וּנְחַיֶּה סוּס וָפֶרֶד וְלוֹא נַכְרִית מֵהַבְּהֵמָה:

Story line 1: 'Many days passed (WAYY.3MS), and the word
of Yhwh came (QTL.3MS) to Elijah, in the third year (of the
drought), saying, "Go (IMPV.MS), present yourself (IMPV.MS) to
Ahab, and I will send (YQTL.1S) rain on face of the land." ²And
Elijah <u>went</u> (WAYY.3MS) to present himself (INF) to Ahab.

Story line 2: 'Now the famine was severe (QTL.3MS) in Samaria.
³And Ahab <u>summoned</u> (WAYY.3MS) Obadiah, who was in charge
of the palace.

Background: 'Now Obadiah greatly feared (QTL.3MS) Yhwh,
⁴and (וַיְהִי)[9] when Jezebel was killing (INF) the prophets of
Yhwh, Obadiah <u>took</u> (WAYY.3MS) a hundred prophets and <u>hid</u>
them (WAYY.3MS), fifty men in (each) cave, and sustained them
(QTL.3MS) with bread and water.

Story line 2 (cont'd.): ⁵'And Ahab <u>said</u> (WAYY.3MS) to Obadiah,
"Go (IMPV.MS) through the land to all the springs of water and
to all the wadis; perhaps we will find (YQTL.1P) grass and keep
the horses and mules alive (QTL.1P), and we will not have to
destroy (YQTL.1P) some of the animals"'.

Example [4.20] reports two concurrent storylines that eventually converge in
the discourse: Elijah's going to appear before Ahab (vv. 1–2); and Ahab and
his servant Obadiah's going out to look for pastureland (vv. 3, 5–6). Within
the second storyline, Obadiah's pious character is described in terms of his
meritorious past actions for God's prophets (vv. 4). This background, however,
is set off from the storyline by a temporal infinitive (בְּהַכְרִית).

Finally, Buth (1994: 142–43) discusses examples of "temporal overlay,"
in which an interrupted storyline is picked up again by verbal repetition or
anaphoric reference to the last reported event in the storyline (see also Talmon
1978). To the example of Lev 6:6–11, which Buth cites, we may add 1 Sam

---

9. The *wayyiqtol* conjugation with היה forms a special case, discussed below (§4.3.4).

14:1–6, 2 Sam 13:29–34, and 1 Kgs 22:35–37 as examples of such temporal overlay, the last of which is given in example [4.21].[10] However, a past perfect sense is not generally required in such instances (e.g., 2 Sam 13:34 in NRSV).

[4.21]   1 Kgs 22:35–37

'[35]And the battle increased (WAYY.3FS) that day, and the king was (QTL.3MS) propped up in the chariot opposite Aram, and he died (wayy.3MS), and the blood of the wound poured (WAYY.3MS) into the bottom of the chariot. [36]And the cry passed through (WAYY.3MS) the camp when the sun went (down) (INF) saying, "Each man to his city and each man to his country!" [37]And (so) the king died (WAYY.3MS) and he came (WAYY.3MS) to Samaria, and they buried (WAYY.3MS) the king in Samaria'.

In summary, a past-perfect meaning cannot be associated with *wayyiqtol*. When it appears in narrative discourse following a leading past-perfect *qatal*, a temporal protasis, or anaphor—all of which signal a break in the default interpretation of the clauses as temporally successive—the *wayyiqtol* conveys continuity within that newly established deictic frame; any apparent past-perfect sense is a pragmatic implicature and not semantic.[11]

Some of the other examples of past perfect *wayyiqtol* offered by Baker (1973; Buth 1994 and Collins 1995 provide a few additional examples) have been misconstrued: in most cases the *wayyiqtol* events are actually temporally successive (e.g., Gen 2:19; 29:12; Exod 2:10; 14:8; 1 Sam 7:13; 9:26; 2 Sam 12:26–29; 13:28; 2 Kgs 6:29); in other cases, a past perfect reading of *wayyiqtol* has been forced as a means of harmonizing redactional difficulties (e.g., Gen 35:7, 15; Exod 4:19; Judg 20:31–47; 2 Sam 4:3, 7; 1 Kgs 7:13); finally, in several of Baker's examples, the initial clause is not intended to be temporally successive with the following *wayyiqtols*, but introduces the discourse topic, as in example [4.22], where a *qatal* form appears in the initial clause (also Num 1:47–49; Judg 11:1).

---

10. See also examples such as 1 Sam 31:4–6, in which the וַיָּמַת (WAYY.3MS) in v. 6 not only creates a temporal overlay of the sort that Buth discusses but serves as a summary statement for the preceding narrative (cited by Harmelink [2004: 134], whose conclusions match my own here, that *wayyiqtol* does not invariably indicate temporal succession; see his discussion and examples on pp. 129–35).

11. Talmon (1978: 17; see pp. 17–26 for other examples) posits three categories into which most of the examples discussed here may be placed: "Cases of complete or almost complete concurrence within a restricted frame of time will be considered under the heading of 'simultaneity' [e.g., [4.17] above]; where a more extensive time element is involved which necessarily results in only partial overlapping, 'contemporaneity' will be used [e.g., [4.19] pp. 291–92]; 'synchroneity' will refer to in-between situations [e.g., [4.20], p. 293, and [4.21] above]."

[4.22] Exod 19:1–2

בַּחֹדֶשׁ הַשְּׁלִישִׁי לְצֵאת בְּנֵי־יִשְׂרָאֵל מֵאֶרֶץ מִצְרָיִם בַּיּוֹם הַזֶּה בָּאוּ מִדְבַּר
סִינָי: וַיִּסְעוּ מֵרְפִידִים וַיָּבֹאוּ מִדְבַּר סִינַי וַיַּחֲנוּ בַּמִּדְבָּר וַיִּחַן־שָׁם יִשְׂרָאֵל
נֶגֶד הָהָר:

'In the third month of the exodus of Israel from the land of
Egypt, on the very day, they came (QTL.3P) to the wilderness of Sinai. They set out (WAYY.3MP) from Raphidim and
came (WAYY.3MP) to the wilderness of Sinai and encamped
(WAYY.3MP) in the wilderness; Israel encamped (WAYY.3MS)
there before the mountain'.

The correlation between *wayyiqtol* and the foreground fairs much better than
the case for temporal succession discussed above. Many languages in the
world feature a *narrative verb* or *tense*, which is employed in narrative discourse to express the basic story line or foreground (see Longacre 1990: 109).
Within BH narrative discourse, there is overwhelming data to support the assertion that *wayyiqtol* is a narrative verb in this sense. In other words, *wayyiqtol*
is the default verb in narrative discourse, and as such, presents (i.e., marks)
foregrounded events.[12]

Recognition of *wayyiqtol* as discourse-pragmatically marking the foreground in narrative is exegetically significant when it occurs in contexts where
we would more naturally expect a background construction to be employed, as
in the account of Jacob's marriage to Laban's daughters, the relevant verses of
which are given in example [4.23].

---

12. Heimerdinger (1999: 223–25) is the only scholar I have found who takes issue with
this view that *wayyiqtol* foregrounds events in Biblical Hebrew narrative. His dissension,
however, is based on a different understanding of foregrounding from the one proposed here.
Heimerdinger defines *foreground* based on Grice's maxims of conversation (i.e., quantity,
quality, relation, and manner; see Levinson 1983: 97–166): the speaker or writer throws
certain events into relief when their inclusion in the discourse violates one of the maxims of
conversation. In Heimerdinger's words (1999: 240), "Foregrounding in Old Hebrew narratives could be described as special salience. In the development of a story, there are special
events which are more arresting than others, because they happen 'out-of-the-blue.'" By
contrast, I am understanding the *foreground* as the default (or unmarked) mode of recounting events in narrative, often marked (as in BH) by means of a dominant narrative verb;
background is marked by departures from the default mode of narration (see §4.2.2 above).
Within the dominant foreground, events may nevertheless be determined to be more or less
important to the development of the theme, as Heimerdinger observes in his criticism of
Longacre (1999: 76–80); but this is a different (literary) matter.

[4.23] a. Gen 29:23–25a

וַיְהִי בָעֶרֶב וַיִּקַּח אֶת־לֵאָה בִתּוֹ וַיָּבֵא אֹתָהּ אֵלָיו וַיָּבֹא אֵלֶיהָ: וַיִּתֵּן
לָבָן לָהּ אֶת־זִלְפָּה שִׁפְחָתוֹ לְלֵאָה בִתּוֹ שִׁפְחָה: וַיְהִי בַבֹּקֶר וְהִנֵּה־הִוא
לֵאָה

'And when it was evening, he took Leah, his daughter, and
brought her to him, and he went in to her. And Laban <u>gave</u>
(WAYY.3MS) Zilpah, his maidservant, to her to be a maid for
Leah, his daughter. And when it was morning, behold, it
was Leah'.

b. Gen 29:28–30a

וַיַּעַשׂ יַעֲקֹב כֵּן וַיְמַלֵּא שְׁבֻעַ זֹאת וַיִּתֶּן־לוֹ אֶת־רָחֵל בִּתּוֹ לוֹ לְאִשָּׁה:
וַיִּתֵּן לָבָן לְרָחֵל בִּתּוֹ אֶת־בִּלְהָה שִׁפְחָתוֹ לָהּ לְשִׁפְחָה: וַיָּבֹא גַּם אֶל־
רָחֵל וַיֶּאֱהַב גַּם־אֶת־רָחֵל מִלֵּאָה

'And Jacob did so and he fulfilled this seven years and he
gave to him Rachel, his daughter, for a wife. And Laban
<u>gave</u> (WAYY.3MS) to Rachel, his daughter, Bilhah his maid
to be a maid for her. And he came in to Rachel also, and he
loved Rachel more than Leah'.

In each of these excerpts, the use of וַיִּתֵּן to report Laban's gift of a maidservant
seems out of place; we may justifiably expect a background construction using *qatal*, such as וְלָבָן נָתַן. Thus, this departure is exegetically significant: by
using *wayyiqtol* forms, and intentionally interrupting the reports of the two
sisters' marriages to Jacob, the narrator highlights and foreshadows the role of
the maidservants as surrogate mothers in the sororial feud between Leah and
Rachel (see Collins 1995: 132–33).

The narrator similarly capitalizes on the unexpected use of a foreground
wayyiqtol in the passage cited above, example [4.16], where Jacob's developed
affection for Rachel might have been portrayed with a *qatal* background construction such as וְיַעֲקֹב אָהַב אֶת־רָחֵל 'Now Jacob was in love with Rachel' in
this context (cf. Gen 37:3). A construction of this sort, however, would obscure
the central motif in the ensuing narrative of Jacob's love for Rachel.

Although the narrative verb *wayyiqtol* consistently marks foregrounded
events, it does not automatically follow that every other verb form is limited
to backgrounded events (cf. Longacre 2003: 65). Notably, *wayyiqtol* and *qatal*
often appear together expressing simultaneous foregrounded events, as illustrated in example [4.24] (e.g., Gen 33:16; 45:14; Exod 17:10; Judg 1:25; see
Talmon 1978: 12; Gross 1981).[13]

---

13. For other examples of *qatal* expressing foreground events, see Heimerdinger 1999:
93–98.

[4.24] Gen 4:3–4

וַיְהִי מִקֵּץ יָמִים וַיָּבֵא קַיִן מִפְּרִי הָאֲדָמָה מִנְחָה לַיהוָה: וְהֶבֶל הֵבִיא גַם־
הוּא מִבְּכֹרוֹת צֹאנוֹ וּמֵחֶלְבֵהֶן וַיִּשַׁע יְהוָה אֶל־הֶבֶל וְאֶל־מִנְחָתוֹ

'And it happened that after some days Cain brought (WAYY.3MS)
some of the produce of the ground as a gift to Yhwh, and Abel
also brought (QTL.3MS) some of the firstborns of his flock and
some of their fat'.

Because Reinhart (1984: 794–95), following Hatav's treatment of BH, identifies *wayyiqtol* as the *only* form that marks temporal succession and foregrounded events in BH narrative, she is forced to identify incorrectly the
wayyiqtol event as foregrounded and the *qatal* event as backgrounded in example [4.24]. Rather, both וַיָּבֵא and הֵבִיא express foregrounded events that are
equally highly salient to the narrative. The motivation for this construction
may have to do with avoiding an implicitly bound interpretation (temporally
successive) of the activity verb [*bring*] expressed by narrative *wayyiqtol*.[14]

In conclusion, there is neither a semantic marking nor a complete discourse
correlation between *wayyiqtol* and temporal succession. The high degree of
coincidence between *wayyiqtol* and temporal succession is explained first of all
by the semantics of *wayyiqtol*; namely, its default perfective aspect regularly
contributes to the expression of temporal succession. Secondly, as the narrative verb, *wayyiqtol* is the preferred form in narrative discourse, in which the
ordo naturalis (i.e., temporal succession) normally holds between successively
described events. The choice of *wayyiqtol* as narrative verb in BH parallels the
preference for simple past verbs for narration in other languages (e.g., English,
French, German) and is motivated by the high saliency of simple past verbs,
which express perfective aspect by default (see table 4.2, p. 284).

By contrast, foregrounding is a discourse-pragmatic feature of *wayyiqtol*;
the form is the narrative verb in Biblical Hebrew, used regularly to express
foregrounded events in narrative discourse. Nevertheless, Biblical Hebrew
does not employ *wayyiqtol* exclusively to express foreground, and neither are
departures from the *wayyiqtol* in narrative always to be construed as marking
background information. Rather, such deviations from *wayyiqtol* (mostly with
perfective *qatal*) may be motivated by any number of factors (or a combination of them), including word order (e.g., focus fronting in Gen 18:7; 25:6),

---

14. Although perfective *qatal* could likewise yield a bounded interpretation, in BH narrative, in which the *ordo naturalis* of temporal succession is generally associated with the default narrative verb, the employment of *qatal* instead of *wayyiqtol* usually implies a departure
from strict temporal sequence—either a simultaneous event or a backgrounded event (mostly
with a perfect or past perfect sense). Distinguishing whether a given instance of *qatal* is temporally successive or not within its context depends to some degree on which interpretation
is the more plausible (see Comrie 1986: 17).

avoidance of temporally successive interpretation (e.g., Gen 37:3, 11), marking of a new discourse section (e.g., Gen 4:1; 39:1), and signaling of backgrounded information (usually with a perfect or pluperfect *qatal*; e.g., Gen 14:3–4).

4.3.2. *Wayyiqtol* in Poetry

The preceding discussion raises questions about the role of *wayyiqtol* outside its "native" context of prose narrative. That the form is indeed native to prose narrative is underscored by its rarity in poetry or (more narrowly) verse.[15] To illustrate, *wayyiqtol* appears as a main predicate in the poetic "sentence" literature of Proverbs only 7 times (11:8, 12:13, 18:22, 20:26, 21:22, 22:12, 25:4; see Cook 2005: 130–32); less than half the occurrences of *wayyiqtol* in Job are in the poetic passages, in chaps. 3–41 (112 of 261 times), where they constitute less than 5 percent of the verbal forms; in the book of Psalms, 89 of the poems lack the form altogether, while 185 of the 332 forms are clustered in Psalms 18, 78, 105, 106, and 107.[16] This distribution of the form in Psalms points to two distinct patterns of use that are particularly enlightening regarding the form's function in poetry. These are examined in turn below.

Outside the 5 poems in which the *wayyiqtol* form is highly concentrated (see below), the *wayyiqtol* form rarely appears in series of 2 or more forms;[17] a notable exception that proves the rule is the passage from Psalm 40 given in example [4.25] below (see also Ps 69:11–12).

[4.25] Ps 40:2–4a

קַוֹּה קִוִּיתִי יְהוָה וַיֵּט אֵלַי וַיִּשְׁמַע שַׁוְעָתִי׃
וַיַּעֲלֵנִי מִבּוֹר שָׁאוֹן מִטִּיט הַיָּוֵן וַיָּקֶם עַל־סֶלַע רַגְלַי כּוֹנֵן אֲשֻׁרָי׃
וַיִּתֵּן בְּפִי שִׁיר חָדָשׁ תְּהִלָּה לֵאלֹהֵינוּ

'I waited (QTL.1s) patiently for Yhwh, and he <u>turned</u> (WAYY.3MS) to me and <u>heard</u> (WAYY.3MS) my cry; he brought me <u>up</u> (WAYY.3MS) from the desolate pit, from the muddy mire,

---

15. I am not strictly distinguishing poetry and verse in my discussion; my main focus is on *wayyiqtol* outside prose narrative, and scholars tend to operate with a simple prose-poetry distinction in mind for biblical literature. The focus on Psalms is convenient inasmuch as it contains exemplary biblical poetry in verse form.

16. Only 11 poems contain 4 or more *wayyiqtol* forms, which together account for almost half of the remaining forms in the book (62 of 139 examples): Ps 7:5, 13, 16 [2×]; 29:5, 6, 9, 10; 37:36 [2×], 40 [2×]; 40:2 [2×], 3 [2×], 4; 44:3 [2×], 10, 19–21; 50:1, 6, 16–18; 64:8–10 [2×]; 69:11 [2×], 12 [2×], 21 [2×], 22; 80:6, 9–10 [2×]; 109:3, 4, 16, 17 [3×], 18 [2×], 28; 119:26, 52, 55, 59–60, 106, 131, 147, 158, 167. Excluded from the statistics are the 8 examples in the prose-narrative titles (i.e., Ps 34:1 [2×]; 52:2 [2×]; 54:2; 59:1; 60:2 [2×]),

17. Excluding the prose-narrative titles that feature multiple *wayyiqtol* forms (i.e., Ps 34:1; 52:2; and 60:1) and the 5 narrative poems, a series of 2 or more *wayyiqtol* forms occur without an intervening predicate only 21 times: Ps 7:16; 29:5–6; 37:36, 40; 40:2–3; 55:6–7; 64:10; 69:11–12, 21; 73:13–14; 80:10; 94:22–23; 97:8; 109:17–18; 144:3.

and he established (WAYY.3MS) my feet upon a rock, he secured
(QTL.3MS) my steps. Then he placed (WAYY.3MS) a new song in
my mouth, a song of praise to our God'.

Rather, in the majority of instances, *wayyiqtol* appears in isolation and expresses a past-time, temporally-successive event following a *qatal* or (in those
few instances) another *wayyiqtol* form, as illustrated by examples [4.26a–b].[18]
In some examples of this sort, the successive relation tends toward more of a
consequential sense, as illustrated by examples [4.26c–d] (see also [3.60b]).

[4.26] a. Ps 7:13b

קַשְׁתּוֹ דָרַךְ וַיְכוֹנְנֶהָ

'He bent his bow and (then) set it'.

b. Ps 81:8a

בַּצָּרָה קָרָאתָ וָאֲחַלְּצֶךָּ

'In distress you called, and (then) I rescued you'.

c. Ps 97:4b

רָאֲתָה וַתָּחֵל הָאָרֶץ

'The earth saw (them), and it writhed'.

d. Ps 33:9

כִּי הוּא אָמַר וַיֶּהִי הוּא־צִוָּה וַיַּעֲמֹד

'For he spoke and it happened; he commanded and it
stood'.

Variants on this pattern include 11 examples in which the *wayyiqtol* follows
successively after a form other than *qatal* or another *wayyiqtol*; some are illustrated in examples [4.27a–d] below. The past temporal context of 3 examples
of this sort suggests that the *yiqtol* form is the archaic preterite (Ps 3:5; 44:3;
80:9); in another 2 passages, the *yiqtols* may be interpreted as past imperfective (Ps 55:18; 94:7); and in Ps 144:3, the 2 *wayyiqtol* forms may be rendered
as past consequential, despite the present-generic rendering of many English
translations (cf. the Septuagint). The *wayyiqtol* forms following a Participle
and *yiqtol* in Ps 34:8 and 59:16, respectively, are more difficult to explain but
are also suspect considering the Future tense translation of the forms in the
Septuagint. The remaining 2 examples (Ps 104:32 and 136:11) appear in praise
psalms that are dominated by relative participial (generic) constructions. As

---

18. This pattern accounts for 79 of the 139 examples (57%) occurring outside the prose
titles and 5 narrative poems: 3:6; 7:13, 16 [וַיִּפֹּל]; 20:9; 22:5, 30; 28:7 [2×]; 30:3, 12; 33:9
[2×]; 37:36 [2×]; 38:13; 39:12; 40:2 [2×], 3 [2×], 4; 41:13; 44:3, 10, 19–21; 45:8; 50:17–18;
55:7; 64:10 [2×]; 65:10; 66:12; 69:11 [2×], 12 [2×], 21 [2×]; 73:13, 16; 75:9; 77:11; 80:10
[2×]; 81:8, 13; 90:10; 94:23; 97:4, 8 [2×]; 102:5, 8, 11; 109:3, 5, 17 [2×], 18, 28; 114:3;
118:21; 119:26, 52, 59, 90, 131, 147, 158; 120:1; 136:4; 138:3; 139:1, 5; 143:4, 6.

such, they underscore the motivation for the use of the *wayyiqtol* in this context
as its overt marking of temporal succession.

[4.27]   a.   Ps 80:9

גֶּפֶן מִמִּצְרַיִם תַּסִּיעַ תְּגָרֵשׁ גּוֹיִם וַתִּטָּעֶהָ

'A vine from Egypt you pulled out; you drove out nations
and planted it'.

b.   Ps 55:18

עֶרֶב וָבֹקֶר וְצָהֳרַיִם אָשִׂיחָה וְאֶהֱמֶה וַיִּשְׁמַע קוֹלִי

'Evening and morning and noonday I was lamenting and
moaning and he heard my voice'.

c.   Ps 144:3

יְהוָה מָה־אָדָם וַתֵּדָעֵהוּ בֶּן־אֱנוֹשׁ וַתְּחַשְּׁבֵהוּ

'Yhwh, what is man that you made yourself known to him,
the son of man that you considered him?

d.   Ps 136:10–11

לְמַכֵּה מִצְרַיִם בִּבְכוֹרֵיהֶם כִּי לְעוֹלָם חַסְדּוֹ׃
וַיּוֹצֵא יִשְׂרָאֵל מִתּוֹכָם כִּי לְעוֹלָם חַסְדּוֹ׃

'(Praise be) to him who struck Egypt in their firstborn—his
steadfast love is everlasting—and brought Israel out from
their midst—his steadfast love is everlasting'.

Above (§4.2.1), I argued that temporal succession is semantically effected
by boundedness but is the pragmatically default interpretation of narrative discourse. What I propose here is that the association of this pragmatic-based
temporally successive meaning with the narrative *wayyiqtol* allows the poets
of Psalms to draw on the form to overtly mark temporal succession within a
context dominated by static (temporally speaking), parallelistic poetry. The
contrast between Hebrew narrative and poetry can be well appreciated in light
of Jakobson's (1960: 358) famous definition of poetic function as transforming
sequence into equivalency: "equivalence is promoted to the constitutive device
of the sequence." In other words, the relationship between predicates in successive lines (i.e., parallel stichs) in poetry is one of equivalency—that is, they
refer to the self-same event—in contrast to prose narrative, in which successive
predicates refer to successive events. Thus, to force a sequential reading of
events in poetry, the *wayyiqtol* form is employed with its implicature meaning
of succession from prose narrative.

As I illustrate below (this section), the overt marking of temporal succession is also the main motivation for the use of *wayyiqtol* in the 5 poems in
which it predominates. But note that the exceptions (i.e., nontemporally successive) among the examples outside these 5 poems, illustrated in example

[4.28a], can mostly be explained by other factors that contribute to the verb choice: in 11 cases, poetic word pairs along with word order and the aesthetics of verb variation dictate the use of *wayyiqtol* in close succession with *qatal* to form a verbal hendiadys or parallel expression (Ps 7:16; 16:9; 29:10; 37:40; 50:1; 73:13; 77:19; 89:20, 39; 90:2; 119:106); similarly, some of the 8 instances of *wayyiqtol* in simple coordination (i.e., nontemporally successive; Ps 7:5; 29:6; 38:3; 45:8; 80:6; 109:16; 119:55, 167) may be explained as motivated by complementary word pairings; finally, in 15 cases, *wayyiqtol* does not "follow" anything (in terms of temporal succession) but introduces an independent past event (8:6; 35:21; 50:6; 64:8–9; 65:9; 76:3; 81:17; 92:11–12; 94:22; 109:17–18; 139:11; 148:14). In some cases, such as example [4.28c], specific discourse concerns may motivate the choice: in Ps 50:6, the *wayyiqtol* interrupts God's speech to make a past report.

[4.28]   a. Ps 77:19

קוֹל רַעַמְךָ בַּגַּלְגַּל הֵאִירוּ בְרָקִים תֵּבֵל רָגְזָה וַתִּרְעַשׁ הָאָרֶץ

'The sound of your thunder (was) in the wheel, lightning lit up the earth, the earth shook and <u>quaked</u>'.

b. Ps 45:8a

אָהַבְתָּ צֶּדֶק וַתִּשְׂנָא רֶשַׁע

'You (have) loved righteousness and <u>hated</u> wickedness'.

c. Ps 50:5–7

אִסְפוּ־לִי חֲסִידָי כֹּרְתֵי בְרִיתִי עֲלֵי־זָבַח׃
וַיַּגִּידוּ שָׁמַיִם צִדְקוֹ כִּי־אֱלֹהִים שֹׁפֵט הוּא סֶלָה׃
שִׁמְעָה עַמִּי וַאֲדַבֵּרָה יִשְׂרָאֵל וְאָעִידָה בָּךְ אֱלֹהִים אֱלֹהֶיךָ אָנֹכִי׃

'"Gather to me my pious ones, those who have cut a covenant over sacrifice." The heavens <u>declared</u> his righteousness, that God is judge. "Listen, my people, and I will speak, O Israel, and I will testify against you. God your God am I'.

The remaining 15 examples of *wayyiqtol* in synonomyous (Ps 29:5; 38:15; 49:15; 50:16; 77:7; 92:8; 136:18) or simple (Ps 29:9; 42:6; 52:9; 55:6; 90:3; 95:10; 118:14, 27) coordination with non-*qatal*/*wayyiqtol* forms may be considered "residue"—passages that may contain textual errors (e.g., the Septuagint renders the *wayyiqtol* in Ps 29:9 with a Future, the form in 42:6 with a Present, and both the *wayyiqtol* and the preceding *yiqtol* as Aorist Indicative in Ps 52:9) or that we do not yet fully understand.[19]

---

19. In any case, the paucity of such examples lends no weight to Michel's view (1960) that *wayyiqtol* expresses consequential action in any temporal sphere (see Gross 1976).

In the 5 poems in which *wayyiqtol* predominates,[20] the form constitutes the "narrative" structure of the poems by its past-tense semantics and its pragmatical implicature of temporal succession, justifying their identification as "narrative poems." In these poems, the form appears in a series of forms either one directly after another (especially Psalm 106) or in successive leading stichs of poetic lines. These two patterns, illustrated in example [4.29], account for about 80% of the instances of *wayyiqtol* in these poems.

[4.29] a. Ps 78:65–69

וַיִּקַ֣ץ כְּיָשֵׁ֣ן ׀ אֲדֹנָ֑י כְּגִבּ֗וֹר מִתְרוֹנֵ֥ן מִיָּֽיִן׃

וַיַּךְ־צָרָ֥יו אָח֑וֹר חֶרְפַּ֥ת ע֝וֹלָ֗ם נָ֣תַן לָֽמוֹ׃

וַיִּמְאַ֥ס בְּאֹ֣הֶל יוֹסֵ֑ף וּֽבְשֵׁ֥בֶט אֶ֝פְרַ֗יִם לֹ֣א בָחָֽר׃

וַ֭יִּבְחַר אֶת־שֵׁ֣בֶט יְהוּדָ֑ה אֶֽת־הַ֥ר צִ֝יּ֗וֹן אֲשֶׁ֣ר אָהֵֽב׃

וַיִּ֣בֶן כְּמוֹ־רָ֭מִים מִקְדָּשׁ֑וֹ כְּ֝אֶ֗רֶץ יְסָדָ֥הּ לְעוֹלָֽם׃

Then the Lord <u>awoke</u> (WAYY.3MS), as a sleeper,
as a strong-man shouting (PTC.MS) because of wine.
He <u>routed</u> (WAYY.3MS) his enemies;
he placed (QTL.3MS) on them enduring disgrace.
He <u>rejected</u> (WAYY.3MS) the tent of Joseph;
he did not choose (QTL.3MS) the tribe of Ephraim.
But he <u>chose</u> (WAYY.3MS) the tribe of Judah,
the Mt. Zion, which he loves (QTL.3MS).
Then he <u>built</u> (WAYY.3MS) his sanctuary like the heights,
like the earth he founded (QTL.3MS) forever.

b. Ps 106:28–30

וַ֭יִּצָּ֣מְדוּ לְבַ֣עַל פְּע֑וֹר וַ֝יֹּאכְל֗וּ זִבְחֵ֥י מֵתִֽים׃

וַיַּ֭כְעִיסוּ בְּמַֽעַלְלֵיהֶ֑ם וַתִּפְרׇץ־בָּ֝֗ם מַגֵּפָֽה׃

וַיַּעֲמֹ֣ד פִּֽינְחָ֣ס וַיְפַלֵּ֑ל וַ֝תֵּעָצַ֗ר הַמַּגֵּפָֽה׃

They attached themselves (WAYY.3MP) to Baal Peor,
and <u>ate</u> (WAYY.3MP) sacrifices to the dead.
Thus they <u>provoked</u> (WAYY.3MP) with their deeds,
and a plague <u>broke out</u> (WAYY.3FS) among them.
Then Phineas <u>stood up</u> (WAYY.3MS) and <u>interceded</u> (WAYY.3MS)
and the plague <u>was halted</u> (WAYY.3FS)

---

20. The *wayyiqtol* occurs 185 times in these 5 poems, whereas the *qatal* and *yiqtol* each occur 145 times, and the Participle occurs 66 times.

Departures from the constitutive narrative *wayyiqtol* in these narrative poems are of two basic sorts: in some cases *wayyiqtol* is avoided at the head of a line for syntactic (i.e., a negative event) or pragmatic (i.e., focus fronting, new section head) reasons (e.g., Ps 78:10, 24–25, 59; 105:14); or for rhetorical or poetic reasons events are reported in an order other than the ordo naturalis of narrative, so the *wayyiqtol* form is avoided, as illustrated by the examples in [4.30].

[4.30] a. Ps 105:16–18

וַיִּקְרָא רָעָב עַל־הָאָרֶץ כָּל־מַטֵּה־לֶחֶם שָׁבָר׃
שָׁלַח לִפְנֵיהֶם אִישׁ לְעֶבֶד נִמְכַּר יוֹסֵף׃
עִנּוּ בַכֶּבֶל רַגְלָיו [רַגְלוֹ] בַּרְזֶל בָּאָה נַפְשׁוֹ׃

Then he <u>summoned</u> (WAYY.3MS) a famine upon the land,
every staff of bread he broke (QTL.3MS).
He <u>had sent</u> (QTL.3MS) a man before them,
Joseph <u>was sold</u> (QTL.3MS) as a slave.
They <u>oppressed</u> (QTL.3MS) his feet with fetters,
his neck <u>entered</u> (QTL.3MS) (a fetter of) iron.

b. Ps 78:44–51

וַיַּהֲפֹךְ לְדָם יְאֹרֵיהֶם וְנֹזְלֵיהֶם בַּל־יִשְׁתָּיוּן׃
יְשַׁלַּח בָּהֶם עָרֹב וַיֹּאכְלֵם וּצְפַרְדֵּעַ וַתַּשְׁחִיתֵם׃
וַיִּתֵּן לֶחָסִיל יְבוּלָם וִיגִיעָם לָאַרְבֶּה׃
יַהֲרֹג בַּבָּרָד גַּפְנָם וְשִׁקְמוֹתָם בַּחֲנָמַל׃
וַיַּסְגֵּר לַבָּרָד בְּעִירָם וּמִקְנֵיהֶם לָרְשָׁפִים׃
יְשַׁלַּח־בָּם חֲרוֹן אַפּוֹ עֶבְרָה וָזַעַם וְצָרָה מִשְׁלַחַת מַלְאֲכֵי רָעִים׃
יְפַלֵּס נָתִיב לְאַפּוֹ לֹא־חָשַׂךְ מִמָּוֶת נַפְשָׁם וְחַיָּתָם לַדֶּבֶר הִסְגִּיר׃
וַיַּךְ כָּל־בְּכוֹר בְּמִצְרָיִם רֵאשִׁית אוֹנִים בְּאָהֳלֵי־חָם׃

He <u>turned</u> (WAYY.3MS) their rivers to blood,
so their streams they were <u>unable to drink</u> (YQTL.3MS).
He <u>sent</u> (PRET.3MS) a swarm among them, and it <u>devoured</u> (WAYY.3MS) them;
and frog(s), and it <u>devastated</u> (WAYY.3MS) them.
Then he <u>gave</u> (WAYY.3MS) their produce to young locust,
and their labor to locust.
He <u>killed</u> (PRET.3MS) their vines with hail,
and their sycamore trees with frost.
And he <u>delivered</u> (WAYY.3MS) to hail their cattle,
and their cattle to lightning.
He <u>sent</u> (PRET.3MS) against them the ferocity of his anger—
wrath, indignation, and distress,
a delegation of messengers of destruction.

> He leveled (PRET.3MS) a path for his anger;
> he did not keep (QTL.3MS) them from death,
> but their lives he delivered (QTL.3MS) to the plague.
> Then he struck (WAYY.3MS) every firstborn in Egypt,
> the firstfruit of their vigor in the tents of Ham.

In conclusion, the a temporally successive meaning that comes to be associated with narrative *wayyiqtol* through pragmatic implicature because of its dominant use in prose narrative is capitalized on in poetic discourse to mark departures form the normal parallelistic, nontemporally successive structure of Hebrew poetry. Thus, this provides a useful illustration of the interaction of semantic and pragmatic meanings for *wayyiqtol*.

4.3.3. Irrealis *Qatal* and Non-narrative Discourse

As already discussed, many scholars view irrealis *qatal* as analogical associated with or derived from *wayyiqtol* (e.g., Bergsträsser 1962: 2.14; Bobzin 1973: 153; Fenton 1973: 39; M. S. Smith 1991: 6–8; Buth 1992: 101).

> The formal analogy of the *wāw*-consecutive perfect [i.e., irrealis *qatal*] to the *wāw*-consecutive imperfect [i.e., *wayyiqtol*] is quite complete: (1) Both are limited to VSO clauses and may not be negated (or otherwise introduced by particles such as *kî* or *ʾîm*). (2) Both report sequential and punctiliar actions/events. (3) Just as *wāw*-consecutive imperfect (preterite) gives way to a perfect when a noun or *lōʾ* 'not' is preposed, so a *wāw*-consecutive perfect gives way to an *imperfect* when a noun or *lōʾ* is preposed to it. Semantically there is a contrast: the *wāw*-consecutive perfect is projected into the future, and the *wāw*-consecutive imperfect is a past tense. (Longacre 1992: 181; cf. Niccacci 1990: 168; Talstra 1992: 272)

Although this analogy extends to both temporal succession and foregrounding, it is only partial in the latter case. Analogous with the case of *wayyiqtol* above, the exclusive and invariable association between irrealis *qatal* and temporal succession and foreground in non-narrative discourse is problematic. Given the discussion of the nature of temporal succession and boundedness, it is unsurprising that the vast number of irrealis *qatal* forms occur in temporally successive constructions: as a perfective gram, the *qatal* effects boundedness even in the irrealis realm (see discussion in §3.3.3.2). However, it is likewise expected that temporally successive expressions may feature other verbal forms, such as in example [4.31a],[21] and that some examples of irrealis *qatal* might not be temporally successive (i.e., the irreversibility property does not hold), as illustrated by וּשְׁמַרְתֶּם in example [4.31b].

---

21. The tendency for future and irrealis expressions to be perfective explains the unexpected use of imperfective *yiqtol* in temporally successive expressions such as this (see Haspelmath 1998: 55; §3.2.3.2 above).

[4.31] a. 1 Kgs 22:20

וַיֹּאמֶר יְהוָה מִי יְפַתֶּה אֶת־אַחְאָב וְיַעַל וְיִפֹּל בְּרָמֹת גִּלְעָד

'Yhwh said, "Who will deceive Ahab that he <u>might go up</u> (JUSS.3MS) and <u>fall</u> (JUSS.3MS) in Ramoth Gilead?"'

b. Exod 19:5 (cf. Deut 26:17 'to keep his statues . . . and to obey his voice')

וְעַתָּה אִם־שָׁמוֹעַ תִּשְׁמְעוּ בְּקֹלִי וּשְׁמַרְתֶּם אֶת־בְּרִיתִי וִהְיִיתֶם לִי סְגֻלָּה

'Now if you will <u>carefully obey</u> my voice and <u>keep</u> (IRR-QTL.2MP) my covenant, then you will be to me a special possession out of all the peoples'.

The association between irrealis *qatal* and foregrounding is far less than in the case of Past Narrative *wayyiqtol*, making the two forms even less analogous than conventionally thought. Longacre (1995: 47; 2003: 79, 106, 121), for example, identifies the irrealis *qatal* as the primary foreground verb in predictive, procedural, and instructional discourse types, but he also recognizes that the form plays a background role ("results/consequences") in hortatory discourse. When we examine typical examples of these discourse types that Longacre identifies, we find that the semantics and pragmatics of this form are varied enough to make his correlations with temporal succession and foregrounding a misleading oversimplification, which is only made more erroneous through the analogies with the *wayyiqtol* form.

Longacre (1994: 51) illustrates predictive discourse with the passage in example [4.32], in which the irrealis *qatal* primarily functions as part of a lengthy temporal protasis-apodosis construction (see also 2 Sam 7:11–17).

[4.32] 1 Sam 10:2–6; irrealis *qatal* in predictive discourse

בְּלֶכְתְּךָ הַיּוֹם מֵעִמָּדִי וּמָצָאתָ שְׁנֵי אֲנָשִׁים עִם־קְבֻרַת רָחֵל בִּגְבוּל בִּנְיָמִן
בְּצֶלְצַח וְאָמְרוּ אֵלֶיךָ נִמְצְאוּ הָאֲתֹנוֹת אֲשֶׁר הָלַכְתָּ לְבַקֵּשׁ וְהִנֵּה נָטַשׁ
אָבִיךָ אֶת־דִּבְרֵי הָאֲתֹנוֹת וְדָאַג לָכֶם לֵאמֹר מָה אֶעֱשֶׂה לִבְנִי: וְחָלַפְתָּ
מִשָּׁם וָהָלְאָה וּבָאתָ עַד־אֵלוֹן תָּבוֹר וּמְצָאוּךָ שָׁם שְׁלֹשָׁה אֲנָשִׁים עֹלִים
אֶל־הָאֱלֹהִים בֵּית־אֵל אֶחָד נֹשֵׂא שְׁלֹשָׁה גְדָיִים וְאֶחָד נֹשֵׂא שְׁלֹשֶׁת כִּכְּרוֹת
לֶחֶם וְאֶחָד נֹשֵׂא נֵבֶל־יָיִן: וְשָׁאֲלוּ לְךָ לְשָׁלוֹם וְנָתְנוּ לְךָ שְׁתֵּי־לֶחֶם וְלָקַחְתָּ
מִיָּדָם: אַחַר כֵּן תָּבוֹא גִּבְעַת הָאֱלֹהִים אֲשֶׁר־שָׁם נְצִבֵי פְלִשְׁתִּים וִיהִי כְבֹאֲךָ
שָׁם הָעִיר וּפָגַעְתָּ חֶבֶל נְבִיאִים יֹרְדִים מֵהַבָּמָה וְלִפְנֵיהֶם נֵבֶל וְתֹף וְחָלִיל
וְכִנּוֹר וְהֵמָּה מִתְנַבְּאִים: וְצָלְחָה עָלֶיךָ רוּחַ יְהוָה וְהִתְנַבִּיתָ עִמָּם וְנֶהְפַּכְתָּ
לְאִישׁ אַחֵר:

'When you <u>go</u> (INF) today from me, (then) you <u>will meet</u> (IRR-QTL.2MS) two men near the tomb of Rachel in the territory of Benjamin in Zelzah, and they <u>will say</u> (IRR-QTL.3P) to you, "The donkeys that you <u>went</u> (QTL.2MS) to look for (INF) have been found (QTL.3P), and behold, your father has abandoned

(QTL.3MS) the matter of the donkeys and is anxious (QTL.3MS)
for you saying, 'What should I do (YQTL.1S) about my son?'"
³And when you pass on (IRR-QTL.2MS) farther from there,
(then) you will come (IRR-QTL.2MS) to the oak of Tabor and
three men will meet you (IRR-QTL.3P) there, going up (PTC.MP)
to God at Bethel, one carrying (PTC.MS) three kids, and one
carrying (ptc.ms) three loaves of bread, and one carrying (PTC.
MS) a skin of wine. ⁴And they will greet (IRR-QTL.3P) you and
give (IRR-QTL.3P) you two (loaves) of bread and you should
take (IRR-QTL.2MS) (them) from their hand. ⁵After that you will
come (YQTL.2MS) to Gibat-elohim, where the Philistine garrison
is. And when you come (INF) there to the city (then) you will
meet (IRR-QTL.2MS) a band of prophets coming down (PTC.MP)
from the high place, with harp, tambourine, and flute, and lyre
before them, and prophesying (PTC.MS). ⁶And the spirit of Yhwh
will rush (IRR-QTL.3FS) upon you so that you will prophesy (IRR-
QTL.2MS) with them so that you are changed (IRR-QTL.2MS) into a
different person'.

Although the events in the apodosis are iconically ordered, they are not temporally successive in quite the same way as the *ordo naturalis* of narrative
discourse inasmuch as they are anchored temporally to the protasis ('When
you go today from me'). The ambiguity about new protases (i.e., v. 3: it seems
preferable to interpret this irrealis *qatal* as beginning a new protasis after the
interruption of the apodosis with direct speech; however, the decision does
not affect the argument made here) and anaphoric adverbial references in the
passage (e.g., 'from there' and 'there' in v. 3; 'after that' and 'there' in v. 5) indicate the need for explicitness to maintain the iconic interpretation of events.
In addition, the form is not restricted to the apodosis foreground, as its deontic
use in v. 4 and its appearance in the two backgrounded result clauses in v. 6
shows.

An even closer correlation between irrealis *qatal* and foreground is found
in procedural and instructional discourse. Longacre (1994: 52, 54; see also
1995) identifies Leviticus 1–5 as procedural discourse and Exodus 25–30 as
instructional discourse. In both discourse types, irrealis *qatal* with a directive
modal meaning expresses the foregrounded procedural or instructional steps
in order. Longacre distinguishes procedural discourse from instructional by
its protasis-apodosis construction (using either irrealis *qatal* or *yiqtol*; cf. Lev
1:10), as illustrated in example [4.33].²²

---

22. Note that, although the procedural steps for the individual sacrifices are introduced
with a protasis-apodosis construction, subsections may have an imperatival introduction
(like instructional discourse) to the protasis-apodosis construction (e.g., Lev 1:2; 4:2).

[4.33] Lev 4:3–7; irrealis *qatal* in procedural discourse

אִם הַכֹּהֵן הַמָּשִׁיחַ יֶחֱטָא לְאַשְׁמַת הָעָם וְהִקְרִיב עַל חַטָּאתוֹ אֲשֶׁר חָטָא
פַּר בֶּן־בָּקָר תָּמִים לַיהוָה לְחַטָּאת: וְהֵבִיא אֶת־הַפָּר אֶל־פֶּתַח אֹהֶל מוֹעֵד
לִפְנֵי יְהוָה וְסָמַךְ אֶת־יָדוֹ עַל־רֹאשׁ הַפָּר וְשָׁחַט אֶת־הַפָּר לִפְנֵי יְהוָה:
וְלָקַח הַכֹּהֵן הַמָּשִׁיחַ מִדַּם הַפָּר וְהֵבִיא אֹתוֹ אֶל־אֹהֶל מוֹעֵד: וְטָבַל הַכֹּהֵן
אֶת־אֶצְבָּעוֹ בַּדָּם וְהִזָּה מִן־הַדָּם שֶׁבַע פְּעָמִים לִפְנֵי יְהוָה אֶת־פְּנֵי פָּרֹכֶת
הַקֹּדֶשׁ: וְנָתַן הַכֹּהֵן מִן־הַדָּם עַל־קַרְנוֹת מִזְבַּח קְטֹרֶת הַסַּמִּים לִפְנֵי יְהוָה
אֲשֶׁר בְּאֹהֶל מוֹעֵד וְאֵת כָּל־דַּם הַפָּר יִשְׁפֹּךְ אֶל־יְסוֹד מִזְבַּח הָעֹלָה אֲשֶׁר־
פֶּתַח אֹהֶל מוֹעֵד:

³'If the anointed priest sins (IRR-YQTL.3MS), to the guilt of the
people, then he should offer (IRR-QTL.3MS) for his sin that he has
committed (QTL.3MS) a bull, son of the herd, without blemish to
Yhwh for a sin offering. ⁴And he should bring (IRR-QTL.3MS) the
bull to the entrance of the tent of meeting before Yhwh, and
he should lay (IRR-QTL.3MS) his hand on the head of the bull,
and he should slaughter (IRR-QTL.3MS) the bull before Yhwh.
⁵And the anointed priest should take (IRR-QTL.3MS) some of
the blood of the bull and bring (IRR-QTL.3MS) it into the tent of
meeting. ⁶And the priest should dip (IRR-QTL.3MS) his finger in
the blood and sprinkle (IRR-QTL.3MS) some of the blood seven
times before Yhwh in front of the curtain of the sanctuary.
⁷And the priest should place (IRR-QTL.3MS) some of the blood
on the horns of the altar of fragrant incense, which is in the tent
of meeting before Yhwh, but all (the rest) of the blood of the
bull he should pour (YQTL.3MS) at the base of the altar of burnt
offering, which is at the entrance of the tent of meeting'.

By contrast, instructional discourse is introduced by an imperative, as in
example [4.34]. In addition, the "step-by-step" characteristic is less evident
than in procedural discourse: in some cases, there is no logical reason for one
instruction to precede the other other (e.g., there is no reason why the instructions for the ark must precede those for the altar).

[4.34] Exod 25:1–3, 8–11; irrealis *qatal* in instructional discourse

וַיְדַבֵּר יְהוָה אֶל־מֹשֶׁה לֵּאמֹר: דַּבֵּר אֶל־בְּנֵי יִשְׂרָאֵל וְיִקְחוּ־לִי תְּרוּמָה
מֵאֵת כָּל־אִישׁ אֲשֶׁר יִדְּבֶנּוּ לִבּוֹ תִּקְחוּ אֶת־תְּרוּמָתִי: וְזֹאת הַתְּרוּמָה אֲשֶׁר
תִּקְחוּ מֵאִתָּם זָהָב וָכֶסֶף וּנְחֹשֶׁת: . . . וְעָשׂוּ לִי מִקְדָּשׁ וְשָׁכַנְתִּי בְּתוֹכָם:
כְּכֹל אֲשֶׁר אֲנִי מַרְאֶה אוֹתְךָ אֵת תַּבְנִית הַמִּשְׁכָּן וְאֵת תַּבְנִית כָּל־כֵּלָיו וְכֵן
תַּעֲשׂוּ: ס וְעָשׂוּ אֲרוֹן עֲצֵי שִׁטִּים אַמָּתַיִם וָחֵצִי אָרְכּוֹ וְאַמָּה וָחֵצִי רָחְבּוֹ
וְאַמָּה וָחֵצִי קֹמָתוֹ: וְצִפִּיתָ אֹתוֹ זָהָב טָהוֹר מִבַּיִת וּמִחוּץ תְּצַפֶּנּוּ וְעָשִׂיתָ
עָלָיו זֵר זָהָב סָבִיב:

'¹Then the Lord spoke to Moses: ²"Instruct (IMPV.MS) the children of Israel that they should take (IRR.YQTL.3P) an offering for me; from everyone whose heart prompts (YQTL.3MS) them, you should receive (IRR-YQTL.2MP) my offering. ³And this is the offering that you should receive (IRR-YQTL.2MP) from them: gold, silver, and bronze. . . . ⁸And they <u>should make</u> (IRR-QTL.3P) a sanctuary so that I <u>may dwell</u> (IRR-QTL.1S) in your midst. ⁹According to all that I am showing you (PTC.MS)—the pattern of the sanctuary and all its furniture—thus you should make (IRR-YQTL.2MP) it. ¹⁰They <u>should make</u> (IRR-QTL.3P) an ark of acacia wood; and its length (should be) two and a half cubits, its width a cubit and a half, and its height a cubit and a half. ¹¹You <u>should overlay</u> (IRR-QTL.2MS) it with pure gold; inside and outside you should overlay (YQTL.2MS) it, and you <u>should make</u> (IRR-QTL.2MS) a molding of gold upon it all around'.

Despite the high degree of correlation in these passages between irrealis *qatal* and foregrounded, iconically ordered procedural/instructional steps, the interaction of verb forms is too varied to allow a simplistic identification of irrealis *qatal* as a temporally successive, foregrounding verb. Other predications appear on the instructional/procedural foreground (e.g., יִשְׁפֹּךְ 'he should pour out' [IRR-YQTL.3MP] דַּבֵּר 'speak' [IMPV.MS] in Exod 25:1) and irrealis *qatal* functions in the background (e.g., וְשָׁכַנְתִּי 'that I may dwell' [IRR-QTL.1CS] in Exod 25:8; so Longacre 1994: 55). In addition, larger syntactic structures such as protasis-apodosis constructions are missed by an analysis of irrealis *qatal* as simply a sequential foregrounding verb in non-narrative discourse. Finally, unlike *wayyiqtol*, which is associated particularly with narrative discourse, non-narrative is too broad and varied to claim as the proper domain of irrealis *qatal*. More-modest claims might be the following: first, irrealis *qatal* is not "native" to narrative discourse as *wayyiqtol* is, though it often occurs in habitual or subordinate modal expressions within prose narrative; rather, it appears primarily in reported speech because its irrealis mood is incompatible with realis past narrative and more appropriate to various statements about alternative events; second, it is found particularly in series of irrealis events that are iconically ordered, because of its bounding capabilities associated with being a perfective gram; third, variation between it and other irrealis forms may in part be attributed to its verb-subject word order and the associated conjunction that appears with most examples of the conjugation. However, this sort of characterization provides minimal explanatory help in the analysis of passages with the form in the Hebrew Bible. In §4.4, I propose a semantic approach to the issue of the temporal shaping of discourse.

4.3.4. Discourse וַיְהִי and וְהָיָה

In light of the above treatments of *wayyiqtol* and irrealis *qatal*, a brief statement is required with regard to the special cases of וַיְהִי and וְהָיָה (i.e., the 3MS of these two conjugations). A number of features shared by these forms make them a special case, foremost of which is that being copular verbs puts them in a special category beside other predications (so Longacre 2003: 64). The narrative form וַיְהִי has especially been the focus of numerous studies (see the survey of previous studies in Harmelink 2004). Here, however, I am narrowly focused on qualifying the status of וַיְהִי and וְהָיָה with respect to the previous discussions of *wayyiqtol* and irrealis *qatal* (§§4.3.1–4.3.3) and, at the same time, clarifying their temporal role in anticipation of the following examination of various discourse specimens, in §4.4.

Hebrew has a zero-copular strategy, and BH evidences at least an incipient "present-parameter" pattern of copular employment: in present temporal expressions, the copula is covert or null; in past or future expressions, it is overt (see §3.2.3.3). Given these analyses, a central function of the copula in BH is simply to provide a "landing site" for TAM marking: the copula appears in the *wayyiqtol* and *qatal* conjugations indicating past tense, in *yiqtol* expressing future tense, and in irrealis *qatal* expressing irrealis mood, as illustrated by examples [4.35a–d].

[4.35] a. 1 Sam 1:1

וַיְהִי אִישׁ אֶחָד מִן־הָרָמָתַיִם צוֹפִים מֵהַר אֶפְרָיִם

'There <u>was</u> a certain man from Ramathaim, a Zophite from the hill country of Ephraim'.

b. Gen 3:1

וְהַנָּחָשׁ הָיָה עָרוּם מִכֹּל חַיַּת הַשָּׂדֶה

'The serpent <u>was</u> craftier than any animal of the field'.

c. Gen 16:12

וְהוּא יִהְיֶה פֶּרֶא אָדָם

'He <u>will be</u> a wild ass of a man'.

d. Gen 2:10

וְנָהָר יֹצֵא מֵעֵדֶן לְהַשְׁקוֹת אֶת־הַגָּן וּמִשָּׁם יִפָּרֵד וְהָיָה לְאַרְבָּעָה רָאשִׁים:

'A river (was) flowing out from Eden to water the garden, and from there it <u>would</u> divide and <u>become</u> four branches'.

The וְהָיָה in [4.35d] is probably best understood habitually, as translated. However, the semantic blurring between irrealis mood and future tense accounts for the ambiguity in other instances of וְהָיָה, such as in example [4.36].

[4.36] Gen 30:32

אֶעֱבֹר בְּכָל־צֹאנְךָ הַיּוֹם הָסֵר מִשָּׁם כָּל־שֶׂה נָקֹד וְטָלוּא וְכָל־שֶׂה־חוּם
בַּכְּשָׂבִים וְטָלוּא וְנָקֹד בָּעִזִּים וְהָיָה שְׂכָרִי:

'I will pass through all of your flock today removing from there
every speckled and spotted sheep and every black sheep among
the lambs and every spotted and speckled (one) among the
goats; (that) <u>will be</u> my pay'.

More importantly, the וַיְהִי and וְהָיָה forms exhibit two distinct functions: a
copular predicate at the clause level, as illustrated above in examples [4.35]–
[4.36]; and a discourse-level TAM signal, often at the opening or closing of a
scene or episode (see especially van der Merwe 1999; Joosten [2009] refers
to it as "narrative *wayhi*"). The distinction between the clause-level and the
discourse-level וַיְהִי/וְהָיָה functions is found in the absence of any arguments
with the latter, as illustrated by example [4.37]: [23] in [4.37a], the first וַיְהִי functions to mark the discourse time in a new episode (note the scene shift here
from vv. 1–3, which also begins with וַיְהִי in v. 1), whereas the second is a full
copular form with an explicit subject (דְּבַר־יְהוָה) and complement (אֶל־נָתָן).
In example [4.37b], the first-occurring וְהָיָה functions as a copula with an expressed subject (יְהוָה) and complement (עִם־הַשֹּׁפֵט), whereas the second וְהָיָה
governs nothing at the clause level but reasserts the habitual sense of the passage at the discourse level (thus avoiding the erroneous interpretation of the
death as describing a specific judge's demise). [24]

[4.37] a. 2 Sam 7:4

וַיְהִי בַּלַּיְלָה הַהוּא וַיְהִי דְּבַר־יְהוָה אֶל־נָתָן לֵאמֹר:

'[PAST] During that night, the word of Yhwh <u>came</u> to
Nathan'.

   b. Judg 2:18–19

וְכִי־הֵקִים יְהוָה לָהֶם שֹׁפְטִים וְהָיָה יְהוָה עִם־הַשֹּׁפֵט וְהוֹשִׁיעָם מִיַּד
אֹיְבֵיהֶם כֹּל יְמֵי הַשּׁוֹפֵט . . . וְהָיָה בְּמוֹת הַשּׁוֹפֵט יָשֻׁבוּ וְהִשְׁחִיתוּ
מֵאֲבוֹתָם לָלֶכֶת אַחֲרֵי אֱלֹהִים אֲחֵרִים לְעָבְדָם וּלְהִשְׁתַּחֲוֹת לָהֶם לֹא
הִפִּילוּ מִמַּעַלְלֵיהֶם וּמִדַּרְכָּם הַקָּשָׁה:

---

23. By making the distinction in this way, my argument is somewhat distinct from and
simpler than van der Merwe's (1999: 113–14); however, I am in basic agreement with him
regarding the temporal functions of the form, which he describes in the following terms:
"וַיְהִי anchors a state of affairs to the time-line (i.e., story-line) of a narrative . . . updating the
current reference time of a subsequent scene."

24. The analysis of these forms in the Accordance syntax (currently includes the books
of Genesis, Joshua, Judges, Joel, Amos, Obadiah, Jonah, Nahum, Habakkuk, Psalms, Proverbs, Ruth, Ecclesiastes, Esther, Daniel, and Ezra) shows that this discourse וַיְהִי occurs about
one and one quarter times more frequently than the copular form with complement and that
discourse וְהָיָה occurs about one and one half times more often than its copular counterpart.

'When Yhwh raised up for them judges, Yhwh would be
with the judge, and he would deliver them from the hand
of their enemies all the days of the judge. . . . [HAB] When
the judge died, they would turn and behave worse than their
fathers'.

These two contrastive pairs point to a proper analysis of each of the neighboring preposition phrases (i.e., בַּלַּיְלָה הַהוּא and בְּמוֹת הַשּׁוֹפֵט) as subordinate to
the *following* verb form rather than to the leading ויהי or והיה. Thus, both syntactically and semantically, at the clause level the discourse-functioning ויהי/
והיה forms are otiose.

That these discourse-functioning forms are otiose is evident from the minimal pairs in examples [4.38a–d],[25] which demonstrate that such temporal
phrases are syntactically subordinate to the following predicate rather than the
leading discourse-level ויהי/והיה, where present.[26]

[4.38]   a.   Gen 22:4

בַּיּוֹם הַשְּׁלִישִׁי וַיִּשָּׂא אַבְרָהָם אֶת־עֵינָיו וַיַּרְא אֶת־הַמָּקוֹם מֵרָחֹק:
'On the third day, Abraham lifted up his eyes and saw the
place from a distance'.

b.   Gen 22:20

וַיְהִי אַחֲרֵי הַדְּבָרִים הָאֵלֶּה וַיֻּגַּד לְאַבְרָהָם לֵאמֹר הִנֵּה יָלְדָה מִלְכָּה גַם־
הִוא בָּנִים לְנָחוֹר אָחִיךָ:
'[PAST] After these things, it was told to Abraham: "Behold,
Milcah also has borne children to Nahor, your brother' ".

c.   Isa 7:20

בַּיּוֹם הַהוּא יְגַלַּח אֲדֹנָי בְּתַעַר הַשְּׂכִירָה בְּעֶבְרֵי נָהָר בְּמֶלֶךְ אַשּׁוּר אֶת־
הָרֹאשׁ וְשַׂעַר הָרַגְלָיִם וְגַם אֶת־הַזָּקָן תִּסְפֶּה:
'On that day, the Lord will shave with a razor hired beyond
the river, the king of Assyra, the head and the hair of the
feet and also the beard it will remove'.

---

25. With respect to וַיְהִי, compare also the parallel passages of 1 Kgs 8:54 // 2 Chr 7:1;
2 Kgs 12:11 // 2 Chr 24:11; 2 Kgs 22:3 // 2 Chr 34:8; and see Waltke and O'Connor 1990:
553–54 for other contrastive examples. On the case of וְהָיָה, compare also Isa 2:2 and 2:20;
and the other alternations with and without וְהָיָה before בַּיּוֹם הַהוּא in Isa 7:18–25.

26. The descriptions in the grammars are often confusing in this regard: Lambdin (1971:
123) discusses "temporal modifiers" that are "introduced" by ויהי/והיה but "modify" the
following predicate; Waltke and O'Connor (1990: 553–54) approvingly cite Lambdin but
introduce relevant examples with the statement: "A circumstantial clause introduced by ויהי
may be followed by a *wayyqtl* form."

d. Isa 7:21

וְהָיָה בַּיּוֹם הַהוּא יְחַיֶּה־אִישׁ עֶגְלַת בָּקָר וּשְׁתֵּי־צֹאן:

'[HAB] On that day, a man will preserve a young cow and
two sheep'.

Minimal pairs such as these, few though they be, not only support the syntactical analysis of the prepositional phrases in examples [4.37a–b] but also support
the need to identify word order in terms of subject and predicate/verb and not
simply clause-initial versus non-clause-initial.

Longacre (2003: 67-68) argues that ויהי never presents foregrounded material, despite being the narrative verb. This sort of view requires revision based
on the analysis presented here of a bifurcated וַיְהִי: the question of foreground
is moot for discourse-functioning וַיְהִי, since it simply (re)asserts the temporal
reference time; but as a copula, despite the stativity of היה (see Gen 29:18 cited
in example [4.16] above), the narrative *wayyiqtol* form foregrounds the predicate, contrasting with the use of היה in *qatal* to express past, backgrounded
events (frequently in negative or subordinate clauses). This foreground-background contrast is illustrated by examples [4.39a–b]: the וַיְהִי forms in [4.39a]
express salient events that move the storyline forward, evident especially from
the ingressive interpretation in one case and also from the fact that 'his master' observes Joseph's condition in the following verse (v. 3); in [4.39b], the
background status of the SV clauses is evident from their contrast with the
neighboring verses (Gen 7:5, 7), both of which contain *wayyiqtol* predicates.

[4.39] a. Gen 39:2

וַיְהִי יְהוָה אֶת־יוֹסֵף וַיְהִי אִישׁ מַצְלִיחַ וַיְהִי בְּבֵית אֲדֹנָיו הַמִּצְרִי:

'Yhwh was with Joseph, and he became a successful man
and stayed in the house of his master, the Egyptian'.

b. Gen 7:6

וְנֹחַ בֶּן־שֵׁשׁ מֵאוֹת שָׁנָה וְהַמַּבּוּל הָיָה מַיִם עַל־הָאָרֶץ:

'Now Noah was six hundred years old, and the flood became water upon the earth'.

The case of וְהָיָה, as with irrealis *qatal*, is almost the reverse: while the
foreground-background distinction does not apply to the discourse-functioning
וְהָיָה, the copular וְהָיָה is almost entirely restricted to background expressions,
no doubt in large measure due to the association of its irrealis meanings with
subordinate types of modality.

4.4. The Temporal and Modal Interpretation of Discourse

Up to this point, the discussion in this chapter has largely been decon-
structive: in §§4.1–4.2, I made the case that a discourse approach devoid of a

semantic foundation is insufficient to the task at hand of analyzing the BHVS; in §4.3, I demonstrated how, specifically, the traditional discourse approach to *wayyiqtol* and irrealis *qatal* is problematic, and I proposed alternative analyses of these conjugations, including the special case of the copula הָיָה in these conjugations. In this section, I turn to the more constructive task of developing a semantics-based alternative to the analysis of the BH verbal conjugations in discourse. I begin, however, with the backdrop of the traditional approach to interclausal relationships and the notion of a multivalent *waw* conjunction.

The coordination of verbal clauses is a standard topic treated in the grammars of Biblical Hebrew, sometimes appearing in more-recent grammars under the heading "verbal sequences" or similar nomenclature (e.g., van der Merwe, Naudé, and Kroeze 1999: 163; Arnold and Choi 2003: 83). There is a high degree of uniformity among all these discussions, despite the long gap of time between some of them with respect to the roles they assign to the *waw* conjunction and to word order regarding the interpretation of verbal sequences. Setting aside the issue of the semantic contrast between the *waw*-prefixed and non-*waw*-prefixed verbal conjugations, which inevitably plays a role in the discussions (e.g., Joüon-Muraoka 2006: §118a, 119a; Arnold and Choi 2003: 83), the grammars minimally distinguish between a conjunctive (or copulative) *waw* and a consecutive (or sequential) *waw*, which are understood to be variants of a single conjunction (e.g., Kautzsch 1910: §49b; Joüon and Muraoka 2006: §115a; Waltke and O'Connor 1999: 650; van der Merwe, Naudé, and Kroeze 1999: 163).

A well-developed analysis of the multivalency of the *waw* conjunction is provided by Waltke and O'Connor (1990: 650), who adopt Lambdin's (1971: 162; see also §§98, 107, 197) taxonomy as their starting point and add to it a fourth category so as to include conjunctive-sequential, disjunctive, epexegetical, and conjunctive varieties of *waw*.[27] Examples [4.40a–b] here are offered in Waltke and O'Connor (1990: 650–54; with their translations) as illustrative of the four meanings that *waw* may express.

[4.40] a. Jer 40:15; conjunctive-sequential *waw*

אֵלְכָה נָּא וְאַכֶּה אֶת־יִשְׁמָעֵאל

'Let me go <u>so that</u> I can kill Ishmael'.

b. Gen 41:54b; disjunctive *waw*

וַיְהִי רָעָב בְּכָל־הָאֲרָצוֹת וּבְכָל־אֶרֶץ מִצְרַיִם הָיָה לָחֶם:

'There was famine in all the (other) lands, <u>but</u> throughout Egypt there was food'.

---

27. The first three derive from Lambdin's grammar, though Waltke and O'Connor mention only the binary distinction of conjunctive-sequential and disjunctive as their starting point.

    c. Exod 24:7b; epexegetical *waw*

וַיֹּאמְרוּ כֹּל אֲשֶׁר־דִּבֶּר יְהוָה נַעֲשֶׂה וְנִשְׁמָע:

    'They said, "All that YHWH has said, we will do; that is, we
    will obey"'.

    d. 1 Kgs 18:41; conjunctive *waw*

עֲלֵה אֱכֹל וּשְׁתֵה

    'Go, eat and drink'.

Because the so-called consecutive/conversive *waw* appears only immediately before a finite verb (see §2.1 for an overview), word order is viewed as
integrally related to the multivalency of the *waw* conjunction.[28] For example,
GKC (Kautzsch 1910: §142a) states that, "[i]n the great majority of instances,
however, the position of the subject at the beginning of a verbal-clause is to be
explained from the fact that the clause is not intended to introduce a new fact
carrying on the narrative, but rather to describe a state." Waltke and O'Connor
(1990: 650) describe word order as "the major device" for distinguishing between the conjunctive (including the conjunctive-sequential) and disjunctive
*waw*s: namely, the conjunctive and conjunctive-sequential *waw*s stand immediately before a verb, whereas the disjunctive *waw* stands immediately before
some word other than a verb.

    This standard treatment is problematic and unsatisfactory. It is problematic
because it places too much semantic weight on the *waw* conjunction and word
order. Steiner (2000) has asked whether the *waw* conjunction has many meanings, one meaning, or no meaning at all. I incline toward the latter view with
respect to verbal coordination: the *waw* conjoins verbal clauses at the same
syntactic level but contributes no real semantic content to the coordinative
construction (as illustrated by the absence of 'and' in many of the gloss translations in the book). The difficulties inherent with placing too much semantic
weight on word order is illustrated by Peckham's article on the Hebrew verbal
system in which he made word order a central component for distinguishing
not only verbal sequence but tense, aspect, and mood in general (Peckham
1997; see §2.4.2.2). This is not to say that word order cannot or does not serve
to signal semantic distinctions; my own argument for a SV : VS distinction
of realis : irrealis mood demonstrates what sort of role word order might play
(see §3.3).

    The traditional treatments of interclausal relationships are likewise unsat-
isfactory, because their accompanying taxonomies of examples illustrate but
fail to *explain* interclausal relationships in Biblical Hebrew—a weakness that

---

    28. Joüon (2006: §115a) states that *waw* is multivalent only when attached to finite ver-
bal forms.

they share with the discourse approaches discussed above (§4.1). The reason that they cannot explain the inner logic of Biblical Hebrew interclausal relationships is precisely because they have focused too exclusively on the *waw* conjunction and word order as determinative of the relationships. In keeping with my prioritization of semantics versus discourse, here I approach the issue from the other direction, by beginning with a taxonomy of temporal relationships (semantics) that may be expressed among successive clauses (discourse). This approach is in keeping with my dismissal of the whole notion of a multivalent *waw* and the accompanying association of *waw* with either TAM distinctions (conversive *waw*) or succession (consecutive *waw*). Although some coordinative functions included in the traditional discussions of interclausal relationships are more than temporal (e.g., epexegetical), they are never less than temporal. That is, temporality can always be measured between successive clauses, and to describe the temporal relationships is to address almost all of the traditional categories of interclausal relationships (at the very least, for prose narrative and narrative poetry).

A useful starting point for developing a semantics-based theory is to study Discourse Representation Theory (DRT; see Kamp and Ryle 1993; Kamp, Genabith, and Ryle 2011; see also §1.5.1 above) as having developed from an interest in the semantic features of the interclausal relationships that traditional semantic theories were unable to treat adequately—namely, anaphor and temporal succession (i.e., movement of the reference time). Two insights related to DRT are particularly relevant here. The first, which lies at the center of DRT as well as other dynamic theories of meaning, is that events need to be interpreted in context and that events and their contexts have a reciprocal relationship. As recently stated by Kamp, Genabith, and Reyle (2011: 125),

> the interaction between context and utterance is reciprocal. Each utterance contributes (via the interpretation which it is given) to the context in which it is made. It modifies the context into a new context, in which this contribution is reflected; and it is this new context which then informs the interpretation of whatever utterance comes next.

The second insight was the reinterpretation of Reichenbach's idea of reference time in ways that demonstrate the complex temporal information contained in TAM grams (e.g., Declerck's [1986] "time of orientation" and "time referred to"; see §1.2.3.4), which pointed the way toward relating events in discourse in terms of reference time (see §1.5).

C. S. Smith's (2003) theory of discourse modes is rooted in DRT and especially focused on the temporal relationships among successive clauses. Thus, her treatment is a useful starting point for an analysis of interclausal temporal relationships in BH. In contrast to Longacre's categories, which are insufficiently different from genre distinctions (so O'Connor personal communication, 2006), Smith focuses on the temporal contours of smaller ("local") stretches of discourse, positing a nonexhaustive list of five discourse modes, given in table 4.4. These five types are distinguished by situation type, temporal deixis, and temporal progression.

Smith's distinction of situation types differs from the standard divisions (state, activities, accomplishment, and achievement). Rather, she notes that the pertinent distinguishing feature in her discourse modes is between eventualities and general statives: the former includes both dynamic and stative predicates, but the statives refer to specific or particular states; by contrast, general statives are habitual and generic expressions, which refer to kinds rather than particulars (see Cook 2005). The latter (general statives) can also include both dynamic and stative predicates.

The three parameters employed by C. S. Smith to distinguish discourse modes—namely, situation type, temporal deixis or anchoring, and temporal progression—lead to Smith's (2003: 93–97) identification of three temporal relationships that may be expressed among successive clauses: continuity, deixis, and anaphor, which are illustrated with her examples in [4.41]–[4.43]. Example [4.41] illustrates *continuity*, in which the events are interpreted as temporally successive with one another. All of the events reported in this brief narrative excerpt (each indicated by a parenthetic, numbered *e*) are interpreted as happening in succession, one after another. Note, however, that the one stative situation (in contrast to the other, dynamic events) in the passage, which is indicated by the parenthetic *s1*, temporally overlaps with the surrounding events in the narrative.

[4.41] Continuity (narrative)
She put on her apron (e1), took a lump of clay from the bin (e2), and weighed enough for a small vase (e3). The clay was wet (s1). Frowning, she cut the lump in half with a cheese-wire to check for air bubbles (e4), then slammed the pieces together much harder than usual (e5). A fleck of clay spun off (e6) and hit her forehead, just above her right eye (e7).

In passages with *deictic* temporality, illustrated by example [4.42], events are interpreted as temporally located with respect to some fixed point such as the narrator's or, more often, the speaker's deictic center. In the example from C. S. Smith in [4.42], the temporal interpretations of the various events are separately related to the speaker's deictic center rather than in any way being temporally located relative to one another.

Table 4.4. Major Discourse Modes
(based on Smith 2003: 19–20)

	Situations	*Temporality*	*Progression*
Narrative	eventualities, specific states	temporally located, dynamic	in narrative time
Report	eventualities, general states		anchored to speech time
Description	states, ongoing events	temporally located, static	spatial: scene or object
Information	general states	atemporal	metaphoric
Argument	abstract entities, general states		

[4.42] Deixis (report; also applies to information and argument)
Downtown Austin will have to live for at least several more months with the half-finished shell of the Intel Corp design center. Intel has postponed a decision on what to do about the project until sometime next year, when the semiconductor company has a better reading on the strength of the economy. Intel decided in March to halt construction on the 10-story center at Fourth and San Antonio streets, as well as other projects around the country, to save money during a chip industry downturn. Intel took heat from critics who called the half-finished concrete skeleton, encircled by a chain-link fence, an eyesore.

Somewhat more complicated is *anaphoric* temporality, illustrated by the excerpt in example [4.43]. C. S. Smith (2003: 96) explains that descriptive passages of this sort are anaphorically anchored by an initial locative reference (in this case, the initial locative phrase *In the passenger car*) and contain a "tacit durative time adverbial."[29] The result is that the events receive a durative, overlapping interpretation despite the fact that the events are mostly dynamic and reported with Simple Past verbs. The anaphoric temporal relation illustrates that the interpretation of discourse modes involves not simply semantics but also discourse pragmatics.

---

29. That is, Smith's "tacit" semantic operator is discourse-pragmatically inferred from the locative adverbial expression that anchors the succeeding events as temporally overlapping descriptions of a single situation.

[4.43] Anaphor (description)

In the passenger car every window was propped open with a stick of kindling wood. A breeze blew through, hot and then cool, fragrant of the woods and yellow flowers and of the train. The yellow butterflies flew in at any window, out at any other. . . . Overhead a black lamp in which a circle of flowers had been cut out swung round and round on a chain as the car rocked from side to side, sending down dainty drifts of kerosene smell.

C. S. Smith's three-way distinction of continuity, deixis, and anaphor provides an excellent starting point for a semantics-based appoach to verbal-sequencing and interclausal relationships in Biblical Hebrew. However, I would like to expand her scheme in two directions to make it more comprehensively applicable to the Biblical Hebrew data. First, while Smith limits herself to indicative modes of discourse, the three-way distinction she proposes seems equally applicable to realis and to irrealis expressions. However, these interpretations apply to each mood in somewhat different ways due to the different temporal character of realis and irrealis moods: in realis expressions, interclausal temporal relations involve the notions of temporal precedence and overlap; by contrast, irrealis expressions additionally include the notion of accessibility of events (see §1.7.5).

Second, I want to propose a fourth category alongside Smith's three temporal interpretations—namely, the category of *generic*. The generic category builds off Smith's distinction between specific states and general states listed in table 4.4 and essentially adds a negative value to the list: in contrast to the various temporal and modal anchorings, generic expressions are unanchored in that they describe situations that are universally valid or accessible (see Cook 2005). The resulting system that I am proposing based on these expansions of Smith's three-way distinction is presented in table 4.5 and includes references to the following examples, which illustrate each category.

These categories are semantic in character, but what I am proposing is a semantics-based explanation of the temporal structure of discourse that also takes into account syntax and pragmatics in place of a *waw*-focused syntactic approach or a correlations-based taxonomic discourse approach. Following Smith's lead, my approach identifies tense, situation aspect, viewpoint aspect, and pragmatics all as contributing to the determination of interclausal relationships. The following examples serve to illustrate each of these categories, as designated in table 4.5.

Continuity refers to the interpretation of events as iconically reflecting their occurrence (see §4.2.1). In each case, the initial event must be anchored in terms of deixis or anaphor, after which the relation expressed is temporal or

Table 4.5. Interpretations of Interclausal Relationships

	Realis Mood: Temporal Relations (Precedence)	*Irrealis Mood: Modal Relations (Accessibility)*
Continuity	One event temporally follows another. [4.44]	One alternative situation is accessible after another. [4.45]–[4.47]
Deixis	An event is temporally anchored in a personal deictic center (speaker or narrator). [4.48]	An event is modally anchored in a personal deictic center (obligation, wish, volition, etc.). [4.49]
Anaphor	An event is temporally anchored by a preceding event in the discourse context. [4.50]	An event is modally anchored by a preceding event in the discourse context. [4.51]
Genericity	An event is true at all times; it is temporally "unanchored." [4.52]	An event is accessible across all situations; it is modally "unanchored." [4.53]

modal succession. *Temporal continuity* or *succession* is the default interpretation of narrative, as illustrated in example [4.44], in which the bracketed event $[e_0 < C_N]$ denotes some past deixis anchoring, prior to the discourse fragment (i.e., some event e_0 precedes the narrator's deictic center C_N).

[4.44] Gen 21:19; temporal continuity

וַיִּפְקַח אֱלֹהִים אֶת־עֵינֶיהָ וַתֵּרֶא בְּאֵר מָיִם וַתֵּלֶךְ וַתְּמַלֵּא אֶת־הַחֵמֶת מַיִם
וַתַּשְׁקְ אֶת־הַנָּעַר׃

'God opened (WAYY.3MS; $[e_0 < C_N]$, $e_0 < e_1$) her eyes and she saw (WAYY.3FS; $e_1 < e_2$) a well of water and she went (WAYY.3FS; $e_2 < e_3$) and filled (WAYY.3FS; $e_3 < e_4$) the skin of water and she gave the lad a drink (WAYY.3FS; $e_4 < e_5$)'.

Modal continuity is the dominant interpretation in irrealis mood procedural materials, in which an agent is obligated to carry out actions in a particular sequence (e.g., tabernacle construction in Exodus 25–31, sacrificial directions in Leviticus 1–6). An example is [4.45], which begins with deixis anchoring of the first event in the series to the speaker's deictic center (God or Moses). Throughout the passage, each event succeeds the previous one, often logically dependent on the previous event's completion. The only exception to this pattern is the overlap between e_2 and e_3 (that is, וְצִפִּיתָ and תְּצַפֶּנּוּ in v. 11): no specific order is given for overlaying the inside and outside of the ark; this temporal overlap is conveyed by the combination of inverted word order, the concomitant switch to irrealis *yiqtol* for e_3, and the repetition of the verbal lexeme צפה. In other words, the departure from the pattern of continuity is effected by a combination of semantic, syntactic, and discourse-pragmatic factors.

[4.45]   Exod 25:10–14, modal continuity, non-conditional instruction

וְעָשׂוּ אֲרוֹן עֲצֵי שִׁטִּים אַמָּתַיִם וָחֵצִי אָרְכּוֹ וְאַמָּה וָחֵצִי רָחְבּוֹ וְאַמָּה וָחֵצִי
קֹמָתוֹ: וְצִפִּיתָ אֹתוֹ זָהָב טָהוֹר מִבַּיִת וּמִחוּץ תְּצַפֶּנּוּ וְעָשִׂיתָ עָלָיו זֵר זָהָב
סָבִיב: וְיָצַקְתָּ לּוֹ אַרְבַּע טַבְּעֹת זָהָב וְנָתַתָּה עַל אַרְבַּע פַּעֲמֹתָיו וּשְׁתֵּי
טַבָּעֹת עַל־צַלְעוֹ הָאֶחָת וּשְׁתֵּי טַבָּעֹת עַל־צַלְעוֹ הַשֵּׁנִית: וְעָשִׂיתָ בַדֵּי עֲצֵי
שִׁטִּים וְצִפִּיתָ אֹתָם זָהָב: וְהֵבֵאתָ אֶת־הַבַּדִּים בַּטַּבָּעֹת עַל צַלְעֹת הָאָרֹן
לָשֵׂאת אֶת־הָאָרֹן בָּהֶם:

'They <u>shall make</u> (QTL.3P; $R_OC_Ne_1$) an ark of acacia wood—two
and a half cubits its length, a cubit and a half its breadth, and
a cubit and a half its height. And you <u>shall overlay</u> (QTL.2MS;
$R_Oe_1 < e_2$) it with pure gold on its inside, and on its outside you
<u>shall overlay it</u> (YQTL.2MS; $R_Oe_3 \cap e_2$). Then you <u>shall make</u>
(QTL.2MS; $R_Oe_3 < e_4$) upon it a gold molding round about. And
you <u>shall cast</u> (QTL.2MS; $R_Oe_4 < e_5$) for it four gold rings and
<u>place</u> (QTL.2MS; $R_Oe_5 < e_6$) (them) upon its four feet—two rings
(shall be) on one of its sides and two (shall be) on the other of
its sides. Then you <u>shall make</u> (QTL.2MS; $R_Oe_6 < e_7$) poles of
acacia wood and <u>overlay</u> (QTL.2MS; $R_Oe_7 < e_8$) them with gold
and <u>insert</u> ($R_Oe_8 < e_9$) the poles into the rings on the sides of
the ark, to lift the ark by them'.

Procedural legal code is frequently casuistic; that is, it is introduced with a
conditional structure, as illustrated by the excerpt from Leviticus 1 in example
[4.46]. In this case, the first three predicates are not successive: the protasis
e_1 is null copular, and thus stative and overlapping with what follows; the
two *yiqtol* forms that begin the apodosis provide further guidelines for the offering—what and where—and a continuous interpretation is avoided by the
topicalizing word order and the repetition of the lexeme and object (יַקְרִיבֶנּוּ
and יַקְרִיב אֹתוֹ 'he must offer it'). The switch from irrealis *yiqtol* to irrealis
qatal in v. 4 begins the procedural portion proper of the lengthy apodosis, in
which the actions must be carried out in the prescribed order. Similar to the
case in example [4.45], in Lev 1:9 in [4.46] the shift to an inverted word order
with irrealis *yiqtol* יִרְחַץ yields a non-successive contrastive statement with the
previous clause: while the priests must arrange some pieces on the altar, they
must wash other specific parts of the animal before burning the entire animal
as a burnt offering.

[4.46] Lev 1:3–9; modal continuity in conditional instruction

אִם־עֹלָה קָרְבָּנוֹ מִן־הַבָּקָר זָכָר תָּמִים יַקְרִיבֶנּוּ אֶל־פֶּתַח אֹהֶל מוֹעֵד יַקְרִיב
אֹתוֹ לִרְצֹנוֹ לִפְנֵי יְהוָה: וְסָמַךְ יָדוֹ עַל רֹאשׁ הָעֹלָה וְנִרְצָה לוֹ לְכַפֵּר עָלָיו:
וְשָׁחַט אֶת־בֶּן הַבָּקָר לִפְנֵי יְהוָה וְהִקְרִיבוּ בְּנֵי אַהֲרֹן הַכֹּהֲנִים אֶת־הַדָּם
וְזָרְקוּ אֶת־הַדָּם עַל־הַמִּזְבֵּחַ סָבִיב אֲשֶׁר־פֶּתַח אֹהֶל מוֹעֵד: וְהִפְשִׁיט אֶת־
הָעֹלָה וְנִתַּח אֹתָהּ לִנְתָחֶיהָ: וְנָתְנוּ בְּנֵי אַהֲרֹן הַכֹּהֵן אֵשׁ עַל־הַמִּזְבֵּחַ וְעָרְכוּ
עֵצִים עַל־הָאֵשׁ: וְעָרְכוּ בְּנֵי אַהֲרֹן הַכֹּהֲנִים אֵת הַנְּתָחִים אֶת־הָרֹאשׁ וְאֶת־
הַפָּדֶר עַל־הָעֵצִים אֲשֶׁר עַל־הָאֵשׁ אֲשֶׁר עַל־הַמִּזְבֵּחַ: וְקִרְבּוֹ וּכְרָעָיו יִרְחַץ
בַּמָּיִם וְהִקְטִיר הַכֹּהֵן אֶת־הַכֹּל הַמִּזְבֵּחָה עֹלָה רֵיחַ־נִיחוֹחַ לַיהוָה: ס

'If his offering (is) (NULL; $R_C C_N e_1$) a burnt offering from the
herd, a male without blemish he must offer it (YQTL.3MS; $R_O e_1$
→ e_2); at the entrance of the tent of meeting he must offer
(YQTL.3MS; $R_O e_2 = e_3$) it for his acceptance before Yhwh. He
should lay (IRR-QTL.3MS; $R_O e_3 < e_4$) his hand upon the head of
the burnt offering, and it will be accepted (IRR-QTL.3MS; $R_O e_4 <$
e_5) on his behalf as atonement for him. Then he shall slaughter
(IRR-QTL.3MS; $R_O e_5 < e_6$) the bull before Yhwh, and Aaron's
sons the priests shall offer (IRR-QTL.3P; $R_O e_6 < e_7$) the blood and
shall dash (IRR-QTL.3MS; $R_O e_7 < e_8$) the blood round about upon
the altar that is at the entrance of the tent of meeting. Then he
shall flay (IRR-QTL.3MS; $R_O e_8 < e_9$) the burnt offering and cut it
up (IRR-QTL.3MS; $R_O e_9 < e_{10}$) into its pieces. Then the sons of
Aaron the priest shall place (IRR-QTL.3P; $R_O e_{10} < e_{11}$) fire upon
the altar and arrange (IRR-QTL.3P; $R_O e_{11} < e_{12}$) wood on the fire.
Then Aaron's sons the priests shall arrange (IRR-QTL.3P; $R_O e_{12} <$
e_{13}) the pieces with the head and the suet upon the wood that is
on the fire on the altar; but its entrails and its legs he shall wash
(IRR-QTL.3MS; $R_O e_{13} \cap e_{14}$) with water. Then the priest shall turn
the whole into smoke (IRR-QTL.3MS; $R_O e_{14} < e_{15}$) on the altar as
a burnt offering, an offering by fire of pleasing odor to Yhwh'.

It is apparent from both of these examples that a simple correlation cannot be
made between verb conjugation and temporal or modal interpretations. Rather,
within a given discourse context, the two irrealis forms contrast in pragmatic
ways that are similar to the *wayyiqtol-qatal* contrast in narrative modes (e.g.,
example [4.24]).

The "future" sense in these two passages (examples [4.45–46]) derives
from the irrealis status of the events: the agents must bring about situations
that are yet to be realized. They are therefore akin to future temporal expressions. However, modal continuity is also present in non-past habitual passages,
which are the irrealis counterpart to realis narrative. In the habitual passage
in example [4.47], the habitual events are temporally anaphorically anchored

by the narrative context in which they appear (i.e., the first irrealis event is modally accessible from some event prior to it in the past-narrative discourse, $[e_0 < C_N]$). After the habitual modal relationship is established by the first irrealis *qatal*, subsequent irrealis forms express the habitual actions in succession, each being related to the preceding event.

[4.47]   Gen 29:3 (modality continuity in habitual narrative)

וְנֶאֶסְפוּ־שָׁמָּה כָל־הָעֲדָרִים וְגָלֲלוּ אֶת־הָאֶבֶן מֵעַל פִּי הַבְּאֵר וְהִשְׁקוּ אֶת־
הַצֹּאן וְהֵשִׁיבוּ אֶת־הָאֶבֶן עַל־פִּי הַבְּאֵר לִמְקֹמָהּ:

'All the flocks <u>would gather</u> (IRR-QTL.3P; $[e_0 < C_N]$, $R_He_0e_1$) there, then they <u>would roll</u> (IRR-QTL.3P; $R_He_1 < e_2$) the stone from upon the mouth of the well; then they <u>would water</u> (IRR-QTL.3P; $R_He_2 < e_3$) the flock; then they <u>would replace</u> (IRR-QTL.3P; $R_He_3 < e_4$) the stone upon the mouth of the well'.

Deixis refers to the anchoring in a personal "deictic center." *Temporal deixis* is associated particularly with the beginning of narrative passages, in which the first event is temporally anchored to the narrator's deictic center (C_N), and with reported speech, in which events are predominantly anchored to the deictic center of the speaker (C_S). Both of these types of temporal deixis are illustrated by example [4.48]: notice that the narrative verbs (e_1 and e_5) are temporally continuous with one another and frame the reported speeches, each of which receives a temporal deixis interpretation: that is, each of the events in the reported speeches is temporally and individually related to the speaker's deictic center.

[4.48]   Gen 24:23–24; temporal deixis in reported speech

וַיֹּאמֶר בַּת־מִי אַתְּ הַגִּידִי נָא לִי הֲיֵשׁ בֵּית־אָבִיךְ מָקוֹם לָנוּ לָלִין: וַתֹּאמֶר
אֵלָיו בַּת־בְּתוּאֵל אָנֹכִי בֶּן־מִלְכָּה אֲשֶׁר יָלְדָה לְנָחוֹר:

'He <u>said</u> (WAYY.3MS; $[e_0 < C_N]$, $e_0 < e_1$), "Whose daughter (<u>are</u>) (NULL; $C_S \subseteq e_2$) you? Please <u>tell</u> (IMPV.FS; $R_Oe_3C_S$) me. <u>Is</u> (EXIST; $C_S \subseteq e_4$) there at your father's house a place for us to spend the night?" She <u>said</u> (WAYY.3FS; $e_1 < e_5$) to him, "I <u>am</u> (NULL; $C_S \subseteq e_6$) the daughter of Bethuel, son of Milcah, whom she <u>bore</u> (QTL.3FS; $e_6 < C_S$) to Nahor"'.

Modal deixis, by analogy with temporal deixis, locates the modal source as the speaker's personal deictic center (C_S)—whether this is the source of obligation, wish, volition, or epistemic judgment. Thus, this discourse mode aligns with epistemic and subjective deontic modality in contrast to dynamic and objective deontic modality (see Verstraete 2007; see table 3.7, p. 255). As argued in §3.3.2 above, the directive system (Imperative and Jussive) in

Biblical Hebrew is restricted to expressing subjective deontic modality. One example of modal deixis using the directive system is the Imperative הַגִּידִי in example [4.48] above. A more extensive example of modal deixis is example [4.49] below.[30]

[4.49] Exod 9:13; modal deixis in directive speech

וַיֹּאמֶר יְהוָה אֶל־מֹשֶׁה הַשְׁכֵּם בַּבֹּקֶר וְהִתְיַצֵּב לִפְנֵי פַרְעֹה וְאָמַרְתָּ אֵלָיו
כֹּה־אָמַר יְהוָה אֱלֹהֵי הָעִבְרִים שַׁלַּח אֶת־עַמִּי וְיַעַבְדֻנִי:

'Yhwh said (WAYY.3MS; [$e_0 < C_N$], $e_0 < e_1$) to Moses, "Get up early (IMPV.MS; $R_Oe_2C_S$) in the morning and station yourself (IMPV.MS; $R_Oe_3C_S$) before Pharaoh, and then say (IRR-QTL.2MS; $R_Oe_3 < e_4$) to him, "Thus says (QTL.3MS; $e_5 \equiv C_S$) Yhwh, the God of the Hebrews, 'Dismiss (IMPV.MS; $R_Oe_6C_S$) my people so that they may serve me (YQTL.3MP; $R_Oe_7C_S$)'"'.

Notice that in this passage the deictic center shifts based on the level of embedded speech or discourse pragmatic considerations. For instance, the direct commands to Moses in e_2 and e_3 are anchored to God's modal deictic center (followed by the modally continuous irrealis *qatal* in e_4),[31] as also is the quotation of God's command in e_6. By contrast, the event in e_7 is an expression of permission anchored to Pharaoh's deictic center.[32]

Anaphor refers to the anchoring (temporal or modal) of an event in some other event reported earlier in the discourse. In *temporal anaphor*, the event is temporally associated with (i.e., included within) a previously established event time, as in the case of static descriptions. Example [4.50] contains two examples of this sort. In this excerpt, the initial וַיְהִי is the discourse marker of past time and not the copular predicate. Note, in support of the discourse analysis, that if it were treated as a copular, as a stative it would require interpreting the event of the sons' names as included within one of the events in the previous verse (see C. S. Smith 2003: 94)—either the appointing of his sons or Samuel's growing old (v. 1)—neither of which makes sense. By contrast, the three null-copula events are anaphorically related to the time set by this discourse וַיְהִי e_1 (i.e., as unbounded events, they include the reference time of e_1). Thus, the discourse וַיְהִי functions in a way that is similar to example [4.50]:

---

30. The messenger formula כֹּה־אָמַר יְהוָה is analyzed here as a performative (the material equivalence sign ≡ indicates that the event time is coincident with the speech); however, a past or perfect interpretation is equally possible: 'Thus Yhwh (has) said . . .'.

31. While e_{2-3} implies the same continuity of modal events as e_{3-4}, that interpretation derives from the pragmatics of the iconic ordering of the events rather than the semantic interpretation signaled by the verbal form.

32. That is, dismissing the people gives them leave or permission to serve Yhwh. Alternatively, this could be analyzed as an (objective) dynamic modal expression (see below on generic modal): 'so that they can (might be able to) serve me'.

[4.50] 1 Sam 8:2–3; temporal anaphor in prose narrative

וַיְהִי שֶׁם־בְּנוֹ הַבְּכוֹר יוֹאֵל וְשֵׁם מִשְׁנֵהוּ אֲבִיָּה שֹׁפְטִים בִּבְאֵר שָׁבַע: וְלֹא־
הָלְכוּ בָנָיו בִּדְרָכָיו וַיִּטּוּ אַחֲרֵי הַבָּצַע וַיִּקְחוּ־שֹׁחַד וַיַּטּוּ מִשְׁפָּט: פ

'[PAST] (WAYY.3MS; $e_1 < C_N$) The name of the firstborn (<u>was</u>)
(NULL; $e_1 \subseteq e_2$) Joel, and the name of his second (<u>was</u>) (NULL;
$e_1 \subseteq e_3$) Abijah; they (<u>were</u>) (NULL; $e_1 \subseteq e_4$) judges in Beersheba. They <u>did</u> not <u>walk</u> (QTL.3P; $e_5 \subseteq e_4$) in his ways but
turned (3MP.WAYY; $e_6 \subseteq e_4$) after unjust gain and <u>took</u> (3MP.
WAYY; $e_7 \subseteq e_4$) bribes and <u>perverted</u> (WAYY.3MP; $e_8 \subseteq e_4$)
justice'.

The last four events ($e_{5–8}$) in example [4.50] are anaphorically related to the
null-copula e_4 '(were) judges' because their reference time is included in the
reference time of this unbound null-copula expression rather than receiving a
continuous interpretation as would be more typical at least for the Past Narrative forms. The null-copula (stative) expression of e_4 thus acts similarly to
C. S. Smith's (2003: 96) "tacit durative time adverbial" in anaphoric discourse,
while the locative phrase "in Beersheba" provides an anaphoric anchor for
events $e_{5–8}$ (C. S. Smith 2003: 95; see example [4.43], p. 318).

Modal anaphor, on analogy with temporal anaphor, is the interpretation of
irrealis events as modally anchored or related to a preceding event in the discourse. The prime example is protasis-apodosis constructions (indicated as R_C
"condition" for protasis, and → for if-then anaphoric relation among events),
in which a protasis event is posited as a condition on which the "accessibility"
of the apodosis is dependent. This is illustrated by example [4.51], excerpted
from [4.46] above.

[4.51] Lev 1:3a; modal anaphor in conditional instructional

אִם־עֹלָה קָרְבָּנוֹ מִן־הַבָּקָר זָכָר תָּמִים יַקְרִיבֶנּוּ . . .

'If his offering (<u>is</u>) (NULL; $R_C C_N e_1$) a burnt offering from the
herd, then a male without blemish he <u>must offer</u> (YQTL.3MS;
$R_O e_1 \rightarrow e_2$) (for) it'.

Generic expressions are temporally or modally "unanchored"—that is, they
are independent of the surrounding discourse (compare with continuity and
anaphor) and of the speaker's deictic center (compare with deixis). The temporal and modal generic modes capture important distinctions in both realis
temporal and irrealis nontemporal expressions. The unanchored character of
generics gives them a "universal" quality, though linguists have struggled to
define precisely the semantics of generic expressions. As outlined in Cook
(2005), there are several different semantic explanations, including that generics express what is prototypically true, what is true about the structure of
reality, or what is true among relevant alternatives.

The association of generics with the structure of reality is suggested particularly by generics that do not refer to actual events but to potentialities, such as "The bishop moves diagonally," spoken in reference to the game of chess (example from Carlson 1995: 225). In turn, examples of this sort suggest that, alongside temporal genericity and on analogy with them, a modal generic mode helpfully distinguishes dynamic and objective deontic modalities from epistemic and subjective deontic modalities: whereas subjective modality is anchored by personal deixis (see above), objective modality leaves the source of modal authority unexpressed or pragmatically implied from the discourse context. As Verstraete (2007: 18) states it, in objective modality, the speaker "merely describes" a modal relation rather than personally committing to it.

In *temporal generic* statements, the events are temporally unanchored and are therefore valid at all temporal locations. For this reason, generic expressions can make use of a variety of different verbal forms (see Cook 2005); this fact in turn demonstrates that verbal conjugations alone do not determine whether an expression is generic or not. While the verbal forms retain their usual TAM contrasts (as argued in Cook 2005), the pragmatics of generic statements (i.e., lack of context, kind-referring noun phrases, etc.) forces a generic interpretation of the events.[33] Thus, the *yiqtol* forms in example [4.52] retain the sense normally associated with them in deictic reported speech, despite receiving a generic interpretation.[34]

[4.52] Prov 10:1–2 (temporal generic in proverbial sentence literature)

בֵּן חָכָם יְשַׂמַּח־אָב וּבֵן כְּסִיל תּוּגַת אִמּוֹ׃

לֹא־יוֹעִילוּ אוֹצְרוֹת רֶשַׁע וּצְדָקָה תַּצִּיל מִמָּוֶת׃

'A wise son will gladden (YQTL.3MS; ∀t: t ⊆ e_1) a father, but a foolish son (is) (NULL; ∀t: t ⊆ e_2) the grief of his mother'.

'The treasures of the wicked will not avail (YQTL.3MP; ∀t: t ⊆ e_3), but righteousness will deliver (YQTL.3FS; ∀t: t ⊆ e_4) from death'.

Modal generics express unrestricted access to all alternative situations; consequently, the situation is universally modally related to every other situation.

---

33. Precisely what all the factors are that lead to generic interpretations is uncertain (see discussion in Carlson 1995). Fortunately, the lack of a clear answer to this perplexing question does not invalidate or detract from the applicability of this theory of interclausal relations.

34. As I have argued elsewhere (in Cook 2005: 124–25; see §3.4.2 above), the analogy of TAM interpretation between reported speech and generic expressions lies in the fact that, in both cases, the deictic center is distinct from the center of the surrounding discourse context: in reported speech, the speaker's deictic center prevails, whereas in generic statements, I am arguing here that the deictic center is essentially "universalized."

As explained above, this category includes objective deontic and dynamic (ability) modal categories, which denote modal relations whose source lies in the "structure" of the world or at least a source other than the speaker, who simply describes this modal relationship. This difference from modal deixis captures the intuitively recognizable distinction between "categorical" commands, such as are found in the Decalogue and illustrated in example [4.53], and the "urgency" of directive commands, as in example [4.49] above.

[4.53]   Exod 20:13–16; modal generic in categorical/apodictic
          commands

ס לֹא תִרְצָח: ס לֹא תִנְאָף: ס לֹא תִגְנֹב: ס לֹא־תַעֲנֶה בְרֵעֲךָ עֵד שָׁקֶר: ס

'You <u>shall</u> not <u>kill</u> (IRR-YQTL.2MS; ∀w: Rwe₁), you <u>shall</u> not
commit adultery (IRR-YQTL.2MS; ∀w: Rwe₂), you <u>shall</u> not steal
(IRR-YQTL.2MS; ∀w: Rwe₃), you <u>shall</u> not <u>testify</u> (IRR-YQTL.2MS;
∀w: Rwe₄) falsely against your companion'.

Having illustrated briefly each of the eight categories, I analyze two lengthier passages in the following two sections that will illustrate how the various modes interact with each other.

4.4.1. 1 Samuel 8 (Prose Narrative)

1 Samuel 8 is a typical prose narrative passage that may be divided into four episodes based on scene shifts (vv. 1–3, 4–6, 7–9, 10–22). The first episode (example [4.54]) begins with two "scene setting" clauses (e_{1-2}): the discourse וַיְהִי deictically locates the episode prior to the narrator's deictic center ($e_1 < C_N$); the null-copula temporal clause e_2 is subordinate to the following clause (e_3) and includes the deictically located time of e_1 in its stative reference time—that of Samuel's being old (e_2).

[4.54]   Episode 1 (1 Sam 8:1–3)

e_1 (WAYY.3MS) ∈ {STA, PFV, DECL}; $e_1 < C_N$	וַיְהִי	8:1a
e_2 (NULL) ∈ {STA, PFV, DECL}; $e_1 \subseteq e_2$	כַּאֲשֶׁר זָקֵן שְׁמוּאֵל	8:1b
e_3 (WAYY.3MS) ∈ {ACC, PFV, DECL}; $e_3 \subseteq e_2$	וַיָּשֶׂם אֶת־בָּנָיו שֹׁפְטִים לְיִשְׂרָאֵל:	8:1c
e_4 (WAYY.3MS) ∈ {STA, PFV, DECL}; $e_4 < C_N$	וַיְהִי	8:2a
e_5 (NULL) ∈ {STA, PFV, DECL}; $e_4 \subseteq e_5$	שֶׁם־בְּנוֹ הַבְּכוֹר יוֹאֵל	8:2b
e_6 (NULL) ∈ {STA, PFV, DECL}; $e_4 \subseteq e_6$	וְשֵׁם מִשְׁנֵהוּ אֲבִיָּה	8:2c
e_7 (NULL) ∈ {STA, PFV, DECL}; $e_4 \subseteq e_7$	שֹׁפְטִים בִּבְאֵר שָׁבַע:	8:2d
e_8 (QTL.3P) ∈ {ACT, PFV, NEG-DECL}; $e_8 \subseteq e_7$	וְלֹא־הָלְכוּ בָנָיו בִּדְרָכָו	8:3a
e_9 (WAYY.3MP) ∈ {ACC, PFV, DECL}; $e_9 \subseteq e_7$	וַיִּטּוּ אַחֲרֵי הַבָּצַע	8:3b
e_{10} (WAYY.3MP) ∈ {ACC, PFV, DECL}; $e_{10} \subseteq e_7$	וַיִּקְחוּ־שֹׁחַד	8:3c
e_{11} (WAYY.3MP) ∈ {ACC, PFV, DECL}; $e_{11} \subseteq e_7$	וַיַּטּוּ מִשְׁפָּט: פ	8:3d

The temporal relationship between e_1 and e_2 is mirrored by that of the second and third clauses (e_{2-3}): the initial "narrative" (i.e., foregrounded) clause (e_3) is interpreted anaphorically as being included within the reference time of e_2.[35] It is important to notice the complex interaction of semantics and context: the narrative *wayyiqtol* in e_3, although past tense, is not interpreted deictically here (as e_1 is), because the context demands an anaphoric interpretation whereby it is temporally included in the previous event reference time (e_2), which also includes the reference time of e_1. Thus, the use of the *wayyiqtol* is motivated by its foregrounding characteristic as well as its consonance with the past temporal context established by the discourse וַיְהִי.

The discourse וַיְהִי in v. 2 "reestablishes" the reference time, which appears somewhat odd in the middle of an episode (note the pronominal anaphor that ties the event in this verse to the preceding verse); however, if e_4 were interpreted as a simple copular clause (rather than the discourse וַיְהִי), it would result in placing the reference time of the event within the temporal expression e_2, which does not make sense (Samuel's sons had names while he was old). As in the case of e_1, the discourse וַיְהִי in e_4 indicates the deictic location of what follows—the pair of verbless clauses in e_{5-6}, in which it is temporally included. Here we see at work C. S. Smith's (2003: 94) principle that unbounded events (e_{5-6}) are temporally interpreted with respect to a previously established reference point (e_4).

The same principle applies to e_7, which consists of a null copula and a Participle (or agentive noun): it includes the reference time of e_4 and, by extension, e_1. In turn, whether interpreted as a stative (agentive noun complement: 'they were judges') or progressive gram (Participle complement: 'they were judging'), this event has scope over the remaining events in this descriptive episode: e_7 temporally includes the events of v. 3 (e_{8-11}). These latter events, which in a different context might be interpreted as temporally successive events (apart from the negative clause of e_8), express the foreground of the description but are interpreted anaphorically in relation to the stative event e_7.

Episode 2, given in example [4.55], consists of a series of narrative events temporally interpreted as simple continuity, within which is embedded a number of deictically interpreted speech events. These latter events are quite similar to Smith's "report mode," which is dynamic and deictically interpreted (see C. S. Smith 2003: 96 and example [4.42] above). Given that there is no

---

35. The idealistic character of her modes is evident in the differences between this passage and her sample description: she notes that, "typically," descriptions have a locative adverbial expression with scope over the whole, and she postulates a "tacit durative time adverbial" with similar scope; by contrast, there is no locative expression here (cf. e_{7-11}, below) but the overt "durative time" reference that "anchors" the anaphorically interpreted e_3 by including the latter within its stative temporal frame.

pronominal anaphor connecting this with the preceding episode, it is possible to argue that the *wayyiqtol* clause at the beginning of this episode should be interpreted deictically as determining the episode time ($e_{12} < C_N$)—and it is important to note that *wayyiqtol* can function in this way over and against the outdated claims that its TAM is dependent on a preceding *qatal* (Kautzsch 1910: §111a). However, it is more likely that the first event in episode 2 (e_{12}) is temporally continuous from the single narrative event in episode 1 (e_3), all of the intervening material between these two events being description rather than narration.

[4.55] Episode 2 (1 Sam 8:4–6)

e_{12} (WAYY.3MP) $\in$ {ACC, PFV, DECL}; $e_3 < e_{12}$	וַיִּתְקַבְּצוּ כֹּל זִקְנֵי יִשְׂרָאֵל	8:4a
e_{13} (WAYY.3MP) $\in$ {ACC, PFV, DECL}; $e_{12} < e_{13}$	וַיָּבֹאוּ אֶל־שְׁמוּאֵל הָרָמָתָה׃	8:4b
e_{14} (WAYY.3MP) $\in$ {ACT, PFV, DECL}; $e_{13} < e_{14}$	וַיֹּאמְרוּ אֵלָיו	8:5a
e_{15} (QTL.2MS) $\in$ {STA, PFV, DECL}; $C_S \subseteq e_{15}$	הִנֵּה אַתָּה זָקַנְתָּ	8:5b
e_{16} (QTL.3P) $\in$ {ACT, PF, DECL}; $e_{16} < C_S$	וּבָנֶיךָ לֹא הָלְכוּ בִּדְרָכֶיךָ	8:5c
e_{17} (IMPV.MS) $\in$ {ACH, DIR}; $R_0 C_S e_{17}$	עַתָּה שִׂימָה־לָּנוּ מֶלֶךְ לְשָׁפְטֵנוּ	8:5d
	כְּכָל־הַגּוֹיִם׃	
e_{18} (WAYY.3MS) $\in$ {STA, PFV, DECL}; $e_{18} < e_{18}$	וַיֵּרַע הַדָּבָר בְּעֵינֵי שְׁמוּאֵל	8:6a
e_{19} (QTL.3P) $\in$ {ACT, PF, DECL}; $e_{19} < e_{18}$	כַּאֲשֶׁר אָמְרוּ	8:6b
e_{20} (IMPV.MS) $\in$ {ACH, DIR}; $R_0 C_S e_{20}$	תְּנָה־לָּנוּ מֶלֶךְ לְשָׁפְטֵנוּ	8:6c
e_{21} (WAYY.3MS) $\in$ {ACT, PFV, DECL}; $e_{21} \subseteq e_7$	וַיִּתְפַּלֵּל שְׁמוּאֵל אֶל־יְהוָה׃ פ	8:6d

The first three events in this episode (e_{12-14}) are therefore typically narrative, being foregrounded, temporally successive events continuously following the narrative event of episode one (e_3): (then) the elders gathered themselves together; then they came to Samuel; then spoke to him.[36] The latter of these events introduces reported speech consisting of three deictically interpreted events (e_{15-17}). However, each of these three events has a different temporal structure. The first (e_{15}) is stative; thus it includes the speaker's deictic center within its reference time. By contrast, the following *qatal* clause (e_{16}) represents a dynamic event, which is given a past temporal interpretation. However, the information from the discourse context—that the sons are serving as judges at this time (e_7)—decides in favor of a perfect interpretation of this *qatal* versus a perfective interpretation. Finally, the last event in the reported speech (e_{17}) is interpreted as modal versus temporal deixis with respect to the

---

36. C. S. Smith (2003: 94) writes of the narrative mode:

> All these situations are temporally located at a time prior to Speech Time, following narrative convention. Otherwise the information conveyed by tense is simple continuity [i.e., temporal succession]. The past tense is not interpreted deictically: if it were the events would be related to Speech Time rather than to each other. Nor do we interpret the past tense as expressing a series of events successively prior to one another. The continuity function of tense holds for narratives in the present or future as well as the past.

speaker; in this case, the speaker's deictic center (C_S) is the speaker's situation (or "world"), to which an alternative situation (or possible world) expressed by the imperative stands in a directive relationship: a speaker-derived obligation is placed on the addressee to bring about the alternative situation. The same relation holds for e_{20} as well.

Event e_{18} reports Samuel's reaction to the speech, thus being successive with the previous narrative (versus reported speech) clause, e_{14}: the elders spoke to Samuel, and then the matter was displeasing to him. Although as a stative, וַיֵּרַע is unbounded, it does not include within its deixis the following event (e_{19}); instead, the latter appearing in a subordinate clause modifying הַדָּבָר, which is anaphorically (i.e., the definite article) linked to the preceding reported speech (e_{14-17}) receives a past perfect interpretation: 'inasmuch as they had said'. The unbounded character of וַיֵּרַע is evident, instead, from its relationship with e_{21}, which though successive with the stative e_{19}, does not wholly follow it but is included within its reference time: what they had said remained grievous to Samuel when he prayed about it.

The third episode, example [4.56], represents the reverse of the type of material found in episode two: in place of continuous narrative with embedded deictic speech, episode three consists of reported speech with a short embedded narrative. The first event in this episode (e_{22}) is successive with the last of the previous episode (e_{21}): the Lord's response to Samuel follows his prayer.

[4.56] Episode 3 (1 Sam 8:7–9)

e_{22} (WAYY.3MS) $\in$ {ACT, PFV, DECL}; $e_{21} < e_{22}$	וַיֹּאמֶר יְהוָה אֶל־שְׁמוּאֵל	8:7a
e_{23} (IMPV.MS) $\in$ {ACT, DIR}; $R_0 C_S e_{23}$	שְׁמַע בְּקוֹל הָעָם לְכֹל	8:7b
e_{24} (YQTL.3MP) $\in$ {ACT, IPFV, DECL}; $C_S \subseteq e_{24}$	אֲשֶׁר־יֹאמְרוּ אֵלֶיךָ	8:7c
e_{25} (QTL.3P) $\in$ {ACH, PF, NEG-DECL}; $e_{25} < C_S$	כִּי לֹא אֹתְךָ מָאָסוּ	8:7d
e_{26} (QTL.3P) $\in$ {ACH, PF, DECL}; $e_{26} < C_S$	כִּי־אֹתִי מָאֲסוּ מִמְּלֹךְ עֲלֵיהֶם:	8:7e
e_{27} (QTL.3P) $\in$ {ACT, PF, DECL}; $e_{27} < C_S$	כְּכָל־הַמַּעֲשִׂים אֲשֶׁר־עָשׂוּ מִיּוֹם הַעֲלֹתִי	8:8a
	אֹתָם מִמִּצְרַיִם וְעַד־הַיּוֹם הַזֶּה	
e_{28} (WAYY.3MP) $\in$ {ACH, PFV, DECL}; $e_{28} \subseteq e_{27}$	וַיַּעַזְבֻנִי	8:8b
e_{29} (WAYY.3MP) $\in$ {ACT, PFV, DECL}; $e_{28} < e_{29}$	וַיַּעַבְדוּ אֱלֹהִים אֲחֵרִים	8:8c
e_{30} (PTC.MP) $\in$ {ACT, PROG, DECL}; $C_S \subseteq e_{30}$	כֵּן הֵמָּה עֹשִׂים גַּם־לָךְ:	8:8d
e_{31} (IMPV.MS) $\in$ {ACT, DIR}; $R_0 C_S e_{31}$	וְעַתָּה שְׁמַע בְּקוֹלָם	8:9a
e_{32} (YQTL.2MS) $\in$ {ACT, DEO}; $R_0 C_S e_{32}$	אַךְ כִּי־הָעֵד תָּעִיד בָּהֶם	8:9b
e_{33} (QTL.2MS) $\in$ {ACT, PFV, DEO}; $R_0 e_{33} = e_{32}$	וְהִגַּדְתָּ לָהֶם מִשְׁפַּט הַמֶּלֶךְ	8:9c
e_{34} (YQTL.3MS) $\in$ {ACT, IPFV, DECL}; $C_S < e_{34}$	אֲשֶׁר יִמְלֹךְ עֲלֵיהֶם: ס	8:9d

The remainder of this third episode is reported speech, which is mostly—for main clauses—interpreted as temporal (e_{24-27}) or modal (e_{23}, e_{31}) deixis. The qatal clauses (e_{25-27}) all receive a perfect (rather than perfective) interpretation in the context. As such, these three clause are not successive; the first two are, in fact, corresponding negative and positive statements. The perfect interpretation of the last (e_{27}) of the three is reinforced by the temporal expression 'from the day . . . until this day'. This clear indication of a perfect meaning lends weight to the otherwise somewhat ambiguous *qatal* forms in the preceding two clauses: '(have) rejected'. In turn, the perfect expression in e_{27} provides the anaphoric reference time for the following short, two-event narrative sequence, interpreted as temporal continuity in e_{28-29}: the people abandoned God and then worshiped other deities (though the two events may be thought to occur relatively simultaneously, they are nevertheless clearly irreversible). Thus this narrative is embedded within a descriptive passage (e_{27-29}), which itself appears within a reportive discourse (e_{25-29}).

The following irrealis event (e_{31}), expressed by the directive imperative, is interpreted as modal deixis, as also is the exceptive clause that follows (e_{32}). The final event in this short series of irrealis events, e_{33}, is identical to the preceding, e_{32}: 'testifying' is further specified in 'informing' them what the king will do. The final event (e_{34}), in the subordinate clause, has a future *yiqtol*, which casts the event after the speaker's deictic reference time.

The fourth and final episode in this narrative is the longest (example [4.57]). It is introduced by the narrative event (e_{34}), which is successive with the previous narrative event of e_{22}. (The narrative events e_{28-29} are excluded from this sequence of events by their embedding in reported speech.) The progressive Participle construction in e_{35} is a relative modifier of the preceding noun, הָעָם, thus containing the event time of e_{34}. The event of e_{36} forms a hendiadys with e_{34}, and by its repetition serves to introduce Samuel's speech directly.

Samuel's predictive speech about the behavior of the king that the people have requested begins with the deictic orienting *yiqtol* copula in e_{37} and a subordinate relative *yiqtol* in e_{38}, which is deictically anchored like e_{37}. The remainder of the description (e_{39-50}) is structured with multiple *yiqtol* forms of לָקַח 'take' (e_{39}, e_{42-43}, e_{47}) and עָשַׂר 'tithe' (e_{45}, e_{49}), each followed by modifying final clauses, with the exception of the last (e_{49}). The final clauses consist of irrealis *qatal*s (e_{40-41}, e_{44}, e_{46}, e_{48}), except for the subordinate infinitive clauses in v. 12, which confirm the final interpretation of the surrounding irrealis *qatal*s. Notably, all of these sequences of *yiqtol*-final irrealis *qatal*, while successive in themselves, are not successive with each other. Rather, each *yiqtol* seems to anchor its own reference time deictically, while the final irrealis *qatal* forms are each interpreted as modally anaphoric with respect to the preceding *yiqtol*s.[37] The description ends with a contrastive *yiqtol* הָיָה clause with overt pronoun (e_{50}): 'But you [in contrast to all that the king will take from you] will be his slaves'.

---

37. Note that the same formal notation is used for a conditional (example [4.51], p. 324) and a final clause here; in both cases, one event modally follows the anchoring event.

[4.57] Episode 4 (1 Sam 8:10–22)

e_{34} (WAYY.3MS) $\in$ {ACT, PFV, DECL}; $e_{22} < e_1$ וַיֹּאמֶר שְׁמוּאֵל אֵת כָּל־דִּבְרֵי יְהוָה 8:10a
אֶל־הָעָם

e_{35} (PTC.MP) $\in$ {ACT, PROG, DECL}; $e_{34} \subseteq e_{35}$ הַשֹּׁאֲלִים מֵאִתּוֹ מֶלֶךְ: ס 8:10b

e_{36} (WAYY.3MS) $\in$ {ACT, PFV, DECL}; $e_{36} = e_{34}$ וַיֹּאמֶר 8:11a

e_{37} (YQTL.3MS) $\in$ {STA, FUT, DECL}; $C_S < e_{37}$ זֶה יִהְיֶה מִשְׁפַּט הַמֶּלֶךְ 8:11b

e_{38} (YQTL.3MS) $\in$ {ACT, FUT, DECL}; $C_S < e_{38}$ אֲשֶׁר יִמְלֹךְ עֲלֵיכֶם 8:11c

e_{39} (YQTL.3MS) $\in$ {ACC, FUT, DECL}; $C_S < e_{39}$ אֶת־בְּנֵיכֶם יִקָּח 8:11d

e_{40} (QTL.3MS) $\in$ {ACH, PFV, FIN}; $Re_{39} \rightarrow e_{40}$ וְשָׂם לוֹ בְּמֶרְכַּבְתּוֹ וּבְפָרָשָׁיו 8:11e

e_{41} (QTL.3P) $\in$ {ACT, PFV, FIN}; $Re_{40} \rightarrow e_{41}$ וְרָצוּ לִפְנֵי מֶרְכַּבְתּוֹ: וְלָשׂוּם לוֹ שָׂרֵי 8:11f
אֲלָפִים וְשָׂרֵי חֲמִשִּׁים וְלַחֲרֹשׁ חֲרִישׁוֹ
וְלִקְצֹר קְצִירוֹ וְלַעֲשׂוֹת כְּלֵי־מִלְחַמְתּוֹ
וּכְלֵי רִכְבּוֹ:

e_{42} (YQTL.3MS) $\in$ {ACC, FUT, DECL}; $C_S < e_{42}$ וְאֶת־בְּנוֹתֵיכֶם יִקָּח לְרַקָּחוֹת וּלְטַבָּחוֹת 8:13a
וּלְאֹפוֹת:

e_{43} (YQTL.3MS) $\in$ {ACC, FUT, DECL}; $C_S < e_{43}$ וְאֶת־שְׂדוֹתֵיכֶם וְאֶת־כַּרְמֵיכֶם וְזֵיתֵיכֶם 8:14a
הַטּוֹבִים יִקָּח

e_{44} (QTL.3MS) $\in$ {ACC, PFV, FIN}; $Re_{43} \rightarrow e_{44}$ וְנָתַן לַעֲבָדָיו: 8:14b

e_{45} (YQTL.3MS) $\in$ {ACC, FUT, DECL}; $C_S < e_{45}$ וְזַרְעֵיכֶם וְכַרְמֵיכֶם יַעְשֹׂר 8:15a

e_{46} (QTL.3MS) $\in$ {ACC, PFV, FIN}; $Re_{45} \rightarrow e_{46}$ וְנָתַן לְסָרִיסָיו וְלַעֲבָדָיו: 8:15b

e_{47} (YQTL.3MS) $\in$ {ACC, FUT, DECL}; $C_S < e_{47}$ וְאֶת־עַבְדֵיכֶם וְאֶת־שִׁפְחוֹתֵיכֶם וְאֶת־ 8:16a
בַּחוּרֵיכֶם הַטּוֹבִים וְאֶת־חֲמוֹרֵיכֶם יִקָּח

e_{48} (QTL.3MS) $\in$ {ACT, PFV, FIN}; $Re_{47} \rightarrow e_{48}$ וְעָשָׂה לִמְלַאכְתּוֹ: 8:16b

e_{49} (YQTL.3MS) $\in$ {ACH, FUT, DECL}; $C_S < e_{49}$ צֹאנְכֶם יַעְשֹׂר 8:17a

e_{50} (YQTL.2MP) $\in$ {STA, FUT, DECL}; $C_S < e_{50}$ וְאַתֶּם תִּהְיוּ־לוֹ לַעֲבָדִים: 8:17b

e_{51} (QTL.2MP) $\in$ {ACT, PFV, FIN}; $R_Ce_{51}e_{50}$ וּזְעַקְתֶּם בַּיּוֹם הַהוּא מִלִּפְנֵי מַלְכְּכֶם 8:18a

e_{52} (QTL.2MP) $\in$ {ACH, PF(V), DECL}; $e_{52} < e_{51}$ אֲשֶׁר בְּחַרְתֶּם לָכֶם 8:18b

e_{53} (YQTL.3MS) $\in$ {ACH, FUT, NEG-DECL};   וְלֹא־יַעֲנֶה יְהוָה אֶתְכֶם בַּיּוֹם הַהוּא: 8:18c
$Re_{51} \rightarrow e_{53}$

e_{54} (WAYY.3MP) $\in$ {ACH, PFV, DECL}; $e_{36} < e_{54}$ וַיְמָאֲנוּ הָעָם לִשְׁמֹעַ בְּקוֹל שְׁמוּאֵל 8:19a

e_{55} (WAYY.3MS) $\in$ {ACH, PFV, DECL}; $e_{54} < e_{55}$ וַיֹּאמְרוּ 8:19b

e_{56} (YQTL.1P) $\in$ {STA, FUT, DECL}; $C_S < e_{56}$ לֹא כִּי אִם־מֶלֶךְ יִהְיֶה עָלֵינוּ: 8:20a

e_{57} (QTL.3MS) $\in$ {ACT, PFV, FIN}; $Re_{56} \rightarrow e_{57}$ וְהָיִינוּ גַם־אֲנַחְנוּ כְּכָל־הַגּוֹיִם 8:20b

e_{58} (QTL.3MS) $\in$ {ACT, PFV, FIN}; $Re_{56} \rightarrow e_{58}$ וּשְׁפָטָנוּ מַלְכֵּנוּ 8:20c

e_{59} (QTL.3MS) $\in$ {ACT, PFV, FIN}; $Re_{56} \rightarrow e_{59}$ וְיָצָא לְפָנֵינוּ 8:20d

e_{60} (QTL.3MS) $\in$ {ACT, PFV, FIN}; $Re_{56} \rightarrow e_{60}$ וְנִלְחַם אֶת־מִלְחֲמֹתֵנוּ: 8:20e

e_{61} (WAYY.3MS) $\in$ {ACC, PFV, DECL}; $e_{55} < e_{61}$ וַיִּשְׁמַע שְׁמוּאֵל אֵת כָּל־דִּבְרֵי הָעָם 8:21a

e_{62} (WAYY.3MS) $\in$ {ACC, PFV, DECL}; $e_{61} < e_{62}$ וַיְדַבְּרֵם בְּאָזְנֵי יְהוָה: פ 8:21b

e_{63} (WAYY.3MS) $\in$ {ACT, PFV, DECL}; $e_{62} < e_{63}$ וַיֹּאמֶר יְהוָה אֶל־שְׁמוּאֵל 8:22a

e_{64} (IMPV.MS) $\in$ {ACT, DIR}; RC_Se_{64} שְׁמַע בְּקוֹלָם 8:22b

e_{65} (QTL.2MS) $\in$ {ACT, PFV, DEO}; $Re_{64} = e_{65}$ וְהִמְלַכְתָּ לָהֶם מֶלֶךְ 8:22c

e_{66} (WAYY.3MS) $\in$ {ACT, PFV, DECL}; $e_{63} < e_{66}$ וַיֹּאמֶר שְׁמוּאֵל אֶל־אַנְשֵׁי יִשְׂרָאֵל 8:22d

e_{67} (IMPV.MP) $\in$ {ACT, DIR}; RC_Se_{67} לְכוּ אִישׁ לְעִירוֹ: פ 8:22e

The warning with which Samuel ends his speech (e_{51-53}) consists of a temporal protasis-apodosis construction, each part of which has an overt adverbial temporal marker בַּיּוֹם הַהוּא 'on that day' that anaphorically links the construction to the stative summary statement in e_{50}: 'when you cry out *on that day*, . . . Yhwh will not answer you *on that day*'. However, while the protasis is interpreted as modally anaphoric to e_{50}, the apodosis is anchored by the protasis itself, just like the conditional construction in example [4.51] (p. 324), absent the obligation modal sense. Intervening between these two events is the *qatal* relative clause, which is interpreted as future perfect in the predictive context (e_{52}): 'whom you will have chosen'.[38]

The response from the people is another reported speech, framed by two narrative events (e_{54-55}) that narratively follow the framing of Samuel's speech (e_{36}). The people's speech consists of a pattern similar to Samuel's: a leading *yiqtol* הָיָה sets the reference time (e_{56}) and is modified by a series of irrealis *qatal* final clauses (e_{57-60}). Samuel conveys the people's response to Yhwh, who responds in turn to Samuel in a series of three narrative clauses (e_{61-63}) that link back as continuous with e_{55}.

Yhwh's brief speech consists of two irrealis clauses: an Imperative (e_{64}) and an irrealis *qatal* (e_{65}). The distinction between these two directive expressions is uncertain. It may be that we should see the second as giving more-precise instructions regarding the former: 'listen to their voice; (that is,) you should make a king for them'. This is followed by one final narrative-reported speech cycle, in which Samuel again addresses the people (e_{66}) and tells them to disband and go home (e_{67}). This final episode nicely illustrates the alternation of narrative and speech, in which each narrative event links successively to the preceding, while each reported speech receives a deictically independent temporal interpretation.

4.4.2. Exodus 12 (Irrealis Instruction)

While irrealis mode interpretations are found scattered throughout the example of narrative discourse above (§4.4.1; e.g., conditional constructions, final clauses, or directive commands), I noted in §4.4 that there are a variety of modes of interpretation in which irrealis forms predominate, mostly with a modal sense of obligation.[39] Rather than focus here on more-monolithic examples (e.g., modal genericity in Exodus 20, the modal continuity of Exodus 25–31 or Leviticus 1–6), I analyze Exodus 12, which contains a more-complex series of irrealis clauses, outlining the directions for observing the Passover and Feast of Unleavened Bread. The "episode" divisions are based on the logic

---

38. This overt future perfect interpretation is not required in English: 'whom you chose' is possible, but within the context in which the people have yet to choose a king, it is implied that it is past with respect to the future deictic context in which it appears.

39. Habitual stands out as the main exception to this and stands somewhere between modal continuity and temporal genericity in its character (see Cook 2005: 118 and sources cited there for discussion of habitual as a subcategory of generics).

of the instructions themselves rather than, for example, scene shifts of the sort used in the analysis of the narrative passage above (§4.4.1). The first episode, Exod 12:1–5, is given in example [4.58].

[4.58] Step 1: Selection of lamb (Exod 12:1–5)

e_1 (WAYY.3MS) $\in$ {ACT, PFV, DECL}; $e_1 < C_N$	וַיֹּאמֶר יְהוָה אֶל־מֹשֶׁה וְאֶל־אַהֲרֹן בְּאֶרֶץ מִצְרַיִם לֵאמֹר:	12:1
e_2 (NULL) $\in$ {STA, PFV, DECL}; $C_S \subseteq_{e2}$	הַחֹדֶשׁ הַזֶּה לָכֶם רֹאשׁ חֳדָשִׁים	12:2a
e_3 (NULL) $\in$ {STA, PFV, DECL}; $C_S \subseteq_{e3}$	רִאשׁוֹן הוּא לָכֶם לְחָדְשֵׁי הַשָּׁנָה:	12:2b
e_4 (MP.IPV) $\in$ {ACT, DEO}; $R_O C_S e_4$	דַּבְּרוּ אֶל־כָּל־עֲדַת יִשְׂרָאֵל לֵאמֹר	12:3a
e_5 (YQTL.3MP) $\in$ {ACC, IPFV, DEO}; $\forall$w: $R_O w e_5$	בֶּעָשֹׂר לַחֹדֶשׁ הַזֶּה וְיִקְחוּ לָהֶם אִישׁ שֶׂה לְבֵית־אָבֹת שֶׂה לַבָּיִת:	12:3b
e_6 (YQTL.3MS) $\in$ {STA, IPFV, COND}; $R_C e_6 e_5$	וְאִם־יִמְעַט הַבַּיִת מִהְיֹת מִשֶּׂה	12:4a
e_7 (QTL.3MS) $\in$ {ACT, PFV, DEO}; $R_O e_6 \rightarrow e_7$	וְלָקַח הוּא וּשְׁכֵנוֹ הַקָּרֹב אֶל־בֵּיתוֹ בְּמִכְסַת נְפָשֹׁת	12:4b
e_8 (YQTL.2MP) $\in$ {ACT, IPFV, DEO}; $R_O e_8 \subseteq e_5$	אִישׁ לְפִי אָכְלוֹ תָּכֹסּוּ עַל־הַשֶּׂה:	12:4c
e_9 (YQTL.3MS) $\in$ {STA, IPFV, DEO}; $R_O e_9 \subseteq e_5$	שֶׂה תָמִים זָכָר בֶּן־שָׁנָה יִהְיֶה לָכֶם	12:5a
e_{10} (YQTL.2MP) $\in$ {ACC, IPFV, DEO}; $R_O e_{10} \subseteq e_5$	מִן־הַכְּבָשִׂים וּמִן־הָעִזִּים תִּקָּחוּ:	12:5b

This instructional section regarding the Passover and Festival of Unleavened bread is framed within narrative; hence, the first event (e_1) is a narrative event that temporally locates the event prior to the deictic center of the narrator. Immediately, the account shifts to reported speech, which then carries through to the end of the account. The verbless clauses of e_2–e_3 are static; the directive meaning often assigned to them (e.g., 'this month shall mark for you . . .' NJPS, NRSV) is a pragmatic implicature (versus a semantic interpretation) based on the directive context. In turn, these static events set the discourse-pragmatic context for the following imperative (e_4): '(Now) speak . . .'.

The following event (e_5) introduces another level of reported speech: the content of what Moses is to say to the people. Notably the verb is prefixed by the *waw* conjunction but also preceded by a temporal subordinate phrase, pointing to the role of conjunction here as indicating irrealis mood VS word order in a manner typical of its customary appearance on irrealis *qatal*. The morphology allows either a deontic *yiqtol* or Jussive interpretation: 'each should take' or 'let each of them take'. One could argue for a Jussive analysis on the basis that the shift from the Imperative is due to the shift to third person, and thus continuity would dictate remaining with directive forms. However, one might equally argue that the shift from the Imperative to the irrealis *yiqtol* is motivated by the shift from subjective modal deixis of God's command to Moses to the objective modality of the instructions for observing Passover.[40] Following the latter tack, I have analyzed e_5 as having a modal generic interpretation,

---

40. This uncertainty illustrates the sometimes difficult and always context-sensitive task of discerning objective versus subjective directive expressions.

though the universal obligation is lexically anchored in the 'tenth day of the month'.

The remainder of this first episode consist of events tied to the lead instruction in e_5. The protasis in e_6 is interpreted as modally anaphorically related to e_5, dealing as it does with a "special case" (family size) regarding the lead obligation in e_5. The apodosis e_7 is then anaphorically related to the protasis, as with other conditional and temporal expressions examined already above. The choice between irrealis *qatal*, as here, and irrealis *yiqtol* for the apodosis seems to be strictly a word-order-motivated choice: in the *yiqtol* apodosis in example [4.51] (p. 324), an adjunct phrase is fronted, whereas here, the irrealis *qatal* is clause initial. (In neither case is there an overt subject.) The final three events, e_{8-10}, are all elaborating the head command in e_5, and hence they are also anaphorically anchored to that event.

In the second episode, in example [4.59], directions are given regarding the cooking and eating of the pascal lamb. The episode begins with the irrealis *qatal* copula וְהָיָה (e_{11}), which is modally continous with the previous event, e_{10}. This interpretation is reinforced by the temporal phrase עַד אַרְבָּעָה עָשָׂר יוֹם לַחֹדֶשׁ הַזֶּה: '(So) it must remain in your care (lit., an obligation to you) *until the fourteenth day of this month*'.

[4.59] Step 2: Cooking and eating a lamb (Exod 12:6–11)

e_{11} (qtl.3ms) $\in$ {STA, PFV, DECL}; $R_OC_Se_{11}$	וְהָיָה לָכֶם לְמִשְׁמֶרֶת עַד אַרְבָּעָה עָשָׂר יוֹם לַחֹדֶשׁ הַזֶּה	12:6a
e_{12} (QTL.3P) $\in$ {ACC, PFV, DEO}; $R_Oe_{11 < }e_{12}$	וְשָׁחֲטוּ אֹתוֹ כֹּל קְהַל עֲדַת־יִשְׂרָאֵל בֵּין הָעַרְבָּיִם:	12:6b
e_{13} (QTL.3P) $\in$ {ACC, PFV, DEO}; $R_Oe_{12 < }e_{13}$	וְלָקְחוּ מִן־הַדָּם	12:7a
e_{14} (QTL.3P) $\in$ {ACC, PFV, DEO}; $R_Oe_{13 < }e_{14}$	וְנָתְנוּ עַל־שְׁתֵּי הַמְּזוּזֹת וְעַל־הַמַּשְׁקוֹף עַל הַבָּתִּים	12:7b
e_{15} (YQTL.3MP) $\in$ {ACT, IPFV, DECL}; $e_{14 < }e_{15}$	אֲשֶׁר־יֹאכְלוּ אֹתוֹ בָּהֶם:	12:7c
e_{16} (QTL.3P) $\in$ {ACT, PFV, DEO}; $R_Oe_{15 < }e_{16}$	וְאָכְלוּ אֶת־הַבָּשָׂר בַּלַּיְלָה הַזֶּה	12:8a
e_{17} (YQTL.3MP) $\in$ {ACT, IPFV, DEO}; $R_Oe_{17 = }e_{16}$	צְלִי־אֵשׁ וּמַצּוֹת עַל־מְרֹרִים יֹאכְלֻהוּ:	12:8b
e_{18} (JUSS.2MP) $\in$ {ACT, NEG-DIR}; $R_OC_Se_{18}$	אַל־תֹּאכְלוּ מִמֶּנּוּ נָא וּבָשֵׁל מְבֻשָּׁל בַּמָּיִם כִּי אִם־צְלִי־אֵשׁ רֹאשׁוֹ עַל־כְּרָעָיו וְעַל־קִרְבּוֹ:	12:9
e_{19} (YQTL.2MP) $\in$ {ACC, NEG-IPFV, DEO}; $R_Oe_{17 < }e_{19}$	וְלֹא־תוֹתִירוּ מִמֶּנּוּ עַד־בֹּקֶר	12:10a
e_{20} (YQTL.2MP) $\in$ {ACT, IPFV, DEO}; $e_{20} \cap e_{19}$	וְהַנֹּתָר מִמֶּנּוּ עַד־בֹּקֶר בָּאֵשׁ תִּשְׂרֹפוּ:	12:10b
e_{21} (YQTL.2MP) $\in$ {ACT, IPFV, DEO}; $R_Oe_{21}e_{19}$	וְכָכָה תֹּאכְלוּ אֹתוֹ מָתְנֵיכֶם חֲגֻרִים נַעֲלֵיכֶם בְּרַגְלֵיכֶם וּמַקֶּלְכֶם בְּיֶדְכֶם	12:11a
e_{22} (QTL.2MP) $\in$ {ACT, PFV, DEO}; $R_Oe_{22}e_{17}$	וַאֲכַלְתֶּם אֹתוֹ בְּחִפָּזוֹן	12:11b
e_{23} (NULL) $\in$ {STA, PFV, DECL}; $C_S \subseteq_{e_{23}}$	פֶּסַח הוּא לַיהוָה:	12:11c

Having begun with the static yet continous copular statement in e_{11}, the episode continues with a series of events interpreted as modal continuity, providing the step-by-step instructions for preparing and eating the lamb ($e_{12-14, 16}$). The *yiqtol* relative clause (e_{15}) interrupting this continuity series anaphorically places the reference time of eating after the application of the blood: 'in which you will be eating it'. Two deontic events also interrupt the series of modal continuity: e_{17} equivalent to e_{16}, providing further details about preparing the lamb in inverted order with the the former (see example [4.51], p. 324, for a similar structure). The following e_{18} stands out from the surrounding discourse as being a negative directive, interpreted as modal deixis. As such, it seems to function as an apostrophe, a sort of annotation to the directions: 'make sure not to eat any of it boiled in water'. The following two events, e_{19-20}, then seem to pick up on the modal continuity mode in unison, as a negative-positive pair of instructions. The last two verbal clauses in the episode also function as a pair (e_{21-22}), anaphorically related to the e_{17}, providing directions on the manner in which the meal is to be eaten, and then ending with the null-copula summary statement, e_{23}.

[4.60] Step 3: Yhwh's Passover (Exod 12:12–13)

e_{24} (QTL.1s) $\in$ {ACC, PFV, COND}; $R_C e_{24} e_{17}$	וְעָבַרְתִּי בְאֶרֶץ־מִצְרַיִם בַּלַּיְלָה הַזֶּה	12:12a
e_{25} (QTL.1s) $\in$ {ACT, PFV, DECL}; $Re_{24} \rightarrow e_{25}$	וְהִכֵּיתִי כָל־בְּכוֹר בְּאֶרֶץ מִצְרַיִם מֵאָדָם וְעַד־בְּהֵמָה	12:12b
e_{26} (QTL.1s) $\in$ {ACT, IPFV, DECL}; $e_{26} \cap e_{25}$	וּבְכָל־אֱלֹהֵי מִצְרַיִם אֶעֱשֶׂה שְׁפָטִים	12:12c
e_{27} (NULL) $\in$ {STA, PFV, DECL}; $C_S \subseteq e_{27}$	אֲנִי יְהוָה׃	12:12d
e_{28} (QTL.3MS) $\in$ {STA, PFV, DECL}; $R_C e_{24} \rightarrow e_{28}$	וְהָיָה הַדָּם לָכֶם לְאֹת עַל הַבָּתִּים	12:13a
e_{30} (NULL) $\in$ {STA, PFV, DECL}; $e_{28} \subseteq e_{30}$	אֲשֶׁר אַתֶּם שָׁם	12:13b
e_{31} (QTL.1s) $\in$ {ACT, PFV, COND}; $R_C e_{28} < e_{31}$	וְרָאִיתִי אֶת־הַדָּם	12:13c
e_{32} (QTL.1s) $\in$ {ACC, PFV, DECL}; $R_C e_{31} < e_{32}$	וּפָסַחְתִּי עֲלֵכֶם	12:13d
e_{33} (YQTL.3MS) $\in$ {ACC, IPFV, NEG-DECL}; $C_S < e_{33}$	וְלֹא־יִהְיֶה בָכֶם נֶגֶף לְמַשְׁחִית בְּהַכֹּתִי בְּאֶרֶץ מִצְרָיִם׃	12:13e

The third episode is notably lacking in deontic expressions. Rather, in balance with the previous series of procedural instructions for observing the Passover, Yhwh informs them what he, for his part, will do on the night when they are observing it. The first event, e_{24}, might be interpreted as temporal continuity with respect to the last-mentioned bounded event (e_{22}). However, the anaphoric temporal expression 'on this night' suggests that the event is also temporally anaphoric, linked to e_{16}, in which that same temporal phrase occurs earlier. At the same time, e_{24} serves as the temporal condition to which the following event (e_{25}) is anaphorically related as its temporal apodosis. The following clause, e_{26}, also relates anaphorically to the preceding: the inverted-order *yiqtol* clause balances with the preceding, expressing the actions that

Yhwh will concurrently ($\cap$) undertake against the Egyptians: striking down their firstborns and passing judgment on their gods.

The null-copula expression of e_{27} is an apostrophe that reads almost like a messenger formula within prophetic discourse ('thus Yhwh has said'). The temporal deixis interpretation anchors the event to the speaker's deictic center of Yhwh's speech to Moses (see e_1). Following this, e_{28} resumes the apodosis anaphorically anchored to e_{24}: 'when I pass . . . I will strike . . . and the blood will be . . .'. The following null-copula stative expression (e_{29}) is included within the reference time of the stative e_{28}, which in turn is anchored to e_{24}. The events in e_{31-32} could be treated as an additional temporal protasis-apodosis series: 'when I see, then I will'; however, it is just as possible and simpler to take them as a continuation of the apodosis that is continuous with e_{28}: 'then I will see, and then I will pass over'. The final negative הָיָה clause (e_{33}) is deictically anchored to the speech time and serves as a summary statement for this portion of the instructions: 'in this way, a plague will not come against you'.

The final episode, given in example [4.61], begins with the copular statement in e_{34} expressing the commemoration as an obligation. As a stative with a temporal expression, this initial statement serves as the anaphoric grounding for what follows. The inverted word order and alternation between irrealis *qatal* and irrealis *yiqtol* in e_{35-36} tie the two events together as referring to the same commemoration: e_{35} is thus anaphorically included in the time of e_{34}, and e_{36} temporally overlaps with e_{35}. The remaining events, e_{37-52}, are all grounded anaphorically to e_{34}, reinforced in particular by the numerous temporal phrases.

[4.61]   Step 4: Commemoration (Exod 20:14–20)

e_{34} (QTL.3MS) $\in$ {STA, PFV, DECL}; $R_0C_Se_{34}$	וְהָיָה הַיּוֹם הַזֶּה לָכֶם לְזִכָּרוֹן	12:14a
e_{35} (QTL.2MP) $\in$ {ACT, PFV, DEO}; $R_0e_{35} \subseteq e_{34}$	וְחַגֹּתֶם אֹתוֹ חַג לַיהוָה	12:14b
e_{36} (QTL.2MP) $\in$ {ACT, IPFV, DEO}; $R_0e_{36} \cap e_{35}$	לְדֹרֹתֵיכֶם חֻקַּת עוֹלָם תְּחָגֻּהוּ:	12:14c
e_{37} (QTL.2MP) $\in$ {ACT, IPFV, DEO}; $R_0e_{37} \subseteq e_{34}$	שִׁבְעַת יָמִים מַצּוֹת תֹּאכֵלוּ	12:15a
e_{38} (QTL.2MP) $\in$ {ACC, IPFV, DEO}; $R_0e_{38} \subseteq e_{34}$	אַךְ בַּיּוֹם הָרִאשׁוֹן תַּשְׁבִּיתוּ שְּׂאֹר מִבָּתֵּיכֶם	12:15b
e_{39} (QTL.3FS) $\in$ {ACC, PFV, DEO}; $R_0e_{39} \subseteq e_{34}$	כִּי כָּל־אֹכֵל חָמֵץ וְנִכְרְתָה הַנֶּפֶשׁ הַהִוא מִיִּשְׂרָאֵל מִיּוֹם הָרִאשֹׁן עַד־יוֹם הַשְּׁבִעִי:	12:15c
e_{40} (NULL) $\in$ {STA, PFV, DEO}; $R_0e_{40} \subseteq e_{34}$	וּבַיּוֹם הָרִאשׁוֹן מִקְרָא־קֹדֶשׁ	12:16a
e_{41} (YQTL.3MS) $\in$ {STA, IPFV, DEO}; $R_0e_{41} \subseteq e_{34}$	וּבַיּוֹם הַשְּׁבִיעִי מִקְרָא־קֹדֶשׁ יִהְיֶה לָכֶם	12:16b
e_{42} (YQTL.3MS) $\in$ {ACT, NEG-IPFV, DEO}; $R_0e_{42} \subseteq e_{34}$	כָּל־מְלָאכָה לֹא־יֵעָשֶׂה בָהֶם	12:16c
e_{43} (YQTL.3MS) $\in$ {ACT, IPFV, DEO}; $R_0e_{43} \subseteq e_{34}$	אַךְ אֲשֶׁר יֵאָכֵל לְכָל־נֶפֶשׁ	12:16d
e_{44} (YQTL.3MS) $\in$ {ACT, IPFV, DEO}; $R_0e_{44} \subseteq e_{34}$	הוּא לְבַדּוֹ יֵעָשֶׂה לָכֶם:	12:16e
e_{45} (QTL.2MP) $\in$ {ACT, PFV, DEO}; $R_0e_{45} \subseteq e_{34}$	וּשְׁמַרְתֶּם אֶת־הַמַּצּוֹת	12:17a
e_{46} (QTL.1S) $\in$ {ACC, PFV, DECL}; $R_0e_{46} \subseteq e_{34}$	כִּי בְּעֶצֶם הַיּוֹם הַזֶּה הוֹצֵאתִי אֶת־צִבְאוֹתֵיכֶם מֵאֶרֶץ מִצְרָיִם	12:17b
e_{47} (QTL.2MP) $\in$ {ACT, PFV, DEO}; $R_0e_{47} \subseteq e_{34}$	וּשְׁמַרְתֶּם אֶת־הַיּוֹם הַזֶּה לְדֹרֹתֵיכֶם חֻקַּת עוֹלָם:	12:17c

[4.61]   Step 4: Commemoration (Exod 20:14–20)

e_{48} (QTL.2MP) $\in$ {ACT, IPFV, DEO}; $R_0e_{48} \subseteq e_{34}$ בָּרִאשֹׁן בְּאַרְבָּעָה עָשָׂר יוֹם לַחֹדֶשׁ   12:18

בָּעֶרֶב תֹּאכְלוּ מַצֹּת עַד יוֹם הָאֶחָד

וְעֶשְׂרִים לַחֹדֶשׁ בָּעָרֶב:

e_{49} (YQTL.3MS) $\in$ {ACC, NEG-IPFV, DEO}; $R_0e_{49} \subseteq e_{34}$ שִׁבְעַת יָמִים שְׂאֹר לֹא יִמָּצֵא בְּבָתֵּיכֶם   12:19a

e_{50} (QTL.3FS) $\in$ {ACC, PFV, DEO}; $R_0e_{50} \subseteq e_{34}$ כִּי כָּל־אֹכֵל מַחְמֶצֶת וְנִכְרְתָה הַנֶּפֶשׁ   12:19b

הַהִוא מֵעֲדַת יִשְׂרָאֵל בַּגֵּר וּבְאֶזְרַח

הָאָרֶץ:

e_{51} (YQTL.2MP) $\in$ {ACT, IPFV, DEO}; $R_0e_{51} \subseteq e_{34}$ כָּל־מַחְמֶצֶת לֹא תֹאכֵלוּ   12:20a

e_{52} (YQTL.2MP) $\in$ {ACT, IPFV, DEO}; $R_0e_{52} \subseteq e_{34}$ בְּכֹל מוֹשְׁבֹתֵיכֶם תֹּאכְלוּ מַצּוֹת: פ   12:20b

4.5. Conclusion

The focus of this chapter is the discourse pragmatics of the BHVS from the perspective of the semantic analysis in chap. 3. In the course of the chapter, I have been concerned with several issues here: first, that semantics be given priority over discourse pragmatics in analyzing the BHVS (§4.1). The passages treated in this chapter illustrate the fact that a variety of factors contribute to the temporal interpretation of the verbal forms and that having the semantics clear first enables the interpreter to distinguish between semantic and discourse-pragmatic elements.

Second, the negative goal of this chapter is my argument against the traditional point of view that BH has verb forms that explicitly indicate temporal succession (i.e., *wayyiqtol* and irrealis *qatal*; §§4.2–4.3). Again, by beginning with semantics, I have shown how properly to attribute the interpretation of temporal succession to semantic and discourse pragmatic factors. In particular, the two domains interact: on the one hand, the semantics of the past perfective *wayyiqtol* makes it the verb of choice in prose narrative, in which discourse-based iconic ordering is the default interpretation; on the other hand, the association of *wayyiqtol* with prose narrative, which is by default temporally successive, leads to the implicature of temporal succession in poetic contexts, where the default mode is static parallelistic rather than successive between events.

Third, I presented a model with which the temporality of interclausal relationships may be approached from a semantic foundation (§4.4). I illustrated the basic scheme with short excerpts (parade examples) and then follow this with examinations of lengthier selections of prose narrative (1 Samuel 8) and instructional material (Exodus 12). At this point, the linguistic investigation fades into philological and literary interpretation. Throughout, my aim has been to illustrate that a methodology that begins with a rigorous semantic analysis and then progresses to discourse-pragmatics and finally to general interpretation (i.e., sensitivity to the literary context) provides a round and comprehensive interpretation of BH texts that conforms to the principle of compositionality: identifying in each case the contributing factor(s) that leads to the most compelling interpretation. In this way, the exercises also produce more-competent readers of the ancient texts of the Bible.

Works Cited

Akman, V.
2006 Situation Semantics. Pp. 98–400 in vol. 10 of *Encyclopedia of Language and Linguistics*, ed. Keith Brown. Amsterdam: Elsevier.

Albright, W. F.
1937 The Egyptian Correspondence of Abimilki, Prince of Tyre. *Journal of Egyptian Archaeology* 23: 190–203.
1942a A Teacher to a Man of Shechem about 1400 B.C. *Bulletin of the American Schools of Oriental Research* 86: 28–31.
1942b A Case of Lèse-Magesté in Pre-Israelite Lachish, with Some Remarks on the Israelite Conquest. *Bulletin of the American Schools of Oriental Research* 87: 32–38.
1943a Two Little Understood Amarna Letters from the Middle Jordan Valley. *Bulletin of the American Schools of Oriental Research* 89: 7–17.
1943b An Archaic Hebrew Proverb in an Amarna Letter from Central Palestine. *Bulletin of the American Schools of Oriental Research* 89: 29–32.

Albright, W. F., and William L. Moran
1948 A Re-interpretation of an Amarna Letter from Byblos. *Journal of Cuneiform Studies* 2: 239–48.

Allen, Joseph Henry, J. B. Greenough, George Lyman Kittredge, Albert Andrew Howard, and Benjamin L. D'Ooge
[1888] 1931 *Allen and Greenough's New Latin Grammar for Schools and Colleges*. Boston: Ginn.

Allen, Robert L.
1966 *The Verb System of Present-Day American English*. The Hauge: Mouton.

Allwood, Jens, Lars-Gunnar Andersson, and Östen Dahl
1977 *Logic in Linguistics*. Cambridge: Cambridge University Press.

Andersen, Francis I., and A. Dean Forbes
2007 The Participle in Biblical Hebrew and the Overlap of Grammar and Lexicon. Pp. 185–212 in *Milk and Honey: Essays on Ancient Israel and the Bible in Appreciation of the Judaic Studies Program at the University of California, San Diego*, ed. Sarah Malena and David Miano. Winona Lake, IN: Eisenbrauns.

Andersen, T. David
2000 The Evolution of the Hebrew Verbal System. *Zeitschrift für Althebräistik* 13: 1–66.

Anderson, J. M.
1973 *An Essay Concerning Aspect*. The Hague: Mouton.

Andrason, Alex
2010   The Panchronic *Yiqtol*: Functionally Consistent and Cognitively Plausible. *Journal of Hebrew Scriptures* 10. http://www.jhsonline.org/.
2011a   Biblical Hebrew *Wayyiqtol*: A Dynamic Definition. *Journal of Hebrew Scriptures* 11. http://www.jhsonline.org/.
2011b   The Biblical Hebrew Verbal System in Light of Grammaticalization. *Hebrew Studies* 52: 19–51.
2011c   The BH *Weqatal*: A Homogenous Form with No Haphazard Functions (Part 1). *Journal of Northwest Semitic Languages* 37/2: 1–26.
forthcoming   The BH *Weqatal*: A Homogenous Form with No Haphazard Functions (Part 2). *Journal of Northwest Semitic Languages*. http://www.sun.ac.za/jnsl.
Anstey, Matthew P.
2009   The Biblical Hebrew *Qatal* Verb: A Functional Discourse Grammar Analysis. *Linguistics* 47: 825–44.
Anttila, Raimo
1989   *Historical and Comparative Linguistics*. 2nd rev. ed. Current Issues in Linguistic Theory. Amsterdam: Benjamins.
Arnold, Bill T., and John H. Choi
2003   *A Guide to Biblical Hebrew Syntax*. New York: Cambridge University Press.
Austin, J. L.
1962   *How to Do Things with Words*. Oxford: Clarendon.
Auwera, Johan van der, Nina Dobrushina, and Valentin Goussev
2005   Imperative-Hortative Systems. Pp. 294–97 in *The World Atlas of Language Structures*, ed. Martin Haspelmath and Hans-Jörg Bibiko. Munich: Max Planck Digital Library.
Baayen, R. Harald
1997   The Pragmatics of the 'Tenses' in Biblical Hebrew. *Studies in Language* 21: 245–85.
Bach, Emmon
1986   The Algebra of Events. *Linguistics and Philosophy* 9: 5–16.
Bache, Carl
1982   Aspect and Aktionsart: Towards a Semantic Distinction. *Journal of Linguistics* 18: 57–72.
1985   *Verbal Aspect: A General Theory and Its Application to Present-Day English*. Odense University Studies in English. Odense: Odense University Press.
1995   *The Study of Tense, Aspect and Action*. Frankfurt am Main: Peter Lang.
Baker, David W.
1973   *The Consecutive Nonperfective as Pluperfect in the Historical Books of the Hebrew Old Testament*. M.A. thesis, Regent College.
Banfield, A.
1982   *Unspeakable Sentences: Narration and Representation in the Language of Fiction*. Boston: Routledge & Kegan Paul.
Barco del Barco, Francisco Javier del
2003   *Profecía y Sintaxis: El Uso de las Formas Verbales en los Profetas Menores Preexílicos* (*Prophecy and Syntax: The Use of the Verbal Forms in the Pre-*

exilic Minor Prophets). Textos y Estudios "Cardenal Cisneros" de la Biblia Palíglota Matritense. Madrid: Instituto de Filología.

Barnes, O. L.
1965   *A New Approach to the Problem of the Hebrew Tenses*. Oxford: Thornton.

Barr, James
1971   Hebrew Linguistic Literature [from the Sixteenth Century to the Present]. Pp. 1390–1401 in vol. 16 of *Encyclopedia Judaica*. Jerusalem: Keter.

Bartelmus, Rüdiger
1982   *HYH: Bedeutung und Funktion eines hebräischen "Allerweltswortes": Zugleich ein Beitrag zur Frage des hebräischen Tempussystems*. Arbeiten zu Text und Sprache im Alten Testament. St. Ottilien: EOS.

Barwise, Jon, and John Perry
1983   *Situations and Attitudes*. Cambridge, MA: MIT Press.

Bauer, Hans
1910   Die Tempora im Semitischen. *Beiträge zur Assyriologie und semitischen Sprachwissenschaft* 81: 1–53.

Bauer, Hans, and Pontus Leander
[1922] 1991   *Historische Grammatik der hebräischen Sprache*. Reprint ed. Hildesheim: Olms.

Bellamy, John
1818   *The Holy Bible Newly Translated from the Original Hebrew with Notes, Critical and Explanatory*. London: Longman, Hurst, Rees, Orme, & Brown, Paternoster Row.

Bender, Lionel
2007   Omotic Morphology. Pp. 729–51 in *Morphologies of Africa and Asia*, ed. Alan S. Kaye. Winona Lake, IN: Eisenbrauns.

Bennett, M., and B. Partee
1978   *Toward the Logic of Tense and Aspect in English*. Bloomington, IN: Indiana University Linguistics Club.

Bennett, Patrick R.
1998   *Comparative Semitic Linguistics: A Manual*. Winona Lake, IN: Eisenbrauns.

Bentinck, Julie
1995   A Comparison of Certain Discourse Features in Biblical Hebrew and Nyaboa and Their Implications for the Translation Process. *Journal of Translation and Textlinguistics* 7/3: 25–47.

Benton, Richard Charles, Jr.
2009   *Aspect and the Biblical Hebrew Niphal and Hitpael*. Ph.D. dissertation, University of Wisconsin.

Benveniste, E.
1966   *Problèmes de linguistique générale*. Paris: Gallimard.

Benveniste, E., and M. E. Meek
1971   *Problems in General Linguistics*. Coral Gables: University of Miami Press.

Bergsträsser, Gotthelf
[1918–29] 1962   *Hebräische Grammatik*. Reprint. Hildesheim: Georg Olms.
1983   *Introduction to the Semitic Languages*, trans. Peter T. Daniels. Winona Lake, IN: Eisenbrauns.

Bhat, D. N. S.
1999   *The Prominence of Tense, Aspect, and Mood.* Studies in Language Companion Series. Amsterdam: Benjamins.
Bickel, Balthasar
2007   Typology in the 21st Century: Major Current Developments. *Linguistic Typology* 11: 239–51.
Bierwisch, M., and R. Schreuder
1992   From Concepts to Lexical Items. *Cognition* 42: 23–60.
Binnick, Robert I.
1991   *Time and the Verb: A Guide to Tense and Aspect.* Oxford: Oxford University Press.
Blake, Frank R.
1944a   The Hebrew *Waw* Conversive. *Journal of Biblical Literature* 63: 271–77.
1944b   Review of *Hebrew Grammar: A New Approach,* by Alexander Sperber. *Journal of Biblical Literature* 63: 195–99.
1946   The Form of Verbs after *Waw* in Hebrew. *Journal of Biblical Literature* 65: 51–57.
1951   *A Resurvey of Hebrew Tenses.* Scripta Pontificii Instituti Biblici 103. Rome: Pontifical Biblical Institute.
Blau, Joshua
1971   Marginalia Semitica I. *Israel Oriental Studies* 1: 1–35.
2010   *Phonology and Morphology of Biblical Hebrew: An Introduction.* Linguistic Studies in Ancient West Semitic 2. Winona Lake, IN: Eisenbrauns.
Bloch, A.
1963   Zur Nachweisbarkeit einer hebräischen Entsprechung der akkadischen Form *iparras. Zeitschrift der Deutschen Morgenländischen Gesellschaft* 113: 41–50.
Bobzin, H.
1973   Überlegungen zum althebräischen 'Tempus' System. *Die Welt des Orients* 7: 141–53.
Bodine, Walter R.
1995   Discourse Analysis of Biblical Literature: What It Is and What It Offers. Pp. 1–18 in *Discourse Analysis of Biblical Literature: What It Is and What It Offers,* ed. Walter R. Bodine. Society of Biblical Literature Semeia Studies. Atlanta: Scholars Press.
Boneh, Nora, and Edit Doron
2008   Habituality and Habitual Aspect. Pp. 321–48 in *Theoretical and Cross-linguistic Approaches to the Semantics of Aspect,* ed. Susan Rothstein. Amsterdam: Benjamins.
2010   Modal and Temporal Aspects of Habituality. Pp. 338–63 in *Syntax, Lexical Semantics, and Event Structure,* ed. Malka Rappaport Hovav, Edit Doron, and Ivy Sichel. Oxford: Oxford University Press.
Bordreuil, Pierre, and Dennis Pardee
2009   *A Manual of Ugaritic.* Linguistic Studies in Ancient West Semitic 3. Winona Lake, IN: Eisenbrauns.

Brockelmann, Carl
1908–13   *Gundriss der Vergleichenden Grammatik der Semitischen Sprachen.* Berlin: Reuther & Richard.
1951   Die 'Tempora' des Semitischen. *Zeitschrift für Phonetik und allgemeine Sprachwissenschaft* 5: 133–54.
1956   *Hebräische Syntax.* Neukirchen-Vluyn: Erziehungsverein.

Brown, Gillian, and George Yule
1983   *Discourse Analysis.* Cambridge Textbooks in Linguistics. Cambridge: Cambridge University Press.

Buccellati, Giorgio
1988   The State of the "Stative." Pp. 153–89 in vol. 58 of *Fucus: A Semitic/Afrasian Gathering in Remembrance of Albert Ehrman,* ed. Yoël L. Arbeitman. Amsterdam Studies in the Theory and History of Linguistic Science. Amsterdam: Benjamins.
1996   *A Structural Grammar of Old Babylonian.* Wiesbaden: Harrassowitz.
1997   Akkadian. Pp. 69–99 in *The Semitic Languages,* ed. Robert Hetzron. London: Routledge.
2003   Akkadian. Pp. 39–42 in vol. 1 of *International Encyclopedia of Linguistics,* ed. William J. Frawley. 2nd ed. New York: Oxford University Press.

Bull, William Emerson
1960   *Time, Tense, and the Verb: A Study in Theoretical and Applied Linguistics, with Particular Attention to Spanish.* University of California Publications in Linguistics. Berkeley: University of California Press.

Buth, Randall
1992   The Hebrew Verb in Current Discussions. *Journal of Translation and Text-linguistics* 5: 91–105.
1994   Methodological Collision between Source Criticism and Discourse Analysis: The Problem of "Unmarked Temporal Overlay" and the Pluperfect/Nonsequential *Wayyiqtol.* Pp. 138–54 in *Biblical Hebrew and Discourse Linguistics,* ed. Robert D. Bergen. Dallas: Summer Institute of Linguistics.

Butler, Christopher S.
2003   *Structure and Function: A Guide to Three Major Structural-Functional Theories, Part I: Approaches to the Simplex Clause.* Studies in Language Companion Series. Amsterdam: Benjamins.

Bybee, Joan L.
1985   *Morphology: A Study of the Relation between Meaning and Form.* Typological Studies in Language. Amsterdam: Benjamins.
1998   "Irrealis" as a Grammatical Category. *Anthropological Linguistics* 40: 257–71.

Bybee, Joan L., and Östen Dahl
1989   The Creation of Tense and Aspect Systems in the Languages of the World. *Studies in Language* 13: 51–103.

Bybee, Joan, Revere Perkins, and William Pagliuca
1994   *The Evolution of Grammar: Tense, Aspect, and Modality in the Languages of the World.* Chicago: University of Chicago Press.

Bybee, Joan, and Suzanne Fleischman
 1995   Modality in Grammar and Discourse: An Introductory Essay. Pp. 1–14 in *Modality in Grammar and Discourse*, ed. Joan Bybee and Suzanne Fleischman. Typological Studies in Language 32. Amsterdam: Benjamins.
Böhl, Franz M. T.
 1909   *Die Sprache der Amarnabriefe*. Leipzig: Hinrichs.
Campbell, Lyle
 2001   What's Wrong with Grammaticalization? *Language Sciences* 23: 113–61.
Cann, Ronnie
 1993   *Formal Semantics: An Introduction*. Cambridge Textbooks in Linguistics. Cambridge: Cambridge University Press.
Carlson, Gregory N.
 1995   Truth Conditions of Generic Sentences: Two Contrasting Views. Pp. 224–37 in *The Generic Book*, ed. Gregory N. Carlson and Francis Jeffry Pelletier. Chicago: University of Chicago Press.
Carroll, Lewis
 2000   *Alice's Adventures in Wonderland and Through the Looking Glass*. New York: Signet.
Chafe, Wallace
 1995   The Realis-Irrealis Distinction in Caddo, the Northern Iroquoian Languages, and English. Pp. 349–65 in *Modality in Grammar and Discourse*, ed. Joan Bybee and Suzanne Fleischman. Typological Studies in Language 32. Amsterdam: Benjamins.
Chomsky, Noam
 1981   *Lectures on Government and Binding*. Dordrecht: Foris.
Chruszczewski, P. P.
 2006   Tarski, Alfred. Pp. 507–9 in vol. 11 of *Encyclopedia of Language and Lingusitics*, ed. Keith Brown. Amsterdam: Elsevier.
Chung, Sandra, and Alan Timberlake
 1985   Tense, Aspect, and Mood. Pp. 202–58 in *Language Typology and Syntactic Description*, vol. 3: *Grammatical Categories and the Lexicon*, ed. Timothy Shopen. Cambridge: Cambridge University Press.
Cochavi-Rainey, Zipora
 1990   Tenses and Modes in Cuneiform Texts Written by Egyptian Scribes in the Late Bronze Age. *Ugarit-Forschungen* 22: 5–23.
Cohen, Marcel
 1924   *Le système verbal sémitique et l'expression du temps*. Paris: Imprimerie nationale.
Collins, Clifford John
 1995   The *Wayyiqtol* as Pluperfect: When and Why? *Tyndale Bulletin* 46: 117–40.
Comrie, Bernard
 1976   *Aspect*. Cambridge Textbooks in Linguistics. Cambridge: Cambridge University Press.
 1985   *Tense*. Cambridge Textbooks in Linguistics. Cambridge: Cambridge University Press.

1986 Tense and Time Reference: From Meaning to Interpretation in the Chronological Structure of a Text. *Journal of Literary Semantics* 15: 12–22.
1994 Tense. Pp. 4558–63 in *The Encyclopedia of Language and Linguistics*, ed. R. E. Asher. Oxford: Pergamon.

Cook, John A.
2001 The Hebrew Verb: A Grammaticalization Approach. *Zeitschrift für Althebräistik* 14: 117–43.
2002 *The Biblical Hebrew Verbal System: A Grammaticalization Approach*. Ph.D. dissertation, University of Wisconsin.
2003a Review of *Focus Structure in Biblical Hebrew*, by Katsuomi Shimasaki. *Catholic Biblical Quarterly* 65: 618–19.
2003b Review of *the Verbal System in Classical Hebrew in the Joseph Story: An Approach from Discourse Analysis*, by Yoshinobu Endo. *Journal of Near Eastern Studies* 62: 62–64.
2004a Review of *Profecía y Sintaxis: El Uso de las Formas Verbales en los Profetas Menores Preexílicos* [Prophecy and Syntax: The Use of the Verbal Forms in the Pre-exilic Minor Prophets], by Francisco Javier del Barco del Barco. *Hebrew Studies* 45: 336–38.
2004b The Semantics of Verbal Pragmatics: Clarifying the Roles of *Wayyiqtol* and *Weqatal* in Biblical Hebrew Prose. *Journal of Semitic Studies* 49: 247–73.
2005 Genericity, Tense, and Verbal Patterns in the Sentence Literature of Proverbs. Pp. 117–33 in *Seeking Out the Wisdom of the Ancients: Essays Offered to Honor Michael V. Fox on the Occasion of His Sixty-Fifth Birthday*, ed. Ronald L. Troxel, Kelvin G. Friebel, and Dennis R. Magary. Winona Lake, IN: Eisenbrauns.
2006a The Finite Verbal Forms in Biblical Hebrew Do Express Aspect. *Journal of the Ancient Near Eastern Society* 30: 21–35.
2006b Review of *Biblical Narrative and the Death of the Rhapsode*, by Robert S. Kawashima. *Hebrew Studies* 47: 439–43.
2006c Review of *Narrative Structure and Discourse Constellations: An Analysis of Clause Function in Biblical Hebrew Prose*, by Roy L. Heller. *Catholic Biblical Quarterly* 68: 116–17.
2008a The Participle and Stative in Typological Perspective. *Journal of Northwest Semitic Languages* 34: 1–19.
2008b The *Vav*-Prefixed Verb Forms in Elementary Hebrew Grammar. *Journal of Hebrew Scriptures* 8. http://www.jhsonline.org/.
2010 Review of a New Understanding of the Verbal System of Classical Hebrew: An Attempt to Distinguish between Semantic and Pragmatic Factors, by Rolf J. Furuli. *Journal of Near Eastern Studies* 69: 249–51.
2012 Detecting Development in Biblical Hebrew Using Diachronic Typology. Pp. 83–95 in *Diachrony in Biblical Hebrew*, ed. Cynthia L. Miller-Naudé and Ziony Zevit. Linguistic Studies in Ancient West Semitic 8. Winona Lake, IN: Eisenbrauns.
forthcoming The Verb in Qoheleth. In *Like Goads: Engaging Qoheleth in the 21st Century*, ed. in Mark J. Boda, Tremper Longman III, and Cristian Rata. Winona Lake, IN: Eisenbrauns.

Croft, William
2003   *Typology and Universals.* 2d ed. Cambridge Textbooks in Linguistics. Cambridge: Cambridge University Press.
Crystal, David
2008   *A Dictionary of Linguistics and Phonetics.* 6th ed. Oxford: Blackwell.
Curtius, Georg
1846   *Die Bildung der Tempora und Modi im Grieschen und Lateinischen sprachvergleichend dargestellt.* Berlin: Wilhelm Besser.
1863   *Erläuterungen zu meiner Griechischen Schulgrammatik.* Prague: Tempsky.
1870   *Elucidations of the Student's Greek Grammar,* trans. Evelyn Abbott. London: John Murray.
Dahl, Östen
1985   *Tense and Aspect Systems.* Oxford: Blackwell.
1994   Aspect. Pp. 240–47 in *The Encyclopedia of Language and Linguistics,* ed. R. E. Asher. Oxford: Pergamon.
1997   Review of *Time in Language,* by Wolfgang Klein. *Studies in Language* 21: 417–28.
2000   *Tense and Aspect in the Languages of Europe.* Empirical Approaches to Language Typology 20-6. Berlin: de Gruyter.
Dallaire, Hélène
2002   *The Syntax of Volitives in Northwest Semitic Prose.* Ph.D. dissertation, Hebrew Union College.
Davidson, A. B.
1901   *Introductory Hebrew Grammar: Hebrew Syntax.* 3rd ed. Edinburgh: T. & T. Clark.
Dawson, David Allan
1994   *Text-Linguistics and Biblical Hebrew.* Journal for the Study of the Old Testament Supplement 177. Sheffield: Sheffield Academic Press.
Decaen, Vincent
1995   *On the Placement and Interpretation of the Verb in Standard Biblical Hebrew Prose.* Ph.D. dissertation, University of Toronto.
1996   Ewald and Driver on Biblical Hebrew 'Aspect'. *Zeitschrift für Althebräistik* 9: 129–51.
1999   A Unified Analysis of Verbal and Verbless Clauses within Government-Binding Theory. Pp. 109–31 in *The Verbless Clause in Biblical Hebrew: Linguistic Approaches,* ed. Cynthia L. Miller. Linguistic Studies in Ancient West Semitic 1. Winona Lake, IN: Eisenbrauns.
Declerck, Renaat
1986   From Reichenbach (1947) to Comrie (1985) and Beyond. *Lingua* 70: 305–64.
1989   Boundedness and the Structure of Situations. *Leuvense Bijdragen* 78: 275–308.
Dekker, P. J. E., and H. L. W. Hendriks
1994   Situation Semantics. Pp. 3954–60 in *The Encyclopedia of Language and Linguistics,* ed. R. E. Asher. Oxford: Pergamon.
DeLancey, Scott
1987   Transitivity in Grammar and Cognition. Pp. 53–68 in *Coherence and Grounding in Discourse,* ed. Russell S. Tomlin. Amsterdam: Benjamins.

Dempster, Stephen G.
1985   *Linguistic Features of Hebrew Narrative: A Discourse Analysis of Narrative from the Classical Period.* Ph.D. dissertation, University of Toronto.
Depraetere, Ilse
1995   On the Necessity of Distinguishing between (Un)Boundedness and (a)Telicity. *Linguistics and Philosophy* 18: 1–19.
DeRouchie, Jason S.
2007   *A Call to Covenant Love: Text Grammar and Literary Structure in Deuteronomy 5–11.* Gorgias Dissertations in Biblical Studies 30. Piscataway, NJ: Gorgias.
Dhorme, Paul (Edouard)
1913–14   La Langue de Canaan. *Revue biblique* 10–11: 369–93, 405–87.
Diakonoff, I. M.
1965   *Semito-Hamitic Languages: An Essay in Classification.* Languages of Asia and Africa. Moscow: Nauka.
1988   *Afrasian Languages.* Languages of Asia and Africa. Moscow: Nauka.
1990   The Importance of Ebla for History and Linguistics. Pp. 3–29 in *Eblaitica: Essays on the Ebla Archives and Eblaite Language*, vol. 2, ed. Cyrus H. Gordon and Gary A. Rendsburg. Winona Lake, IN: Eisenbraun.
Dik, Simon
1997   *The Theory of Functional Grammar, Part 1: The Structure of the Clause.* 2nd ed. Functional Grammar Series. Berlin: de Gruyter.
Dillmann, August
[1899] 1974   *Ethiopic Grammar*, trans. James A. Chrichton. 2nd ed. Amsterdam: Philo.
Dobbs-Allsopp, F. W.
2004–7   (More) on Performatives in Semitic. *Zeitschrift für Althebräistik* 17–20: 36–81.
Donner, Herbert, and Wolfgang Röllig
2002   *Kanaanäische und aramäische Inschriften*, vol. 1. 5th ed. Wiesbaden: Harrassowitz.
Downing, Pamela
1995   Word Order in Discourse: By Way of Introduction. Pp. 1–27 in *Word Order in Discourse*, ed. Pamela Downing and Michael Noonan. Typological Studies in Language 30. Amsterdam: Benjamins.
Dowty, David R.
1977   Semantic Analysis of Verb Aspect and the English Imperfective Progressive. *Linguistics and Philosophy* 1: 45–77.
1979   *Word Meaning and Montague Grammar.* Synthese Language Library. Dordrecht: Reidel.
1986   The Effect of Aspectual Classes on the Temporal Structure of Discourse: Semantics or Pragmatics? *Linguistics and Philosophy* 9: 37–61.
Driver, G. R.
1936   *Problems of the Hebrew Verbal System.* Edinburgh: T. & T. Clark.

Driver, S. R.
[1892] 1998   *A Treatise on the Use of the Tenses in Hebrew and Some Other Syn-*
                tactical Questions. 3rd ed., with an Introductory Essay by W. Randall Garr.
                Grand Rapids, MI: Eerdmans.
Dry, Helen Aristar
1981   Sentence Aspect and the Movement of Narrative Time. *Text* 1: 233–40.
1983   The Movement of Narrative Time. *Journal of Literary Semantics* 12/2: 19–53.
Dryer, Matthew S.
2005   Order of Subject and Verb. Pp. 334–37 in *The World Atlas of Language Struc-*
        tures, ed. Martin Haspelmath and Hans-Jörg Bibiko. Munich: Max Planck
        Digital Library.
Dyk, J. W.
1994   *Participles in Context: A Computer-Assisted Study of Old Testament Hebrew.*
        Amsterdam: Vrije Universiteit Press.
Dyk, Janet W., and Eep Talstra
1999   Paradigmatic and Syntagmatic Features in Identifying Subject and Predicate
        in Nominal Clauses. Pp. 133–85 in *The Verbless Clause in Biblical Hebrew:*
        Linguistic Approaches, ed. Cynthia L. Miller. Linguistic Studies in Ancient
        West Semitic 1. Winona Lake, IN: Eisenbrauns.
Ebeling, Erich
1910   Das Verbum der El-Amarna-Briefe. *Beiträge zur Assyriology* 10: 39–79.
Edelheit, Amos
1944   Blake's Review of "Hebrew Grammar: A New Approach" by Alexander
        Sperber. *Journal of Biblical Literature* 63: 438–39.
Emerton, J. A.
1994a   New Evidence for the Use of *Waw* Consecutive in Aramaic. *Vetus Testa-*
        mentum 44: 255–58.
1994b   What Light Has Ugaritic Shed on Hebrew? Pp. 53–69 in *Ugarit and the Bible:*
        Proceedings of the International Symposium on Ugarit and the Bible, Man-
        chester, September 1992, ed. George J. Brooke, Adrian Curtis, and John F.
        Healey. Ugaritisch-Biblische Literatur 11. Münster: Ugarit-Verlag.
1997   Further Comments on the Use of Tenses in the Aramaic Inscription from Tel
        Dan. *Vetus Testamentum* 47: 429–40.
Endo, Yoshinobu
1996   *The Verbal System of Classical Hebrew in the Joseph Story: An Approach*
        from Discourse Analysis. Studia Semitica Neerlandica. Assen: Van Gorcum.
Erbaugh, Mary S.
1987   A Uniform Pause and Error Strategy for Native and Non-Native Speakers.
        Pp. 109–30 in *Coherence and Grounding in Discourse,* ed. Russell S. Tomlin.
        Typological Studies in Language 11. Amsterdam: Benjamins.
Eskhult, Mats
1990   *Studies in Verbal Aspect and Narrative Technique in Biblical Hebrew Prose.*
        Studia Semitica Upsaliensia. Uppsala: Almqvist & Wiksell.
Ewald, Heinrich
1870   *Ausführliches Lehrbuch der hebräischen Sprache des Alten Bundes.* 8th ed.
        Göttingen: Dieterichschen Buchhandlung.

1879 *Syntax of the Hebrew Language of the Old Testament*, trans. James Kennedy. Edinburgh: T. & T. Clark.

Exter Blokland, A. F. den
1995 *In Search of Text Syntax: Towards a Syntactic Text-Segmentation Model for Biblical Hebrew*. Amsterdam: Vrije Universiteit Press.

Faber, Alice
1997 Genetic Subgroupings of the Semitic Languages. Pp. 3–15 in *The Semitic Languages*, ed. Robert Hetzron. London: Routledge.

Fassberg, Steven E.
1999 The Lengthened Imperative קָטְלָה in Biblical Hebrew. *Hebrew Studies* 40: 7–13.

Fensham, F. C.
1978 The Use of the Suffix Conjugation and the Prefix Conjugation in a Few Old Hebrew Poems. *Journal of Northwest Semitic Languages* 6: 9–18.

Fenton, Terry L.
1970 The Absence of a Verbal Formation *Yaqattal* from Ugaritic and North-West Semitic. *Journal of Semitic Studies* 15: 31–41.
1973 The Hebrew "Tenses" in the Light of Ugaritic. Pp. 31–39 in *Proceedings of the Fifth World Congress of Jewish Studies*, vol. 4: *Hebrew and Semitic Language, Folklore, Art and Music*. Jerusalem: World Union of Jewish Studies.

Fernald, Theodore B.
2000 *Predicates and Temporal Arguments*. New York: Oxford University Press.

Fitzgerald, Aloysius
1972 A Note on G-Stem ינצר Forms in the Old Testament. *Zeitschrift für die alttestamentliche Wissenschaft* 84: 90–92.

Fleischman, Suzanne
1990 *Tense and Narrativity*. Austin: University of Texas Press.

Folmer, Margaretha L.
1991 Some Remarks on the Use of the Finite Verb Form in the Protasis of Conditional Sentences in Aramaic Texts from the Achaemenid Period. Pp. 56–78 in *Studies in Hebrew and Aramaic Syntax*, ed. K. Jongeling, H. L. Murre-Van Ven Berg, and L. Van Rompay. Leiden: Brill.
1995 *The Aramaic Language of the Achaemenid Period: A Study in Linguistic Variation*. Orientalia Lovaniensia Analecta. Leuven: Peeters.

Forsyth, J.
1970 *A Grammar of Aspect*. Cambridge: University of Cambridge Press.

Furuli, Rolf J.
2006 *A New Understanding of the Verbal System of Classical Hebrew: An Attempt to Distinguish between Semantic and Pragmatic Factors*. Oslo: Awatu.

Gai, Amikam
1982 The Reduction of Tense (and Other Categories) of the Consequent Verb in North-West Semitic. *Orientalia* 51: 254–56.

Garr, W. Randall
1998 Driver's *Treatise* and the Study of Hebrew: Then and Now. Pp. xviii–lxxxvi in *A Treatise on the Use of the Tenses in Hebrew and Some Other* Syntactical *Questions*. 3rd ed. The Biblical Resource Series. Grand Rapids, MI: Eerdmans.

2004   *Dialect Geography of Syria–Palestine, 1000–586 B.C.E.* Reprint ed. Winona Lake, IN: Eisenbrauns.

Gell, Philip

1818   *Observations on the Idiom of the Hebrew Language.* London: n.p.

Geller, Stephen A.

1991   Cleft Sentences with Pleonastic Pronoun: A Syntactic Construction of Biblical Hebrew and Some of Its Literary Uses. *Journal of the Ancient Near Eastern Society of Columbia University* 20: 15–33.

Gentry, Peter J.

1998   The System of the Finite Verb in Classical Biblical Hebrew. *Hebrew Studies* 39: 7–39.

Gesenius, Wilhelm, Thomas Jefferson Conant, and Emil Roediger

1855   *Gesenius' Hebrew Grammar.* 17th ed. New York: Appleton.

Gibson, J. C. L.

1994   *Davidson's Introductory Hebrew Grammar: Syntax.* 4th ed. Edinburgh: T. & T. Clark.

Ginsberg, H. L.

1939   Two Religious Borrowings in Ugaritic Literature, I: A Ḫurrian Myth in Semitic Dress. *Orientalia* 8: 317–23.

Givón, Talmy

1984   *Syntax: A Functional-Typological Introduction.* Amsterdam: Benjamins.

1987   Beyond Foreground and Background. Pp. 175–88 in *Coherence and Grounding in Discourse*, ed. Russell S. Tomlin. Typological Studies in Language 11. Amsterdam: Benjamins.

Glinert, Lewis

1989   *The Grammar of Modern Hebrew.* Cambridge: Cambridge University Press.

Goedsche, C. R.

1940   Aspect versus Aktionsart. *Journal of English and Germanic Philology* 39: 189–97.

Goerwitz, Richard L.

1992   The Accentuation of the Hebrew Jussive and Preterite. *Journal of the American Oriental Society* 112: 198–203.

Goetze, Albrecht

1936   The *T*-Form of the Old Babylonian Verb. *Journal of the American Oriental Society* 56: 297–334.

1938   The Tenses of Ugaritic. *Journal of the American Oriental Society* 58: 266–309.

1941a   The Nikkal Poem from Ras Shamra. *Journal of Biblical Literature* 60: 353–74.

1941b   Is Ugaritic a Canaanite Language? *Language* 17: 127–38.

1942   The So-Called Intensive of the Semitic Languages. *Journal of the American Oriental Society* 62: 1–8.

Goldfajn, Tal

1998   *Word Order and Time in Biblical Hebrew Narrative.* Oxford Theological Monographs. New York: Oxford University Press.

Gordon, Amnon
1982   The Development of the Participle in Biblical, Mishnaic, and Modern Hebrew. *Afroasiatic Linguistics* 8/3: 1–59.
Gordon, Cyrus H.
1938   The Accentual Shift in the Perfect with *Waw* Consecutive. *Journal of Biblical Literature* 57: 319–26.
1965   *Ugaritic Textbook*. Analecta Orientalia. Rome: Pontifical Biblical Institute.
1997   Amorite and Eblaite. Pp. 100–113 in *The Semitic Languages*, ed. Robert Hetzron. London: Routledge.
Greenberg, Joseph H.
1952   The Afro-Asiatic (Hamito-Semitic) Present. *Journal of the American Oriental Society* 72: 1–9.
Greenstein, Edward L.
1988   On the Prefixed Preterite in Biblical Hebrew. *Hebrew Studies* 29: 7–17.
1998   On a New Grammar of Ugaritic. *Israel Oriental Society* 18: 397–420.
2006   Forms and Functions of the Finite Verb in Ugaritic Narrative Verse. Pp. 75–102 in *Biblical Hebrew in Its Northwest Semitic Setting: Typology and Historical Perspectives*, ed. Steven E. Fassberg and Avi Hurvitz. Institute for Advanced Studies 1. Jerusalem: Magnes / Winona Lake, IN: Eisenbrauns.
Grice, H. P.
1975   Logic and Conversation. Pp. 41–58 in *Syntax and Semantics*, vol. 3: *Speech Acts*, ed. P. Cole and J. L. Morgan. New York: Academic Press.
Gropp, Douglas M.
1991   The Function of the Finite Verb in Classical Biblical Hebrew. *Hebrew Annual Review* 13: 45–62.
Gross, Walter
1976   *Verbform und Funktion: Wayyiqtol für Gegenwart? Ein Beitrag zur Syntax poetischer althebräischer Texte*. Münchener Universitätsschriften. St. Ottilien: EOS.
1981   Syntaktische Ersheinungen am Anfang althebräischer Erzählungen: Hintergrund und Vordergrund. Pp. 131–45 in *Congress Volume: Vienna, 1980*, ed. J. A. Emerton. Vetus Testamentum Supplement 32. Leiden: Brill
Hale, Mark
2007   *Historical Linguistics: Theory and Method*. Blackwell Textbooks in Linguistics. Oxford: Blackwell.
Hamori, A.
1973   A Note on *Yaqtulu* in East and West Semitic. *Archiv Orientální* 41: 319–24.
Hare, Richard Mervyn
1952   *The Language of Morals*. Oxford: Clarendon.
1970   Meaning and Speech Acts. *The Philosophical Review* 79/1: 3–24.
Harmelink, Bryan L.
2004   *Exploring the Syntactic, Semantic, and Pragmatic Uses of* וַיְהִי *in Biblical Hebrew*. Ph.D. dissertation, Westminster Theological Seminary.
Harris, Zellig S.
1939   *Development of the Canaanite Dialects: An Investigation in Linguistic History*. New Haven, CT: American Oriental Society.

1952a Discourse Analysis. *Language* 28: 1–30.
1952b Discourse Analysis: A Sample Text. *Language* 28: 474–94.

Haspelmath, Martin
1998   The Semantic Development of Old Presents: New Futures and Subjunctives without Grammaticalization. *Diachronica* 15/1: 29–62.

Hatav, Galia
1989   Aspects, *Aktionsarten*, and the Time Line. *Linguistics* 27: 487–516.
1993   The Aspect System in English: An Attempt at a Unified Analysis. *Linguistics* 31: 209–37.
1997   *The Semantics of Aspect and Modality: Evidence from English and Biblical Hebrew*. Studies in Language Companion Series. Amsterdam: Benjamins.
2004   Anchoring World and Time in Biblical Hebrew. *Journal of Linguistics* 40: 491–526.

Haug, Dag
2008   From Resultatives to Anteriors in Ancient Greek. Pp. 285–305 in *Grammatical Change and Linguistic Theory: The Rosendal Papers*, ed. Thórhallur Eythórsson. Linguistik Aktuell. Amsterdam: Benjamins.

Haupt, Paul
1878   Studies on the Comparative Grammar of the Semitic Languages with Special Reference to Assyrian: The Oldest Semitic Verb-Form. *Journal of the Royal Asiatic Society* 10: 244–51.

Heimerdinger, Jean-Marc
1999   *Topic, Focus and Foreground in Ancient Hebrew Narratives*. Journal for the Study of the Old Testament Supplement 295. Sheffield: JSOT Press.

Heine, Bernd, Ulrike Claudi, and Friederike Hünnemeyer
1991   From Cognition to Grammar: Evidence from African Languages. Pp. 149–87 in *Approaches to Grammaticalization*, ed. Elizabeth Closs Traugott and Bernd Heine. Typological Studies in Language 19. Amsterdam: Benjamins.

Heine, Bernd, and Tania Kuteva
2002   *World Lexicon of Grammaticalization*. Cambridge: Cambridge University Press.

Heinrichs, E.
1986   Temporal Anaphora in Discourses of English. *Linguistics and Philosophy* 9: 62–82.

Held, Moshe
1962   The *YQTL-QTL (QTL-YQTL)* Sequence of Identical Verbs in Biblical Hebrew and in Ugaritic. Pp. 281–90 in *Studies and Essays in Honor of Abraham A. Neuman*, ed. M. Ben-Horin et al. Leiden: Brill.

Heller, Roy L.
2004   *Narrative Structure and Discourse Constellations: An Analysis of Clause Function in Biblical Hebrew Prose*. Harvard Semitic Studies 55. Winona Lake, IN: Eisenbrauns.

Hendel, Ronald S.
1996   In the Margins of the Hebrew Verbal System. *Zeitschrift für Althebräistik* 9: 152–81.

Hetzron, Robert
1969 The Evidence for Perfect **Yáqtul* and Jussive **Yaqtúl* in Proto-Semitic. *Journal of Semitic Studies* 14: 1–21

Hoffman, G.
1887 Review of "Semitic Languages," by Theodor Nöldeke. *Literarisches Centralblatt für Deutschland* 18: 605.

Hoftijzer, J.
1985 *The Function and Use of the Imperfect Forms with* Nun Paragogicum *in Classical Hebrew*. Studia Semitica Neerlandica. Assen: Van Gorcum.
1991 A Preliminary Remark on the Study of the Verbal System in Classical Hebrew. Pp. 645–51 in *Semitic Studies in Honor of Wolf Leslau on the Occasion of His Eighty-Fifth Birthday*, ed. Alan S. Kaye. Wiesbaden: Harrassowitz.

Hoftijzer, J., and K. Jongeling
1995 *Dictionary of the North-West Semitic Inscriptions*. Handbuch der Orientalistik. Leiden: Brill.

Holmstedt, Robert D.
2002 *The Relative Clause in Biblical Hebrew: A Linguistic Analysis*. Ph.D. dissertation, University of Wisconsin.
2003 Adjusting Our Focus: A Review of *Focus Structure in Biblical Hebrew: A Study of Word Order and Information Structure*, by Katsuomi Shimasaki. *Hebrew Studies* 44: 101–13.
2005 Word Order in the Book of Proverbs. Pp. 135–54 in *Seeking Out the Wisdom of the Ancients: Essays Offered to Honor Michael V. Fox on the Occasion of His Sixty-Fifth Birthday*, ed. Ronald L. Troxel, Kelvin G. Friebel, and Dennis R. Magary. Winona Lake, IN: Eisenbrauns.
2009 Word Order and Information Structure in Ruth and Jonah. *Journal of Semitic Studies* 59: 111–39.
2011 The Typological Classification of the Hebrew of Genesis: Subject-Verb or Verb-Subject? *Journal of Hebrew Scriptures* 11. http://www.jhsonline.org/.

Hopper, Paul J.
1979 Aspect and Foregrounding in Discourse. Pp. 213–41 in *Discourse and Syntax*, ed. Talmy Givón. Syntax and Semantics 12. New York: Academic Press.
1982 Aspect between Discourse and Grammar: An Introductory Essay for the Volume. in *Tense-Aspect: Between Semantics and Pragmatics*, ed. Paul J. Hopper. Typological Studies in Language. Amsterdam: Benjamins.
1987 Emergent Grammar. Pp. 139–57 in *Grammar and Cognition*, ed. Jon Aske, Natasha Beery, and Laura Michaelis. Berkeley Linguistic Society 13. Berkeley: University of California Press.

Hopper, Paul J., and Sandra A. Thompson
1980 Transitivity in Grammar and Discourse. *Language* 56: 251–99.

Hopper, Paul J., and Elizabeth Closs Traugott
1993 *Grammaticalization*. Cambridge Textbooks in Linguistics. Cambridge: Cambridge University Press.
2003 *Grammaticalization*. 2nd ed. Cambridge Textbooks in Linguistics. Cambridge: Cambridge University Press.

Hornstein, Norbert
1977   Towards a Theory of Tense. *Linguistic Inquiry* 8: 521–57.
1990   *As Time Goes By: Tense and Universal Grammar.* Cambridge, MA: MIT Press.
Huehnergard, John
1987a "Stative," Predicative, Pseudo-Verb. *Journal of Near Eastern Studies* 46: 215–32.
1987b *Ugaritic Vocabulary in Syllabic Transcription.* Harvard Semitic Studies 32. Atlanta: Scholars Press. [Rev. ed., Winona Lake, IN: Eisenbrauns, 2008.]
1988   The Early Hebrew Prefix-Conjugations. *Hebrew Studies* 29: 19–23.
1989   *The Akkadian of Ugarit.* Harvard Semitic Studies 34. Atlanta: Scholars Press.
1991   Remarks on the Classification of Northwest Semitic Languages. Pp. 282–93 in *The Balaam Text from Deir ʿAlla Re-evaluated: Proceedings of the International Symposium Held at Leiden, 21–24 August 1989,* ed. J. Hoftijzer and G. van der Kooij. Leiden: Brill.
1992   Languages: Introductory Survey. Pp. 155–70 in vol. 4 of *Anchor Bible Dictionary,* ed. David Noel Freedman et al. New York: Doubleday.
2002   Comparative Semitic Linguistics. Pp. 119–50 in *Semitic Linguistics: The State of the Art at the Turn of the 21st Century,* ed. Shlomo Izre'el. Israel Oriental Studies 20. Winona Lake, IN: Eisenbrauns.
2004   Afro-Asiatic. Pp. 138–59 in *The Cambridge Encyclopedia of the World's Ancient Languages,* ed. Roger D. Woodard. Cambridge: Cambridge University Press.
2005   *A Grammar of Akkadian.* 2nd ed. Harvard Semitic Museum Studies 45. Winona Lake, IN: Eisenbrauns.
Huehnergard, John, and Christopher Woods
2004   Akkadian and Eblaite. Pp. 218–80 in *The Cambridge Encyclopedia of the World's Ancient Languages,* ed. Roger D. Woodard. Cambridge: Cambridge University of Press.
Hughes, James A.
1955   *The Hebrew Imperfect with Waw Conjunctive and Perfect with Waw Consecutive and Their Interrelationship.* M.A. thesis, Faith Theological Seminary.
1962   *Some Problems of the Hebrew Verbal System with Particular Reference to the Uses of the Tenses.* Ph.D. dissertation, University of Glasgow.
1970   Another Look at the Hebrew Tenses. *Journal of Near Eastern Studies* 29: 12–24.
Isaksson, Bo
1987   *Studies in the Language of Qoheleth, with Special Emphasis on the Verbal System.* Studia Semitica Upsaliensia. Uppsala: Almqvist & Wiksell.
Izre'el, Shlomo
1978   The Gezer Letters of the El-Amarna Archive. *Israel Oriental Studies* 8: 13–90.
Izre'el, Shlomo, with an appendix by Itamar Singer
1991   *Amurru Akkadian: A Linguistic Study.* 2 vols. Harvard Semitic Studies 40–41. Atlanta: Scholars Press.

Jakobson, Roman
1932   Zur Struktur des Russischen Verbums. Pp. 74–84 in *Charisteria Gvilelmo Mathesio qvinqvagenario a discipulis Et Circuli Lingvistici Pragensis sodalibus oblata*. Prague: Cercle Linguistique de Prague.
1960   Closing Statement: Linguistics and Poetics. Pp. 350–77 in *Style and Language*, ed. Thomas A. Sebeok. Cambridge: MIT Press.

Janssen, T. M. V.
2006   Montague Semantics. Pp. 244–55 in vol. 7 of *Encyclopedia of Language and Linguistics*, ed. Keith Brown. Amsterdam: Elsevier.

Janssens, G.
1972   The Present-Imperfect in Semitic. *Bibliotheca Orientalis* 29: 3–7.
1980   Review of *Hebräisches Perfekt und Imperfekt mit vorangehendem We*, by Bo Johnson. *Bibliotheca Orientalis* 37: 73–74.

Jespersen, Otto
1924   *The Philosophy of Grammar*. New York: Holt.

Johnson, Bo
1979   *Hebräisches Perfekt und Imperfekt mit Vorangehendem We*. Coniectanea Biblica: Old Testament Series. Lund: Gleerup.

Johnson, Marion R.
1977   *A Semantic Analysis of Kikuyu Tense and Aspect*. Ph.D. dissertation, Ohio State University.
1981   A Unified Temporal Theory of Tense and Aspect. Pp. 145–75 in *Syntax and Semantics*, vol. 14: *Tense and Aspect*, ed. Philip J. Tedeschi and Annie Zaenen. New York: Academic Press.

Joosten, Jan
1989   The Predicative Participle in Biblical Hebrew. *Zeitschrift für Althebräistik* 2: 128–59.
1992   Biblical *Weqatal* and Syriac *Waqtal* Expressing Repetition in the Past. *Zeitschrift für Althebräistik* 5: 1–14.
1997a The Indicative System of the Biblical Hebrew Verb and Its Literary Exploitation. Pp. 51–71 in *Narrative Syntax and the Hebrew Bible: Papers of the Tilburg Conference 1996*, ed. Ellen van Wolde. Leiden: Brill.
1997b Workshop: Meaning and Use of the Tenses in 1 Samuel 1. Pp. 72–83 in *Narrative Syntax and the Hebrew Bible: Papers of the Tilburg Conference 1996*, ed. Ellen van Wolde. Leiden: Brill.
1998   The Functions of the Semitic D Stem: Biblical Hebrew Materials for a Comparative-Historical Approach. *Orientalia* 67: 202–30.
1999   The Long Form of the Prefixed Conjugation Referring to the Past in Biblical Hebrew Prose. *Hebrew Studies* 40: 15–26.
2002   Do the Finite Verbal Forms in Biblical Hebrew Express Aspect? *Journal of the Ancient Near Eastern Society of Columbia University* 29: 49–70.
2005   The Distinction between Classical and Late Biblical Hebrew as Reflected in Syntax. *Hebrew Studies* 46: 327–39.
2006   The Disappearance of Iterative *Weqatal* in the Biblical Hebrew Verbal System. Pp. 135–53 in *Biblical Hebrew in Its Northwest Semitic Setting: Typology and*

Historical Perspectives, ed. Steven E. Fassberg and Avi Hurvitz. Institute for Advanced Studies 1. Jerusalem: Magnes / Winona Lake, IN: Eisenbrauns.

2009　Diachronic Aspects of Narrative *Wayhi* in Biblical Hebrew. *Journal of Northwest Semitic Languages* 35/2: 43–61.

Joseph, Brian D., and Richard D. Janda

1988　The How and Why of Diachronic Morphologization and Demorphologization. Pp. 193–210 in *Theoretical Morphology: Approaches to Modern Lingusitics*, ed. Michael Hammond and Michael Noonan. New York: Academic Press.

Joüon, Paul

1923　*Grammaire de l'Hébrew Biblique*. Rome: Pontifical Biblical Institute.

2006　*A Grammar of Biblical Hebrew*, trans. Takamitsu Muraoka. Subsidia Biblica 27. Rome: Pontifical Biblical Institute.

Kahan, J.

1889　*Über die verbalnominale Doppelnatur der hebräischen Participien und Infinitive und ihre darauf beruhende verschiedene Konstruktion*. Leipzig: Vollrath.

Kamp, Hans

1981　A Theory of Truth and Semantic Representation. Pp. 277–322 in *Formal Methods in the Study of Language*, ed. Jeroen A. G. Groenendijk, T. M. V. Janssen, and Martin B. J. Stokhof. Mathmatical Centre Tract 135. Amsterdam: Mathmatisch Centrum.

Kamp, Hans, Josef van Genabith, and Uwe Reyle

2011　Discourse Representation Theory. Pp. 125–394 in vol. 15 of *Handbook of Philosophical Logic*, ed. Dov M. Gabby and Franz Guenthner. 2nd ed. Dordrecht: Springer.

Kamp, Hans, and Uwe Reyle

1993　*From Discourse to Logic: An Introduction to Modeltheoretic Semantics of Natural Language, Formal Logic and Discourse Representation Theory*. Boston: Kluwer Academic.

Kamp, Hans, and Christian Rohrer

1983　Tense in Texts. Pp. 250–69 in *Meaning, Use, and Interpretation of Language*, ed. Rainer Bäuerle, Christoph Schwarze, and Arnim Von Stechow. Berlin: de Gruyter.

Kanizsa, Gaetano

1979　*Organization in Vision: Essays on Gestalt Perception*. New York: Praeger.

Kaufmann, Stefan

2005　Conditional Predictions: A Probabilistic Account. *Linguistics and Philosophy* 28: 181–231.

Kautzsch, Emil, ed.

1910　*Gesenius' Hebrew Grammar*, trans. A. E. Cowley. 2nd English ed. Oxford: Clarendon.

Kawashima, Robert S.

2004　*Biblical Narrative and the Death of the Rhapsode*. Indiana Studies in Biblical Literature. Bloomington, IN: Indiana University Press.

Kenny, Anthony

1963　*Action, Emotion, and Will*. London: Routledge and Kegan Paul.

Khan, Geoffrey
2006   Some Aspects of the Copula in North West Semitic. Pp. 155–76 in *Biblical Hebrew in Its Northwest Semitic Setting: Typological and Historical Perspectives*, ed. Steven E. Fassberg and Avi Hurvitz. Jerusalem: Magnes / Winona Lake, IN: Eisenbrauns.
2007   The Morphology of Babylonian Jewish Aramaic. Pp. 107–19 in *Morphologies of Africa and Asia*, vol. 1, ed. Alan S. Kaye. Winona Lake, IN: Eisenbrauns.

Kiefer, Ferenc
1987   On Defining Modalty. *Folia Linguistica* 21: 67–94.

Kienast, Burkhart
2001   *Historische semitische Sprachwissenschaft, mit Beiträgen von Erhart Graefe (Altaegyptisch) und Gene B. Gragg (Kuschitisch)*. Wiesbaden: Harrossowitz.

Kittel, Bonnie Pedrotti, Vicki Hoffer, and Rebecca Abts Wright
2004   *Biblical Hebrew: A Text and Workbook*. 2nd ed. New Haven, CT: Yale University Press.

Klaiman, M. H.
1991   *Grammatical Voice*. Cambridge Studies in Linguistics. Cambridge: Cambridge University Press.

Klein, G. L.
1990   The 'Prophetic Perfect'. *Journal of Northwest Semitic Languages* 16: 45–60.

Klein, Wolfgang
1994   *Time in Language*. London: Routledge.

Knudsen, Ebbe E.
1991   Amorite Grammar: A Comparative Statement. Pp. 866–85 in *Semitic Studies: in Honor of Wolf Leslau on the Occassion of His Eighty-Fifth Birthday, November 14th, 1991*, vol. 1, ed. Alan S. Kaye. Wiesbaden: Harrassowitz.

Knudtzon, J. A.
1892   Zur assyrischen und allgemein semitischen Grammatik. *Zeitschrift für Assyriologie* 7: 33–63.
1915   *Die El-Amarna-Tafeln*. Leipzig:

Koehler, Ludwig, Walter Baumgartner, and Johann Jakob Stamm, eds.
1994–2000   *The Hebrew and Aramaic Lexicon of the Old Testament*, trans. and ed. M. E. J. Richardson. 5 vols. Leiden: Brill.

Koffka, K.
1935   *Principles of Gestalt Psychology*. New York: Harcourt, Brace & World.

Kouwenberg, N. J. C.
2000   Nouns as Verbs: The Verbal Nature of the Akkadian Stative. *Orientalia* 69: 21–71.
2010   *The Akkadian Verb and Its Semitic Background*. Languages of the Ancient Near East 2. Winona Lake, IN: Eisenbrauns.

Krahmalkov, Charles R.
1986   The *Qatal* with Future Tense Reference in Phoenician. *Journal of Semitic Studies* 31: 5–10.

Kratzer, Angelika
1995   Stage-Level and Individual-Level Predicates. Pp. 125–75 in *The Generic Book*, ed. Gregory N. Carslon and Francis Jeffry Pelletier. Chicago: University of Chicago Press.

Kummerow, David
2007   How Can the Form יִקְטֹל Be a Preterite, Jussive, and a Future/Imperfective? *Kleine Untersuchungen zur Sprache des Alten Testaments und seiner Umwelt* 8/9: 63–95.
2007   On the Biblical Hebrew Verbal System: A Linguistic Critique in Defense of the Mostly Traditional. *Journal of Asia Adventist Seminary* 10: 107–34.

Kürschner, Wilfried
1996   Die Lehre des Grammatikers Dionysios (Dionysios Thrax, *Tekhne Grammatike*—Deutsch). Pp. 177–215 in *Ancient Grammar: Content and Context*, ed. Pierre Swiggers and Alfons Wouters. Orbis Supplementa 7. Leuven: Peeters.

Kurylowicz, Jerzy K.
1961   *Lápophonie en Sémitique*. Prace Jezykoznawcze. Wrocław: Zakad Narodowy im. Ossolinskich Wydawn.
1972   *Studies in Semitic Grammar and Metrics*. Warsaw: Polkiej Akademii Nauk.
1973   Verbal Aspect in Semitic. *Orientalia* 42: 114–20.

Kustár, Péter
1972   *Aspekt in Hebräischen*. Basel: Reinhardt.

Kuteva, Tania
2001   *Auxiliation: An Enquiry into the Nature of Grammaticalization*. Oxford: Oxford University Press.

Kutscher, Eduard Yechezkel
1982   *A History of the Hebrew Language*. Jerusalem: Magnes.

Labov, William
1972   The Transformation of Experience in Narrative Syntax. in *Language in the Inner City*. Philadelphia: University of Pennsylvania Press.

Lakoff, R. T.
1971   If's, And's and But's about Conjunctions. Pp. 114–49 in *Studies in Linguistic Semantics*, ed. C. J. Fillmore and D. T. Langendoen. New York: Rinehart.

Lambdin, Thomas O.
1971   *Introduction to Biblical Hebrew*. New York: Scribner's.

Lambert, M.
1893   Le vav conversif. *Revue des études juives* 26: 47–62.

Leo, C.
1818   An Examination of the Fourteen Verses Selected from Scripture, by Mr. J. Bellamy, as a Specimen of His Emendation of the Bible. *Classical Journal* 17: 221–40.

Lessau, Donald A., ed.
1994   *A Dictionary of Grammaticalization*. Bochum: Universitätsverlag Dr. N. Brockmeyer.

Levinson, Stephen C.
1983   *Pragmatics.* Cambridge Textbooks in Linguistics. Cambridge: Cambridge University Press.

Li, Charles N., and Sandra A. Thompson
1977   A Mechanism for the Development of Copula Morphemes. Pp. 419–44 in *Mechanisms of Syntactic Change,* ed. Charles N. Li. Austin: University of Texas Press.

Li, Tarsee
1999   *The Expression of Sequence and Non-sequence in Northwest Semitic Narrative Prose.* Ph.D. dissertation, Hebrew Union College–Jewish Institute of Religion.

Liddell, Henry, and Robert George Scott
1984   *Greek-English Lexicon.* Oxford: Clarendon.

Lindblom, K.
2006   Cooperative Principle. Pp. 176–83 in vol. 3 of *Encyclopedia of Language and Linguistics,* ed. Keith Brown. 2nd ed. Amsterdam: Elsevier.

Lindstedt, Jouko
2001   Tense and Aspect. Pp. 768–83 in *Language Typology and Language Universals: An International Handbook,* vol. 1, ed. Martin Haspelmath et al. Berlin: de Gruyter.

Longacre, Robert E.
1972   *Hierarchy and Universality of Discourse Constituents in New Guinea Languages.* Washington, DC: Georgetown University Press.

1985   Sentences as Combinations of Clauses. Pp. 235–86 in *Language Typology and Syntactic Description,* vol. 2: *Complex Constructions,* ed. Timothy Shopen. Cambridge: Cambridge University Press.

1990   *Storyline Concerns and Word Order Typology.* Studies in African Linguistics Supplement 10. Los Angeles: University of California Press.

1992   Discourse Perspective on the Hebrew Verb: Affirmation and Restatement. Pp. 177–89 in *Linguistics and Biblical Hebrew,* ed. Walter R. Bodine. Winona Lake, IN: Eisenbrauns.

1994   *Weqatal* Forms in Biblical Hebrew Prose: A Discourse-Modular Approach. Pp. 50–98 in *Biblical Hebrew and Discourse Linguistics,* ed. Robert D. Bergen. Dallas: Summer Institute of Linguistics.

1995   Building for the Worship of God: Exodus 25:1–30:10. Pp. 21–49 in *Discourse Analysis of Biblical Literature: What It Is and What It Offers,* ed. Walter R. Bodine. Atlanta: Scholars Press.

1996   *The Grammar of Discourse.* 2nd ed. Topics in Language and Linguistics. New York: Plenum.

2003   *Joseph: A Story of Divine Providence—A Text Theoretical and Textlinguistic Analysis of Genesis 37 and 39–48.* 2nd ed. Winona Lake, IN: Eisenbrauns.

Loprieno, Antonio
1986   *Das Verbalsystem im Ägyptischen und im Semitischen: Zur Grundlegung einer Aspekttheorie.* Wiesbaden: Harrossowitz.

Lyons, John
1968 *Introduction to Theoretical Linguistics.* Cambridge: Cambridge University Press.
1977 *Semantics.* Cambridge: Cambridge University Press.
Madvig, Johan Nicolai
1895 *A Latin Grammar*, trans. George Woods. Boston: Ginn.
Marchese, Lynell
1988 Sequential Chaining and Discourse Structure in Godie. Pp. 247–73 in *Clause Combining in Grammar and Discourse*, ed. John Haiman and Sandra A. Thompson. Typological Studies in Language 18. Amsterdam: Benjamins.
Matheus, Frank
2011 *Ein jegliches hat seine Zeit: Tempus und Aspekt im biblisch-hebräischen Verbalsystem.* Kleine Untersuchungen zur Sprache des Alten Testaments und seiner Umwelt Supplement B/1. Kamen: Hartmut Spenner.
Matthews, Peter
2001 *A Short History of Structural Linguistics.* Cambridge: Cambridge University Press.
McCawley, James D.
1993 *Everything That Linguists Have Always Wanted to Know about Logic.* 2nd ed. Chicago: University of Chicago Press.
McCoard, Robert W.
1978 *The English Perfect: Tense-Choice and Pragmatic Inferences.* Amsterdam: North-Holland.
McFall, Leslie
1982 *The Enigma of the Hebrew Verbal System.* Historic Texts and Interpreters in Biblical Scholarship 2. Sheffield: Almond.
Melnik, N.
2010 Modal Predicates in Modern Hebrew. *The Proceedings of the 17th International Conference on HPSG.* Stanford, CA: CSLI.
Merwe, Christo H. J. van der
1999 The Elusive Biblical Hebrew Term ויהי: A Perspective in Terms of Its Syntax, Semantics, and Pragmatics in 1 Samuel. *Hebrew Studies* 40: 83–114.
Merwe, Christo H. J. van der, Jackie A. Naudé, and Jan H. Kroeze
1999 *A Biblical Hebrew Reference Grammar.* Biblical Languages: Hebrew 3. Sheffield: Sheffield Academic Press.
Mettinger, Tryggve N. D.
1974 The Hebrew Verbal System: A Survey of Recent Research. *Annual of the Swedish Theological Institute* 9: 64–84.
Meulen, Alice G. B. ter
1995 *Representing Time in Natural Language: The Dynamic Interpretation of Tense and Aspect.* Cambridge, MA: MIT Press.
Meyer, Rudolf
1953 Zur Geschichte des hebräischen Verbums. *Vetus Testamentum* 3: 225–35.
1958 Spuren eines westsemitischen Präsens-Futur in den Texten von Chirbet Qumran. Pp. 118–28 in *Von Ugarit nach Qumran: Beiträge zur alttestamentlichen Forschung, Otto Eissfeldt zum 1. September 1957 dargebracht*

von Freunden und Schülern. Beiheft zur Zeitschrift für die altestamentliche Wissenschaft 77. Berlin: Alfred Töpelmann.

1960   Das hebräische Verbalsystem im Licht der gegenwärtigen Forschung. Pp. 309–17 in *Congress Volume: Oxford, 1959.* Vetus Testamentum Supplementum 7. Leiden: Brill

1964   Aspekt und Tempus im althebräischen Verbalsystem. *Orientalistische Literaturzeitung* 59: 117–26.

1966   Zur Geschichte des hebräischen Verbums. *Forshungen und Forschritte* 40: 241–43.

[1969–72] 1992   *Hebräische Grammatik.* 3d ed. 3 vols. Berlin: de Gruyter.

Michaelis, Laura A.
1997   *Aspectual Grammar and Past-Time Reference.* New York: Routledge.

Michel, Diethelm
1960   *Tempora und Satzstellung in den Psalmen.* Bonn: Bouvier.

Mill, J. S.
1843   *A System of Logic.* London: Longmans.

Miller, Cynthia L.
2003   *The Representation of Speech in Biblical Hebrew Narrative: A Linguistic Analysis.* Harvard Semitic Monograph 55. Rev. ed. Winona Lake, IN: Eisenbrauns.

Mithun, Marianne
1995   On the Relativity of Irreality. Pp. 367–88 in *Modality in Grammar and Discourse,* ed. Joan Bybee and Suzanne Fleishman. Typological Studies in Language 32. Amsterdam: Benjamins.

1999   *The Languages of Native North America.* Cambridge: Cambridge University Press.

Moens, Marc
1987   *Tense, Aspect and Temporal Reference.* Edinburgh: University of Edinburgh.

Molendijk, Arie
1994   Tense Use and Temporal Orientation: The *Passé Simple* and the *Imparfait* of French. Pp. 21–48 in *Tense and Aspect in Discourse,* ed. Co Vet and Carl Vetters. Trends in Linguistics. Studies and Monographs 75. Berlin: de Gruyter.

Montague, Richard
1974   *Formal Philosophy: Selected Papers of Richard Montague.* New Haven, CT: Yale University Press.

Moran, William L.
1950   *A Syntactical Study of the Dialect of Byblos as Reflected in the Amarna Tablets.* Ph.D. dissertation, Johns Hopkins University.

1960   Early Canaanite *Yaqtula. Orientalia* 29: 1–19.

1992   *The Amarna Letters.* Baltimore: Johns Hopkins University Press.

2003   *Amarna Studies: Collected Writings.* Harvard Semitic Studies 54. Winona Lake, IN: Eisenbrauns.

Moran, William L., Dominique Collon, and Henri Cazelles
1987   *Les lettres d'El-Amarna: Correspondance diplomatique du pharaon.* Littératures Anciennes du Proche-Orient. Paris: Cerf.

Moravcsik, Edith A.
2007   What Is Universal about Typology? *Lingusitic Typology* 11: 27–41.

Moreno Cabrera, J. C.
1998   On the relationship between grammaticalization and lexicalization. Pp. 211–27 in *Limits of Grammaticalization*, ed. Anna Giacalone Ramat and Paul J. Hopper. Typological Studies in Language 37. Amsterdam: Benjamins.

Moscati, Sabatino, ed.
1980   *An Introduction to the Comparative Grammar of the Semitic Languages: Phonology and Morphology*. Porta Linguarum Orientalium 6. Wiesbaden: Harrassowitz.

Mourelatos, Alexander P. D.
1981   Events, Processes, and States. Pp. 191–212 in *Syntax and Semantics*, vol. 14: *Tense and Aspect*, ed. Philip J. Tedeschi and Annie Zaenen. New York: Academic Press.

Muraoka, Takamitsu
1995   Linguistic Notes on the Aramaic Inscription from Tel Dan. *Israel Exploration Journal* 45: 19–21.
1997a The Alleged Final Function of the Biblical Syntagm <Waw + a Volitive Verb Form>. Pp. 229–41 in *Narrative Syntax and the Hebrew Bible: Papers of the Tilburg Conference 1996*, ed. Ellen van Wolde. Leiden: Brill.
1997b *Classical Syriac: A Basic Grammar with a Chrestomathy*. Porta Linguarum Orientalium. Wiesbaden: Harrassowitz.
1998   Again on the Tel Dan Inscription and the Northwest Semitic Verb Tenses. *Zeitschrift für Althebräistik* 11: 74–81.
1999a The Participle in Qumran Hebrew with Special Reference to Its Periphrastic Use. Pp. 188–204 in *Sirach, Scrolls, and Sages: Proceedings of a Second International Symposium on the Hebrew of the Dead Sea Scrolls, Ben Sira, and the Mishnah, Held at Leiden University, 15–17 December 1997*, ed. Takamitsu Muraoka and J. F. Elwolde. Leiden: Brill.
1999b The Tripartite Nominal Clause Revisited. Pp. 187–214 in *The Verbless Clause in Biblical Hebrew: Linguistic Approaches*, ed. Cynthia L. Miller. Linguistic Studies in Ancient West Semitic 1. Winona Lake, IN: Eisenbrauns.

Müller, Hans-Peter
1983   Zur Geschichte des hebräischen Verbs: Diachronie der Konjugationsthemen. *Biblische Zeitschrift* 27: 34–57.
1984   Ebla und das althebräische Verbalsystem. *Biblica* 65: 145–67.
1986   Polysemie im semitischen und hebräischen Konjugationssystem. *Orientalia* 55: 365–89.
1991   Wa-, ha- und das Imperfectum consecutivum. *Zeitschrift für Althebräistik* 4: 144–60.
1995a Die aramäische Inschrift von Tel Dan. *Zeitschrift für Althebräistik* 8: 121–39.
1995b Ergative Constructions in Early Semitic Languages. *Journal of Near Eastern Studies* 54: 261–71.
1998   Zu den semitisch-hamitischen Konjugationsystemen. *Zeitschrift für Althebräistik* 11: 140–52.

Newmeyer, Fredrick J.
1998   *Language Form and Language Function*. Cambridge, MA: MIT Press.

Niccacci, Alviero
1987 A Neglected Point of Hebrew Syntax: *Yiqtol* and Position in the Sentence. *Liber Annuus* 37: 7–19.
1989 An Outline of the Biblical Hebrew Verbal System in Prose. *Liber Annuus* 39: 7–26.
1990 *The Syntax of the Verb in Classical Hebrew Prose*, trans. W. G. E. Watson. Journal for the Study of the Old Testament Supplement 86. Sheffield: JSOT Press.
1993 Simple Nominal Clause (Snc) or Verbless Clause in Biblical Hebrew Prose. *Zeitschrift für Althebräistik* 6: 216–27.
1994a Analysis of Biblical Narrative. Pp. 175–98 in *Biblical Hebrew and Discourse Linguistics*, ed. Robert D. Bergen. Dallas: Summer Institute of Linguistics.
1994b On the Hebrew Verbal System. Pp. 117–37 in *Biblical Hebrew and Discourse Linguistics*, ed. Robert D. Bergen. Dallas: Summer Institute of Linguistics.
1995 Essential Hebrew Syntax. Pp. 111–25 in *Narrative and Comment: Contributions to Discourse Grammar of Biblical Hebrew*, ed. Eep Talstra. Amsterdam: Societas Hebraica Amstelodamensis.
1996 Finite Verb in Second Position of the Sentence: Coherence of the Hebrew Verbal System. *Zeitschrift für die Alttestamentliche Wissenschaft* 108: 434–40.
1997 Basic Facts and Theory of the Biblical Hebrew Verb System in Prose. Pp. 167–202 in *Narrative Syntax and the Hebrew Bible: Papers of the Tilburg Conference 1996*, ed. Ellen van Wolde. Leiden: Brill.
1999 Types and Functions of the Nominal Sentence. Pp. 215–48 in *The Verbless Clause in Biblical Hebrew: Linguistic Approaches*, ed. Cynthia L. Miller. Linguistic Studies in Ancient West Semitic 1. Winona Lake, IN: Eisenbrauns.
2006 The Biblical Hebrew Verbal System in Poetry. Pp. 247–68 in *Biblical Hebrew in Its Northwest Semitic Setting: Typology and Historical Perspectives*, ed. Steven E. Fassberg and Avi Hurvitz. Institute for Advanced Studies 1. Jerusalem: Magnes / Winona Lake, IN: Eisenbrauns.
Nichols, Johanna
2007 What, if Anything, is Typology? *Linguistic Typology* 11: 231–38.
Nöldeke, Theodor
[1904] 2001 *Compendious Syriac Grammar*, trans. James A. Crichton. Reprint. Winona Lake, IN: Eisenbrauns.
Notarius, Tania
2010 The Active Predicative Participle in Archaic and Classical Biblical Poetry: A Typological and Historical Investigation. *Ancient Near Eastern Studies* 47: 241–69.
Nuyts, Jan
2001 *Epistemic Modality, Language, and Conceptualization: A Cognitive-Pragmatic Perspective*. Human Cognitive Processing. Amsterdam: Benjamins.
O'Connor, M.
2002 Discourse Linguisitics and the Study of Biblical Hebrew. Pp. 17–42 in *Congress Volume: Basel, 2001*, ed. A. Lemaire. Vetus Testamentum Supplement 92. Leiden: Brill.

Olsen, Mari Broman
1997   *A Semantic and Pragmatic Model of Lexical and Grammatical Aspect*. New York: Garland.
Palmer, Frank R.
1986   *Mood and Modality*. Cambridge Textbooks in Linguistics. Cambridge: Cambridge University Press.
2001   *Mood and Modality*. 2nd ed. Cambridge Textbooks in Linguistics. Cambridge: Cambridge University Press.
Pardee, Dennis
1997   Ugaritic. Pp. 131–44 in *Semitic Languages*, ed. Robert Hetzron. London: Routledge.
1999   Review of *Canaanite in the Amarna Dialects: A Linguistic Analysis of the Mixed Dialect Used by Scribes from Canaan*, vol. 1: *Orthography, Phonology, Morphosyntactic Analysis of the Pronouns, Nouns, Numerals*. Vol. 2: *Morphosyntactic Analysis of the Verbal System*. Vol. 3: *Morphosyntactic Analysis of the Particles and Adverbs*. Vol. 4: *References and Indexes of Texts Cited*, by Anson F. Rainey. *Journal of Near Eastern Studies* 58: 313–17.
2003–4 Rezension von J. Tropper, Ugaritische Grammatik. *Archiv für Orientforschung* 50: 1–404.
2004a   Canaanite Dialects. Pp. 386–90 in *The Cambridge Encyclopedia of the World's Ancient Languages*, ed. Roger D. Woodard. Cambridge: Cambridge University Press.
2004b   Ugaritic. Pp. 288–318 in *The Cambridge Encyclopedia of the World's Ancient Languages*, ed. Roger D. Woodard. Cambridge: Cambridge University Press.
Partee, Barbara
1984   Nominal and Temporal Anaphora. *Linguistics and Philosophy* 7: 243–86.
Peckham, Brian
1997   Tense and Mood in Biblical Hebrew. *Zeitschrift für Althebräistik* 10: 139–68.
Peled, Yishai
1992   *Conditional Structures in Classical Arabic*. Studies in Arabic Language and Literature. Wiesbaden: Harrassowitz.
Penner, Ken
2006   *Verb Form Semantics in Qumran Hebrew Texts: Tense, Aspect, and Modality between the Bible and the Mishnah*. Ph.D. dissertation, McMaster University.
Pentiuc, Eugen J.
2001   *West Semitic Vocabulary in the Akkadian Texts from Emar*. Harvard Semitic Studies 49. Winona Lake, IN: Eisenbrauns.
Pérez Fernández, Miguel
1997   *An Introductory Grammar of Rabbinic Hebrew*, trans. John Elwolde. Leiden: Brill.
Pike, Kenneth Lee
1967   *Language in Relation to a Unified Theory of the Structure of Human Behavior*. 2nd ed. Janua Linguarum: Series Maior. The Hague: Mouton.
Polzin, Robert
1976   *Late Biblical Hebrew: Toward an Historical Typology of Biblical Hebrew Prose*. Harvard Semitic Monograph 12. Missoula, MT: Scholars Press.

Porten, Bazalel, and Ada Yardeni
1986   *Textbook of Aramaic Documents from Ancient Egypt*, vol. 1: *Letters*. 4 vols. Texts and Studies for Students. Jerusalem: Hebrew University Department of the History of the Jewish People.

Portner, Paul
2009   *Modality*. Oxford Linguistics. Oxford: Oxford University Press.

Pratico, Gary D., and Miles V. Van Pelt
2001   *Basics of Biblical Hebrew Grammar*. Grand Rapids, MI: Zondervan.

Prince, Ellen F.
1988   Discourse Analysis: A Part of the Study of Linguistic Competence. Pp. 164–82 in *Linguistics: The Cambridge Survey*, vol. 2: *Lingusitic Theory: Extensions and Implications*, ed. Fredrick J. Newmeyer. Cambridge: Cambridge University Press.

Prior, Arthur N.
1967   *Past, Present and Future*. Oxford: Clarendon.

Qimron, Elisha
1997   A New Approach to the Use of Forms of the Imperfect without Personal Endings. Pp. 174–81 in *Hebrew of the Dead Sea Scrolls and Ben Sira: Proceedings of a Symposium Held at Leiden University*, ed. T. Muraoka and J. F. Elwolde. Studies on the Texts of the Desert of Judah 26. Leiden: Brill.

Rabin, Chaim
2000   *The Development of the Syntax of Post-biblical Hebrew*. Studies in Semitic Languages and Linguistics. Leiden: Brill.
2007   Semitic Languages. Pp. 280–84 in vol. 18 of *Encyclopedia Judaica*, ed. Fred Skolnik. 2nd ed. Detroit: Thomson Gale.

Rabinowitz, Isaac
1984   ʾ*Az* Followed by Imperfect Verb-Form in Preterite Contexts: A Redactional Device in Biblical Hebrew. *Vetus Testamentum* 34: 53–62.

Radden, Günter
2004   The Metaphor TIME AS SPACE across Languages. Pp. 226–39 in *Übersetzen, Interkulturelle Kommunikation, Spracherwerb und Sprachvermittlung—das Leben mit mehreren Sprachen: Festschrift für Juliane House zum 60. Geburtstag*, ed. Nicole Baumgarten, Claudia Böttger, Markus Motz, and Julia Probst. Zeitschrift für Interkulturellen Fremdsprachenunterricht 8(2/3). Bochum: AKS.

Rainey, Anson F.
1971   Verbal Forms with Infixed -*T*- in the West Semitic El-Amarna Lettters. *Israel Oriental Studies* 1: 86–102.
1973   Reflections on the Suffix Conjugation in West Semitized Amarna Tablets. *Ugarit-Forschungen* 5: 235–62.
1975   Morphology and the Prefix-Tenses of West Semitized El-ʾAmarna Tablets. *Ugarit-Forschungen* 7: 395–426.
1978   *El Amarna Tablets 359–379*. 2nd ed. Alter Orient und Altes Testament. Kevelaer: Butzon & Bercker / Neukirchen-Vluyn: Neukirchener Verlag.
1986   The Ancient Hebrew Prefix Conjugation in the Light of Amarnah Canaanite. *Hebrew Studies* 27: 4–19.

1988   Further Remarks on the Hebrew Verbal System. *Hebrew Studies* 29: 35–42.

1990   The Prefix Conjugation Patterns of Early Northwest Semitic. Pp. 407–20 in *Lingering over Words: Studies in Ancient Near Eastern Literature in Honor of William L. Moran*, ed. Tzvi Abusch, John Huehnergard, and Piotr Steinkeller. Harvard Semitic Studies 37. Atlanta: Scholars Press.

1991–93 Is There Really a *Yaqtula* Conjugation Pattern in the Canaanite Amarna Tablets? *Journal of Cuneiform Studies* 43–45: 107–18.

1993   The Use of the Precative by Canaanite Scribes in the Amarna Letters. Pp. 331–41 in *Mesopotamia – Ugaritica – Biblica: Festschrift für Kurt Bergerhof zur Vollendung seines 70. Lebensjahres am 7. Mai 1992*, ed. Manfried Dietrich and Oswald Loretz. Alter Orient und Altes Testament 232. Neukirchen-Vluyn: Neukirchener Verlag / Kevelaer: Butzon & Bercker.

1996a   *Canaanite in the Amarna Tablets: A Linguistic Analysis of the Mixed Dialect Used by the Scribes from Canaan*, vol. 1: *Orthography, Phonology, Morphosyntactic Analysis of the Pronouns, Nouns, Numerals*. Handbuch der Orientalistik. Leiden: Brill.

1996b   *Canaanite in the Amarna Tablets: A Linguistic Analysis of the Mixed Dialect Used by the Scribes from Canaan*, vol. 2: *Morphosyntactic Analysis of the Verbal System*. Handbuch der Orientalistik. Leiden: Brill.

1996c   *Canaanite in the Amarna Tablets: A Linguistic Analysis of the Mixed Dialect Used by the Scribes from Canaan*, vol. 3: *Morphosyntactic Analysis of the Particles and Adverbs*. Handbuch der Orientalistik. Leiden: Brill.

1996d   *Canaanite in the Amarna Tablets: A Linguistic Analysis of the Mixed Dialect Used by the Scribes from Canaan*, vol. 4: *References and Index of Texts Cited*. Handbuch der Orientalistik. Leiden: Brill.

2003a   The Suffix Conjugation Pattern in Ancient Hebrew: Tense and Modal Functions. *Ancient Near Eastern Studies* 40: 3–42.

2003b   The *Yaqtul* Preterite in Northwest Semitic. Pp. 395–407 in *Hamlet on a Hill: Semitic and Greek Studies Presented to Professor T. Muraoka on the Occasion of His Sixty-Fifth Birthday*, ed. M. F. J. Baasten and W. T. van Peursen. Orientalia Lovaniensia Analecta 118. Leuven: Peeters.

Rattray, Susan
1992   *The Tense-Mood-Aspect System of Biblical Hebrew, with Special Emphasis on 1 and 2 Samuel*. Ph.D. dissertation, University of California.

Reichenbach, Hans
1947   *Elements of Symbolic Logic*. London: Collier-Macmillan.

Reinhart, Tanya
1984   Principles of Gestalt Perception in the Temporal Organization of Narrative Texts. *Linguistics* 22: 779–809.

Revell, E. J.
1984   Stress and the *Waw* "Consecutive" in Biblical Hebrew. *Journal of the American Oriental Society* 104: 437–44.

1985   The Conditioning of Stress Position in *Waw* Consecutive Perfect Forms in Biblical Hebrew. *Hebrew Annual Review* 9: 277–300.

1989   The System of the Verb in Standard Biblical Prose. *Hebrew Union College Annual* 60: 1–37.

Richardson, M. E. J.
1991   Tense, Aspect and Mood in Ugaritic YQTL. Pp. 283–89 in *Proceedings of the Fifth International Hamito-Semitic Congress*, ed. Hans G. Mukarovsky. Veröffentlichungen der Institute für Afrikanistik und Ägyptologie der Universität Wien 57. Beiträge zur Afrikanistik 41. Vienna: Afro-Pub.

Ridzewski, Beate
1992   *Neuhebräische Grammatik auf Grund der ältesten Handschriften und Inschriften*. Heidelberger Orientalistische Studien. Frankfurt: Peter Lang.

Robins, R. H.
1995   The Authenticity of the *Tékhnee:* The *Status Quaestionis*. Pp. 13–26 in *Dionysius Thrax and the Tékhnee Grammatikee*, ed. Vivian Law and Ineke Sluiter. The Henry Sweet Society Studies in the History of Linguistics. 1. Münster: Nodus.
1997   *A Short History of Linguistics*. 4th ed. New York: Longman.

Rogland, Max
2003   *Alleged Non-past Uses of Qatal in Classical Hebrew*. Studia Semitica Neerlandica. Assen: Van Gorcum.

Romaine, Suzanne
1995   The Grammaticalization of Irrealis in Tok Pisin. Pp. 389–427 in *Modality in Grammar and Discourse*, ed. Joan Bybee and Suzanne Fleischman. Typological Studies in Language 32. Amsterdam: Benjamins.

Rosén, Haiim B.
1969   The Comparative Assignment of Certain Hebrew Tense Forms. Pp. 212–34 in *Proceedings of the International Conference on Semitic Studies Held in Jerusalem 1965*. Leiden: Brill.

Rössler, Otto
1950   Verbalbau und Verbalflexion in den Semitohamitischen Sprachen. *Zeitschscrift der deutschen morgenländischen Gesellschaft* 100: 461–514.
1961   Eine bisher unbekannte Tempusform im Althebräischen. *Zeitschrift der Deutschen Morgenländischen Gesellschaft* 111: 445–51.
1962   Die Präfixkonjugation *Qal* der Verba Iae *nûn* im Althebräischen und das Problem der sogenannten Tempora. *Zeitschrift für die Alttestamentliche Wissenschaft* 74: 125–41.
1981   The Structure and Inflexion of the Verb in the Semito-Hamitic Languages. Pp. 679–748 in *Bono Homini Donum: Essays in Historical Linguistics*. Amsterdam: Benjamins.

Rothstein, Susan
2004   *Structuring Events: A Study in the Semantics of Lexical Aspect*. Explorations in Semantics. Oxford: Blackwell.

Rubinstein, A.
1952   A Finite Verb Continued by an Infinitive Absolute in Hebrew. *Vetus Testamentum* 1: 362–67.

Rundgren, Frithiof
1961   *Das althebräische Verbum: Abriss der Aspektlehre*. Stockholm: Almquist & Wiksell.

1963 *Erneuerung des Verbalaspekts im Semitischen: Funktionell-diachronische Studien zur Semitischen Verblehre*. Uppsala: Almqvist & Wiksells.

Ryle, Gilbert
1949 *The Concept of Mind*. New York: Hutchinson.

Sáenz-Badillos, Angel
1993 *A History of the Hebrew Language*. Translated by John Elwolde. Cambridge: Cambridge University Press.

Sasson, Victor
1997 Some Observations on the Use and Original Purpose of the *Waw* Consecutive in Old Aramaic and Biblical Hebrew. *Vetus Testamentum* 47: 111–27.

2001 The *Waw* Consecutive/*Waw* Contrastive and the Perfect: Verb Tense, Context, and Texture in Old Aramaic and Biblical Hebrew, with Comments on the Deir ʿAlla Dialect and Post-biblical Hebrew. *Zeitscrift für die alttestamentliche Wissenschaft* 113: 602–17.

Satzinger, Helmut
2002 The Egyptian Connection: Egyptian and the Semitic Languages. Pp. 227–64 in *Semitic Linguistics: The State of the Art at the Turn of the 21st Century*, ed. Shlomo Izreʾel. Israel Oriental Studies 20. Winona Lake, IN: Eisenbrauns.

Saussure, Ferdinand de
1959 *Course in General Linguistics*, ed. Charles Bally and Albert Sechehaye, trans. Wade Baskin. New York: Philosophical Library.

Saussure, Ferdinand de,
1995 *Cours de Linguistique Générale,* ed. Charles Bally, Albert Sechehaye, and Tullio De Mauro. Paris: Payot.

Schneider, Wolfgang
1982 *Grammatik des biblischen Hebräisch*. 5th ed. Munich: Claudius.

Schoors, A.
1992 *The Preacher Sought to Find Pleasing Words: A Study of the Language of Qoheleth*. Orientalia Lovaniensia Analecta. Leuven: Peeters.

Schroeder, N. W.
1824 *Insititutiones ad Fundamenta Linguae Hebraicae*. 4th ed. Glasgow: Prelum Academicum.

Schuh, Russell G.
2007 Bade Morphology. Pp. 587–639 in *Morphologies of Africa and Asia*, ed. Alan S. Kaye. Winona Lake, IN: Eisenbrauns.

Schwarzwald, Ora
2001 *Modern Hebrew*. Languages of the World. Munich: Lincom Europa.

Searle, J. R.
1983 *Intentionality*. Cambridge: Cambridge University Press.

Segal, M. H.
1927 *A Grammar of Mishnaic Hebrew*. Oxford: Clarendon.

Segert, Stanislav
1984 *A Basic Grammar of the Ugaritic Language: With Selected Texts and Glossary*. Los Angeles: University of California Press.

Sellin, E.
1889 *Die Verbal-nominale Doppelnatur der hebräischen Participien und Infinitive und ihre darauf beruhende verschiedene Construktion.* Leipzig: Ackermann & Glaser.

Seow, C. L.
1995 *A Grammar for Biblical Hebrew.* 2nd ed. Nashville: Abingdon.

Sheehan, John F. X.
1970 Conversive *Waw* and Accentual Shift. *Biblica* 51: 545–48.

Shimasaki, Katsuomi
2002 *Focus Structure in Biblical Hebrew: A Study of Word Order and Information Structure.* Bethesda, MD: CDL.

Shlonsky, Ur
1997 *Clause Structure and Word Order in Hebrew and Arabic: An Essay in Comparative Semitic Syntax.* Oxford Studies in Comparative Syntax. Oxford: Oxford University Press.

Shulman, Ahouva
1996 *The Use of Modal Verb Forms in Biblical Hebrew Prose.* Ph.D. dissertation, University of Toronto.
1999 The Particle אֲ in Biblical Hebrew Prose. *Hebrew Studies* 40: 57–82.
2000 The Function of the 'Jussive' and 'Indicative' Imperfect Forms in Biblical Hebrew Prose. *Zeitschrift für Althebräistik* 13: 168–80.

Siedl, Suitbert H.
1971 *Gedanken zum Tempussystem im Hebräischen und Akkadischen.* Wiesbaden: Harrassowitz.

Silverman, M. H.
1973 Syntactic Notes on the *Waw* Consecutive. Pp. 167–75 in vol. of *Orient and Occident: Essays Presented to Cyrus H. Gordon,* ed. H. A. Hoffner Jr. Alter Orient und Altes Testament 22. Kevelaer: Butzon und Bercker.

Sivan, Daniel
1997 *A Grammar of the Ugaritic Language.* Handbook of Oriental Studies. Leiden: Brill.
1998 The Use of *QTL* and *YQTL* Forms in the Ugaritic Verbal System. Pp. 89–103 in *Past Links: Studies in the Languages and Cultures of the Ancient Near East,* Dedicated to Professor Anson F. Rainey, ed. Shlomo Izre'el, Itamar Singer, and Ran Zadok. Israel Oriental Studies 18. Winona Lake, IN: Eisenbrauns.

Sivan, Daniel, and Zipora Cochavi-Rainey
1992 *West-Semitic Vocabulary in Egyptian Script of the 14th to the 10th Centuries BCE.* Beer-Sheva: Ben-Gurion University of the Negev Press.

Smith, Carlota S.
1997 *The Parameter of Aspect.* 2nd ed. Studies in Linguistics and Philosophy. Dordrecht: Kluwer Academic.
1999 Activities: States or Events? *Linguistics and Philosophy* 22: 479–508.
2003 *Modes of Discourse: The Local Structure of Texts.* Cambridge Studies in Linguistics. Cambridge: Cambridge University Press.

2006 The Pragmatics and Semantics of Temporal Meaning. Pp. 92–106 in *Proceedings, Texas Linguistic Forum 2004*, ed. P. Denis, E. Mccready, A. Palmer, and B. Reese. Somerville, MA: Cascadilla.

2007 Time in Navajo: Direct and Indirect Interpretation. *International Journal of American Linguistics* 73/1: 40–71.

2008 Time with and without Tense. Pp. 227–50 in *Time and Modality*, ed. Jacqueline Guéron and Jacqueline Lecarme. Studies in Natural Language and Linguistic Theory. Dordrecht: Springer.

Smith, Carlota S., and Mary S. Erbaugh
2005 Temporal Interpretation in Mandarin Chinese. *Linguistics* 43: 713–56.

Smith, Mark S.
1991 *The Origins and Development of the Waw-Consecutive: Northwest Semitic Evidence from Ugarit to Qumran*. Harvard Semitic Studies 39. Atlanta: Scholars Press.

1995 The *qatala Form in Ugaritic Narrative Poetry. Pp. 789–803 in *Pomegranates and Golden Bells: Studies in Biblical, Jewish, and Near Eastern Ritual, Law, and Literature in Honor of Jacob Milgrom*, ed. D. P. Wright, D. N. Freedman, and A. Hurvitz. Winona Lake, IN: Eisenbrauns.

Smyth, Herbert Weir
1956 *Greek Grammar*. Cambridge: Harvard University Press.

Soden, Wolfram von
1995 *Grundriss der Akkadischen Grammatik*. 3rd ed. Analecta Orientalia. Rome: Pontifical Biblical Institute.

Sperber, Alexander
1943 Hebrew Grammar: A New Approach. *Journal of Biblical Literature* 62: 137–262.

1966 *A Historical Grammar of Biblical Hebrew: A Presentation of Problems with Suggestions to Their Solution*. Leiden: Brill.

Stassen, Leon
1997 *Intransitive Predication*. Oxford Studies in Typology and Linguistic Theory. Oxford: Clarendon.

Steiner, George
1998 *After Babel: Aspects of Language and Translation*. 3rd ed. New York: Oxford University Press.

Swiggers, Pierre, and Alfons Wouters
1998 *De Tékhnee Grammatikée van Dionysius Thrax: De Oudste Spraakkunst in Het Westen*. Orbis Linguarum. Leuven: Peeters.

Sáenz-Badillos, Angel
1993 *A History of the Hebrew Language*, trans. John Elwolde. Cambridge: Cambridge University Press.

Talmon, Shemaryahu
1978 The Presentation of Synchroneity and Simultaneity in Biblical Narrative. Pp. 9–26 in Studies in Hebrew Narrative Art throughout the Ages, ed. J. Heinemann and S. Werses. Scripta Hierosolymitana 27. Jerusalem: Magnes.

Talstra, Eep
1978   Text Grammar and Hebrew Bible I: Elements of a Theory. *Bibliotheca Orientalis* 35: 168–75.
1982   Text Grammar and Hebrew Bible II: Syntax and Semantics. *Bibliotheca Orientalis* 39: 26–38.
1992   Text Grammar and Biblical Hebrew: The Viewpoint of Wolfgang Schneider. *Journal of Translation and Textlinguistics* 5: 269–97.
1997   Tense, Mood, Aspect and Clause Connections in Biblical Hebrew: A Textual Approach. *Journal of Northwest Semitic Languages* 23: 81–103.

Taylor, John R.
2003   *Linguistic Categorization.* 3rd ed. Oxford Textbooks in Linguistics. New York: Oxford University Press.

Testen, David D.
1993   On the Development of the Energic Suffixes. Pp. 293–311 in *Perspectives on Arabic Linguistics V: Papers from the Fifth Annual Symposium on Arabic Linguistics,* ed. Mushira Eid and Clive Holes. Current Issues in Linguistic Theory. Amsterdam: Benjamins.
1994   On the Development of the Arabic Subjunctive. Pp. 151–66 in *Perspectives on Arabic Linguistics VI: Papers from the Sixth Annual Symposium on Arabic Linguistics.* Current Issues in Linguistic Theory. Amsterdam: Benjamins.
1998   *Parallels in Semitic Linguistics: The Development of Arabic* La- *and Related Semitic Particles.* Studies in Semitic Languages and Linguistics. Leiden: Brill.

Thacker, T. H.
1954   *The Relationship of the Semitic and Egyptian Verbal Systems.* Oxford: Clarendon.

Thompson, Sandra A.
1987   "Subordination" and Narrative Structure. Pp. 435–54 in *Coherence and Grounding in Discourse,* ed. Russell S. Tomlin. Typological Studies in Language 11. Amsterdam: Benjamins.

Tigay, Jeffrey H.
1996   *Deuteronomy.* The JPS Torah Commentary. Philadelphia: The Jewish Publication Society.

Timberlake, Alan
2007   Aspect, Tense, Mood. Pp. 280–333 in *Language Typology and Syntactic Description,* vol. 3: *Grammatical Categories and the Lexicon,* ed. Timothy Shopen. Cambridge: Cambridge University Press.

Tomlin, Russell
1995   Focal Attention, Voice, and Word Order: An Experimental, Cross-Linguistic Study. Pp. 517–54 in *Word Order in Discourse,* ed. Pamela Downing and Michael Noonan. Typological Studies in Language 30. Amsterdam: Benjamins.

Traugott, Elizabeth C.
1978   On the Expression of Spatio-Temporal Relations in Language. Pp. 369–400 in *Universals of Human Language,* vol. 3: *Word Structure,* ed. Joseph H. Greenberg. Stanford, CA: Stanford University Press.

Tropper, Josef

1991   Finale Sätze und *yqtla*- Modus im Ugaritischen. *Ugarit-Forschungen* 23: 341–52.

1992   Das ugaritische Verbalsystem. *Ugarit-Forschungen* 24: 313–37.

1995   Das Altkanaanäische und Ugaritische Verbalsystem. Pp. 159–70 in *Ugarit: Ein Ostmediterranes Kulturzentrum im Alten Orient: Ergebnisse und Perspektiven der Forschung*, ed. Manfried Dietrich and Oswald Loretz. Abhandlungen zur Literatur Alt-Syrien-Palästinas 7. Münster: Ugarit-Verlag.

1996   Aramäisches *wyqtl* und hebräisches *wayyiqtol*. *Ugaritic-Forschungen* 28: 633–45.

1998a   Althebraisches und semitisches Aspektsystem. *Zeitschrift für Althebräistik* 11: 153–90.

1998b   Das Verbalsystem der Amarnabriefe aus Jerusalem. *Ugarit-Forschungen* 30: 665–78.

1999a   Die Endungen der semitischen Suffixkonjugation und der Absolutivkasus. *Journal of Semitic Studies* 44: 175–93.

1999b   Tempusmarkierung durch Wortstellung? *Zeitschrift für Althebräistik* 12: 104–6.

1999c   Ugaritic Grammar. Pp. 91–121 in *Handbook of Ugaritic Studies*, ed. Wilfred G. E. Watson and N. Wyatt. Handbuch der Orientalistik. Erste Abteilung, Nahe und der Mittlere Osten. Leiden: Brill.

2000   *Ugaritische Grammatik*. Alter Orient und Altes Testament. Münster: Ugarit-Verlag.

Trubetzkoy, Nicolai S.

1958   *Grundzüge der Phonologie*. Reprint. Travaux du Cercle Linguistique de Prague. Göttingen: Vandenhoeck & Ruprecht.

1969   *Principles of Phonology*, trans. C. A. M. Baltaxe. Berkeley: University of California Press.

Turner, William

1876   The Tenses of the Hebrew Verb. Pp. 338–407 in *Studies Biblical and Oriental*. Edinburgh: Black.

Van Valin, R. D., Jr., and R. J. LaPolla

1997   *Syntax: Structure, Meaning and Function*. Cambridge: Cambridge University Press.

Vendler, Zeno

1957   Verbs and Times. *Philosophical Review* 66: 143–60.

1967   *Linguistics in Philosophy*. Ithaca, NY: Cornell University Press.

Verkuyl, Henk J.

1993   *A Theory of Aspectuality: The Interaction between Temporal and Atemporal Structure*. Cambridge Studies in Linguistics. Cambridge: Cambridge University Press.

Verstraete, Jean-Christophe

2001   Subjective and Objective Modality: Interpersonal and Ideational Functions in the English Modal Auxiliary System. *Journal of Pragmatics* 33: 1505–28.

2007   *Re-thinking the Coordinate-Subordinate Dichotomy: Interpersonal Grammar and the Analysis of Adverbial Clauses in English.* Topics in English Linguistics. Berlin: de Gruyter.

Voigt, Rainer M.
1987   The Classification of Central Semitic. *Journal of Semitic Studies* 32: 1–19.
1990   The Tense-Aspect System of Biblical Hebrew. Pp. 1–8 in *Proceedings of the Tenth World Congress of Jewish Studies*, division D/vol. 1: *The Hebrew Language*. Jerusalem: World Union of Jewish Studies.
2002   The Hamitic Connection: Semitic and Semitohamitic. Pp. 265–90 in *Semitic Linguistics: The State of the Art at the Turn of the 21st Century*, ed. Shlomo Izre'el. Israel Oriental Studies 20. Winona Lake, IN: Eisenbrauns.

Wald, Benji
1987   Cross-Clause Relations and Temporal Sequence in Narrative and Beyond. Pp. 481–512 in *Coherence and Grounding in Discourse*, ed. Russell S. Tomlin. Typological Studies in Language 11. Amsterdam: Benjamins.

Waltke, Bruce K., and M. O'Connor
1990   *An Introduction to Biblical Hebrew Syntax.* Winona Lake, IN: Eisenbrauns.

Warren, Andrew
1998   Did Moses Permit Divorce? Modal *Wqatal* as Key to New Testament Readings of Deuteronomy. *Tyndale Bulletin* 49: 39–56.

Washburn, David L.
1994   Chomsky's Separation of Syntax and Semantics. *Hebrew Studies* 35: 27–46.

Waterhouse, Viola Grace
1974   *The History and Development of Tagmemics.* Janua Linguarum: Series Critica. The Hague: Mouton.

Watson, Wilfred G. E., and N. Wyatt
1999   *Handbook of Ugaritic Studies.* Handbuch der Orientalistik. Erste Abteilung, Nahe und der Mittlere Osten. Boston: Brill.

Weinrich, Harald
2001   *Tempus: Besprochene und erzählte Welt.* 6th ed. Sprache und Literatur. Stuttgart: Kohlhammer.

Wierzbicka, Anna
1990   Prototypes Save. Pp. 347–67 in *Meanings and Prototypes: Studies in Linguistic Categorization*, ed. Savas L. Tsohatzidis. London: Routledge.

Williams, Ronald J.
1972   Energic Verbal Forms in Hebrew. Pp. 75–85 in *Studies on the Ancient Palestinian World Presented to Professor F. V. Winnett*, ed. Wevers J. W. and D. B. Redford. Toronto: University of Toronto Press.

Wittgenstein, Ludwig
2003   *Philosophical Investigations: The German Text, with a Revised English Translation*, trans. G. E. M. Anscombe. 3rd ed. Malden, MA: Blackwell.

Wright, G. H. von
1951   *An Essay in Modal Logic.* Amsterdam: North-Holland.

Wright, William
[1896–98] 1962   *A Grammar of the Arabic Language.* 3rd ed. 2 vols. Cambridge: Cambridge University Press.

Yon, Marguerite
2006   *The City of Ugarit at Tell Ras Shamra.* Winona Lake, IN: Eisenbrauns.
Zevit, Ziony
1988   Talking Funny in Biblical Henglish and Solving a Problem of the *Yaqtúl* Past Tense. *Hebrew Studies* 29: 25–33.
1998   *The Anterior Construction in Classical Hebrew.* Society of Biblical Literature Monograph Series. Atlanta: Scholars Press.
Zewi, Tamar
1996   The Definition of the Copula and the Role of Third Independent Personal Pronouns in Nominal Sentences of Semitic Languages. *Folia Linguistica Historica* 17/1–2: 41–55.
Zuber, Beat
1986   *Das Tempussystem des biblischen Hebräisch.* Beiheft zur Zeitschrift für die altestamentliche Wissenshaft. Berlin: de Gruyter.

Index of Authors

Akman, V. 38
Albright, W. F. 111
Allen, R. L. 3, 4, 5, 9, 10
Allwood, J. 43, 56, 70
Andersen, F. I. 223
Andersen, T. D. 104, 105, 197, 206, 209, 220
Anderson, J. M. 59
Andersson, L.-G. 43, 56, 70
Andrason, A. 149, 174, 178, 182, 184, 200, 220, 221, 245, 246, 251, 263
Anstey, M. P. 202, 218
Anttila, R. 93
Aristotle 1, 5, 7, 19, 20, 57, 59, 180, 181, 194
Arnold, B. T. 313
Austin, J. L. 44, 45, 52, 317
Auwera, J. van der 241

Baayen, R. H. 157, 158, 171, 274
Bach, E. 21
Bache, C. 18, 19, 26, 27, 73, 74, 75, 145, 152, 273
Baker, D. W. 291, 294
Banfield, A. 170
Barco, F. J. del 160, 161
Barnes, O. L. 135, 136
Barr, J. 97
Barwise, J. 38
Bauer, H. 96, 100, 101, 102, 103, 104, 105, 108, 109, 114, 120, 122, 125, 130, 131, 132, 164, 209, 220, 257, 263
Bellamy, J. 85
Bender, L. 95
Bennett, M. 29, 60
Bennett, P. R. 94
Bentinck, J. 161, 163
Bergsträsser, G. 79, 80, 94, 95, 120, 201, 203, 206, 209, 218, 241, 257, 304
Bhat, D. N. S. 121, 200, 205, 260
Bickel, B. 186
Bierwisch, M. 181
Binnick, R. I. 1, 2, 3, 4, 5, 6, 7, 9, 13, 18, 19, 20, 22, 25, 26, 27, 68, 81, 82, 87, 88, 126, 134, 137, 262

Blake, F. R. 82, 105, 120, 130, 131, 132, 210
Blau, J. 132
Bloch, A. 98
Bobzin, H. 120, 209, 304
Bodine, W. R. 150
Böhl, F. M. T. 98, 111
Boneh, N. 143, 222
Bordreuil, P. 106, 107, 110
Borger, R. 203
Brockelmann, C. 77, 95, 102, 122, 125, 127, 130, 132, 202
Brown, G. 149, 276, 281
Buccellati, G. 98, 99, 112, 113
Bull, W. E. 12, 13, 15, 16, 18, 135, 136
Buth, R. 120, 161, 162, 163, 165, 166, 174, 200, 209, 291, 293, 294, 304
Butler, C. S. 21, 49, 180
Bybee, J. L. 27, 45, 46, 51, 52, 54, 61, 68, 74, 134, 137, 138, 139, 143, 145, 146, 176, 177, 178, 181, 182, 185, 186, 190, 199, 200, 201, 202, 204, 205, 206, 207, 208, 209, 218, 220, 221, 222, 230, 232, 234, 235, 245, 250, 263, 265, 266, 278

Campbell, L. 186
Cann, R. 29, 37, 43, 44, 55, 56, 58, 182, 183
Carlson, G. N. 325
Carroll, L. 9, 27, 48, 51, 52, 64, 65, 67, 68, 70, 72
Cazelles, H. 111
Chafe, W. 53
Choi, A. H. 313
Chomsky, N. 144
Chruszczewski, P. P. 56
Chung, S. 20, 45, 46, 65
Claudi, U. 177, 178, 246, 251, 252, 283
Cohen, M. 120, 122
Collins, C. J. 291, 294, 296
Collon, D. 111
Comrie, B. 12, 13, 14, 15, 16, 17, 18, 26, 36, 67, 68, 134, 143, 163, 173, 200, 202, 221, 232, 256, 274, 278, 297

Cook, J. A.   41, 54, 71, 72, 83, 128, 129,
    139, 141, 143, 148, 149, 150, 151, 159,
    163, 166, 167, 169, 170, 173, 178, 180,
    191, 193, 197, 203, 214, 215, 216, 219,
    221, 222, 223, 224, 229, 232, 233, 235,
    240, 256, 259, 263, 282, 289, 298, 316,
    318, 324, 325, 332
Croft, W.   185, 186, 187, 188, 189
Crystal, D.   11, 34, 55, 136
Curtius, G.   87, 91, 92

Dahl, Ö   19, 30, 32, 33, 43, 56, 62, 68, 69,
    70, 74, 138, 139, 145, 146, 179, 180,
    181, 182, 185, 200, 201, 211, 214, 221,
    266
Dallaire, H.   238, 244
Daniels, P. T.   206
Davidson, A. B.   201, 202, 218, 241, 257
Dawson, D. A.   153, 154
DeCaen, V.   86, 87, 88, 91, 93, 133, 143,
    144, 145, 146, 147, 148, 149, 169, 236,
    258, 259
Declerck, R.   8, 15, 16, 17, 18, 28, 33, 41,
    42, 69, 315
Dekker, P. J. E.   38
DeLancey, S.   273, 283
Dempster, S. G.   77, 167, 168
Depraetere, I.   22, 41, 59, 60, 169, 266
DeRouchie, J. S.   167, 168, 172
Dhorme, E.   98, 111
Diakonoff, I. M.   95, 119, 197, 203, 220
Dik, S.   21, 49, 52, 68
Dillmann, A.   120, 250
Dionysius Thrax   1, 2, 3
Dobbs-Allsopp, F. W.   208
Dobrushina, N.   241
Donner, H.   251
Doron, E.   143, 222
Downing, P.   273
Dowty, D. R.   19, 22, 29, 38, 58, 60, 68, 278,
    281, 284
Driver, G. R.   102, 103, 104, 105
Driver, S. R.   77, 83, 86, 90, 91, 92, 93, 97,
    102, 105, 115, 120, 122, 130, 138, 148,
    201, 202, 115, 214, 218, 121, 223, 224,
    130, 131, 238, 241, 250, 131
Dry, H. A.   38, 41, 275, 277, 286
Dryer, M. S.   186, 236
Dyk, J. W.   83, 223, 228, 230

Ebeling, E.   98, 111
Edelheit, A.   82
Emerton, J. A.   107, 119

Endo, Y.   77, 161, 163, 164, 166, 200, 262
Erbaugh, M. S.   266, 283
Eskhult, M.   124, 144
Ewald, H.   77, 79, 80, 83, 86, 87, 88, 89, 90,
    92, 93, 97, 102, 105, 114, 120, 121, 122,
    127, 130, 131, 148, 171, 202, 209, 224,
    238, 258, 289

Faber, A.   95, 96
Fassberg, S. E.   239
Fensham, F. C.   93
Fenton, T. L.   98, 108, 120, 209, 304
Fernald, T. B.   24
Fitzgerald, A.   98
Fleischman, S.   46, 51, 52, 234, 274, 275,
    276, 285, 288
Folmer, M. L.   120, 250, 251
Forbes, A. D.   223
Forsyth, J.   25
Frege, G.   44, 55, 56, 179, 180, 185
Furuli, R.   128, 129, 148, 149, 184, 256

Gai, G.   276
Garr, W. R.   90, 119, 220
Gelb, I. J.   119
Gell, P.   85
Geller, S. A.   226
Genabith, J. van   37, 315
Gentry, P. J.   133, 164, 165, 166, 239, 240
Gesenius, W.   97, 105, 131, 184, 195
Gibson, J. C. L.   79, 80, 201, 202, 218, 241,
    257
Ginsberg, H. L.   98
Givón, T.   45, 275, 283
Glinert, L.   225, 229
Goedsche, C. R.   18
Goerwitz, R. L.   96
Goetze, A.   98, 100, 106, 108, 109
Goldfajn, T.   77, 169, 170, 202
Gordon, A.   223, 228, 229
Gordon, C. H.   95, 106, 107, 108, 109, 112,
    107
Goussev, V.   241
Greenberg, J. H.   98, 100, 178
Greenough, J. B.   3, 4, 5, 8
Greenstein, E. L.   107, 110, 125, 260
Grice, H. P.   34, 267, 295
Grimm, J.   87
Gropp, D. M.   161, 162, 163, 165, 169, 244
Gross, W.   296, 301

Hale, M.   269
Hamori, A.   97

Hare, R. M.   44, 45
Harmelink, B. L.   294, 309
Harris, Z. S.   108, 109, 149
Haspelmath, M.   185, 221, 267, 304
Hatav, G.   20, 21, 41, 46, 60, 66, 68, 77, 148,
   152, 168, 169, 202, 247, 259, 260, 265,
   273, 277, 278, 279, 290, 297
Haug, D.   206
Haupt, P.   99, 100
Heimerdinger, J.-M.   295, 296
Heine, B.   177, 178, 220, 221, 246, 251, 252,
   282, 283
Heinrichs, E.   15, 38, 277, 281
Held, M.   108, 215
Heller, R. L.   77, 158, 159, 160, 161, 169,
   185
Hendel, R. S.   165, 174, 216, 262, 263
Hetzron, R.   96
Hoffer, V.   83
Hoffman, G.   100, 102
Hoftijzer, J.   223, 240, 241
Holmstedt, R. D.   54, 114, 235, 236, 237, 258
Hopper, P. J.   150, 151, 186, 188, 189, 259,
   273, 274, 275, 276, 288
Hornstein, N.   10, 11, 12, 15, 16, 18
Huehnergard, J.   95, 96, 97, 98, 99, 102, 106,
   107, 110, 111, 112, 113, 114, 119, 203,
   206, 220, 228, 241, 257, 258
Hughes, J. A.   102, 105, 120, 130, 131, 132,
   219
Hünnemeyer, F.   177, 178, 246, 251, 252,
   283

Isaksson, B.   124
Izre'el, S.   98, 111, 115

Jahn, J.   86
Jakobson, R.   18, 179, 181, 184, 300
Janssen, T. M. V.   37, 55
Janssens, G.   98, 103, 128
Jespersen, O.   4, 5, 6, 7, 8, 9, 13, 14, 27, 42,
   179
Johnson, B.   127, 130
Johnson, M. R.   28, 29, 30, 67, 69
Joosten, J.   120, 134, 141, 142, 143, 144,
   146, 147, 148, 149, 168, 195, 196, 199,
   200, 218, 219, 223, 224, 237, 310
Joüon, P.   79, 80, 83, 128, 130, 162, 173,
   184, 195, 197, 198, 201, 202, 213, 217,
   218, 224, 232, 236, 238, 241, 244, 257,
   313, 314

Kahan, J.   223

Kamp, H.   37, 38, 39, 41, 277, 315
Kanizsa, G.   66
Kaufmann, S.   252, 253
Kautzsch, E.   79, 80, 102, 131, 201, 217,
   218, 229, 232, 238, 241, 249, 257, 261,
   263, 313, 314, 328
Kawashima, R. S.   169, 170
Kennedy, J.   86, 87
Kenny, A.   19, 20
Khan, G.   201, 226, 229
Kiefer, F.   43, 45, 46, 52, 72
Kienast, B.   102, 204, 220
Kittel, B. P.   83
Klaiman, M. H.   196, 197
Klein, C. L.   216
Klein, W.   30, 31, 32, 36, 65, 66, 67, 68
Knudsen, E. E.   119
Knudtzon, J. A.   98, 100, 102, 111,
   119
Koehler, L.   197
Koffka, K.   284, 285, 286
Kouwenberg, N. G. C.   98, 99, 203, 206,
   220, 263
Krahmalkov, C. R.   120, 250, 251
Kratzer, A.   24
Kroeze, J. H.   184, 313
Kummerow, D.   128, 238, 257
Kuryłowicz, J.   97, 134, 136, 137, 138,
   139, 141, 146, 147, 149, 170, 201, 203,
   220
Kustár, P.   127, 173
Kuteva, T.   220, 221, 229
Kutscher, E. Y.   198

Labov, W.   275, 277
Lakoff, R. T.   277
Lambdin, T. O.   83, 158, 311, 313
LaPolla, R. J.   21
Leander, P.   96, 100, 105, 109, 114
Lessau, D. A.   259
Levinson, S. C.   34, 44, 45, 295
Levita, E.   83, 89
Li, C. N.   226
Li, T.   166, 167
Liddell, H.   57
Lindblom, K.   267
Lindstedt, J.   177, 179, 181
Lipiński, E.   107, 203, 220, 238
Longacre, R. E.   150, 152, 153, 154, 155,
   156, 158, 160, 162, 167, 171, 272, 273,
   275, 276, 282, 287, 288, 295, 296, 304,
   305, 306, 308, 309, 312, 315
Loprieno, A.   103, 140

Lyons, J.   18, 43, 44, 45, 49, 52, 53, 75, 122, 140, 170, 179

Madvig, J. N.   3, 4, 5, 6, 7, 9
Matheus, F.   268
Matthews, P.   176, 179, 181
McCawley, J. D.   43, 44, 56, 70, 75
McCoard, R. W.   13
McFall, L.   77, 79, 80, 83, 85, 86, 88, 89, 90, 92, 103, 127, 239, 258, 276
Meillet, A.   186
Melnik, N.   234
Merwe, C. H. J. van der   184, 310, 313
Mettinger, T. N. D.   77, 122, 124, 125
Meulen, A. G. B. ter   38, 39, 40, 277, 278, 281
Meyer, R.   98, 122, 124, 125, 130, 132, 202, 257, 260
Michaelis, L. A.   19
Michel, D.   126, 127, 130, 173, 301
Mill, J. S.   179
Miller, C. L.   199, 267, 291
Mithun, M.   54
Moens, M.   68
Molendijk, A.   151
Montague, R.   37, 38, 55, 56
Moran, W. L.   94, 98, 103, 105, 110, 111, 112, 113, 114, 115, 116, 117, 118, 120, 184, 207, 238, 240, 250, 251
Moravcsik, E. A.   178, 186, 187
Moreno Cabrera, J. C.   188
Moscati, S.   94, 95, 203
Moshavi, A.   235
Mourelatos, A. P. D.   20, 21
Müller, H.-P.   97, 119, 125, 126, 197, 203, 126
Muraoka, T.   119, 130, 162, 173, 201, 226, 229, 244, 313

Naudé, J. A.   184, 313
Newmeyer, F. J.   177, 180, 185, 186
Niccacci, A.   133, 152, 156, 157, 158, 160, 171, 244, 272, 158
Nichols, J.   186
Nöldeke, T.   120, 201, 250
Notarius, T.   223, 233
Nuyts, J.   50, 51

O'Connor, M.   77, 79, 80, 86, 89, 90, 127, 150, 161, 162, 171, 184, 202, 213, 218, 219, 224, 232, 241, 249, 257, 260, 264, 274, 311, 313, 314, 316
Olsen, M. B.   19, 21, 22, 23, 24, 28, 33, 34, 35, 36, 58, 59, 61, 69, 73, 74

Pagliuca, W.   27, 51, 52, 54, 61, 68, 74, 137, 143, 145, 176, 177, 178, 181, 182, 185, 186, 190, 199, 200, 201, 202, 204, 205, 206, 207, 208, 209, 218, 220, 221, 222, 230, 245, 250, 263, 265, 266, 278
Palmer, F. R.   42, 45, 46, 47, 48, 49, 50, 52, 53, 54, 72, 75, 234
Pardee, D.   94, 96, 105, 106, 107, 110, 116, 213
Partee, B.   29, 38, 57, 60
Peckham, B. J.   134, 135, 314, 134
Peled, Y.   251, 253
Penner, K.   147, 148, 149, 184
Pentiuc, E. J.   111
Pérez Fernández, M.   198, 208, 221, 229, 246
Perkins, R.   27, 51, 52, 54, 61, 68, 74, 137, 143, 145, 176, 177, 178, 181, 182, 185, 186, 190, 199, 200, 201, 202, 204, 205, 206, 207, 208, 209, 218, 220, 221, 222, 230, 232, 245, 250, 263, 265, 266, 278
Perry, J.   38
Pike, K. L.   153
Polzin, R.   204, 240
Porten, B.   251
Portner, P.   42, 45, 46, 47, 48, 49, 50, 51, 53, 54, 55, 70
Pratico, G. D.   83
Prince, E. F.   149
Prior, A. N.   10, 12, 15, 16, 97
Priscian Caesariensis   2

Qimron, E.   240

Rabin, C.   97, 229
Rabinowitz, I.   261
Rainey, A. F.   98, 107, 109, 110, 111, 112, 113, 114, 115, 116, 117, 118, 120, 133, 166, 174, 184, 203, 207, 238, 250, 256, 260, 265
Rattray, S.   140, 240, 241
Reichenbach, H.   4, 6, 7, 8, 9, 10, 11, 12, 13, 15, 16, 17, 18, 29, 36, 37, 38, 131, 135, 170, 202, 315
Reinhart, T.   38, 275, 276, 283, 284, 285, 286, 287, 297
Revell, E. J.   132, 133, 144, 165, 210, 236, 261
Reyle, U.   37, 315
Richardson, M. E. J.   107, 108, 109
Ridzewski, B.   198
Robins, R. H.   1, 2, 3, 4, 87, 88
Rogland, M.   214, 216, 217
Rohrer, C.   37, 38, 39, 41, 277

Röllig, W.   251
Romaine, S.   53
Rosén, H. B.   98, 133, 236
Rössler, O.   96, 98, 124
Rothstein, S.   20, 22, 23, 24, 25, 58, 59, 61,
   64, 194
Rubinstein, A.   276
Rundgren, F.   122, 123, 124, 125, 130, 140,
   143, 144, 123
Ryle, G.   19, 315

Sapir, E.   129
Sasson, V.   119
Satzinger, H.   103
Saussure, F. de   176, 177, 178, 179
Schneider, W.   121, 152, 154, 155, 156, 157,
   158, 171, 172
Schoors, A.   124
Schreuder, R.   181
Schroeder, N. W.   84, 85
Schuh, R. G.   199
Schwarzwald, O.   229
Scott, R. G.   57
Searle, J. R.   44, 45, 213
Segal, M. H.   198, 200
Segert, S.   106, 107, 109, 112, 116
Sellin, E.   223
Seow, C. L.   257
Sheehan, J. F. X.   210
Shimasaki, K.   235
Shlonsky, U.   229
Shulman, A.   133, 165, 184, 236, 238, 239,
   240, 244, 246, 247
Siedl, S. H.   98
Silverman, M. H.   132, 133
Singer, I.   98, 111, 115
Sivan, D.   106, 107, 109, 111, 112, 116
Smith, C. S.   19, 20, 21, 22, 23, 26, 34, 35,
   41, 59, 60, 73, 74, 168, 169, 181, 183,
   201, 211, 266, 267, 278, 279, 280, 20,
   292, 315, 316, 317, 318, 323, 324, 74, 75
Smith, M. S.   107, 119, 120, 209, 304
Smyth, H. W.   133, 240
Soden, W. von   98, 99, 112, 113, 114, 203,
   220, 239, 258
Sperber, A.   82, 219
Stassen, L.   197, 225, 226, 228, 229, 230
Steiner, G.   314
Swiggers, P.   2

Talmon, S.   292, 293, 294, 296
Talstra, E.   150, 152, 154, 155, 157, 171,
   172, 230, 272, 304

Taylor, J. R.   176, 179, 180, 181
Testen, D. S.   240, 258, 259
Thacker, T. H.   77, 103, 104
Thompson, S. A.   151, 226, 273, 275, 151
Timberlake, A.   20, 45, 46, 65
Tolkien, J. R. R.   287
Tomlin, R.   273
Traugott, E. C.   8, 57, 186, 188, 189, 259,
   275, 276
Tropper, J.   105, 106, 107, 109, 110, 112,
   116, 119, 135, 195, 197, 203
Trubetzkoy, N. S.   34

Van Pelt, M. V.   83
Van Valin, R. D.   21
Varro, Marcus Terentius   3
Vendler, Z.   19, 20, 22, 23
Verkuyl, H. J.   20, 21, 22, 59
Verstraete, J.-C.   49, 50, 51, 237, 242, 247,
   254, 322, 325
Voigt, R. M.   95, 96, 97, 133

Wald, B.   275, 282
Waltke, B. K.   77, 79, 80, 86, 89, 90, 127,
   161, 162, 184, 202, 213, 218, 219, 224,
   232, 241, 249, 257, 260, 264, 311, 313,
   314
Warren, A.   146, 147
Washburn, D. L.   258
Waterhouse, V. G.   153
Watson, W. G. E.   105
Weinrich, H.   121, 151, 152, 154, 155, 156,
   170, 272, 273, 274
Wierzbicka, A.   180, 181
Williams, R. J.   240
Wittgenstein, L.   179, 180
Woods, C.   95, 98, 99, 119
Wouters, A.   2
Wright, G. H. von   43
Wright, R. A.   83
Wright, W.   89, 97, 102, 120, 195, 240, 250,
   251, 258
Wyatt, N.   105

Yardeni, A.   251
Yon, M.   105
Yule, G.   149, 276, 281

Zevit, Z.   133, 134, 170, 202, 219, 260
Zewi, T.   117, 184, 226, 241
Zuber, B.   139, 140, 141, 142, 144, 147

Index of Scripture

Genesis
1:1 78
1:3 243
2:5 261
2:6 78, 193
2:10 309
2:19 294
2:24 81
3:1 309
3:3 246
3:15 224
4:1 298
4:2–3 133
4:3–4 159, 297
4:18 203
4:26 191, 261
5:24 212
6:1 191
6:4 218, 226
6:13 232
6:17 232
7:5 312
7:6 312
7:7 312
8:20 263
9:10 192
10:8 191, 192
10:24 203
11:6 191
11:8 192
11:30 227
14:3–4 298
14:22 207
16:8 218
16:12 309
17:20 203, 214
17:22 192
18:7 297
18:11 192, 224
18:22 231
18:26 253
18:33 192
19:1 142
19:8 238

Genesis (cont.)
19:13 232
19:19 264
19:28–29 292
21:19 319
22:4 311
22:16 207
22:19 242
22:20 311
23:10–11 214
24:1 224
24:15 192
24:19 192
24:22 192
24:23–24 322
24:30 231
24:33 232
24:39 247
24:45 192, 262
25:6 193, 297
25:15 262
25:34 291
26:10 202
26:13 192
27:30 192
28:15 207
29:2 248
29:2–3 255
29:3 322
29:12 294
29:14–18 290
29:18 312
29:21 238
29:23–25 296
29:28–30 296
29:31 227
29:34 203
30:7 193
30:8 203
30:32 310
31:9 264
31:32 78
31:39 193
32:5 264

Genesis (cont.)
32:6 239
33:16 296
35:7 294
35:15 294
37–47 158
37:2 229
37:3 296, 298
37:11 298
37:15 79, 218
37:15–16 268
37:17 243
37:30 232
39:1 298
39:2 312
39:13–14 265
39:22 229
40:23 159
41:11 239
41:49 192
41:54 191, 313
42:7 79
42:37 248
43:2 192
43:4 228
43:10 202
43:14 207
43:21 239
44:33 236
45:14 296
47:4 243
48:10 212, 227
49:33 192
50:9 227

Exodus
2:10 294
3:1 229
4:1 79
4:19 294
5:14 192
6:2 291
7:17 231
8:20 218

Exodus (cont.)
9:13 254, 323
9:17–18 232
10:4 232
10:28 241
12 332, 337
12:1–5 333
12:6–11 334
12:12–13 335
14:8 294
15:1 261, 263
15:5–6 260
15:26 84
17:9 232
17:10 296
17:12 227
19:1–2 295
19:5 305
19:19 218
20 332
20:10 82
20:12 249
20:13 79
20:13–16 326
20:14–20 336
23:5 192
24:7 314
25–30 306
25–31 319, 332
25:1 308
25:1–3 307
25:8 308
25:8–11 307
25:10–14 254
25:11 319
29:2–3 193
31:16 84
31:18 192
33:7 193
34:33 192
40:36 193

Leviticus
1–5 306

Leviticus (cont.)
1–6   319, 332
1:2   306
1:3   324
1:3–9   321
1:9   320
4:2   306
4:3–7   307
6:6–11   293
10:19   84
16:20   192
19:2   246
19:9   192
23:22   192
26:44   192

Numbers
1:47–49   294
7:1   192
8:19   239, 240
9:13   192
9:18   193
16:31   192
20:3   202
21:17   261, 263
25:1   191
27:9   252
32:17   207

Deuteronomy
1:10   212
1:12   245, 248
1:22   240
1:30   267
2:9   241
2:12   260
2:31   191
3:24   191
4:11   240
4:22   233
4:33   265
4:41   261
5:23   240
5:27   203
7:12   84
7:22   192
8:3   289
8:10   207
8:19   207
9:24   229
16:9   191
20:9   192
23:23   192

Deuteronomy (cont.)
26:12   192
26:17   305
31:3   227
31:21   261
31:24   192
32:8   260
32:8–13   118
32:10   260
32:11   260
32:13   260
32:15   192
32:29   202
32:45   192

Joshua
2:8   261
2:15–16   290
2:23   289
3:14   224
3:15   224
3:17   224
4:24   248
5:5   229
7:7   202
8:4   290
8:24   192
8:30   78, 261,
           263
9:8   79, 218
11:6   232
13:8–33   291
18:8   290
19:47   264
19:49   192
19:51   192
22:34   226
23:2   212, 224
24:8   239

Judges
1:7   229
1:25   296
1:30   192
1:33   192
1:35   192
2:1   260
3:18   192
5:1   263
6:9   240
6:9–10   239
6:10   239
6:13   226

Judges (cont.)
6:39   243
8:1   240
8:19   202
9:38   78, 218
10:12   239
10:18   191
11:1   294
11:18   240
12:3   239
13:5   191
13:16   249
13:23   202, 250
13:25   191
14:4   231
14:18   202, 250
15:1   238
15:2   240
15:17   192
16:19   191
16:21   229
16:22   191
19:24   238
20:31   191
20:31–47   294
20:39–40   191

1 Samuel
1:1   309
1:3   194
1:7   193
1:10   218
1:23   195
2:11   229
2:15   261
2:19   193
2:28   239, 240
3:2   191
3:3   261
3:24   267
4:1   192
7:13   294
7:15–16   193
7:16   193
8   326
8:1–3   326
8:2–3   324
8:4–6   328
8:7–9   329
8:10–22   331
8:11   194
9:3   261
9:26   294

1 Samuel (cont.)
10:2–6   305
10:8   241
10:13   192
11:3   253
12:23   192
13:10   192
13:17–18   218
14:1–6   294
14:35   191, 263
18:1   192
19:11   232
20:22   207
22:15   191
22:23   218
23:13   192
24:17   192
25:34   202
28:15   239
31:4–6   294

2 Samuel
2:27   202
3:6   229
4:3   294
4:4   292
4:7   294
4:10   239
5:5   211
6:18   192
7:1–3   310
7:4   310
7:9   239
7:11–17   305
7:16   228
11:17   289
12:8   239, 240
12:26–29   294
13:12   240
13:19   159
13:28   294
13:29–34   294
13:34   294
13:36   192
13:39   192
14:5   259
15:32   193
15:37   218
17:11   207
17:17   193
19:7   202
19:30   207
20:6   248

2 Samuel (cont.)
22   260
22:12   260
22:14   260
22:16   260
22:24   239
23:10   218
24:4   204
24:14   241
24:22–23   207

1 Kings
1:9–10   159
1:25   205
1:41   192
3:1   192
5:1   204
5:25   193
6:1   129
6:8   218
7:13   294
7:40   192
8:1   261, 263
8:4   204
8:54   192, 311
9:1   192
11:7   261, 263
11:15–22   292
12:16   204
12:18   261
13:1   227
14:21   204
15:13   204
15:16   261
15:21   192
16:5   261
18:1–5   293
18:41   314
20:33   218
20:39   228
22:20   305
22:35–37   294
22:41   204

2 Kings
2:9   261
2:16   248
3:4   193
5:6   252
6:29   294
7:6–7   291
7:15–20   291
8:27   204

2 Kings (cont.)
9:33   240
10:25   192
10:32   191
12:11   311
13:13–20   291
13:19   202
14:1–16   292
15:5   204
15:37   191
16:17   204
18:3–4   282
18:4   204, 232
18:36   81
19:15   226
19:23   238
20:12   81
22:3   311

Isaiah
1:9   202
1:16   192
1:21   218
2:2   311
2:9   265
2:20   311
5:13   216
5:15   265
5:19   239
5:25   265
6:1   84
7:18–25   311
7:20   311
7:21   312
10:18   192
11:9   78, 207,
      216
19:7   216
24:18   265
36:21   81
39:1   81, 259
41:4   84
41:5   240
44:12–13   265
48:18   250
49:7   264
63:19   250
66:7   261

Jeremiah
1:16   84
4:16   265
5:3   192

Isaiah (cont.)
7:17   230
8:3   207
8:6   264
8:16   265
11:18   239
17:18   241
18:18   241
25:7   248
25:10–14   320
25:29   191
26:8   192
28:3   231
29:14   207
29:18   207
31:29   79
31:36   192
32:9   239
33:22   223
40:15   313
43:1   192
44:18   192
47:1   261
48:41   216
51:30   192
51:63   192

Ezekiel
3:3   239, 241
3:19   78
9:8   239
16:11   239, 240
16:57   261
18:2   79
23:16   239
23:20   239
31:5   192
33:4   265
33:6   265
43:23   192
44:8   240

Hosea
2:1   218
12:11   84

Joel
2:23   265

Amos
1:4   210
1:4–5   80
1:5   210

Amos (cont.)
1:7–8   80
4:7–8   161, 193
6:3   240
7:2   192
9:15   207

Jonah
1:2   242
3:4   191

Micah
2:13   265
5:2   207

Zephaniah
3:2   197

Zechariah
3:3   229
7:5   276
10:6   202
11:13   239

Psalms
2:2   216
3:5   299
3:6   239, 299
4:2   250
7:5   239, 298,
      301
7:7   78, 250
7:13   265, 298,
      299
7:16   298, 299,
      301
8:6   301
9:3   243
16:9   301
18   260, 298
18:12   260
18:14   260
18:16   260
20:9   265, 299
22:5   299
22:30   265, 299
24:2   216, 260
25:2   241, 243
27:13   202
28:7   299
29:5   298, 301
29:5–6   298
29:6   298, 301

Psalms (cont.)
29:9 298, 301
29:10 298,
   301
30:3 299
30:12 299
31:2 241
31:18 241
33:9 299
34:1 298
34:8 299
35:21 301
36:4 192
37:36 298, 299
37:40 265, 298,
   301
38:3 301
38:13 299
38:15 301
39:12 299
40 298
40:2 298, 299
40:2–3 298
40:2–4 298
40:3 298, 299
40:4 298, 299
41:13 299
42:6 301
43:4 238
44:3 298, 299
44:10 298, 299
44:19–21 298,
   299
45:8 299, 301
49:15 265, 301
50:1 298, 301
50:5–7 301
50:6 298, 301
50:16 301
50:16–18 298
50:17–18 299
52:2 298
52:9 301
54:2 298
55:6 301
55:6–7 298
55:7 299
55:18 299, 300
59:1 298
59:16 299
60:1 298
60:2 298
64:8–9 301

Psalms (cont.)
64:8–10 265,
   298
64:10 298, 299
65:9 301
65:10 299
66:12 299
69:11 298, 299
69:11–12 298
69:12 239, 240,
   298, 299
69:15 241
69:21 239, 298,
   299
69:22 298
71:1 241
71:21 241
73:13 299, 301
73:13–14 298
73:16 239, 299
75:9 299
76:3 301
77:7 301
77:11 299
77:19 301
78 298
78:10 303
78:24–25 303
78:44–51 303
78:59 303
78:65–69 302
80:6 298, 301
80:9 299, 300
80:9–10 298
80:10 298, 299
81:8 299
81:13 299
81:17 301
89:20 301
89:39 301
90:2 301
90:3 301
90:10 239, 299
92:8 301
92:11–12 301
94:7 299
94:22 301
94:22–23 265,
   298
94:23 299
95:10 301
97:4 299
97:8 298, 299

Psalms (cont.)
102:5 299
102:8 299
102:11 299
104:31 243
104:32 299
105 298
105:14 303
105:16–18 303
106 298
106:28–30 302
107 298
109:3 298, 299
109:4 298
109:5 299
109:16 298, 301
109:17 298, 299
109:17–18 298,
   301
109:18 298, 299
109:28 265, 298,
   299
114:3 299
118:14 301
118:21 299
118:27 301
119:26 298, 299
119:52 298, 299
119:55 239, 298,
   301
119:59 239, 299
119:59–60 298
119:67 261
119:90 265, 299
119:106 239,
   298, 301
119:131 239,
   298, 299
119:147 239,
   298, 299
119:158 239,
   298, 299
119:167 298,
   301
120:1 299
136:4 299
136:10–11 300
136:11 299
136:18 301
138:3 299
139:1 299
139:5 299
139:11 301

Psalms (cont.)
143:4 299
143:6 299
144:3 298, 299,
   300
148:14 301

Job
1:5 79, 194
1:14 229
1:15–17 239
1:19 239
3–4 298
3:6 243
3:13 202
5:15–16 265
6:2 202
9:34 240
10:14 253
10:19 202
13:21 240
14:17 265
19:20 239
29:17 239
31:15 240
33:24 240
36:7 265

Proverbs
7:15 264
10:1 222
10:1–2 325
11:4 223
11:6 222
11:8 298
11:11 222
11:13 232
11:31 222
12:13 298
12:21 215
12:25 222
13:13 222
13:16 222
13:20 223
14:1 215
14:11 222
14:17 222
15:1 222
15:2 222
15:20 79
16:23 222
17:2 223
17:20 223

Proverbs (cont.)
18:1 222
18:22 298
19:5 223
19:9 223
20:12 215
20:26 298
21:11 223
21:22 215, 298
22:12 298
22:13 78
25:4 298
26:24 222
27:18 223
28:18 223
29:2 222
29:8 222
29:23 223

Ruth
1:6–7 289
1:9 242
1:18 192
2:7 82
2:21 207
3:3 192
4:9 207

Song of Songs
2:7 207

Qoheleth
1:3 223
1:17 239, 240
1:18 223
2:3 223
2:16 223
2:21 223
3:14 223
3:15 223
3:17 223
4:10 223
4:11 223
4:12 223
5:9 223
5:11 223
5:17 223

Qoheleth (cont.)
6:7 223
6:12 223
7:3 223
7:7 223
7:9 223
7:12 223
7:18 223
7:19 223
7:20 223
7:26 223
8:1 223
8:3 223
8:5 223
8:12 223
8:13 223
8:15 223
9:4 223
9:11 223
10:1 223
10:8 223
10:9 223
10:12 223
10:14 223
10:15 223
10:18 223
10:19 223
10:20 223
11:3 223
11:4 223
11:5 223

Lamentations
1:13 240
1:18 227
1:21 250

Esther
6:13 191
9:23 191

Daniel
8:13 239
8:15 239
8:17 239
9:3 240
9:3–4 239

Daniel (cont.)
9:4 239
9:24 192
10:2 229
10:16 239
10:19 239
12:7 192
12:8 239

Ezra
3:6 191
7:28 239
8:15–17 239
8:23 239
8:24–26 239
8:28 239
8:31 239
9:3 239
9:5–6 239
9:6 239

Nehemiah
1:4 229, 239
2:1 239, 240
2:6 239, 240
2:9 239, 240
2:13 239
4:1 191
5:7 240
5:7–8 239
5:13 239
6:3 239
6:8 239
6:11 240
6:11–12 239
7:5 239
8:13 240
12:31 239
13:7–11 239
13:9 240
13:11 240
13:13 239
13:17 239, 240
13:19 192, 239,
    240
13:21 240
13:21–22 239

Nehemiah (cont.)
13:22 240
13:30 239

1 Chronicles
1:10 191, 192
1:18 203
1:26 204
2:48–49 203
5:2 263
13:2 240
13:3 240
14:15 207, 212
16:2 192
17:2 228
19:13 240
21:2 240
21:4 204
21:13 240
22:5 240
27:24 191

2 Chronicles
1:10 238, 240
3:1–2 191
4:11 192
5:2 261, 263
5:5 204
7:1 192, 311
7:12 203
10:16 204
12:13 204
15:16 204
16:5 192
18:6 240
20:9 240
20:31 204
22:3 204
24:11 311
26:20 204
28:16 204
29:29 192
31:1 204
31:7 191
31:10 191
34:3 191
34:8 311